Ordnance Survey

STREET ATLAS
Edinburgh
and East Central Scotland

Contents

III   *Key to map symbols*

IV-V   *Key to map pages*

VI-VII   *Route planning*

VIII   *Administrative and post code boundaries*

1   *Street maps*

232   *Extra-large-scale map of Edinburgh town centre*

234   *Index of hospitals, industrial estates, railway stations, schools, shopping centres, street names and universities*

PHILIP'S

First edition published 1995
First colour edition published 1999 by

Ordnance Survey®   and   George Philip Ltd., a division of
Romsey Road   Octopus Publishing Group Ltd
Maybush   2-4 Heron Quays
Southampton   London
SO16 4GU   E14 4JB

ISBN 0-540-07653 8 (hardback)
ISBN 0-540-07654 6 (spiral)

To the best of the Publishers' knowledge, the information in this atlas was
correct at the time of going to press. No responsibility can be accepted
for any errors or their consequences.

The representation in this atlas of a road, track or path is no evidence
of the existence of a right of way.

**The mapping between pages 1 and 233 (inclusive) in this atlas is
derived from Ordnance Survey® Large Scale and Landranger®
mapping, and revised using OSCAR® and Land-Line® data.**

Ordnance Survey, OSCAR, Land-line and Landranger are registered trade
marks of Ordnance Survey, the national mapping agency of Great Britain.

Printed and bound in Spain by Cayfosa

Digital Data

The exceptionally high-quality mapping
found in this book is available as digital
data in TIFF format, which is easily
convertible to other bit-mapped (raster)
image formats.

The index is also available in digital form
as a standard database table. It contains
all the details found in the printed index
together with the National Grid reference
for the map square in which each entry
is named and feature codes for places
of interest in eight categories such as
education and health.

For further information and to discuss
your requirements, please contact the
Ordnance Survey Solutions Centre on
01703 792929.

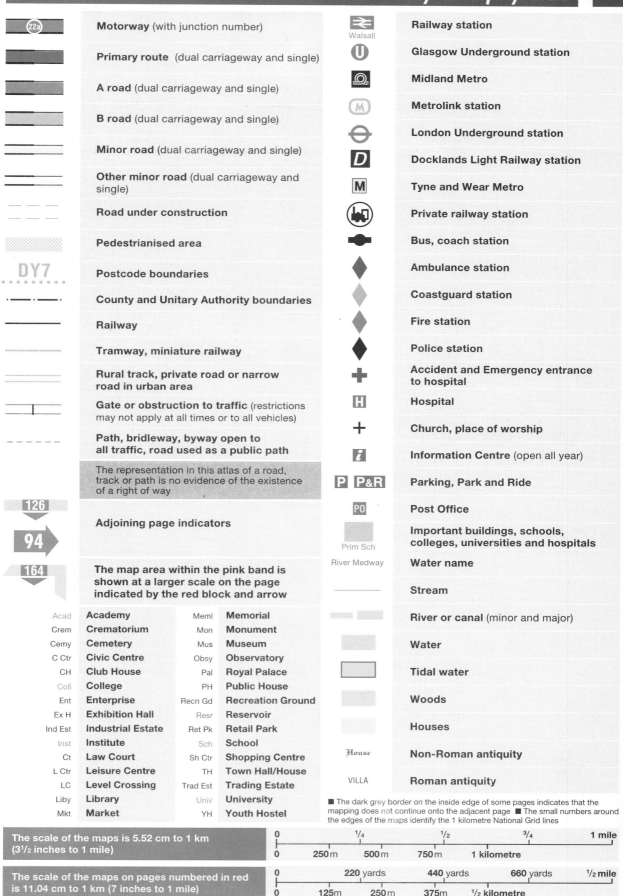

Motorway (with junction number)	Railway station
Primary route (dual carriageway and single)	Glasgow Underground station
A road (dual carriageway and single)	Midland Metro
B road (dual carriageway and single)	Metrolink station
Minor road (dual carriageway and single)	London Underground station
Other minor road (dual carriageway and single)	Docklands Light Railway station
Road under construction	Tyne and Wear Metro
Pedestrianised area	Private railway station
Postcode boundaries	Bus, coach station
County and Unitary Authority boundaries	Ambulance station
Railway	Coastguard station
Tramway, miniature railway	Fire station
Rural track, private road or narrow road in urban area	Police station
Gate or obstruction to traffic (restrictions may not apply at all times or to all vehicles)	Accident and Emergency entrance to hospital
Path, bridleway, byway open to all traffic, road used as a public path	Hospital
The representation in this atlas of a road, track or path is no evidence of the existence of a right of way	Church, place of worship
	Information Centre (open all year)
Adjoining page indicators	Parking, Park and Ride
	Post Office
The map area within the pink band is shown at a larger scale on the page indicated by the red block and arrow	Important buildings, schools, colleges, universities and hospitals

Acad	Academy	Meml	Memorial
Crem	Crematorium	Mon	Monument
Cemy	Cemetery	Mus	Museum
C Ctr	Civic Centre	Obsy	Observatory
CH	Club House	Pal	Royal Palace
Coll	College	PH	Public House
Ent	Enterprise	Recn Gd	Recreation Ground
Ex H	Exhibition Hall	Resr	Reservoir
Ind Est	Industrial Estate	Ret Pk	Retail Park
Inst	Institute	Sch	School
Ct	Law Court	Sh Ctr	Shopping Centre
L Ctr	Leisure Centre	TH	Town Hall/House
LC	Level Crossing	Trad Est	Trading Estate
Liby	Library	Univ	University
Mkt	Market	YH	Youth Hostel

The scale of the maps is 5.52 cm to 1 km (3½ inches to 1 mile)

The scale of the maps on pages numbered in red is 11.04 cm to 1 km (7 inches to 1 mile)

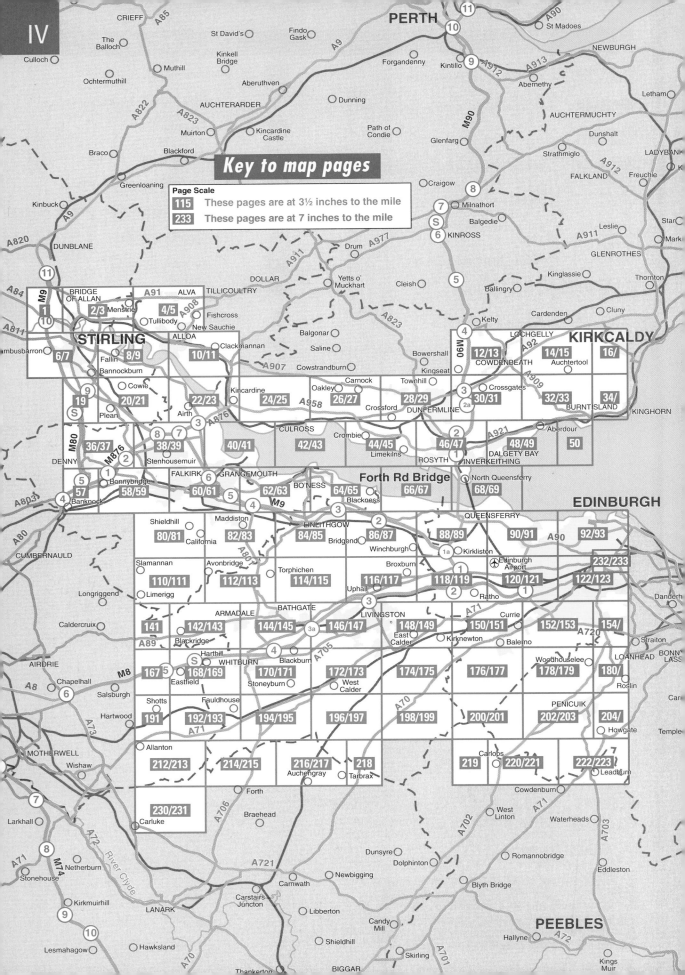

ST ANDREWS

NEWBURGH

Luthrie

A92

Balmullo

Leuchars

Moonzie

Strathkinness

Blebocraigs

Boarhills

CUPAR

A91

Letham

Pitscottie

Kingsbarns

TERMUCHTY

Springfield

Craigrothie

Ceres

Stravithie

Dunshalt

Peat Inn

CRAIL

ALKLAND

A912

LADYBANK

A914

Kingskettle

A915

Freuchie

Largoward

A917

Montrave

Arncroach

KILRENNY

Langdyke

A916

Colinsburgh

ANSTRUTHER

PITTENWEEM

Leslie

Star

Lower Largo

ST MONANCE

A911

Kennoway

Markinch

ELIE

EARLSFERRY

GLENROTHES

LEVEN

A955

Methil

Thornton

BUCKHAVEN

Cluny

East Wemyss

West Wemyss

Firth of Forth

/17 18

/35

RNTISLAND

KINGHORN

tool

NORTH BERWICK

Dirleton

51 52/53 A198 54/55 56

Gullane

Kingston Scoughall

Whitekirk

70/71 72/73 74/75 76/77 78/79

Aberlady Drem Tyninghame DUNBAR

COCKENZIE AND PORT SETON Longniddry Athelstaneford EAST LINTON

96/97 98/99 100/101 102/103 104/105 106/107 108/109

PRESTONPANS Elvingston A1 Stenton Spott Thorntonloch

94/95 Pitcox

MUSSELBURGH TRANENT A199 HADDINGTON Halls Innerwick

124/125 126/127 128/129 130/131 132/133 134/135 136/137 138/139 140

Danderhall New Town Garvald Oldhamstocks Cockbur

Elphinstone Bolton

Ormiston Pencaitland A6093 Gifford Carfrae Ecclaw

/155 156/157 158/159 160/161 162/163 164/165 166

Straiton DALKEITH Peastonbank Danskine Grantshouse

LOANHEAD BONNYRIGG & LASSWADE Pathhead Gilchriston Longyester

/181 182/183 184/185 186/187 188/189 190

Roslin Humbie Cranshaws

Carrington Gorebridge Fala Blegbie Abbey St Bathans

/205 206/207 208/209 210/211

Howgate Temple Middleton Tynehead Ellemford

Leadburn Gilston Longformacus Preston

224/225 226/227 228/229

Falahill

Heriot A7 A68 DUNS

Gavinton

Fountainhall Oxton Blythe Fogo

A703 Torquhan LAUDER A697 Leitholm

Eddleston Killochyett Houndslow Greenlaw

Stow A6105

Nether Blainslie Gordon Lambden

A6089 Hume Eccles

Kings Muir Walkerburn Bowland Langshaw Buckholm Fans Earlston Stichill

Key map scale

0 1 2 3 4 5 6 7 8 Km

0 1 2 3 4 5 Miles

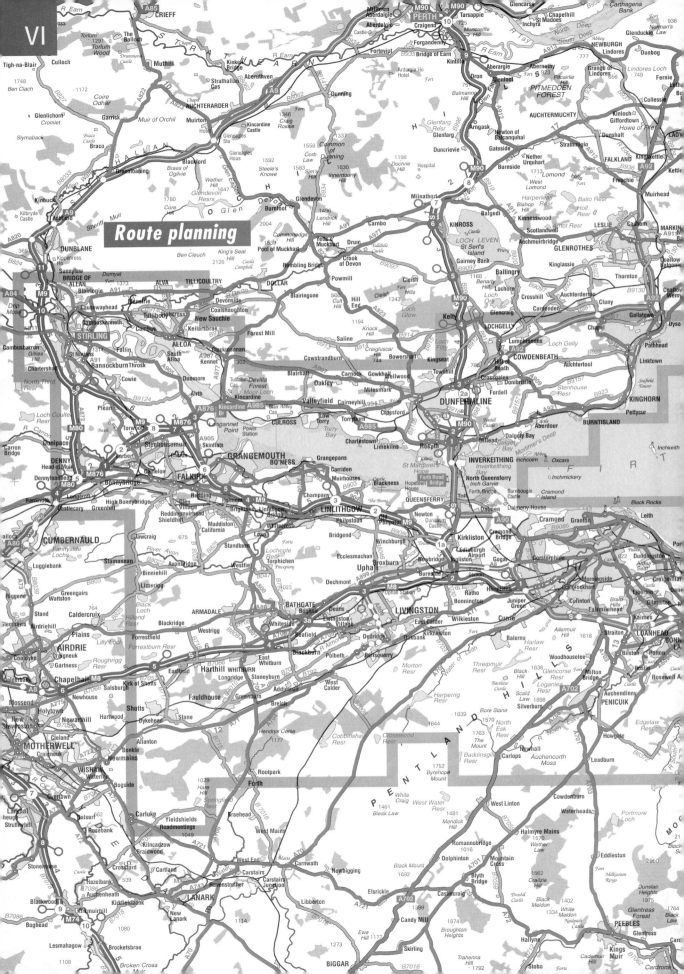

Route planning

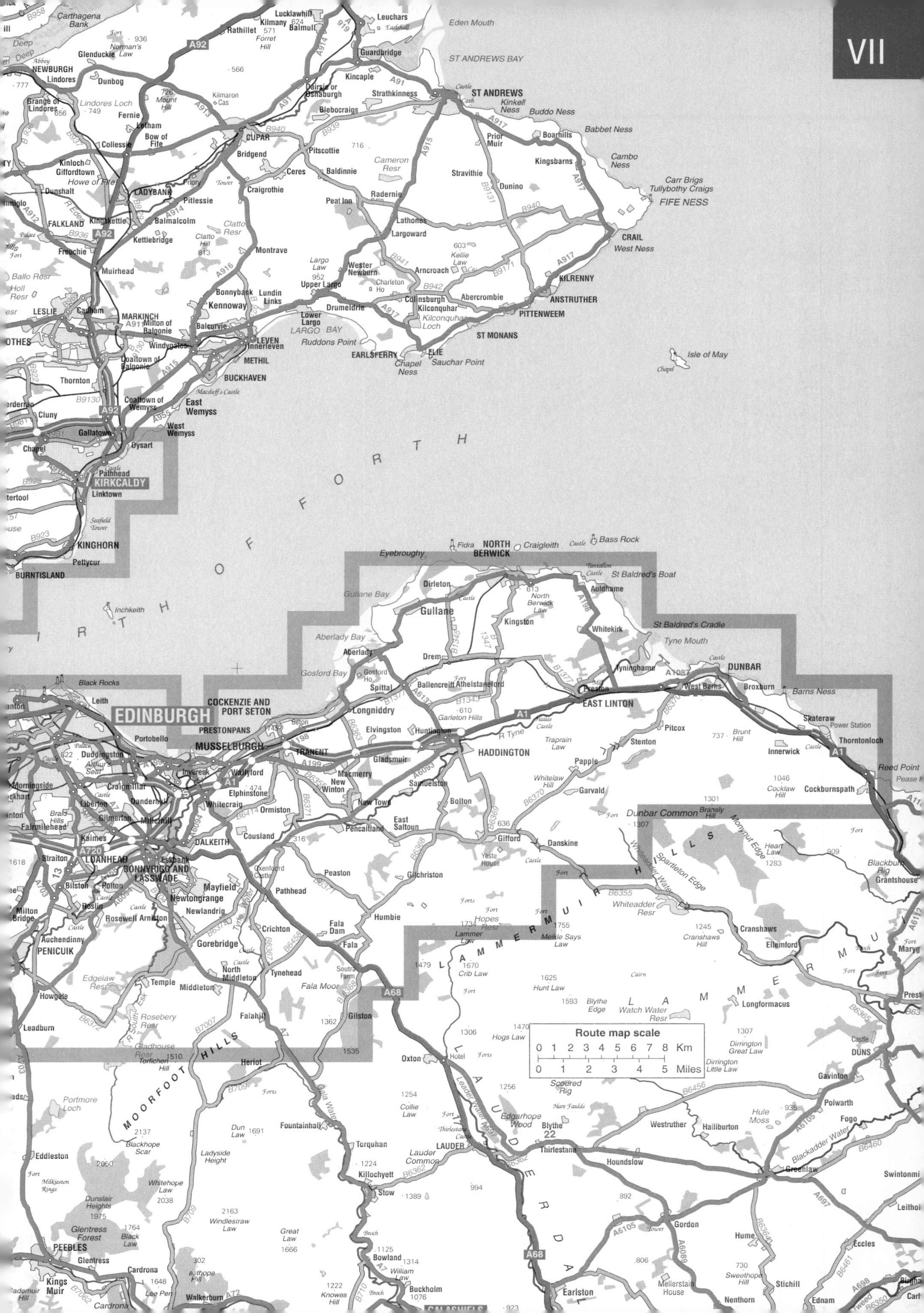
Carthagena Bank
Lucklawhill
Kilmany
Balmullo
Leuchars
Earlshall
Eden Mouth
Rathillet
Forret Hill
Norman's Law
Glenduckie
NEWBURGH
Lindores
Dunbog
A92
A919
A914
Guardbridge
ST ANDREWS BAY
Kincaple
A91
Dairsie or Osnaburgh
Strathkinness
ST ANDREWS
Kinkell Ness
Buddo Ness
Kilmaron Cas
Mount Hill
Lindores Loch
Grange of Lindores
Fernie
Letham
Blebocraigs
A917
Boarhills
Babbet Ness
CUPAR
Bow of Fife
Collessie
Bridgend
Pitscottie
Cameron Resr
A915
Prior Muir
Kingsbarns
Cambo Ness
Kinloch
Giffordtown
Howe of Fife
Ceres
Baldinnie
Stravithie
Dunino
Carr Brigs
Tullybothy Craigs
FIFE NESS
Dunshalt
LADYBANK
Priory
Craigrothie
Radernie
Pitlessie
Peat Inn
FALKLAND
Kingskettle
Balmalcolm
Clatto Resr
Lathones
Largoward
CRAIL
West Ness
Kettlebridge
Clatto Hill
Freuchie
Montrave
Kellie Law
Muirhead
Largo Law
Wester Newburn
Arncroach
Charleton Ho
KILRENNY
Ballo Resr
Holl Resr
Bonnybank
Lundin Links
Upper Largo
Colinsburgh
Abercrombie
ANSTRUTHER
LESLIE
Cadham
Kennoway
Kilconquhar
Kilconquhar Loch
PITTENWEEM
MARKINCH
Milton of Balgonie
Drumeldrie
Lower Largo
LARGO BAY
ST MONANS
Balcurvie
LEVEN
Innerleven
Windygates
Ruddons Point
EARLSFERRY
ELIE
Saucher Point
Chapel Ness
Isle of May
Coaltown of Balgonie
METHIL
BUCKHAVEN
Thornton
Macduff's Castle
Coaltown of Wemyss
East Wemyss
Cluny
Gallatown
West Wemyss
Dysart
Chapel
Pathhead
KIRKCALDY
Linktown
Seafield Tower
KINGHORN
Pettycur
BURNTISLAND
F I R T H   O F   F O R T H
Inchkeith
Fidra
NORTH BERWICK
Craigleith
Bass Rock
Eyebroughy
Tantallon Castle
St Baldred's Boat
Dirleton
Auldhame
Gullane Bay
Gullane
North Berwick Law
Kingston
A198
Whitekirk
St Baldred's Cradle
Aberlady Bay
Tyne Mouth
Aberlady
Drem
Gosford Bay
Gosford Ho
Tyninghame
A1087
DUNBAR
Black Rocks
Spittal
Ballencrieff
Athelstaneford
Preston
West Barns
Broxburn
Barns Ness
Leith
EDINBURGH
COCKENZIE AND PORT SETON
Longniddry
EAST LINTON
Garleton Hills
A1
Skateraw
Power Station
PRESTONPANS
Seton
Elvingston
Huntington
Hailes Castle
Pitcox
Brunt Hill
Thorntonloch
Portobello
MUSSELBURGH
TRANENT
Traprain Law
Stenton
Innerwick
Duddingston
Arthur's Seat
Gladsmuir
HADDINGTON
Reed Point
Inveresk
Wallyford
Macmerry
Papple
Morningside
Craigmillar
Elphinstone
New Winton
Samuelston
Whitelaw Hill
Garvald
Cocklaw Hill
Cockburnspath
Liberton
Danderhall
Whitecraig
Ormiston
New Town
Bolton
Braid Hills
Fairmilehead
Gilmerton
Millerhill
Pencaitland
East Saltoun
Dunbar Common
Bransly Hill
Kaimes
DALKEITH
Cousland
Gifford
Danskine
Monynut Edge
Heart Law
A720
Straiton
LOANHEAD
Eskbank
Yester House
Blackburn Rig
Grantshouse
BONNYRIGG AND LASSWADE
Oxenfoord Castle
Peaston
Gilchriston
Spartleton Edge
Whiteadder Water
Bilston
Polton
Mayfield
Pathhead
Roslin
Newtongrange
Newlandrig
Whiteadder Resr
Milton Bridge
Rosewell
Arniston
Hopes Resr
Crichton
Fala Dam
Humbie
Meikle Says Law
Cranshaws
Cranshaws Hill
Ellemford
Auchendinny
Lammer Law
PENICUIK
Gorebridge
Fala
Crib Law
North Middleton
Tynehead
Soutra Farm
L A M M E R M U I R   H I L L S
Edgelaw Resr
Temple
Middleton
Fala Moor
A68
Hunt Law
Howgate
Blythe Edge
Watch Water Resr
Longformacus
Rosebery Resr
Leadburn
Falahill
Gilston
Hogs Law
Route map scale
0 1 2 3 4 5 6 7 8 Km
0 1 2 3 4 5 Miles
Dirrington Great Law
Dirrington Little Law
Gladhouse Resr
Torfichen Hill
Heriot
Oxton
Hotel
DUNS
Gavinton
MOORFOOT HILLS
Scoured Rig
Portmore Loch
Collie Law
Leader Water
Edgarhope Wood
Hule Moss
Polwarth
Fogo
Dun Law
Fountainhall
Thirlestane
Blythe
Westruther
Halliburton
Blackadder Water
Blackhope Scar
Torquhan
LAUDER
Lauder Common
Thirlestane
Houndslow
Greenlaw
Eddleston
Ladyside Height
Killochyett
Swintonmill
Milkieston Rings
Whitehope Law
Stow
L A U D E R D A L E
Leitholm
Dunslair Heights
Windlestraw Law
Gordon
Glentress Forest
Black Law
Great Law
Hume
Eccles
PEEBLES
Bowland
Glentress
Cardrona
William Law
Mellerstain House
Sweethope Hill
Stichill
Kings Muir
Lee Pen
Walkerburn
Knowes Hill
Buckholm
Earlston
Nenthorn
Ednam
GALASHIELS

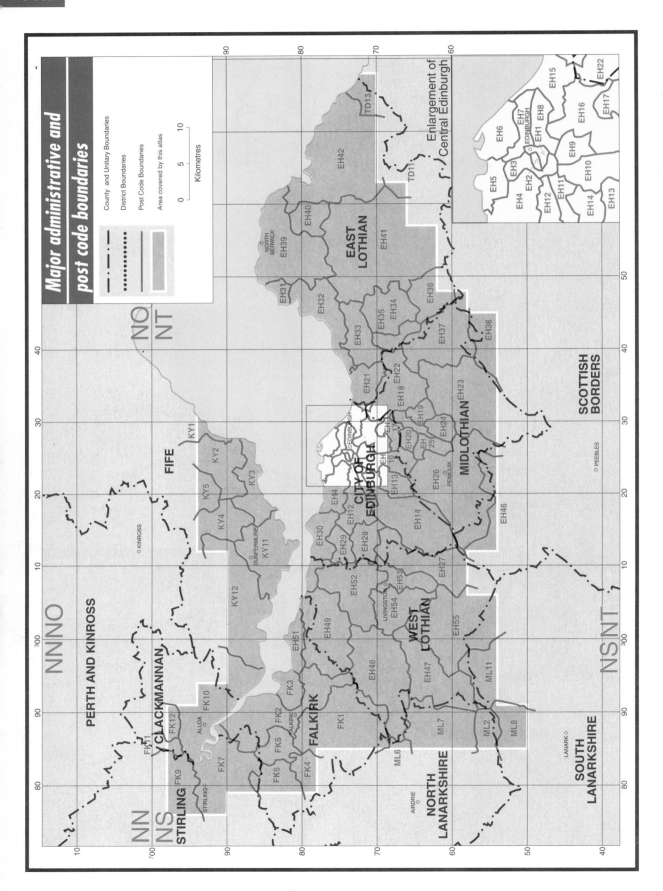

Major administrative and post code boundaries

County and Unitary Boundaries
District Boundaries
Post Code Boundaries
Area covered by this atlas

Kilometres

0   5   10

Enlargement of Central Edinburgh

EH15
EH7 EH8
EH6   EDINBURGH EH1
EH5 EH3 EH1 EH9 EH16
EH4 EH2 EH10 EH17 EH22
EH12 EH11 EH14 EH13
EH13

PERTH AND KINROSS

NN
NS
STIRLING

FK11
FK12
FK9
FK7
FK10
ALLOA
STIRLING
FK8
FK6
FK5
FK4
FK2
FALKIRK
FK1
FK3
FALKIRK

NORTH LANARKSHIRE
AIRDRIE

ML6
ML7
ML2
ML8
LANARK
SOUTH LANARKSHIRE

FIFE

KINROSS

KY1
KY2
KY5
KY4
KY3
DUNFERMLINE
KY11
KY12

NN NO
NS NT

EH30
EH29
EH28
EH12
EH4
EH14

EH52
EH54
EH53
EH55
LIVINGSTON
WEST LOTHIAN
EH47
EH48
EH49
EH51
ML11

CITY OF EDINBURGH
EDINBURGH

EH21
EH18
EH22
EH19
EH20
EH25
EH26
EH27
MIDLOTHIAN
EH23
PENICUIK
EH24
EH37
EH38
EH46
PEEBLES

SCOTTISH BORDERS

EH31
EH32
EH33
EH35
EH34
EH36
EH39
EH40
EH41
EH42
NORTH BERWICK
EAST LOTHIAN

TD13
TD11

NO
NT

NS NT

40
300
90
300
10
20
30
40
50
60
70
80
90
60
70
80
90
700
80
90
50
40
10

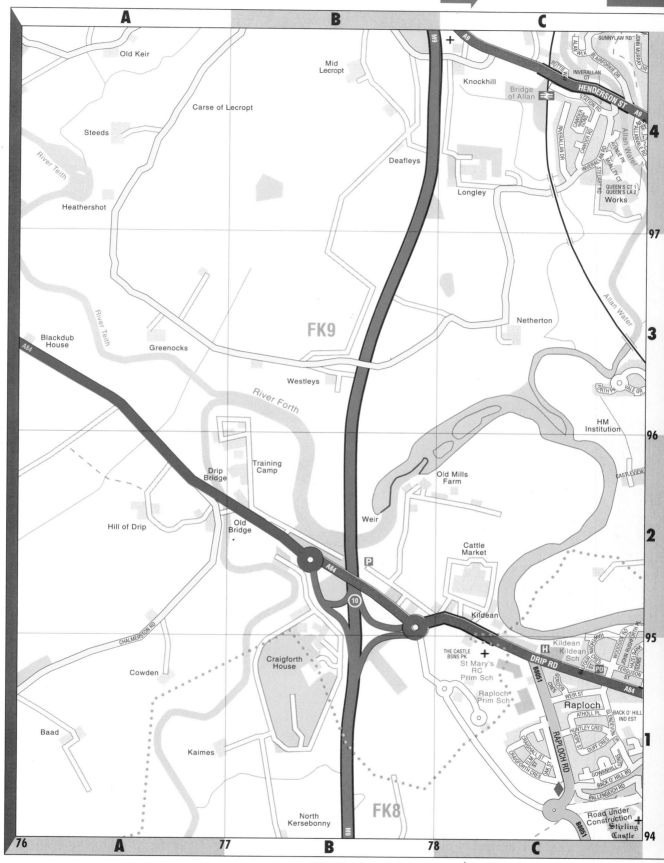

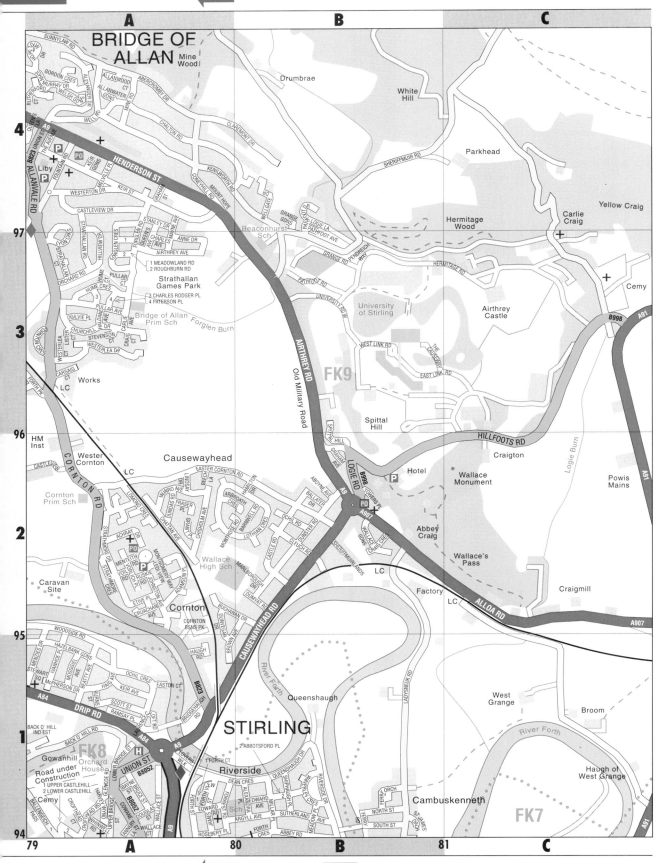

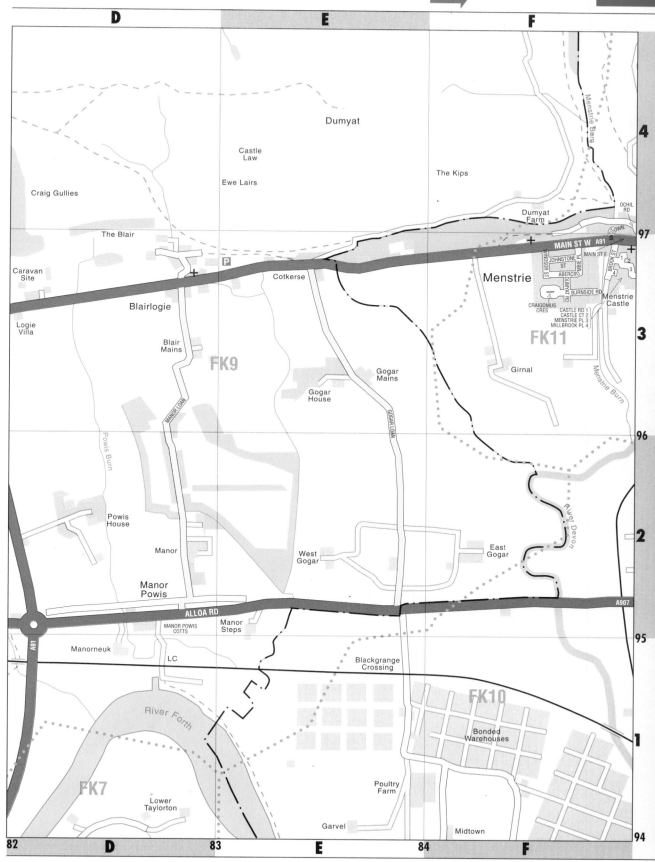

Dumyat

Castle
Law

Ewe Lairs

Craig Gullies

The Kips

Menstrie Braa

OCHIL
RD

Dumyat
Farm

The Blair

97

MAIN ST W   A91

Caravan
Site

Cotkerse

WINDSOR RD
JOHNSTONE
ST
ABERCRO
BURNSIDE RD

MAIN ST E

BROOK ST

MIDTOWN

1
2

3

Menstrie

Blairlogie

Logie
Villa

Blair
Mains

FK9

Gogar
Mains

CRAIGOMUS
CRES

CASTLE RD 1
CASTLE CT 2
MENSTRIE PL 3
MILLBROOK PL 4

Menstrie
Castle

FK11

Girnal

Gogar
House

MANOR LOAN

Powis Burn

GOGAR LOAN

Menstrie Burn

96

Powis
House

River Devon

Manor

West
Gogar

East
Gogar

2

Manor
Powis

ALLOA RD

A907

MANOR POWIS
COTTS

Manor
Steps

95

Manorneuk

A91

LC

Blackgrange
Crossing

FK10

River Forth

Bonded
Warehouses

1

FK7

Poultry
Farm

Lower
Taylorton

Garvel

Midtown

94

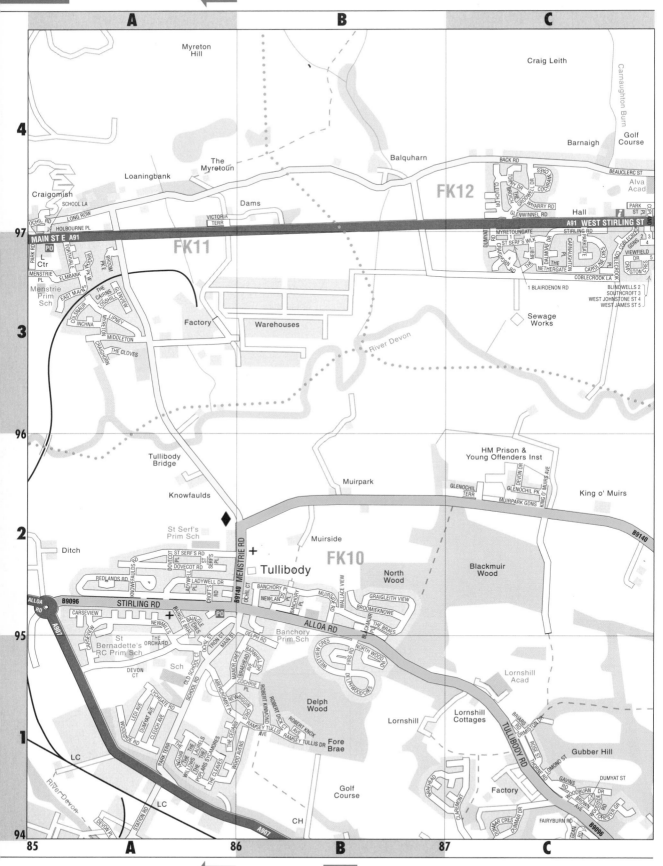

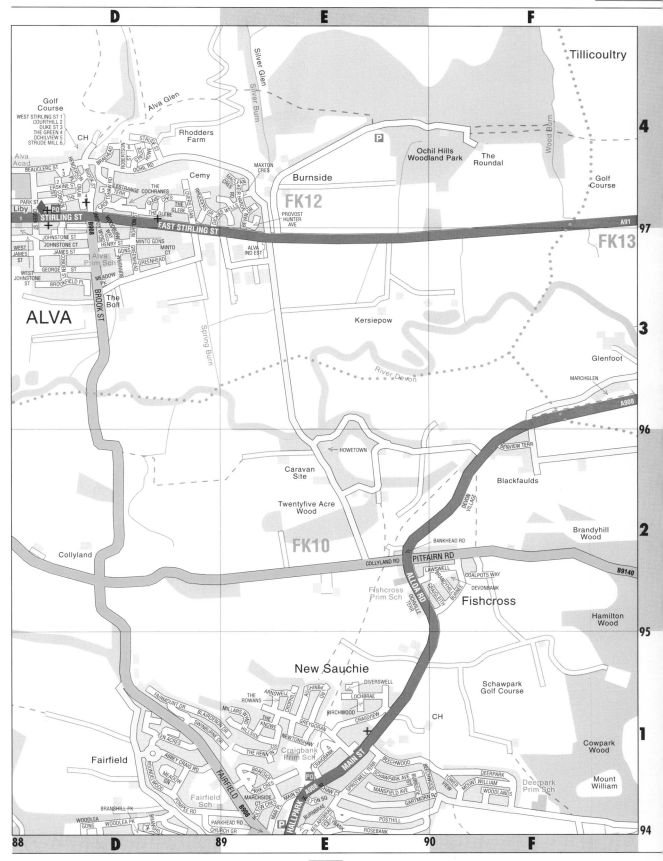

ALVA

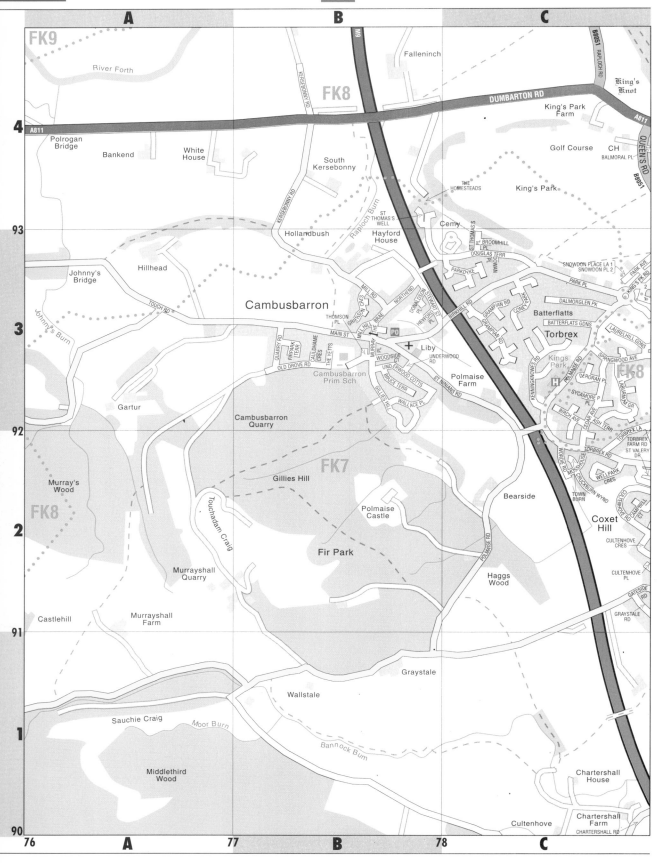

A B C

FK9

River Forth

Falleninch

KERSEBONNY RD

M9

FK8

DUMBARTON RD

King's Knot

A811

4

A811

Polrogan Bridge

Bankend

White House

South Kersebonny

King's Park Farm

Golf Course

CH

BALMORAL PL

QUEEN'S RD

B8051

RAPLOCH RD

B8051

King's Park

THE HOMESTEADS

93

Hollandbush

St Thomas's Well

Hayford House

Cemy

ST THOMAS'S

BROOMHILL PL

DOUGLAS TERR

SNOWDON PLACE LA 1
SNOWDON PL 2

PARK AVE

KING'S PK RD

Johnny's Bridge

Hillhead

TOUCH RD

Cambusbarron

Raploch Burn

Kersebonny Rd

MILL RD

NORTHEND

STEWART ST

HEYFORD PL

DONALDSON PL

BIRKHILL RD

GRAMPIAN RD

PARK DYKE

CONEY PARK

GOWAN

DALMORGLEN PK

Batterflatts

BATTERFLATS GDNS

LAURELHILL GDNS

PARK PL

Johnny's Burn

THOMSON PL

GRIERSON CRES

MILL HILL

THE BRAE

Liby

Torbrex

FK8

SPRINGWOOD AVE

3

QUARRY RD

PAPARK TERR

CAULDHAME CRES

THE YETTS

MAIN ST

MURRAY PL

WOODSIDE

PO

UNDERWOOD RD

UNDERWOOD

Kings Park

H

DEROBAN PL

PIO MAISE RD

LABURNUM GR

Gartur

OLD DROVE RD

Cambusbarron Prim Sch

UNDERWOOD COTTS

BRUCE TERR

GILLIES HILL

ST NINIANS RD

Polmaise Farm

KENNINGKNOWES RD

SYCAMORE PL

CEDAR AVE

ASH TERR

BIRCH AVE

TORBREX LA

92

Cambusbarron Quarry

WALLACE PL

TORBREX FARM RD

ST VALERY DR

TORBREX RD

WYNDFORD RD

MOSSGIEL CRES

CRAIGBURN WYND

WELLPARK CRES

Murray's Wood

FK7

Gillies Hill

Bearside

TOWN BURN

GATEHAVE CAMPBELL

Coxet Hill

CULTENHOVE CRES

FK8

2

Touchadam Craig

Polmaise Castle

POLMAISE RD

CULTENHOVE PL

Murrayshall Quarry

Fir Park

Haggs Wood

GATESIDE RD

GRAYSTALE RD

91

Castlehill

Murrayshall Farm

Graystale

1

Sauchie Craig

Moor Burn

Wallstale

Bannock Burn

Chartershall House

90

Middlethird Wood

Cultenhove

Chartershall Farm

CHARTERSHALL RD

76 A 77 B 78 C

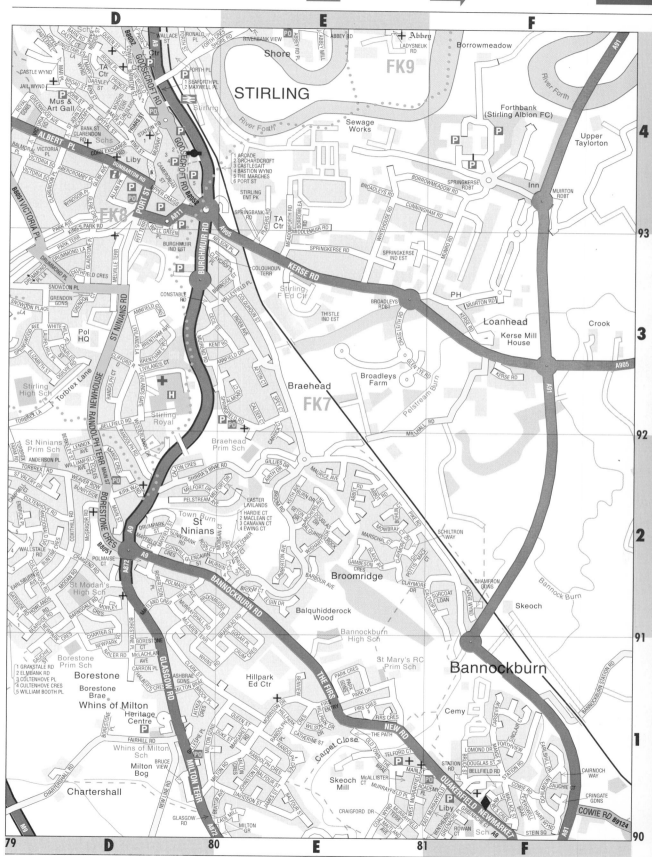

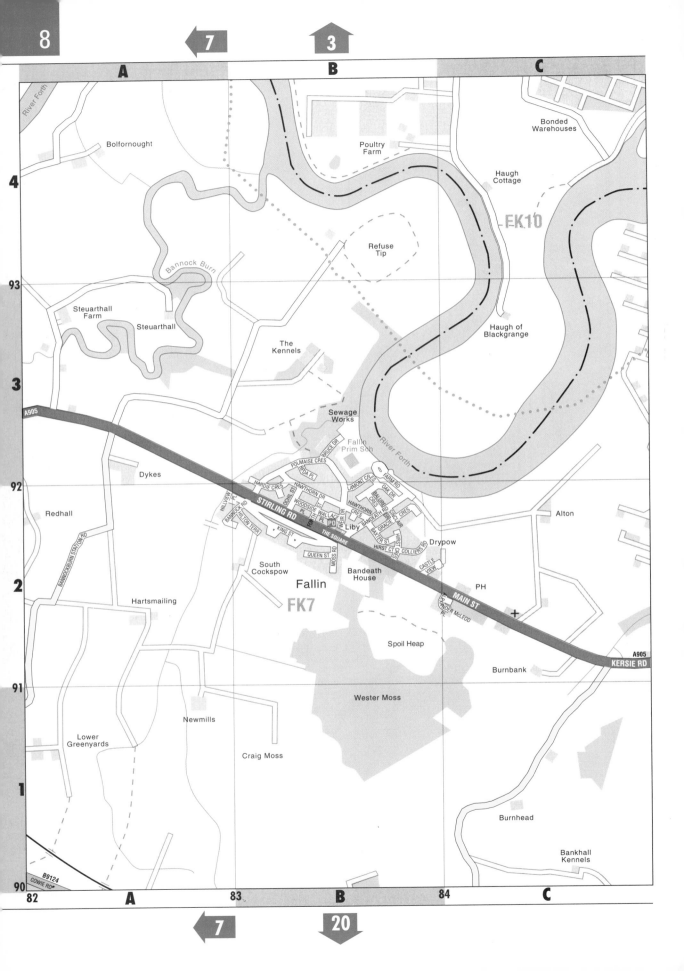

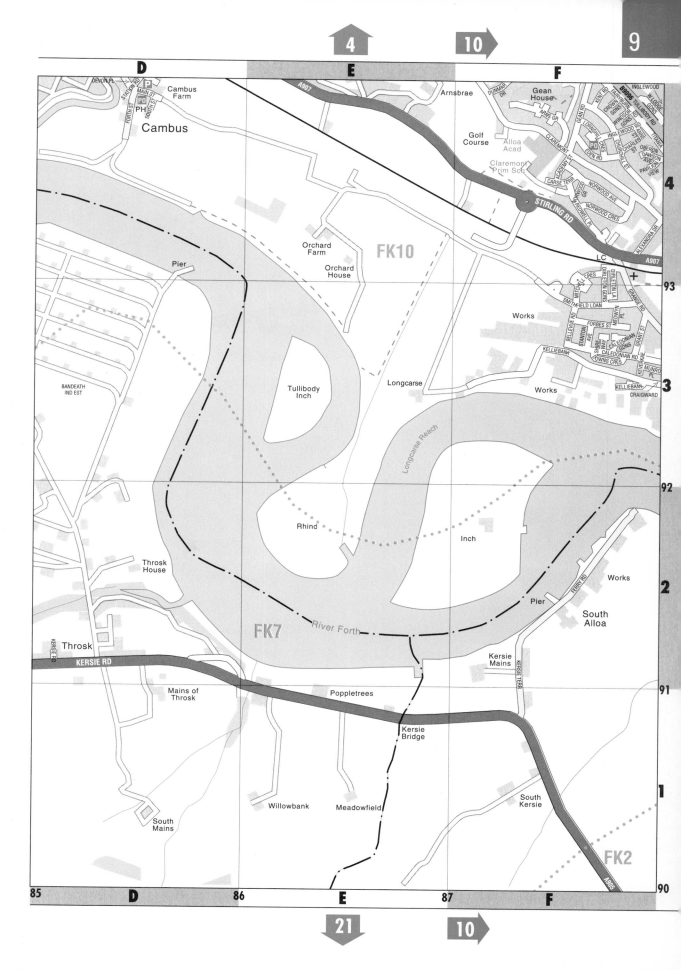

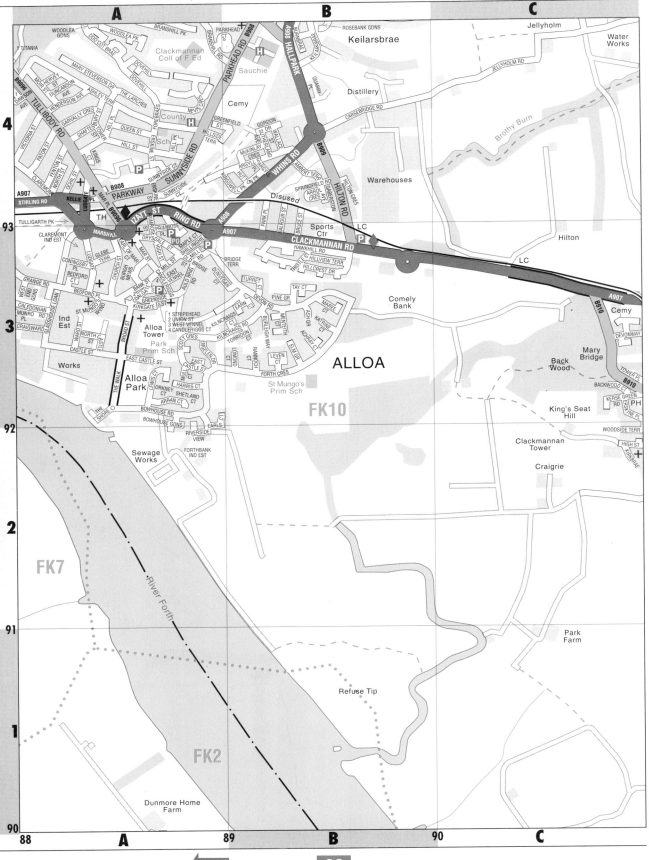

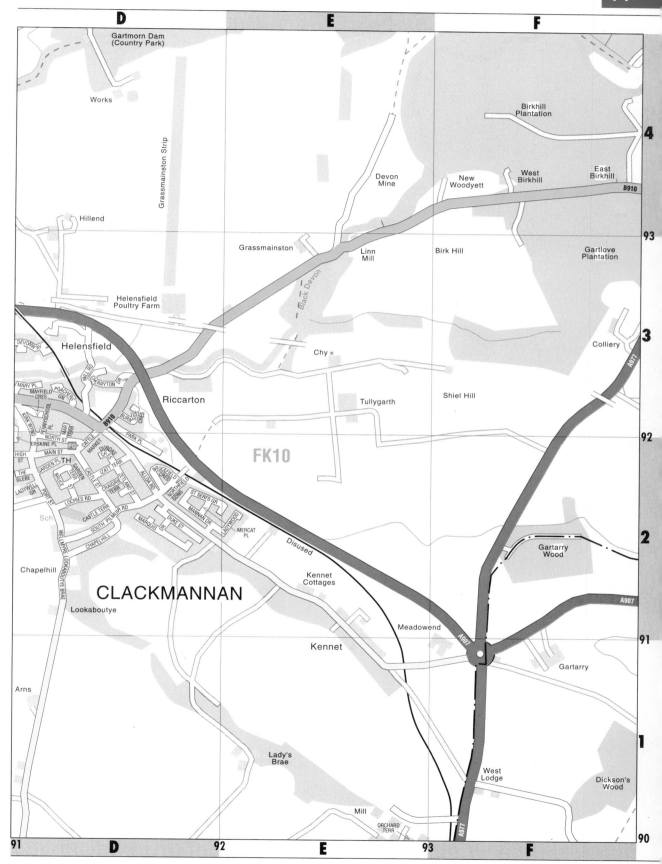

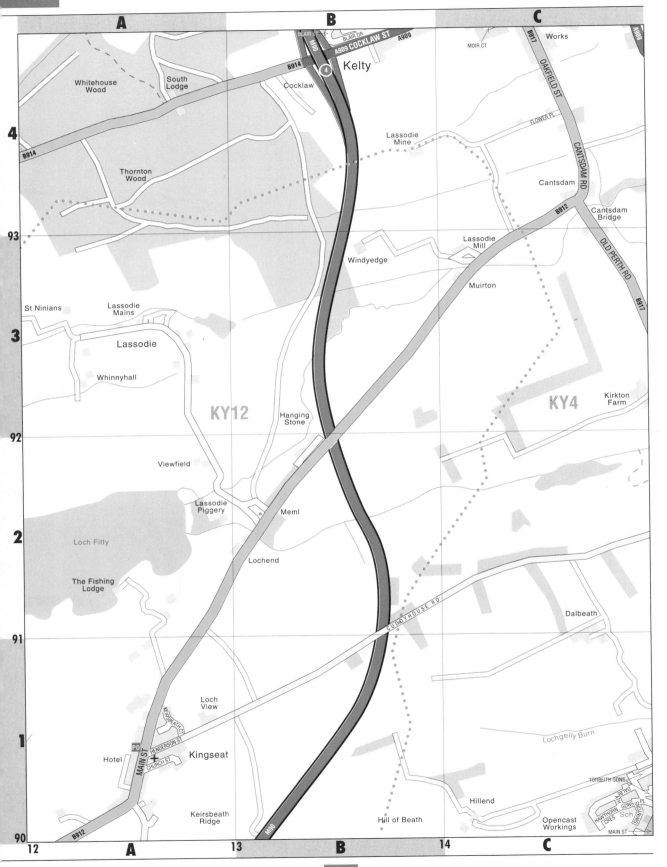

A B C

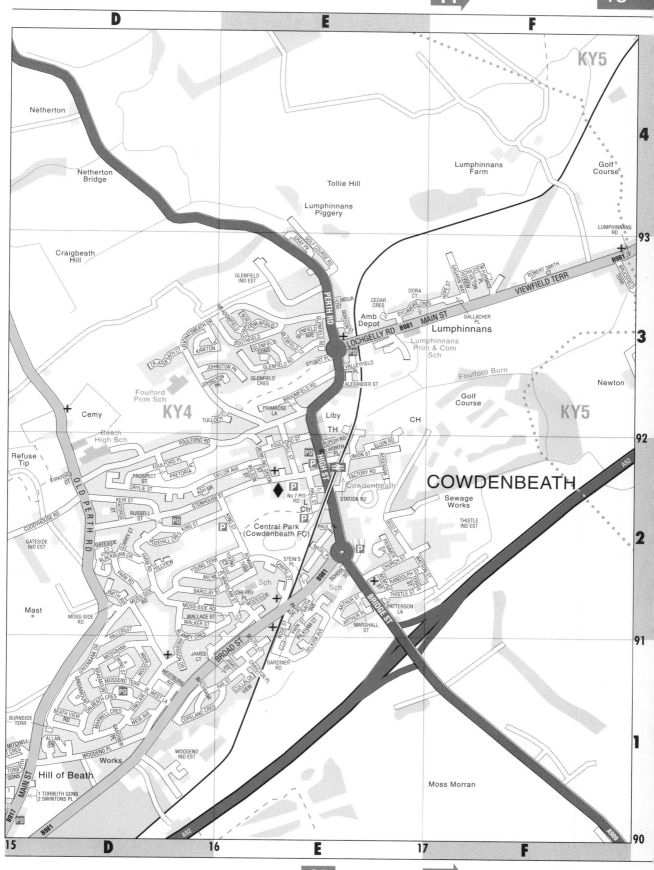

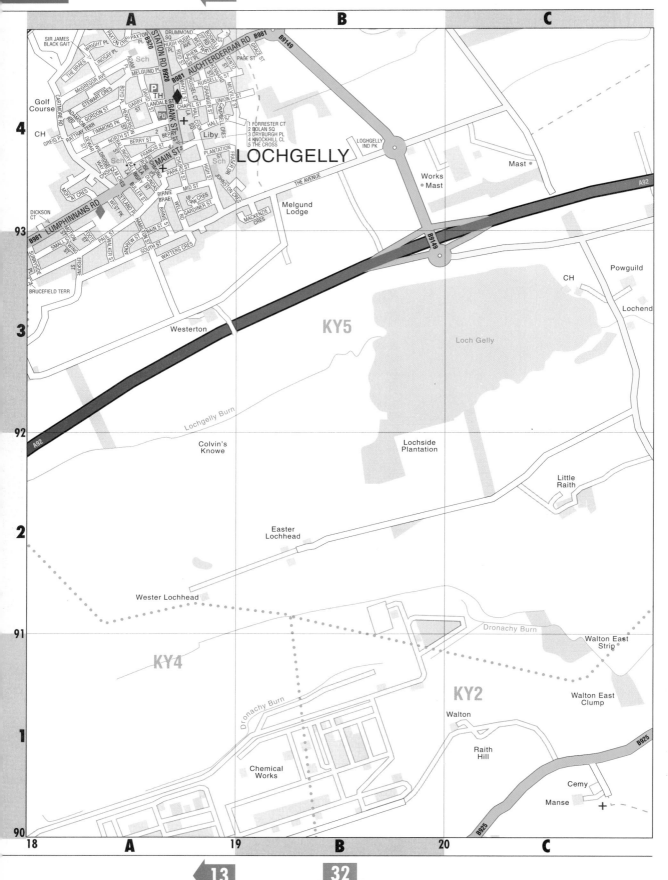

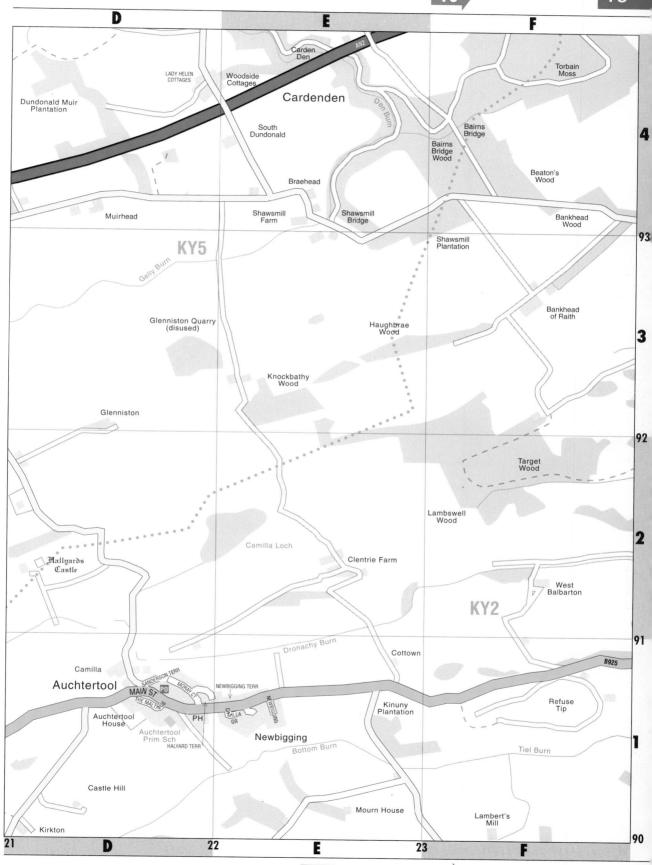

Carden Den

A92

Torbain Moss

LADY HELEN COTTAGES

Woodside Cottages

Cardenden

Dundonald Muir Plantation

Den Burn

Bairns Bridge

4

South Dundonald

Bairns Bridge Wood

Beaton's Wood

Braehead

Muirhead

Shawsmill Farm

Shawsmill Bridge

Shawsmill Bridge

Bankhead Wood

93

KY5

Gelly Burn

Shawsmill Plantation

Glenniston Quarry (disused)

Haughbrae Wood

Bankhead of Raith

3

Knockbathy Wood

Glenniston

92

Target Wood

Lambswell Wood

2

Camilla Loch

Clentrie Farm

Hallyards Castle

West Balbarton

KY2

91

Dronachy Burn

Cottown

Camilla

B925

Auchtertool

SANDERSON TERR

MORAY CT

NEWBIGGING TERR

MAIN ST

PO

THE MALTINGS

CAMILLA GR

NEWBIGGING

Kinuny Plantation

Refuse Tip

Auchtertool House

PH

Newbigging

Auchtertool Prim Sch

HALYARD TERR

Bottom Burn

Tiel Burn

1

Castle Hill

Mourn House

Lambert's Mill

Kirkton

90

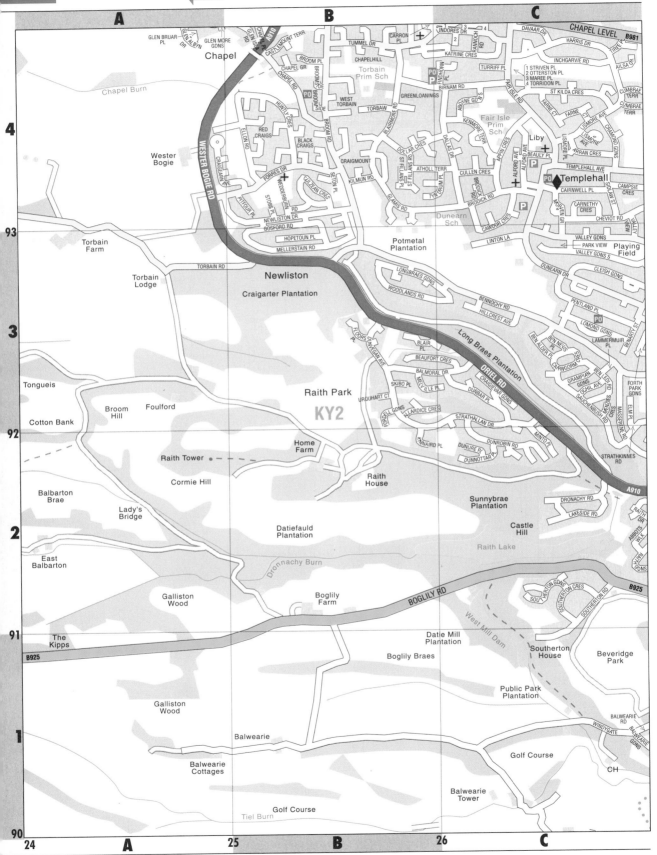

A   B   C

CHAPEL LEVEL   B981

Chapel

Chapel Burn

Wester Bogie

WESTER BOGIE RD

A810

Glen Bruar Pl   Glen More Gdns   Glen Albyn Dr

Castlemount Terr   Glen Pk Rd

Chapel Gr   Chapel Rd   Broomside   Brooms Pl   Broom Pl

West Torbain   Torbain   Torbaw

Tummel Dr   Chapelhill   Carron Pl   Findores Dr   Bannoch   Katrine Cres   Davaar Dr   Harris Pl   Inchgarvie Rd   Tiree   Ailsa Cr

Torbain Prim Sch   Greenloanings   Birnam Rd   Turriff Pl   St Kilda Cres   Cumbrae Terr   Cumbrae Terr

Huntly Cres   Red Craigs   Black Craigs   Craigmount   Elton Rd   Broom Rd   Seton Pl   Kilmun Rd

Blairmore Rd   Aboyne Gdns   Kenmore Terr   Fair Isle Prim Sch   Lismore Ave   Ormond Gdns   Liby   Arran Cres

Torres Dr   Wedderburn Rd   Culzean Cres   Pitfour Pl   Storrs Pl   Newliston Dr   Gosford Rd   Hopetoun Pl   Mellerstain Rd   Torbain Rd

St Ninians   St Fillans Rd   Atholl Terr   Cullen Cres   Dollar Cres   Dallas Dr   Glamis Rd   Tyrum Pl   Brodick Rd   Cawdor Cres   Dunearn Sch   Alford Ave   Appin Pl   Beauly Pl   Templehall Ave   Cairnwell Pl   Carnethy Cres   Campsie Cres   Cheviot Rd   Valley View

Templehall

Moven Gr   Sidlaw St

Potmetal Plantation   Linton La   Valley Gdns   Park View   Valley Gdns S   Cleish Gdns   Playing Field

Torbain Farm

Torbain Lodge

Newliston   Craigarter Plantation   Torbain Rd

Longbraes Gdns   Woodlands Rd   Bennochy Rd   Hillcrest Ave   Dunearn Dr   Pentland Pl   Lomond Gdns   Lammermuir Pl

Long Braes Plantation   Oriel Rd

Blair Pl   Beaufort Cres   Balmoral Dr   Niecy Ile Pl   Skibo Pl   Urquhart Ct   Dunvegan Ave   Floors Pl   Craigievar Gdns   Dunbar Pl   Ben Nevis   Ben Alder Pl   Cairngorm   Ben Ledi Rd   Grampian Gdns   Ochil Ave   Menzies Rd   Elm Pl   Forth Park Gdns   Beatty Pl

Raith Park   KY2   Fernie Gdns   Allardice Cres   Strathallan Dr   Dunure Pl   Dunrobin Rd   Minto Pl   Salt.Saucharnbush Rd   Masserene Rd   Strathkinnes Rd

Tongueis   Broom Hill   Foulford   Kinnaird Pl   Dunnottar Pl   A910

Cotton Bank   Home Farm

Raith Tower   Cormie Hill   Raith House   Sunnybrae Plantation   Dronachy Rd   Lakeside Rd   Raith Dr   Abbots Wlk

Balbarton Brae   Lady's Bridge   Datiefauld Plantation   Castle Hill   Raith Path Gdns

East Balbarton   Raith Lake   Dronnachy Burn

Galliston Wood   Boglily Farm   BOGLILY RD   B925   Southerton Gdns   Souherton Cres   Sou   West Mill Dam   Southerton Rd

The Kipps   B925   Datie Mill Plantation   Southerton House   Beveridge Park

Boglily Braes   Public Park Plantation   Balwearie Rd   Balwearie Gdns   Windygate

Galliston Wood   Balwearie   Golf Course   CH

Balwearie Cottages   Balwearie Tower   Golf Course   Tiel Burn

24   A   25   B   26   C   90

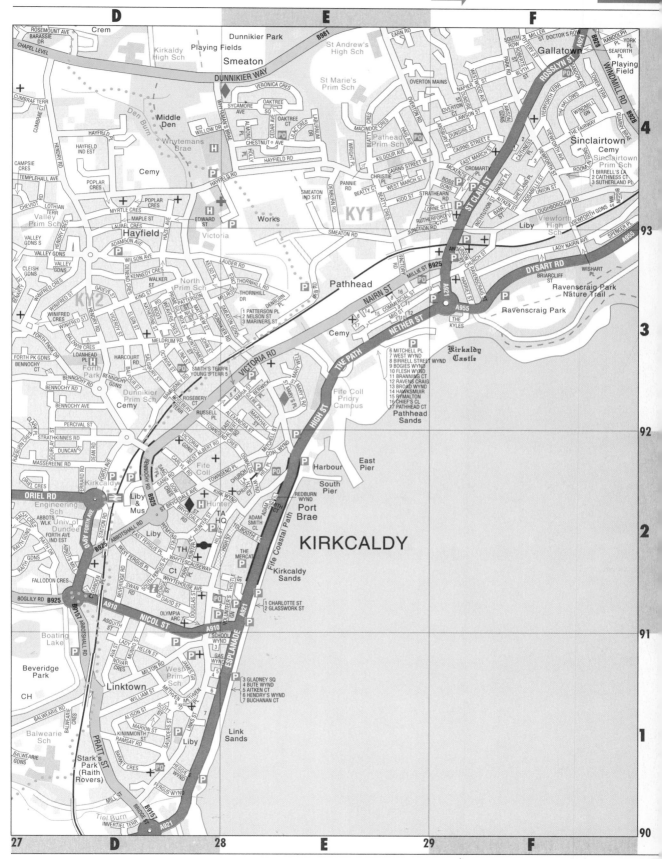

KIRKCALDY

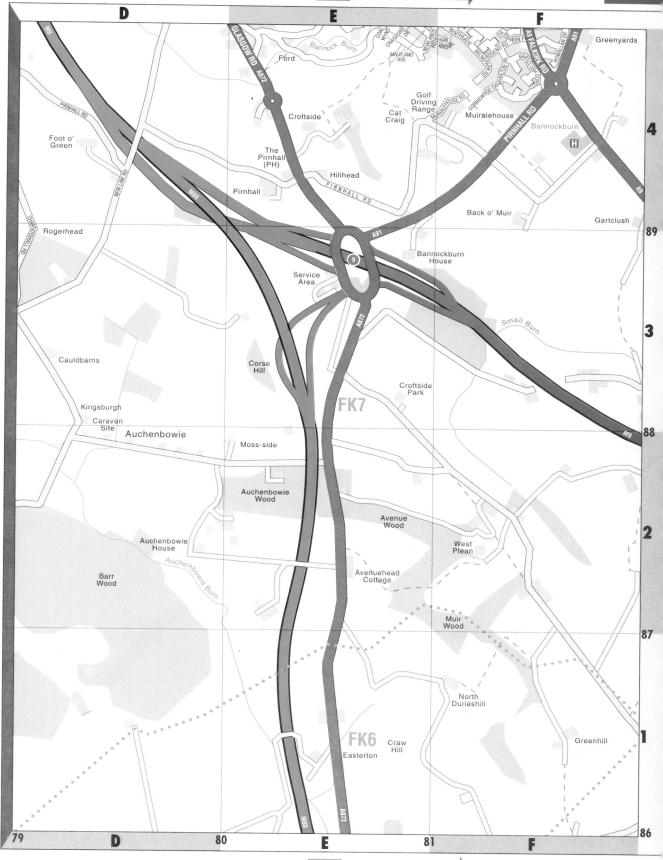

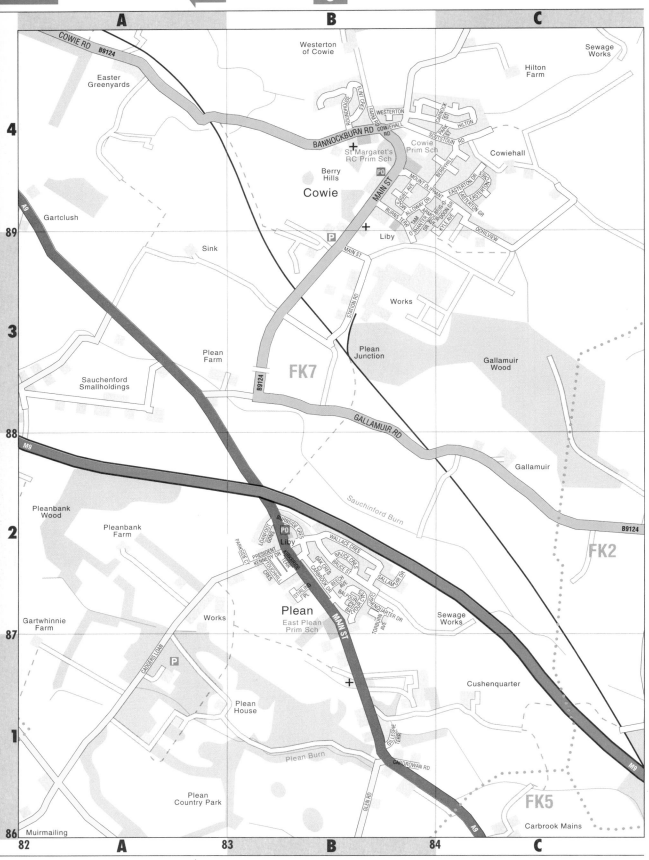

A

B

C

COWIE RD B9124

Easter
Greenyards

Westerton
of Cowie

Hilton
Farm

Sewage
Works

A9

Gartclush

BANNOCKBURN RD

COWIEHALL
RD

ROUNDHOUSE
FLINT CRES
FARM RD
WESTERTON

CARNOCK
PARK ST
HILTON

SCOTSTOUN RD

Cowie
Prim Sch

Cowiehall

St Margaret's
RC Prim Sch

Berry
Hills

PO

MAIN ST

MOUNT OLIPHANT

BERRYHILL

EASTERTON DR
EASTERTON GR
EASTERTON

SELGIE AVE
LYON
ALLOWAY DR
FAM
ARMOUR
BIGG-O
O SHANTER
ADAM
DR
KYLE AVE

Cowie

4

Liby

OCHILVIEW

89

Sink

MAIN ST

P

STATION RD

Works

3

Plean
Farm

B9124

Plean
Junction

Plean
Junction

FK7

Gallamuir
Wood

Sauchenford
Smallholdings

GALLAMUIR RD

88

M9

Gallamuir

B9124

Pleanbank
Wood

Sauchinford Burn

FK2

Pleanbank
Farm

BURNSIDE CRES

PO
Liby

WALLACE CRES

2

LOANFOOT
GDNS
PARKSIDE CT
PRESIDENT
KENNEDY DR
CHURCHILL
CRES

DUMBRIDGE
TERR
CARBROOK DR
OAK CRES
BEECH
AVE
BALFOUR
CT
BALFOUR
AVE

BAUCE ST
BRUCE ST
GALLAM'R DR
CUSHENQUARTER DR
TORBURN
AVE

Gartwhinnie
Farm

Works

STIRLING
PL

Plean

East Plean
Prim Sch

Sewage
Works

87

P

CADGERS LOAN

Cushenquarter

MAIN ST

Plean
House

GILLESPIE
TERR

1

A9

GLEN RD

CARDROWAN RD

M9

Plean
Country Park

Plean Burn

FK5

86

Muirmailing

Carbrook Mains

82

A

83

B

84

C

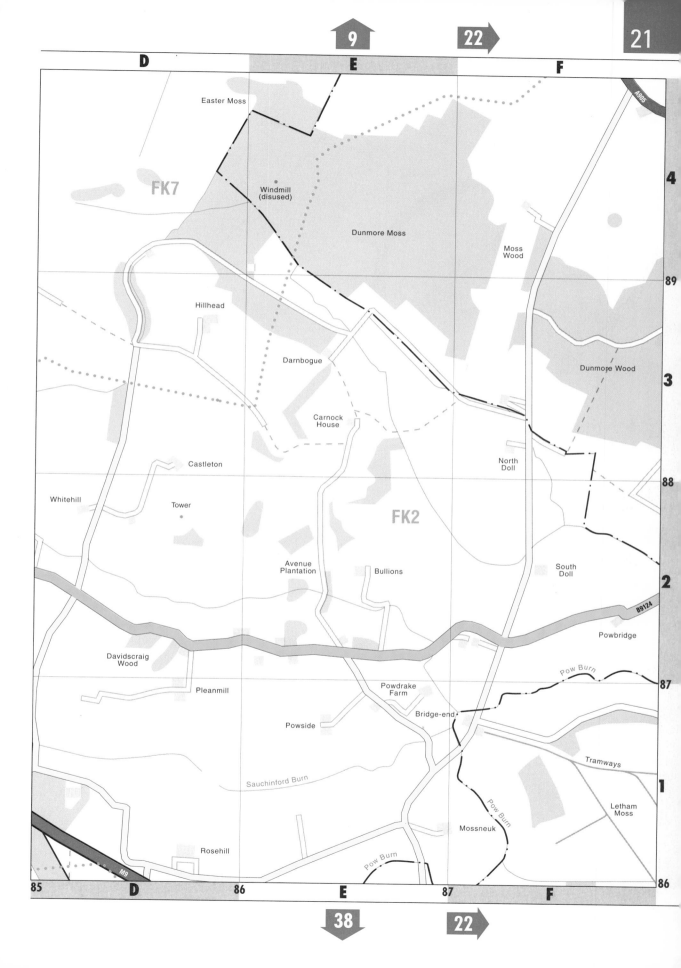

D
E
F

A905

FK7

Easter Moss

Windmill
(disused)

Dunmore Moss

Moss
Wood

4

89

Hillhead

Darnbogue

Dunmore Wood

3

Carnock
House

Castleton

North
Doll

88

Whitehill

Tower

FK2

Avenue
Plantation

Bullions

South
Doll

2

Powbridge

B9124

Davidscraig
Wood

Pow Burn

Pleanmill

87

Powdrake
Farm

Powside

Bridge-end

Tramways

Sauchinford Burn

1

Pow Burn

Letham
Moss

Mossneuk

M9

Rosehill

Pow Burn

86

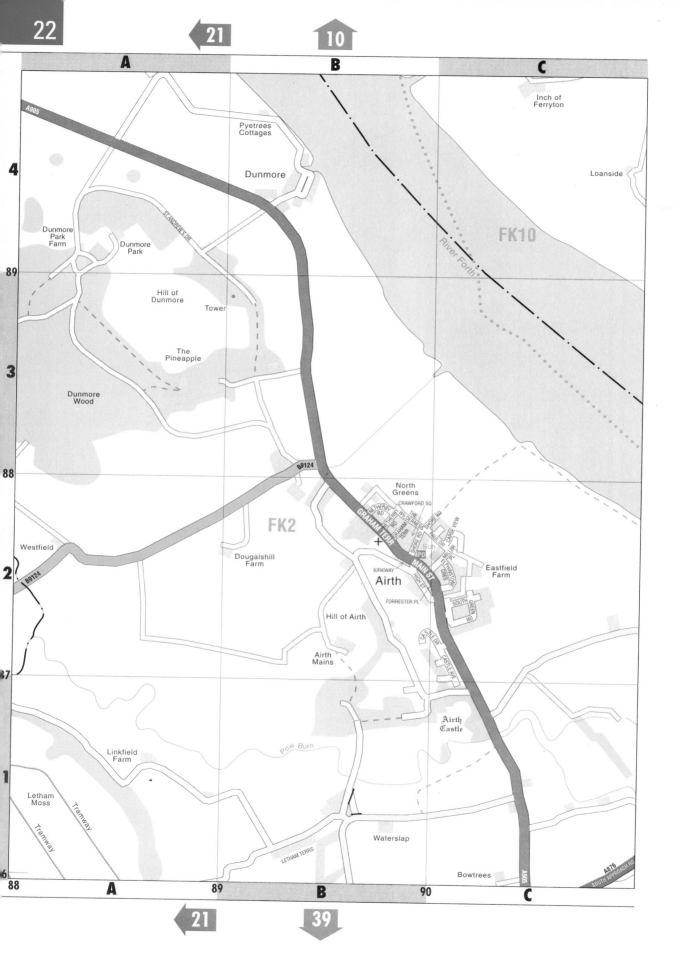

A B C

4

89

3

88

2

87

1

6

88 A 89 B 90 C

A905

Pyetrees
Cottages

Dunmore

ST ANDREWS DR

Inch of
Ferryton

Loanside

FK10

River Forth

Dunmore
Park
Farm

Dunmore
Park

Hill of
Dunmore

Tower

The Pineapple

Dunmore
Wood

B9124

North
Greens

CRAWFORD SQ

NETHERBY RD
NETHERBY RD
THE WILDERNESS
SHORE RD
SHORE Rd
PAUL DR
CARSE VIEW

FK2

Westfield

B9124

Dougalshill
Farm

GRAHAM TERR
GRAHAM TERR

Sch

PO

MAIN ST

Airth

KIRKWAY

HIGH ST

FORRESTER PL

ELPHINSTONE CRES

MILL RD
MILL PL

Eastfield
Farm

SOUTH GREEN DR

Hill of Airth

Airth
Mains

CASTLE DR

CASTLE AVE

Airth
Castle

Pow Burn

Linkfield
Farm

Letham
Moss

Tramway

Tramway

Tramway

Waterslap

LETHAM TERRS

Bowtrees

A905

A876
SOUTH APPROACH RD

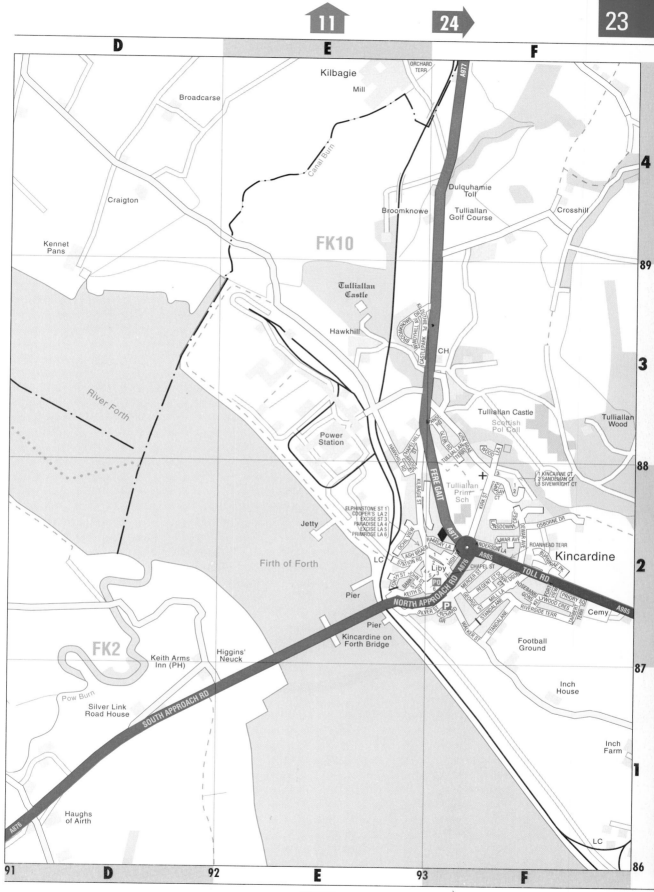

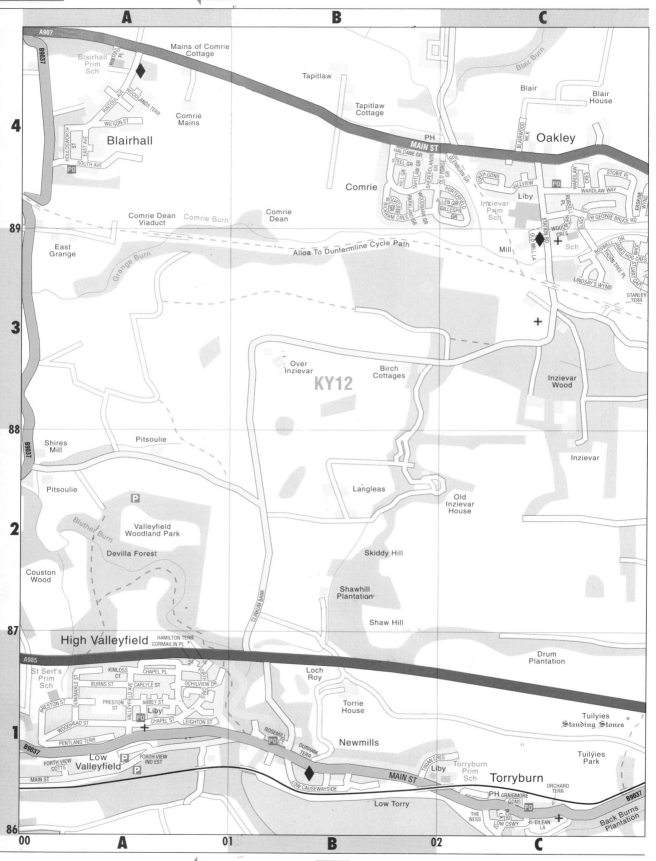

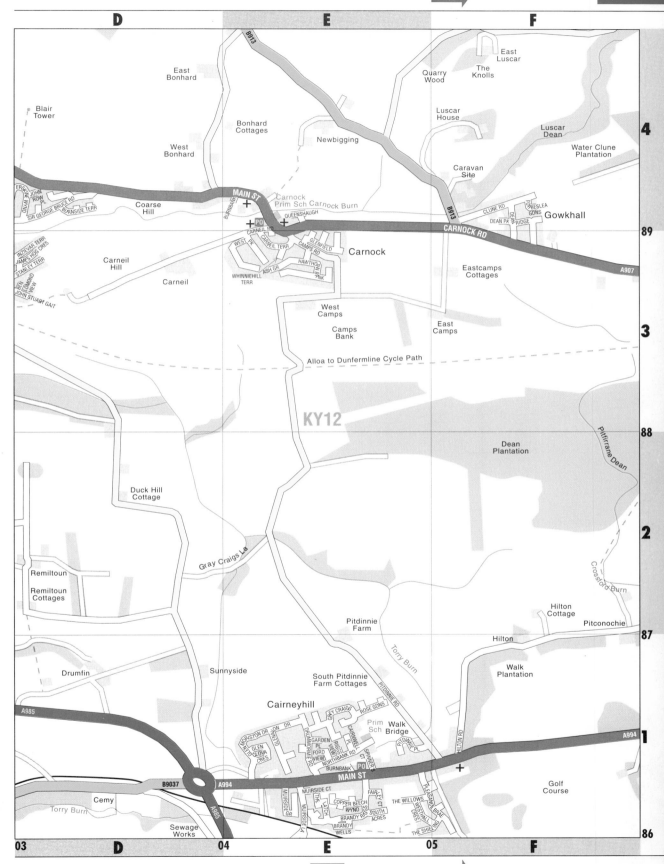

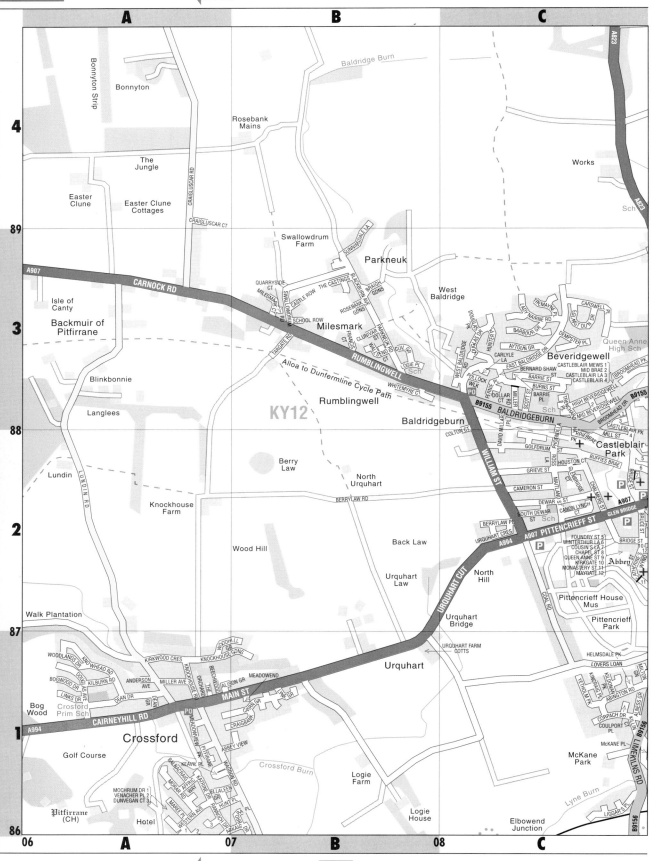

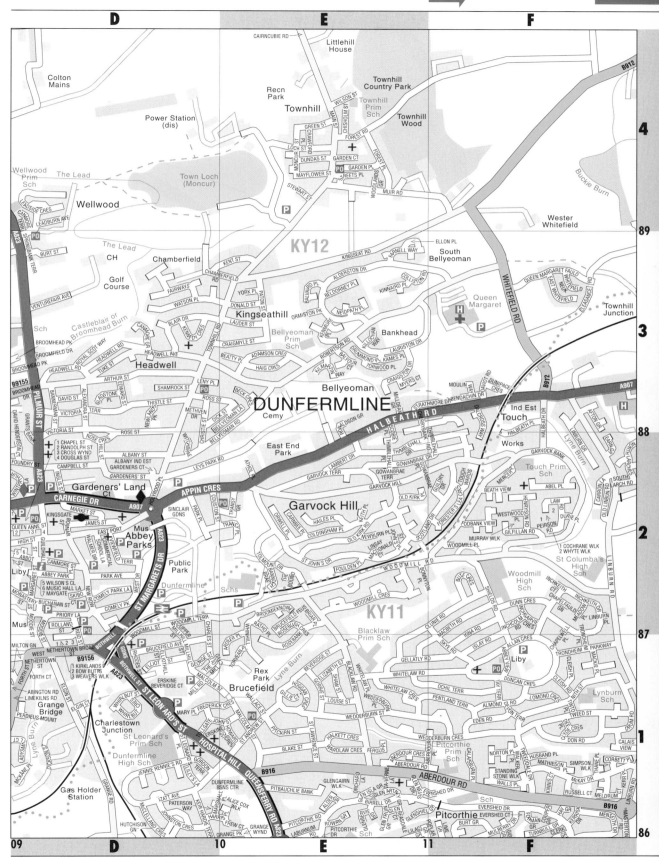

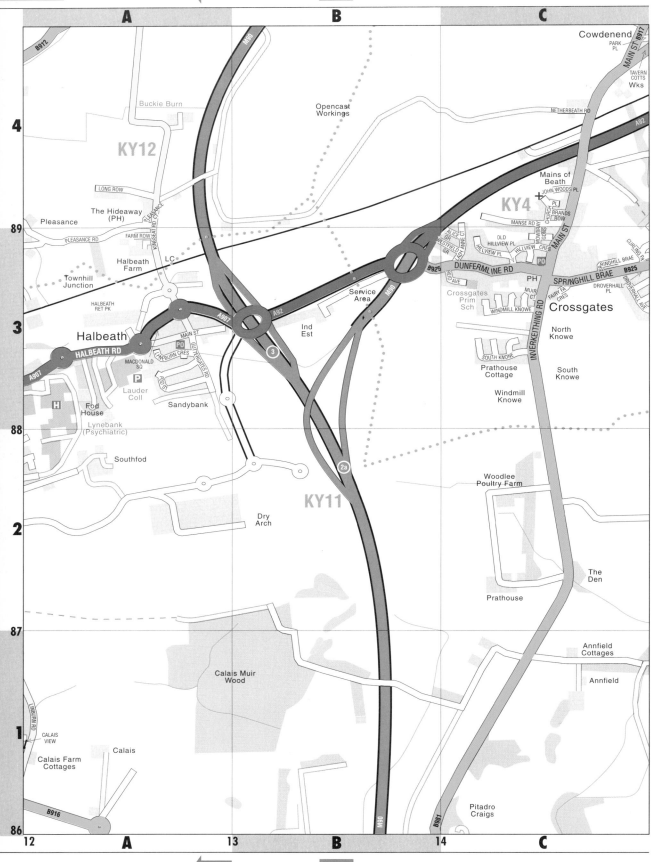

29
12

A   B   C

B972

Cowdenend

PARK PL

MAIN ST B917

TAVERN COTTS Wks

Buckie Burn

Opencast Workings

NETHERBEATH RD

A92

4

M90

KY12

LONG ROW

Mains of Beath

JOHN WOODS PL

KY4

CHURCH PL

BRANDS BOW

The Hideaway (PH)

PLEASANCE RD CHANGE

MANSE RD

MOWBRAY GDNS

89

Pleasance

FARM ROW

KINGSEAT RD

ALICE GR

LADY ANNE CT

OLD HILLVIEW PL

HILLVIEW CRES

MAIN ST

CURLING PK

PLEASANCE RD

WESTFIELD GR

HILLVIEW PL

PO

RINGHILL BRAE

B925

Halbeath Farm

LC

DUNFERMLINE RD

B925

SPRINGHILL BRAE

DROVERHALL PL

DROVERHALL AVE

Townhill Junction

HALBEATH RET PK

A907

Service Area

RED AVE

PH

FAIRY FA CRES

Crossgates

3

Halbeath

A92

Ind Est

Crossgates Prim Sch

MUIR CT

INVERKEITHING RD

North Knowe

HALBEATH RD

MAIN ST

3

WINDMILL KNOWE

A907

LYNEBURN CRES

MACDONALD SQ

GUTTERGATES RD

PO

SOUTH KNOWE

Prathouse Cottage

South Knowe

P

Sandybank

Lauder Coll

Windmill Knowe

Fod House

H

Lynebank (Psychiatric)

88

Southfod

Woodlee Poultry Farm

KY11

Dry Arch

The Den

2

Prathouse

87

Annfield Cottages

Calais Muir Wood

Annfield

LINBURN RD

1

CALAIS VIEW

Calais

Calais Farm Cottages

M90

B981

Pitadro Craigs

86

B916

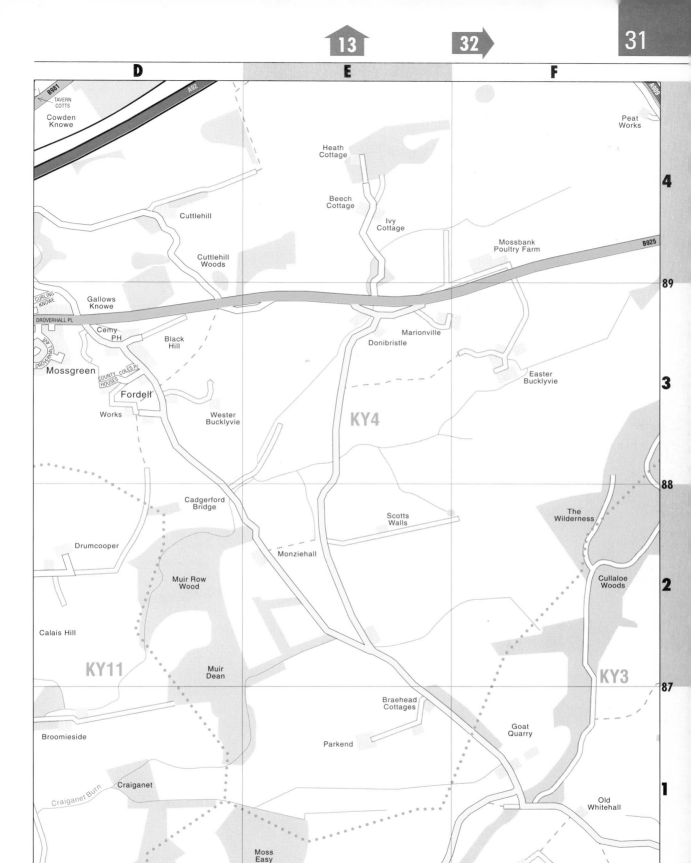

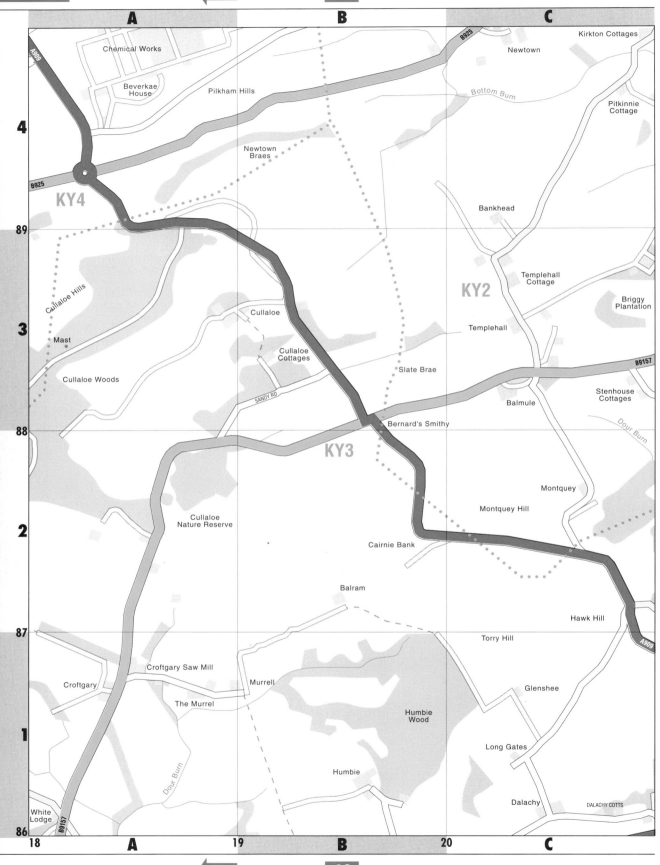

A

B

C

Chemical Works

Beverkae House

Pilkham Hills

B925

Kirkton Cottages

Newtown

Bottom Burn

Pitkinnie Cottage

4

Newtown Braes

A909

B925

KY4

89

Bankhead

Cullaloe Hills

Templehall Cottage

KY2

Briggy Plantation

3

Cullaloe

Mast

Cullaloe Cottages

Templehall

B9157

Cullaloe Woods

SANDY RD

Slate Brae

Balmule

Stenhouse Cottages

Dour Burn

88

Bernard's Smithy

KY3

Montquey

Montquey Hill

Montquey

2

Cairnie Bank

Cullaloe Nature Reserve

Hawk Hill

87

Balram

Torry Hill

A909

Croftgary Saw Mill

Murrell

Glenshee

Croftgary

The Murrel

Humbie Wood

1

Long Gates

Dour Burn

Humbie

Dalachy

DALACHY COTTS

White Lodge

B9157

86

18

A

19

B

20

C

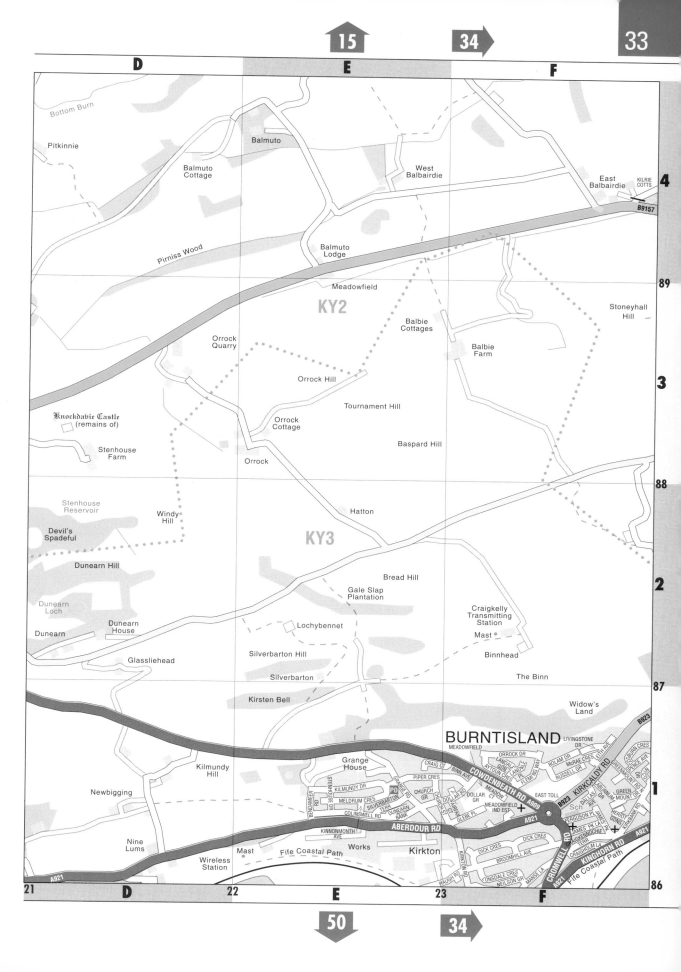

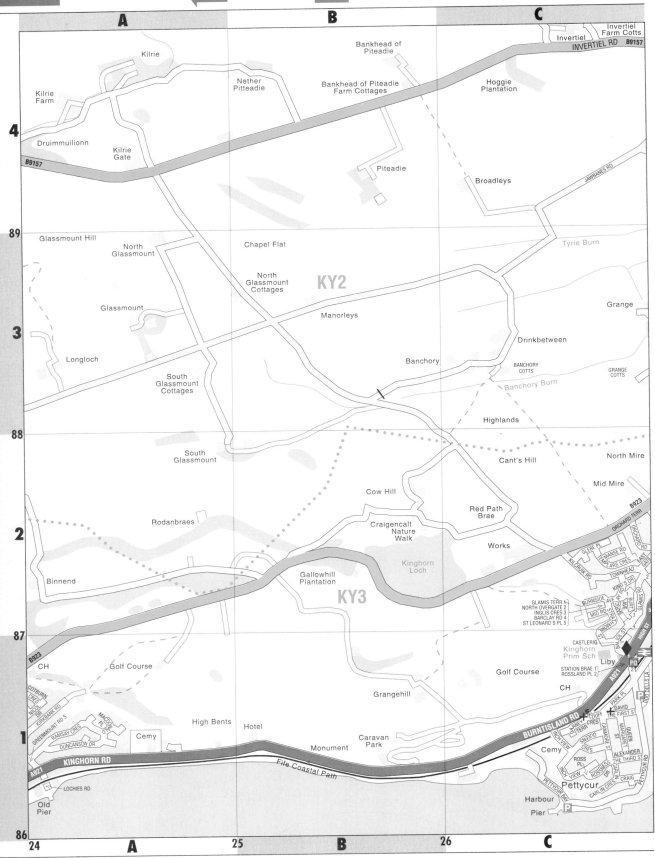

A B C

4

89

3

88

2

87

1

86

24 A 25 B 26 C

Invertiel
Farm Cotts
Invertiel
INVERTIEL RD B9157

Kilrie

Kilrie
Farm

Druimmuilionn

Kilrie
Gate

Nether
Pitteadie

Bankhead of
Piteadie

Bankhead of Piteadie
Farm Cottages

Piteadie

Hoggie
Plantation

Broadleys

B9157

Glassmount Hill

North
Glassmount

Chapel Flat

Tyrie Burn

North
Glassmount
Cottages

KY2

Grange

Glassmount

Manorleys

Drinkbetween

Longloch

Banchory

BANCHORY
COTTS

GRANGE
COTTS

South
Glassmount
Cottages

Banchory Burn

Highlands

South
Glassmount

Cant's Hill

North Mire

Mid Mire

Rodanbraes

Cow Hill

Craigencalt Nature
Walk

Red Path
Brae

Works

B923

ORCHARD TERR

GLEBE PL

Binnend

Gallowhill
Plantation

KY3

Kinghorn
Loch

KILCRUIK RD

TEMPLARS CRES

MANSE RD

ORCHARD
RD

TOWNHEAD
KING'S DR

GLAMIS TERR 1
NORTH OVERGATE 2
INGLIS CRES 3
BARCLAY RD 4
ST LEONARD'S PL 5

BURNSIDE
AVE

MID RD

KING
RD

GLAMIS RD
HIGH ST

87

B923

CH

Golf Course

CASTLERIG
Kinghorn
Prim Sch

Liby

STATION BRAE 1
ROSSLAND PL 2

CH

Golf Course

DAVID
THE FIRST ST

PARK PL

LOW DELL'S LA

BURNTISLAND RD

A921

COTBURN
CRES

NICOL
DR

KIRKBANK RD

GREENMOUNT RD S

MACDONALD DR

RAMSAY CRES

DUNCANSON DR

Cemy

High Bents

Hotel

Monument

Caravan
Park

Grangehill

COUFF

ARNEY
TERR CRES

QUEEN'S
CRES

INCH VIEW

CANMORE ST

MARGARET
ST

ALEXANDER
ST

QUEEN
ST

THE THIRD ST

PETTYCUR RD

KINGHORN RD

A921

LOCHIES RD

Old
Pier

Fife Coastal Path

Cemy

ROSS
PL

INCH
VIEW

ROSSNESS
DR

CARLIN CRES

CARLIN
CRAIG

PETTYCUR BAY

Pettycur

Harbour
Pier

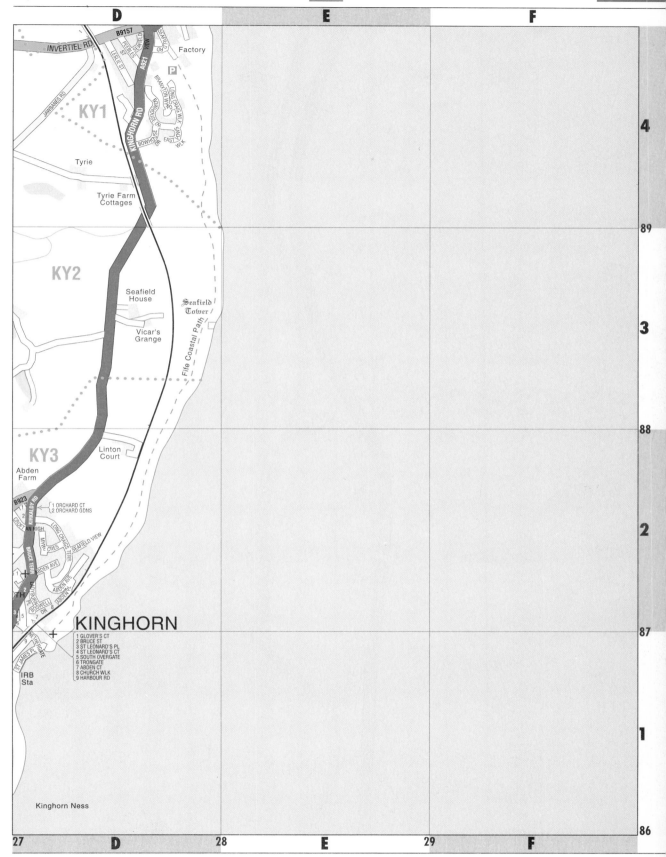

INVERTIEL RD
B9157
Factory
P
KY1
Tyrie
Tyrie Farm
Cottages
KY2
Seafield
House
Seafield
Tower
Vicar's
Grange
Fife Coastal Path
KY3
Linton
Court
Abden
Farm
B923
1 ORCHARD CT
2 ORCHARD GDNS
SEAFIELD VIEW
LONG CRAIGS TERR
MYRE CRES.
ABDEN AVE
KINGHORN

1 GLOVER'S CT
2 BRUCE ST
3 ST LEONARD'S PL
4 ST LEONARD'S CT
5 SOUTH OVERGATE
6 TRONGATE
7 ABDEN CT
8 CHURCH WLK
9 HARBOUR RD

IRB
Sta

Kinghorn Ness

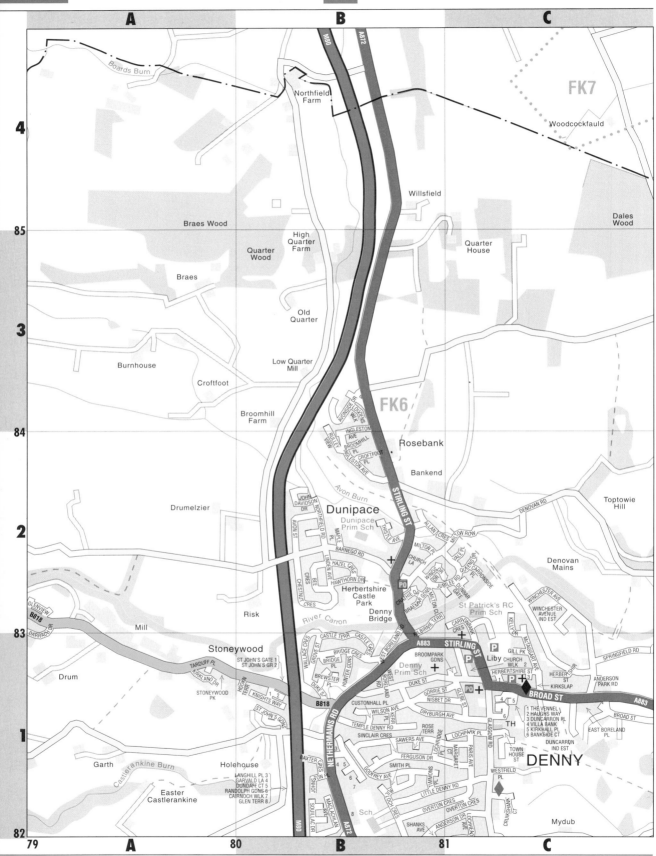

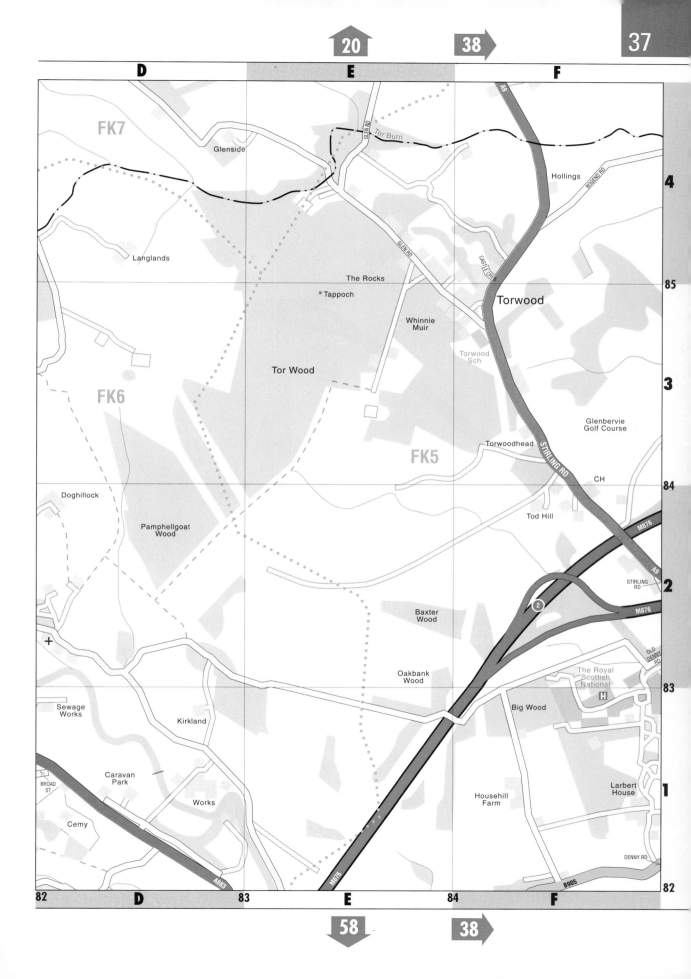

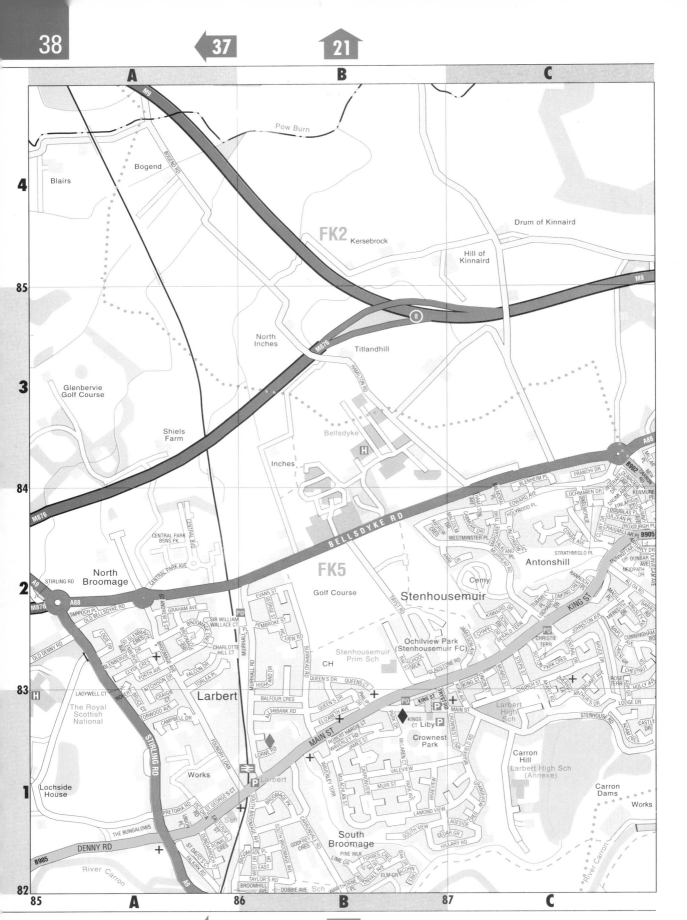

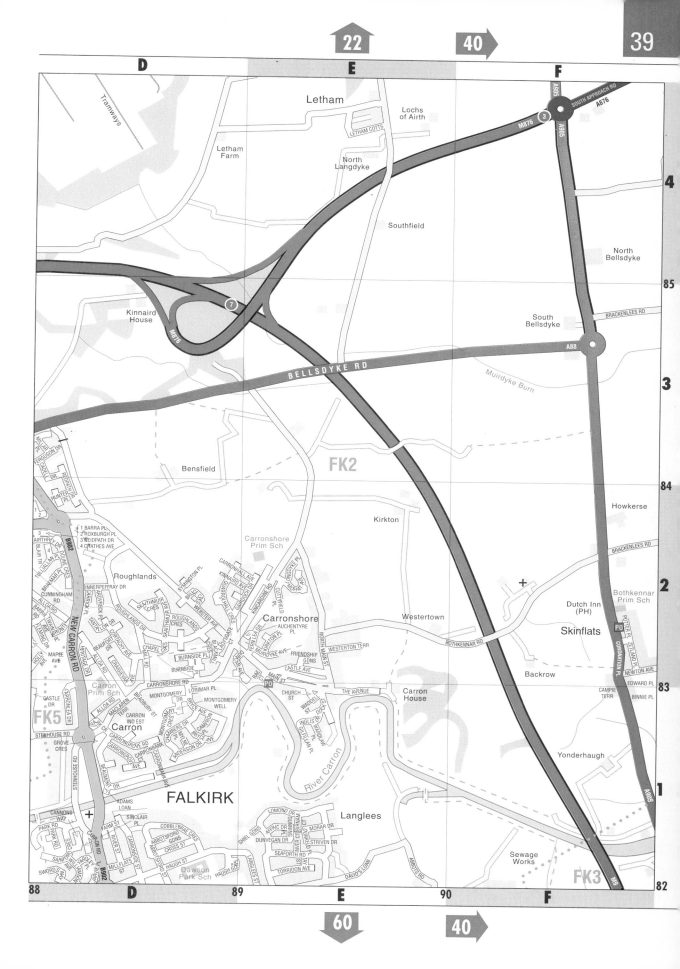

A   B   C

FK10

Greendyke

Powfoulis
Manor Hotel

4

Mains of
Powfoulis

Pocknave

Brackenlees

85

Hardlands

Stonehouse
Farm

Firth of Forth

3

FK2

BRACKENLEES RD

Orchardhead

84

Newton Mains
Farm

2

Skinflats

NEWTON AVE

NEWTON RD

83

Grangemouth Harbour
& Docks

NORTH SHORE RD

Western Channel

Carron Dock

CENTRAL DOCK RD

River Carron

1

LC

MIDDLE ST LA

NORTH ST

SOUTH BRIDGE ST

GRANGE LA

SOUTH ST

FK3

Glensburgh

WEST CHURCH LA

DALGRAIN RD

1 YORK LA
2 YORK SQ
3 YORK ARC
4 LA PORTE PREC
5 LIBRARY LA
6 CHARING CROSS

1 BELL CT
2 TAYLOR CT
3 NELSON GDNS

LC's

A905

GLENSBURGH RD

DEVON ST

BANK ST

CLYDE ST

AVON ST

DON ST

TWEED ST

KELVIN ST

TAY ST

STATION RD

EARL'S RD

A904

UNION RD

DOCK RD

BO'NESS RD

A904

TH

PO

Liby

ALLAN CT

WHITESMITH ST

PARK ST

NELSON ST

GRANGEBURN RD

GEORGE

ALBERT

KINGS ST

SOUTH SHORE RD

BOWDYKE RD

AVE

82

91   A   92   B   93   C

D E F

Blair
Castle

FK10

KY12

4

LC's

Longannet
Point

Power Station

Chy

85

Jetty

3

Firth of Forth

84

Breakwater

2

Eastern Channel

83

NORTH SHORE RD

FK3

SOUTH SHORE RD

Grange
Dock

CENTRAL DOCK RD

LC

1

LC

Grange Burn

BEACH RD

Oil Refinery

7TH ST

8TH ST

CANDIE RD

MAIN RD

BATTERY RD

9TH ST

TARGET RD

OLD REFINERY
RD

82

94 D 95 E 96 F

KY12

Mus

Dunimarle Castle

BALGOWNIE W

Sch

Palace Mus

BACK CSWY

LOW CAUSEWAYSIDE

LC

Sch

P

PH

PO

Blairburn

CULROSS

1 TANHOUSE BRAE
2 MID CSWY
3 LITTLE CSWY
4 LITTLE SANDHAVEN
5 BACK ST

Firth of Forth

1 TANHOUSE BRAE
2 MID CSWY
3 LITTLE CSWY
4 LITTLE SANDHAVEN
5 BACK ST

West Pier

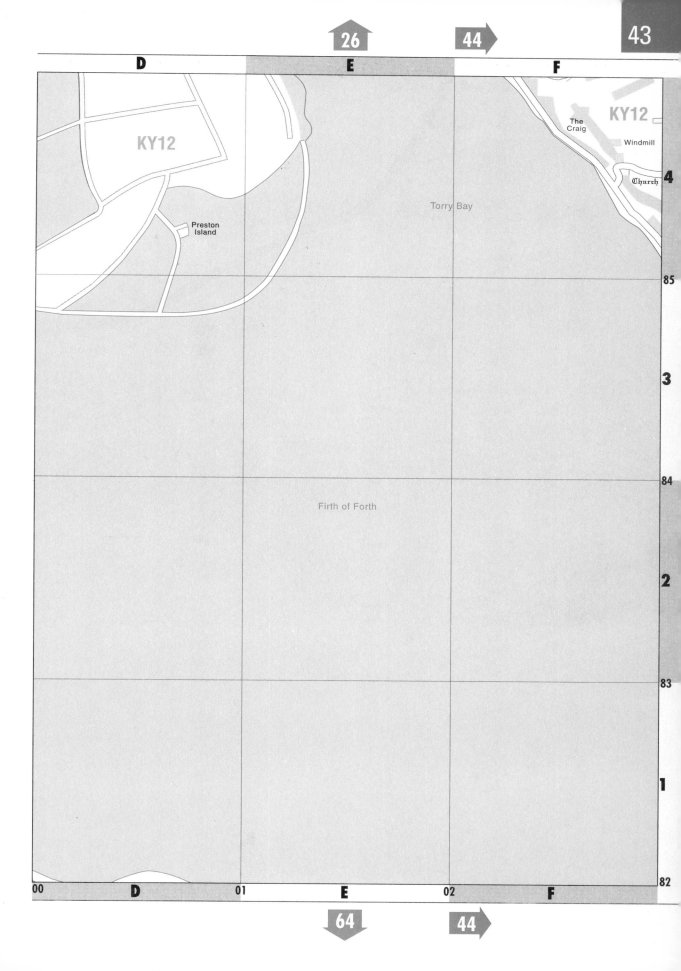

D E F

KY12

KY12

The
Craig

Windmill

4

Church

Preston
Island

Torry Bay

85

3

84

Firth of Forth

2

83

1

82

00 D 01 E 02 F

A   B   C

Muirside
Cottage
MUIRSIDE LA
Muirside

Mire
End

KY11

A985

Bankhead

4

CRAIGWELL PATH

Crombie

Crombie
Prim Sch

MAIN RD

Shoreside

Bullions Farm
Cottages

CENTRAL RD

FARM RD

ORDNANCE RD

LITTLE FD

WORN

85

Stripeside

Bullions

Crombie
Farm

PO

Waukmill
Cottages

Kiln
Hill

Crombie
Point

A985

Crombie
Pier

3

CAMP RD

Waukmill

KY12

Kinniny Braes

KY11

Ironmill
Bay

84

Crombie
Pier

2

Jetty

Firth of Forth

83

1

82

03   04   05

A   B   C

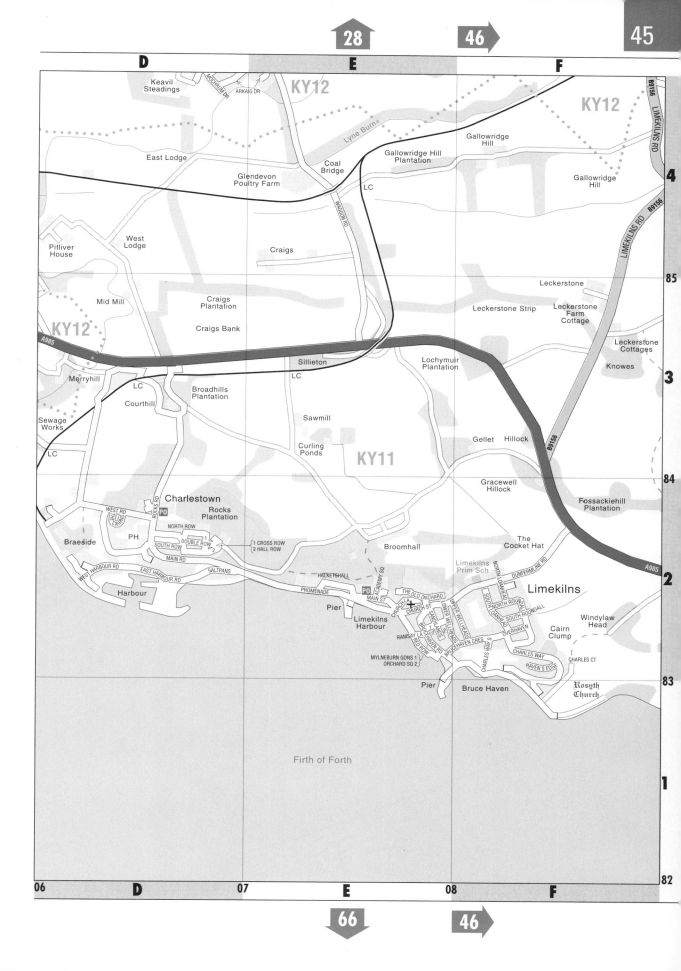

D
E
F

KY12

B9156

Keavil
Steadings

MOCHRUM DR

ARKAIG DR

KY12

Lyne Burn

Gallowridge
Hill

East Lodge

Coal
Bridge

Gallowridge Hill
Plantation

LC

Gallowridge
Hill

4

LIMEKILNS RD

B9156

Glendevon
Poultry Farm

WAGGON RD

Pitliver
House

West
Lodge

Craigs

LIMEKILNS RD

B9156

Leckerstone

85

Mid Mill

Craigs
Plantation

Leckerstone Strip

Leckerstone
Farm
Cottage

KY12

A985

Craigs Bank

Sillieton

Lochymuir
Plantation

Leckerstone
Cottages

Knowes

LC

Merryhill

LC

Broadhills
Plantation

LC

Sawmill

KY11

Gellet

Hillock

B9156

3

Courthill

Curling
Ponds

84

Sewage
Works

Gracewell
Hillock

Fossackiehill
Plantation

LC

Charlestown

Rocks
Plantation

PO

ROCKS RD

WEST RD

The
Cocket Hat

A985

Braeside

PH

NORTH ROW

1
DOUBLE ROW

2

1 CROSS ROW
2 HALL ROW

Broomhall

Limekilns
Prim Sch

NORTH LOANHEAD

DUNFERMLINE RD

Limekilns

2

SOUTH ROW

SOUTH ROUNDALL

SOUTH LOANHEAD

NORTH ROW

MAIN RD

Windylaw
Head

WEST HARBOUR RD

EAST HARBOUR RD

SALTPANS

HALKETSHALL

ACADEMY SQ

PROMENADE

PO

MAIN ST

THE OLD ORCHARD

UPPER WELLHEADS

Cairn
Clump

CHARLES CT

Harbour

Pier

Limekilns
Harbour

CHURCH LA

CHURCH ST

SANDLANDS

LOWER WELLHEADS

OVERHAVEN

CHARLES WAY S

CHARLES WAY

HAVEN'S EDGE

RAMSAY LA

RED ROW

BRUCEHAVEN RD

BRUCEHAVEN CRES

MYLNEBURN GDNS 1
ORCHARD SQ 2

Pier

Bruce Haven

Rosyth
Church

83

Firth of Forth

1

82

06
D
07
E
08
F

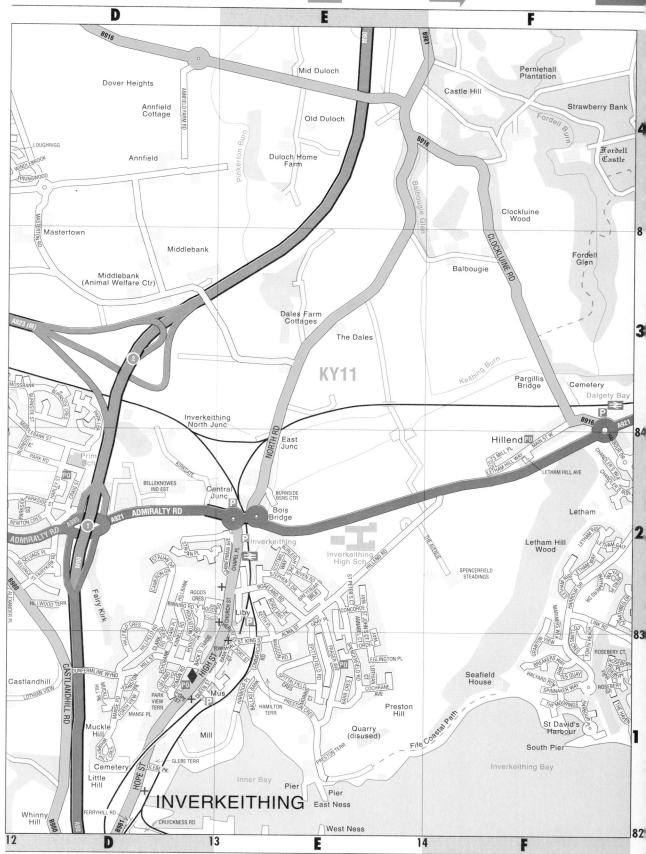

INVERKEITHING

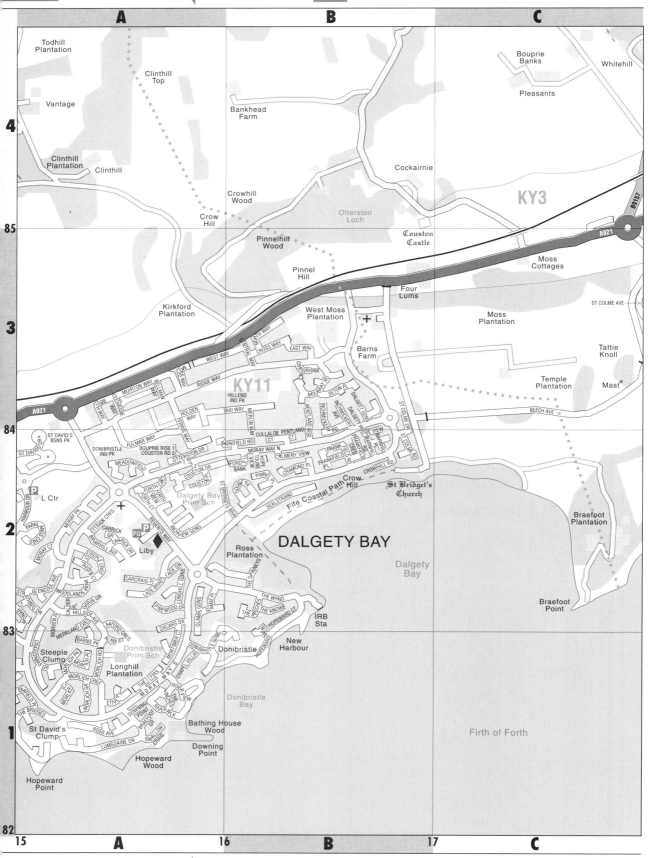

Todhill
Plantation

Clinthill
Top

Vantage

Clinthill
Plantation

Clinthill

Bankhead
Farm

Bouprie
Banks

Whitehill

Pleasants

Cockairnie

KY3

4

Crowhill
Wood

Crow
Hill

Otterston
Loch

Pinnelhill
Wood

Couston
Castle

Moss
Cottages

A921

B9157

85

Pinnel
Hill

Four
Lums

St Colme Ave

Kirkford
Plantation

West Moss
Plantation

Moss
Plantation

Tattie
Knoll

3

Barns
Farm

Temple
Plantation

Mast

A921

BEECH AVE

CENTRAL WAY

WEST WAY

CROSS WAY

EAST WAY

RIDGE WAY

CRAIGRIDGE

MOIRA RD

SETON PL

DALGETY GDNS

St COLME DR

KY11

HILLEND
IND PK

TAXI WAY

MERLIN WAY

HOLDEN
WAY

FERNS WAY

MUIRTON WAY

BELLMAN WAY

COCHRANE WAY

CTH WAY

FULMAR WAY

INCHMICKERY

PENTLAND RISE

INCHCOLM

DALGETY

SEA VIEW

84

St David's
BSNS PK

St DAVID'S DR

DONIBRISTLE
IND PK

BOUPRIE RISE 1
COUSTON RD 2

MEADOWFIELD

OTTERSTON GR

PARKFIELD RD

CULLALOE PENTLAND
CT

MORAY WAY S

KARKFIELD
RD

FRANK
FIELD PL

FRANKFIELD RD

St COLME RD

L Ctr

FORTH GR

FORTH DRV

FORTH CT

COUSTON DR

FORD
BANK

HOPE
TOUNE
VIEW

MORAY WAY N

PINN

CRAMOND PL

KILMENY VIEW

FRANKFIELD
PL

CROWHILL RD

2

HARBOUR DR

PARKL

MORAY CT

MORAY PK

ETTRICK CRES

BRAEHILL AVE

CARRICK
GR

CARRICK DR

REGENTS WAY

INCH

NEW GDNS

St BRIDGET'S BRAE

SEALSTRAND

Fife Coastal Path

Crow
Hill

St Bridget's
Church

Braefoot
Plantation

Liby

Dalgety Bay
Prim Sch

DALGETY BAY

Ross
Plantation

Dalgety
Bay

STRATHBEG DR

GLENCOL AVE

CALDER
PL

GRUN GR

WOODLAND

HILLSIDE AVE

ALKFORD CRES

CARCRAIG PL

LADE BRAES

LADE GRN

LONGHILL GDNS

PINEWOOD DR

OXCARS DR

GLAMIS GDNS

THE SPINNEYS

AIMS PL

THE BEECHES

THE KNOWE

THE WYND

KIRK

Braefoot
Point

83

MORVEN

MERKLAND CRES

BARNS PK

ALNE CT

MORTIMER CT

DONIBRISTLE GDNS

CHAPEL VILLAS

Donibristle

HOPEWARD

New
Harbour

IRB
Sta

Steeple
Clump

CRAIGDIMAS GR

MORLICH PK

PORT

MORLICH CRES

THE FIRS

MORAY WAY S

RIVER VIEW

RIVER GR

Donibristle
Prim Sch

Longhill
Plantation

Donibristle
Bay

Firth of Forth

1

SCAFIELD

THE BRIDGES

CALDER

MORLICH CRES

MORLICH

ETN

DOWNING
POINT

BRAEFOOT GR

SWALLOW

RIVER WLK

Bathing House
Wood

St David's
Clump

ROSS AVE

LUMSDAINE DR

CRAIG

Downing
Point

Hopeward
Wood

Hopeward
Point

82

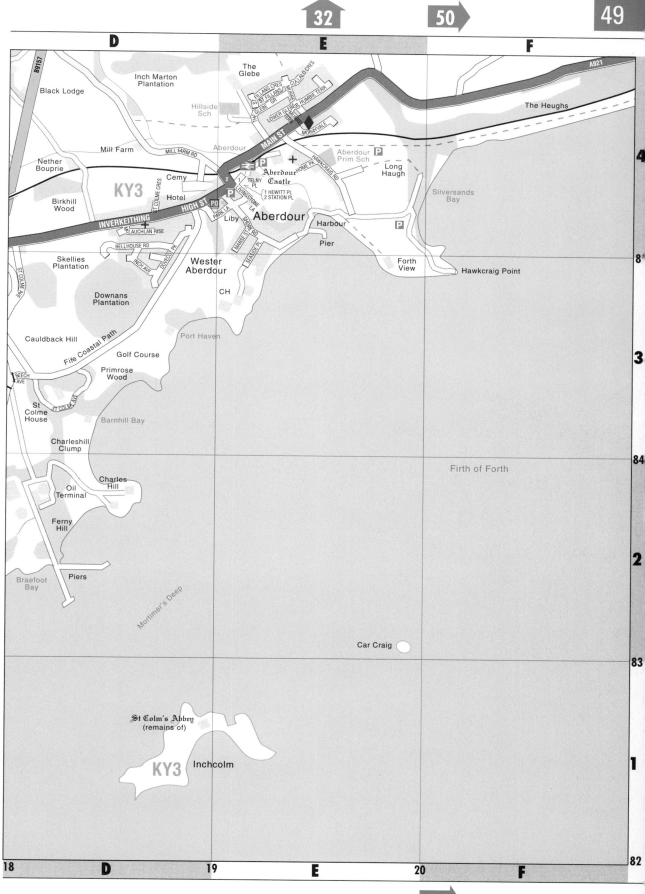

D

B9157

Black Lodge

Inch Marton
Plantation

The Glebe

ST FILLANS CRES
ST FILLANS
GR

THE GLEBE RD
LOWER GLEBE RD

CULALLO CRES

HUMBIE TERR

A921

Hillside
Sch

The Heughs

Mill Farm

MILL FARM RD

Aberdour

MAIN ST

MORAYVALE

Nether
Bouprie

Cemy

Aberdour
Prim Sch

P

4

HAWKCRAIG RD

HOME PK

Long
Haugh

Aberdour
Castle

KY3

ST COLME CRES

Hotel

P

TELNY
PL

2

Silversands
Bay

Birkhill
Wood

LIVINGSTONE LA

1 HEWITT PL
2 STATION PL

HIGH ST

PO

P

INVERKEITHING

PARK LA

Liby

Aberdour

M'LAUCHLAN RISE

Harbour

Pier

8

BELLHOUSE RD

T MANSE ST
SEASIDE PL
SHORE RD

Wester
Aberdour

Forth
View

Hawkcraig Point

Skellies
Plantation

INCH AVE

DOVECOT PK

CH

ST COLME AVE

Downans
Plantation

Port Haven

Cauldback Hill

Fife Coastal Path

Golf Course

3

BEECH
AVE

Primrose
Wood

ST COLM AVE

St
Colme
House

Barnhill Bay

Charleshill
Clump

Firth of Forth

84

Charles
Hill

Oil
Terminal

Ferny
Hill

Braefoot
Bay

Piers

2

Mortimer's Deep

Car Craig

83

St Colm's Abbey
(remains of)

KY3

Inchcolm

1

82

49
33

A   B

A921

Fife Coastal Path

KY3

Carron
Harbour

HAUGH RD
HADDOW GR
ROSSEND
TERR
DURIE
ST
SHEPHERD CRES
PARK
GDNS
SAILORS WLK
MELVILLE
SEAFORTH PL
WEST
BROOMHILL
BROOMHILL
EAST BROOMHILL
THISTLE ST
MANSE LA
KIRKTON
RD
CROMWELL RD
ROSE ST
KIRKGATE
HIGH ST
LINKS PL
LOTHIAN ST
SOMERVILLE ST
EAST LEVEN ST
NORTH VIEW
LAMMERLAWS RD
SOUTH VIEW
P
P
P
TH
Liby
Beacon
L Ctr

Ross
Point

Fife Coastal
Path

Works

Dock

KY3

BURNTISLAND

Outer
Harbour

Dock

SCHOLARS BRAE

Burntisland

SOUTH HILLS

HARBOUR PL
FORTH
WEST
LEVEN ST
SOMERVILLE SQ

4

85

3

84

Firth of Forth

2

83

1

82

21   22   23

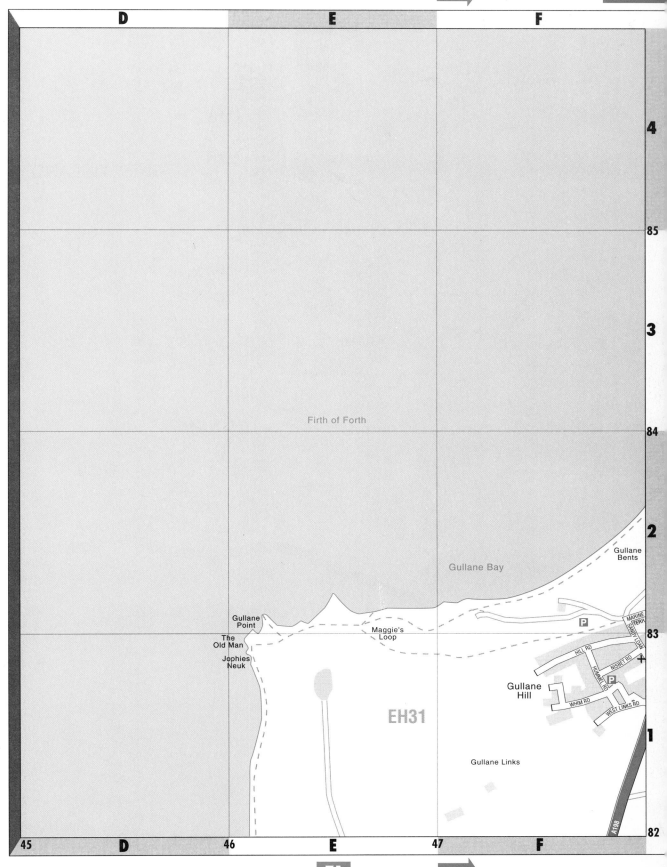

Firth of Forth

Gullane Bay

Gullane
Bents

Gullane Point

MARINE TERR

SANDY LOAN

P

The
Old Man

Maggie's
Loop

HILL RD

NISBET RD

Jophies
Neuk

HIMMEL RD

P

Gullane
Hill

WHIM RD

WEST LINKS RD

EH31

Gullane Links

A198

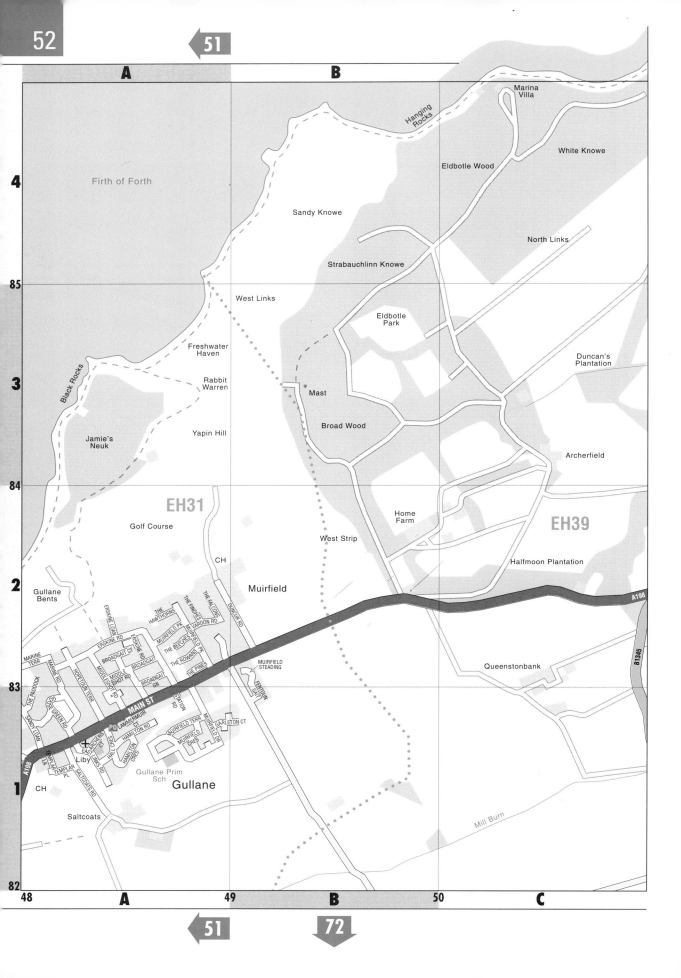

A B

4

Firth of Forth

Marina
Villa

Hanging
Rocks

White Knowe

Eldbotle Wood

Sandy Knowe

North Links

Strabauchlinn Knowe

85

West Links

Eldbotle
Park

Duncan's
Plantation

Freshwater
Haven

3

Rabbit
Warren

Black Rocks

Mast

Broad Wood

Archerfield

Jamie's
Neuk

Yapin Hill

84

EH31

Golf Course

West Strip

Home
Farm

EH39

Halfmoon Plantation

CH

2

Muirfield

Gullane
Bents

A198

B1345

MARINE
TERR

THE HAWTHORNS

THE FINCHES

THE FALCONS

ERSKINE LOAN RD

MUIRFIELD PK

THE BEECHES

MUIRFIELD PK

VARDON RD

DUNCAR RD

Queenstonbank

MARINE RD

HOPETOUN TERR

BROADGAIT CT

ERSKINE ROAD

BROADGAIT

THE ROWANS

MUIRFIELD STEADING

THE PADDOCK

MIDDLESHOT RD

MIDDLE
SHOT RD

BROADGAIT
GN

THE PINES

83

GREEN RD

LINKS RD

MAIN ST

STATION
RD

FENTON
GAIT

DAVID
COXS

LAMMERMUIR
CT

HAMILTON RD

MUIRFIELD TERR

MUIRFIELD DR

CARLETON CT

MUIRFIELD
CRES

TEMPLAR
PL

SALTCOATS RD

EAST LINKS RD

HALL CRES

HAMILTON
TERR

PO

ARCHERS
CT

TEMPLAR
LA

Liby

CH

1

Gullane Prim
Sch

Gullane

Saltcoats

Mill Burn

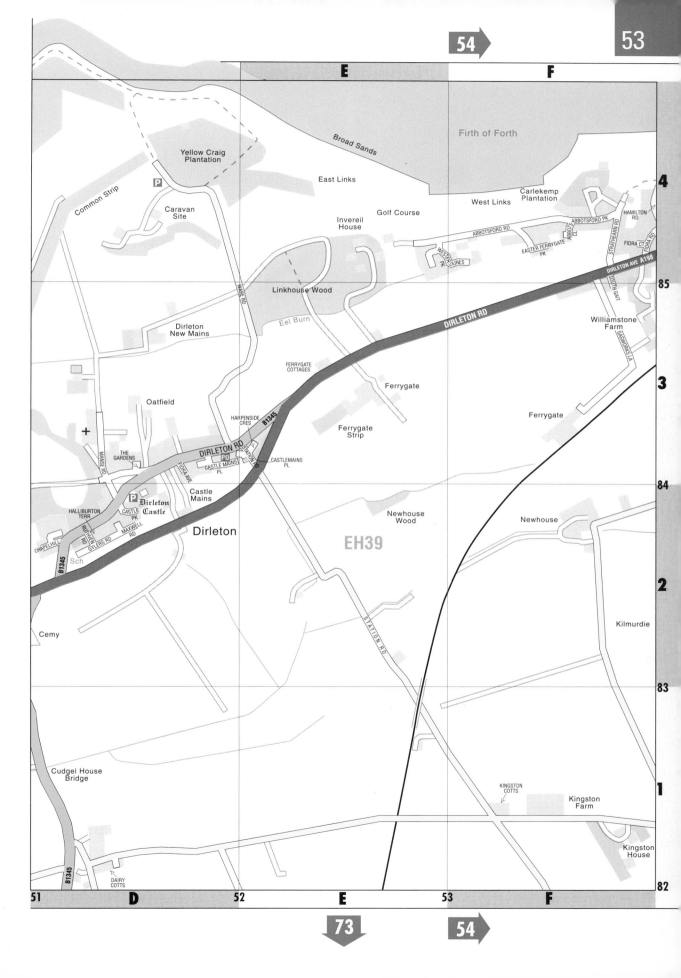

E   F

Firth of Forth

Broad Sands

Yellow Craig
Plantation

P

East Links

Carlekemp
Plantation

West Links

Common Strip

Caravan
Site

Golf Course

Invereil
House

4

Abbotsford Rd

Abbotsford Pk

Hamilton
Rd

Easter Ferrygate
Pk

Abbots
Cl

Strathearn Rd

Fidra Ct Rd

Fidra Rd

West Fecunes

Dirleton Ave A198

85

Ware Rd

Linkhouse Wood

Dirleton Rd

South Gait

Williamstone
Farm

Gasworks La

Dirleton
New Mains

Eel Burn

Ferrygate
Cottages

Ferrygate

3

Oatfield

Harpenside
Cres

B1345

Ferrygate
Strip

Ferrygate

+

Manse Rd

The
Gardens

Dirleton Rd

Fidra Ave

Castle Mains
Pl

Castlemains
Pl

Station Rd

PO

84

Castle
Mains

Newhouse
Wood

Newhouse

Halliburton
Terr

Castle
Pk

Dirleton
Castle

P

Chapelhill

Ruthven
Rd

Gylers Rd

Maxwell
Rd

Dirleton

EH39

2

B1345

Sch

Kilmurdie

Cemy

Station Rd

83

Cudgel House
Bridge

Kingston
Cotts

1

Kingston
Farm

B1345

Dairy
Cotts

Kingston
House

82

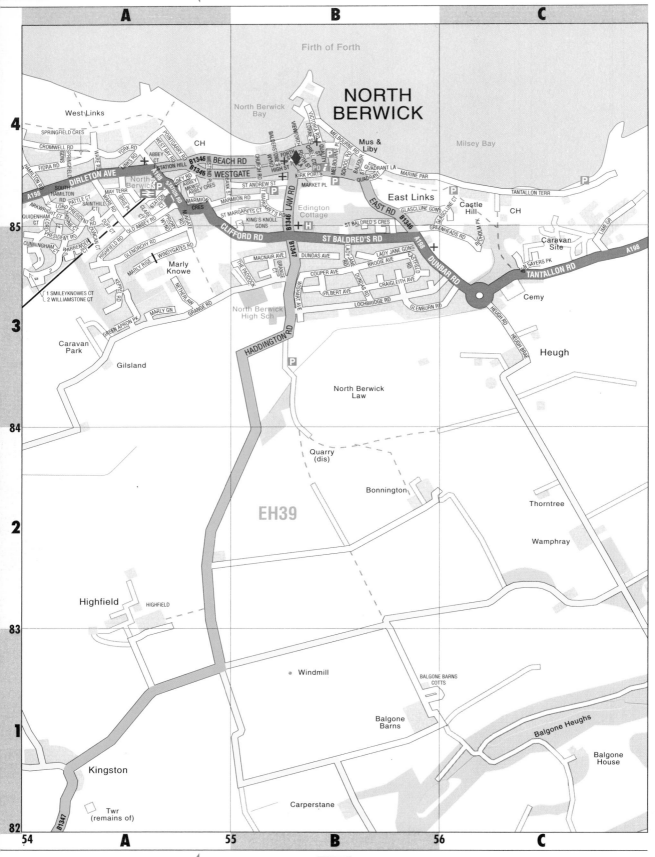

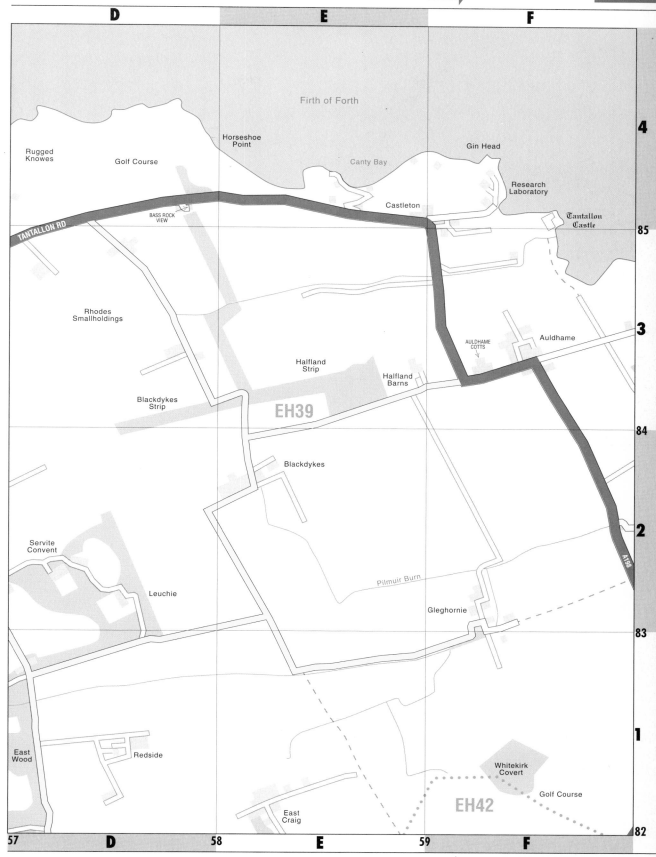

Firth of Forth

Horseshoe
Point

Gin Head

Rugged
Knowes

Canty Bay

Golf Course

Research
Laboratory

Castleton

4

Tantallon
Castle

TANTALLON RD

BASS ROCK
VIEW

85

Rhodes
Smallholdings

AULDHAME
COTTS

Auldhame

3

Halfland
Strip

Halfland
Barns

Blackdykes
Strip

EH39

84

Blackdykes

Servite
Convent

A198

2

Leuchie

Pilmuir Burn

Gleghornie

83

East
Wood

Redside

1

Whitekirk
Covert

Golf Course

EH42

East
Craig

82

55

A   B   C

4

85

3   Cave

SEACLIFF →   Seacliff

84   Chapel
Brae

Crow
Wood

2   EH39   Pilmuir Burn

Scoughall

83   Coastguard
Lookout

New
Mains   Scoughall
Links

1   Peffer Burn   Peffer
Sands
Pefferside

EH42

82
60   A   61   B   62   C

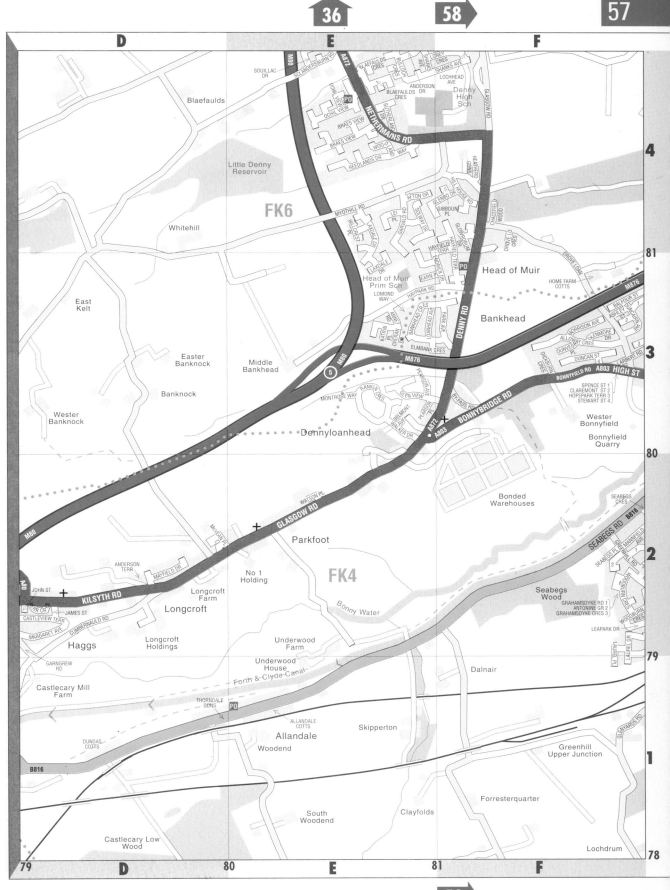

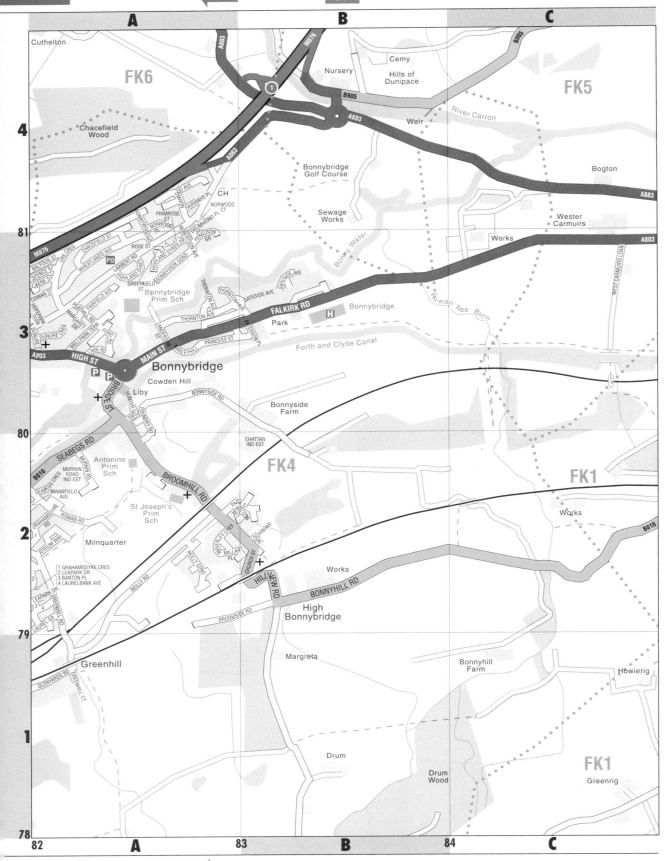

A   B   C

Cuthelton

FK6

Nursery

Cemy

Hills of
Dunipace

FK5

Chacefield
Wood

4

Weir

River Carron

A883

Bogton

Bonnybridge
Golf Course

A883

81

Sewage
Works

Wester
Carmuirs

Works

A803

WEST CARMUIRS LOAN

Bonny Water

CH

Bonnybridge
Prim Sch

FALKIRK RD

H

Bonnybridge

3

Park

Rowan Tree Burn

HIGH ST

A803

MAIN ST

Bonnybridge

Forth and Clyde Canal

Cowden Hill

Liby

BONNYSIDE RD

Bonnyside
Farm

Bonnybridge
Prim Sch

FK4

Works

FK1

80

SEABEGS RD

Antonine
Prim Sch

CHATTAN
IND EST

B816

MURNIN
ROAD IND EST

BROOMHILL RD

Works

B816

Milnquarter

St Joseph's
Prim Sch

2

1 GRAHAMSDYKE CRES
2 LEAPARK DR
3 BANTON PL
4 LAURELBANK AVE

Works

BONNYHILL RD

HILLVIEW RD

High
Bonnybridge

79

BROOMSIDE RD

Greenhill

Margreta

Bonnyhill
Farm

Howierig

1

Drum

Drum
Wood

FK1

Greenrig

78

82   A   83   B   84   C

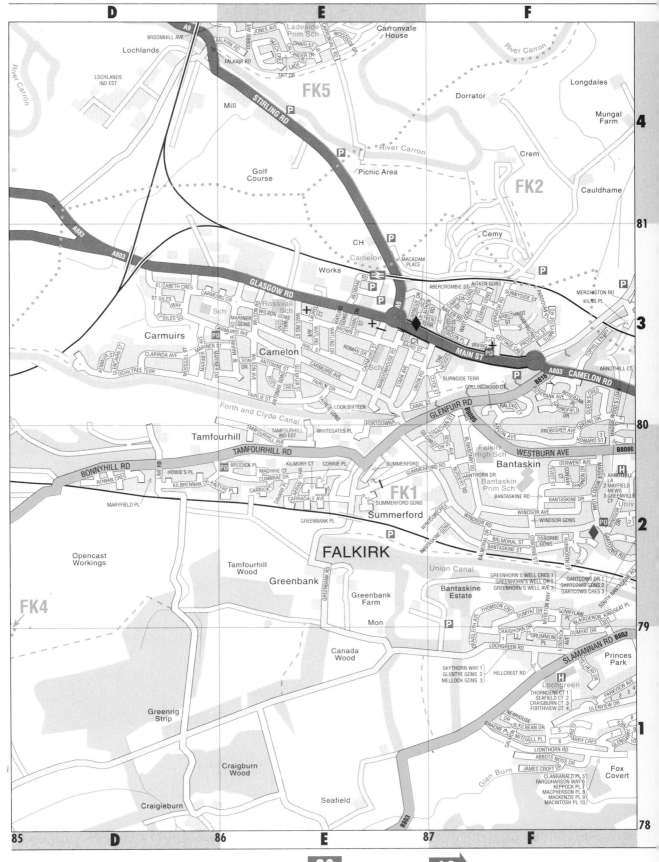

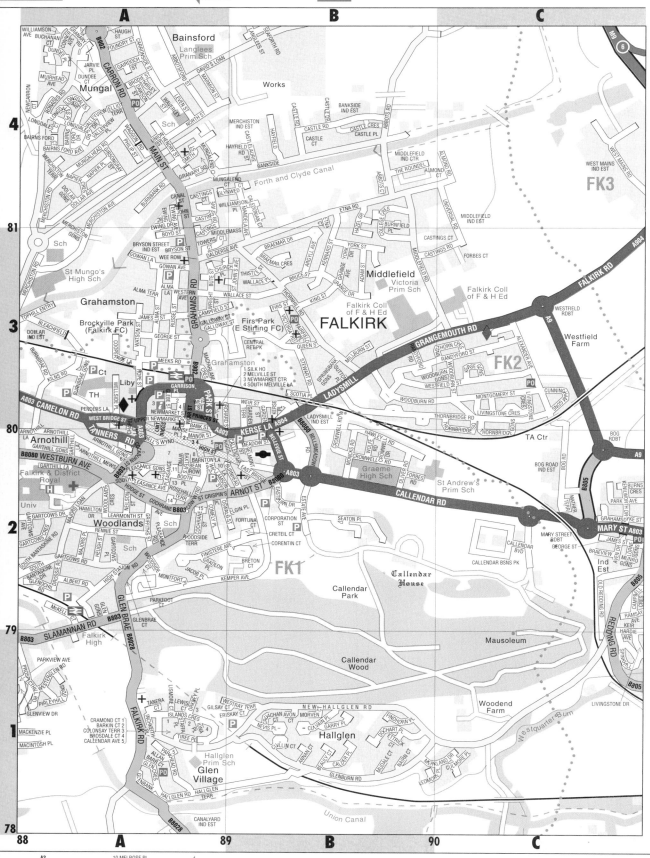

A2
1 BURNFOOT LA
2 KIRK WYND
3 TOLBOOTH ST
4 WOOER ST
5 CALLENDAR SQUARE SH CTR
6 ARNOTHILL BANK
7 HOWGATE SH CTR
8 KINGS CT
9 MISSION LA

10 MELROSE PL
11 ST ANDREWS PL
12 PLEASANCE SQ
13 PLEASANCE CT
14 ST MODANS CT
15 COMELY PARK TERR

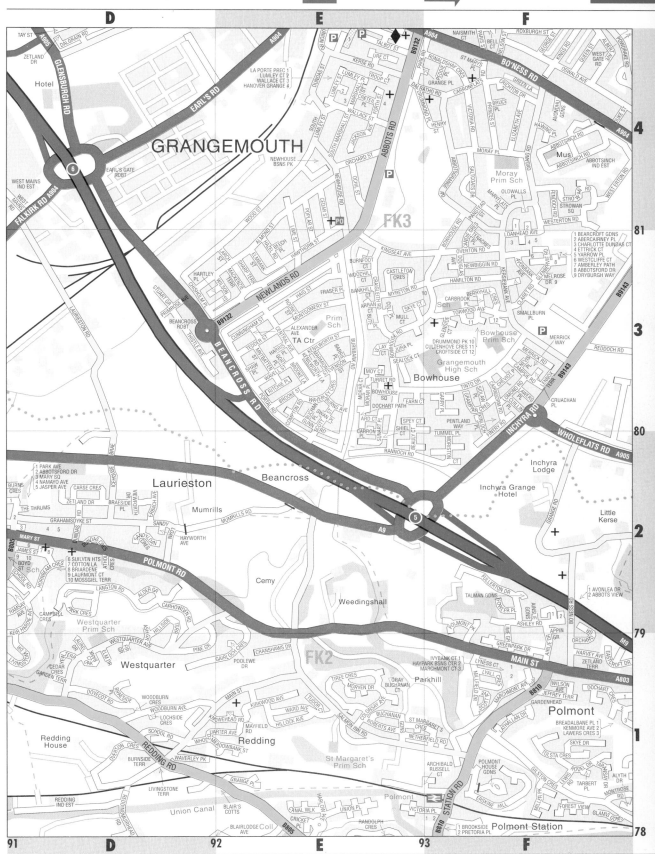

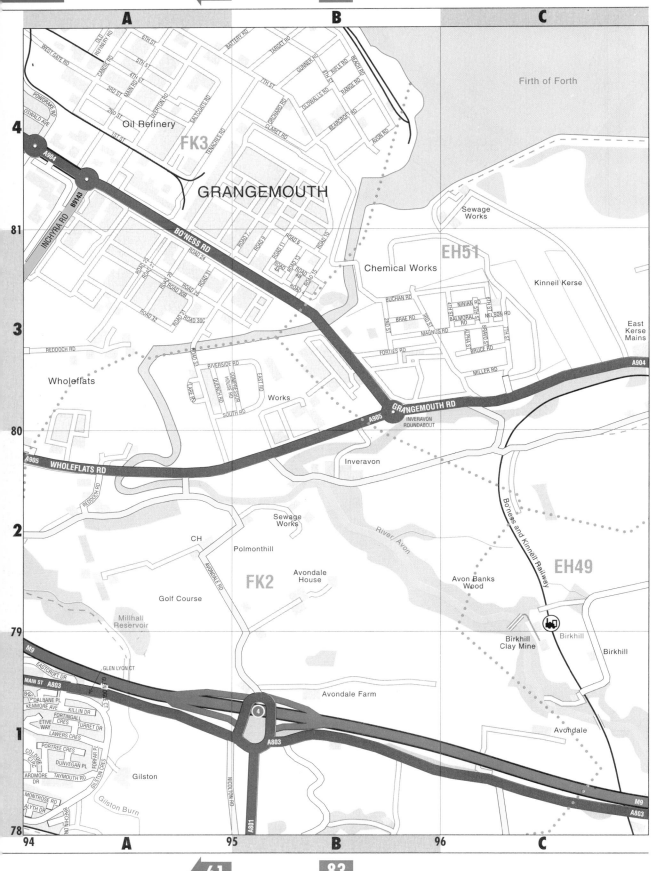

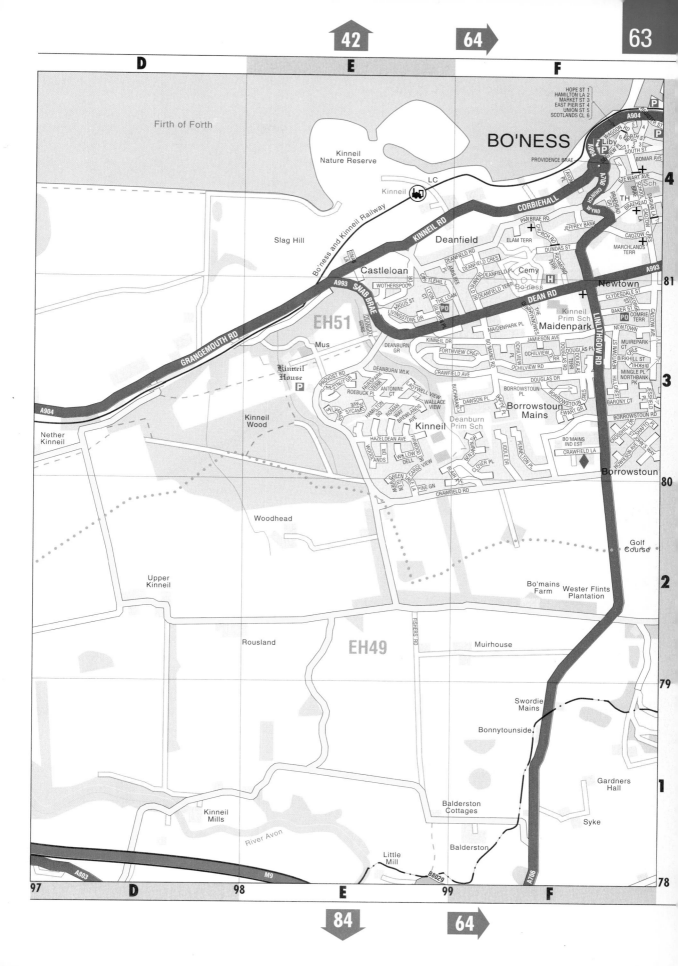

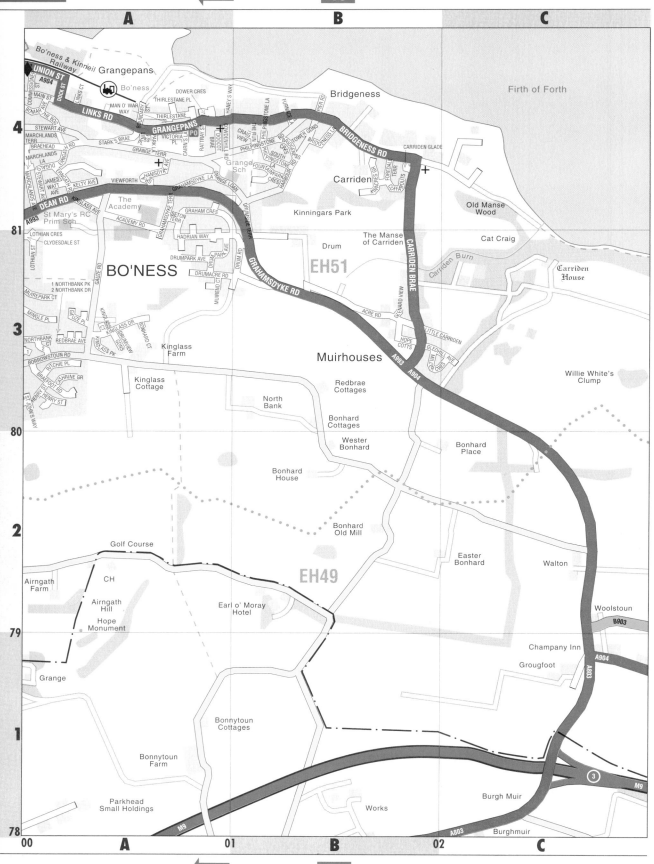

Bo'ness & Kinneil Railway
Grangepans

UNION ST
A904
Bo'ness
MAN O' WAR WAY
LINKS RD
GRANGEPANS

DOWER CRES
THIRLESTANE PL
THIRLESTANE

Bridgeness

HANEY'S WAY
PIPER RD

BRIDGENESS RD

Carriden Glade

4

STEWART AVE
MARCHLANDS TERR
BRAEHEAD
MARCHLANDS LA
JAMES WATT AVE
KELTY AVE
VIEWFORTH

GRAHAMSDYKE LA
GRANGE LOAN

Grange Sch

Carriden

Old Manse Wood

DEAN RD
A993
St Mary's RC Prim Sch

The Academy
ACADEMY RD
GRAHAM CRES
HADRIAN WAY

DRUMSIDE TERR

Kinningars Park

The Manse of Carriden

Cat Craig

81

LOTHIAN CRES
CLYDESDALE ST
LOTHIAN ST

DRUMPARK AVE
PARK AVE
DRUMACRE RD

GRAHAMSDYKE RD

Drum

EH51

CARRIDEN BRAE

Carriden Burn

Carriden House

BO'NESS

KINGLASS AVE
1 NORTHBANK PK
2 NORTHBANK DR

MUIREND RD

ACRE RD

GLENARD VIEW

LITTLE CARRIDEN
HOPE COTTS
GLEDHILL AVE
MILLER CRES

3

MINGLE PL
NORTHBANK CT
BORROWSTOUN RD
GAUZE PL
REDBRAE AVE
KINGLASS PK
KINGLASS GDNS
BONHARD CT

Kinglass Farm

Muirhouses

A993
A904

Willie White's Clump

BRAEFOOT RD
SHRINE GR
RITCHIE PL
HENRY ST
ST JOHN'S WAY

Kinglass Cottage

North Bank

Redbrae Cottages

80

Bonhard Cottages

Wester Bonhard

Bonhard Place

Bonhard House

2

Golf Course

Bonhard Old Mill

Easter Bonhard

Walton

Airngath Farm
CH

EH49

Airngath Hill
Hope Monument

Earl o' Moray Hotel

Woolstoun
B903

79

Grange

Champany Inn
Grougfoot

A904
A803

1

Bonnytoun Cottages

Bonnytoun Farm

Burgh Muir

3
M9

Parkhead Small Holdings

Works

78

M9

A803

Burghmuir

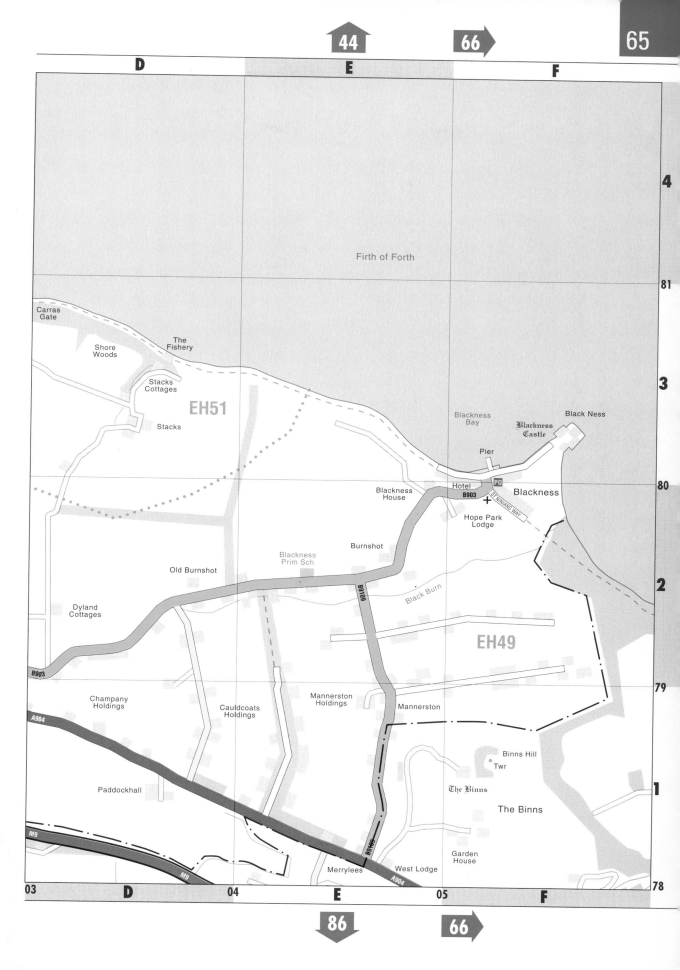

D E F

4

Firth of Forth

81

Carras
Gate

Shore
Woods

The
Fishery

3

Stacks
Cottages

EH51

Blackness
Bay

Black Ness

Stacks

Blackness
Castle

Pier

Blackness House

Hotel

PO

Blackness

B903

ST NINIANS WAY

80

Hope Park
Lodge

Burnshot

Old Burnshot

Blackness
Prim Sch

Black Burn

2

Dyland
Cottages

B9109

EH49

B903

79

Champany
Holdings

Cauldcoats
Holdings

Mannerston
Holdings

Mannerston

A904

Binns Hill
Twr

The Binns

1

Paddockhall

The Binns

M9

Garden
House

Merrylees

West Lodge

A904

78

03 D 04 E 05 F

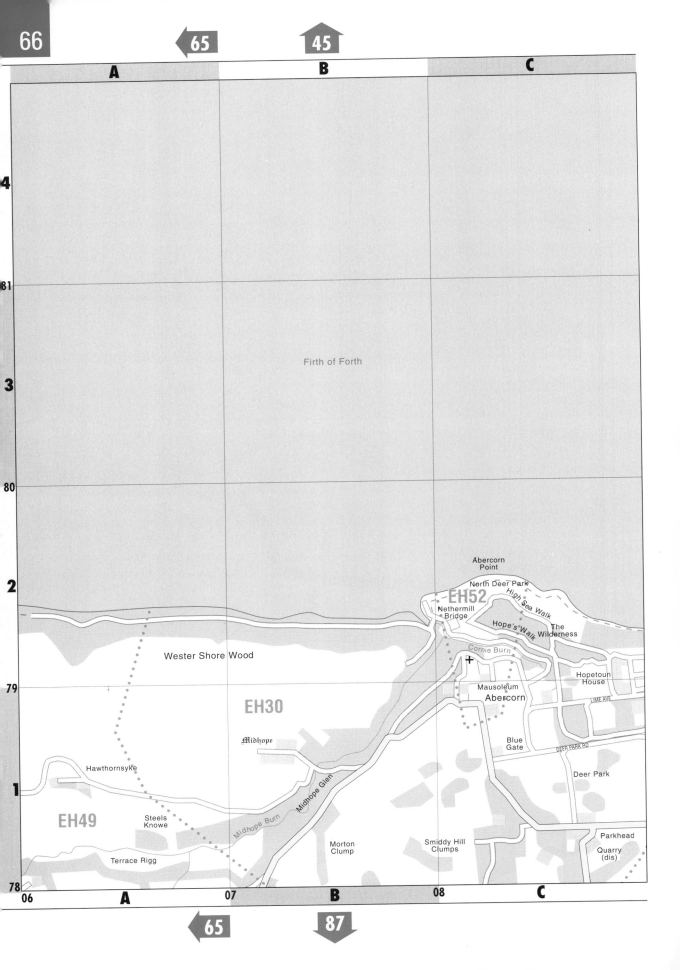

A
B
C

4

81

Firth of Forth

3

80

2

Abercorn
Point

North Deer Park

EH52

High Sea Walk

Nethermill
Bridge

Hope's Walk

The
Wilderness

Cornie Burn

Wester Shore Wood

Hopetoun
House

79

EH30

Mausoleum
Abercorn

LIME AVE

Midhope

Blue
Gate

DEER PARK RD

Hawthornsyke

Deer Park

1

Midhope Glen

EH49

Steels
Knowe

Midhope Burn

Parkhead

Morton
Clump

Smiddy Hill
Clumps

Quarry
(dis)

Terrace Rigg

78

06
A
07
B
08
C

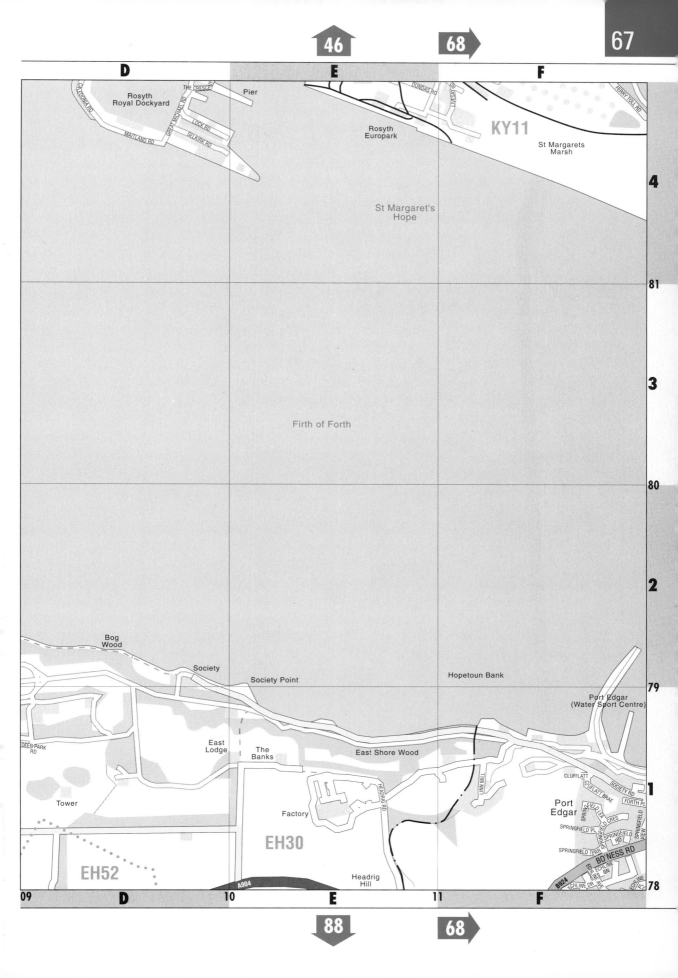

Rosyth
Royal Dockyard

THE CRESCENT

Pier

CALEDONIA RD

GREAT MICHAEL RD

LOCK RD

SELKIRK RD

MAITLAND RD

DUNDAS RD

LYNN RD

FERRY TOLL RD

Rosyth
Europark

KY11

St Margarets
Marsh

4

St Margaret's
Hope

81

3

Firth of Forth

80

2

Bog
Wood

Society

Society Point

Hopetoun Bank

79

Port Edgar
(Water Sport Centre)

DEER PARK RD

East
Lodge

The
Banks

East Shore Wood

HEADRIG RD

LINN MILL

CLUFFLATT

CLUFFLATT BRAE

SOCIETY RD

FORTH PL

Port
Edgar

SPRINGFIELD LEA

SPRINGFIELD CRES

SPRINGFIELD VIEW

1

Tower

Factory

SPRINGFIELD PL

SPRINGFIELD RD

SPRINGFIELD TERR

EH30

EH52

Headrig
Hill

BO'NESS RD

ECHLINE DR

ECHLINE AVE

ECHLINE GN

ECHLINE VIEW

B924

A904

78

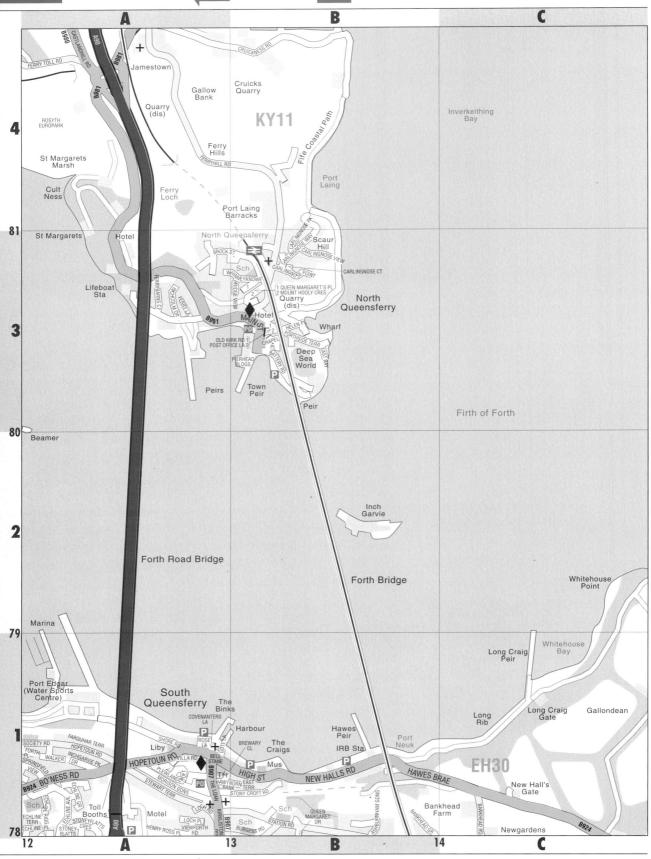

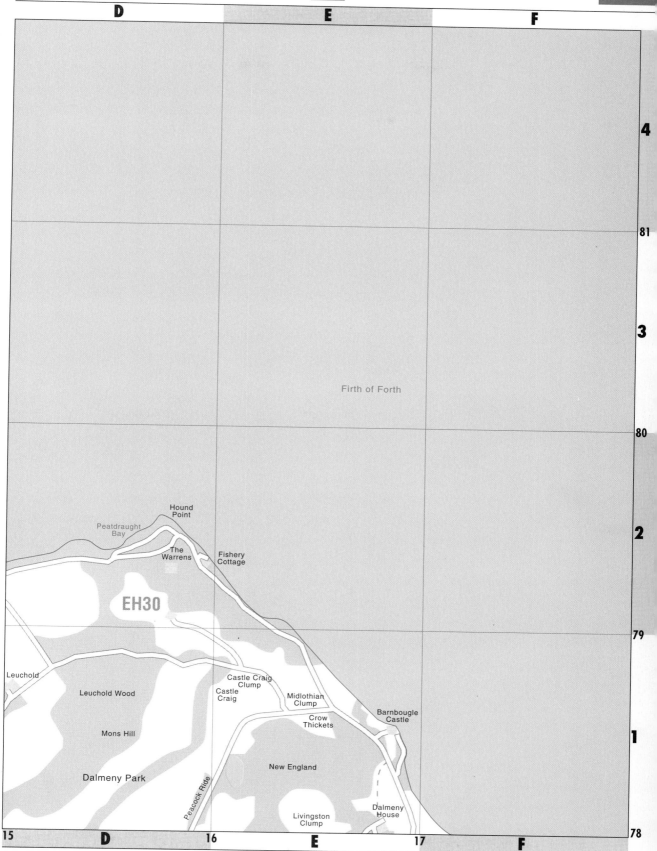

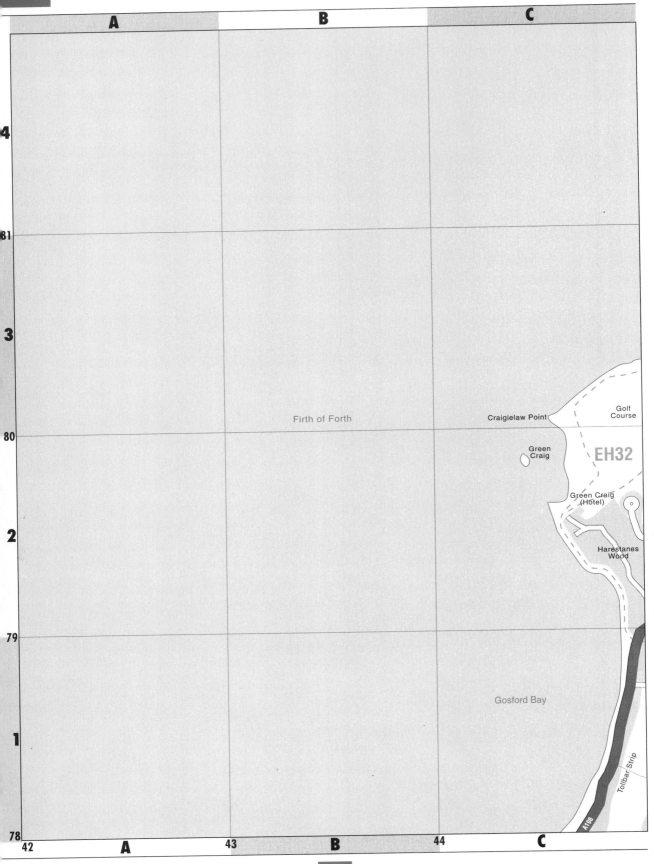

A   B   C

4

81

3

Firth of Forth   Craigielaw Point   Golf Course

80   **EH32**

Green Craig

Green Craig (Hotel)

2   Harestanes Wood

79

Gosford Bay

1   Tollbar Strip

A198

78
42   A   43   B   44   C

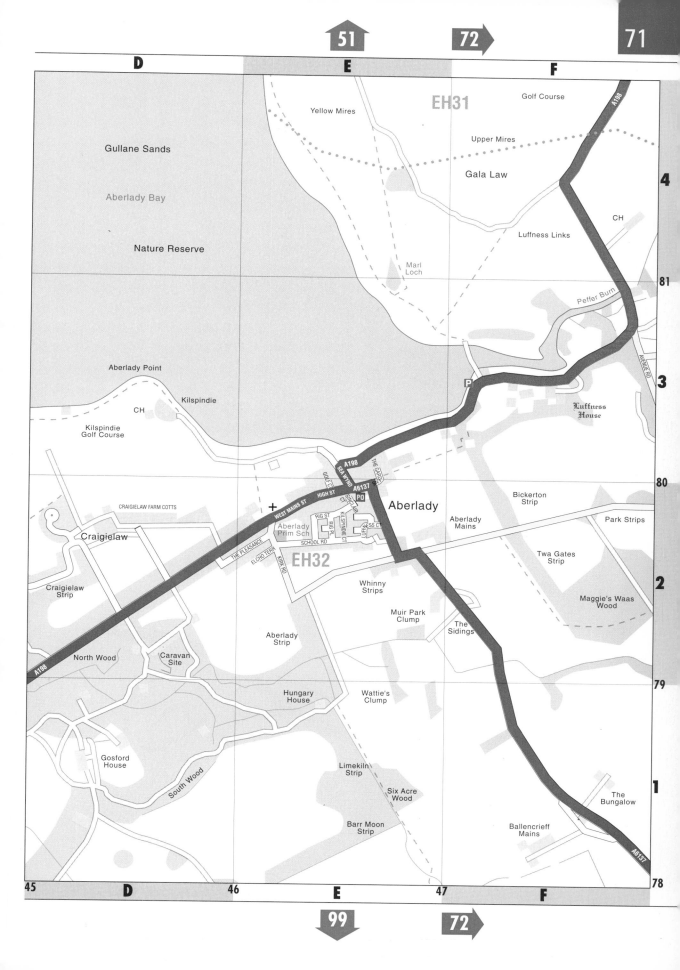

EH31

Golf Course

Yellow Mires

Upper Mires

Gullane Sands

Gala Law

Aberlady Bay

Luffness Links

CH

Nature Reserve

Marl Loch

Peffer Burn

4

81

Aberlady Point

Kilspindie

P

3

CH

Luffness House

Kilspindie Golf Course

A198

THE GARDEN

80

CRAIGIELAW FARM COTTS

GOLF CT

SEAWYND

A6137

PO

Aberlady

Bickerton Strip

Craigielaw

WEST MAINS ST

HIGH ST

SINCLAIR

KILSPINDIE CT

UFFNESS CT

Aberlady Mains

Park Strips

Aberlady Prim Sch

RIG ST

RIG PL

THE PLEASANCE

ELCHO TERR

SCHOOL RD

KIRK RD

EH32

Twa Gates Strip

2

Craigielaw Strip

Whinny Strips

Maggie's Waas Wood

Muir Park Clump

Aberlady Strip

The Sidings

A198

North Wood

Caravan Site

79

Hungary House

Wattie's Clump

Gosford House

Limekiln Strip

South Wood

Six Acre Wood

The Bungalow

1

Barr Moon Strip

Ballencrieff Mains

A6137

71
52

A   **B**   **C**

EH31

West Fenton

WEST FENTON COTTS

Craighead Cottage

New Mains

4

Peffer Bank Wood

Depot

81

Luffness Mill House

Hatty's Plantation

Park Hills

Peffer Burn

Drem Ride

3

B1345

AVENUE RD

Floors Strip

Coldhame Wood

EH39

EH32

80

Luffness Mains

LUFFNESS MAINS COTTS

Mungoswells Rough Strip

Drem Farm

PO

2

B1377

Motor Museum

LC

79

Poultry Farm

Mungoswells

Bridgend

Sixpence Strip

Foster Law

1

Tighnablair

Ballencrieff House

Dalvreck Farm

The Chesters

BALLENCRIEFF COTTS

Camptoun Holdings

A8137

B1377

Ballencrieff

78

48   **A**   49   **B**   50   **C**

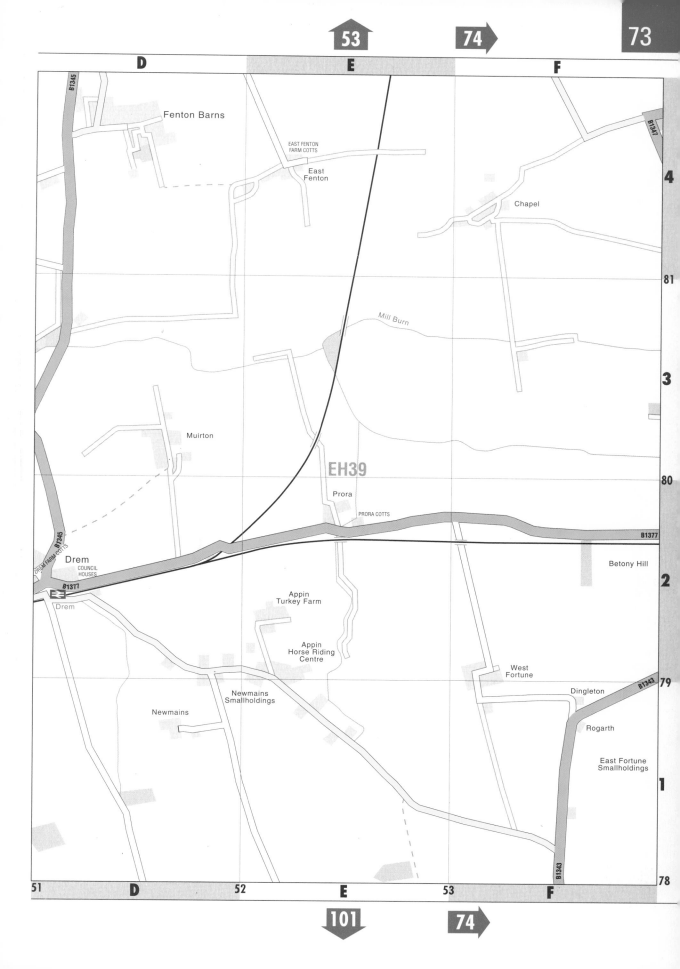

D E F

B1345
B1347

Fenton Barns

EAST FENTON
FARM COTTS

East
Fenton

Chapel

4

81

Mill Burn

3

Muirton

EH39

80

Prora

PRORA COTTS

B1377

DREM FARM COTTS
B1345

Drem

COUNCIL
HOUSES

Betony Hill

B1377

2

Drem

Appin
Turkey Farm

Appin
Horse Riding
Centre

West
Fortune

Dingleton

B1343

79

Newmains
Smallholdings

Newmains

Rogarth

East Fortune
Smallholdings

1

B1343

51 D 52 E 53 F 78

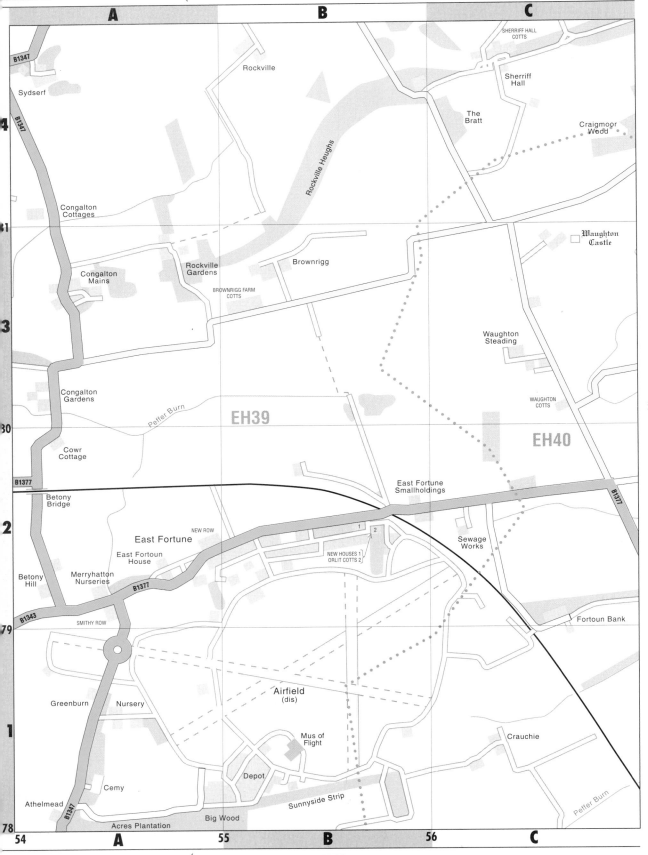

A
B
C

B1347

Sydserf

B1347

4

SHERRIFF HALL
COTTS

Rockville

Sherriff
Hall

The
Bratt

Craigmoor
Wood

Congalton
Cottages

Rockville Heughs

31

Waughton
Castle

Congalton
Mains

Rockville
Gardens

Brownrigg

BROWNRIGG FARM
COTTS

3

Waughton
Steading

Congalton
Gardens

Peffer Burn

EH39

WAUGHTON
COTTS

30

EH40

Cowr
Cottage

B1377

Betony
Bridge

East Fortune
Smallholdings

B1377

2

East Fortune

NEW ROW

1

2

Sewage
Works

East Fortoun
House

NEW HOUSES 1
ORLIT COTTS 2

Betony
Hill

Merryhatton
Nurseries

B1377

Fortoun Bank

B1343

79

SMITHY ROW

Greenburn

Nursery

Airfield
(dis)

1

Crauchie

Mus of
Flight

Athelmead

B1347

Cemy

Depot

Sunnyside Strip

Peffer Burn

78

Big Wood

Acres Plantation

D
E
F

EH39

Whitekirk Hill

Craig
Wood

Pleasants

Whitekirk

4

Whitekirk
Mains

BINNING WOOD RD

A198

A198

EH42

Merrylaws

Old
Stonelaws

81

STONELAWS
COTTS

BANKHEAD
COTTS

Bankhead

Duncanson's
Wood

Gildswell
Wood

Stonelaws

3

Stonelaws

Angus Wood

Newbyth

Howden

Newbyth Farm
Steading

Crow
Wood

Howden Burn

Old Mansion
House

Inch
Wood

80

Ashfield House

Kamehill

Birkhill

Peffer Burn

2

Black's Park
Wood

Oak Wood

EH40

LAWHEAD
COTTS

Cauldside

79

Smeaton
Farm

Smeaton
House

Nursery

1

Preston
Mains

Drylaw
Hill

B1377

DRYLAWHILL

THE DEAN

B1407

78

57
D
58
E
59
F

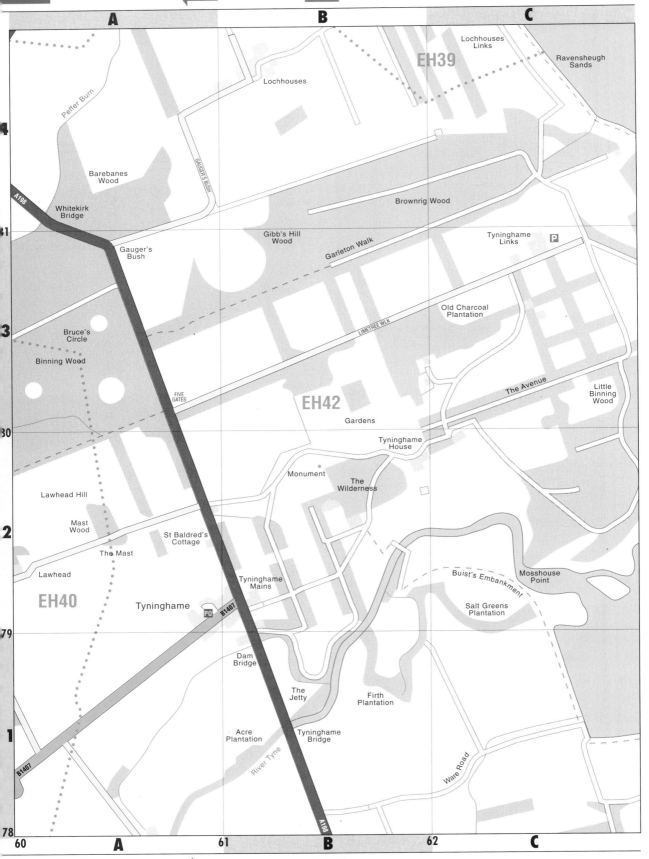

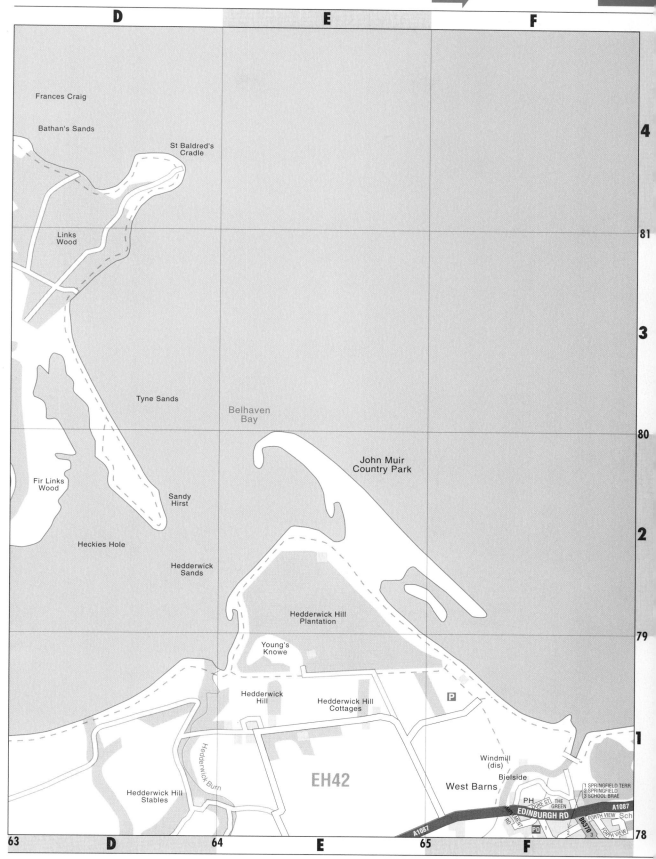

D
E
F

Frances Craig

Bathan's Sands

St Baldred's
Cradle

4

81

Links
Wood

3

Tyne Sands

Belhaven
Bay

John Muir
Country Park

80

Fir Links
Wood

Sandy
Hirst

2

Heckies Hole

Hedderwick
Sands

Hedderwick Hill
Plantation

79

Young's
Knowe

Hedderwick
Hill

Hedderwick Hill
Cottages

P

1

Hedderwick Burn

Windmill
(dis)

Bielside

EH42

West Barns

1 SPRINGFIELD TERR
2 SPRINGFIELD
3 SCHOOL BRAE

Hedderwick Hill
Stables

PH

DUKE ST

THE
GREEN

A1087

EDINBURGH RD

FORTH VIEW

Sch

A1087

B6370

FORTH VIEW

PO

78

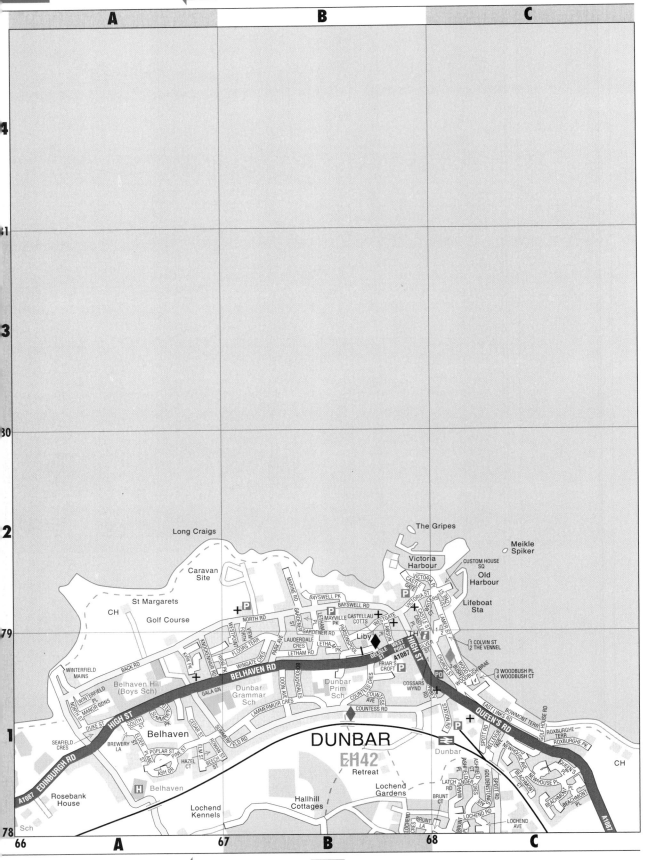

4

81

3

80

2

79

1

78

Golf Course

West Links

Sports & Social
Centre

Fluke
Dub

EH42

Lawrie's
Den

The
Vaults

Vaults Wood

Mill Stone
Neuk

69   **D**   70   **E**   71   **F**

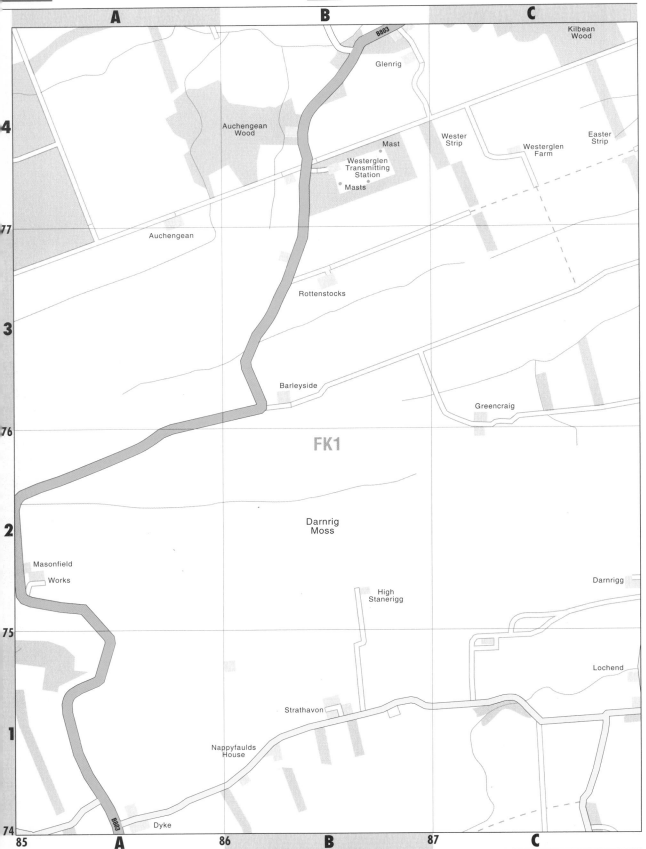

A
B
C

Kilbean
Wood

B803

Glenrig

4

Auchengean
Wood

Mast

Westerglen
Transmitting
Station

Wester
Strip

Westerglen
Farm

Easter
Strip

Masts

77

Auchengean

3

Rottenstocks

Barleyside

Greencraig

76

FK1

Darnrig
Moss

2

Masonfield

Darnrigg

Works

High
Stanerigg

75

Lochend

Strathavon

1

Nappyfaulds
House

74

B803

Dyke

A
B
C

D
E
F

Mavisbank

Glen Farm

Cleuch Plantation

Mavisbank Wood

Wester Newlands

FK2

B8028

B810

Easter Pirleyhill

Reddingrig Muir

4

Westquarter Burn

Wester Pirleyhill

Shieldhill

Pirleyhill Bridge

BELMONT AVE

Belmont Ave

Patrick Dr

Carmond Pl

77

OCHIL VIEW

EASTON DR

Paterson Dr

GARDRUM GDNS

LEDI PL

VORLICH DR

WALLACE VIEW

HIGH VIEW

BRAES VIEW

RANNOCH PL

ANDERSON CRES

PARK LODGE

HEATHER AVE

GREENCRAIG AVE

HERDSHILL AVE

DRUCKSHANK DR

PIRLEYHILL DR

MUIRPARK DR

GREENMUIR DR

B810

MAVISBANK AVE

CROSS BRAE

PO

MAIN ST

Easter Shieldhill

B8028

Redding Muir

BRAESIDE

Shieldhill

3

ELIM DR

Greenwells

Burnside

Shieldhill Prim Sch

ROSEMEAD TERR

MAIN ST

Church Rd

The Three Kings (PH)

Polmont Burn

California Prim Sch

MAMRES DR

Wester Shieldhill Lands

California

CHURCH ST

MERVILLE CRES

QUEEN ST

Summerhouse

EBENEZER ST

PRINCES ST

ST ANDREWS ST

CALIFORNIA TERR

Quarryhead

FK1

Recn Gd

PO

76

MERVILLE TERR

Works

Gardrum

Blackbraes

Gardrum Moss

Mast

2

Craigmad

Loch Ellrig

Grayrigg Inn (PH)

75

Heathery Knowe

Blackbrigs

Greyrigg Farm

Mast
Resr

1

Boxtonrighead

Broom

Boxton Burn

Glen Ellrig

B8028

Greencraig Cottages

74

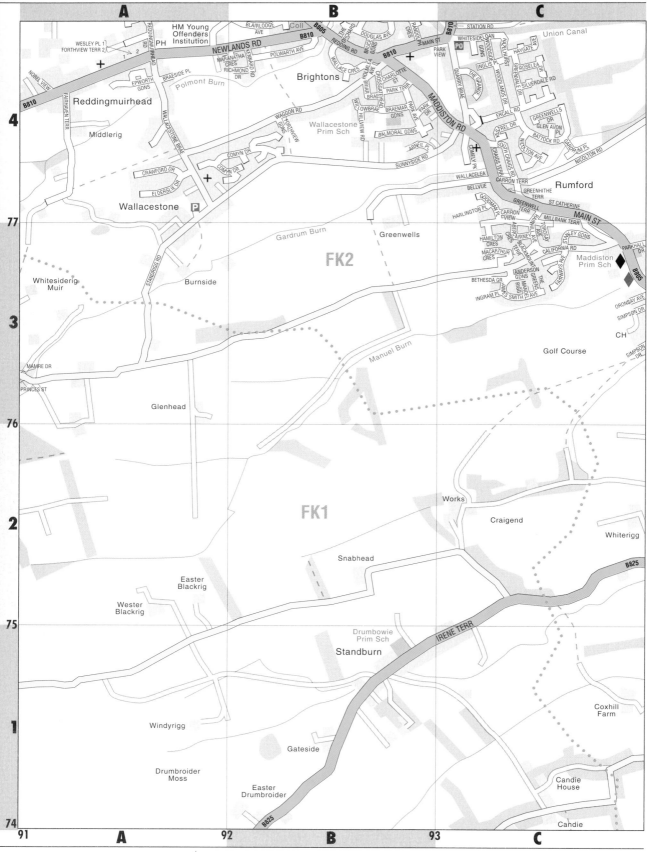

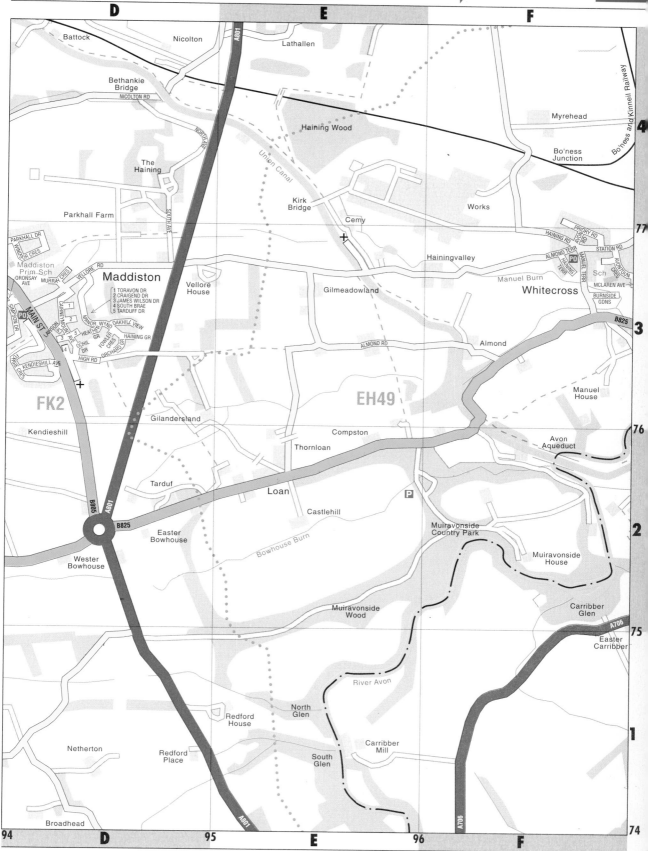

Battock
Nicolton
Lathallen
Myrehead
Bethankie Bridge
NICOLTON RD
Haining Wood
Bo'ness Junction
Bo'ness and Kinneil Railway
The Haining
Union Canal
NORTH AVE
SOUTH AVE
A801
4
Parkhall Farm
Kirk Bridge
Cemy
Works
HAINING RD
PRIORY RD
STATION RD
ALMOND TERR
77
PARKHALL DR
WINDSOR CRES
VELLORE RD
Maddiston Prim Sch
ORONSAY AVE
MURRA
CAIRNGMOUNT AVE
Maddiston
1 TORAVON DR
2 CRAIGEND DR
3 JAMES WILSON DR
4 SOUTH BRAE
5 TARDUFF DR
Vellore House
Hainingvalley
Manuel Burn
HAINING
MANUEL TERR
ALMOND TERR
Sch
MCLAREN AVE
AUCHOUN CRES
BURNSIDE GDNS
Whitecross
Gilmeadowland
POT
SIMPSON DR
MAIN ST
LAWSON DR
HEATHER GR
OCHIL DR
FOWLER CRES
ORCHARD GR
OAKHILL VIEW
HAINING GR
HIGH RD
MANOR WYND
B825
3
Almond
ALMOND RD
FK2
+
Kendieshill
Gilandersland
EH49
Compston
Thornloan
Manuel House
Avon Aqueduct
76
B805
Tarduf
Loan
Castlehill
P
Muiravonside Country Park
Muiravonside House
2
Easter Bowhouse
A801
B825
Bowhouse Burn
Carribber Glen
A706
75
Wester Bowhouse
Muiravonside Wood
Easter Carribber
Redford House
River Avon
North Glen
Carribber Mill
1
Netherton
Redford Place
South Glen
A706
Broadhead
A801

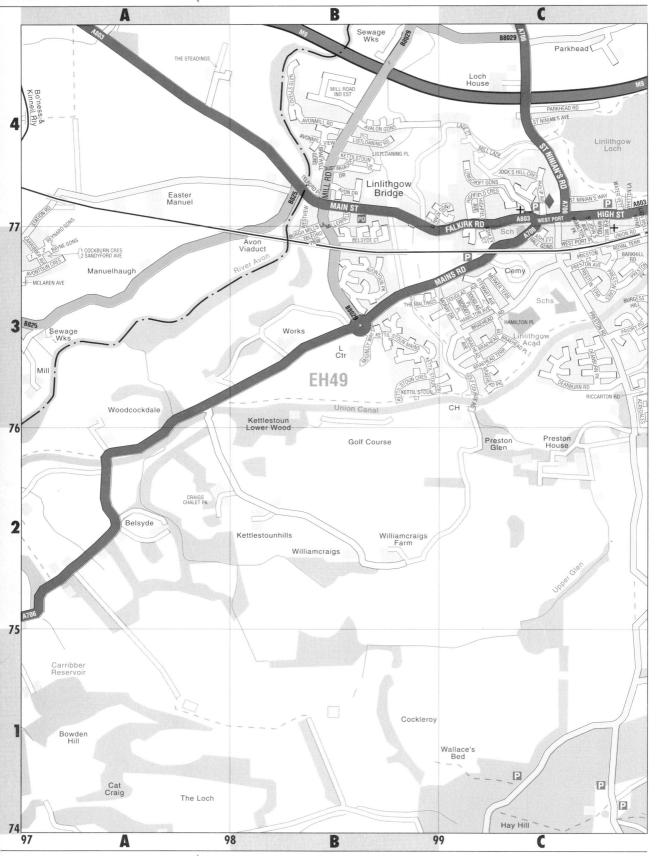

A   B   C

A803

THE STEADINGS

M9

Sewage Wks

B8029

B8029

A706

Parkhead

Loch House

Bo'ness & Kinneil Rly

MILL ROAD IND EST

Parkhead Rd

St Ninian's Ave

4

AVONMILL RD

AVALON GDNS

LISTLOANING RD

Linlithgow Loch

AVONMILL VIEW

LISTLOANING PL

MILL LADE

Jock's Hill Cres

LONGCROFT GDNS

PHILIP AVE

ST NINIAN'S RD

Easter Manuel

B825

MILL RD

KETTILSTOUN RD

AVON DR

Linlithgow Bridge

HIGHFIELD CRES

ST NINIAN'S WAY

WATER YETT

WHITTEN LA

A803

MAIN ST

77

WESTVIEW

PO

FALKIRK RD

A803

WEST PORT

HIGH ST

Sch

A706

West Port Pl

Royal Terr

Avon Viaduct

BURGH MILLS LA

TELFORD VIEW

BELSYDE CT

ASHLEY HALL GDNS

Barkhill Rd

Manuelhaugh

River Avon

MAINS RD

Cemy

Preston Ave

Burgess Hill

MCLAREN AVE

1 COCKBURN CRES
2 SANDYFORD AVE

AVONTOUN PK

THE MALTINGS

Schs

Priory Rd

3

B825

Works

L Ctr

KETTILSTOUN MAINS

Braehead

Hamilton Pl

Linlithgow Acad

Deanburn Pk

Sewage Wks

MCGINLEY WAY

KETTILSTOUN CRES

KETTILSTOUN DR

Deanburn Rd

Riccarton Rd

Mill

EH49

KETTILSTOUN CT

GOLF COURSE RD

CH

Woodcockdale

Kettlestoun Lower Wood

Union Canal

Preston Glen

Preston House

76

Golf Course

CRAIGS CHALET PK

2

Belsyde

Kettlestounhills

Williamcraigs

Williamcraigs Farm

Upper Glen

A706

75

Carribber Reservoir

Cockleroy

1

Bowden Hill

Wallace's Bed

Cat Craig

The Loch

Hay Hill

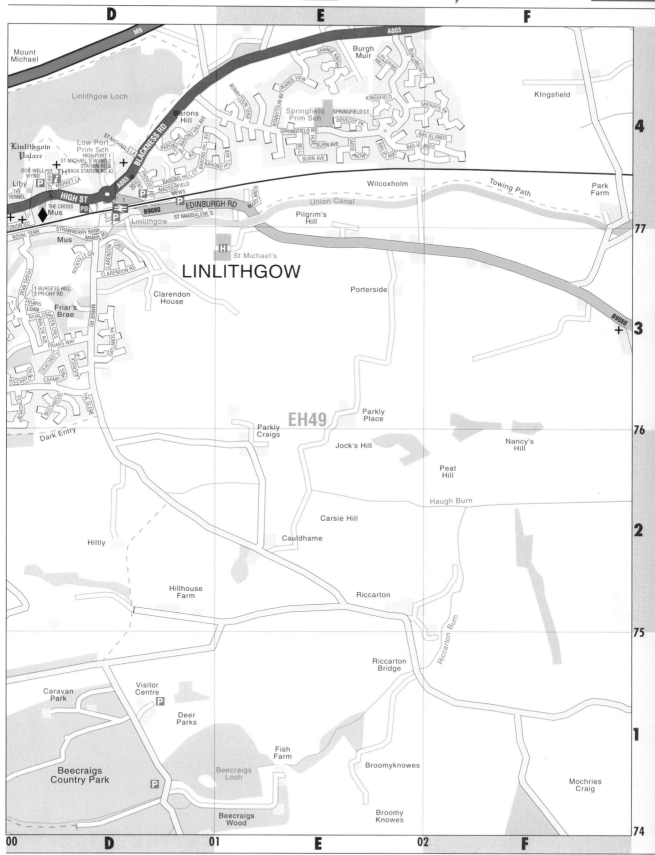

D E F

64 86

85

Mount Michael

M9

A803

Linlithgow Loch

Burgh Muir

GRANGE KNOWE

PILGRIMS HILL

BURGHMUIR CT

KIngsfield

Barons Hill

BLACKNESS RD

BONNYTOUN TERR

GRANGE VIEW

BONNYTOUN AV

Springfield Prim Sch

KINGSFIELD

SPRINGFIELD CT

SHERIFFS PK

St Michael's La

BARONS HILL AVE

BARONS HILL

BARONS HILL AVE

SPRINGFIELD RD

DOVECOT PK

BAILIELANDS

4

Low Port Prim Sch

HIGH PORT 1

ST MICHAEL'S WYND 2

STATION RD 3

BACK STATION RD 4

A803

BARONS HILL CT

BARONS HZ LAVE

HUN

BELLS

BURN AVE

CARSE

KNOW

BAILIE LANDS

BAILIELANDS

Linlithgow Palace

DOG WELL WYND

MARKET LA

PROVOST RD

MADDERFIELD MEWS

Liby

THE VENNEL

P

P

TH

Wilcoxholm

Towing Path

Park Farm

HIGH ST

PO

B9080

EDINBURGH RD

ST MAGDALENE S

MANS LANDS

Union Canal

77

Royal Terr

UNION RD

Mus

P

Linlithgow

Pilgrim's Hill

B9080

STRAWBERRY BANK

MANSE RD

Mus

ROCKVILLE GR

CLARENDON CRES

H

St Michael's

ROYAL TERR

FRIARS BRAE

1 BURGESS HILL

2 PRIORY RD

CLARENDON RD

Porterside

LINLITHGOW

Clarendon House

FRIARS LOAN

1

2

Friar's Brae

RIVALDSG

RIVALDE AVE

GREEN CRES

MANSE RD

FRIARS WAY

OATLANDS PK

Parkly Place

DEACONS PL

PADDOCKH

RICCARTON

CARMEL

SMIL

PK

BECHWOOD

THE GLEBE

EH49

Parkly Craigs

Jock's Hill

Nancy's Hill

76

Dark Entry

Peat Hill

Haugh Burn

2

Carsie Hill

Hiltly

Cauldhame

Hillhouse Farm

Riccarton

Riccarton Burn

75

Riccarton Bridge

Visitor Centre

P

Caravan Park

Deer Parks

Fish Farm

Broomyknowes

1

Beecraigs Country Park

P

Beecraigs Loch

Broomy Knowes

Mochries Craig

Beecraigs Wood

74

00 D 01 E 02 F

EH30

Philpstoun House

Hopetoun Wood

Woodville

The Manse

A904

B8020

Woodend

4

East Philpstoun

EH49

Galascrook

Abercorn Prim Sch

WHITEQUARRIES IND EST

Duntarvie

77

Philpstoun Mill

Bailies Muir

Philpstoun Muir

Craigton

Fawnspark

Craigton House

3

Union Canal

EH52

M9

B8046

Mounthooly

The Den

Myre

76

Trinlaymire

2

Garage

Lampinsdub

TIPPET KNOWES CT

AULDCATHIE PL

MAIN ST B9080

Bennett WOOD TERR

Glendevon

Winchburgh Prim Sch

CHESTNUT GR

ABERCORN PL

NIDDRY VIEW

MIDHOPE PL

CRAIGTON PL

75

Glendevon Cottages

Holy Family RC Prim Sch

NIDDRY RD

Winchburgh

Tippet Knowes

Millcraig

BELL'S MILL TERR

GLASS PL GLASS CRES GLASS RD

Cemy

1

Niddry Burn

Kirklands

Fauchel Dean

B8020

Niddry

74

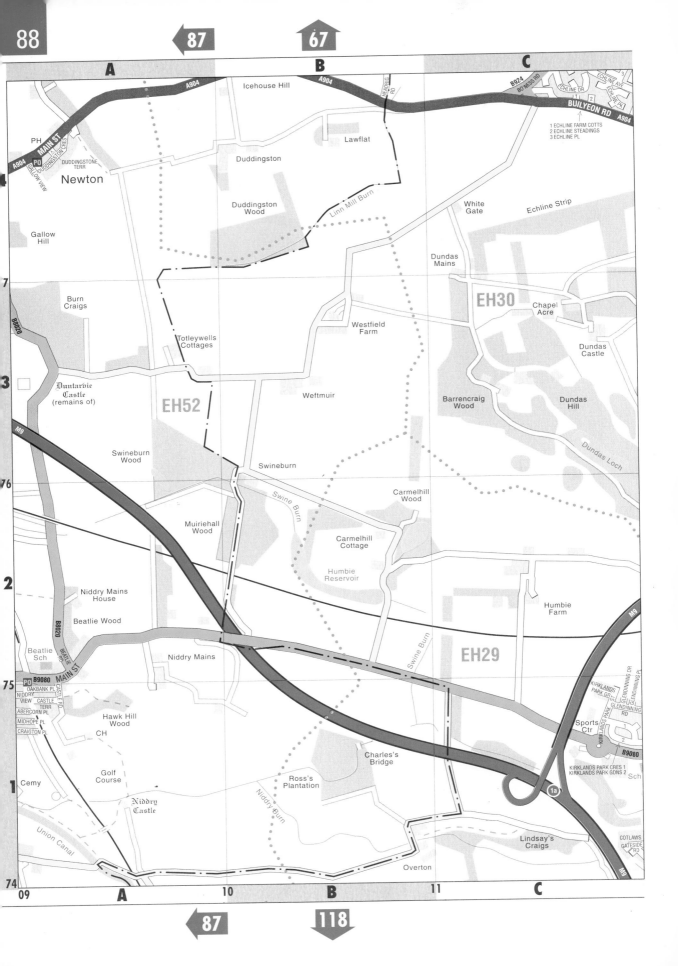

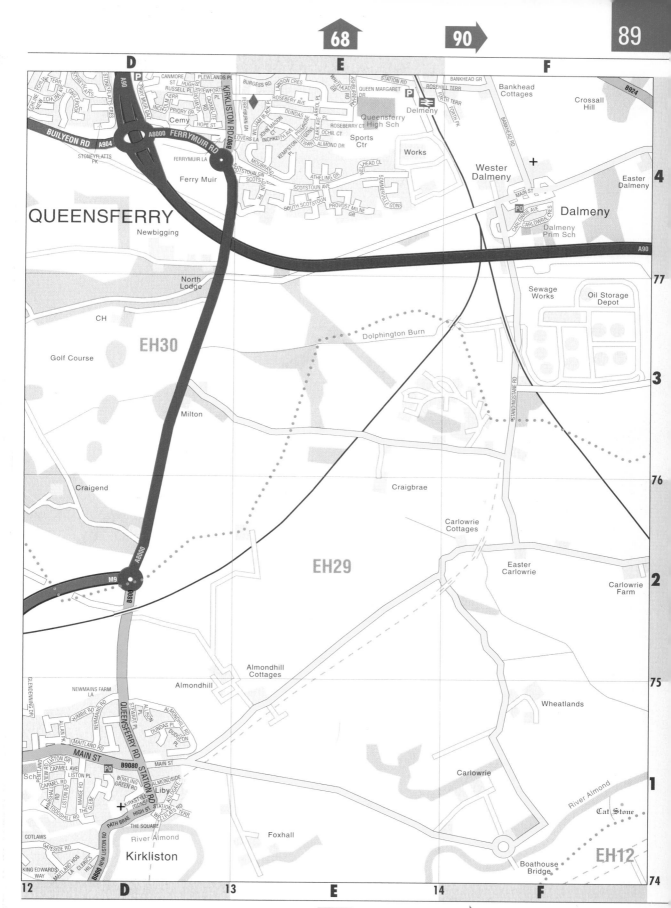

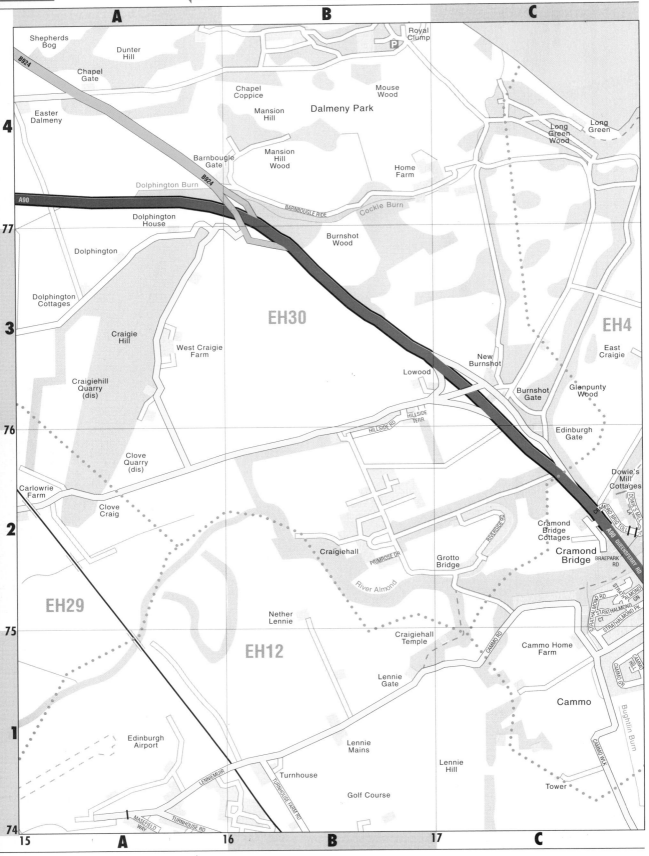

Shepherds Bog

B924

Dunter Hill

Chapel Gate

Royal Clump

P

Chapel Coppice

Mouse Wood

Dalmeny Park

Long Green Wood

Long Green

Easter Dalmeny

Mansion Hill

4

Barnbougle Gate

Mansion Hill Wood

Home Farm

Dolphington Burn

A90

B924

BARNBOUGLE RIDE

Cockle Burn

77

Dolphington House

Burnshot Wood

Dolphington

EH30

EH4

Dolphington Cottages

Craigie Hill

West Craigie Farm

New Burnshot

East Craigie

3

Lowood

Burnshot Gate

Glenpunty Wood

Craigiehill Quarry (dis)

76

HILLSIDE RD

HILLSIDE TERR

Edinburgh Gate

Clove Quarry (dis)

Dowie's Mill Cottages

Carlowrie Farm

CRAMOND BRIG TOLL

DOWIE'S MILL LA

Clove Craig

Cramond Bridge Cottages

A90 QUEENSFERRY RD

2

Craigiehall

PRIMROSE DR

Grotto Bridge

RIVERSIDE RD

Cramond Bridge

BRAEPARK RD

EH29

River Almond

STRATHALMOND RD

STRATHALMOND GN

STRATHALMOND RD CT

STRATHALMOND PK

Nether Lennie

Cammo Home Farm

CAMMO RD

CAMMO HILL

CAMMO CR

75

Craigiehall Temple

EH12

Lennie Gate

Cammo

1

Edinburgh Airport

Lennie Mains

Lennie Hill

CAMMO WLK

Bughtlin Burn

Tower

LENNIEMUIR

Turnhouse

Golf Course

74

MASSFIELD WAY

TURNHOUSE RD

TURNHOUSE FARM RD

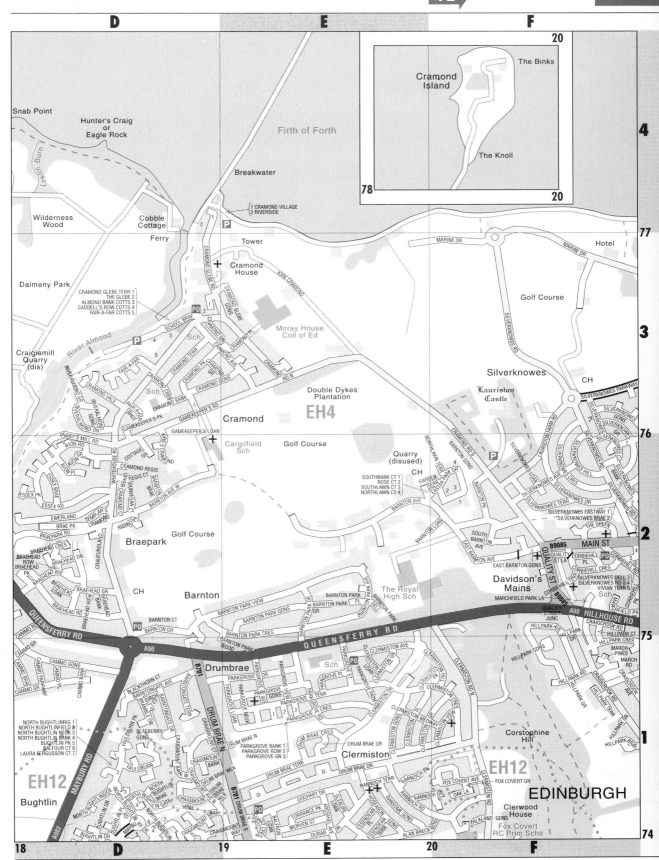

D · E · F

20

Cramond Island

The Binks

The Knoll

78 · 20

4

Snab Point

Hunter's Craig or Eagle Rock

Firth of Forth

Breakwater

1 CRAMOND VILLAGE
2 RIVERSIDE

MARINE DR

Hotel

77

Wilderness Wood

Cobble Cottage

Ferry

Tower

Cramond House

MARINE DR

Golf Course

SILVERKNOWES RD

Dalmeny Park

CRAMOND GLEBE TERR 1
THE GLEBE 2
ALMOND BANK COTTS 3
CADDELL'S ROW COTTS 4
FAIR-A-FAR COTTS 5

KIRK CRAMOND

Moray House Coll of Ed

Silverknowes

CH

3

Craigiemill Quarry (dis)

River Almond

Sch

Sch

Double Dykes Plantation

EH4

Lauriston Castle

SILVERKNOWES PARKWAY

76

Cramond

Cargilfield Sch

Golf Course

Quarry (disused)

CH

SOUTHBANK CT 1
ROSE CT 2
SOUTHLAWN CT 3
NORTHLAWN CT 4

SILVERKNOWES EASTWAY 1
SILVERKNOWES BRAE 2
THE GREEN

MAIN ST

2

Essex Pk

Essex Rd

Ewerland

Braepark

Golf Course

Barnton

CH

Braehead

South Barnton Ave

EAST BARNTON GDNS

Davidson's Mains

MARCHFIELD PARK LA

CORBIEHILL PL
CORBIEHILL CRES

SILVERKNOWES DELL 3
SILVERKNOWES RD S 4
VIVIAN TERR S

Sch

QUALITY ST

B9085

HILLHOUSE RD

CRAIGCROOK RD

75

QUEENSFERRY RD

A90

Barnton Park View

BARNTON PARK

The Royal High Sch

QUEENSFERRY RD

HILLPARK AVE

HILLPARK GDNS

MARCH PINES

MARCH RD

CAMMO RD

CAMMO GR

Drumbrae

B701

PARKGROVE DR

Sch

PO

CLERMISTON AVE

CLERMISTON RD

HILLPARK DR

HILLPARK TERR

CRAIGCROOK AVE

Corstophine Hill

1

NORTH BUGHTLINRIG 1
NORTH BUGHTLINFIELD 2
NORTH BUGHTLIN NEUK 3
NORTH BUGHTLIN BANK 4
BUGHTLIN PK 5
BALFOUR CT 6
LAURA FERGUSSON CT 7

EH12

Bughtlin

MAYBURY RD

DRUM BRAE N

B701

Clermiston

PARKGROVE BANK 1
PARKGROVE ROW 2
PARKGROVE GN 3

DRUM BRAE GR

Fox Covert Ave

EH12

Fox Covert Gr

Clerwood House

Fox Covert RC Prim Schs

EDINBURGH

74

18 · D · 19 · E · 20 · F

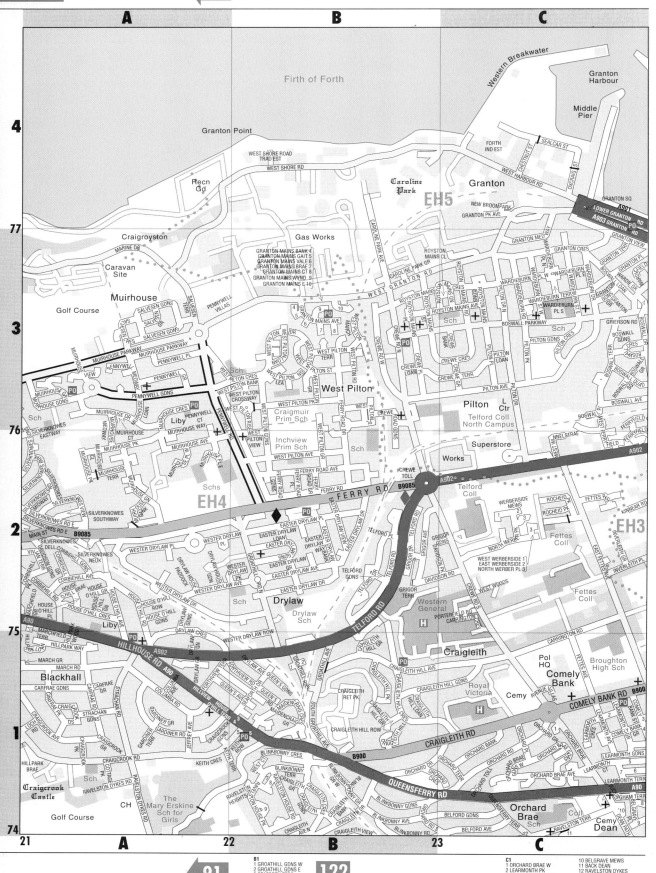

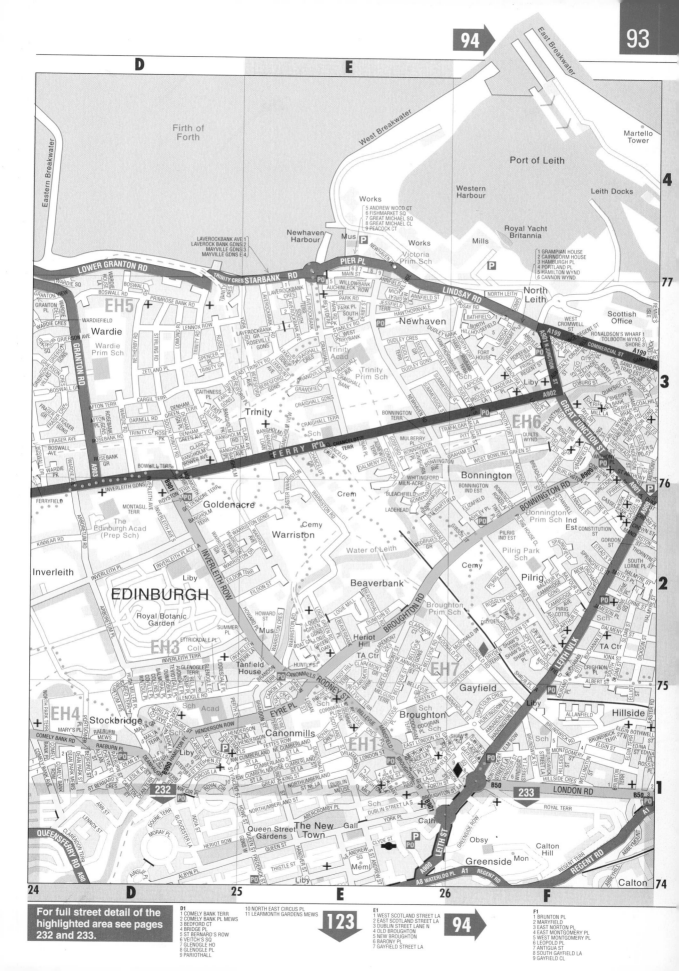

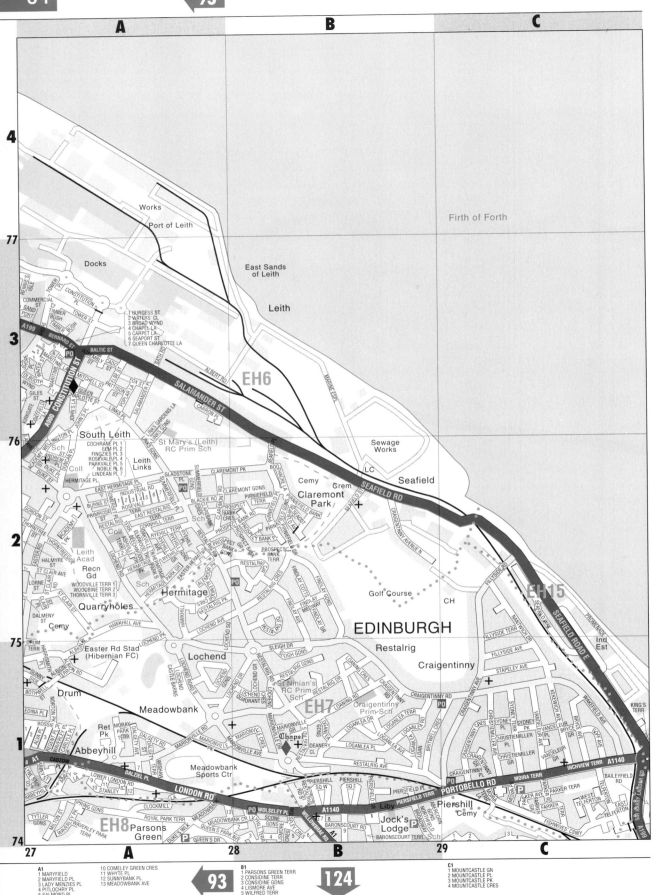

A   B   C

4

77

Firth of Forth

Works
Port of Leith

Docks

East Sands
of Leith

Leith

1 BURGESS ST
2 WATERS CL
3 BROAD WYND
4 CHAPEL LA
5 CARPET LA
6 SEAPORT ST
7 QUEEN CHARLOTTE LA

3

A199

BALTIC ST

SALAMANDER ST   EH6

ALBERT RD

South Leith

COCHRANE PL 1
ELM PL 2
FINGZIES PL 3
ROSEVALE PL 4
PARKVALE PL 5
NOBLE PL 6
LINDEAN PL 7

St Mary's (Leith)
RC Prim Sch

Leith
Links

Sewage
Works

76   Coll

Claremont Park

Claremont
Park

Cemy

Crem

LC

Seafield

SEAFIELD RD

Leith
Acad

2   Coll

Prospect
Bank
Sch

Golf Course

CH

EH15

Recn
Gd

WOODVILLE TERR 1
WOODBINE PL 2
THORNVILLE TERR 3

Hermitage

Quarryholes

EDINBURGH

Restalrig

Craigentinny

FILLYSIDE

SEAFIELD ROAD E

Ind
Est

King's
Terr

Dalmeny
Cemy

75   DRUM
TERR

Easter Rd Stad
(Hibernian FC)

Lochend

Sleigh Dr

St Ninian's
RC Prim
Sch

EH7

Craigentinny
Prim Sch

Drum

Meadowbank

Chapel

Meadowbank
Sports Ctr

PORTOBELLO RD

Moira Terr

INCHVIEW TERR   A1140

Baileyfield
Rd

1   A1

CADZOW

Abbeyhill

DALZIEL PL

LOWER LONDON RD

STANLEY

LONDON RD

CLOCKMILL

Piershill

Piershill
SQ W

Piershill
SQ E

Liby

Piershill
Cemy

WOLSELEY PL   A1140

Jock's
Lodge

Piershill

EH8   Parsons
Green

Royal Park
Park

Meadowbank

Jock's
Lodge

74
27   A   28   B   29   C

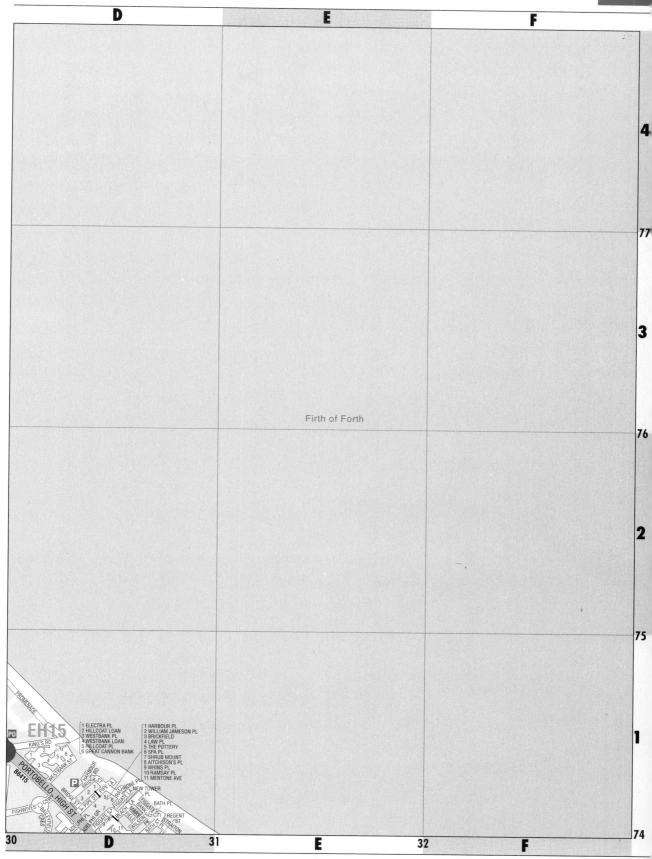

Firth of Forth

D   E   F

4

77

3

76

2

75

1

74

EH15

PROMENADE

PO

KING'S RD

WESTBANK ST

PORTOBELLO HIGH ST
B6415

FISHWIVES
CSWY
BALEFIELD
CRES

1 ELECTRA PL	1 HARBOUR PL
2 HILLCOAT LOAN	2 WILLIAM JAMESON PL
3 WESTBANK PL	3 BRICKFIELD
4 WESTBANK LOAN	4 LAW PL
5 HILLCOAT PL	5 THE POTTERY
6 GREAT CANNON BANK	6 SPA PL
	7 SHRUB MOUNT
	8 AITCHISON'S PL
	9 WHINS PL
	10 RAMSAY PL
	11 MENTONE AVE

HARBOUR
BRIDGE RD

P

BRIDGE ST

PIPE ST

RATHBONE PL

FIGGATE LA

NEW TOWER
PL

BATH PL

FIGGATE BANK

BATH ST

REGENT
ST

STRATTON

ADELPHI PL

ADELPHI GR

BEACH LA

FIELD

MARL

PK

WILSON'S

Sch

30   D   31   E   32   F

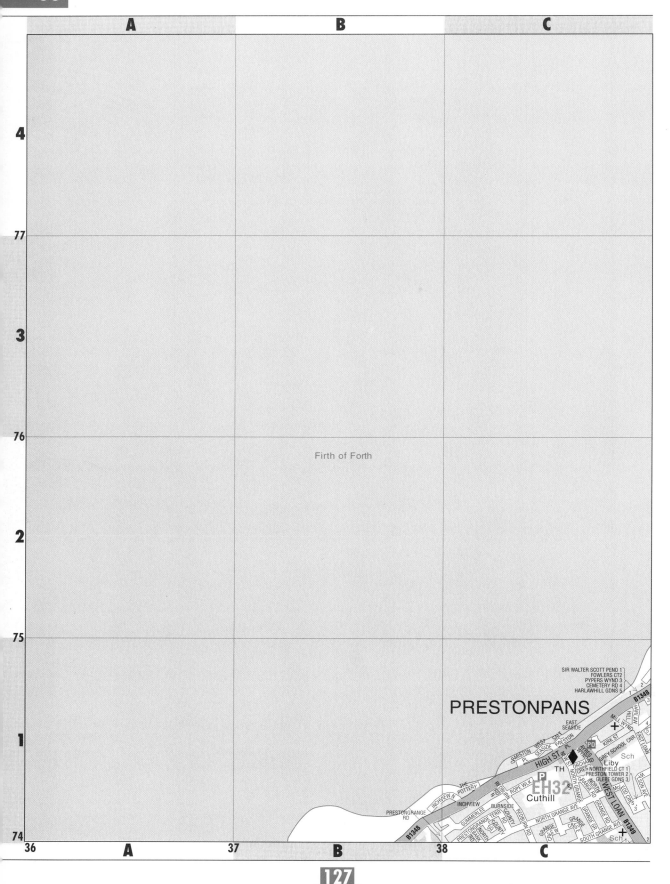

A   B   C

4

77

3

76

Firth of Forth

2

75

SIR WALTER SCOTT PEND 1
FOWLERS CT 2
PYPERS WYND 3
CEMETERY RD 4
HARLAWHILL GDNS 5

PRESTONPANS

EAST
SEASIDE

1

HIGH ST

Liby
NORTHFIELD CT 1
PRESTON TOWER 2
GLEBE GDNS 3

EH32

Cuthill

PRESTONGRANGE
RD

74

36   A   37   B   38   C

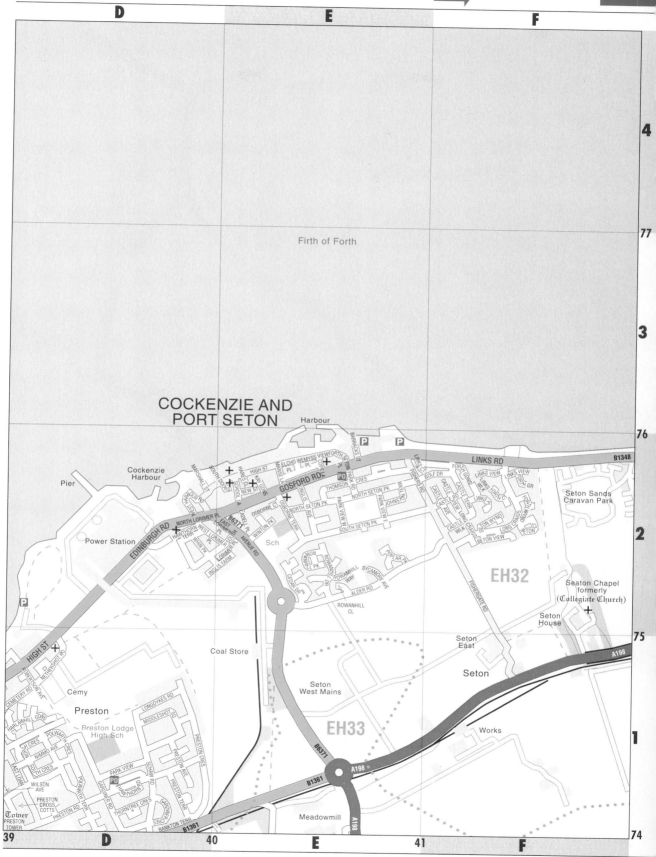

D · E · F

Firth of Forth

COCKENZIE AND PORT SETON

Harbour

Cockenzie Harbour

Pier

Power Station

Seton Sands Caravan Park

LINKS RD

B1348

GOSFORD RD

EDINBURGH RD

EH32

Seaton Chapel formerly (Collegiate Church)

Seton House

Coal Store

HIGH ST

Cemy

Preston

Preston Lodge High Sch

Seton East

Seton

Seton West Mains

EH33

Works

Tower
PRESTON TOWER

Meadowmill

A198

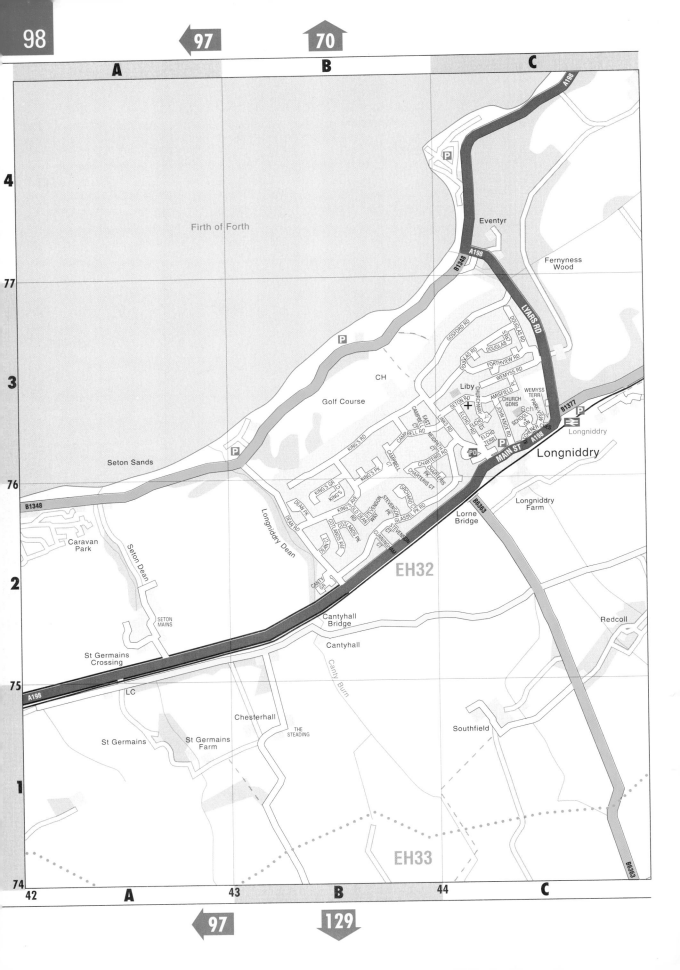

Firth of Forth

Golf Course

CH

Seton Sands

Liby

SCH
Longniddry

Longniddry

MAIN ST

A198

B1377

Eventyr

Fernyness
Wood

LYARS RD

B1348

A198

GOSFORD RD

DOUGLAS RD

DOUGLAS

DOUGLAS RD

FORTHVIEW RD

WEMYSS RD

WEMYSS
TERR

AMISFIELD

CHURCH
GDNS

PARK VIEW

GARDENER CRES

SETON RD

CHURCHWAY

JOHN KNOX RD

ELCHO RD

ELCHO TERR

ELCHO

EAST
CAMPBELL
CT

NEWPATH
CT

LINKS RD

CHARTERS RD

CHARTERS CT

CHARTERS
PK RD

CHARTERS CT

CAMPBELL RD

CAMPBELL
CT

KING'S RD

KING'S PK

KING'S AVE

KING'S GR

KING'S
PK

KING'S
RD

KING'S
OLD RD

ORCHARD CT

STEVENSON
WAY

STEVENSON
PK

GLASSEL PK RD

STEVENSON

DEAN PK

DEAN RD

COTLANDS PK

COTLANDS AVE

COTLANDS
CT

CUNNINGHAM

CANTY
GR

Longniddry Dean

Lorne
Bridge

Longniddry
Farm

B6363

EH32

Caravan
Park

Seton Dean

SETON
MAINS

Cantyhall
Bridge

Cantyhall

Redcoll

St Germains
Crossing

LC

A198

Canty Burn

Chesterhall

THE
STEADING

Southfield

St Germains

St Germains
Farm

EH33

B6363

B1348

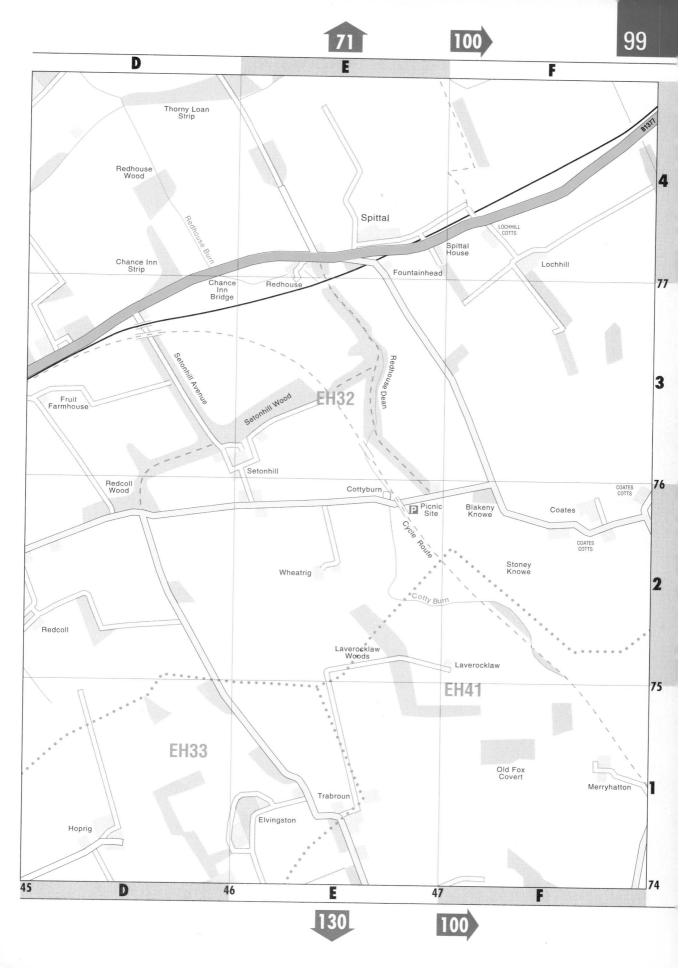

A **B** **C**

B1377
A6137

Ballencrieff
Corn Hill
Viewmont
Poultry Farm
Glenarrol
Gallows Law
Camptoun
Camptoun House

4

Poultry Farm
Garleton
EH32
EH39
East Garleton

77

Byres
B1343
EAST GARLETON COTTS

Rye Hill
Jinging Hill
Hopetoun Monument
Garleton Hills
Skid Hill

3

West Garleton Farm
B1343
Byres Hill
Picnic Site
Score Hill

West Garleton House

76

West Garleton Holdings
Phantassie Hill

Bangly Hill

Blackmains Toll

BANGLY BRAE
Woodlea

2

EH41
Alderston Mains

Bangly Quarry

Alderston Hill
Harperdean

75

Huntington

Alderston Mains Dairy
A1

UGSTON COTTS
Ugston
Crow Wood
Alderston
A199
PEPPERCRAIG QUARRY IND SITE

1

Merryhatton Cottages
Aldeston Burn
HARPERDEAN TERR 1
GARLETON DR 2
A199
A6137
H

South Lodge
Cycle Route
HALDANE AVE
QUEENS AVE
LESTER PL
DAVIDSON TERR
DUNPENDER DR
ABERLADY RD
BAIRD TERR
CAPONFLAT CRES
BEECHWOOD RD
ALDERSTON PL
HAWTHORNBANK RD
HOSPITAL RD
H Roodlands General
Works
HOPETOUN DR

74

48 **A** 49 **B** 50 **C**

A1
A199
GATESIDE AVE
ALDERSTON MOWS
LWR ALDERSTON RD

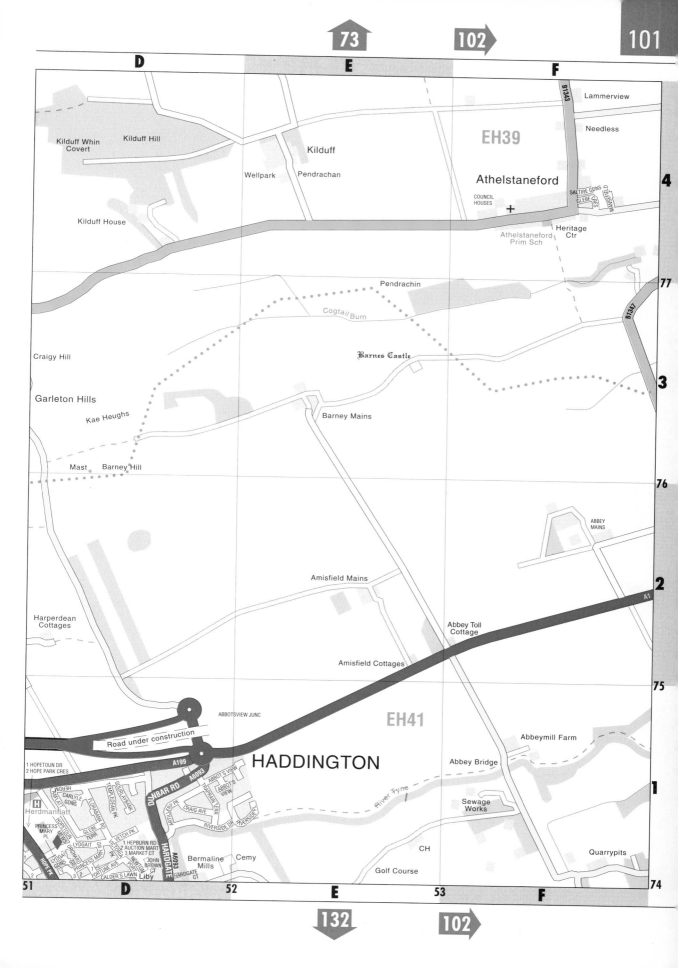

Lammerview
B1343
EH39
Needless

Kilduff Whin
Covert
Kilduff Hill
Kilduff

Wellpark
Pendrachan
Athelstaneford

SALTIRE GDNS
MANSFIELD
COUNCIL
HOUSES
GLEBE CRES
4

Kilduff House
+

Heritage
Ctr
Athelstaneford
Prim Sch

77

Pendrachin
B1347

Cogtail Burn

Craigy Hill
Barnes Castle

Garleton Hills
3

Kae Heughs
Barney Mains

Mast   Barney Hill

76

ABBEY
MAINS

Amisfield Mains
2
A1

Harperdean
Cottages
Abbey Toll
Cottage

Amisfield Cottages

75

EH41

Abbeymill Farm

Road under construction
ABBOTSVIEW JUNC
Abbey Bridge

A199
HADDINGTON

1 HOPETOUN DR
2 HOPE PARK CRES
A6093
ABBOT'S VIEW
ABBOT'S
VIEW
River Tyne

DUNBAR RD
H
Herdmanflatt
CRAIG AVE
RIVERSIDE DR
1
Sewage
Works

PRINCESS
MARY
PL
1 HEPBURN RD
AUCTION MART
3 MARKET CT
CH

HOPE PK
HARDGATE
A6093
Bermaline
Mills
Cemy
Golf Course
Quarrypits

Liby
HARDGATE
CT

101
74

A
B
C

B1347

Kennel
Strip

Gilmerton
House

Home
Farm

EH40

EH39

Markle
Mains

Peffer Burn

4

Athelstaneford
Mains

Sewage
Works

Cogtail
Bridge

B1347

77

Markle Mains Heights

Markle
Quarry

Beanston
Mains

Pencraig
Wood

3

A1

B1347

Beanston

Monksmuir
Caravan Park

76

Crockers Hedges

Brown Knowe
Plantation

EH41

2

B1347

Beanston
Mill

A1

Sandy's
Mill

Nether
Hailes

Mill Lade

River Tyne

75

Stevenson
House

Bearford
Bridge

East
Bearford

1

Lady's
Wood

Stevenson
Mains

Bearford Burn

Stevenson
Wood

74

54
A
55
B
56
C

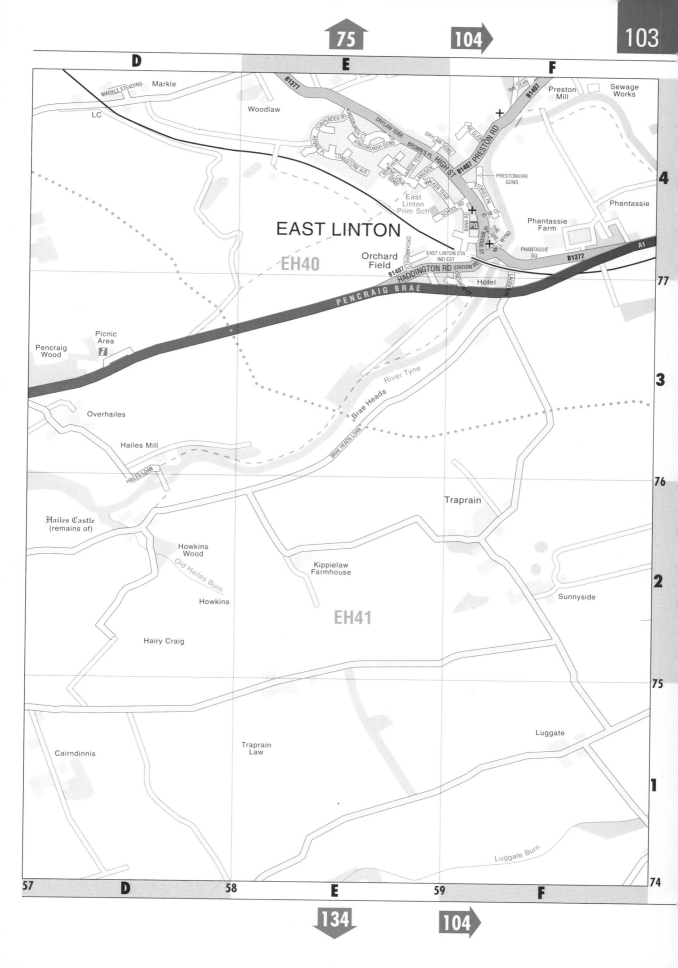

D · E · F

MARKLE STEADING · Markle
Woodlaw
LC
B1377
DUMPENDER RD · KINGSBURY CT · DRYLAW TERR · DRYLAW GDNS · THE DEAN · B1407 · Preston Mill · Sewage Works
RENNIE PL · KINGSBURGH GDNS · BROWN'S PL · HIGH ST · THE GLEBE · PRESTON RD
LONGSTONE AVE · BRAE VIEW · MC CALL GDNS · HARDIE TERR · LANGSIDE · KEIR TERR · WALKER TERR · SCHOOL RD · B1407 · STORES PL · PRESTONKIRK GDNS
East Linton Prim Sch · BANK RD · TYNE CL · Phantassie
PO · THE SQUARE · Phantassie Farm

EAST LINTON

ORCHARDFIELD · BRIDGE ST · MILL WYND · Phantassie

EH40 · Orchard Field · EAST LINTON STA IND EST · PHANTASSIE SQ · B1377 · A1
B1407 · HADDINGTON RD · STATION RD · LAUDER RD · Hotel

PENCRAIG BRAE · ORCHARD CT · 77

Picnic Area
Pencraig Wood
River Tyne
Overhailes · Brae Heads
Hailes Mill · BRAE HEADS LOAN
HAILES LOAN · 76

Traprain

Hailes Castle (remains of)
Howkins Wood
Old Hailes Burn
Kippielaw Farmhouse
Howkins · Sunnyside · 2

EH41

Hairy Craig
75

Luggate

Cairndinnis · Traprain Law
1

Luggate Burn
74

57 · D · 58 · E · 59 · F

103
76

A   B   C

Knowes Mill
Ford
Knowes
Kirklandhill
A198
Tynefield
Kirklandhill Cottages
River Tyne
A1
The North Lodge
4
LC
Ninewar
A1
EH40
Ninewar Wood
77
Howmuir
Pudlum
EH42
3
Beesknowe
76
West Lodge
Biel Water
Bielmill
Grangelea
Biel Park Cottage
2
Bielgrange
Grangemuir
Whittingehame Water
Ginglet House
75
Ginglet Hill
East Lodge
Newbarns
B6370
MILL RD
Quarry Hill
Sauchet Water
Luggate Burn
1
PO
ROOD WELL COTTS
EH41
Ruchlaw Mains
THE CROFTS
Eastfield
Stenton
Luggate Burn
Whittingehame Water
Ruchlaw
Stenton House
Redcliff
B6370
Sch
Loanhead
STENTON LOAN
74

60   A   61   B   62   C

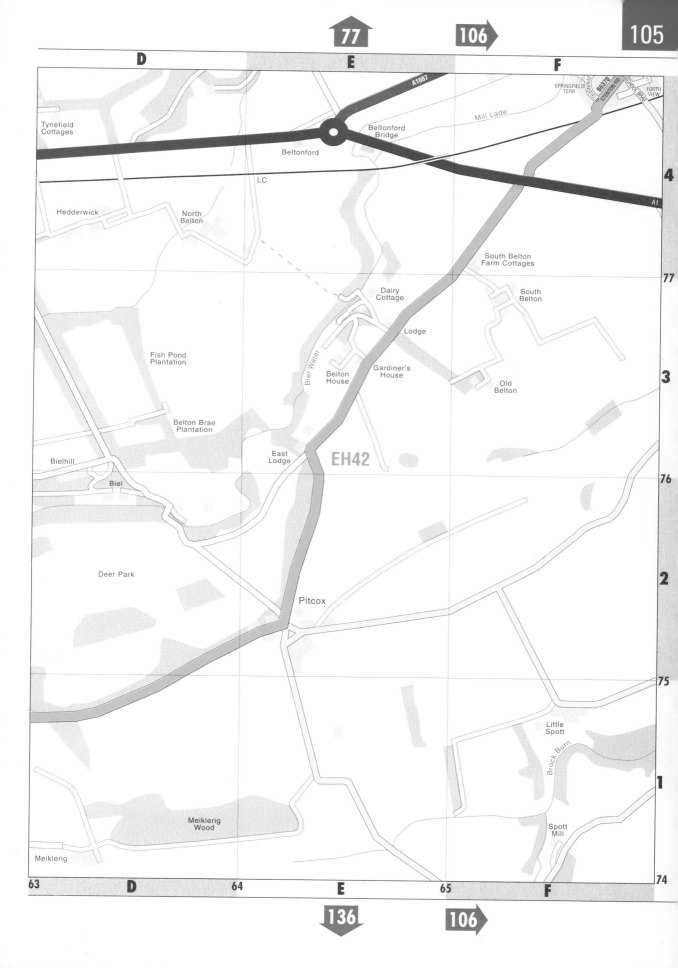

D
E
F

A1087

Springfield
Terr
B6370
Stenton Rd
School Brae
Forth
View

Tynefield
Cottages

Beltonford
Bridge

Mill Lade

Beltonford

LC

4

A1

Hedderwick

North
Belton

South Belton
Farm Cottages

77

Dairy
Cottage

South
Belton

Biel Water

Fish Pond
Plantation

Lodge

Belton
House

Gardiner's
House

Old
Belton

3

Belton Brae
Plantation

Bielhill

East
Lodge

EH42

76

Biel

Deer Park

2

Pitcox

75

Little
Spott

Brock Burn

1

Meiklerig
Wood

Spott
Mill

Meiklerig

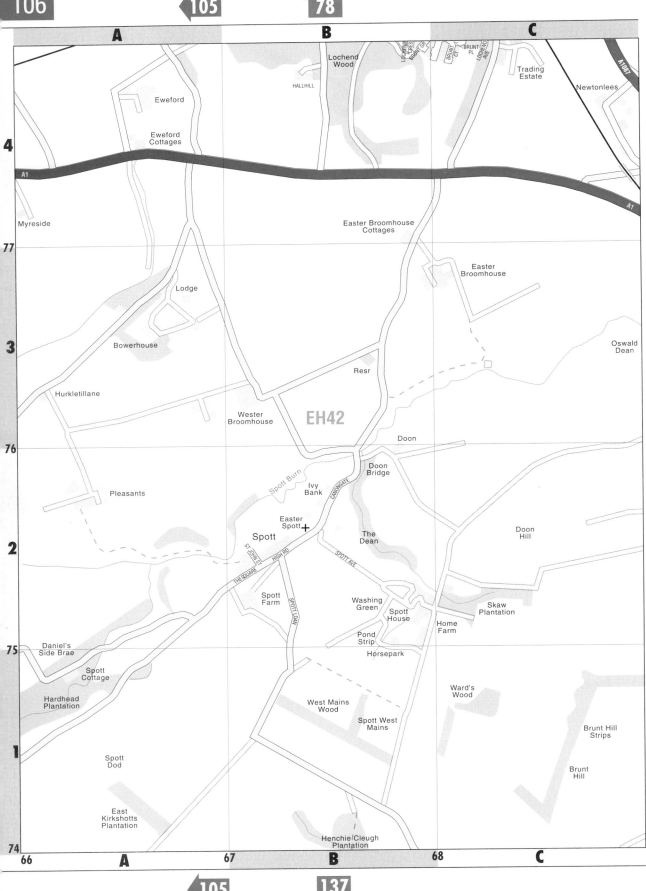

A1

4

Eweford

Eweford
Cottages

Lochend
Wood

HALLHILL

LOCHEND
CRES

BRUNT GR

BRUNT
PL

BRUNT
CT

BRUNT
AVE

LOCHEND
AVE

Trading
Estate

Newtonlees

A1087

A1

Myreside

Easter Broomhouse
Cottages

77

Lodge

Easter
Broomhouse

3

Bowerhouse

Resr

Oswald
Dean

Hurkletillane

Wester
Broomhouse

EH42

Doon

76

Doon
Bridge

Pleasants

Spott Burn

Ivy
Bank

CANONGATE

Easter
Spott

Doon
Hill

Spott

The
Dean

2

ST JOHN'S ST

HIGH RD

SPOTT AVE

THE SQUARE

Spott
Farm

SPOTT LOAN

Washing
Green

Spott
House

Skaw
Plantation

Home
Farm

Daniel's
Side Brae

Pond
Strip

75

Spott
Cottage

Horsepark

Hardhead
Plantation

West Mains
Wood

Ward's
Wood

Spott West
Mains

Brunt Hill
Strips

1

Spott
Dod

Brunt
Hill

East
Kirkshotts
Plantation

Henchie Cleugh
Plantation

74

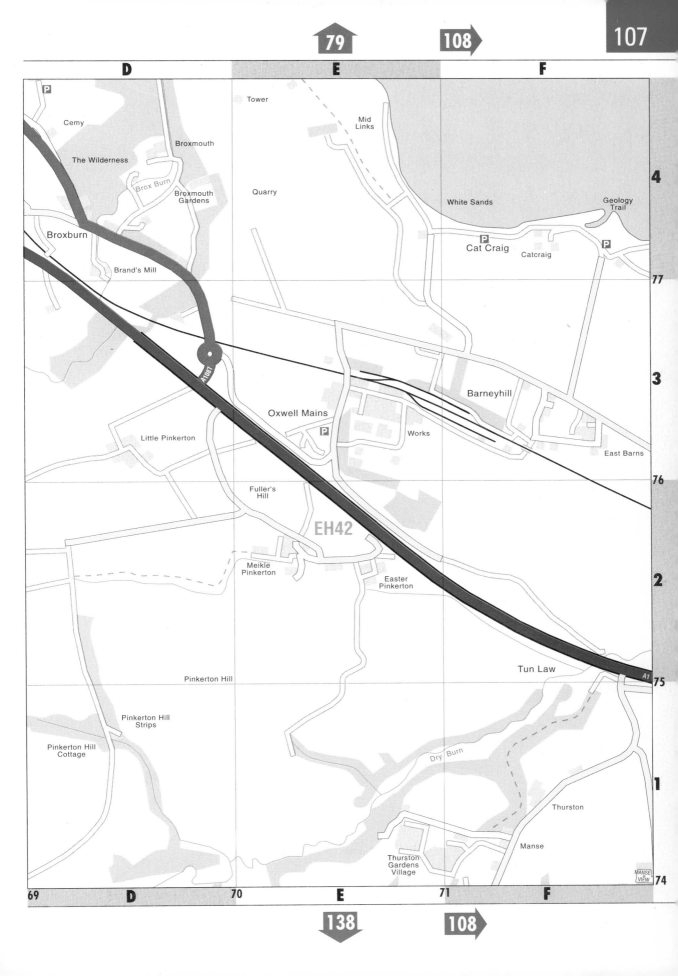

D

E

F

4

Tower

Mid Links

Cemy

Broxmouth

The Wilderness

Brox Burn

Quarry

White Sands

Geology Trail

Broxmouth Gardens

P Cat Craig

Catcraig

P

77

Broxburn

Brand's Mill

A1087

3

Barneyhill

Oxwell Mains

Little Pinkerton

P

Works

East Barns

76

Fuller's Hill

EH42

2

Meikle Pinkerton

Easter Pinkerton

Tun Law

A1

75

Pinkerton Hill

Pinkerton Hill Strips

Dry Burn

1

Pinkerton Hill Cottage

Thurston

Manse

Thurston Gardens Village

MANSE VIEW

74

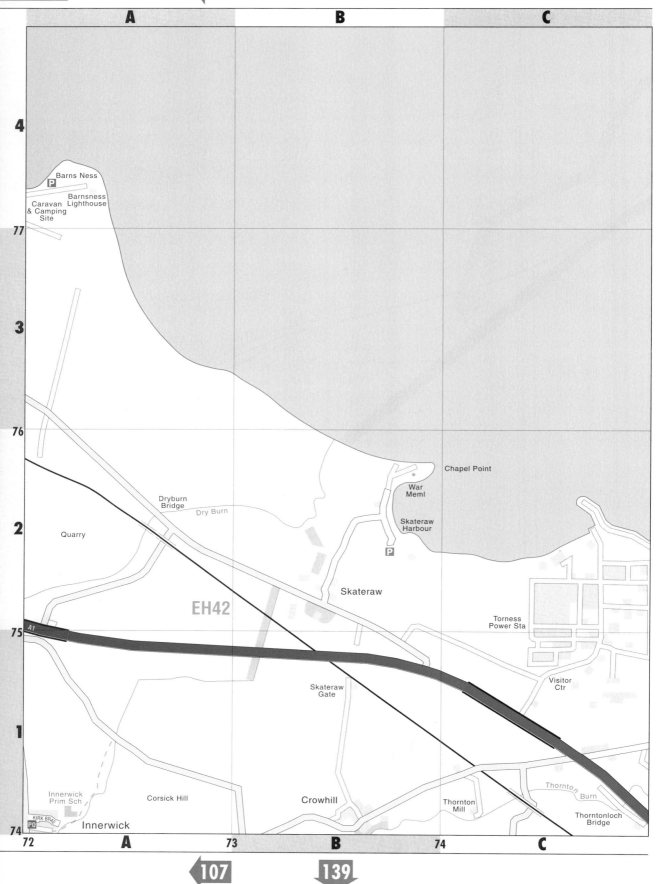

A

B

C

4

Barns Ness

P

Barnsness
Lighthouse
Caravan
& Camping
Site

77

3

76

Chapel Point

Dryburn
Bridge

Dry Burn

War
Meml

Skateraw
Harbour

Quarry

P

2

EH42

Skateraw

Torness
Power Sta

A1

75

Skateraw
Gate

Visitor
Ctr

1

Innerwick
Prim Sch

Corsick Hill

Crowhill

Thornton
Mill

Thornton Burn

KIRK BRAE

PO

Innerwick

Thorntonloch
Bridge

72

A

73

B

74

C

74

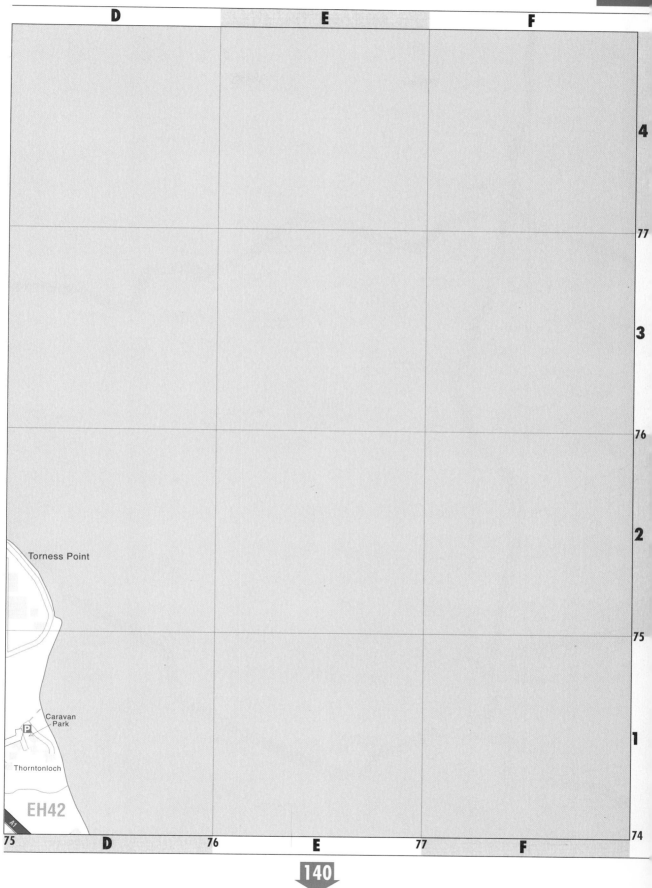

Torness Point

Caravan
Park

Thorntonloch

EH42

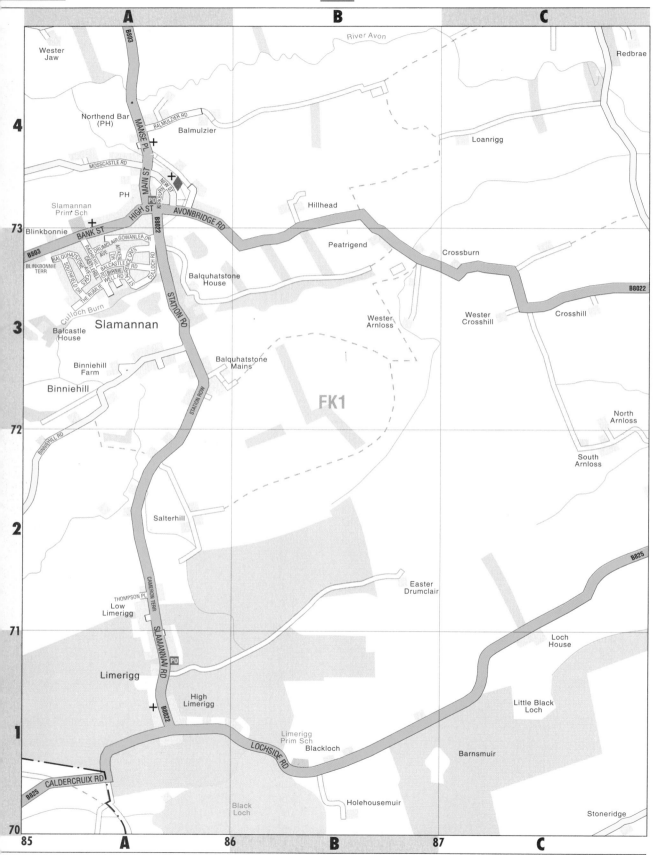

Boxton

Boagstown

Hareburn

B8028

North Bankhead

4

Balmitchell

Windy-yett

Avonview

Manse

South Bankhead

Whinny Knowes

B8028

73

River Avon

Bogo

Neucks

THE NEUCKS

FK1

AVON PK

SLAMANNAN RD

B825

3

Summerhouse

Babbithill

B8022

Crossroads

Craigend

Bulliondale

72

Dykehead

Wester Holehouse

North East Holehouse

Holehouse

Redhall

Lin Mill Burn

2

South Holehouse

Easter Greenhill

Linhouse Farm

Elrigside Wood

East Plantation

Wester Greenhill

Drumtassie Burn

71

Barns

North Rhodens Plantation

1

70

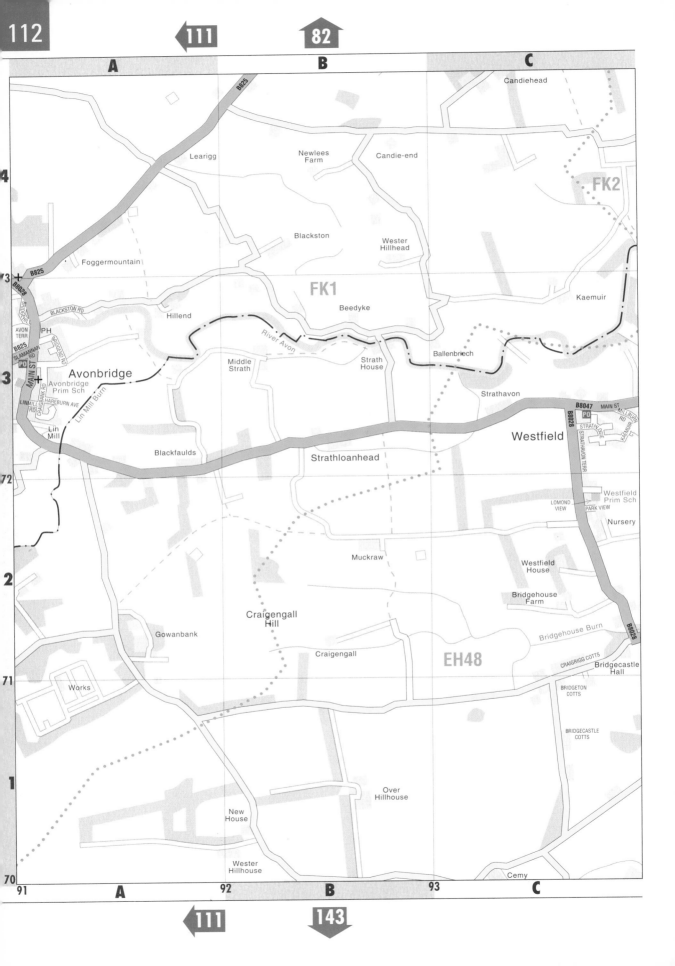

111
82

A B C

4

FK2

Candiehead

Learigg

Newlees Farm

Candie-end

Blackston

Wester Hillhead

73

B825

B8028

FK1

Beedyke

Kaemuir

Foggermountain

BLACKSTON RD

Hillend

River Avon

Ballenbriech

BRIDGEHILL

AVON TERR

SPRINGHOLL RD

PH

Middle Strath

Strath House

Strathavon

B825

SLAMANNAN RD

MAIN ST

PO

3

Avonbridge

Avonbridge Prim Sch

B8047 MAIN ST

B8028

PO

MILLBURN RD

KAEMUIR CT

STRATHAVON TERR

LINMILL RD

CRAIGBANK RD

HAREBURN AVE

Lin Mill Burn

Westfield

STRATHDIKE

Lin Mill

Blackfaulds

Strathloanhead

LOMOND VIEW

PARK VIEW

Westfield Prim Sch

72

Nursery

Muckraw

Westfield House

2

Bridgehouse Farm

Craigengall Hill

Gowanbank

Bridgehouse Burn

B8028

Craigengall

EH48

CRAIGRIGG COTTS

Bridgecastle Hall

71

Works

BRIDGETON COTTS

BRIDGECASTLE COTTS

1

Over Hillhouse

New House

Wester Hillhouse

Cemy

70

91 A 92 B 93 C

111
143

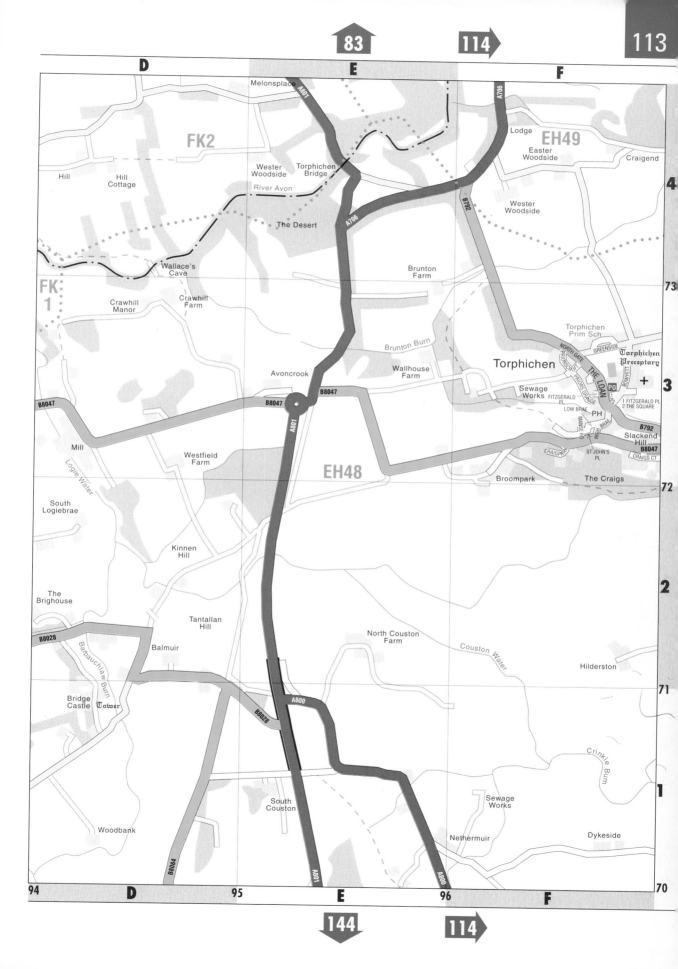

D

E

F

Melonsplace

A801

A706

Lodge

EH49

FK2

Easter
Woodside

Craigend

Hill

Hill
Cottage

Wester
Woodside

Torphichen
Bridge

River Avon

B792

4

Wester
Woodside

The Desert

A706

Brunton
Farm

73

Wallace's
Cave

Torphichen
Prim Sch

GREENSIDE

Crawhill
Manor

Crawhill
Farm

Brunton Burn

Torphichen
Preceptory

FK
1

NORTH GATE

PRIORSCROFT

THE LOAN

BONNYETT

+

3

Avoncrook

B8047

Wallhouse
Farm

Torphichen

PRIORS GRANGE

PO
1

B8047

B8047

Sewage
Works

FITZGERALD
PL

1 FITZGERALD PL
2 THE SQUARE

LOW BRAE

PH

B792

Mill

Westfield
Farm

A801

EH48

MANSE RD

HIGH BRAE

Slackend
Hill

B8047
CRAIGS CT

Logie Water

CRAIGPARK

ST JOHN'S
PL

South
Logiebrae

Broompark

The Craigs

72

Kinnen
Hill

2

The
Brighouse

Tantallan
Hill

North Couston
Farm

Couston Water

Hilderston

B8028

Balmuir

Barbauchlaw Burn

71

Bridge
Castle Tower

B8028

A800

Crinkle Burn

A801

A800

1

South
Couston

Sewage
Works

B8084

Woodbank

Nethermuir

Dykeside

D
E
F

113
84

A   **B**   **C**

Cow Hill

EH49

Tower

Lochcote Resr

Kipps (remains of)

Kipps Hill

Kipps Farm

EH49

Beecraigs Wood

Beecraigs Country Park

4

Refuge Stone

Wairdlaw

Gormyre

73

Witch Craig Wood

Hanging Rock Plantation

Gormyre Hill

3

Stoney Manuel Plantation

Torpichen Hills

Craigmailing

Cathlaw House

Slackend

B792

B8047

CRAIGS CT

MALLENS BRAE

CATHLAW LA

EH48

Cathlawhill

North Mine Plantation

72

Bishopbrae Strips

Cairnpapple Henge & Cairn

Cairnpapple Hill

Mast

2

P

The Glebe

Hilderston Hills

Knock

Bishopbrae

P The Knock

71

Resr

Crinkle Burn

Crinkle Bridge

Ballencrieff Mains

Sheddon Braes

Raven Craig Wood

1

Bathgate Hills

Resr

Golf Course

B792

TORPICHEN RD

BALLENCRIEFF TOLL

Galabraes

Wester Drumcross

70

97   **A**   98   **B**   99   **C**

113
145

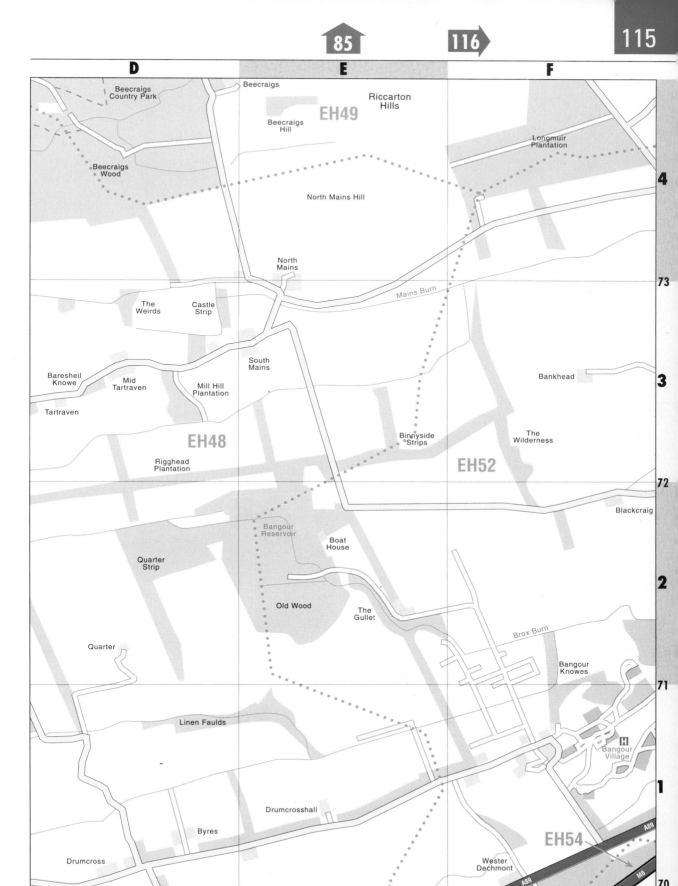

D
E
F

Beecraigs
Country Park
Beecraigs
Riccarton
Hills
EH49
Beecraigs
Hill
Longmuir
Plantation
Beecraigs
Wood

4

North Mains Hill

North
Mains

73

The
Weirds
Castle
Strip
Mains Burn

South
Mains

Baresheil
Knowe
Mid
Tartraven
Mill Hill
Plantation
EH48
Bankhead

3

Tartraven

The
Wilderness

Binnyside
Strips

Righead
Plantation
EH52

72

Blackcraig

Bangour
Reservoir
Boat
House

Quarter
Strip

2

Old Wood
The
Gullet
Brox Burn

Quarter
Bangour
Knowes

71

Linen Faulds

H
Bangour
Village

1

Drumcrosshall

Byres
EH54
A89

Drumcross
Wester
Dechmont
A89
M8

70

A B C

Ecclesmachan Burn

Ochiltree Mill

EH49

Oatridge

Ecclesmachan Covert

B8046

WELLPARK

BYBURN

Hangingside

Binny Craig

Oatridge Ag Coll

Mains Burn

4

West Broadlaw

Mausoleum

Binny House

Binny Park

Ecclesmachan

Lodge

73

East Broadlaw

West Binny

Binny Burn

Upper Uphall

ECCLESMACHAN RD

MANSE PK

3

EH52

Law

Law Wood

72

St ANDREW S DR

BIRKDALE DR

MUIRFIELD DR

ROSSMOUNT DR

Thomson CT

Thomson GR

FERNLEA

GLEBE AV

B8046

Craigbeg

Craig Binning

Forkneuk Farm

FORKNEUK STEADINGS

SCHOOL PL

STRATHBROCK PL

Uphall

HOWIESON GN

MUIR'S

JOHNSTON

PO

WEST MAIN ST

A899

Rench

CH

P

B8046

MILLBANK PL

MACFARLANE PL

HOUSTOUN GDNS

JOHNSTONE AV

FORREST WLK

2

Burnhouse

Hotel

Golf Course

MACLARDY CT

STANKARDS RD

A89

Brox Burn

STATION RD

71

BURNHOUSE RD

A899

B8046

BURNHOUSE DR

GOODALL CRES

MAIN ST

DEER WOOD

ACTON CT

1 KNIGHTSRIDGE CT

2 GRAIGLAW PL

Beugh Burn

Bangour Village

H

GOODALL PL

1

CRAIGLAW

Houstoun Mains Holdings

BURNSIDE

PO

KNIGHTSRIDGE RD

DEER HILL

2

Dechmont

NETTLEHILL RD

1

Dechmont Inf Sch

Hotel

DEER PARK DR

LIVINGSTON E RD A899

DECHMONT RD T

M8

KINGSTHORNE PK

EH54

Deer Hill

DEER PARK BSNS CAMPUS

DEER PARK RD

MOSS RD

Hotel

3

LIVINGSTONE E RD

A899

HOUSTOUN IND EST

NETTLEHILL RD

TODD SQ

HUNTING PK

M8

A89

KNIGHTSRIDGE RD

70

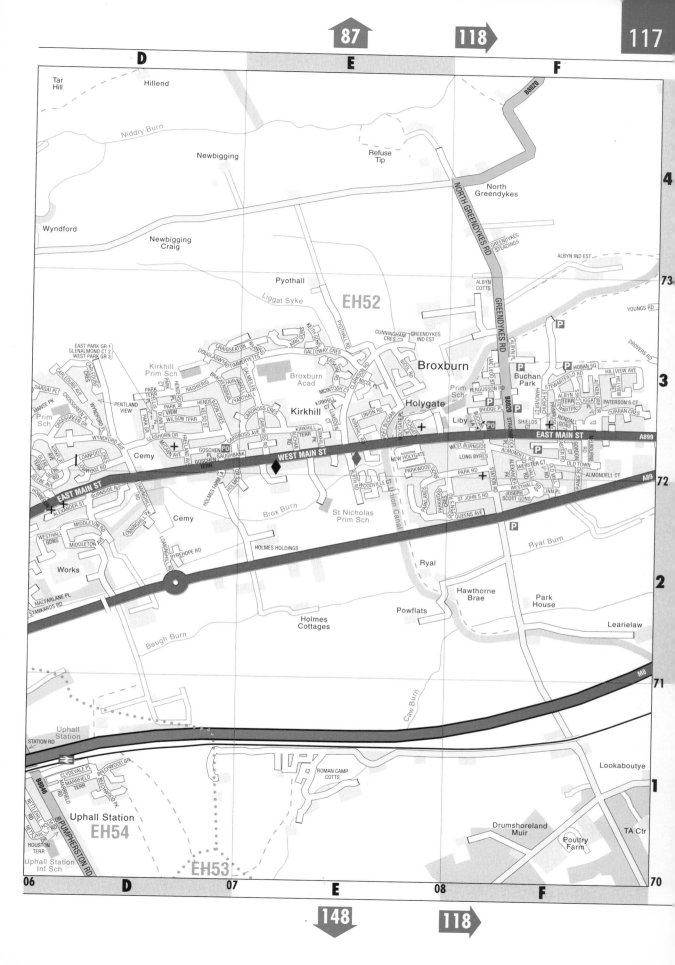

D
E
F

Tar Hill

Hillend

Niddry Burn

Newbigging

Refuse Tip

B8020

North Greendykes

4

Wyndford

Newbigging Craig

NORTH GREENDYKES RD

ALBYN IND EST

73

Pyothall

Liggat Syke

EH52

ALBYN COTTS

GREENDYKES RD

GREENDYKES STEADINGS

YOUNGS RD

DROVERS RD

P

East Park Gr 1
Glenalmond Ct 2
West Park Gr 3

CARLEDUBS CRES

DARGAI PL

CROSSGREEN DR

WYNDFORD PL

WYNDFORD AVE

Prim Sch

Kirkhill Prim Sch

CRAIGSEATON

DOUGLASWD

WYNRIG

TIMMERYETTS

LAING GDNS

KEITH GDNS

PYOTHALL RD

GALLOWAY CRES

ERSKINE

CUNNINGHAM CRES

GREENDYKES IND EST

Broxburn Acad

Broxburn

CLARKSON RD

NICOL PL

Prim Sch

ALBYN PL

McLEOD GDNS

B8020

FERGUSSON RD

Buchan Park

STEWARTFIELD RD

HOBAN SQ

HILLVIEW AVE

HANOVER CT

ST JOSEPHS

ALBYN TERR

PRIMROSE CT

LIGGAT PL

HILLVIEW PL

AITKEN DR

PATERSON'S CT

CURRAN CRES

P

3

Kirkhill

PARK TERR

HENDERSON PL

RASHIERIG

FAIRNIE PL

C'APTHALL

BRACKENSBRAE

GALMEILEN

KELSO ST

CARDROSS CRES

McINTOSH CT

CARDROSS AVE

CARDROSS RD

KIRKHILL TERR

KIRKHILL RD

LUMSDEN

BUCHAN RD

UNION RD

KIRKHILL PK

KIRKHILL RD

NICOL PL

PORT BUCHAN

HOLYGATE PL

Holygate

Liby

P

RENDALL GDNS

SHIELDS CT

EAST MAIN ST

MELBOURNE

A899

PENTLAND VIEW

PARK GR

PARK VIEW

WILSON TERR

CLEGHORN DR

FREELAND AVE

McCAIN WAY

SAUGHBANK

GOSCHEN PL

GOSCHEN TERR

HOLMES FARM LA

HOLMES

WEST MAIN ST

BLYTH RD

WOODVILLE CT

NEW HOLYGATE

WEST BURNSIDE

LONG BYRES

STRATHBROCK PL

ALMONDELL RD

WEBSTER CT

ALEXANDER

OLD MILL

STER

GORDON PL

OLD TOWN

P

ALMONDELL CT

A89

72

MANSE PK

CARLEDUBS CRES

CROSSGREEN PL

Prim Sch

GLEBE PL

KIRKLA

GLEBE RD

GLEBE AVE

LOANFOOT RD

LOANFOOT CRES

HOWIESHILL

ALEXANDER ST

BURNSIDE RD

EAST MAIN ST

Cemy

DANKINHILL

LONGINGHILL PK

LOANINGHILL RD

Cemy

Brox Burn

St Nicholas Prim Sch

PARKWOOD

SNODS

PARKLANDS

PARK RD

PARKWOOD RD

ST JOHN'S RD

QUEEN'S RD

QUEENS AVE

STATION RD

JOSEPH SCOTT GDNS

LINN PL

WESTHALL RD

P

Union Canal

WESTHALL GDNS

MIDDLETON RD

MIDDLETON AVE

Works

LOANINGHILL RD

BYREHOPE RD

HOLMES HOLDINGS

Ryal

Ryal Burn

Hawthorne Brae

Park House

2

MACFARLANE PL

STANKARDS RD

Holmes Cottages

Powflats

Learielaw

Beugh Burn

Caw Burn

M8

71

Uphall Station

STATION RD

Lookaboutye

B8046

CLYDEVALE PL

MARRFIELD RD

MARRFIELD TERR

BEECHWOOD GR

BEECHWOOD PK

ROMAN CAMP COTTS

1

NETTLEHILL RD

NETTLEHILL

HOUSTON RD

HOUSTON TERR

PUMPHERSTON RD

Uphall Station

EH54

Drumshoreland Muir

Poultry Farm

TA Ctr

Uphall Station Inf Sch

EH53

70

06

D

07

E

08

F

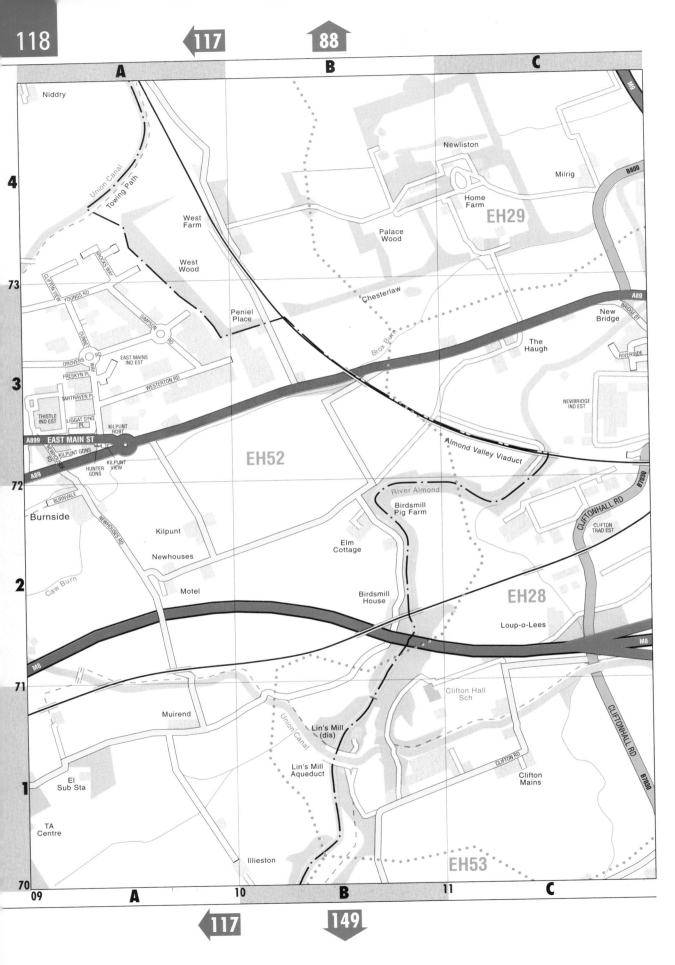

117
88

A B C

4

Niddry

Union Canal

Towing Path

West Farm

West Wood

Newliston

Milrig

Home Farm

EH29

B800

Palace Wood

A89

BRIDGE ST

73

CLIFTON VIEW

BROCKS WAY

YOUNGS RD

SIMPSON RD

Peniel Place

Chesterlaw

New Bridge

RIVERSIDE

DUNNET

The Haugh

Brox Burn

3

DROVERS WAY

FRESKYN PL

EAST MAINS IND EST

WESTERTON RD

NEWBRIDGE IND EST

TARTRAVEN PL

LIGGAT SYKE PL

THISTLE IND EST

KILPUNT RDBT

Almond Valley Viaduct

A899 EAST MAIN ST

KILPUNT GDNS

EH52

BT030

A89

HUNTER GDNS

KILPUNT VIEW

72

River Almond

CLIFTONHALL RD

BURNVALE

Birdsmill Pig Farm

CLIFTON TRAD EST

Burnside

NEWHOUSES RD

Kilpunt

Elm Cottage

Newhouses

Caw Burn

2

Motel

Birdsmill House

EH28

Loup-o-Lees

M8

M8

71

Clifton Hall Sch

Muirend

CLIFTONHALL RD

BT030

Union Canal

Lin's Mill (dis)

CLIFTON RD

Clifton Mains

1

El Sub Sta

Lin's Mill Aqueduct

TA Centre

Illieston

EH53

70

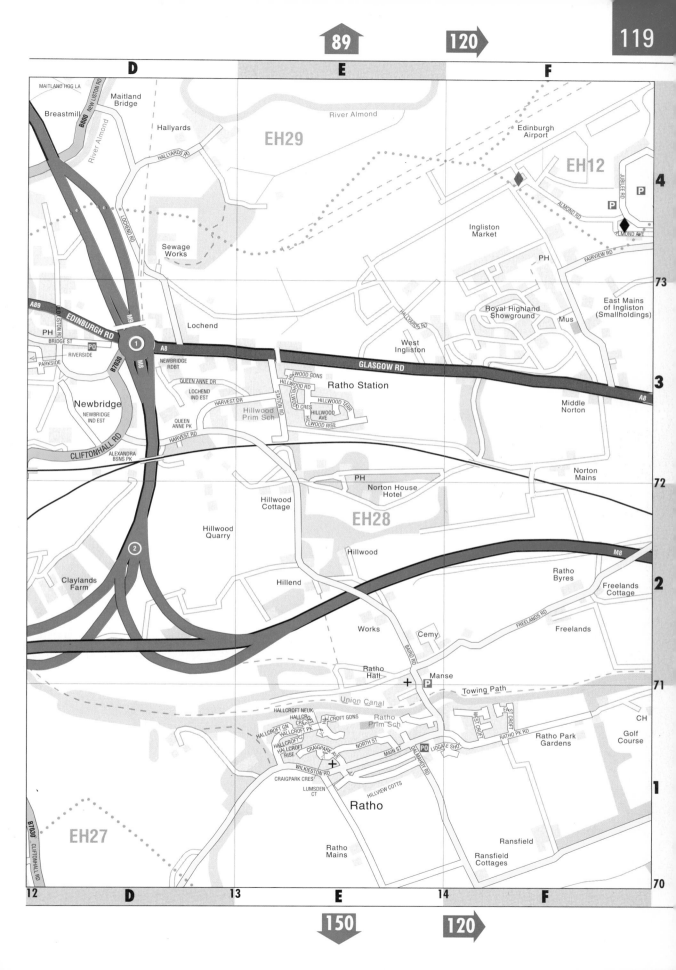

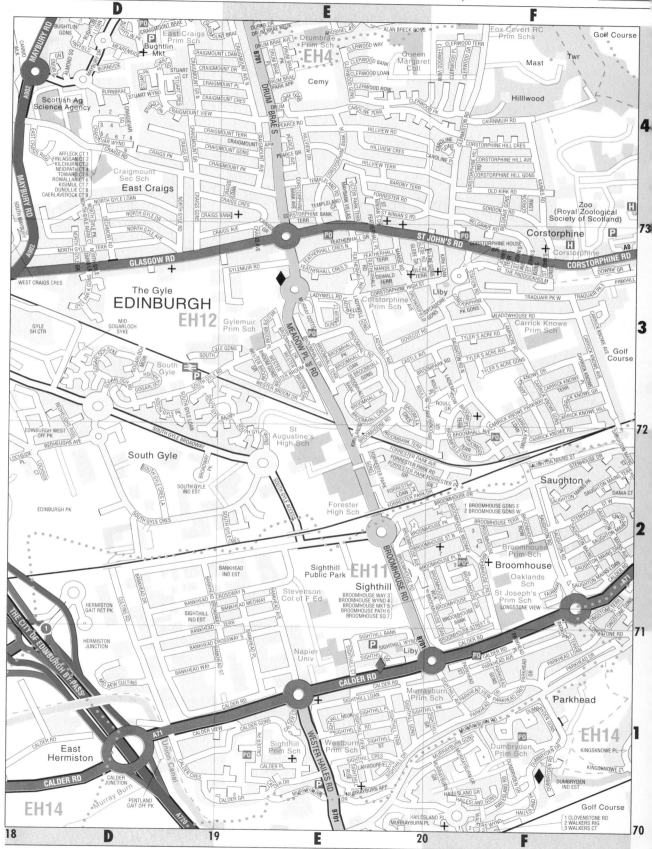

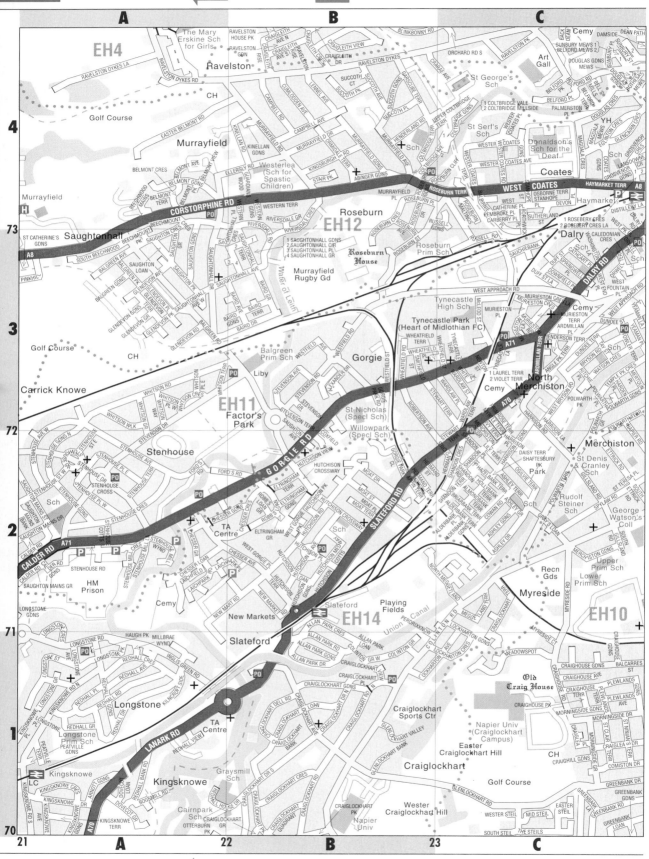

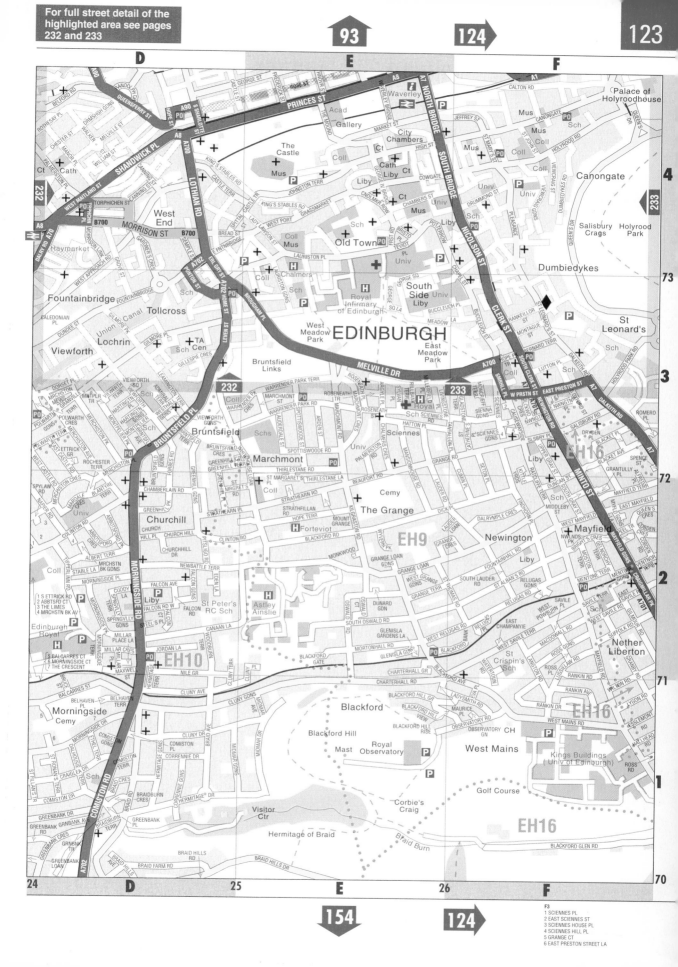

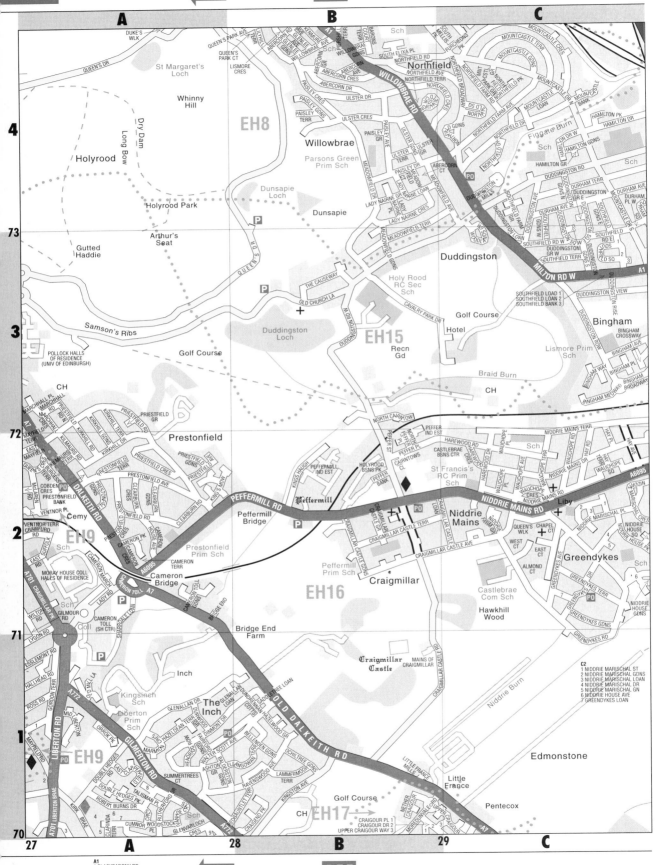

A1
1 BLACKBARONY RD
2 BRAEFOOT TERR
3 ORCHARDHEAD RD
4 MOSSGIEL WLK
5 ALLOWAY LOAN
6 JEAN ARMOUR AVE
7 SHANTER WAY
8 TRESSILIAN GDNS
9 GREENMANTLE LOAN

C2
1 NIDDRIE MARISCHAL ST
2 NIDDRIE MARISCHAL GDNS
3 NIDDRIE MARISCHAL LOAN
4 NIDDRIE MARISCHAL DR
5 NIDDRIE MARISCHAL GN
6 NIDDRIE HOUSE AVE
7 GREENDYKES LOAN

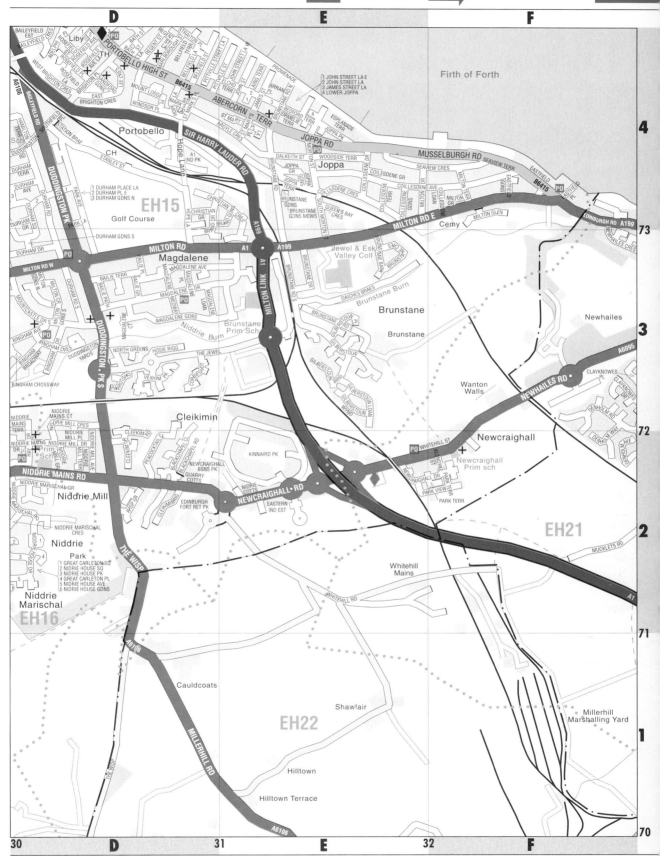

D4
1 ADELPHI GR
2 WILLIAMFIELD SQ
3 BEACH LA

D   E   F

Firth of Forth

1 JOHN STREET LA E
2 JOHN STREET LA
3 JAMES STREET LA
4 LOWER JOPPA

BAILEYFIELD EST
BAILEYFIELD CRES
WEST BRIGHTON CRES
BRIGHTON CRES
EAST BRIGHTON CRES
Liby
Portobello
PORTOBELLO HIGH ST
ABERCORN TERR

B6415

Portobello
CH
EH15
Golf Course

1 DURHAM PLACE LA
2 DURHAM PL E
3 DURHAM GDNS N

DUDDINGSTON PK
A6106
BAILEYFIELD RD
SOUTHFIELD
DURHAM TERR
DURHAM AVE
DURHAM GR
DURHAM SQ
DURHAM RD
PARK AVE
PARK LA

MOUNT LODGE
WINDSOR PL

SIR HARRY LAUDER RD
Hope Lane

DALKEITH ST
JOPPA GR
JOPPA TERR
Joppa
JOPPA RD

MUSSELBURGH RD   SEAVIEW TERR   EASTFIELD
SEAVIEW CRES
B6415
EDINBURGH RD A199
NEWHAILES CRES
73

MILTON RD E
Cemy
MILTON GLEN

DURHAM DR
MILTON RD W
MILTON RD
Magdalene
A1   A199

Jewel & Esk
Valley Coll

Brunstane Burn
Brunstane
Brunstane

Newhailes
3

MILTON LINK
A1

BAILIE TERR
MAGDALENE AVE
MAGDALENE
MAGDALENE GDNS

Niddrie Burn
Brunstane
Prim Sch

DAICHES BRAES

GILBERSTOWN
Wanton
Walls

NEWHAILES RD
A6095
CLAYKNOWES PL
DENHOLM
72

BINGHAM AVE
BINGHAM BROADWAY
BINGHAM CRES
BINGHAM CROSSWAY

DUDDINGSTON PK S

NORTH GREENS
HOSIE RIGG
THE JEWEL
VEXHM

Cleikimin
KINNAIRD PK
NEWCRAIGHALL
BSNS PK
QUARRY
COTTS

WHITEHILL ST
PO
Newcraighall
Newcraighall
Prim sch

EH21
MUCKLETS RD

NIDDRIE
MAINS
TERR
NIDDRIE MAINS
Prim Sch
PO

NIDDRIE MAINS RD
Niddrie Mill
NIDDRIE MARISCHAL GR

NIDDRIE
MARISCHAL RD
Niddrie
Park
Niddrie
Marischal
EH16

NIDDRIE MARISCHAL CRES

1 GREAT CARLETON SQ
2 NIDRIE HOUSE SQ
3 NIDRIE HOUSE PK
4 GREAT CARLETON PL
5 NIDRIE HOUSE AVE
6 NIDRIE HOUSE GDNS

THE WISP
A6106

NEWCRAIGHALL RD
NIDRIE
COTTS
Edinburgh
Fort Ret Pk
EASTERN
IND EST

A1
71

Cauldcoats
Whitehill
Mains
WHITEHILL RD

EH22
Shawfair

Millerhill
Marshalling Yard
1

MILLERHILL RD

Hilltown

THE WISP

Hilltown Terrace

A6106
70

125

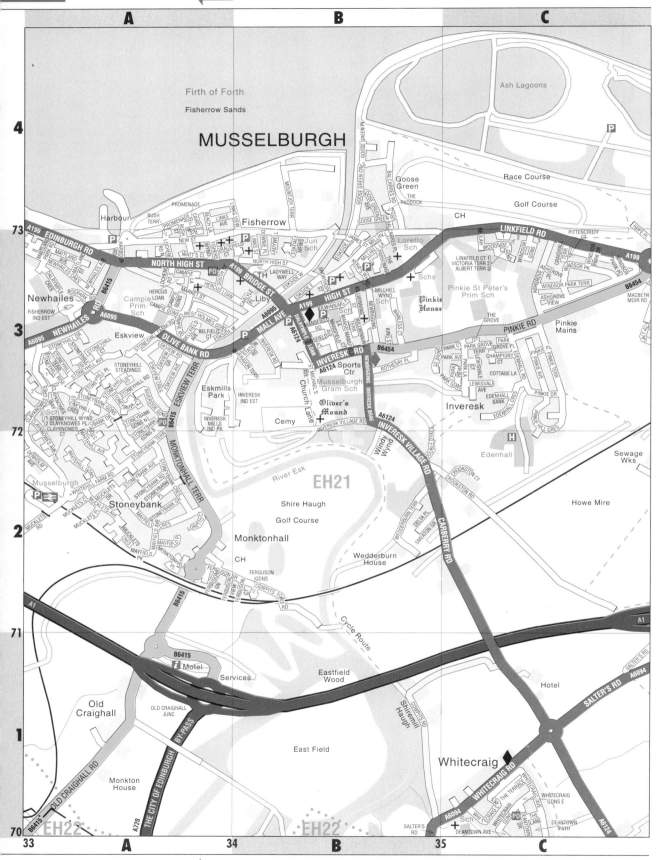

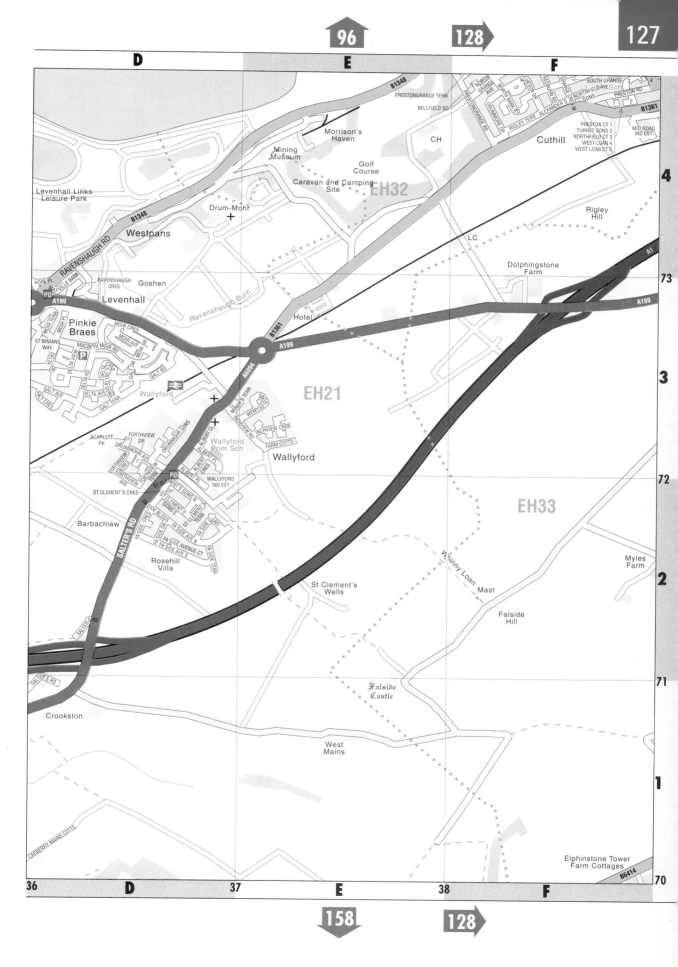

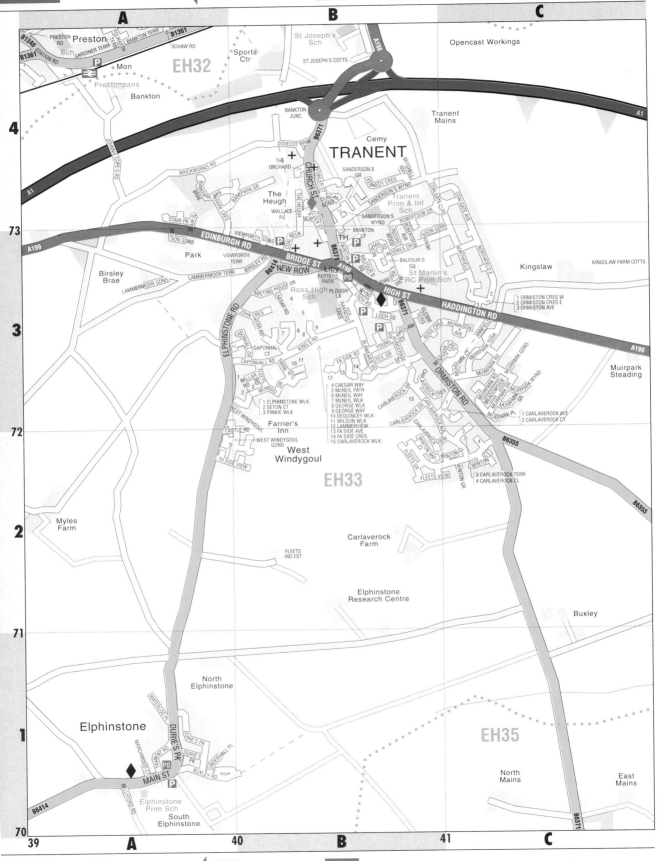

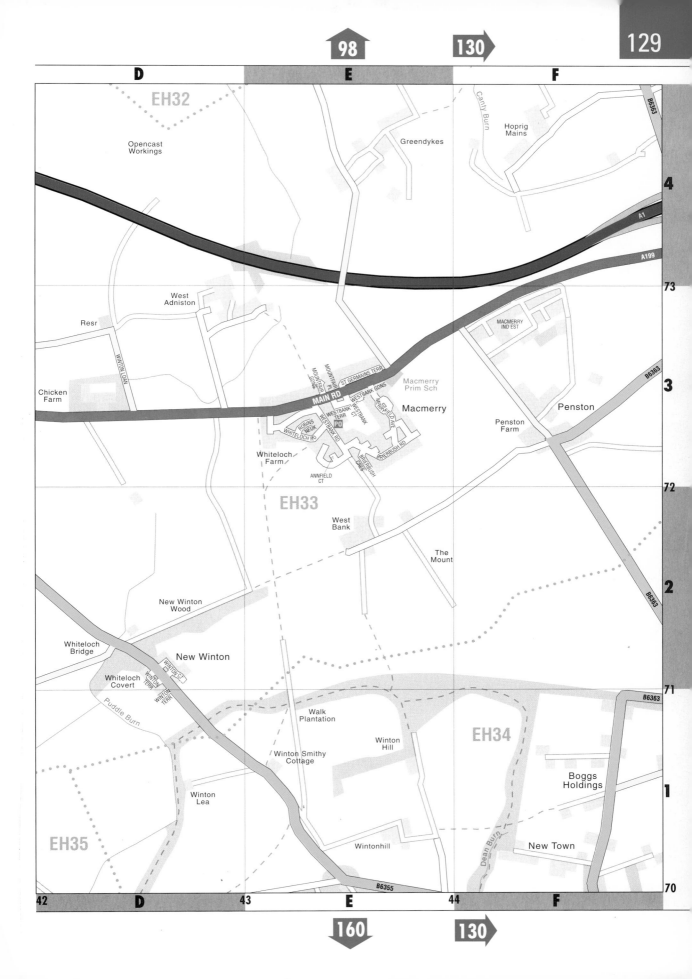

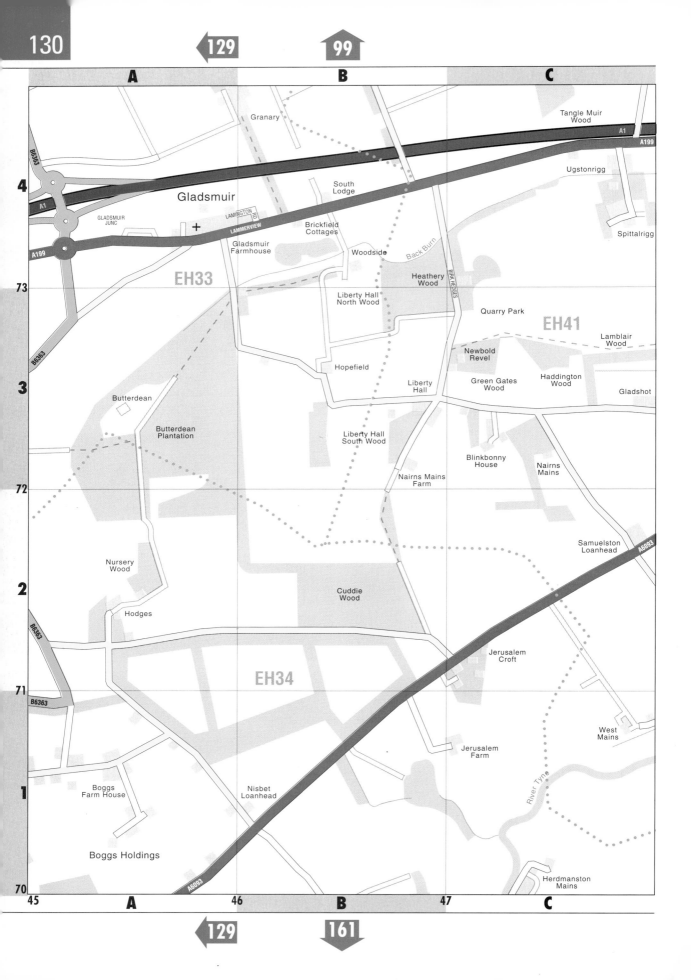

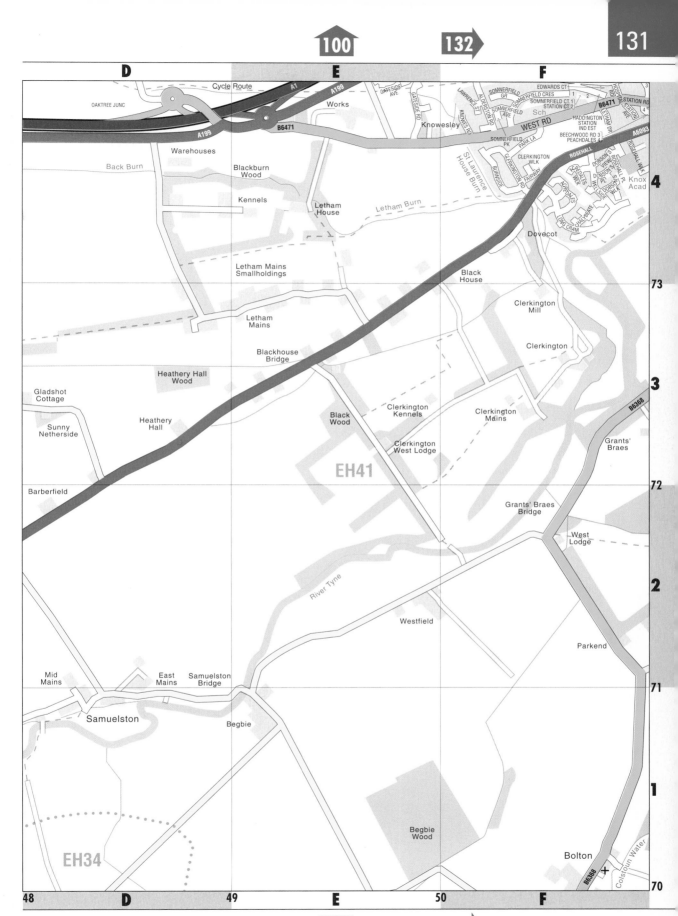

D
E
F

Cycle Route
OAKTREE JUNC
A1
A199
A199
B6471

GATESIDE AVE
GATESIDE RD
Works
Knowesley

SOMNERFIELD GR
LAWRENCE ST
ALDERSTON RD
SOMNERFIELD CRES
SOMNERFIELD CT 1
STATION CT 2
Sch
EDWARDS CT
HADDINGTON STATION RD
HOSPITAL RD
STATION RD
ELTHAM DR
B6471
Warehouses
Back Burn

WEST RD
SOMNERFIELD PK
PARK LA
HADDINGTON STATION IND EST
BEECHWOOD RD 3
PEACHDALES 4
A6093

Blackburn Wood
St Laurence House Burn
BURNSIDE
CLERKINGTON RD
CLERKINGTON WLK
FAIRWAY
ROSEHALL
ROSEHALL PL
ROSEHALL WLK
Knox Acad
VIEWS
DOBSON'S
DOBSON'S WLK

Kennels
Letham House
Letham Burn
ACREVIEW
ACREDALES
HALFGATE
DMG CRAM
Dovecot

4

Letham Mains Smallholdings
Black House

73

Clerkington Mill

Letham Mains

Clerkington

Blackhouse Bridge

Heathery Hall Wood
Black Wood
Clerkington Kennels
Clerkington Mains
B6368

3

Gladshot Cottage
Heathery Hall
Clerkington West Lodge
Grants' Braes

Sunny Netherside

EH41

Barberfield
72

Grants' Braes Bridge

West Lodge

2

River Tyne
Westfield
Parkend

Mid Mains
East Mains
Samuelston Bridge
71

Samuelston
Begbie

1

Begbie Wood
Bolton
B6368
Colstoun Water

EH34
70

48
D
49
E
50
F

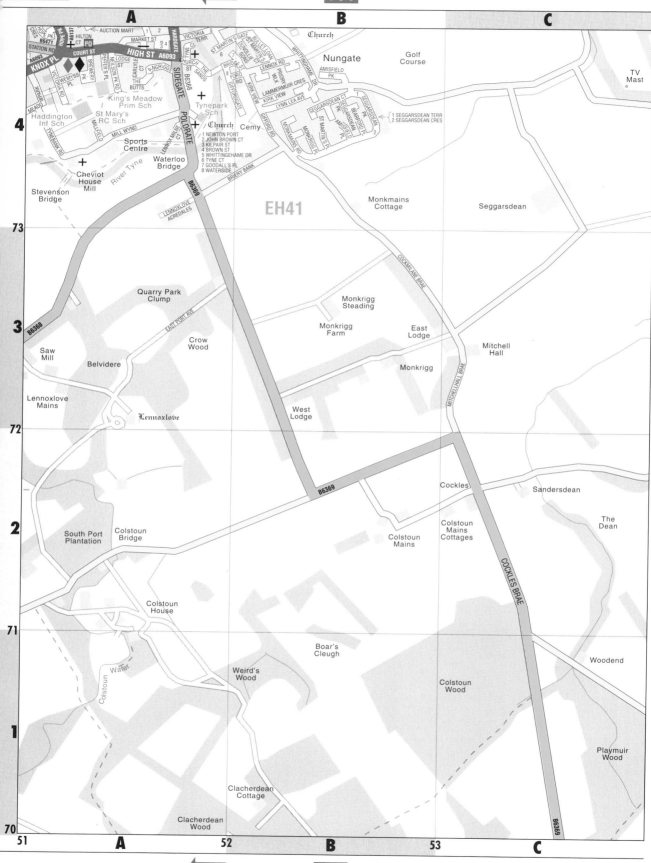

EH41

A

AUCTION MART
HILTON
MARKET ST
HIGH ST A6093
COURT ST
KNOX PL
STATION RD
B6471
B6137
PO
LODGE
B6093
MEADO
HADDINGTON
Inf Sch
St Mary's
RC Sch
King's Meadow
Prim Sch
Tynepark
Sch
VICTORIA RD
MILLFIELD
MILL WYND
TYNEBANK RD
THE BUTTS
Sports
Centre
Cheviot
House
Mill
SIDEGATE
POLDRATE
B6368
LENNOX MILNE CT
Waterloo
Bridge
River Tyne
Church
Cemy
Stevenson
Bridge
LENNOXLOVE
ACREDALES
B6369

B

Church
Nungate
Golf
Course
AMISFIELD
PK
St MARTIN'S GATE
WHITTINGHAME DR
LENNOX RD
VICTORIA TERR
St MARTIN'S
THE SANDS
CHURCH ST
BRIDGE
FORD
KIRK VIEW
GIFFORD RD
LAMMERMUIR CRES
PRIORY WLK
LYNN LEA AVE
MONKMAINS RD
SEGGARSDEAN CT
SEGGARSDEAN PK
BEARFORD PL
AMISFIELD PL
St MARTIN'S PL

1 SEGGARSDEAN TERR
2 SEGGARSDEAN CRES

1 NEWTON PORT
2 JOHN BROWN CT
3 KILPAIR ST
4 BROWN ST
5 WHITTINGEHAME DR
6 TYNE CT
7 GOODALL'S PL
8 WATERSIDE

BRIERY BANK

Monkmains
Cottage
Seggarsdean

COCKMILANE BRAE

Monkrigg
Steading
Monkrigg
Farm
East
Lodge
Monkrigg
Mitchell
Hall

MITCHELL HALL BRAE

C

TV
Mast

Quarry Park
Clump
EAST PORT AVE
Crow
Wood
B6368
Saw
Mill
Belvidere
Lennoxlove
Mains
Lennoxlove
West
Lodge
B6369
Cockles
Sandersdean
The
Dean
South Port
Plantation
Colstoun
Bridge
Colstoun
Mains
Colstoun
Mains
Cottages
COCKLES BRAE
Colstoun
House
Boar's
Cleugh
Colstoun
Wood
Woodend
Colstoun Water
Weird's
Wood
Playmuir
Wood
Clacherdean
Cottage
Clacherdean
Wood
B6369

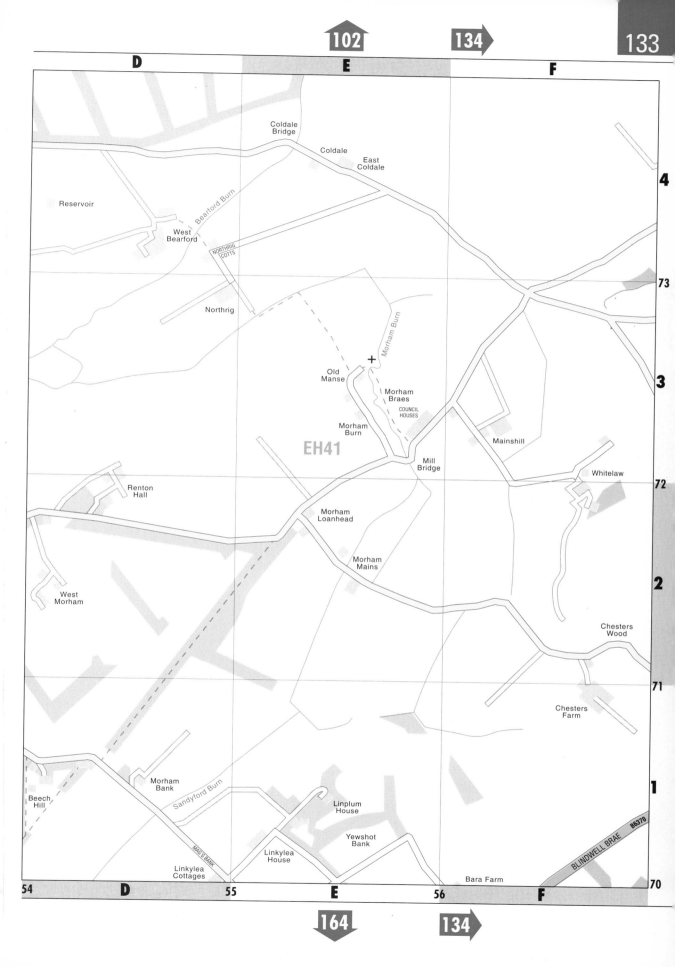

D
E
F

4
73
3
72
2
71
1
70

Coldale
Bridge
Coldale
East
Coldale

Reservoir

Bearford Burn

West
Bearford

NORTHRIG
COTTS

Northrig

Morham Burn

Old
Manse

Morham
Braes
COUNCIL
HOUSES

Morham
Burn

Mainshill

EH41

Mill
Bridge

Whitelaw

Renton
Hall

Morham
Loanhead

Morham
Mains

West
Morham

Chesters
Wood

Chesters
Farm

Morham
Bank

Sandyford Burn

Beech
Hill

Linplum
House

Yewshot
Bank

MAG'S BANK

Linkylea
House

Linkylea
Cottages

Bara Farm

BLINDWELL BRAE
B6370

54
D
55
E
56
F

133
103

A

B

C

4

Standingstone

Whittingehame
Mains

North
Lodge

Luggate Burn

73

Mon

Blaikie
Heugh

Lawhead
Plantation

Clartyside
Plantation

North Bank
Wood

3

West
Mains

Lawhead
Hill

Papple

Whittingehame Water

Papple Farm Cotts.

Oakbank
Wood

EH41

Dunstane
Plantation

Papple
Bridge

Overfield

B6370

72

Black Knowe
Plantation

Overfield
Plantation
Birks
Plantation

2

Whitelaw
Hill

Mould
Bridge

Garvald
Grange

Stoneypath
Tower

Ninewells Burn

Tanderlane

Papana Water

71

Garvald

PO

Nunraw

Thornter Burn

1

BLINDWELL BRAE

B6370

Priest Bank

Papana Cotts

Burnside
Ct.

Nunraw
Barns

Nunraw
Wood

Sled
Hill

Nunraw
Abbey

70

57

A

58

B

59

C

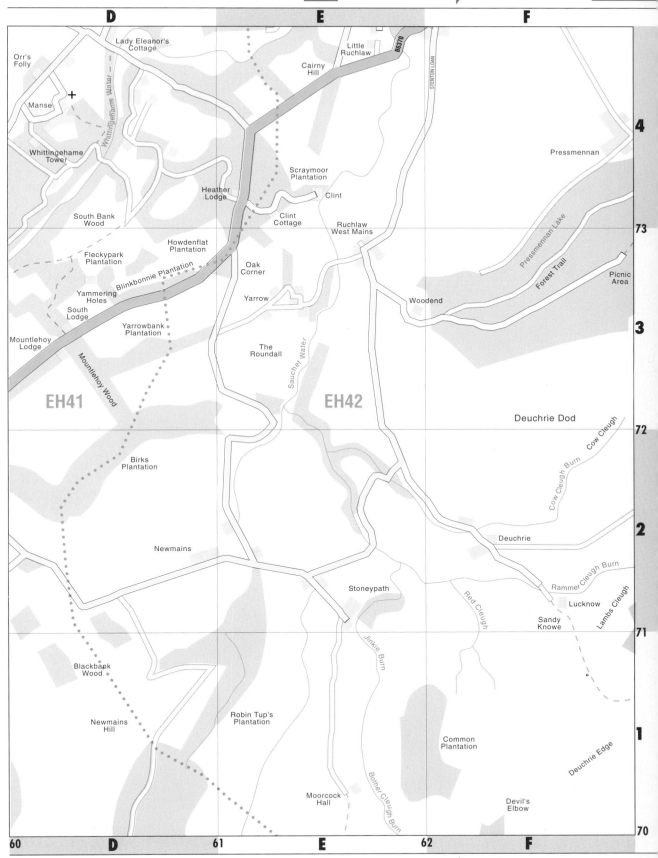

A **B** **C**

4

Bennet's Burn

Ford

Burnhead
Wood

Frizzels
Wood

Ice
Cleugh

Channel
Wood

CHANNEL BRAE

73

The
Sneep

Pressmennan
Wood

Pathhead

Halls

Staneshal
Wood

Cauld Burn

Gallows
Law

Gairy Burn

3

Well Hill

Rottenraw Burn

EH42

Hartside

72

Deuchrie
Wood

Hartside
Law

Hartside Burn

Lint Burn

Herring Road

Sleepy
Knowe

Rammer
Wood

Mearns Cleugh

2

Halls Edge

Lothian Edge

Ox Cleugh

Redscar Burn

Herring Road

Rammer
Dodd

Wester Hartside
Edge

Rammer Cleugh

71

Crow
Cleugh

Rammer Cleugh Burn

Rammer Moss

1

Mossy Burn

Lodge Burn

Watch
Law

70

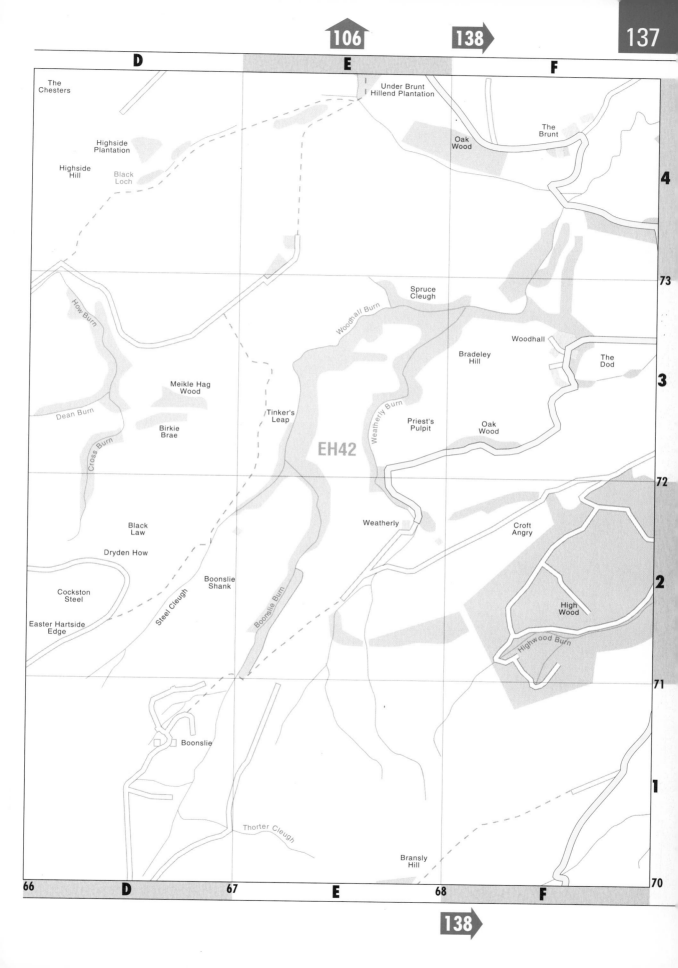

The Chesters

Highside Plantation

Highside Hill

Black Loch

Under Brunt Hillend Plantation

Oak Wood

The Brunt

How Burn

Spruce Cleugh

Woodhall Burn

Woodhall

Meikle Hag Wood

Dean Burn

Tinker's Leap

Weatherly Burn

Bradeley Hill

The Dod

Cross Burn

Birkie Brae

Priest's Pulpit

Oak Wood

EH42

Black Law

Weatherly

Croft Angry

Dryden How

Boonslie Shank

Cockston Steel

Boonslie Burn

High Wood

Easter Hartside Edge

Steel Cleugh

Highwood Burn

Boonslie

Thorter Cleugh

Bransly Hill

D

E

F

4

73

3

72

2

71

1

70

66

D

67

E

68

F

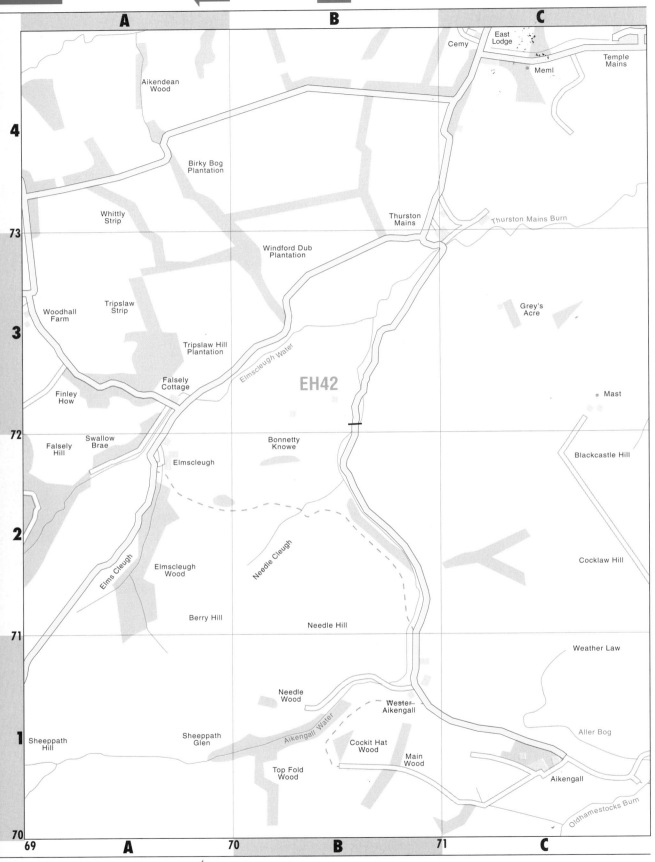

A

B

C

4

Aikendean
Wood

Birky Bog
Plantation

Cemy

East
Lodge

Meml

Temple
Mains

Whittly
Strip

Thurston
Mains

Thurston Mains Burn

73

Windford Dub
Plantation

Woodhall
Farm

Tripslaw
Strip

Grey's
Acre

3

Tripslaw Hill
Plantation

Elmscleugh Water

EH42

Falsely
Cottage

Mast

Finley
How

Swallow
Brae

72

Falsely
Hill

Elmscleugh

Bonnetty
Knowe

Blackcastle Hill

2

Elms Cleugh

Elmscleugh
Wood

Needle Cleugh

Cocklaw Hill

Berry Hill

Needle Hill

71

Weather Law

Needle
Wood

Wester-
Aikengall

Aller Bog

1

Sheeppath
Hill

Sheeppath
Glen

Aikengall Water

Cockit Hat
Wood

Main
Wood

Aikengall

Top Fold
Wood

Oldhamestocks Burn

70

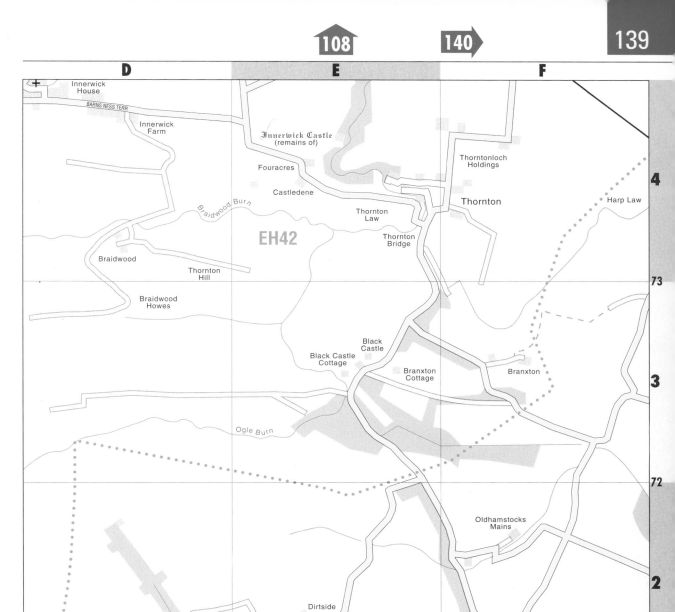

D   E   F

Innerwick
House

BARNS NESS TERR

Innerwick
Farm

Innerwick Castle
(remains of)

Fouracres

Castledene

Thornton
Law

Thornton
Bridge

Thorntonloch
Holdings

Thornton

Harp Law

4

Braidwood Burn

EH42

Braidwood

Thornton
Hill

Braidwood
Howes

73

Black
Castle

Black Castle
Cottage

Branxton
Cottage

Branxton

3

Ogle Burn

72

Oldhamstocks
Mains

2

Dirtside

Battens
Cleugh

Cocklaw

TD13

Cockit Hat
Strip

71

Oldhamstocks Burn

Broom Hill

Rowans
Cleugh

The
Haystall

Ford

Oldhamstocks

Haystall
Knowe

Cromwell
Cottages

Oldhamstocks
Bridge

1

Stottencleugh

Ford

Oldhamstocks
Mill

Browgates

Woollands

70

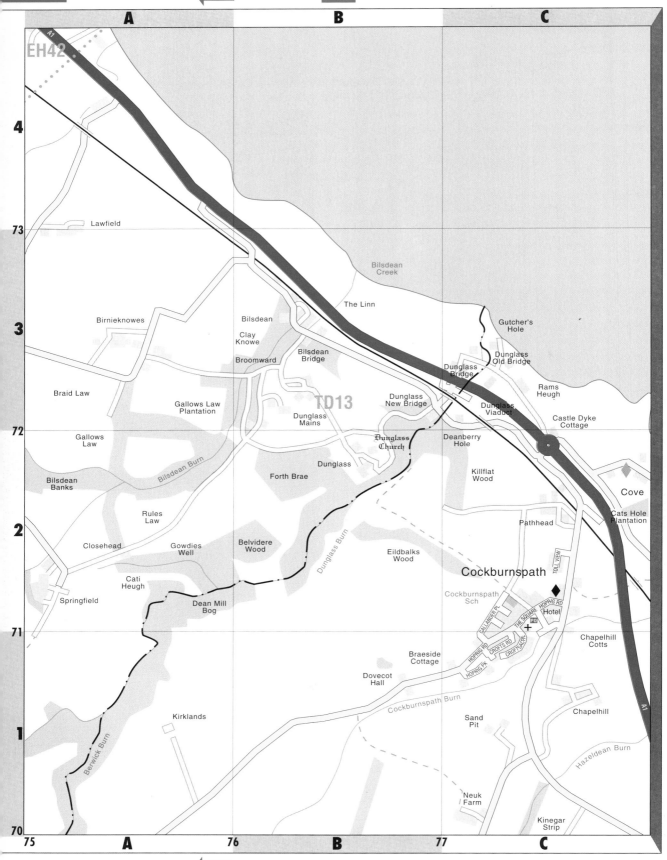

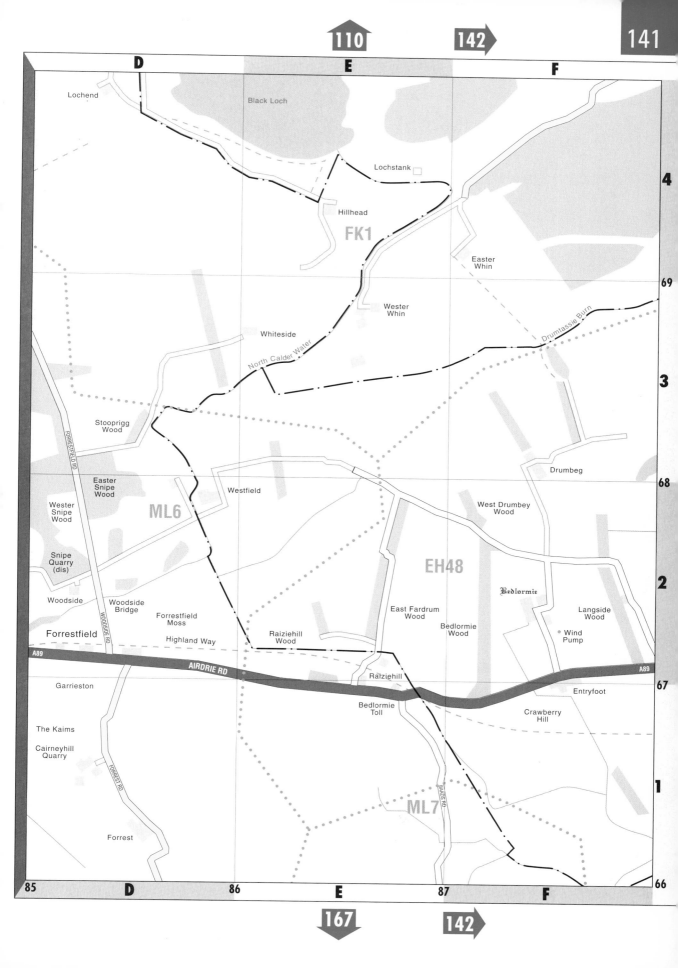

141
111

A **B** **C**

Burnhead
Moss

Burnhead

Croft
Plantation

Wester Burnhead
Wood

Drum Park
Plantation

Drumtassie Burn

4

Opencast
Workings

FK1

Heights

Tawnycraw
Hill

West Rhodens
Plantation

69

Drumelzie

East Backmuir
Wood

Blawhorn Moss

Reservoir

3

Eastcraigs
Hill

68

Crowns
Hill

Blawhorn
Wood

EH48

Craigs

1 CRAIGHILL VIEW
2 BLACKHILL RD
3 SUNNYDALE RD

Barn
Wood

Westcraigs
Hill

GREENHILL
RD

SUNNYDALE
DR

2

Heatherhouse
Wood

Wester
Redburn

Easter
Redburn

Blackridge

PARK RD

CRAIG ST

A89

Bedlormie
House

LANGSIDE DR

WOODHILL RD

FARQUHAR
SQ

Blackridge
Prim Sch

DRUMMOND PL

HILLSIDE DR

HILLSIDE PL

HEIGHTS RD

CRAIGINN
CT

CRAIGINN TERR

FLEMING PL

Westrigg

+PH

+

WESTCRAIGS
PK

MAIN ST

MACLEAN TERR

A89

PO

LOUBURN

Liby
CT

CRAIG LEA

B718

WESTCRAIGS RD

67

BEDLORMIE
DR

REDBURN RD

OGILFACE
CRES

STANDHILL
Farm

STATION
RD

HARTHILL RD

Spoil
Heap

Mosshouse

Bathgate Airdrie Railway Path

Cycle Track

Standhill
Farm

WHITELAW ST

1

Torrance
Farm

B718

Bogend
Farm

ML7

66

88 **A** **89** **B** **90** **C**

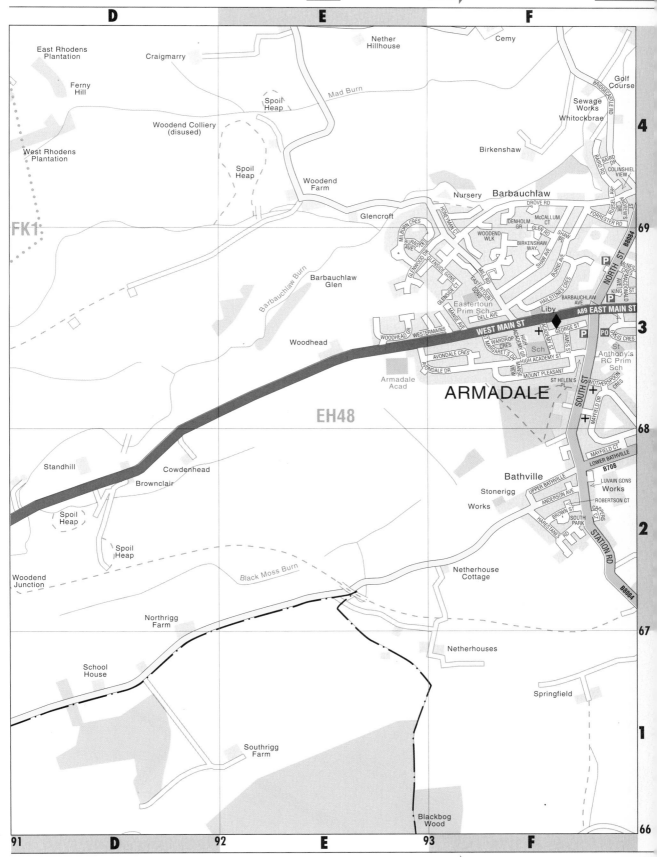

East Rhodens
Plantation

Craigmarry

Nether
Hillhouse

Cemy

Ferny
Hill

Mad Burn

Golf
Course

BRIDGECASTLE RD

Spoil
Heap

Sewage
Works

Whitockbrae

4

Woodend Colliery
(disused)

Birkenshaw

BAIRD RD

COLINSHIEL
VIEW

West Rhodens
Plantation

Spoil
Heap

Woodend
Farm

Nursery

Barbauchlaw

JW TISSDIE

ST ANDREW'S ST

DROVE RD

McCALLUM
CT

FORRESTER RD

FK1

Glencroft

HOMEMAIN CT

DENHOLM
GR

GLEN RD

SHAW

McNEIL
CRES

69

BR084

MILBURN CRES

WOODEND
WLK

BIRKENSHAW
WAY

SHAW
AVE

KING

MACDONALD
AVE

P

NORTH ST

BURNSIDE

GLENWOOD DR

GLENSIDE GDNS CT

MIL RD

EASTERTOUN
GDNS

BURNS CRES

P

Barbauchlaw
Glen

Barbauchlaw Burn

GLENSIDE DR

GLENSIDE AVE

EASTERTOUN
GDNS

HAILSTONES CRES

Barbauchlaw
AVE

Eastertoun
Prim Sch

MANSE AVE

DELL AVE

Liby

A89 EAST MAIN ST

PO

P

3

Woodhead

WEST MAIN ST

WESTERMAINS

WARDROP
CRES

HIGH
ACADEMY
ST GR

George St

ACADEMY ST

JAMES ST

St
Anthony's
RC Prim
Sch

CRAIG CRES

WOODHEAD DR

ST MARGARET'S DR

AVONDALE CRES

MANSE
VIEW

HIGH ACADEMY ST

Sch

WOTHERSPOON
CRES

SOUTH ST

AVONDALE DR

MOUNT PLEASANT

ST HELEN'S
PL

Armadale
Acad

ARMADALE

MAYFIELD DR

68

EH48

MAYFIELD CT

Standhill

Cowdenhead

LOWER BATHVILLE

B708

LUVAIN GDNS

Brownclair

Bathville

UPPER BATHVILLE

Works

ROBERTSON CT

Spoil
Heap

Stonerigg

ANDERSON AVE

SOPERS CT

2

Spoil
Heap

Works

BROWN ST

SOUTH
PARK

HARESTANES RD

STATION RD

Woodend
Junction

Black Moss Burn

Netherhouse
Cottage

BR084

67

Northrigg
Farm

Netherhouses

School
House

Springfield

1

Southrigg
Farm

Blackbog
Wood

66

A   **B**   **C**

Belvedere Wood

Belvedere

BALLENCRIEFF MILL

Bathgate Water

Golf Course

4

Eastoun Farm

BALMUIR RD A800

Works

Colinshiel

EASTON RD

BURNSIDE RD

COLINSHIEL AVE 1
HAMILTON LA 2

RACE RD

TRAPRAIN

BUCHAN RD

NORTH ST

69

Middlerig

WOODHEAD PL

HOPE PARK GDNS

HAMILTON RD

CRES

MONKLAND RD

IRVINE CRES

MILBURN RD

McNEIL CRES

BARLAW

BIRKDALE PK.

Heatherfield

Windyknowe Prim Sch

HOPEPARK

ASHBANK CT

GLASGOW RD

A89

KING ST

EAST MAIN ST

A89

THE MARCHES

Windyknowe Prim Sch

WINDYKNOWE CRES

WINDYKNOWE PK

B708

BRIDGEND PK

BRIDGEND CT

Windyknowe

3

WOOD TERR

FERRY

MARCHES DR

CHURCH PL

Armadale Stadium

Hardhill

DURHAM DR

HARDHILL RD

LANGRAULD

GREIG CRES

EWART AVE

ST PAUL'S DR

SIBBALDS BRAE

HARDHILL TERR

BOGHEAD CRES

FALSIDE CRES

Cemy

BARBAUCHLAW AVE

TEMPLE AVE

GRACIE'S WYND

CATHERVAL

Kenbog

Garden Cottage

FALSIDE TERR

MALCOLM CT

MEADOWPARK RD

YOUNG CRES

Mayfield

WATT AVE

WOODLANDS COTTS

HARDHILL PL

WOODLANDS GR

ROBERTSON AVE

SYLVAN WAY

DALLING RD

B7002

BATHVILLE BSNS CTR

Falside

WHITESIDE

MAYFIELD DR

CALDER CRES

LOWER BATHVILLE

EH48

68

B708

Works

Reyssie Law

WHITESIDE IND EST

RD

FAC

BIRNIEHILL AVE

STANDHILL CT

Boghead Burn

Whiteside

Teepit Hill

BIRNIEHILL CRES

BIRNIEHILL DR

2

Tarrareoch

BIRNIEHILL TERR

INCHCROSS

WHITBURN RD

Trees

West Mains

INCHCROSS IND EST

Standhill Farm

67

STATION RD

B8084

Inchcross

A7066

Torbane

Hall Torbane Farm

Standhill

Half Loaf Pond

1

B7002

A7066

Inchmore

66

Tippethill **H** B8084

94   **A**   95   **B**   96   **C**

A706

A801

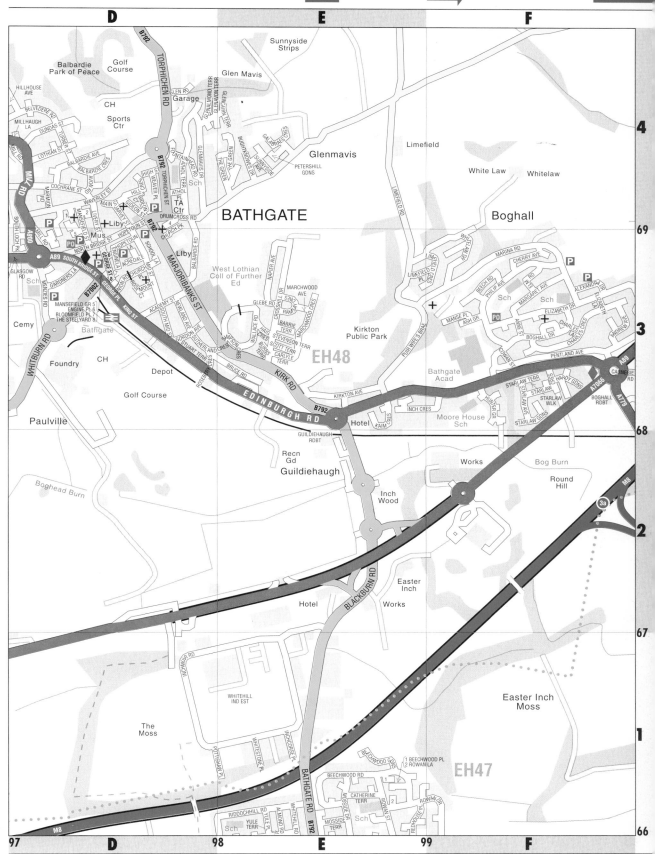

114
146
171
146

D4
1 WAVERLEY STREET IND UNITS
2 MANSEFIELD CT
3 GLEN WAY
4 HATFIELD PL

D   E   F

Sunnyside
Strips

Balbardie
Park of Peace

Golf
Course

HILLHOUSE
AVE

Glen Mavis

CH

Garage

GLEN RD

Sports
Ctr

Limefield

Glenmavis

White Law   Whitelaw

PETERSHILL
GDNS

BATHGATE

Boghall

BELVEDERE RD

MILLHAUGH
LA

DUNDAS ST

Liby

Mus

PO

Sch

Liby

West Lothian
Coll of Further
Ed

MARCHWOOD
AVE

MARCHWOOD CRES

Kirkton
Public Park

Sch   Sch

PO

GLASGOW
RD

Sch

MANSEFIELD GR 5
ENGINE PL 6
BLOOMFIELD PL 7
THE STEELYARD 8

Cemy

Bathgate

EH48

PVIR WIFE'S BRAE

Bathgate
Acad

CARNEGIE
RD

Paulville

Foundry

CH

Depot

Golf Course

EDINBURGH RD

KIRK RD

KIRKTON AVE

Hotel

KAIM CRES

INCH CRES

Moore House
Sch

STARLAW GDNS

BOGHALL
RDBT

GUILDIEHAUGH
RDBT

Recn
Gd

Guildiehaugh

Inch
Wood

Works

Bog Burn

Round
Hill

Boghead Burn

3a

Easter
Inch

Hotel

BLACKBURN RD

Works

WHITEHILL
IND EST

The
Moss

Easter Inch
Moss

EH47

Beechwood
1 BEECHWOOD PL
2 ROWAN LA

BATHGATE RD

BEECHWOOD RD

CATHERINE
TERR

MOSSIDE
TERR

Sch

RIDDOCHHILL RD

ALMOND RD

WHITEHILL RD

YULE TERR

MOSSIDE
TERR

Sch

M8

D   E   F

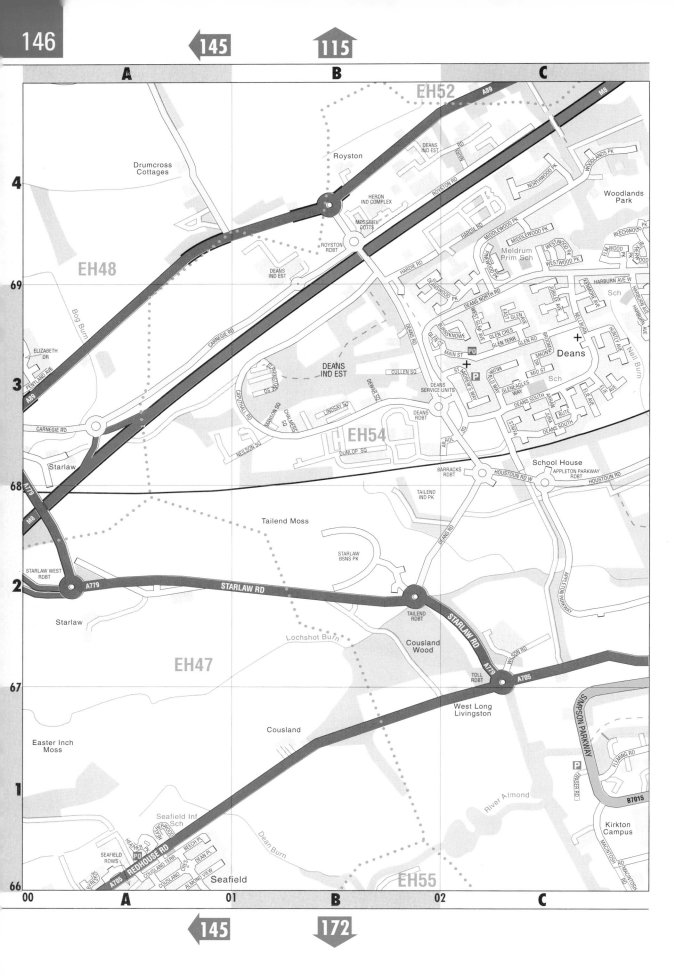

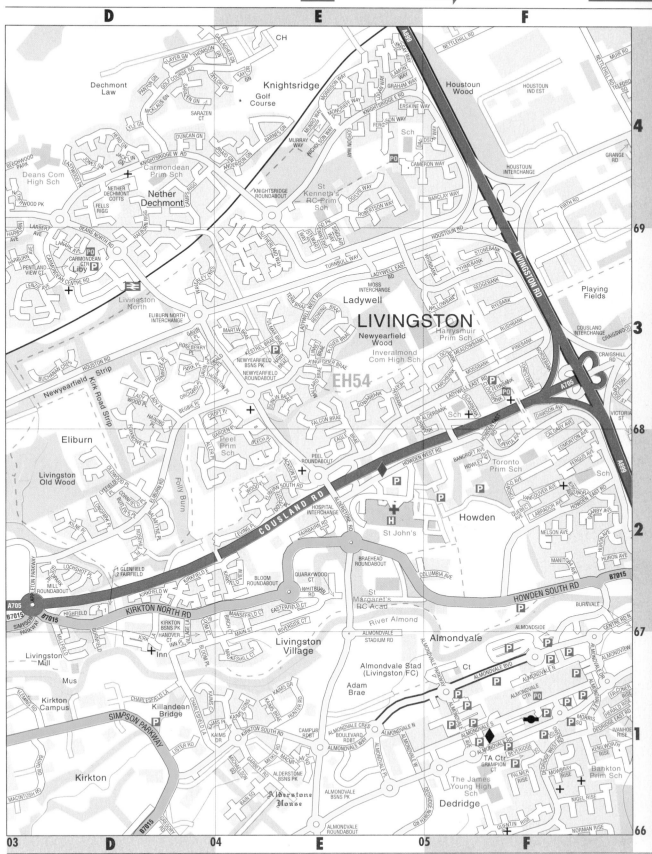

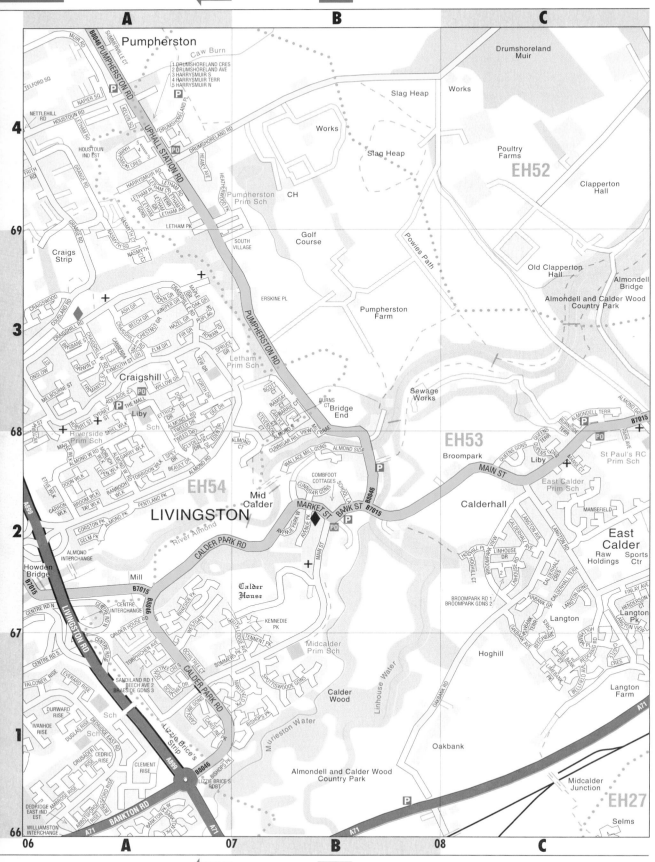

Pumpherston

Caw Burn

1 DRUMSHORELAND CRES
2 DRUMSHORELAND AVE
3 HARRYSMUIR S
4 HARRYSMUIR TERR
5 HARRYSMUIR N

Slag Heap

Works

Drumshoreland Muir

Works

Slag Heap

Poultry Farms

EH52

Clapperton Hall

Golf Course

Powies Path

Old Clapperton Hall

Almondell Bridge

Almondell and Calder Wood Country Park

Pumpherston Prim Sch

CH

South Village

ERSKINE PL

Pumpherston Farm

Craigs Strip

Letham Prim Sch

Sewage Works

EH53

Almondell Terr

B7015

Craigshill

BURNS CT
Bridge End

Broompark

Liby

St Paul's RC Prim Sch

Riverside Prim Sch

The Mall
Liby Sch

Almond Side

Main St

East Calder Prim Sch

Calderhall

EH54

Mid Calder

Combfoot Cottages

Market St
Bank St
B0046

LIVINGSTON

Avenue Park W

East Calder

Raw Holdings

Sports Ctr

Howden Bridge

Mill

Calder Park Rd

River Almond

Broompark Rd 1
Broompark Gdns 2

Langton

Langton Pk

Almond Interchange

Centre Interchange

Calder House

Calder House Rd

Midcalder Prim Sch

Hoghill

Langton Farm

Kennedie Pk

A71

Sandiland Rd
Beech Ave 2
Braeside Gdns 3

Calder Wood

Linhouse Water

Oakbank

Midcalder Junction

EH27

Lizzie Brice's Strip

Calder Park Rd

Murieston Water

Almondell and Calder Wood Country Park

Selms

Dedridge East Ind Est

Williamston Interchange

Bankton Rd

A71

Lizzie Brice's Rdbt

A71

B0046

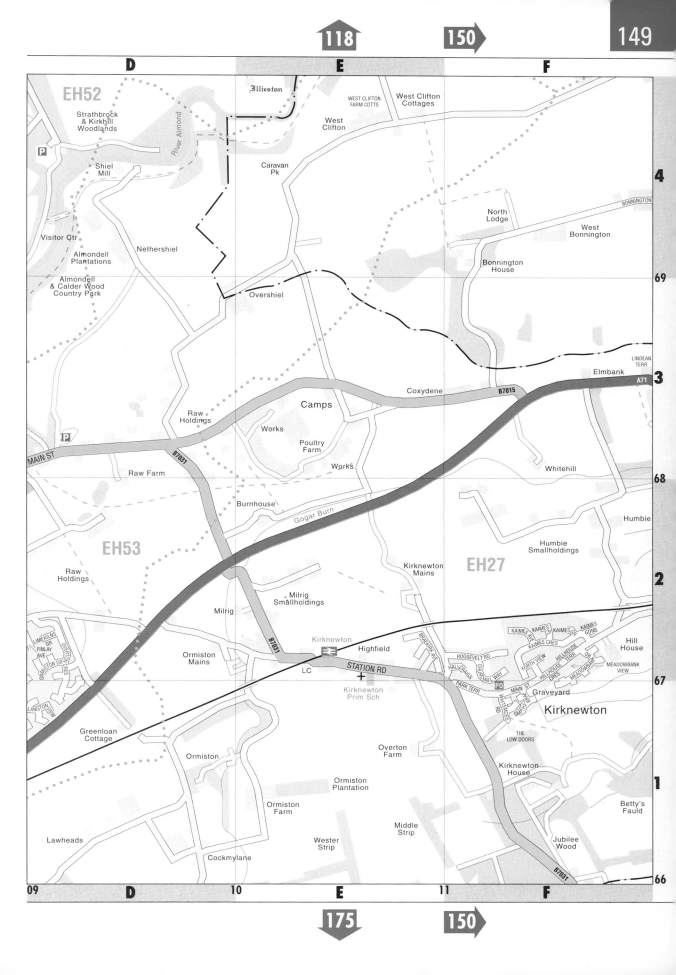

D
E
F

EH52

Illieston

WEST CLIFTON
FARM COTTS

West Clifton
Cottages

Strathbrock
& Kirkhill
Woodlands

West
Clifton

River Almond

P

Shiel
Mill

Caravan
Pk

North
Lodge

West
Bonnington

4

BONNINGTON

Visitor Ctr

Almondell
Plantations

Nethershiel

Bonnington
House

Almondell
& Calder Wood
Country Park

Overshiel

69

LINDEAN
TERR

Elmbank

Coxydene

B7015

A71

3

Camps

Raw
Holdings

Works

Poultry
Farm

Whitehill

P

MAIN ST

B7031

Raw Farm

Works

68

Burnhouse

Gogar Burn

Humbie

Humbie
Smallholdings

EH53

Raw
Holdings

Kirknewton
Mains

EH27

2

Milrig
Smallholdings

Milrig

LIMEKILNS
GR
FINLAY
AVE

OVERTON DR CRES

ORMISTON DR CRES

Ormiston
Mains

B7031

Kirknewton

Highfield

KAIMES
ANE
KAIMES
PL

KAIMES
CR

KAIMES
GDNS

Hill
House

KAIMES CRES

FORTH VIEW

HILLHOUSE
TERR

HILLHOUSE
CRES

MEADOWBANK
VIEW

MEADOWBANK

LANGTON VIEW

STATION RD

LC

ROOSEVELT RD

HALL CRAIGS

CHURCHILL WAY

BRAEKIRK AVE

PARK TERR

MAIN ST

WHITMOSS RD

PO

Graveyard

67

Greenloan
Cottage

Kirknewton
Prim Sch

Kirknewton

Ormiston

THE
LOW DOORS

Kirknewton
House

1

Ormiston
Farm

Overton
Farm

Betty's
Fauld

Ormiston
Plantation

Lawheads

Wester
Strip

Middle
Strip

Jubilee
Wood

Cockmylane

B7031

66

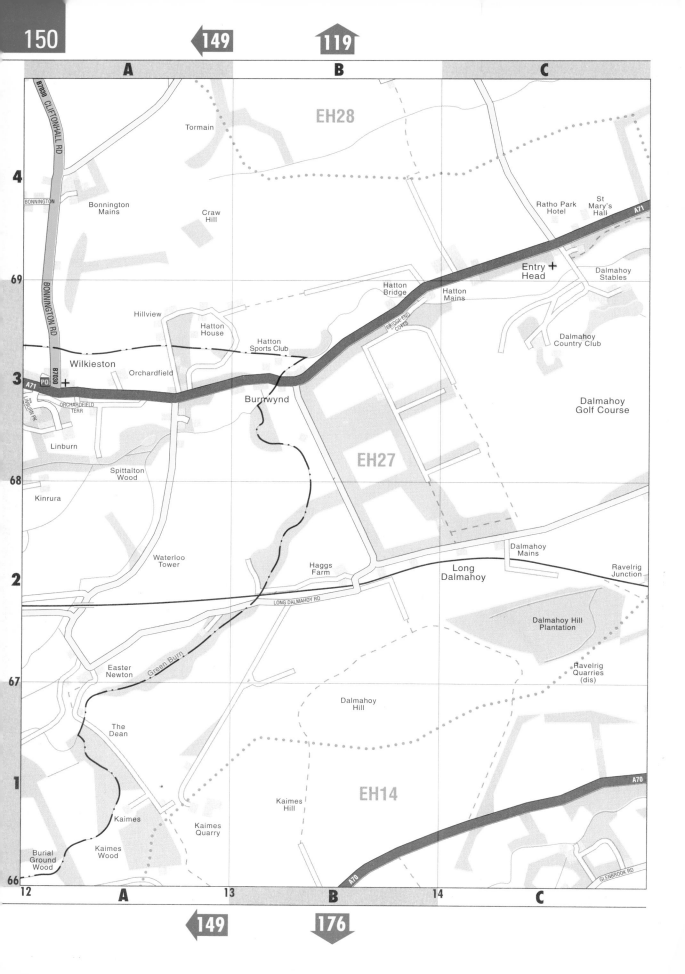

EH28

Tormain

Bonnington

Bonnington
Mains

Craw
Hill

B7030 CLIFTONHALL RD

BONNINGTON RD

Ratho Park
Hotel

St
Mary's
Hall

A71

Entry
Head

Dalmahoy
Stables

Hatton
Bridge

Hatton
Mains

Dalmahoy
Country Club

Hillview

Hatton
House

BRIDGE END COTTS

Hatton
Sports Club

Wilkieston

Orchardfield

Burnwynd

Dalmahoy
Golf Course

A71

PO

B7030

ORCHARDFIELD
TERR

LINBURN PK

Linburn

EH27

Spittalton
Wood

Kinrura

Waterloo
Tower

Haggs
Farm

Long
Dalmahoy

Dalmahoy
Mains

Ravelrig
Junction

LONG DALMAHOY RD

Dalmahoy Hill
Plantation

Easter
Newton

Green Burn

Ravelrig
Quarries
(dis)

Dalmahoy
Hill

The
Dean

A70

EH14

Kaimes
Hill

Kaimes

Kaimes
Quarry

Burial
Ground
Wood

Kaimes
Wood

A70

GLENBROOK RD

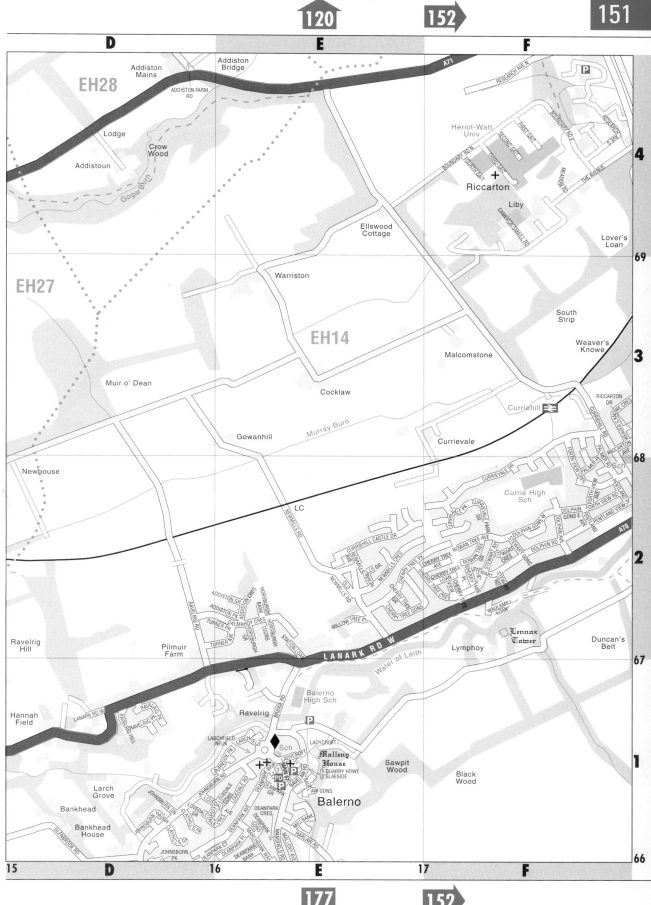

D   E   F

EH28

Addiston
Mains
Addiston
Bridge
ADDISTON FARM
RD
A71

Lodge
Crow
Wood
Addistoun
Gogar Burn

4

Heriot-Watt
Univ
Riccarton
Liby

RESEARCH AVE N
FIRST GAIT
SECOND GAIT
THIRD GAIT
FOURTH GAIT
BOUNDARY RD N
BOUNDARY RD E
RESEARCH
RESEARCH
PARK
MEADOW RD
THE AVENUE
CAMERON SMAIL RD

Lover's
Loan

EH27

Ellswood
Cottage

69

Warriston

South
Strip
Weaver's
Knowe

EH14

Malcomstone

3

Muir o' Dean

Cocklaw

Curriehill

RICCARTON
DR
NINE CRES

Gowanhill
Murray Burn
Currievale

ANNE'S BRIDGE
CURRIEHILL RD
PALMER RD
PALMER
FORTH VIEW CRES
FORTH VIEW
RD
Sch

68

Newbouse

Currievale Dr
Currie High
Sch

LC
CURRIEVALE PARK
DOLPHIN
DOLPHIN
GDNS E
PENTLAND
PENTLAND VIEW

A70

CURRIEHILL CASTLE DR
CURRIE VALE PK
CURRIE VALE GR
CHERRY TREE
AVE
ROWAN TREE AVE
STEWART AVE
DOLPHIN GDNS W
DOLPHIN AVE
DOLPHIN RD

2

Addiston Gr.
ADDISTON CRES
HORSBURGH
BANK
HORSBURGH
GDNS
NEWMILLS RD
OLD
NEWMILLS
NEWMILLS CRES
NEWMILLS GR
CHERRY TREE PK
CHERRY TREE
LOAN
CHERRY TREE
VIEW
CHERRY TREE
PL
ROWAN TREE
GR
STEWART
CRES
STEWART
GDNS
STEWART
PL
STEWART

Ravelrig
Hill
Pilmuir
Farm
RAVELRIG RD
TURNER PK
TURNER AVE
DALMAHOY CRES
HORSBURGH
GR
STATION LOAN
WILLOW TREE PL
CHERRY TREE GR
CHERRY TREE GDNS
CHERRY TREE CRES

Lymphoy
Lennox
Tower
Duncan's
Belt

WAULKMILL
LOAN

67

LANARK RD W
Water of Leith

Hannah
Field
LANARK RD W
RAVELRIG HILL
RAVELRIG
RAVELRIG PK
Ravelrig

Balerno
High Sch

BRIDGE RD

Black
Wood

Sawpit
Wood

1

Larchfield
Neuk
Sch
LARCHFIELD
LADYCROFT
Malleny
House
1 QUARRY HOWE
2 SLAESIDE

Larch
Grove
Bankhead
Bankhead
House

JOHNSBURN RD
AVENSOR RD
LOVEDALE
LOVEDALE GDNS
LOVEDALE AVE
LOVEDALE CRES
LOVEDALE GR
CLAYTHILS
CLAYTHILS PK
CLAYTHILS GR
MAIN ST
DEANPARK AVE
DEANPARK
CRES
DEANPARK GDNS
DEANPARK BANK
MANSFIELD RD
MALLENY
MALLENY AVE
HARLAW RD
MILLBANK
MARCHBANK WAY
BAVELAW RD
AW GDNS
Balerno

JOHNSBURN GN
WHINGHILL
RALPH
JOHNSBURN
PK
GLENBROOK RD
DEANPARK CT
DEANPARK
PK

15   16   17

D   E   F

66

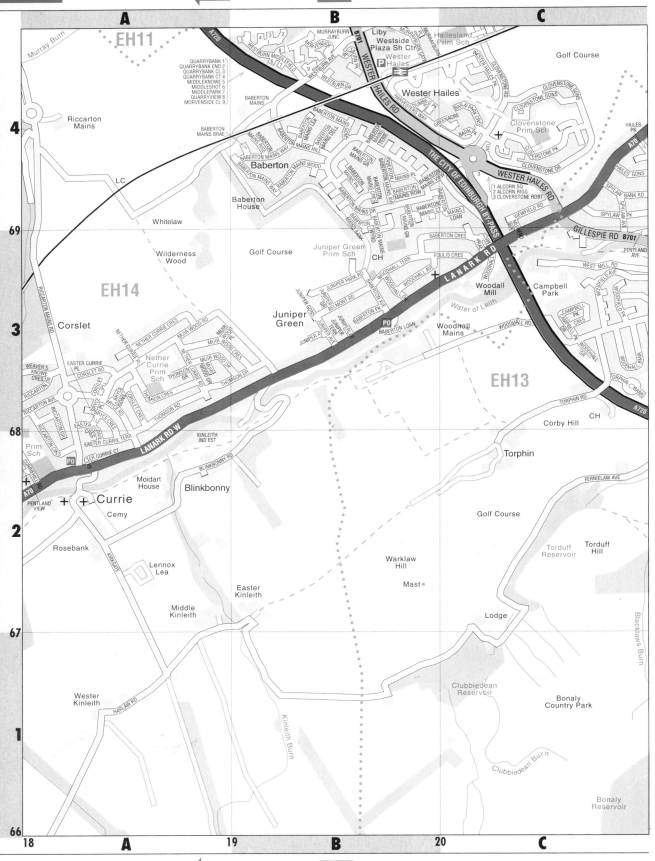

EH11

A720

Murray Burn

QUARRYBANK 1
QUARRYBANK END 2
QUARRYBANK CL 3
QUARRYBANK CT 4
MIDDLEKNOWE 5
MIDDLESHOT 6
MIDDLEPARK 7
QUARRYVIEW 8
MORVENSIDE CL 9

Riccarton Mains

LC

Baberton Mains

BABERTON MAINS BRAE

Baberton

Baberton House

Whitelaw

Murrayburn Junc

Westburn Middlefield

Liby Westside Plaza Sh Ctr

Hailesland Prim Sch

Golf Course

Wester Hailes

Wester Hailes

WESTER HAILES RD

THE CITY OF EDINBURGH BY-PASS

Clovenstone Prim Sch

HAILES PK

A70

Clovenstone Dr

WESTER HAILES RD

1 ALCORN SQ
2 ALCORN RIGG
3 CLOVENSTONE RDBT

GILLESPIE RD   B701

SPYLAW BANK RD

HAILES GDNS

PENTLAND AVE

SPYLAW PK

EH14

69

Wilderness Wood

Golf Course

Juniper Green Prim Sch

CH

VIEWFIELD RD

Woodall Mill

LANARK RD

WEST MILL RD

Corslet

Nether Currie Prim Sch

MUIR WOOD RD

Juniper Green

Belmont Rd

Baberton Pk

PO
Baberton Loan

Water of Leith

Woodhall Mains

Campbell Park

WOODHALL RD

EH13

WOODFIELD AVE

WOODHALL GR

WOODHALL BANK

Weaver's Knowe Cres

Easter Currie Pl

RICCARTON AVE

CORSLET RD

BRYCE

THOMSON

THOMSON DR

KINLEITH IND EST

Torphin Bk

TORPHIN RD

Corby Hill   CH

A720

Prim Sch

PO

LANARK RD W

Easter Currie Terr

BLINKBONNY RD

Torphin

Pentland View

Currie

Cemy

Moidart House

Blinkbonny

FERNIELAW AVE

Rosebank

KIRKGATE

Lennox Lea

Easter Kinleith

Warklaw Hill

Mast

Golf Course

Torduff Reservoir

Torduff Hill

Blacklaws Burn

Middle Kinleith

67

Lodge

Wester Kinleith

HARLAW RD

Kinleith Burn

Clubbiedean Reservoir

Bonaly Country Park

Clubbiedean Burn

Bonaly Reservoir

66

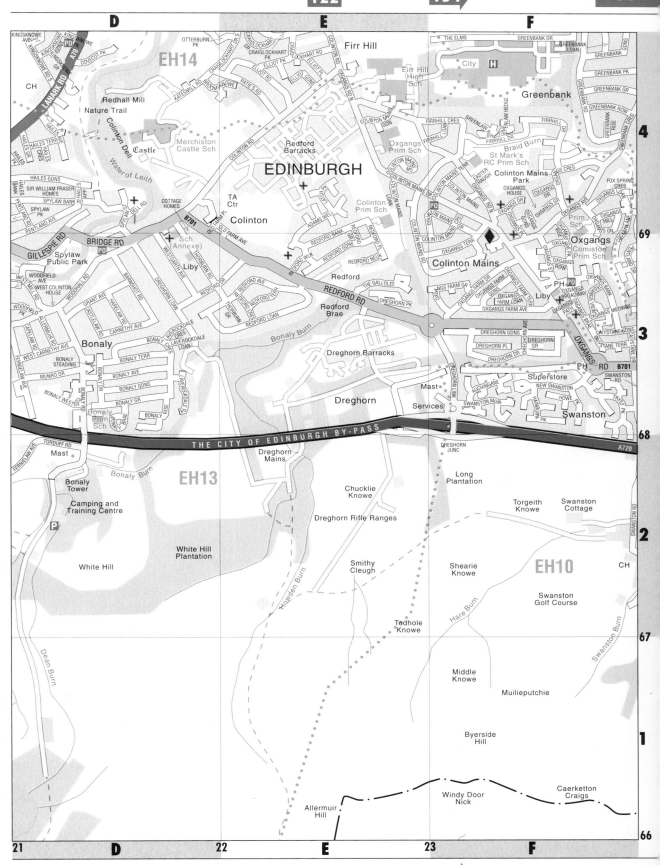

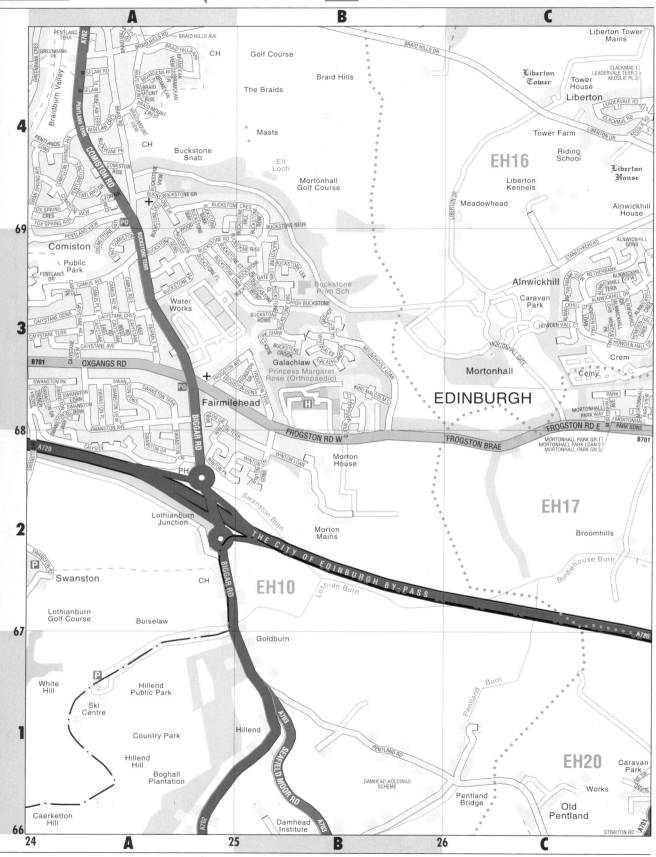

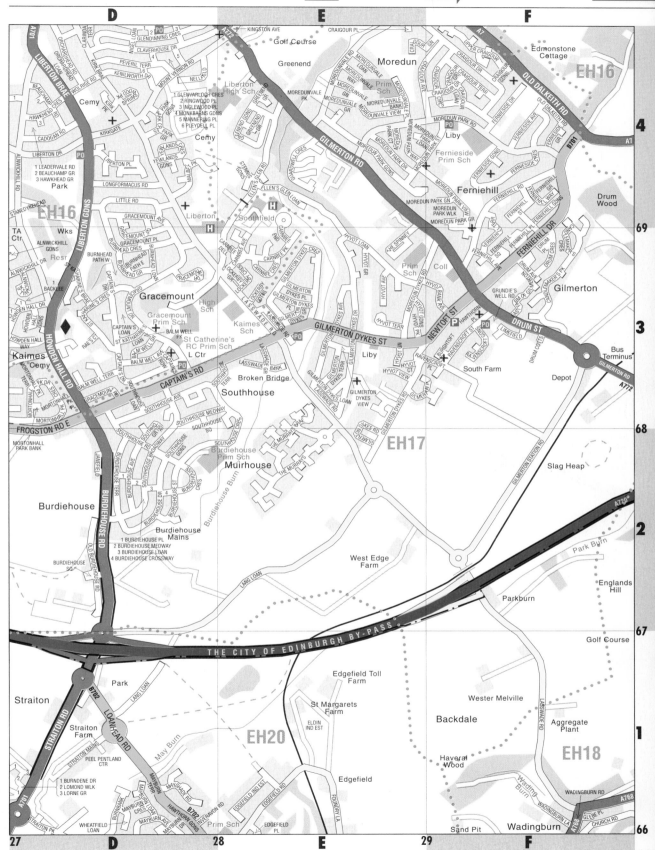

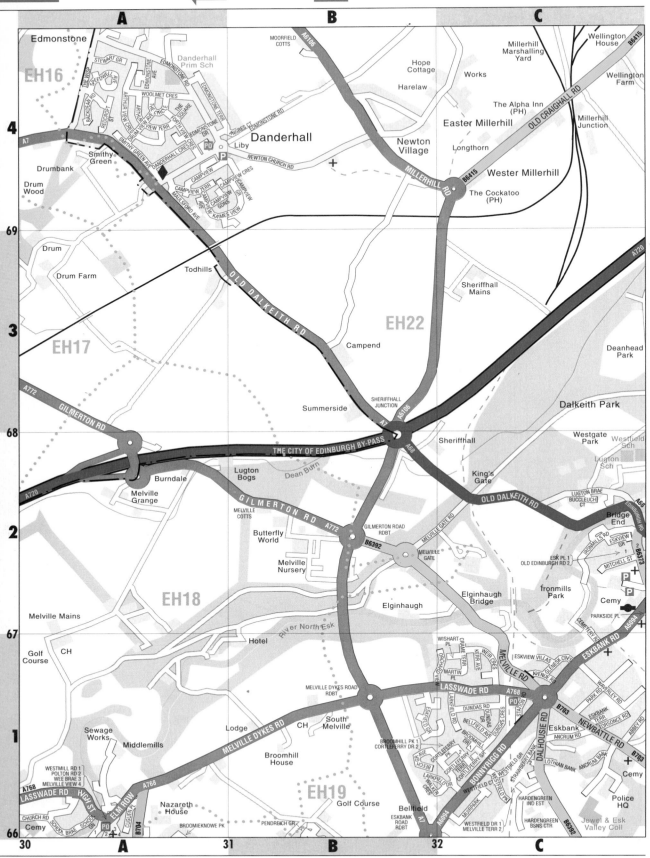

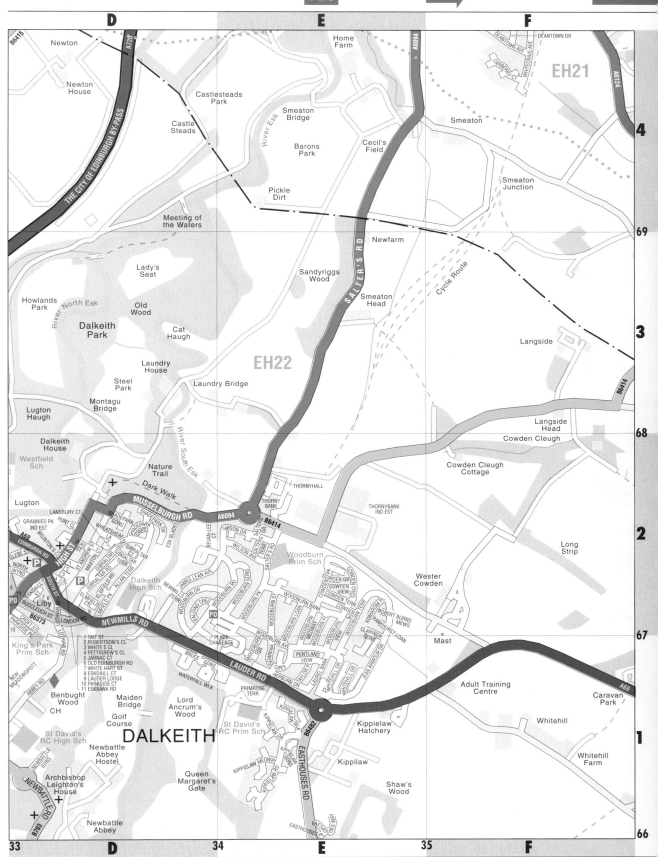

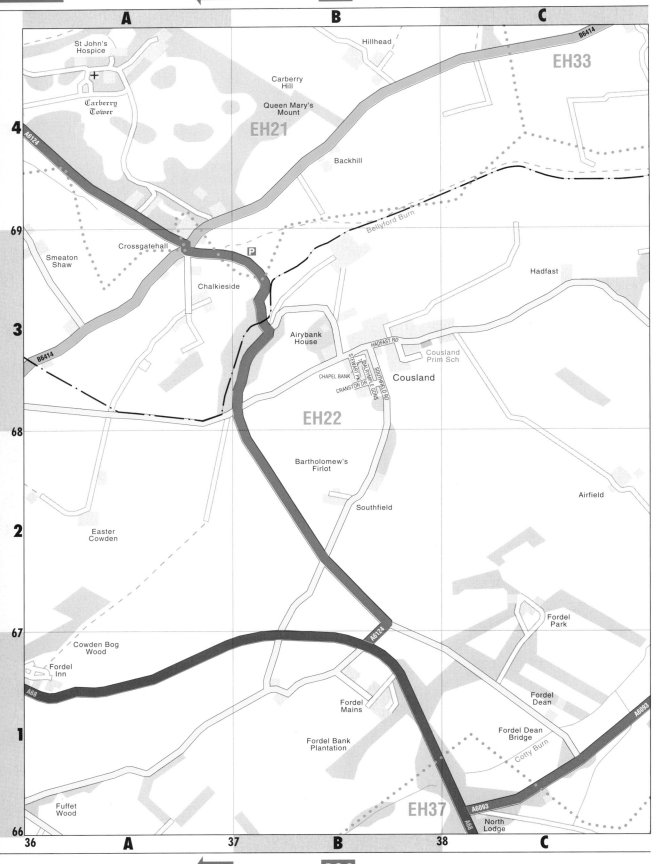

A   B   C

EH33

B6414

St John's
Hospice

Carberry
Hill

Hillhead

Carberry
Tower

Queen Mary's
Mount

4

EH21

A6124

Backhill

Hadfast

Bellyford Burn

69

Crossgatehall

Smeaton
Shaw

P

Chalkieside

3

B6414

Airybank
House

HADFAST RD

Cousland
Prim Sch

Cousland

CHAPEL BANK

STEWART PK

DALRYMPLE GDNS

CRANSTON DR

SOUTHFIELD RD

68

EH22

Bartholomew's
Firlot

Southfield

Airfield

2

Easter
Cowden

Fordel
Park

67

A6124

Cowden Bog
Wood

Fordel
Inn

Fordel
Dean

A68

Fordel
Mains

Fordel
Dean
Bridge

A6093

1

Fordel Bank
Plantation

Cotty Burn

Fuffet
Wood

EH37

A6093

North
Lodge

A68

66

36   A   37   B   38   C

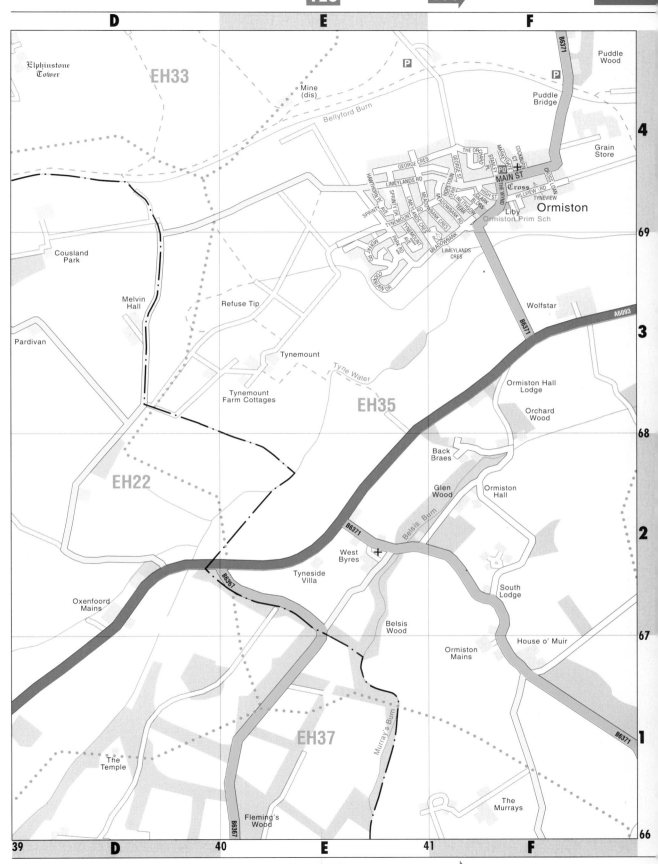

159
129

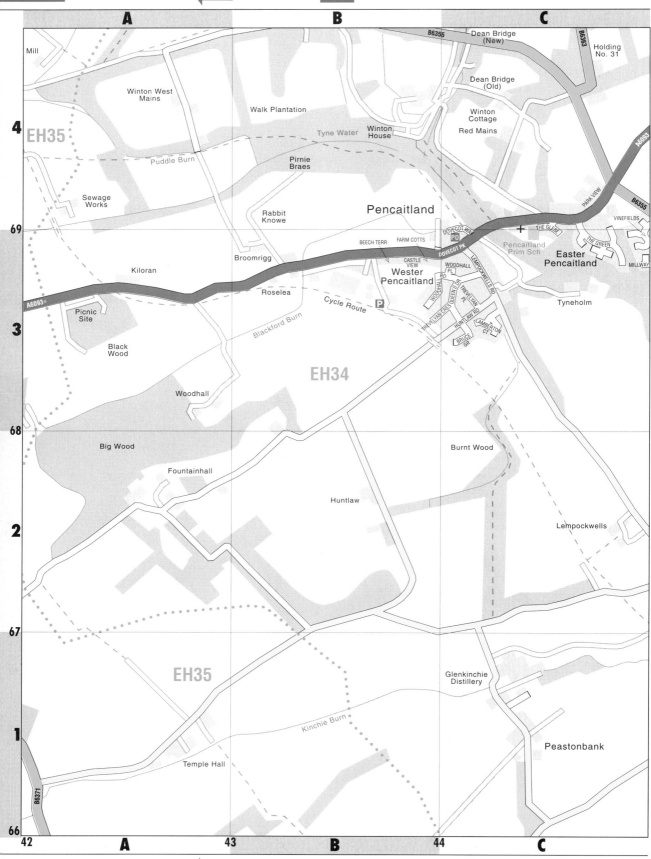

159
186

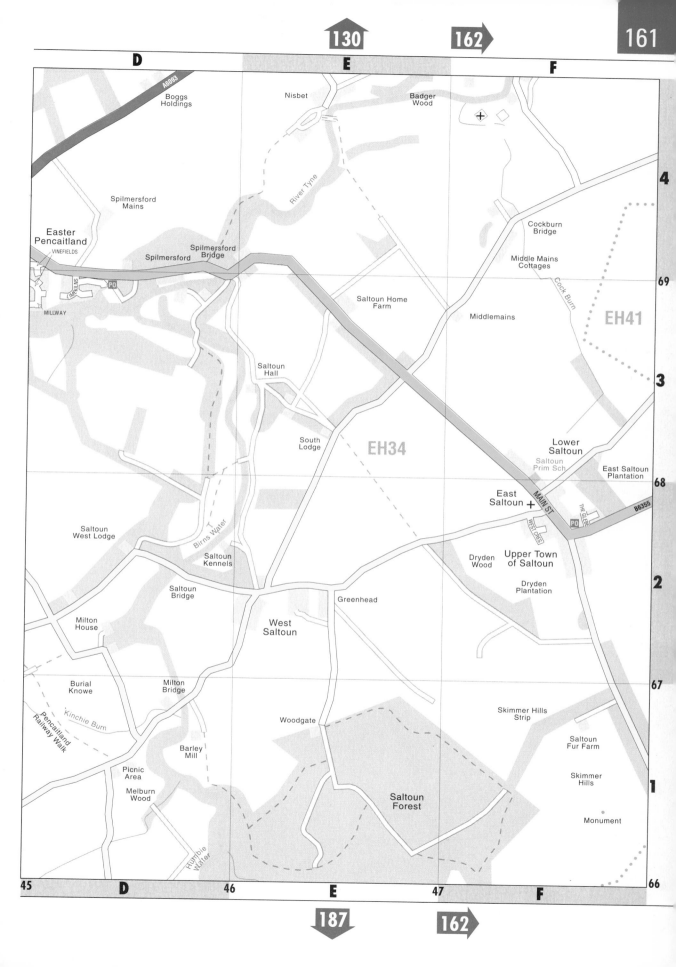

130
162
187
162

D
E
F

4
69
3
68
2
67
1

45
46
47
66

Boggs
Holdings

Nisbet

Badger
Wood

A6093

Spilmersford
Mains

Easter
Pencaitland

VINEFIELDS

Spilmersford
Bridge

Spilmersford

River Tyne

Cockburn
Bridge

Middle Mains
Cottages

Cock Burn

EH41

PO

MILLWAY

Saltoun Home
Farm

Middlemains

Saltoun
Hall

South
Lodge

EH34

Lower
Saltoun

Saltoun
Prim Sch

East Saltoun
Plantation

Saltoun
West Lodge

Birns Water

Saltoun
Kennels

East
Saltoun

MAIN ST

WEST CRES

Upper Town
of Saltoun

THE GLEBE

PO

B6355

Dryden
Wood

Dryden
Plantation

Saltoun
Bridge

Greenhead

Milton
House

West
Saltoun

Burial
Knowe

Milton
Bridge

Kinchie Burn

Pencaitland Railway Walk

Woodgate

Skimmer Hills
Strip

Saltoun
Fur Farm

Barley
Mill

Picnic
Area

Melburn
Wood

Saltoun
Forest

Skimmer
Hills

Monument

Humbie Water

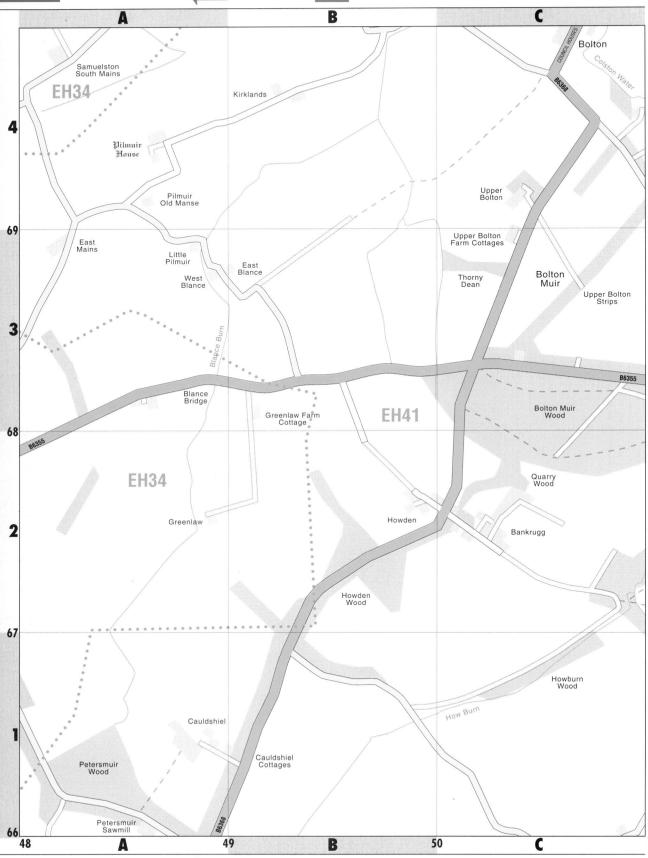

A   **B**   **C**

Bolton

Colston Water

B6368

Samuelston
South Mains

EH34

Kirklands

4

Pilmuir
House

Upper
Bolton

Pilmuir
Old Manse

69

Upper Bolton
Farm Cottages

East
Mains

Little
Pilmuir

East
Blance

Thorny
Dean

Bolton
Muir

West
Blance

Upper Bolton
Strips

3

Blance Burn

B6355

Blance
Bridge

Greenlaw Farm
Cottage

EH41

Bolton Muir
Wood

68

B6355

EH34

Quarry
Wood

Greenlaw

Howden

Bankrugg

2

Howden
Wood

67

Howburn
Wood

How Burn

Cauldshiel

1

Petersmuir
Wood

Cauldshiel
Cottages

B6368

66

Petersmuir
Sawmill

48   **A**   49   **B**   50   **C**

D E F

Gowks Hill

Clacherdean Wood

Brounshill

B6369

Playmuir Wood

Dalgowrie Brae

Colstoun Old Mill

Crown Wood

Myreside

Haydean

Eaglescairnie

Ewelie Wood

Colstoun Water

South Lodge

4

Hay Dean

Home Farm

Slateford

69

Eaglescairnie Mains

Sandyford Burn

Beugh Banks

Beugh Burn

Fawn Wood

The Common

Heather Wood

Sewage Works

Gifford Vale

3

Membland

Inglisfield

Bell's Wood

Broadwoodside

Speedy Wood

STATION RD

OLD MILL LA

Hotel TH THE SQUARE

MAIN ST

DUNS RD

B6369

LILLIES LA

B6355

Bolton Muir Wood

EH41

TWEEDDALE CRES

TWEEDDALE GR

TWEEDDALE TER

PO

THE WYND

HIGH ST

BAILLINS WYND

WALDEN DR

WALDEN TERR

WALDEN PL

68

Newhall Burn

Pyotshaw

Speedy Burn

Holynbank

THE AVENUE

Gifford

Yester Prim Sch

Craises Roundall

Gifford Bank

Lady's Wood

Port Wood

Newhall Port

Blawearie Wood

CH

Carter's Haugh

Broad Wood

Gifford Water

Beechbank Wood

2

Golf Course

Trafalgar

Meg's Bridge

Bents Wood

Bailie's Hag Wood

Newhall Wood

67

Well Hag Wood

Foxes Wood

Bankhead Bridge

Bankhead Wood

Woodhead

Yester Mains

1

Smithy Cottage

Skedsbush Bridge

Kidlaw Burn

Dean Wood

Bonny Wood

Wester Wood

Saugh Wood

Green Wood

Redshill

Scarhill Wood

66

51 D 52 E 53 F

A   **B**   **C**

Sandyford Burn

B6370

Bara Farm

Bara

4

Bara Wood

Sounding Burn

Bara Loch

69

Winding Law

3

Townhead

Townhead Wood

B6370

Duncanlaw

B6355

Cross Hill

EH41

68

Duncanlaw Strip

Sheriffside Roundall

Danskine Loch

Sunnyside

Sheriffside

Walden

2

Sunnyside Strip

Kailrig Wood

Danskine Lodge

Danskine

Sheriffside Clough

B6355

Yester House

Duncan's Bog

Thicket Wood

Walden Lea

Danskine Burn

Hattie Braes

67

Gifford Water

Castle Wood

Swallow Cleugh

Shank Lea Wood

Newlands Burn

Newlands

Gamuelston Burn

Castle

Hopes Water

1

Black Basin

Newlands Strip

Todlaw Bog Wood

Castle Mains House

Park

66

Castle Mains

54   **A**   55   **B**   56   **C**

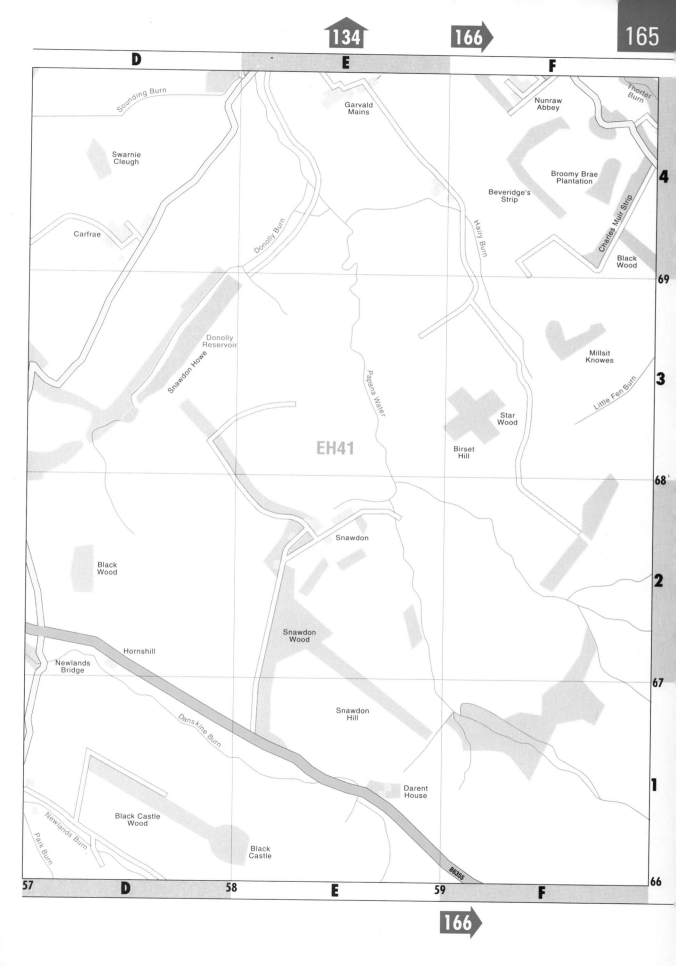

165

135

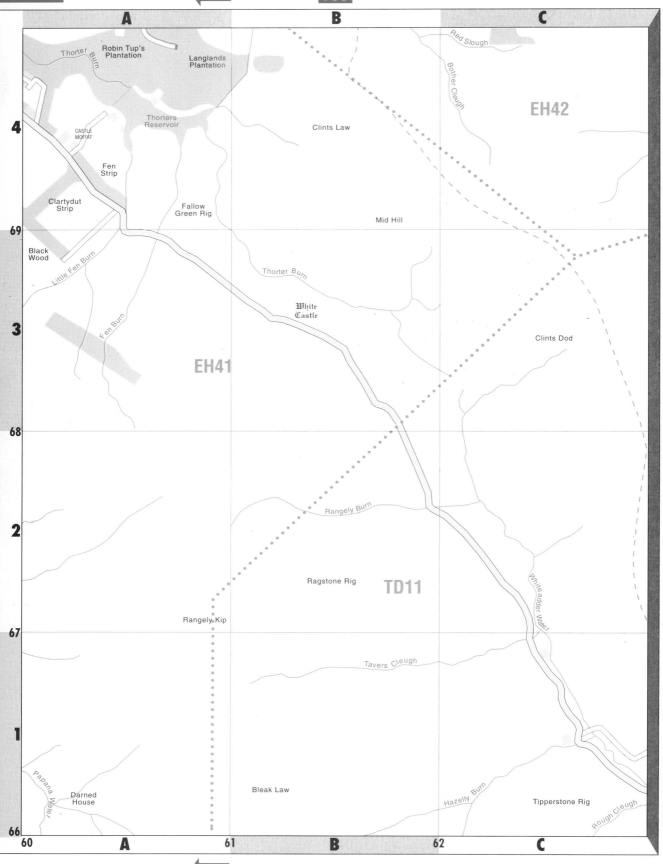

Thorter Burn

Robin Tup's Plantation

Langlands Plantation

Red Slough

Bother Cleugh

EH42

Clints Law

4

Thorters Reservoir

CASTLE MOFFAT

Fen Strip

Mid Hill

69

Clartydut Strip

Fallow Green Rig

Black Wood

Little Fen Burn

Thorter Burn

White Castle

Fen Burn

3

EH41

Clints Dod

68

Rangely Burn

2

Ragstone Rig

TD11

White adder Water

Rangely Kip

67

Tavers Cleugh

1

Papana Water

Darned House

Bleak Law

Hazelly Burn

Tipperstone Rig

Rough Cleugh

66

60   **A**   **61**   **B**   **62**   **C**

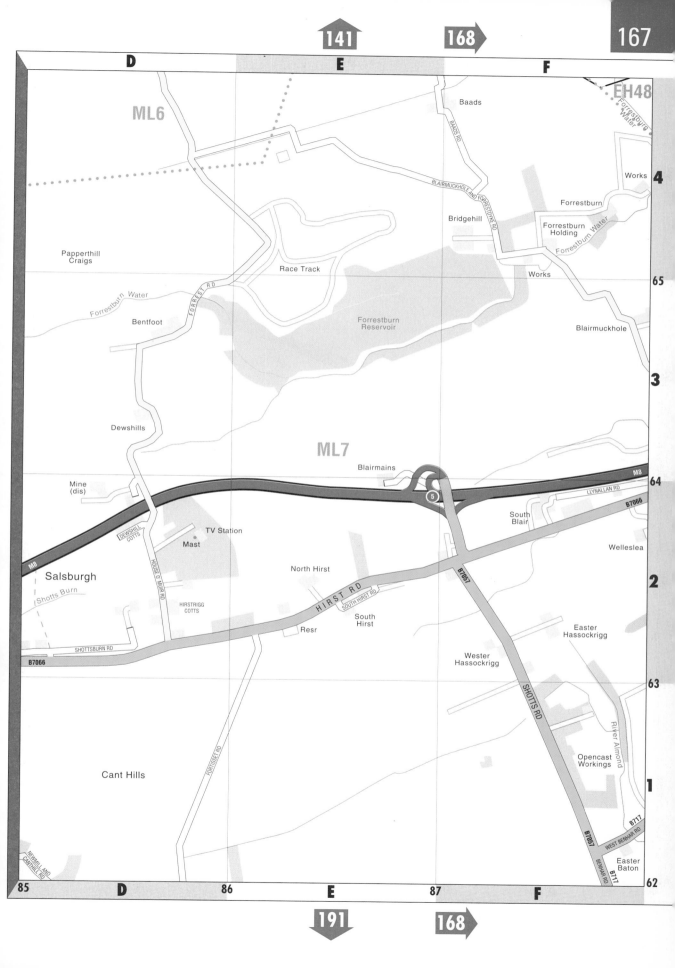

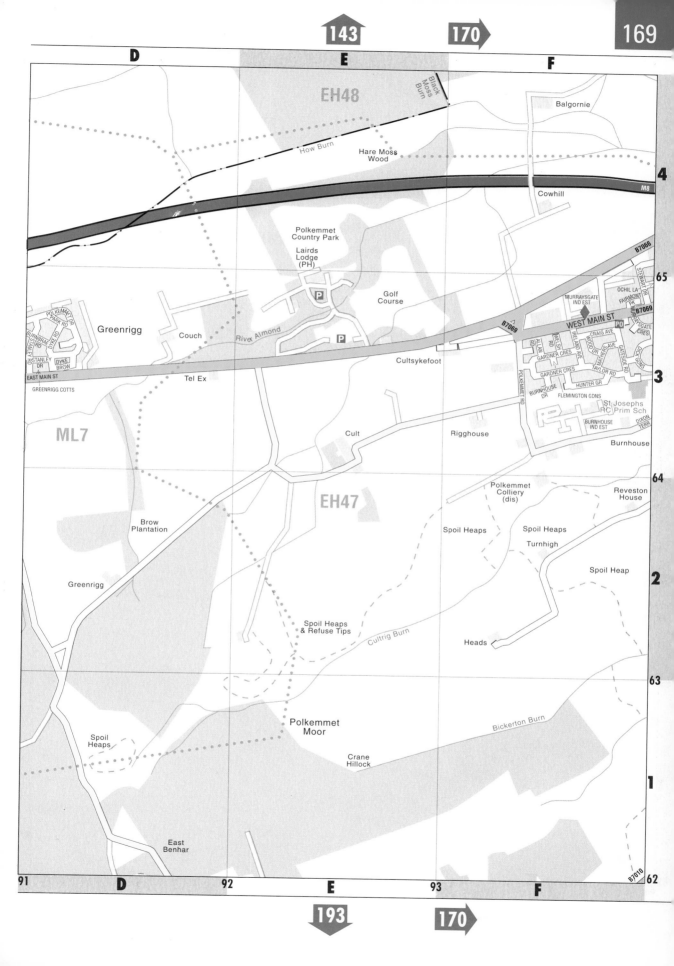

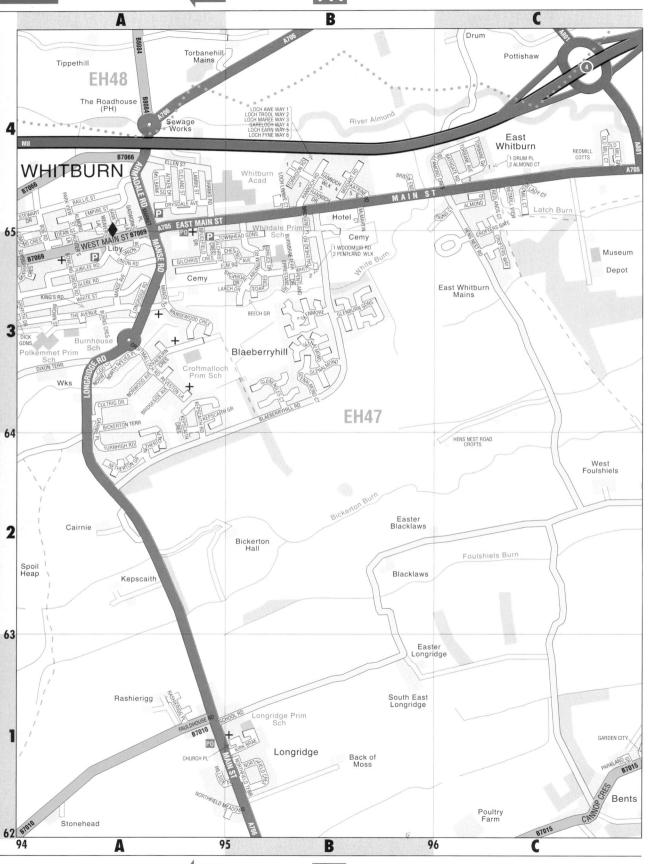

A • B • C

Tippethill
Torbanehill Mains
Drum
Pottishaw
4
EH48
The Roadhouse (PH)
Sewage Works
River Almond
East Whitburn
REDMILL COTTS
OLD MILL GR
OLD MILL CT
1 DRUM PL
2 ALMOND CT

4

M8

WHITBURN

Whitburn Acad

LOCH AWE WAY 1
LOCH TROOL WAY 2
LOCH MAREE WAY 3
LOCH EARN WAY 4
LOCH EARN WAY 5
LOCH FYNE WAY 6

RANNOCH WLK

MAIN ST

Latch Burn

65

EAST MAIN ST

WEST MAIN ST

Liby

Whitdale Prim Sch

Hotel

Cemy

1 WOODMUIR RD
2 PENTLAND WLK

CROFTERS GATE

Museum Depot

Cemy

Cemy

White Burn

East Whitburn Mains

3

Polkemmet Prim Sch

Burnhouse Sch

Blaeberryhill

Croftmalloch Prim Sch

EH47

BLAEBERRYHILL RD

HENS NEST ROAD CROFTS

West Foulshiels

64

Cairnie

Bickerton Hall

Bickerton Burn

Easter Blacklaws

Foulshiels Burn

Blacklaws

2

Spoil Heap

Kepscaith

Easter Longridge

63

Rashierigg

South East Longridge

GARDEN CITY

PARKLAND ST

Bents

1

Longridge Prim Sch

Longridge

Back of Moss

Poultry Farm

Stonehead

Northfield Meadows

62

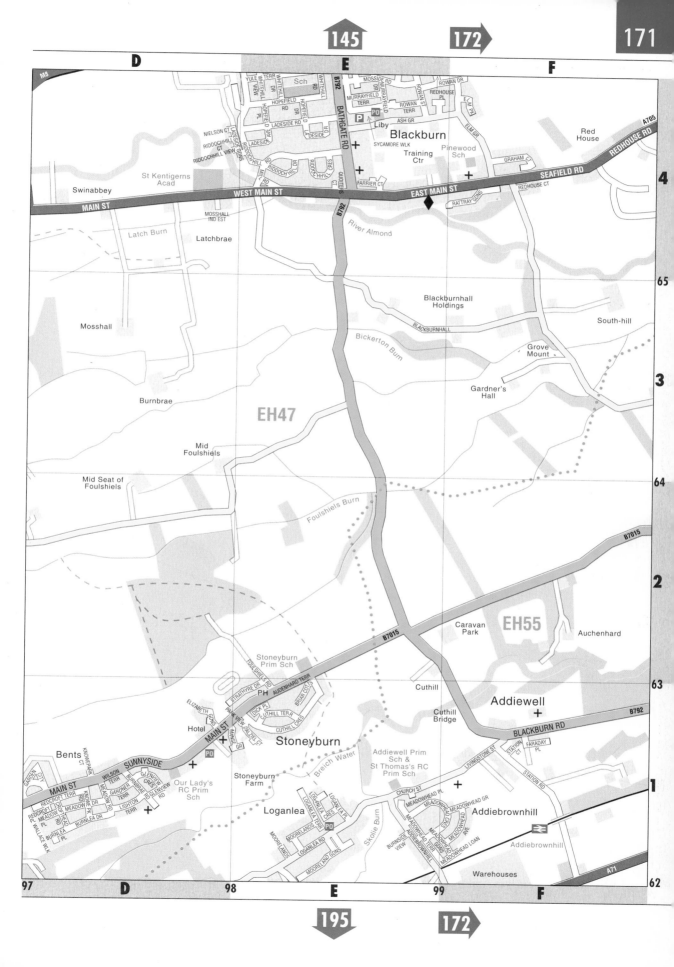

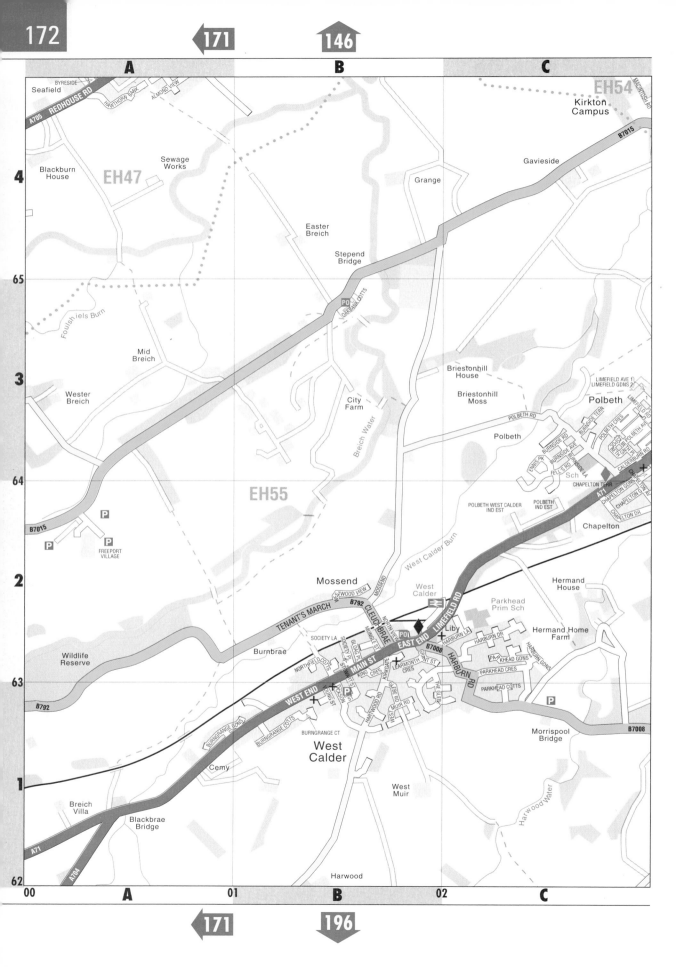

171
146

A   B   C

Seafield
BYRESIDE
REDHOUSE RD
A705
HAWTHORN BANK
ALMOND VIEW

Blackburn House
EH47
Sewage Works

4

Easter Breich

Grange

EH54

Kirkton Campus

Gavieside

B7015

65

PO
OAKBANK COTTS

Stepend Bridge

Foulshiels Burn

Mid Breich

Briestonhill House

Briestonhill Moss

LIMEFIELD AVE 1
LIMEFIELD GDNS 2

Polbeth

POLBETH RD

3

Wester Breich

City Farm

Breich Water

Polbeth

EMNS PK
BURNSIDE RD
BURNSIDE AVE
BURNSIDE LA
FELL'S RD
Sch

BURNSIDE RD
POLBETH CRES
POLBETH TERR
POLBETH AVE
CALDERBURN RD

CHAPELTON TERR

64

EH55

POLBETH WEST CALDER IND EST

POLBETH IND EST

CHAPELTON GDNS
CHAPELTON G
CHAPELTON DR

A71

Chapelton

B7015
A705
P
P
P
FREEPORT VILLAGE

West Calder Burn

Hermand House

2

Mossend

West Calder

Parkhead Prim Sch

Hermand Home Farm

TWOOD VIEW
B792
CLEUCHBRAE
MOSSEND

Liby
HARBURN LA
HARBURN DR
PA KHEAD GDNS
HARBURN GDNS

TENANT'S MARCH

Burnbrae

SOCIETY LA
NORTHFIELD COTTS
SOCIETY PL
ST JAMES ST
GLOUG PL
MUIRLEE CT
MAIN ST
KING CRES
KIRKGATE
LEARMONTH CRES
GRANT ST
PO
EAST END
LIMEFIELD RD
B7008
HARBURN RD

PARKHEAD CRES

P

Wildlife Reserve

HARTWOOD RD
JEBB RD
MUIR RD
THE GLEBE

PARKHEAD COTTS

Morrispool Bridge

63

B792

WEST END
DICKSON
YOUNG ST

BURNGRANGE GDNS
BURNGRANGE COTTS
BURNGRANGE CT

West Calder

West Muir

B7008

Cemy

Breich Villa

Blackbrae Bridge

Harwood Water

1

A71

Harwood

A704

62

00   A   01   B   02   C

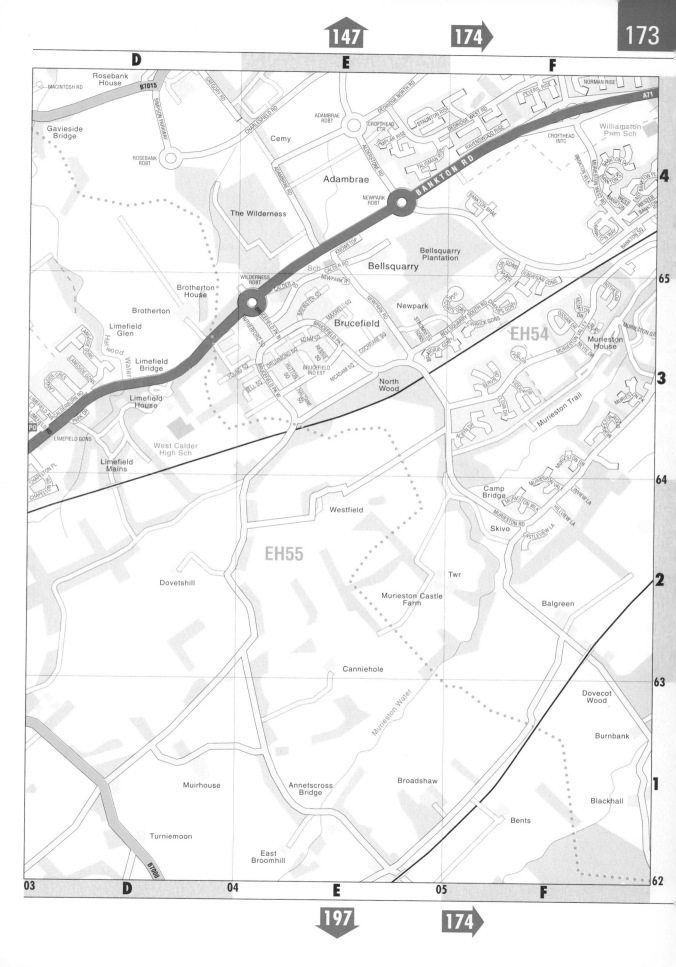

173
148

A **B** **C**

BANKTON RD
DEDRIDGE EAST RD
BANKTON GDNS
EASTER BANKTON
EASTER BANKTON GR
BANKTON EAST RD
BANKTON PK E
Sch
BANKTON GR GLADE
Bankton House
EAST BANKTON
WESTER BANKTON
BANKTON GR

A71
Manse Covert
OAKBANK RDBT
Williamston Bridge
OAKBANK PARK WAY
OAKBANK PARK
OAKBANK PARK RD
OAKBANK PARK DR

A71
Red Craig

Selms Tops

4

P
Livingston South
MURIESTON WEST RD
MURIESTON SOUTH

Murieston
Nether Williamston

Blackraw

Selm Muir Reservoir (dis)

65

MURIESTON WAY
MURIESTON VALLEY
MURIESTON GDNS
MURIESTON DR
MURIESTON RD
MURIESTON CT

EH54

Selm Muir Wood

MURIESTON GR

3

Wellhead Farm

Linhouse Water

EH53

64

Corston

2

Linn Caldron

Morton Reservoir

Linnhouse Cottages

63

Morton
Mortonhill
Morton Burn
Morton Reservoir
Morton Burn

Linnhous

1

Linnhouse

Camilty Water

EH27

62

06 **A** 07 **B** 08 **C**

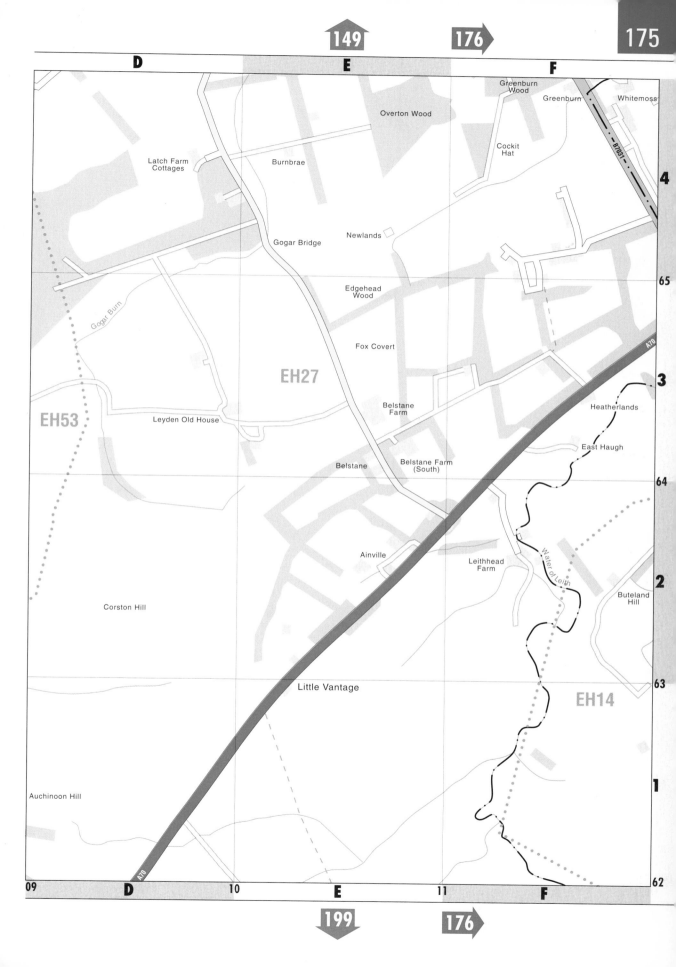

D
E
F

Greenburn
Wood

Overton Wood

Greenburn

Whitemoss

B7031

Cockit
Hat

Latch Farm
Cottages

Burnbrae

4

Gogar Bridge

Newlands

65

Edgehead
Wood

A70

Fox Covert

EH27

3

Heatherlands

Belstane
Farm

Leyden Old House

EH53

East Haugh

Gogar Burn

Belstane

Belstane Farm
(South)

64

Ainville

Leithhead
Farm

Water of Leith

2

Buteland
Hill

Corston Hill

63

Little Vantage

EH14

1

Auchinoon Hill

A70

62

09
D
10
E
11
F

175
150

A　　　　　　　　　　B　　　　　　　　　　C

Airfield

Boll-o-Bere

A70

Whelpside

Glenbrook
House

GLENBROOK

Glenbrook

Beechgrove
Farm

House of
Cockburn

4

B7031

Cockburn

Haughhead
Farm

65

Inveroe

Ford

Water of Leith

COCKBURNHILL RD

Pirnie
Hall

A70

House-o-Muir

Buteland
Farm

Cock Burn

3

EH27

Buteland
House

Temple
House

Cockburnhill

64

EH14

2

63

1

Bavelaw Burn

62

12　　　　　A　　　　　13　　　　　B　　　　　14　　　　　C

175
200

D E F

Malleny Mills

GLENBROOK RD
JOHNSBURN PK
DEANPARK CT
Dean Park Sch
Hotel
HARLAW MARCH
Harlaw Farm
Harlaw Sch
Balleny Farm
Goodtrees
CROSSWOOD AVE
CROSSWOOD CRES
CAIRNS DR
CAIRNS GDNS
HIGHLEA CIRC
COCKBURNHILL RD
COCKBURN CRES
WHITELEA CRES
WHITELEA RD
MARCHBANK GDNS
MARCHBANK PL
MARCHBANK GR
THREIPMUIR PL
THREIPMUIR AVE
THREIPMUIR GDNS
GREENFIELD CRES
GREENFIELD GDNS
MALLENY AVE
MANSFIELD RD
MALLENY MILLGATE
HARLAW RD
Bavelaw Burn

Cockdurno

Upper Dean Park

6

Harlaw Reservoir

3

Marchbank Hotel

Threipmuir

EH14

64

The Common
Wildlife Reserve

P

Threipmuir Reservoir

East Rigg

Redford Wood
Redford Bridge

2

Easter Bavelaw

Bavelaw Burn

63

West Rigg

Wester Bavelaw

Bavelaw Castle

Eastertown Burn

Bavelaw Mill Farm

1

Green Cleugh

Hare Hill

62

177
152

A

B

C

HARLAW RD

Bonaly Country Park

Bonaly Resr

Whiteside Plantations

Kinleith Burn

EH13

4

Harbour Hill

P

Cock Rig

Harlaw House

Malleny Rifle Range (dis)

65

Harlaw Reservoir

Craigentarrie

3

EH14

Bell's Hill

Threipmuir Reservoir

King's Hill

White Cleugh Burn

White Cleugh

White Cleugh Burn

2

White Cleugh Burn

EH26

Logan Cottage

Black Hill

Logan House

Logan Burn

63

Gask Hill

1

Howlet's House

Flesh Cleugh

Loganlea Reservoir

Green Cleugh

The Pinnacle

The Howe

62

18

A

19

B

20

C

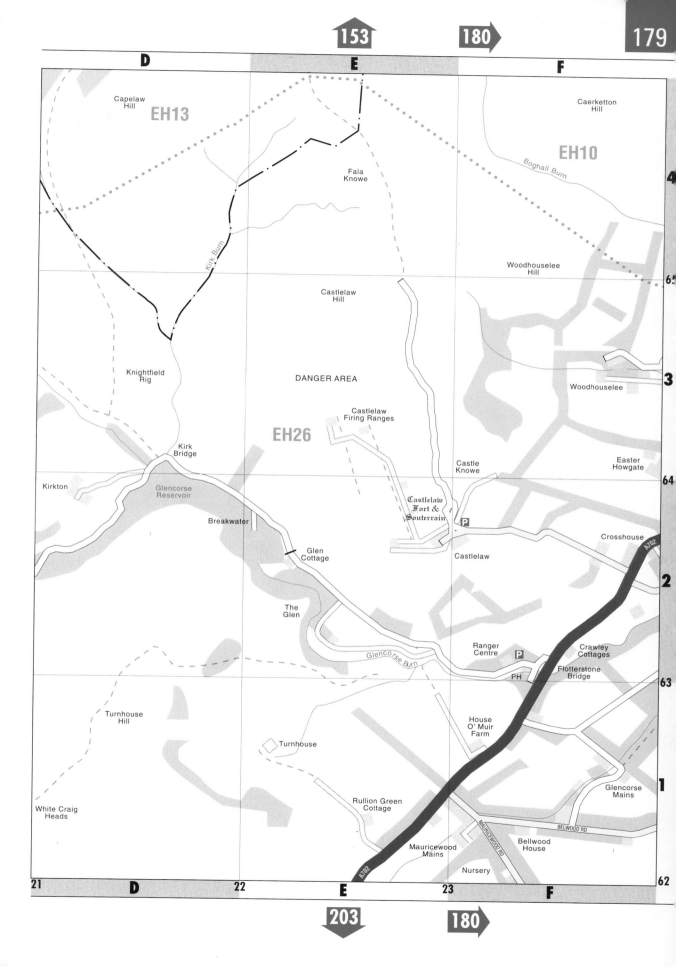

D

E

F

Capelaw
Hill

EH13

Fala
Knowe

Caerketton
Hill

EH10

Boghall Burn

4

Kirk Burn

Castlelaw
Hill

Woodhouselee
Hill

65

Knightfield
Rig

DANGER AREA

Woodhouselee

3

Castlelaw
Firing Ranges

EH26

Kirk
Bridge

Kirkton

Glencorse
Reservoir

Castle
Knowe

Castle
Knowe

Easter
Howgate

64

Breakwater

Castlelaw
Fort &
Souterrain

P

Crosshouse

A702

Glen
Cottage

Castlelaw

2

The
Glen

Glencorse Burn

Ranger
Centre

P

Crawley
Cottages

Turnhouse
Hill

PH

Flotterstone
Bridge

63

Turnhouse

House
O' Muir
Farm

White Craig
Heads

Rullion Green
Cottage

Glencorse
Mains

1

BELWOOD RD

MAURICEWOOD RD

Mauricewood
Mains

Bellwood
House

A702

Nursery

62

21

D

22

E

23

F

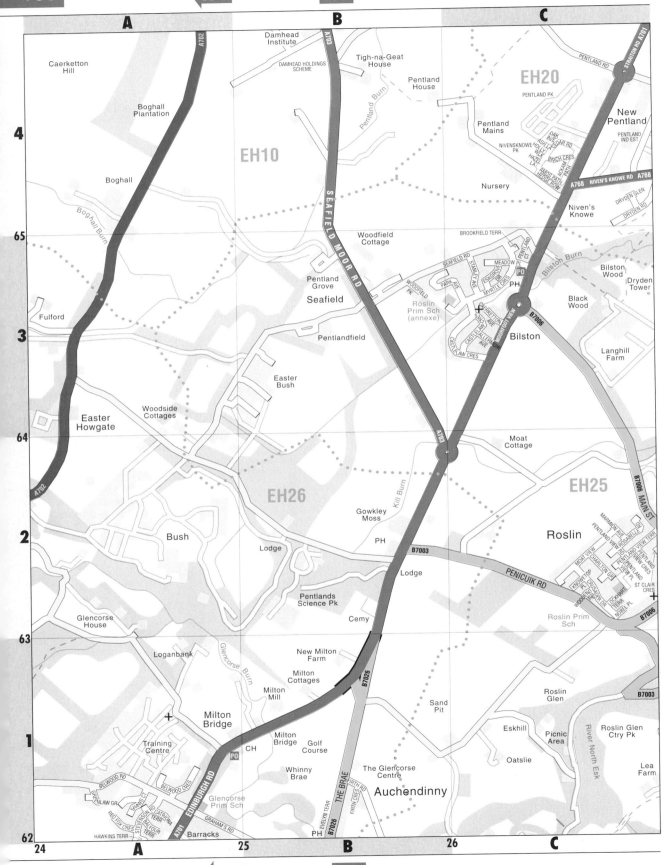

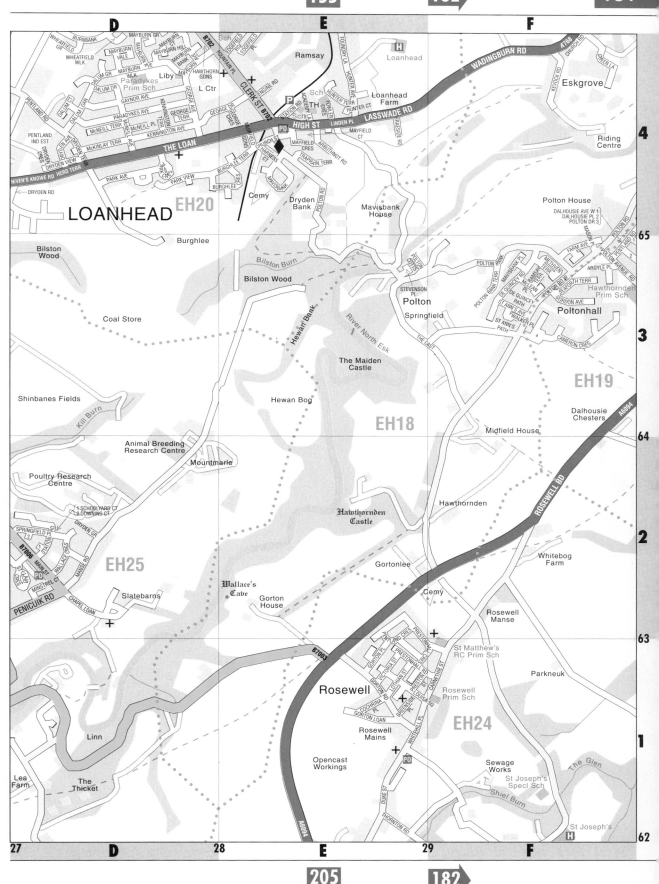

D E F

27 D 28 E 29 F

4
65
3
64
2
63
1
62

LOANHEAD EH20

Loanhead

Ramsay

Wheatfield WLK
BURNBANK
MAYBURN GR
MAYBURN CT
MAYBURN VALE
MAYBURN HILL
MAYBURN BANK
WHEATFIELD GR
Paradykes Prim Sch
Liby
L Ctr
DALUM GR
DALUM PK
DALUM CT
DALUM LOAN
GAYNOR AVE
GEORGE AVE
GEORGE CRES
GEORGE TERR
PENTLAND RD
McNEILL TERR
McNEILL PL
McNEILL AVE
KENNINGTON TERR
KENNINGTON AVE
Paradykes Ave
McKINLAY TERR
PENTLAND IND EST
DRYDEN CRES
DRYELAW
DRYDEN VIEW
DRYDEN TERR
HERD TERR
Niven's Knowe Rd
Dryden Rd
THE LOAN
PARK AVE
PARK VIEW
BURGHLEE TERR
BURGHLEE CRES
Cemy
MAVISBANK
HAWTHORN PL
HARNESS
CHURCH ST
MURFIELD
GOWN
Burghlee
Dryden Bank

EDGEFIELD RD
EDGEFIELD PL
FOUNTAIN RD
CLERK ST B702
B702
Sch
Engine Rd
ACADEMY LA
TH
Sch
Fowler Cres
HUNTER TERR
HUNTER CT
P
STATION RD
PO
HIGH ST
LINDEN PL
LASSWADE RD
FOUNDRY LA
HUNTER AVE
Loanhead Farm
BRAESIDE RD
MAYFIELD CT
MAYFIELD CRES
ARBUTHNOT RD
TRAPRAIN TERR
POLTON RD

Mavisbank House

Polton Mains
POLTON COURTS
Stevenson PL
Polton
Springfield
THE CAST
WALKER PL

Polton House
DALHOUSIE AVE W 1
DALHOUSIE PL 2
POLTON DR 3
FARM AVE
MASSON RD
POLTON AVENUE RD
POLTON RD
PENTLAND RD
POLTON BANK
POLTON BANK TERR
MAVISBANK RD
DE QUINCEY RD
DE QUINCEY PL
CLYDE PL
RAMSAY PL
McLEAN PL
METHVEN PL
ST ANN'S AVE
ST ANN'S PATH
WALKER PL
GORDON AVE
SEAFORTH TERR
ARGYLE PL
CAMERON CRES
Hawthornden Prim Sch
Poltonhall

EH19

WADINGBURN RD
A768
KEVOCK RD
CHURCH LA
GREEN LA
ORCHARD
Eskgrove

Riding Centre

Bilston Wood
Bilston Wood
Bilston Burn

Hewan Bank
River North Esk
The Maiden Castle
Hewan Bog

Coal Store

Shinbanes Fields
Kill Burn

Animal Breeding Research Centre
Mountmarle

Poultry Research Centre
1 SCHOOLYARD CT
2 DOWNING CT
DRYDEN GR
SPRINGFIELD PL
STATION RD
MANSE RD
WALLACE CRES
MAIN ST
B7006
CRES
MINSTREL CT
PENICUIK RD
CHAPEL LOAN
PO

EH25

Slatebarns

Wallace's Cave
Gorton House

EH18

Midfield House

Hawthornden
Hawthornden Castle

Gortonlee
Cemy

Dalhousie Chesters
A6094
ROSEWELL RD

Whitebog Farm
Rosewell Manse

Linn

Lea Farm
The Thicket

B7003
Opencast Workings
A6094

PENTLAND CRES
PRESTONHALL CRES
GORTON PL
VICTORIA ST
LOTHIAN ST
PRESTON RD
GREENSIDE PL
GREENSIDE DR
CARNETHIE ST
PRESTONHALL SQ
St Matthew's RC Prim Sch
Parkneuk
Rosewell
COCHRINA PL
GORTON LOAN
WHITEHILL PL
Rosewell Prim Sch
Rosewell Mains
DUKE ST
PO
THORNTON RD

EH24

Sewage Works
St Joseph's Specl Sch
Shiel Burn
The Glen
St Joseph's
H

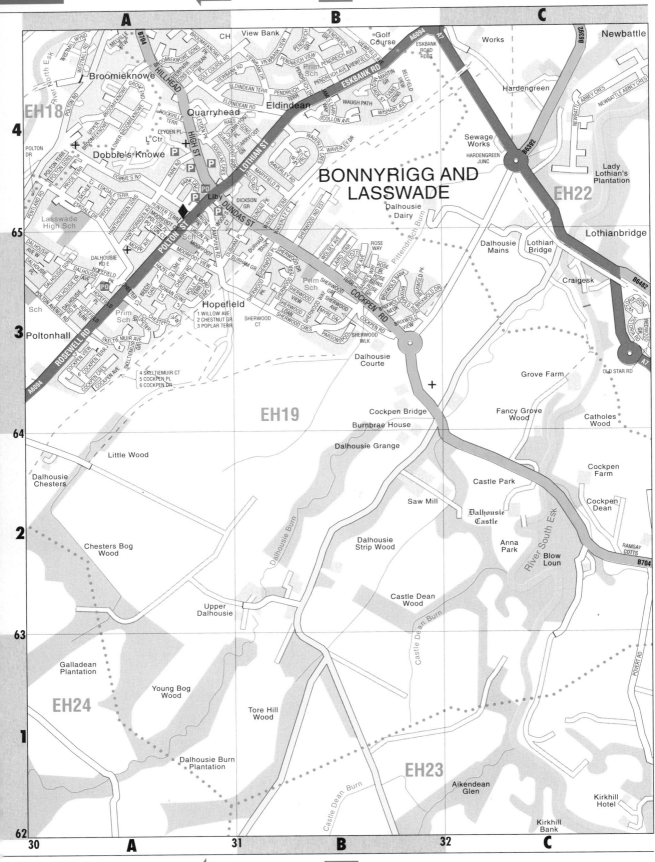

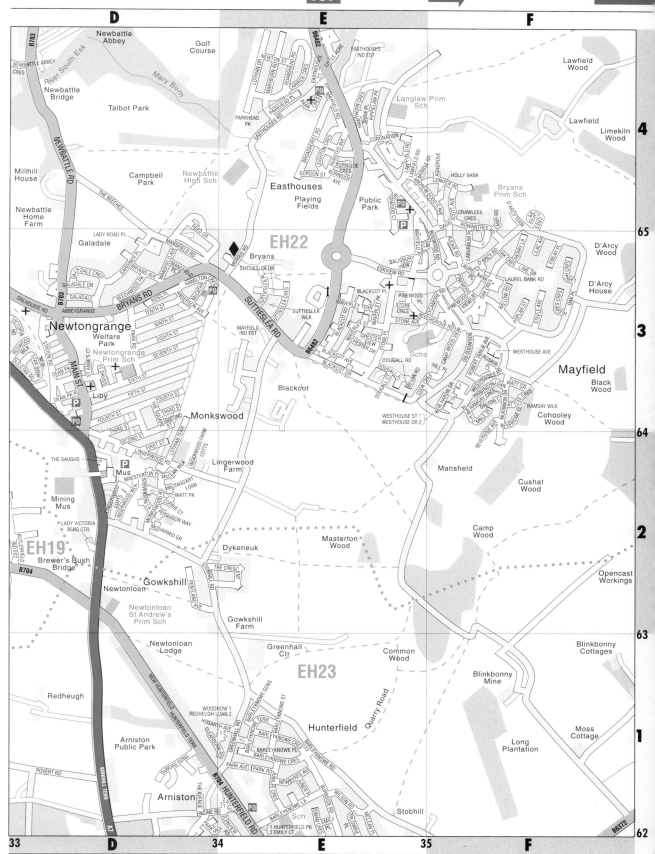

A **B** **C**

Cotty Burn

Coldwells

Green Drive
Wood

Byres Loan

Cranston
Riddel

4

Edgehead

Oxenford
Castle

EH22

Chesterhill

Beech Clump

Blackwood
Farm

EH37

A68

B6372

THE LOAN

Chesterhill
Wood

65

EDGEHEAD RD

Windmill
Wood

Cranston
Prim Sch

Cemy

Stair Arms
Hotel

Spy Law
Wood

Sauchenside

3

Dewar Town
Glen

Dewar Town Burn

The Dowery
House

Ford

MAIN ST

Ford Glen

64

Dewartown

Woodhead

Southside

B6367

EH23

2

Vogrie Burn

Crow Wood

Turniedykes
Strip

Chesters
Wood

Vogrie Estate
Country Park

Tyne Water

Nursery

Vogrie
House

P

Turniedykes

63

Alderdean

Tynebank

Blinkbonny

Vogrie
Grange

Golf Course

Vogrie Burn

1

Newlandburn
House

Newlandrig

Tile Works
Wood

Currie
Lee

Newlandburn
Farm

Stretchendean

Crichton

B6372

COLEGATE RD

B6367

62

36 **A** **37** **B** **38** **C**

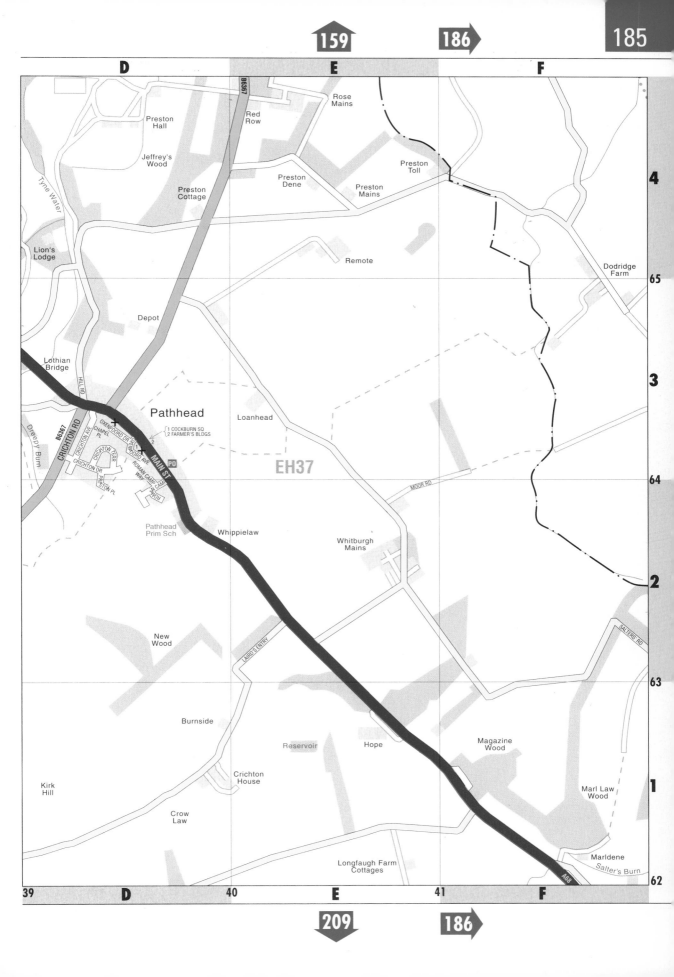

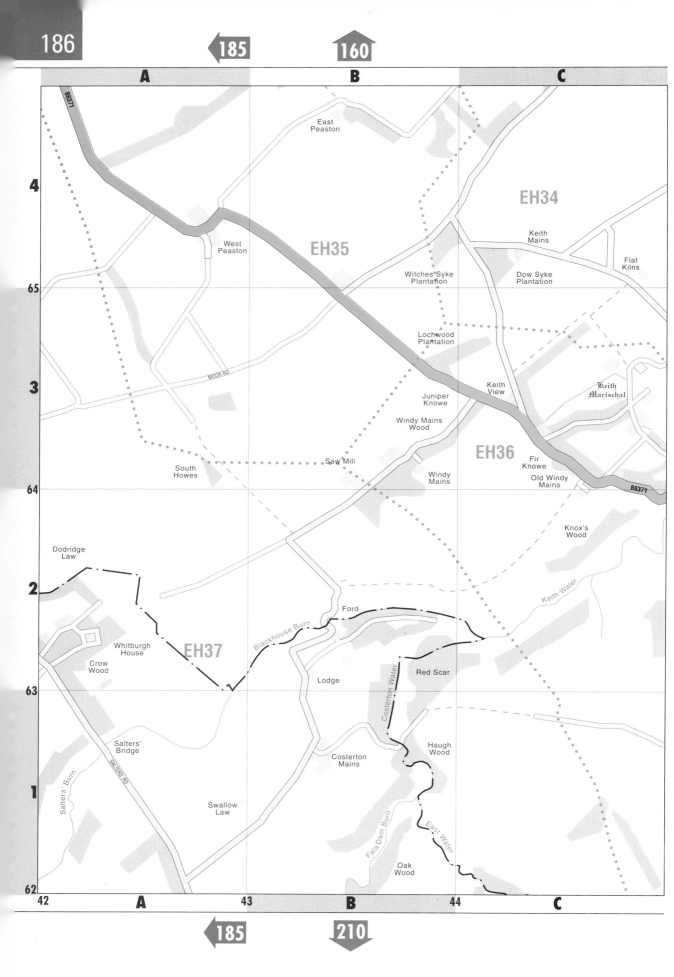

185
160

A **B** **C**

B6371

East
Peaston

4

EH34

Keith
Mains

West
Peaston

EH35

Flat
Kilns

Witches Syke
Plantation

Dow Syke
Plantation

65

Lochwood
Plantation

MOOR RD

3

Keith
View

Keith
Marischal

Juniper
Knowe

Windy Mains
Wood

EH36

Fir
Knowe

Saw Mill

South
Howes

Windy
Mains

Old Windy
Mains

B6371

64

Knox's
Wood

Dodridge
Law

Keith Water

2

Ford

EH37

Blackhouse Burn

Whitburgh
House

Red Scar

Crow
Wood

Costerton Water

Lodge

63

Salters'
Bridge

Haugh
Wood

Salters' Burn

SALTERS RD

Costerton
Mains

1

Swallow
Law

Fala Dam Burn

East Water

Oak
Wood

62

42 **A** 43 **B** 44 **C**

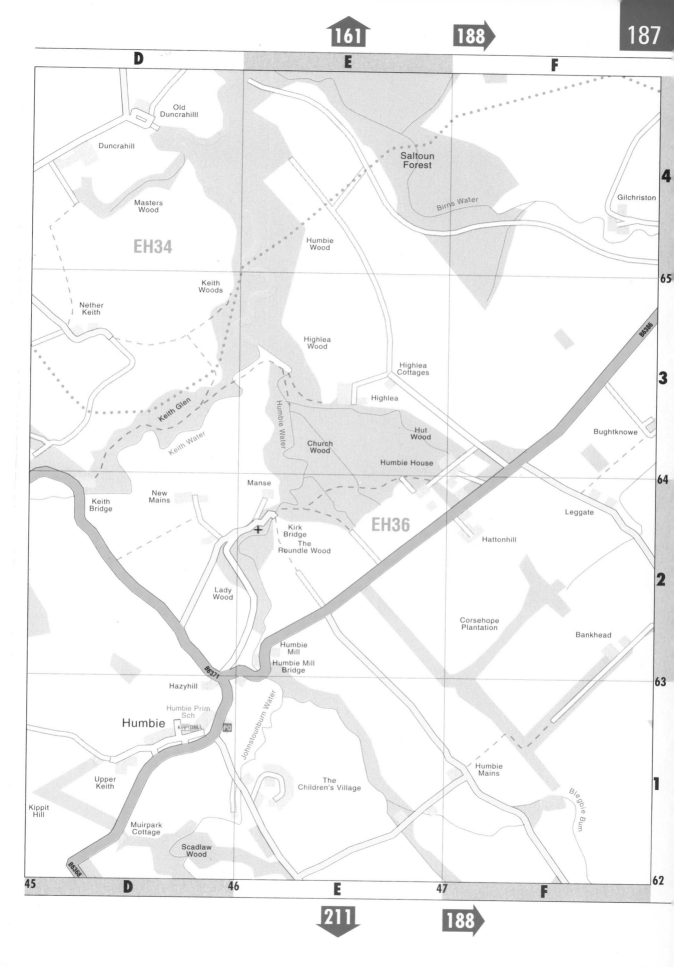

187
162

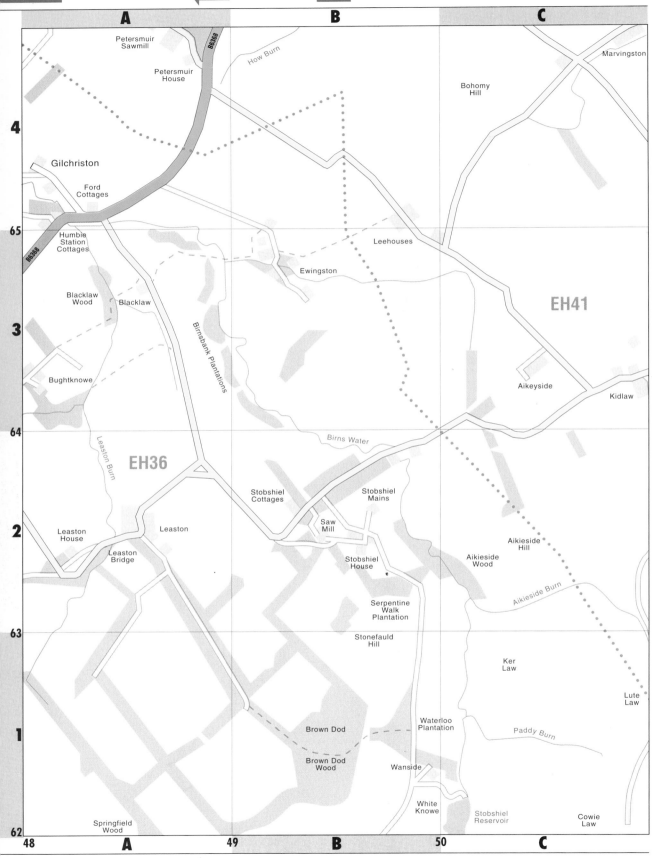

187

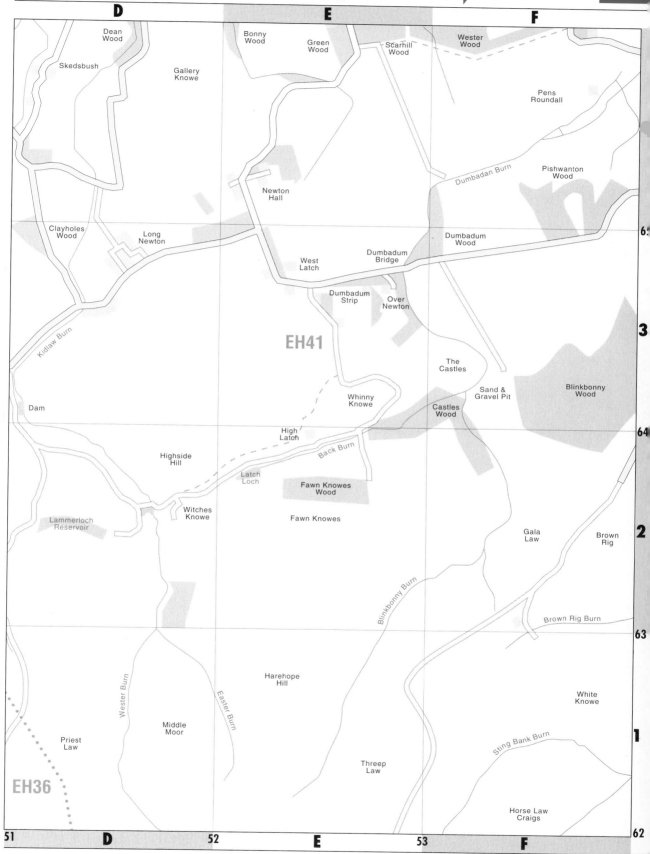

Dean Wood
Skedsbush
Gallery Knowe
Bonny Wood
Green Wood
Scarhill Wood
Wester Wood
Pens Roundall
Newton Hall
Dumbadan Burn
Pishwanton Wood
Clayholes Wood
Long Newton
Dumbadum Wood
West Latch
Dumbadum Bridge
Kidlaw Burn
Dumbadum Strip
Over Newton
EH41
The Castles
Dam
Whinny Knowe
Sand & Gravel Pit
Blinkbonny Wood
Castles Wood
High Latch
Back Burn
Highside Hill
Latch Loch
Fawn Knowes Wood
Lammerloch Reservoir
Witches Knowe
Fawn Knowes
Gala Law
Brown Rig
Blinkbonny Burn
Brown Rig Burn
Wester Burn
Harehope Hill
White Knowe
Easter Burn
Priest Law
Middle Moor
Sting Bank Burn
EH36
Threep Law
Horse Law Craigs

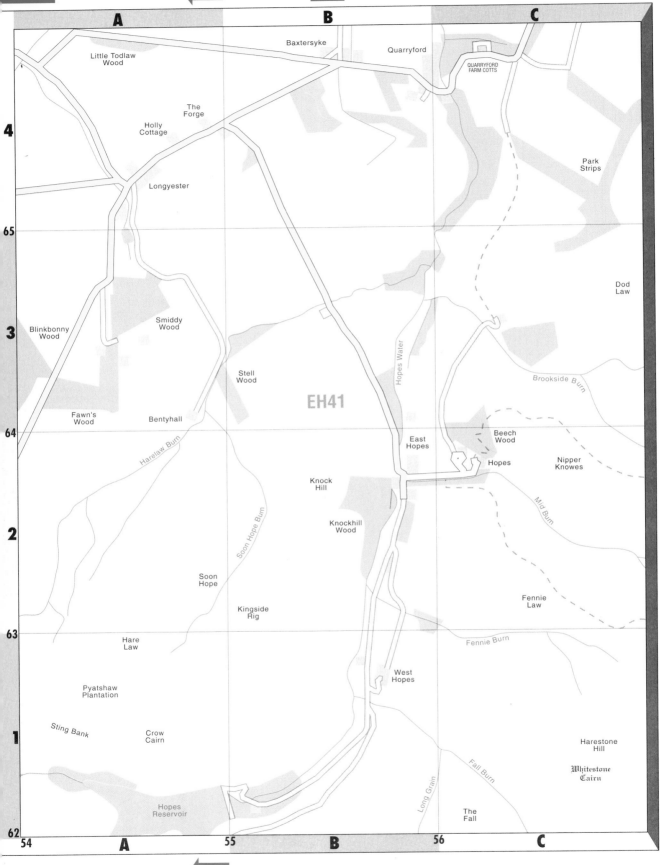

A   B   C

Little Todlaw
Wood

Baxtersyke

Quarryford

QUARRYFORD
FARM COTTS

The
Forge

Holly
Cottage

4

Park
Strips

Longyester

65

Blinkbonny
Wood

Smiddy
Wood

Dod
Law

3

Stell
Wood

Hopes Water

Brookside Burn

EH41

Fawn's
Wood

Bentyhall

East
Hopes

Beech
Wood

64

Harelaw Burn

Hopes

Nipper
Knowes

Knock
Hill

Soon Hope Burn

Knockhill
Wood

Mid Burn

2

Soon
Hope

Fennie
Law

Kingside
Rig

63

Hare
Law

Fennie Burn

Pyatshaw
Plantation

West
Hopes

Sting Bank

Crow
Cairn

Harestone
Hill

1

Whitestone
Cairn

Long Grain

Fall Burn

Hopes
Reservoir

The
Fall

62

54   A   55   B   56   C

191
168

A
B
C

4

61

Golf
Course

CH

B717

BENHAR RD

3

B717

Spoil
Heap

Stane

STABLE RD

Starryshaw
Farm

South Calder Water

Stanebent

Cairneyhead

ML7

60

GRAY ST
HIGH ST

Torbothie

CEDAR WYND
TAN CRES

HAZEL
GR

CHARLES ST

TORBOTHIE RD

CLYDE DR

KELVIN DR

CALDER DR

HAWTHORN DR

SOUTHFIELD
RD

SOUTHFIELD CRES

SOUTHFIELD AVE

Torbothie

Stane
Prim Sch

CEMETERY RD

2

MARSE RD

CHARLOTTE ST

NEVIS PL

1
GARTEN
DR
2
3

Cemy

1 ETIVE WLK
2 ULG WAY
3 GAIR WYND
4 BOWMORE WLK
5 TORRIN LOAN
6 SPRINGHILL VIEW
7 DORNIE WYND
8 MORAR WAY
9 COIRE LOAN
10 SUNA PATH
11 SALEN LOAN

EH47

B7010
MAIN ST

REDHAWS RD

SANDYVALE
AVE
1
2

SANDYVALE
PL

Stane

BLINNY CT 1
TARBRAX PATH 2

BRIDGE
PL

KNOLL CROFT RD

SHIEL GDNS

MANSE CT

LOCHABER
CRES
4
5
7
6
8

TULLOCH RD

APPIN TERR

LANSDOWNE CRES

MELFORD AVE

WYVIS PL

11
10

OMICH PL

LAGGAN AVE

HUNTLY
TERR

SPRINGHILL RD

Springhill

B7010

59

BLACKHALL
ST

BELMONT
PL

LARCHFIELD LA

BROWN ST

BERRYHILL
PL

MULDRON
TERR CT

BEECHMOUNT

NORTHFIELD AVE

ELMWOOD RD

SPRINGHILL AND LEADLOCH RD

B715 HEADLESSCROSS RD
B715

Works

STANE RD

Springhill

Knowton
Farm

A71

A71

Lingore Linn

Works

1

58

88
A
89
B
90
C

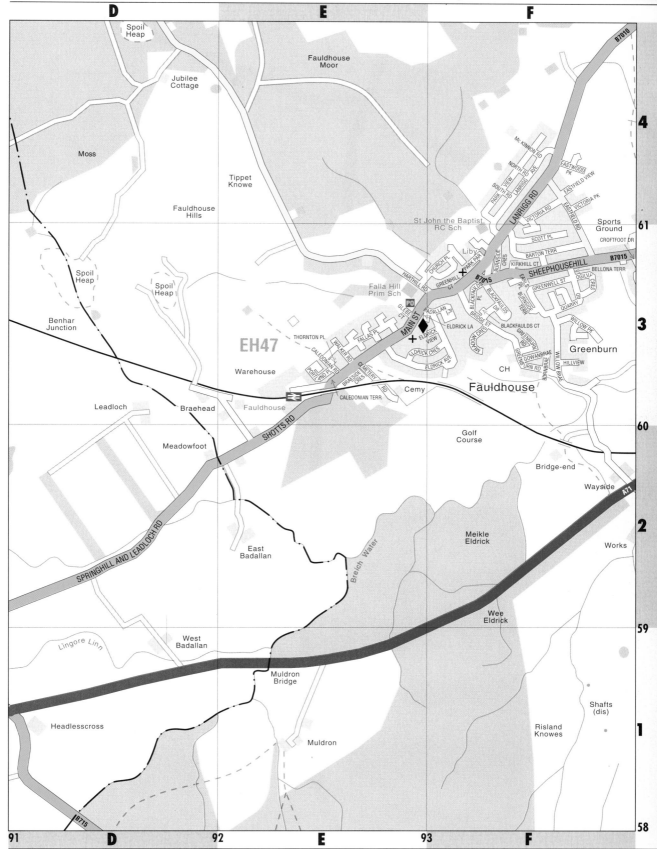

193
170

A **B** **C**

B7010

Northfield

Burnhead

B7015

STONEHEAP
CROFTS

Stoneheap

Blackhill

4

Nursery

Holehouseburn

Blackhill
Bridge

A706

Breich Water

Rashiehill

61

SHEEPHOUSEHILL B7015

A71

Breich
Bridge

Glenhutch

PO

RASHIEHILL TERR

RASHIEHILL CRES

Craighead

Breich

BREICH TERR

WOODMUIR PL

Breich

CROFTFOOT DR

East
Handaxwood

Hotel

Woodmuir
Prim Sch

WOODMUIR RD

3

Croftfoot

EH55

Sewage
Works

Woodmuir Burn

Woodmuir
Farm

60

West
Handaxwood

Rashiehill
Muir
(ruin)

A71

A704

EH47

2

Leven
Seat

Works

A704

Levenseat
House

Longford Burn

Woodmuir
Plantation

59

Linn
Bridge

Miller's
Moss

Rashiehill
Muir

1

ML11

A704

A706

58

94 **A** 95 **B** 96 **C**

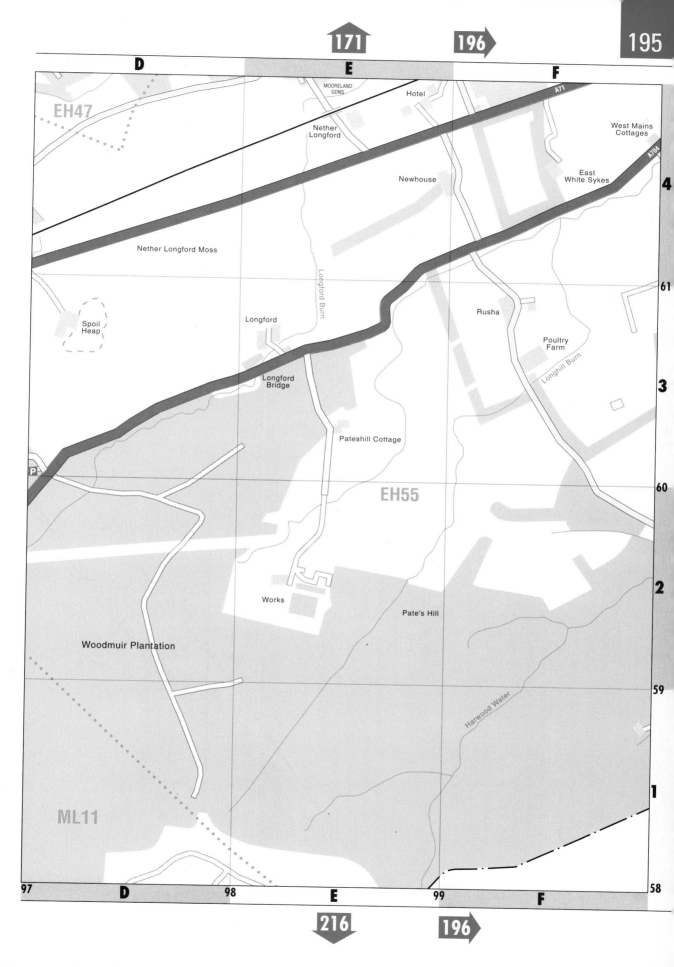

D
E
F

EH47

MOORELAND GDNS

Hotel

Nether Longford

West Mains Cottages

A71

Newhouse

East White Sykes

A704

4

Nether Longford Moss

Longford Burn

61

Longford

Rusha

Poultry Farm

Spoil Heap

Longhill Burn

3

Longford Bridge

Pateshill Cottage

EH55

P

60

Works

Pate's Hill

2

Woodmuir Plantation

Harwood Water

59

ML11

1

97
D
98
E
99
F
58

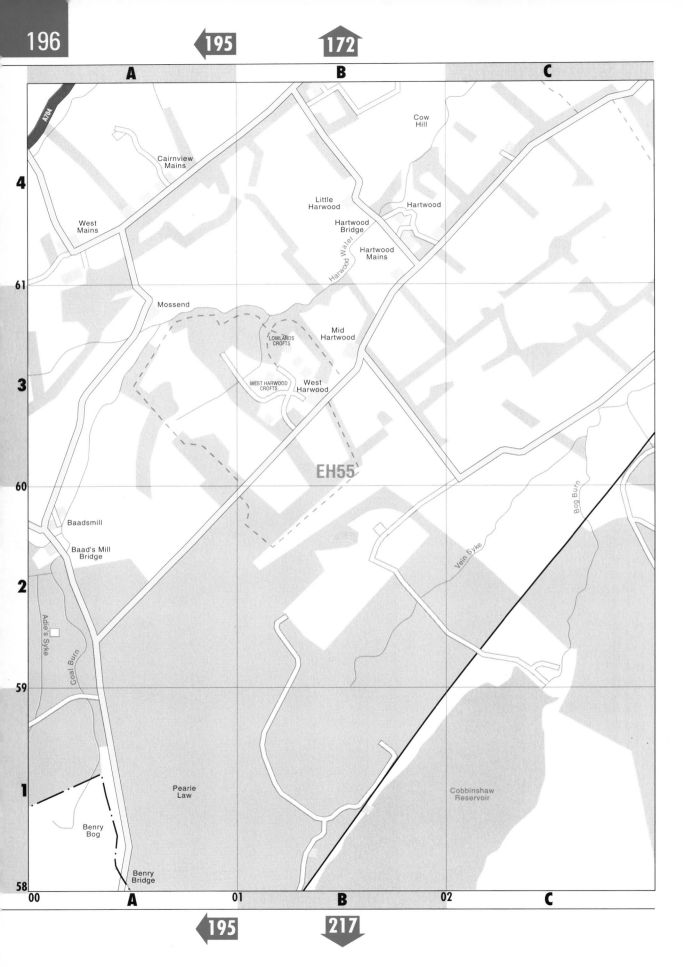

A   B   C

4

61

3

60

2

59

1

58

00   01   02

A   B   C

A704

Cairnview
Mains

Cow
Hill

Hartwood

West
Mains

Little
Harwood

Hartwood
Bridge

Harwood Water

Hartwood
Mains

Mossend

Mid
Hartwood

LOWLANDS
CROFTS

WEST HARWOOD
CROFTS

West
Harwood

EH55

Bog Burn

Baadsmill

Baad's Mill
Bridge

Vein Syke

Adie's Syke

Coal Burn

Pearie
Law

Cobbinshaw
Reservoir

Benry
Bog

Benry
Bridge

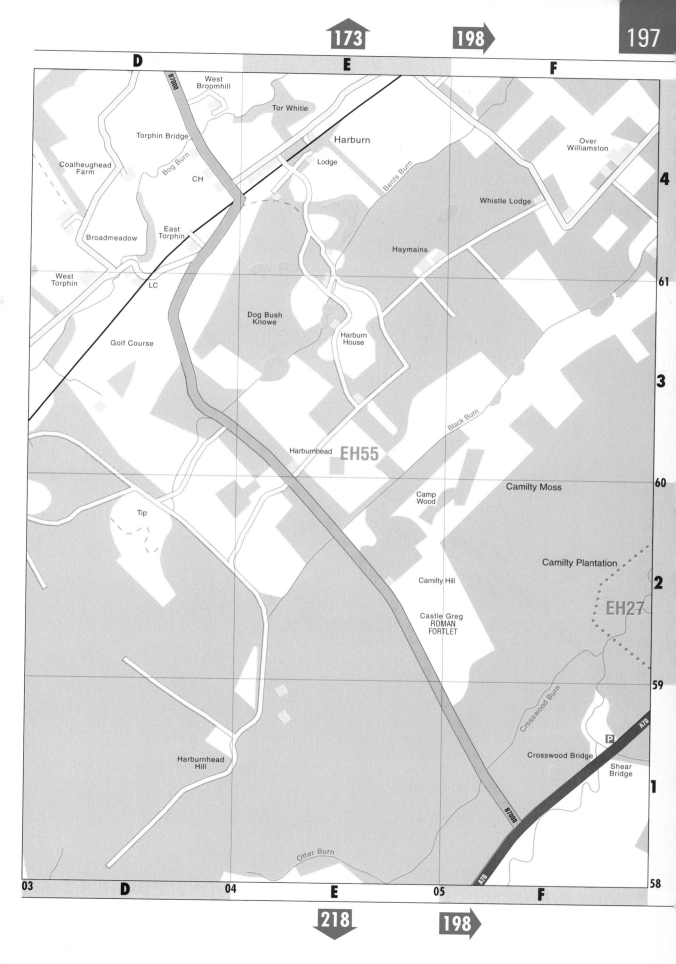

D   E   F

West Broomhill

Tor Whitie

Harburn

B7008

Torphin Bridge

Lodge

Over Williamston

Coalheughead Farm

Bog Burn

CH

Bents Burn

Whistle Lodge

4

Broadmeadow

East Torphin

Haymains

West Torphin

LC

61

Dog Bush Knowe

Golf Course

Harburn House

3

Black Burn

Harburnhead

EH55

Camilty Moss

60

Tip

Camp Wood

Camilty Plantation

Camilty Hill

EH27

2

Castle Greg
ROMAN FORTLET

Crosswood Burn

59

P

A70

Crosswood Bridge

Harburnhead Hill

Shear Bridge

B7008

1

Otter Burn

A70

03   D   04   E   05   F   58

A

B

C

EH53

Morton Hill

Rae Burn

4

Camilty Mill
Cottage

Camilty
Lodge

Camilty Water

A70

Causewood

61

High Camilty

EH55

Camilty
Bridge

Wester
Causewayend

Berry Knowe

Whitelea Burn

3

EH27

West
Cairns

60

Brookbank

Water of Leith

Halfway
House

2

Kelly Syke

Sinkie Syke

59

A70

West Colzium

Colzium

West Burn

Mid Burn

1

Shear Burn
Plantation

EH55

Plea
Knowe

Fauch
Hill

58

06

A

07

B

08

C

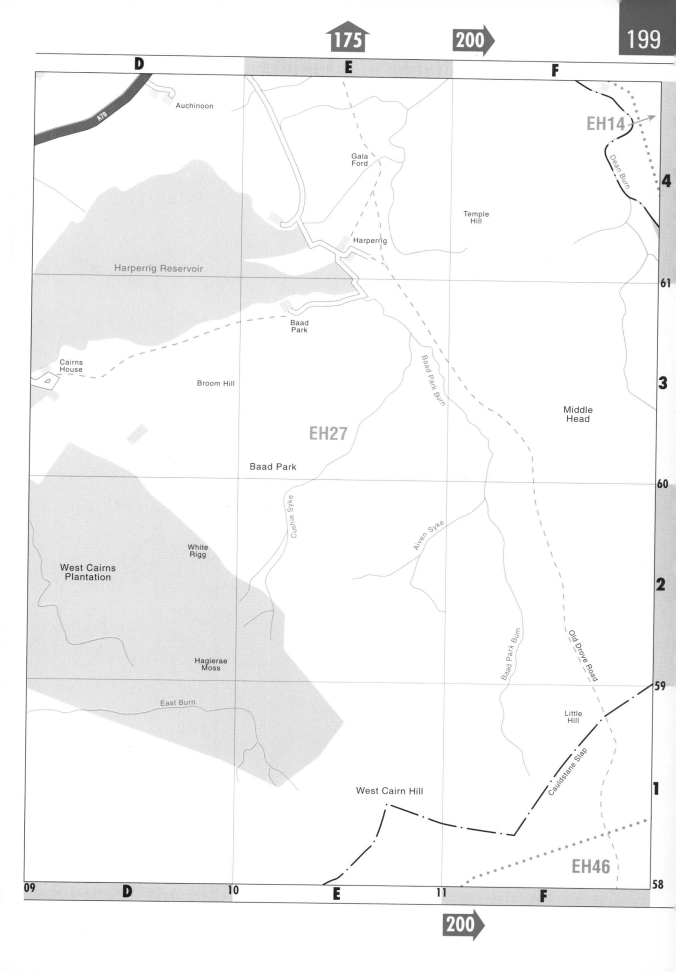

D
E
F

Auchinoon

A70

EH14

Gala
Ford

Dean Burn

Temple
Hill

Harperrig

4

Harperrig Reservoir

61

Baad
Park

Cairns
House

Baad Park Burn

3

Broom Hill

Middle
Head

EH27

Baad Park

60

Cushie Syke

Aiven Syke

White
Rigg

West Cairns
Plantation

2

Hagierae
Moss

Baad Park Burn

Old Drove Road

59

East Burn

Little
Hill

Cauldstane Slap

West Cairn Hill

1

EH46

199
176

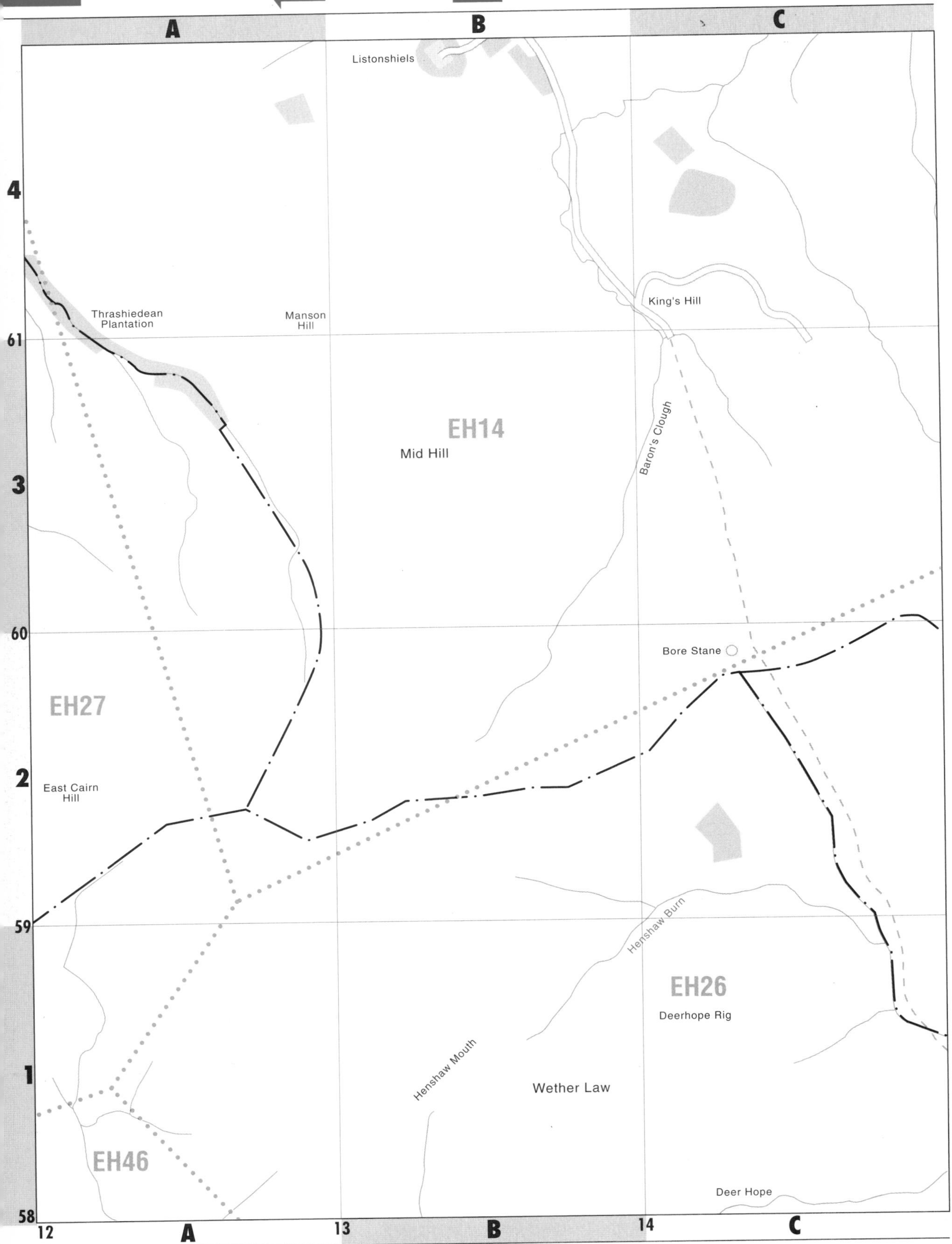

A   B   C

4

Listonshiels

Thrashiedean
Plantation

61

Manson
Hill

King's Hill

EH14

Mid Hill

Baron's Clough

3

EH27

60

Bore Stane ○

East Cairn
Hill

2

EH26

Deerhope Rig

59

Henshaw Burn

1

Henshaw Mouth

Wether Law

Deer Hope

EH46

58

12   A   13   B   14   C

D

E

F

4

61

EH14

Pentland Hills
Regional Park

Rowantree Burn

Logan Burn

West Kip

3

Kitchen Moss

Eastside Burn

60

Cap Law

2

Green Law

EH26

Font Stone

Cock Rig

Gutterford Burn

59

Spittal Hill

Monks Burn

Greystone Head

Scroggy Hill

1

North Esk
Reservoir

15

D

16

E

17

F

58

201
178

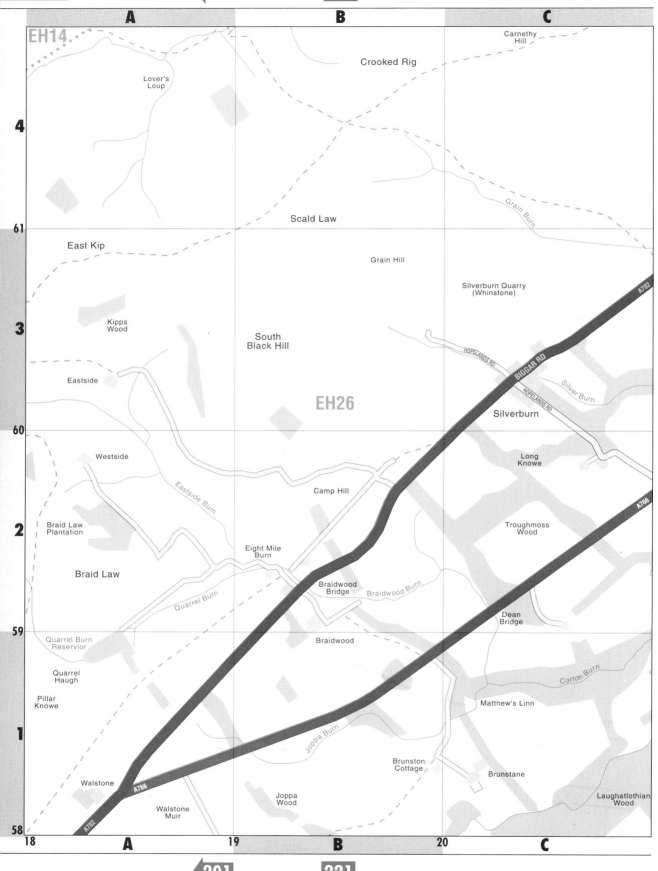

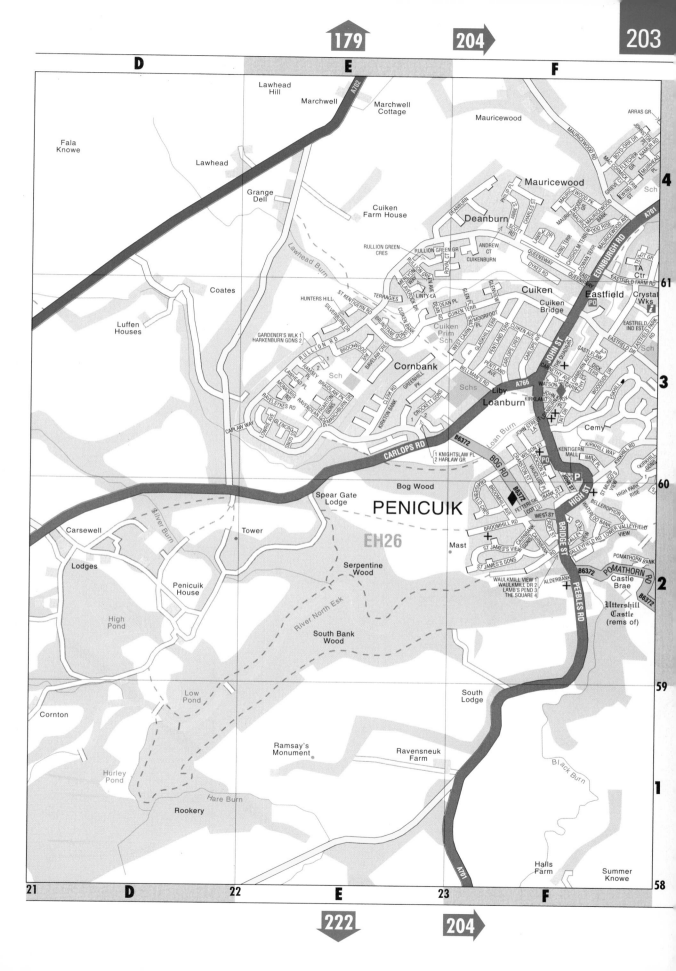

D

E

F

Fala
Knowe

Lawhead
Hill

Marchwell

Marchwell
Cottage

Mauricewood

Lawhead

ARRAS GR

Mauricewood

Deanburn

4

Grange
Dell

Cuiken
Farm House

RULLION GREEN
CRES

Rullion Green Gr

Andrew
Ct

Cuikenburn

Queensway

61

Coates

HUNTERS HILL

TERRAGIES

Cuiken
Bridge

Cuiken

Eastfield
PO

Crystal
Wks

Luffen
Houses

GARDENER'S WLK 1
HARKENBURN GDNS 2

Cuiken
Prim
Sch

Eastfield
Ind Est Park

Sch

RULLION RD

Sch

Cornbank

JOHN ST

3

Schs

Liby
Loanburn

A766

Cemy

CARLOPS RD

B6372

1 KNIGHTSLAW PL
2 HARLAW GR

BOG RD

Bog Wood

Kirkhill Way

60

Spear Gate
Lodge

PENICUIK

P

Carsewell

Silver Burn

Tower

EH26

Mast

POMATHORN RD

Castle
Brae

Pomathorn Bank

Lodges

Penicuik
House

Serpentine
Wood

B6372

PEEBLES RD

Uttershill
Castle
(rems of)

B6372

2

High
Pond

River North Esk

South Bank
Wood

Cornton

Low
Pond

South
Lodge

59

Hurley
Pond

Ramsay's
Monument

Ravensneuk
Farm

Black Burn

1

Rookery

Hare Burn

A701

Halls
Farm

Summer
Knowe

58

21

D

22

E

23

F

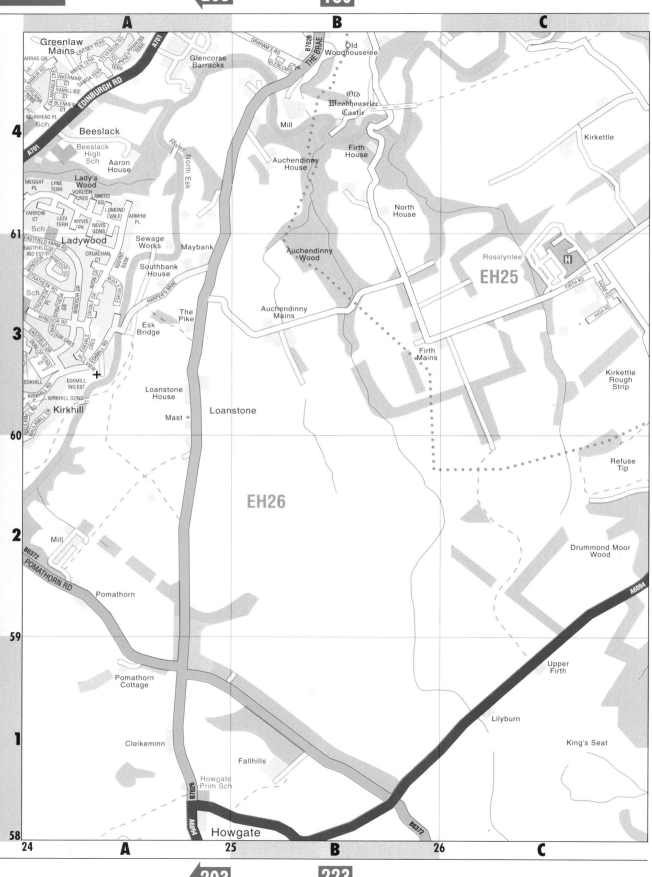

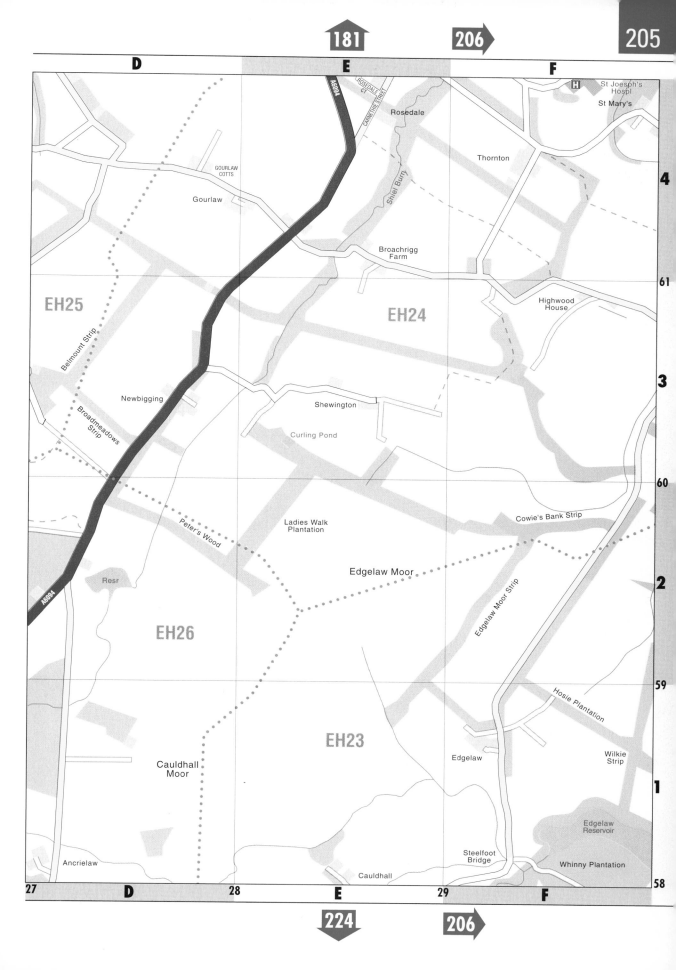

A6094

ROSEDALE CT

CARNETHIE STREET

Rosedale

Thornton

St Joesph's
Hospl

St Mary's

GOURLAW
COTTS

Gourlaw

Shiel Burn

4

Broachrigg
Farm

EH25

EH24

61

Highwood
House

Belmount Strip

Newbigging

Shewington

3

Broadmeadows
Strip

Curling Pond

Peter's Wood

Ladies Walk
Plantation

60

Cowie's Bank Strip

Resr

Edgelaw Moor

2

A6094

EH26

Edgelaw Moor Strip

Hosie Plantation

59

EH23

Edgelaw

Wilkie
Strip

1

Cauldhall
Moor

Edgelaw
Reservoir

Ancrielaw

Steelfoot
Bridge

Whinny Plantation

58

Cauldhall

205 182

A B C

Capielaw

Aikendean Bridge

Aikendean

Aikendean Cottages

Castle Dean Burn

4

Whitehill Aisle

Carrington Barns

61

Parduvine

EH24

Stonefieldhill Farm

Carrington

PRIMROSE GDNS

MAIN ST

CARRINGTON MAINS COTTS

Carrington Mains

MANSE RD

Deadman Lies

3

Hendean Wood

Carrington Hill

60

EH23

Long Wood

Cottage Bank

Ducks Pond Strip

Carrington Mill

Carrington Bridge

Arniston

2

Redside

Lodge

The Wilderness

BEECH AVE

B6372

River South Esk

Redside Burn

Purvies Hill

59

Old Planation

Braidwood Bridge

Saw Mill

Purvies Hill Burn

Birken Craig

Braidwood

Temple Prim Sch

1

Mitchell Strip

Temple

TEMPLE PK

Shaw Knowe

PO

Edgelaw Reservoir

Great Law

B6372

Temple Farm

58

30 A 31 B 32 C

Trotter's Bridge
Picnic Area
Millbank House
Arniston Engine
Playing Fields
Gorebridge
Liby
Sch
Stobhill
Stobhill Prim Sch
Monteith Houses
Shank Tongue
Newbyres Gdns
Castle P
Mossend
Millstone Brow Cottages
Saw Mill
Stobs
Shank
Shank Bridge
Millbank Gr
Castle View
Moorfoot View
Sewage Wks
Harvieston Villas
Lady Brae
River South Esk
Stobs Mills
Glenview
John Bernard Way
Robertsons Bank
Ashbank
Mount Cottage
Robert Adams Wood
Harvieston Mains
Roseberry Cres
Brackenside
Gore Water
Shank Avenue
B6372
Harvieston House
Harvieston Farm
Catcune Mills Cotts
Portland Clump
Baker's Avenue Wood
Bells Mains
Bellsmains
EH23
Arniston Mains
Cemy
Catcune House
Catcune
Haughhead
Eastwood
Home Farm
Lodge
Carlisle Wood
Lodge
Castle Law
Black Bog Wood
Edinburgh Castle Walk
Carlisle Approach
North Middleton
Crow Wood
Middleton North Burn Bridge
Sheil Knowe
Borthwick Castle Terr
Borthwick Castle Rd
Cleuch Rd
PH
Rylaw Knowe
Guildie Howes Rd
Castleton
William Wood
Guildie Howes
Lime Works
Castleton Strip
Halk Law
Halkerston
Middleton North Burn
A7

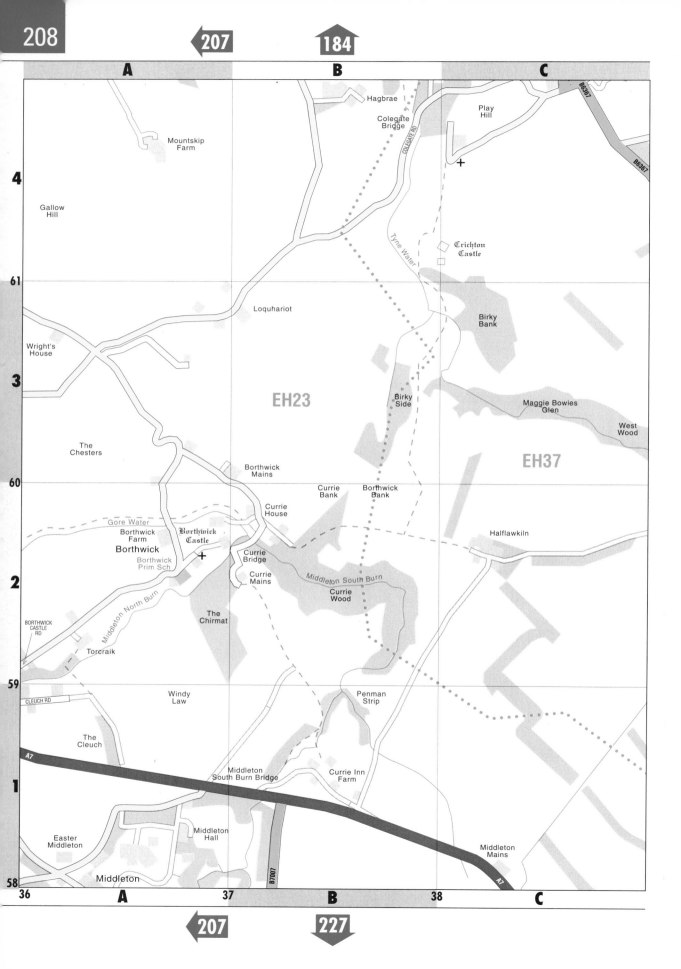

207
184

A
B
C

Hagbrae

Colegate
Bridge

Play
Hill

Mountskip
Farm

COLEGATE RD

B6367

B6367

4

Gallow
Hill

Crichton
Castle

Tyne Water

61

Loquhariot

Birky
Bank

Wright's
House

3

EH23

Birky
Side

Maggie Bowies
Glen

West
Wood

The
Chesters

EH37

Borthwick
Mains

60

Currie
Bank

Borthwick
Bank

Gore Water

Currie
House

Borthwick
Farm

Borthwick
Castle

Halflawkiln

Borthwick

Currie
Bridge

Borthwick
Prim Sch

Currie
Mains

Middleton South Burn

2

BORTHWICK
CASTLE
RD

The
Chirmat

Currie
Wood

Middleton North Burn

Torcraik

59

Windy
Law

Penman
Strip

CLEUCH RD

The
Cleuch

A7

1

Middleton
South Burn Bridge

Currie Inn
Farm

Easter
Middleton

Middleton
Hall

B7007

Middleton
Mains

58

Middleton

A7

36
A
37
B
38
C

209
186

A   **B**   **C**

Hough Head House

Gardiner's Hall Wood

Fala Dam Wood

Fala Mill

Fala Dam Burn

Routhenhill

A68

B6458

Fala Hall

East Water

EH36

4

Bleak Law

Fala Dam

Fala Brae Dam

SALTERS RD

Routing Burn

Routing Glen

Watergate Toll

B6457

Fala

61

Cakemuir Burn

B6457

Blackshiels

PO

+

3

Frostineb

Fala Mains Wood

MOOR RD

Woodcote Bridge

Juniperlea Hotel

Fala Mains

60

EH37

Black Burn

Partridge Burn

New Salvandi

A68

Deanburn House

2

Mains Wood

North Wood

High Wood

Salvandi

59

Fala Luggie

Dean Burn

1

Fala Flow Loch

Fala Moor

58

42   **A**   43   **B**   44   **C**

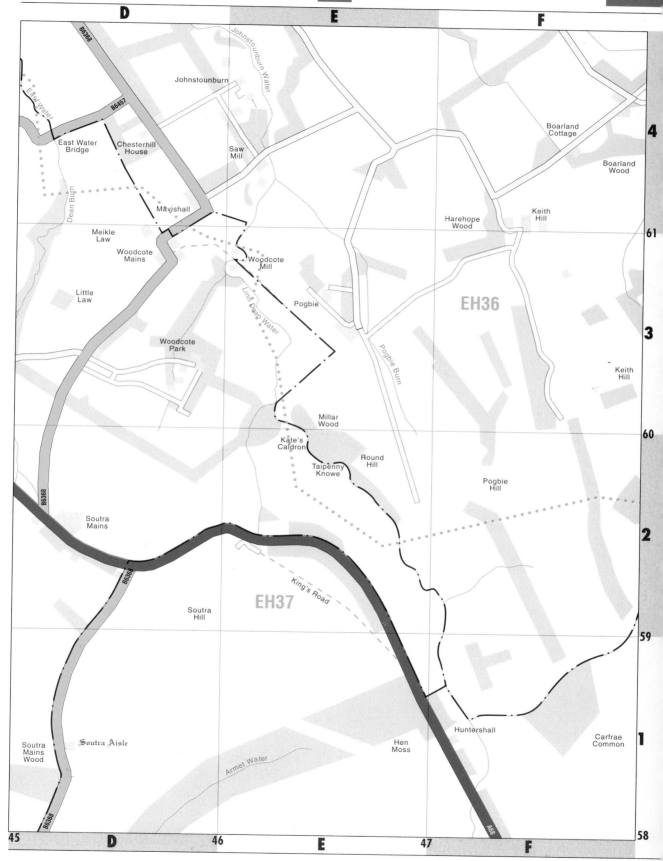

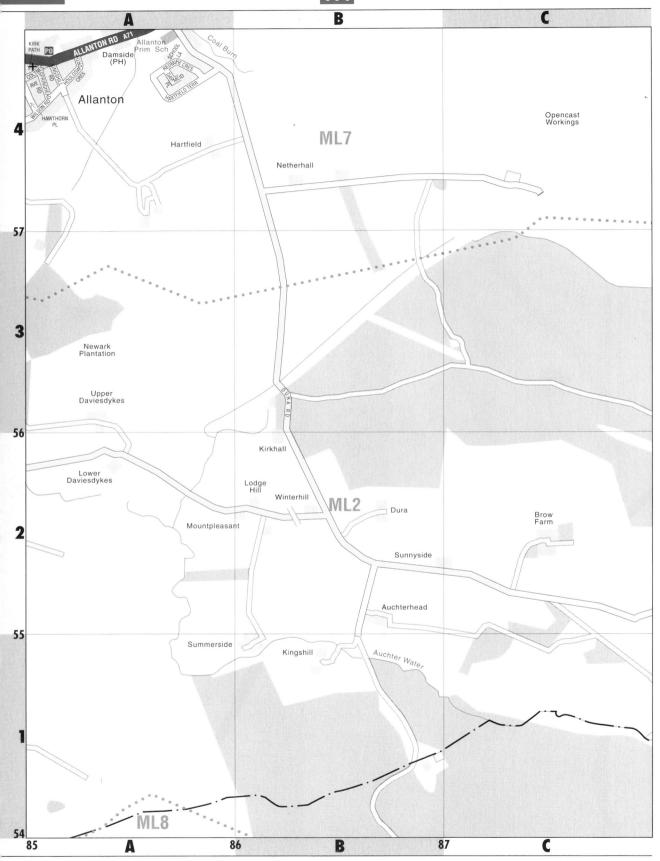

KIRK PATH
PO
ALLANTON RD A71
Damside (PH)
Allanton Prim Sch
Coal Burn
SCHOOL LA
REDMIRE CRES
DURMEJO
HARTFIELD TERR
COLTNESS
AVE RD
KINGSHILL
SPRINGHEAD RD
HOULDSWORTH CRES
WILSON RD
HAWTHORN PL
Allanton

ML7

Hartfield

Netherhall

Opencast Workings

57

Newark Plantation

3

Upper Daviesdykes

DURA RD

56

Kirkhall

Lower Daviesdykes

Lodge Hill

Winterhill

ML2

Dura

Brow Farm

Mountpleasant

2

Sunnyside

Auchterhead

55

Summerside

Kingshill

Auchter Water

1

ML8

54

D E F

ML7

EH47

Opencast Workings

Causeyhill

57

3

Lark Law

ML11

56

ML2

2

Cairney

Spoutcross

DURA RD

Mon

55

Auchterhead Muir

Auchterhead

1

ML8

88 D 89 E 90 F 54

4

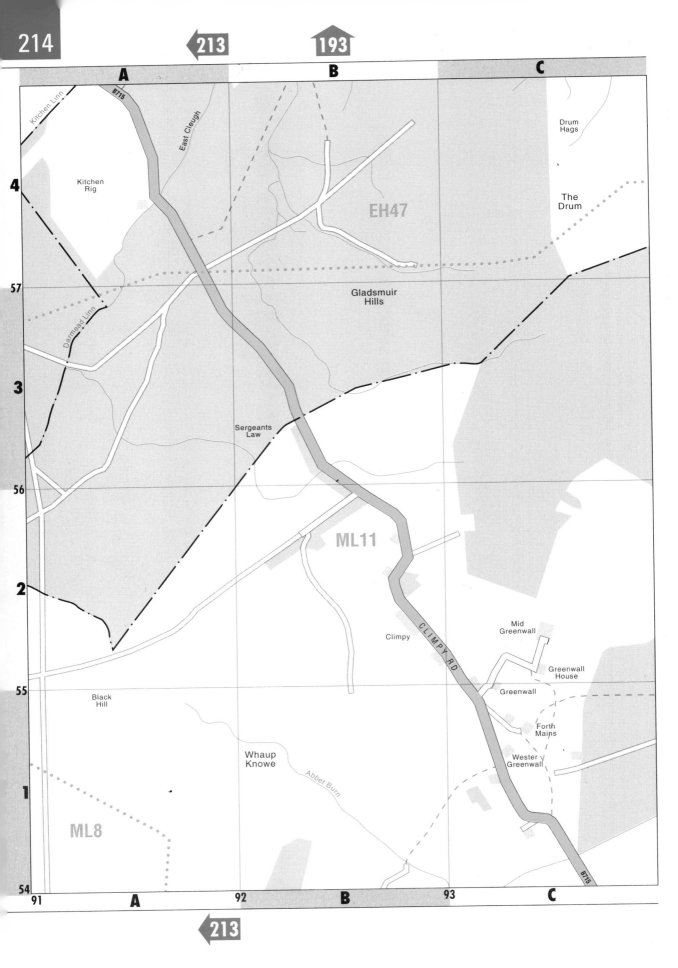

213
193

A B C

Kitchen Linn

B715

East Cleugh

Kitchen
Rig

4

EH47

Drum
Hags

The
Drum

57

Gladsmuir
Hills

Darmead Linn

3

Sergeants
Law

56

ML11

2

Climpy

CLIMPY RD

Mid
Greenwall

Greenwall
House

Greenwall

55

Black
Hill

Forth
Mains

Whaup
Knowe

Abbet Burn

Wester
Greenwall

1

ML8

B715

54

91 A 92 B 93 C

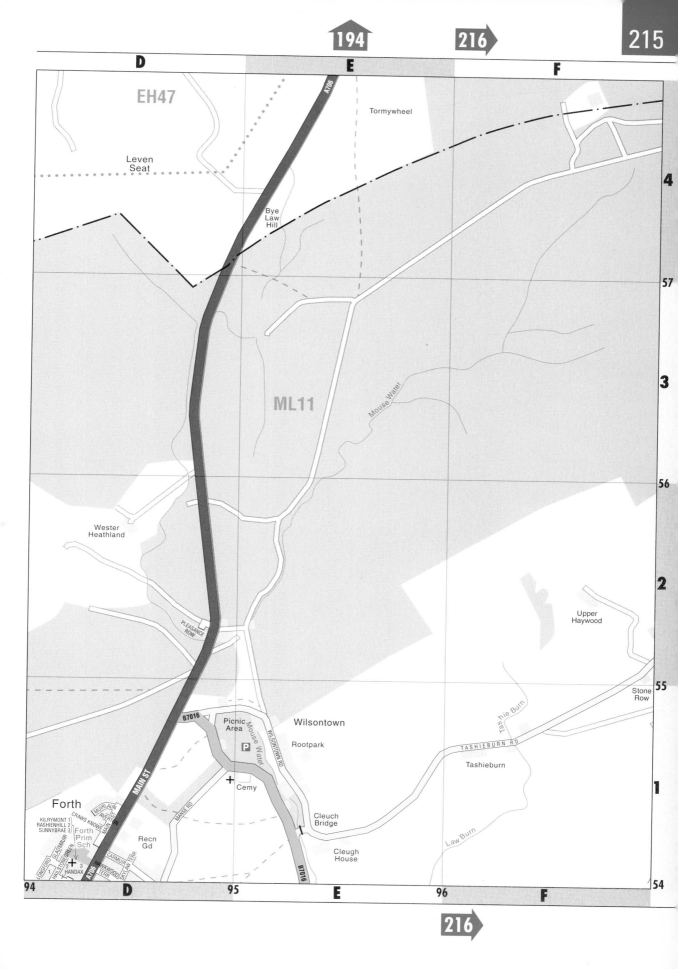

215
195

A B C

Hendry's
Corse

4

57

Worm Law

3

EH55

Wormlaw Burn

Mosshat Burn

Mountainblaw
Farm

Easter
Mosshat

56

ML11

Wester Mosshat

MOSSHAT RD

2

Burnfoot Poultry
Farm

Burnfoot

Dippool Water

Bughtknowes

Old Manse

TASHIEBURN RD

55

Crooklands

Lawhead
View

Pentland View

Haywood

Greenbank

Memorial

1

AUCHENGRAY RD

Auchengray Inn
(PH)

Mid
Auchengray

Auchengray

Hillhead of
Auchengray

54

97 A 98 B 99 C

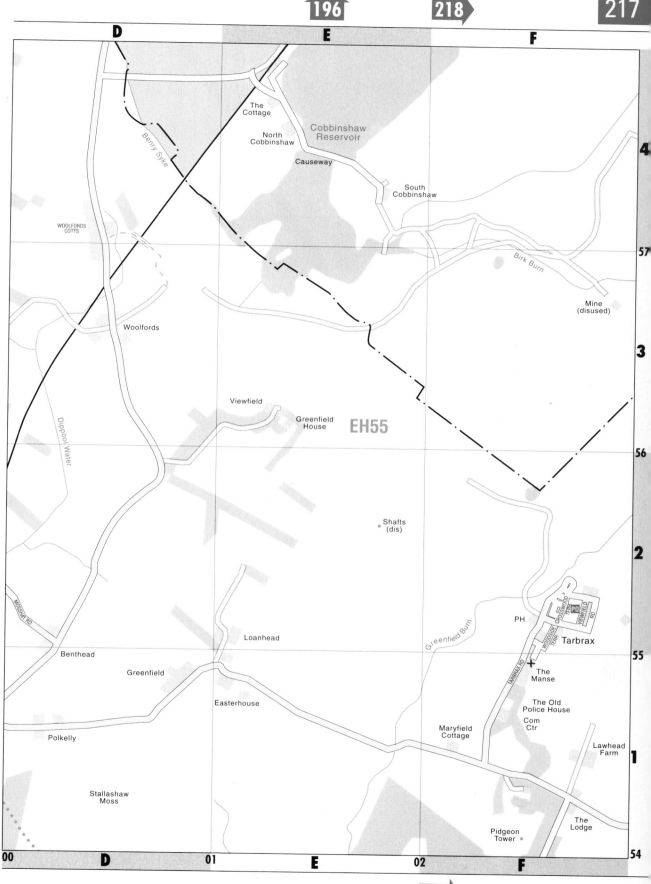

The Cottage

North Cobbinshaw

Cobbinshaw Reservoir

Causeway

South Cobbinshaw

Benry Syke

WOOLFORDS COTTS

Woolfords

Birk Burn

Mine (disused)

4

57

3

Dippool Water

Viewfield

Greenfield House

EH55

56

Shafts (dis)

2

Tarbrax

PO

WOODSIDE TERR

CROSSWOOD

VIEWFIELD RD

PH

Loanhead

Greenfield Burn

TARBRAX RD

The Manse

55

Benthead

MOSSHAT RD

Greenfield

Easterhouse

The Old Police House

Com Ctr

Maryfield Cottage

Lawhead Farm

Polkelly

1

Stallashaw Moss

Pidgeon Tower

The Lodge

54

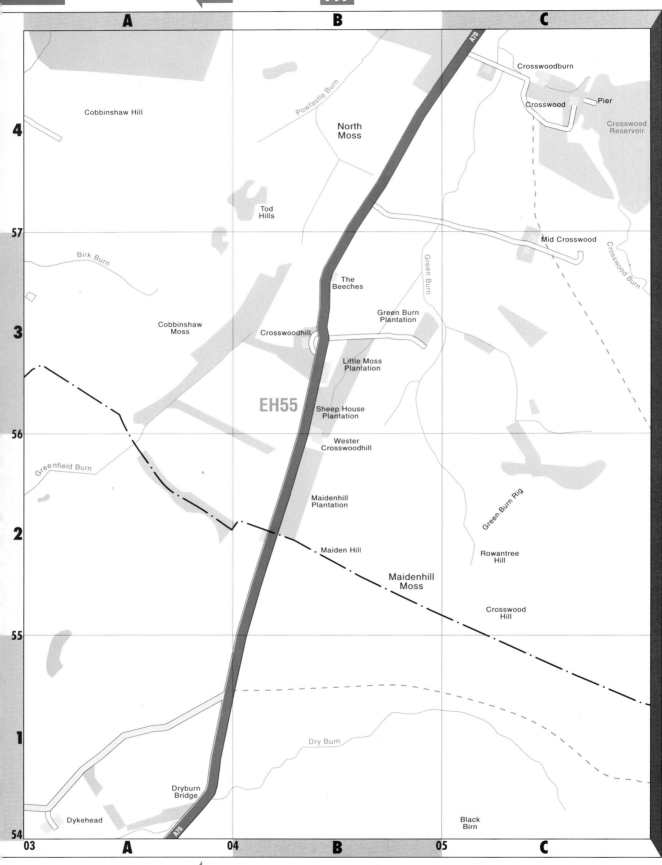

EH55

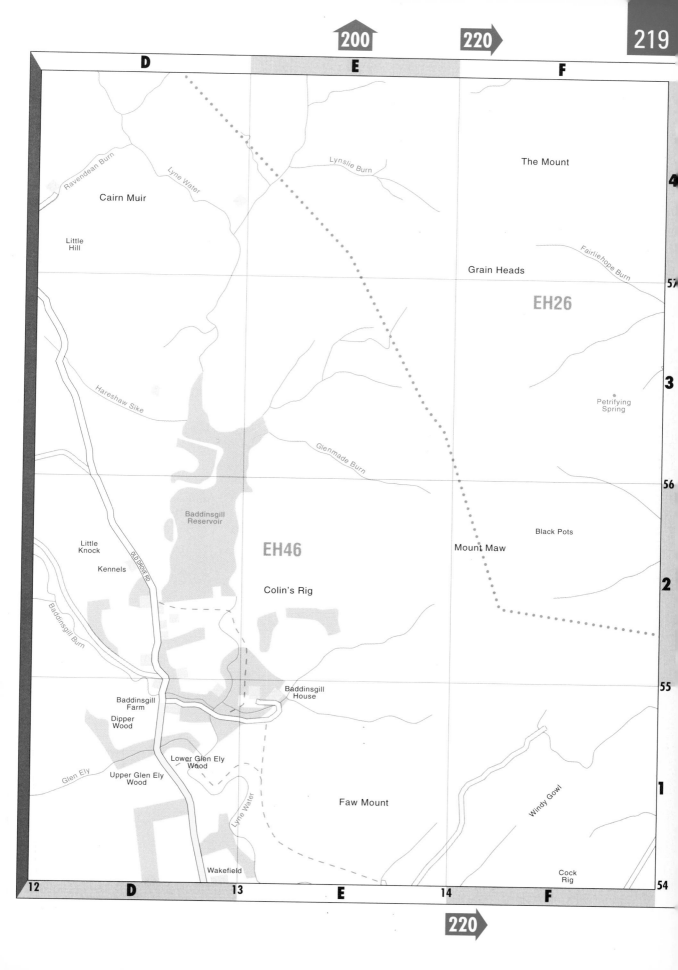

200

220

D E F

The Mount

Ravendean Burn

Lyne Water

Lynslie Burn

Cairn Muir

Little
Hill

Grain Heads

Fairliehope Burn

57

EH26

4

Hareshaw Sike

Petrifying
Spring

3

Glenmade Burn

56

Baddinsgill
Reservoir

Black Pots

EH46

Little
Knock

OLD DROVE RD

Mount Maw

Kennels

Colin's Rig

2

Baddinsgill Burn

Baddinsgill
House

55

Baddinsgill
Farm

Dipper
Wood

Windy Gowl

Lower Glen Ely
Wood

Glen Ely

Upper Glen Ely
Wood

Lyne Water

Faw Mount

1

Wakefield

Cock
Rig

54

12 D 13 E 14 F

220

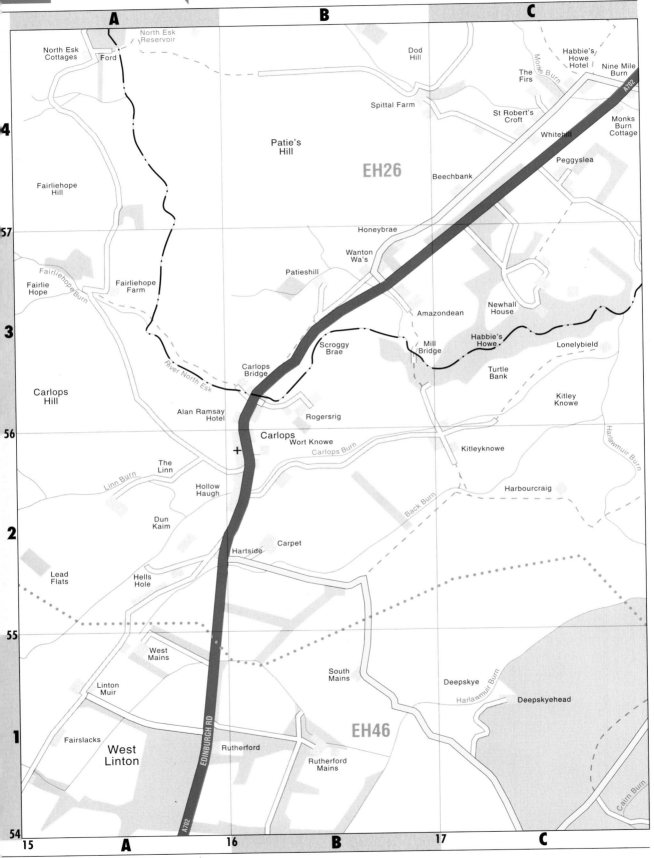

North Esk
Reservoir

A

North Esk
Cottages

Ford

B

Dod
Hill

C

Habbie's
Howe
Hotel

Nine Mile
Burn

The
Firs

Monks Burn

4

Patie's
Hill

Spittal Farm

St Robert's
Croft

Whitehill

Monks
Burn
Cottage

EH26

Beechbank

Peggyslea

Fairliehope
Hill

57

Honeybrae

Wanton
Wa's

Fairlie
Hope

Fairliehope Burn

Fairliehope Farm

Patieshill

Amazondean

Newhall
House

3

Carlops
Hill

River North Esk

Scroggy
Brae

Mill
Bridge

Habbie's
Howe

Lonelybield

Carlops
Bridge

Turtle
Bank

Kitley
Knowe

Alan Ramsay
Hotel

Rogersrig

56

Carlops

Wort Knowe

Kitleyknowe

Harlawmuir Burn

The
Linn

Carlops Burn

Linn Burn

Hollow
Haugh

Harbourcraig

Back Burn

2

Dun
Kaim

Carpet

Hartside

Lead
Flats

Hells
Hole

South
Mains

Deepskye

Deepskyehead

55

West
Mains

Harlawmuir Burn

Linton
Muir

EDINBURGH RD

1

Fairslacks

West
Linton

Rutherford

EH46

Rutherford
Mains

Cairn Burn

A702

54

A **B** **C**

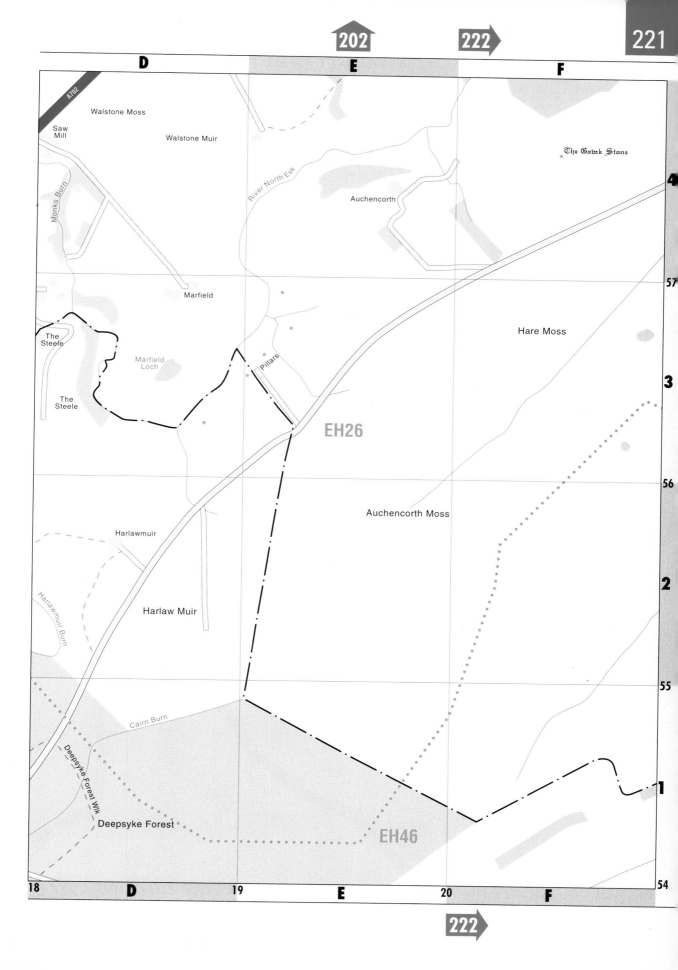

A702

Walstone Moss

Saw
Mill

Walstone Muir

The Gawk Stone

River North Esk

Auchencorth

Monks Burn

Marfield

57

The
Steele

Hare Moss

Marfield
Loch

Pillars

3

The
Steele

EH26

56

Auchencorth Moss

Harlawmuir

Harlawmuir Burn

2

Harlaw Muir

55

Cairn Burn

Deepsyke Forest Wlk

1

Deepsyke Forest

EH46

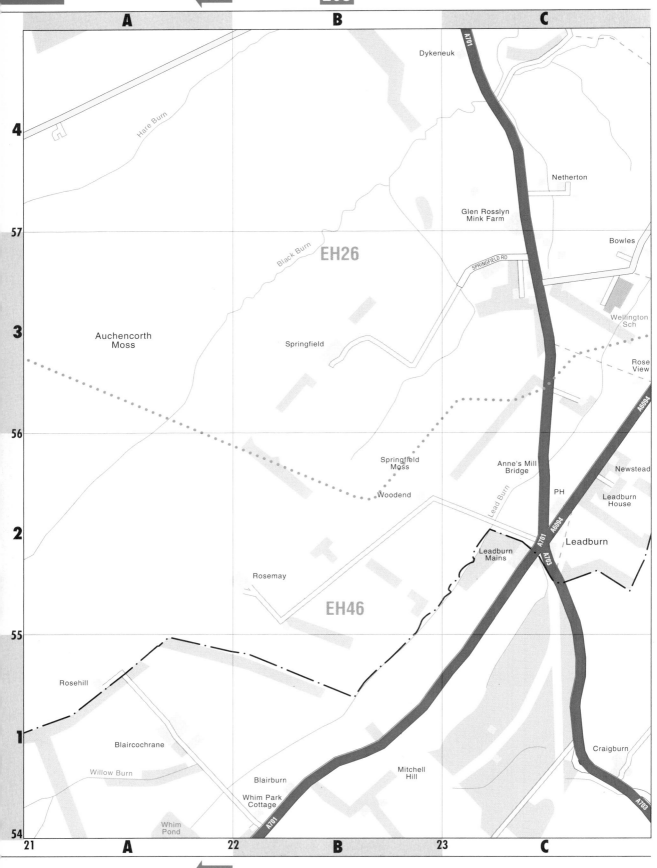

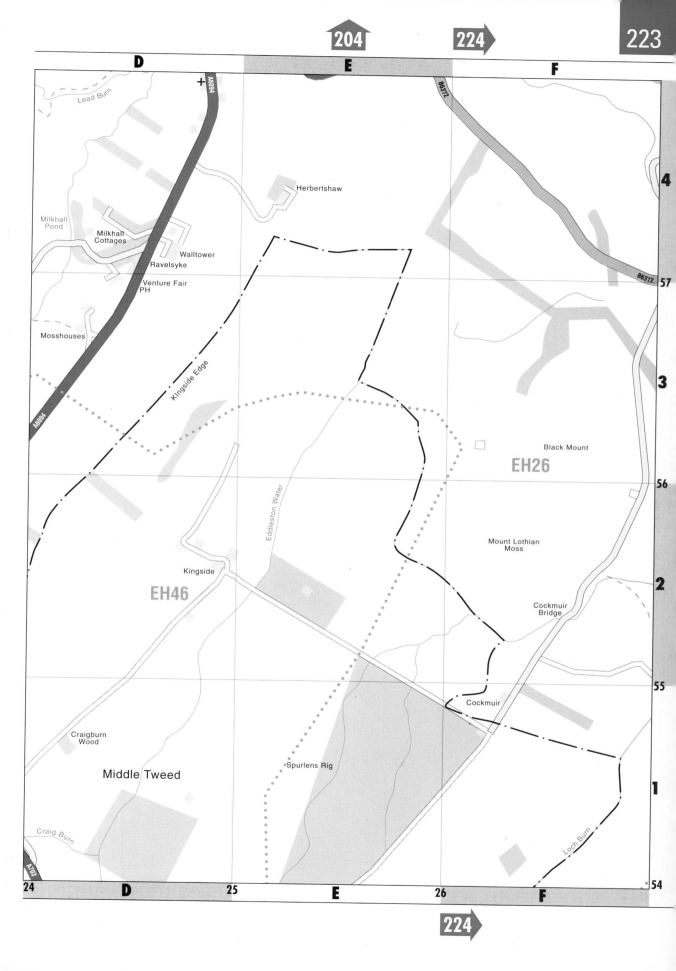

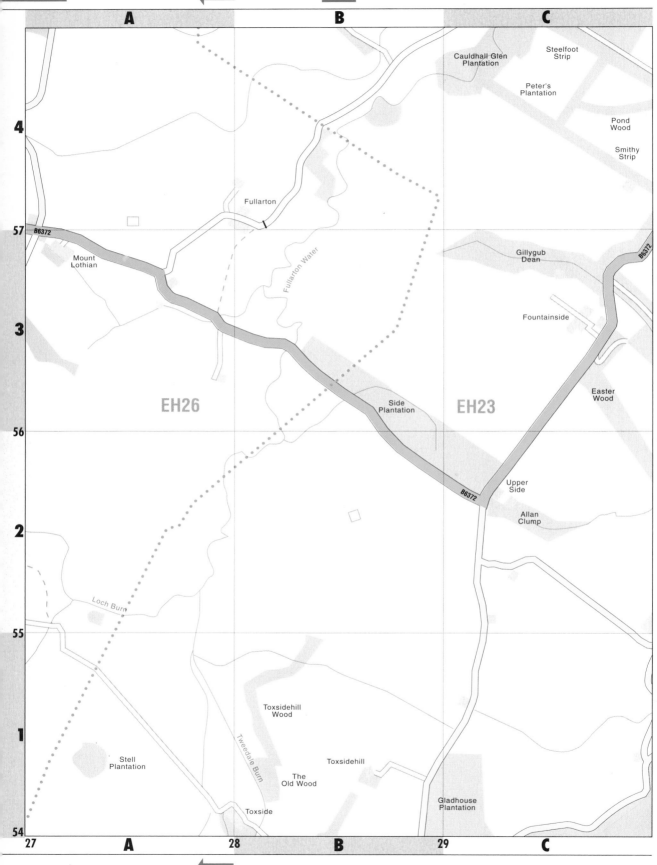

A
B
C

Cauldhall Glen Plantation

Steelfoot Strip

Peter's Plantation

Pond Wood

4

Smithy Strip

Fullarton

57
B6372

Mount Lothian

Gillygub Dean

B6372

Fullarton Water

Fountainside

3

EH26

Side Plantation

EH23

Easter Wood

56

Upper Side

B6372

2

Allan Clump

Loch Burn

55

Toxsidehill Wood

1

Tweedale Burn

Toxsidehill

Stell Plantation

The Old Wood

Gladhouse Plantation

Toxside

54
27
A
28
B
29
C

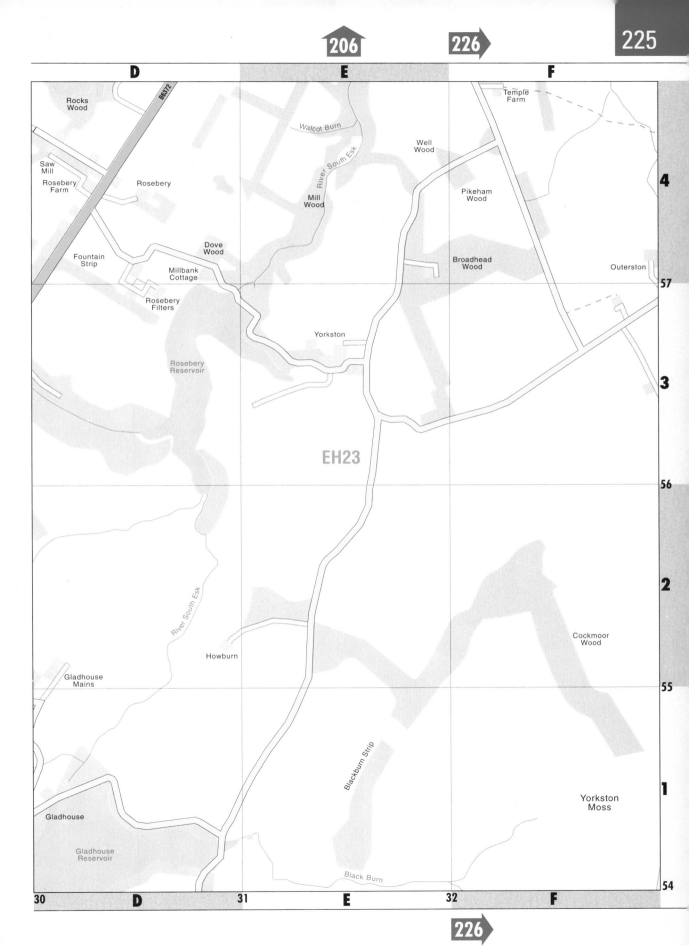
D E F

Rocks
Wood

B6372

Walcot Burn

Well
Wood

Temple
Farm

Saw
Mill

Rosebery
Farm

Rosebery

Mill
Wood

Pikeham
Wood

4

Fountain
Strip

Dove
Wood

Millbank
Cottage

Broadhead
Wood

Outerston

57

Rosebery
Filters

Yorkston

Rosebery
Reservoir

River South Esk

3

EH23

56

River South Esk

2

Cockmoor
Wood

Howburn

Gladhouse
Mains

55

Blackburn Strip

1

Gladhouse

Yorkston
Moss

Gladhouse
Reservoir

Black Burn

54

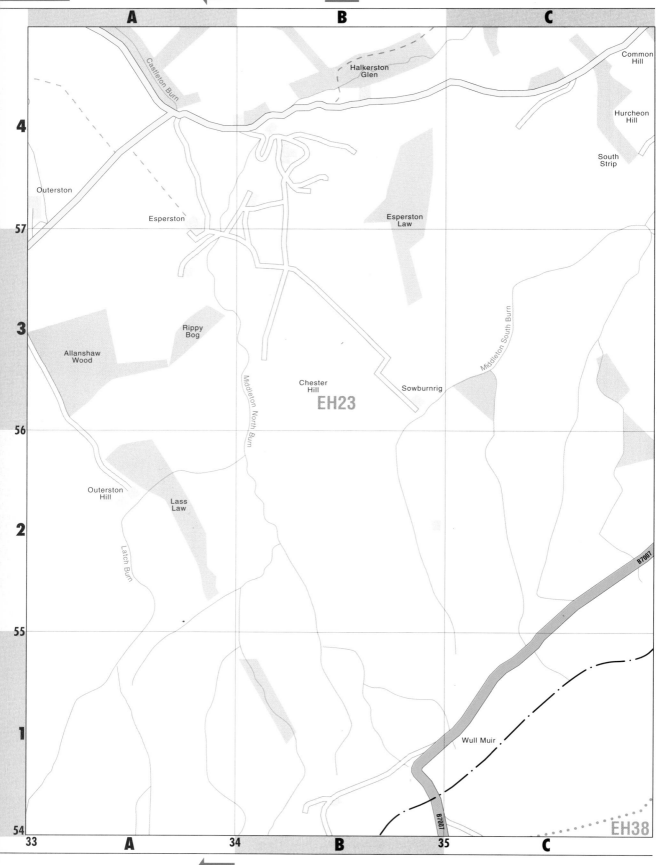

A   B   C

Common Hill

Castleton Burn

Halkerston Glen

Hurcheon Hill

4

South Strip

Outerston

Esperston

Esperston Law

57

Middleton South Burn

3

Rippy Bog

Allanshaw Wood

Chester Hill

Sowburnrig

EH23

Middleton North Burn

56

Outerston Hill

Lass Law

2

Latch Burn

B7007

55

1

Wull Muir

B7007

EH38

54

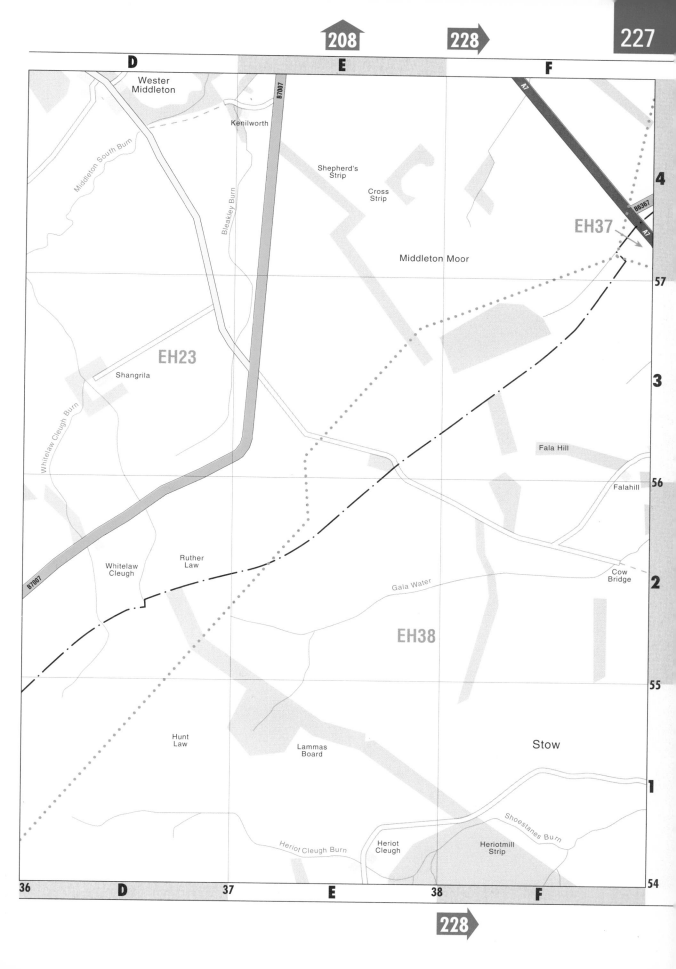

D
E
F

Wester
Middleton

Kenilworth

B7007

A7

Middleton South Burn

Bleakley Burn

Shepherd's
Strip

Cross
Strip

B6367

EH37

A7

4

Middleton Moor

57

Whitelaw Cleugh Burn

EH23

Shangrila

Fala Hill

3

Falahill

56

B7007

Whitelaw
Cleugh

Ruther
Law

Cow
Bridge

2

Gala Water

EH38

55

Hunt
Law

Lammas
Board

Stow

1

Shoestanes Burn

Heriot Cleugh Burn

Heriot
Cleugh

Heriotmill
Strip

36
D
37
E
38
F
54

B6367

Cowbraehill

Cakemuir
Hill

Cakemuir
Edge

EH37

4

A7

57

54

Cakemuir Burn

Sandy
Knowe

3

Falahill

FALAHILL
COTTS

56

Nettlingflat

EH38

2

Gala Water

55

Heriot

Robertston

Hangingshaw
Hill

SHOESTANES RD

SHOESTANES
TERR

HERIOT WAY B709

Shoestanes

1

Shoestanes Burn

Heriot
House

SHOESTANE S RD

B709

A7

Sandyknowe

Crookston North
Mains Hill

54

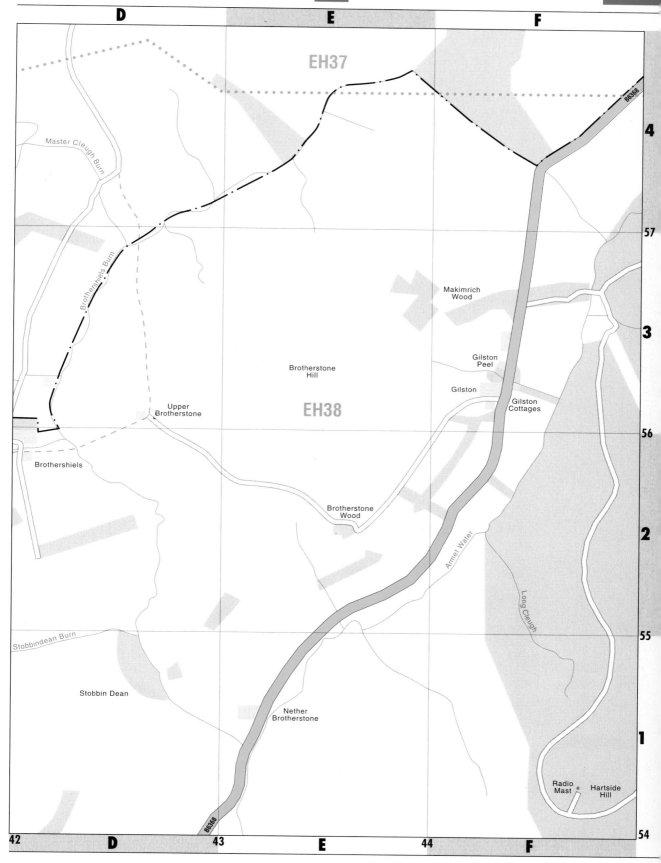

EH37

EH38

D

E

F

Master Cleugh Burn

Brothershiels Burn

Brotherstone
Hill

Upper
Brotherstone

Brothershiels

Makimrich
Wood

Gilston
Peel

Gilston

Gilston
Cottages

Brotherstone
Wood

Arnet Water

Long Cleugh

Stobbindean Burn

Stobbin Dean

Nether
Brotherstone

Radio
Mast

Hartside
Hill

B6368

B6368

42

43

44

4

57

3

56

2

55

1

54

212

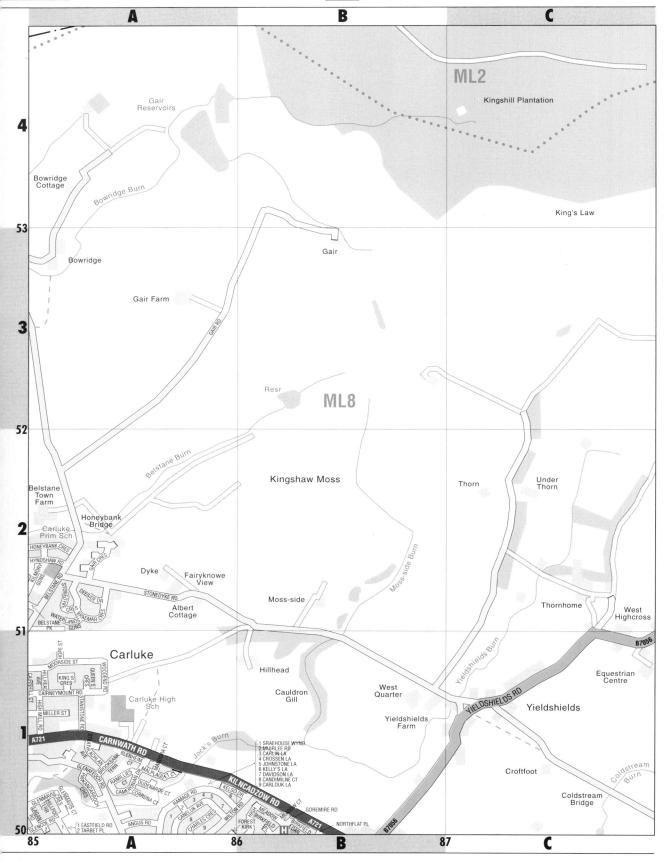

230

A B C

ML2

Kingshill Plantation

King's Law

4

Bowridge Cottage

Gair Reservoirs

Bowridge Burn

53

Bowridge

Gair

Gair Farm

GAIR RD

3

Resr

ML8

52

Belstane Burn

Kingshaw Moss

Thorn

Under Thorn

Belstane Town Farm

Honeybank Bridge

Carluke Prim Sch

HONEYBANK CRES

HYNDSHAW RD

KILMORY GDNS

BELSTANE RD

STONEDYKE CRES

GAIR CRES

2

Dyke

Fairyknowe View

DEESIDE DR

STONEDYKE RD

Moss-side Burn

Moss-side

Thornhome

West Highcross

CRES

BRAEMAR CRES

WATERLANDS GDNS

BELSTANE PK

Albert Cottage

51

Yieldshields Burn

B7056

Carluke

MOORSIDE ST

HIGH ST

KING'S CRES

QUEEN'S CRES

CRES

WOODEND RD

Hillhead

Cauldron Gill

West Quarter

Equestrian Centre

Yieldshields

YIELDSHIELDS RD

CAIRNEYMOUNT RD

STANISTONE RD

Carluke High Sch

HILLHEAD

HIGH MILL RD

CARTFELL CT

MILLER ST

Yieldshields Farm

1

A721

CARNWATH RD

Jock's Burn

1 SRAEHOUSE WYND
2 MUIRLEE RD
3 CARLIN LA
4 CROSSEN LA
5 JOHNSTONE LA
6 KELLY'S LA
7 DAVIDSON LA
8 CANDIMILNE CT
9 CARLOUK LA

Croftfoot

Coldstream Burn

STRATHACHLAN AVE

BROOKBANK TERR

BLENHEIM CT

MALPLAQUET CT

MANORIA CT

GLENAFEOCH RD

RAMILLIES CT

CAMERONIAN

OUDENARDE CT

CORRUNA CT

RAMAGE RD

KELSO DR

WILTON RD

HIGH MEADOW

MEADOW CT

BIRKFIELD CT

GOREMIRE RD

KILNCADZOW RD

A721

NORTHFLAT PL

B7056

Coldstream Bridge

GLENMAVIS DR

HILLFOOT TERR

GLENMARS CT

TAXANDAROCH

GLENCOE RD

CARGLEN

ANGUS RD

CANELUK AVE

CHARLES CRES

FOREST KIRK

1 EASTFIELD RD
2 TARBET PL

50

85 A 86 B 87 C

ML2

Black Law

ML8

Thornmuir

Birniehall

Netherton Burn

Springfield
Reservoir

Hill of
Westerhouse

Middlehope
Farm

Easterseat

Springfield

Knowehead

Middlehouse

YIELDSHIELDS RD

B7056

Westerhouse

Netherton Burn

Damhead

East
Highcross

Coldstream Burn

Candymill Burn

Mid
Coldstream

Craigend

ML11

88   D   89   E   90   F   50

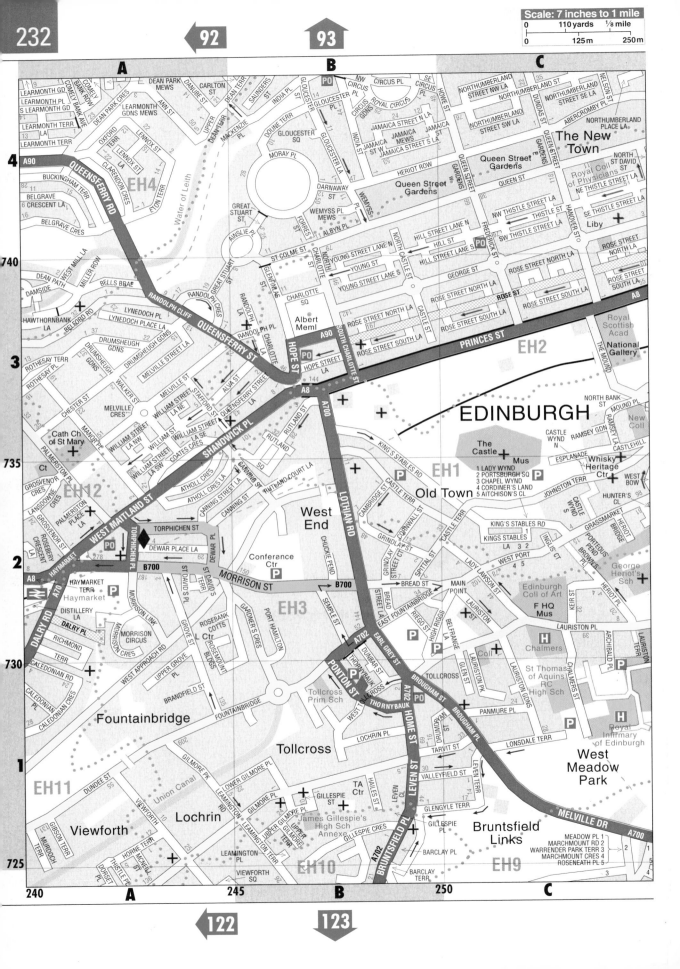

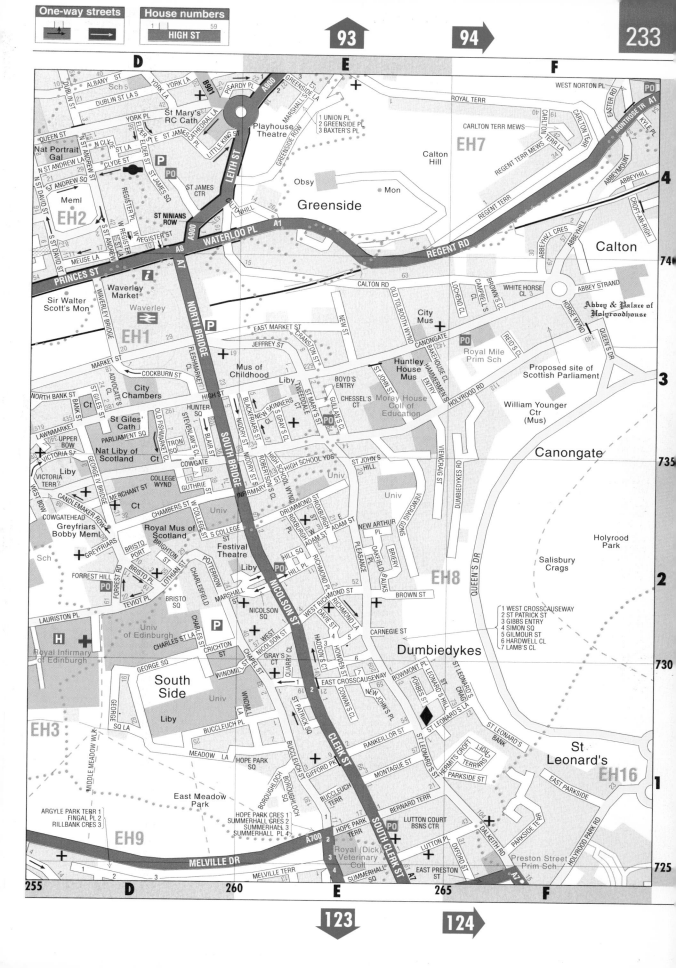

Index

Street names are listed alphabetically and show the locality, the Postcode District, the page number and a reference to the square in which the name falls on the map page

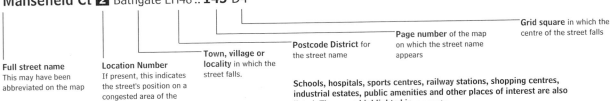

Mansefield Ct 2 Bathgate EH48 .. **145** D4

Full street name
This may have been abbreviated on the map

Location Number
If present, this indicates the street's position on a congested area of the map instead of the name

Town, village or locality in which the street falls.

Postcode District for the street name

Page number of the map on which the street name appears

Grid square in which the centre of the street falls

Schools, hospitals, sports centres, railway stations, shopping centres, industrial estates, public amenities and other places of interest are also listed. These are highlighted in magenta

Abbreviations used in the index

App	Approach	Cl	Close	Espl	Esplanade	Mdw	Meadows	S	South
Arc	Arcade	Comm	Common	Est	Estate	N	North	Sq	Square
Ave	Avenue	Cnr	Corner	Gdns	Gardens	Orch	Orchard	Strs	Stairs
Bvd	Boulevard	Cotts	Cottages	Gn	Green	Par	Parade	Stps	Steps
Bldgs	Buildings	Ct	Court	Gr	Grove	Pk	Park	St	Street, Saint
Bsns Pk	Business Park	Ctyd	Courtyard	Hts	Heights	Pas	Passage	Terr	Terrace
Bsns Ctr	Business Centre	Cres	Crescent	Ho	House	Pl	Place	Tk	Track
Bglws	Bungalows	Dr	Drive	Ind Est	Industrial Estate	Prec	Precinct	Trad Est	Trading Estate
Cswy	Causeway	Dro	Drove	Intc	Interchange	Prom	Promenade	Wlk	Walk
Ctr	Centre	E	East	Junc	Junction	Ret Pk	Retail Park	W	West
Circ	Circle	Emb	Embankment	La	Lane	Rd	Road	Yd	Yard
Cir	Circus	Ent	Enterprise	Mans	Mansions	Rdbt	Roundabout		

Town and village index

Abercorn	66	C1
Aberdour	49	E4
Aberlady	71	E2
Addiewell	171	F1
Airth	22	B2
Allandale	57	E1
Alloa	10	B3
Alva	5	D3
Armadale	143	F3
Athelstaneford	101	F4
Auchendinny	180	B1
Auchengray	216	C1
Auchtertool	15	D1
Avonbridge	112	A3
Balerno	151	E1
Bankhead	57	F3
Bannockburn	7	F1
Bathgate	145	E4
Bilston	180	C3
Blackburn	171	E4
Blackness	65	F2
Blackridge	142	B2
Blairhall	26	A4
Bo'ness	63	F4
Bolton	162	C4
Bonnybridge	58	A3
Bonnyrigg and Lasswade	182	B4
Borthwick	208	A2
Breich	194	C3
Bridge of Allan	2	A4
Bridgend	86	B2
Brightons	82	B4
Broxburn	117	E3
Burntisland	50	C4
Cairneyhill	27	E1
California	81	F3
Cambus	9	D4
Cambusbarron	6	B3
Cardenden	15	E4
Carluke	230	A1
Carnock	27	E3
Carrington	206	B3
Charlestown	45	D2
Clackmannan	11	D2
Cockburnspath	140	C2
Cockenzie and Port Seton	97	E3
Comrie	26	B4
Cousland	158	B3
Cowdenbeath	13	F2
Cowie	20	B4
Craigiehall	90	B2
Crombie	44	B4
Crossford	28	A1
Crossgates	30	C3
Culross	42	B4
Currie	152	A2
Dalgety Bay	48	B2
Dalkeith	157	D1
Dalmeny	89	F4
Danderhall	156	B4
Dechmont	116	B1
Denny	36	C1
Dennyloanhead	57	E3
Dirleton	53	D2
Drem	73	D2
Dunbar	78	B1
Dunfermline	29	E3
Dysart	18	A4
East Calder	148	C2
East Fortune	74	A2
East Linton	103	E4
East Saltoun	161	F2
East Whitburn	170	C4
Easthouses	183	E4
Ecclesmachan	116	C4
Edinburgh	123	E3
Edinburgh	232	C3
Elphinstone	128	A1
Fala	210	B4
Falkirk	60	B3
Fallin	8	B2
Fauldhouse	193	F3
Fishcross	5	F2
Fordell	31	D3
Forrestfield	141	D2
Forth	215	D1
Garvald	134	B1
Gifford	163	F2
Gladsmuir	130	A4
Gorebridge	207	E4
Gowkhall	27	F4
Grangemouth	61	E4
Gullane	52	A1
Haddington	101	E1
Haggs	57	D2
Halbeath	30	A3
Harthill	168	C3
Hartwood	191	D1
Heriot	228	B1
High Bonnybridge	58	B2
High Valleyfield	26	A1
Hillend	47	F2
Howgate	204	A1
Humbie	187	D1
Innerwick	108	A1
Inverkeithing	47	D1
Kelty	12	B4
Kincardine	23	F2
Kinghorn	35	D2
Kingseat	12	A1
Kirkcaldy	17	E2
Kirkliston	89	D1
Kirknewton	149	F1
Larbert	38	A1
Laurieston	61	D2
Letham	39	E4
Limekilns	45	F2
Linlithgow	85	D3
Livingston	147	E3
Loanhead	181	D4
Lochgelly	14	B4
Longcroft	57	D2
Longniddry	98	C3
Longridge	170	B1
Macmerry	129	E3
Maddiston	83	D3
Manor Powis	3	D2
Mayfield	183	F3
Menstrie	3	F3
Mid Calder	148	B2
Musselburgh	126	B4
New Winton	129	D2
Newbridge	119	D3
Newcraighall	125	F2
Newmills	26	B1
Newton	88	A4
Newtongrange	183	D3
North Berwick	54	B4
North Middleton	207	F2
North Queensferry	68	B3
Oakley	26	C4
Ormiston	159	F4
Pathhead	185	D3
Pencaitland	160	B4
Penicuik	203	E2
Philpstoun	86	B3
Plean	20	B2
Polbeth	172	C3
Polmont	61	F1
Prestonpans	96	C1
Pumpherston	148	A4
Queensferry	89	D4
Ratho	119	E1
Ratho Station	119	E3
Redding	61	E1
Reddingmuirhead	82	A4
Rosewell	181	E1
Roslin	180	C2
Rosyth	46	C2
Salsburgh	167	D2
Seafield	146	A1
Shieldhill	81	E3
Shotts	191	F3
Silverburn	202	C3
Skinflats	39	F2
Slamannan	110	A3
South Alloa	9	F2
Spittal	99	E4
Spott	106	B2
Standburn	82	B1
Stenhousemuir	38	B2
Stenton	104	C1
Stirling	7	E4
Stoneyburn	171	E1
Straiton	155	D1
Tarbrax	217	F2
Temple	206	B1
Threemiletown	86	C2
Throsk	9	D2
Torphichen	113	F3
Torryburn	26	C1
Torwood	37	F3
Townhill	29	E4
Tranent	128	B4
Tullibody	4	B2
Tyninghame	76	A2
Uphall	116	C2
Uphall Station	117	D1
Wallacestone	82	A4
Wallyford	127	E3
Wellwood	29	D4
West Barns	77	F1
West Calder	172	B1
West Linton	220	A1
Westfield	112	C3
Westquarter	61	D1
Whitburn	170	A4
Whitecraig	126	C3
Whitecross	83	F3
Whitekirk	75	F4
Wilkieston	150	A3
Winchburgh	87	F1

1st St FK3 .... 62 A4
2nd St
  Grangemouth, Chemical Works
  EH51 .... 62 B3
  Grangemouth, Oil Refinery
  FK3 .... 62 A4
3rd St
  Grangemouth, Chemical Works
  EH51 .... 62 C3
  Grangemouth, Oil Refinery
  FK3 .... 62 A4
4th St
  Grangemouth, Chemical Works
  EH51 .... 62 C3
  Grangemouth, Oil Refinery
  FK3 .... 62 A4
5th St
  Grangemouth, Chemical Works
  EH51 .... 62 C3
  Grangemouth, Oil Refinery
  FK3 .... 62 A4
6th St
  Grangemouth, Oil Refinery
  FK9 .... 41 D1
  EH51 .... 62 C3
7th St
  Grangemouth, Chemical Works
  EH51 .... 62 B4
  Grangemouth, Oil Refinery
  FK3 .... 62 B4
8th St FK3 .... 62 B4
A1 Ind Pk EH15 .... 125 D4
Abbey Craig Rd FK10 ...... 5 D1
Abbey Cres EH39 .... 54 A4
Abbey Ct EH39 .... 54 A4
Abbey La EH8 .... 94 A1
Abbey Mains EH41 .... 101 F2
Abbey Mews EH39 .... 54 A4
Abbey Mill FK8 .... 7 E4
Abbey & Palace of
  Holyroodhouse EH8 .... 233 F3
Abbey Park Pl KY12 .... 29 D1
Abbey Rd Dalkeith EH22 .. 157 D1
  Dunbar EH42 .... 78 B1
  North Berwick EH39 ...... 54 A4
  Stirling FK8 .... 2 B1
Abbey Rd Pl FK8 .... 7 E4
Abbey St Edinburgh EH7 ... 94 A1
  High Valleyfield KY12 ..... 26 A1
Abbey Strand EH8 .... 233 F3
Abbey View
  Crossford KY12 .... 28 B1
  Dunfermline KY11 .... 29 F1
Abbeygrange EH22 .... 183 D3
Abbeyhill EH8 .... 233 F4
Abbeyhill Cres EH8 .... 233 F4
Abbeyhill Prim Sch EH7 ... 94 A1
Abbeymount EH8 .... 233 F4
Abbot Rd FK7 .... 7 E2
Abbot St KY12 .... 29 D2
Abbot's View EH41 .... 101 D1
Abbots Cl EH39 .... 53 F4
Abbots Ct FK2 .... 60 B4
Abbots Mill KY2 .... 17 D2
Abbots Moss Dr FK1 .... 59 F1
Abbots Rd Falkirk FK2 ..... 60 B4
  Grangemouth FK3 .... 61 E4
Abbots View FK2 .... 61 F2
Abbots Wlk KY2 .... 16 C2
Abbotsford Cres
  Edinburgh EH10 .... 123 D2
  Shotts ML7 .... 191 F3
Abbotsford Ct EH10 ...... 123 D2
Abbotsford Dr
  Grangemouth 61 F3
  Laurieston FK2 .... 61 D2
Abbotsford Gdns FK2 ..... 39 D1
Abbotsford Pk
  Edinburgh EH10 .... 123 D2
  North Berwick EH39 ...... 53 F4
Abbotsford Pl FK8 .... 2 B1
Abbotsford Rd EH39 .... 53 F4
Abbotsford Rise EH54 .... 148 A1
Abbotsford St FK2 .... 60 A4
Abbotsgrange Rd FK3 ..... 61 F4
Abbotshall Rd KY2, KY1 ... 17 D1
Abbotsinch Ind Est EH54 .. 61 F4
Abbotsinch Rd FK3 .... 61 F4
Abbotsview Junc EH41 ... 101 D1
Abden Av KY3 .... 35 D2
Abden Ct KY3 .... 35 D2
Abden Pl KY3 .... 35 D2
Abel Pl KY11 .... 29 F2
Abercairney Cres FK1 ..... 82 C3
Abercairney Pl FK1 .... 61 F4
Abercorn Ave EH8 .... 124 B4
Abercorn Cres EH8 .... 124 B4
Abercorn Ct EH8 .... 124 B4
Abercorn Dr EH8 .... 124 B4
Abercorn Gdns EH8 .... 94 B1
Abercorn Gr EH8 .... 124 B4
Abercorn Pl EH52 .... 87 F1
Abercorn Prim Sch
  EH52 .... 87 E4
Abercorn Rd EH8 .... 124 B4
Abercorn Terr EH15 ...... 125 E4
Abercrombie Pl FK11 .... 3 F3
Abercromby Pl
  Stirling FK8 .... 59 F3
Abercromby Dr FK9 .... 2 A4
Abercromby Pl
  Edinburgh EH3 .... 232 C4
  Stirling FK8 .... 7 D4
  Tullibody FK10 .... 4 A1
Aberdour Castle KY3 ...... 49 E4
Aberdour Cres KY11 .... 29 E1
Aberdour Pl KY11 .... 29 E1
Aberdour Prim Sch KY3 ... 49 E4

Aberdour Rd
  Burntisland KY3 .... 33 E1
  Dunfermline KY11 .... 29 F1
Aberdour Sta KY3 .... 49 E4
Aberlady Prim Sch EH32 .. 71 E2
Aberlady Rd EH41 .... 100 C1
Aberlour St KY11 .... 46 C2
Abinger Gdns EH12 .... 122 B4
Abington Rd KY12 .... 28 C1
Aboyne Ave FK9 .... 2 B2
Aboyne Gdns KY2 .... 16 C4
Academy La EH20 .... 181 E4
Academy Pk EH6 .... 94 A2
Academy Pl KY7 .... 7 F1
Academy St
  Bo'ness EH51 .... 64 A4
  Stirling FK8 .... 7 D4
Academy Sq KY11 .... 45 E2
Academy St Alloa FK10 .... 9 F4
  Armadale EH48 .... 143 F3
  Bathgate EH48 .... 145 D3
  Edinburgh EH6 .... 94 A2
Academy The EH51 .... 64 A4
Acheson Dr EH32 .... 127 F4
Achray Ct FK10 .... 10 B3
Achray Dr FK9 .... 2 A2
Ackam Path EH20 .... 180 C4
Acorn Cres FK5 .... 38 B1
Acre Rd EH14 .... 64 B3
Acredale Bathgate EH48 .. 145 D3
  Linlithgow EH49 .... 85 D3
Acredales EH41 .... 131 F4
Acredales Wlk EH41 ...... 131 F4
Adam Cres FK5 .... 38 C1
Adam Pl KY5 .... 14 A4
Adam Smith Cl KY1 .... 17 E2
Adam Smith St KY1 .... 17 E2
Adam Sq FK2 .... 173 E3
Adam St FK2 .... 60 B3
Adambrae Rd EH54 .... 173 E4
Adambrae Rdbt EH54 .... 173 E4
Adams Loan FK2 .... 39 D1
Adams Well EH13 .... 153 E4
Adamson Ave KY2 .... 17 D3
Adamson Cres KY12 .... 29 E3
Adamson Pl FK9 .... 2 A2
Adamson Rd KY5 .... 14 A4
Addiebrownhill EH55 ..... 171 E1
Addiebrownhill Sta
  EH55 .... 171 F1
Addiewell Prim Sch &
St Thomas's RC Prim Sch
  EH55 .... 171 E1
Addiston Cres EH14 ...... 151 E2
Addiston Farm Rd
  EH28 .... 120 A1
Addiston Gr EH14 .... 151 E2
Addiston Pk EH14 .... 151 E2
Adelaide St EH54 .... 148 A3
Adelphi Gr **1** EH15 .... 125 D4
Adelphi Pl EH15 .... 125 D4
Admiral Terr EH10 .... 123 D2
Admiralty Rd
  Inverkeithing KY11 .... 47 E2
  Rosyth KY11 .... 46 B2
Admiralty St EH6 .... 93 F3
Advocate's Cl EH1 .... 233 D3
Affleck Ct EH12 .... 121 D4
Affric Dr FK2 .... 39 E1
Affric Loan ML7 .... 191 E1
Affric Way KY12 .... 28 A1
Afton Ct Dechmont EH52 .. 116 B1
  Stirling FK7 .... 7 E3
Afton Dr FK6 .... 57 E4
Afton Gr KY11 .... 29 F3
Afton Pl EH5 .... 93 D3
Afton Terr EH5 .... 93 D3
Agnew Terr EH6 .... 93 E3
Ailsa Gr KY2 .... 16 C4
Ainslie Gdns FK2 .... 61 F2
Ainslie Pl EH3 .... 232 B4
Airdrie Rd ML6 .... 141 D2
Airlie Dr FK2 .... 61 F1
Airth Dr FK7 .... 7 E2
Airth Prim Sch FK2 .... 22 C2
Airthrey Ave FK9 .... 2 A3
Airthrey Dr FK5 .... 39 D2
Airthrey Rd FK9 .... 2 B3
Aitchison Dr FK5 .... 38 A2
Aitchison's Cl EH1 .... 232 C2
Aitchison's Pl EH15 .... 95 D1
Aitken Cres FK7 .... 7 D1
Aitken Ct KY1 .... 17 D1
Aitken Dr Slamannan FK1 .. 110 A3
  Whitburn EH47 .... 170 A4
Aitken Gdns FK1 .... 59 F3
Aitken Orr Dr EH52 .... 117 F3
Aitken Rd FK1 .... 59 E3
Aitken St KY1 .... 17 F4
Aitken Terr FK1 .... 59 E3
Akarit Rd FK5 .... 38 C1
Alan Breck Gdns EH4 ...... 91 E1
Alan Wlk FK5 .... 1 C4
Albany Ind Est KY12 .... 29 D2
Albany La EH1 .... 93 E1
Albany St
  Dunfermline KY12 .... 29 D2
  Edinburgh EH1 .... 233 D4
Albert Ave FK3 .... 61 F4
Albert Cl EH21 .... 127 D3
Albert Cres EH21 .... 127 D3
Albert Pl Stirling FK8 .... 7 D4
  Wallyford EH21 .... 127 D3
Albert Rd Edinburgh EH6 .. 94 A3
  Falkirk EH51 .... 60 A2
  Harthill ML7 .... 168 C3
Albert St Edinburgh EH7 ... 93 F2
  Rosyth KY11 .... 46 C2

Albert Terr
  Edinburgh EH10 .... 123 D2
  Musselburgh EH21 ...... 126 C3
Alberta Ave EH54 .... 147 F2
Albion Pl EH7 .... 94 A1
Albion Rd EH7 .... 94 A1
Albion Terr EH7 .... 94 A1
Albyn Cotts EH52 .... 117 F3
Albyn Dr EH52 .... 173 F3
Albyn Ind Est EH52 .... 117 F4
Albyn Pl Broxburn EH52 .. 117 F3
  Edinburgh EH2 .... 232 B4
Albyn Terr EH52 .... 117 F3
Alcorn Rigg EH14 .... 152 C4
Alcorn Sq EH14 .... 152 C4
Alder Gr Dunfermline KY11 .. 29 E1
  Westquarter FK2 .... 61 D2
Alderbank
  Livingston EH54 .... 147 F3
  Penicuik EH26 .... 203 F2
Alderbank Gdns EH11 .... 122 C2
Alderbank Pl EH11 .... 122 C2
Alderbank Terr EH11 ..... 122 C2
Alderston Dr KY12 .... 29 E3
Alderston Mdws EH41 ... 100 C1
Alderston Pl EH41 .... 100 C1
Alderston Rd EH41 .... 131 F4
Alderstone Bsns Pk
  EH54 .... 147 E1
Alderstone Rd
  Livingston, Adambrae EH54 .. 173 E1
  Livingston, Howden EH54 .. 147 E2
Alemoor Cres EH7 .... 94 A2
Alemoor Pk EH7 .... 94 A2
Alexander Ave
  Falkirk FK2 .... 60 C3
  Grangemouth FK3 .... 61 E3
Alexander Dr
  Bridge of Allan FK9 .... 2 A4
  Edinburgh EH11 .... 122 B3
  Prestonpans EH32 .... 127 F4
Alexander McLeod Pl
  FK7 .... 8 C2
Alexander Pk EH52 .... 117 F2
Alexander Pl KY11 .... 46 C2
Alexander Rd ML7 .... 191 E3
Alexander St
  Cowdenbeath KY4 .... 13 E3
  Dysart KY1 .... 18 A4
  Uphall EH52 .... 117 D2
Alexander The Third St
  KY3 .... 34 C1
Alexandra Bsns Pk
  EH28 .... 119 D3
Alexandra Dr Alloa FK10 ... 9 F4
  Bathgate EH48 .... 145 F3
Alexandra Pl FK8 .... 2 B1
Alexandra St
  Dunfermline KY12 .... 29 D3
  Kirkcaldy KY1 .... 17 E3
Alford Ave KY2 .... 16 C4
Alfred Pl EH9 .... 123 F2
Alice Cox Wlk KY11 .... 29 E1
Alice Gr KY4 .... 30 C3
Aline Ct KY11 .... 48 A1
Alison Gr KY12 .... 28 A1
Alison St KY1 .... 17 D1
Allan Barr Ct FK1 .... 60 A1
Allan Cres Denny FK6 ..... 36 B2
  Dunfermline KY11 .... 29 F1
Allan Ct FK3 .... 40 C1
Allan Park Cres EH14 .... 122 B2
Allan Park Dr EH14 .... 122 B1
Allan Park Gdns EH14 .... 122 B1
Allan Park Loan EH14 .... 122 B1
Allan Park Rd EH14 ...... 122 B1
Allan Pk
  Cowdenbeath KY4 .... 13 D1
  Kirkliston EH29 .... 89 D1
  Stirling FK8 .... 7 D4
Allan Rd EH47 .... 169 F3
Allan St EH4 .... 93 D1
Allan Terr EH22 .... 157 D2
Allan's Prim Sch FK8 .... 7 D4
Allanbank Rd FK5 .... 38 B1
Allandale Cotts FK4 .... 57 E1
Allanfield EH7 .... 93 F1
Allanton Prim Sch
  ML7 .... 212 A4
Allanton Rd ML7 .... 191 E1
Allanvale Rd FK9 .... 1 C4
Allanwater Gdns FK9 ...... 2 A4
Allanwood Ct FK9 .... 2 A4
Allardice Cres KY2 .... 16 B3
Allen Gr KY12 .... 26 C4
Aller Pl EH54 .... 147 D2
Allermuir Ave EH25 ...... 180 C3
Allermuir Rd EH13 .... 153 D3
Allison Pl EH29 .... 89 D1
Alloa Acad FK10 .... 9 F4
Alloa Rd
  Clackmannan FK10 .... 11 D2
  Falkirk FK2 .... 39 D2
  Fishcross FK10 .... 5 E2
  Manor Powis FK9 .... 3 D2
  Stenhousemuir FK5 ...... 38 C2
  Tullibody FK10 .... 4 B2
Alloa Twr FK10 .... 10 A3
Alloway Cres FK4 .... 57 F3
Alloway Dr KY2 .... 16 B4
Alloway Loan **5** EH16 ... 124 A1
Alma La FK2 .... 60 A3
Alma St Falkirk FK2 .... 60 A3
  Inverkeithing KY11 .... 47 E2
Alma Terr FK2 .... 60 A3
Almond Ave HE12 .... 119 F4
Almond Bank Cotts EH4 ... 91 D3
Almond Cres EH19 .... 182 A3

Almond Ct
  East Whitburn EH47 ..... 170 C4
  Edinburgh EH16 .... 124 C2
  Falkirk FK2 .... 60 C4
  Livingston EH54 .... 148 B2
  Stirling FK7 .... 7 E3
Almond East EH54 .... 148 A3
Almond Gn EH12 .... 121 D4
Almond Gr
  East Calder EH53 .... 148 C3
  Queensferry EH30 .... 89 E4
Almond Intc EH54 .... 148 A2
Almond Pk EH54 .... 148 A2
Almond Pl KY11 .... 17 E4
Almond Rd
  Blackburn EH47 .... 145 E1
  Dunfermline KY11 .... 29 E1
  Falkirk FK2 .... 60 C4
  Livingston EH54 .... 148 A2
  Maddiston FK2 .... 83 E3
  Newbridge HE12 .... 119 F4
Almond S EH53 .... 148 B3
Almond Side EH53 .... 148 B2
Almond Sq
  East Whitburn EH47 ..... 170 C4
  Edinburgh EH12 .... 121 D4
Almond St
  Grangemouth FK3 .... 61 E3
  Whitburn EH47 .... 170 A4
Almond Terr
  Harthill ML7 .... 168 B3
  Whitecross EH49 .... 83 F3
Almond View EH47 .... 146 A1
Almond West Rd EH47 ... 146 A1
Almondbank Prim Sch
  EH54 .... 148 A3
Almondbank Terr EH11 .. 122 C2
Almondell & Calder Wood
  Ctry Pk EH52 .... 149 D4
Almondell Ct EH52 .... 117 F3
Almondell Rd EH52 ...... 117 F3
Almondell Terr EH53 ..... 148 C3
Almondhill Rd EH29 ...... 89 D1
Almondside
  Kirkliston EH29 .... 89 D1
  Livingston EH54 .... 147 F1
Almondvale Ave EH54 ... 147 F1
Almondvale Bsns Pk
  EH54 .... 147 F1
Almondvale Bvd EH54 ... 147 E1
Almondvale Cres EH54 .. 147 E1
Almondvale Ctr EH54 .... 147 F1
Almondvale Dr EH54 ..... 147 F1
Almondvale E EH54 ...... 147 F1
Almondvale N
  Livingston EH54 .... 147 F1
  Livingston EH54 .... 147 F1
Almondvale Parkway
  EH54 .... 147 F1
Almondvale Rd EH54 .... 147 E1
Almondvale Rdbt EH54 .. 147 F1
Almondvale S EH54 ...... 147 F1
Almondvale Stad
  (Livingston FC) EH54 ... 147 E1
Almondvale Stadium Rd
  EH54 .... 147 F1
Almondvale W EH54 ..... 147 F1
Almondvale Way EH54 .. 147 E1
Almondview EH54 .... 147 F1
Alness St KY12 .... 28 C1
Alnwickhill Cres EH16 ... 154 C3
Alnwickhill Ct EH16 ...... 154 C3
Alnwickhill Dr EH16 ...... 154 C3
Alnwickhill Gdns EH16 .. 154 C3
Alnwickhill Gr EH16 ...... 154 C3
Alnwickhill Loan EH16 ... 154 C3
Alnwickhill Pk EH16 ...... 155 D3
Alnwickhill Rd EH16 ..... 155 D4
Alnwickhill Terr EH16 .... 154 C3
Alnwickhill View EH16 ... 154 C3
Alpha St EH51 .... 62 C3
Alva Acad FK12 .... 5 D3
Alva Glen FK12 .... 5 D4
Alva Ind Est FK12 .... 5 E3
Alva Pl EH7 .... 94 A1
Alva Prim Sch FK12 .... 5 D3
Alva St EH2 .... 232 A4
Alyth Dr FK2 .... 62 A1
Amberley Path FK3 .... 61 F3
Ambrose Rise EH54 ...... 148 A1
Amisfield Pk EH41 .... 132 B4
Amisfield Pl
  Haddington EH41 .... 132 B4
  Longniddry EH32 .... 98 C3
Amos Path EH20 .... 180 C4
Amulree Pl EH51 .... 63 E4
Ancrum Bank EH22 .... 156 C1
Ancrum Rd EH22 .... 156 C1
Anderson Ave
  Armadale EH48 .... 143 F2
  Crossford KY12 .... 28 A1
  Newtongrange EH22 .... 183 D3
Anderson Cres FK1 .... 81 F3
Anderson Dr
  Cowdenbeath KY4 .... 13 D1
  Denny FK6 .... 36 C1
  Falkirk FK2 .... 39 D1
Anderson Gdns FK2 .... 82 C3
Anderson La
  Kincardine FK10 .... 23 F2
  Rosyth KY11 .... 46 B3
Anderson Park Rd
  FK6 .... 36 C1
Anderson Pl
  Edinburgh EH6 .... 93 F3
  Stirling FK7 .... 7 D2

Anderson St
  Bonnybridge FK4 .... 58 A3
  Dysart KY1 .... 18 A4
  Kirkcaldy KY1 .... 17 F3
Anderson Terr FK4 .... 57 D2
Andrew Ave EH48 .... 145 F3
Andrew Cres FK5 .... 38 B2
Andrew Ct EH26 .... 203 F4
Andrew Dodd's Ave
  EH22 .... 183 F4
Andrew St KY5 .... 14 A3
Andrew Wood Ct EH6 ..... 93 E3
Angle Park Terr EH11 .... 122 C3
Angres Ct EH22 .... 156 B4
Angus Rd ML8 .... 230 A1
Angus St EH51 .... 63 E3
Ann St EH4 .... 232 A4
Annabel Ct KY11 .... 47 E1
Annan Ct FK1 .... 60 B1
Annandale Side EH7 ...... 93 F1
Annandale Street La
  EH7 .... 93 F1
Anne Dr Bridge of A FK9 ... 2 A3
  Stenhousemuir FK5 ...... 38 C2
Anne St Alloa FK10 .... 9 F4
  Bathgate EH48 .... 145 F3
  Penicuik EH26 .... 203 F4
Annet Rd FK6 .... 57 E3
Annfield Edinburgh EH6 ... 93 E3
  Tranent EH33 .... 128 C3
Annfield Ct EH33 .... 129 E3
Annfield Dr FK7 .... 7 E3
Annfield Farm Rd KY11 ... 47 D4
Annfield Gdns FK8 .... 7 D3
Annfield St EH6 .... 93 E3
Anson Ave FK1 .... 59 F2
Antigua St **7** EH1 .... 93 F1
Antonine Ct FK1 .... 63 E3
Antonine Gdns FK1 .... 59 E3
Antonine Gr FK4 .... 57 F2
Antonine Prim Sch FK4 ... 58 A2
Antonine St FK1 .... 59 E3
Appin Cres
  Dunfermline KY12 .... 29 D2
  Kircaldy KY2 .... 16 C4
Appin Gr FK2 .... 61 F2
Appin Terr
  Edinburgh EH14 .... 122 B2
  Shotts ML7 .... 192 A2
Appleton Parkway
  EH54 .... 146 C2
Appleton Parkway Rdbt
  EH54 .... 146 C3
Arboretum Ave EH4 .... 93 D1
Arboretum Pl EH3 .... 93 D2
Arboretum Rd EH3 .... 93 D2
Arbroath Cres FK9 .... 2 A2
Arbuthnot Rd EH20 ...... 181 E4
Arbuthnot St FK1 .... 59 F3
Arcade FK8 .... 7 D4
Archers Ave KY7 .... 7 E2
Archers Ct EH31 .... 52 A1
Archibald Pl EH3 .... 232 C2
Archibald Russell Ct FK2 .. 61 F1
Ard Ct FK3 .... 61 E3
Ardeer Pl KY11 .... 29 E1
Arden St EH9 .... 123 E3
Ardgowan Pl ML7 .... 191 E1
Ardmillan Pl EH11 .... 122 C3
Ardmillan Terr EH11 ..... 122 C3
Ardmore Pk FK2 .... 62 A1
Ardshiel Ave EH4 .... 91 E1
Ardvreck Pl FK2 .... 39 E2
Argyle Cres EH15 .... 125 E4
Argyle Park Terr EH9 ..... 233 D1
Argyle Pl
  Bonnyrigg and Lasswade
  EH19 .... 181 F3
  Edinburgh EH9 .... 123 E3
Argyle St FK8 .... 93 F3
Argyll Ave Falkirk FK2 ..... 60 B3
  Stirling FK8 .... 2 B1
Argyll Pl FK10 .... 10 B4
Argyll St FK10 .... 10 B4
Arkaig Dr KY12 .... 28 B1
Arkwright Ct EH39 .... 54 A4
Armadale Acad EH48 .... 143 F3
Armadale Prim Sch
  EH48 .... 143 F3
Armadale Rd EH47 .... 170 A4
Armine Pl EH26 .... 204 A4
Armour Ave FK7 .... 20 B4
Arneil Pl FK2 .... 82 B4
Arnot St FK1 .... 60 A2
Arnothill FK1 .... 60 A2
Arnothill Bank **6** FK1 ... 60 A2
Arnothill Ct FK1 .... 59 F3
Arnothill Gdns FK1 .... 60 A2
Arnothill La FK1 .... 59 F2
Arnothill Mews FK1 .... 60 A2
Arnott Gdns EH14 .... 122 A1
Arnprior Rd EH23 .... 207 E4
Arns Gr FK10 .... 9 F4
Arnswell FK10 .... 5 E1
Arran FK10 .... 146 C3
Arran Cres KY2 .... 16 C4
Arran Ct Alloa FK10 .... 10 A3
  Grangemouth FK3 .... 61 E3
Arran Pl FK1 .... 125 E4
Arran Terr FK1 .... 59 E2
Arras Gr FK10 .... 204 A4
Arrol Cres FK10 .... 10 B4
Arrol Pl EH30 .... 89 E4
Arrol Sq EH54 .... 146 C3
Arthur Pl KY4 .... 13 E2

1st – Art **235**

Arthur St
Cowdenbeath KY4 .... 13 E2
Dunfermline KY12 .... 29 D3
Edinburgh EH6 .... 93 F2
Arthur Street La EH6 .... 93 F2
Arthur View Cres
EH22 .... 156 A4
Arthur View Terr EH22 .... 156 A4
Arthur's Dr FK5 .... 38 C1
Artillery Pk EH41 .... 101 C1
Ash Braes FK10 .... 23 E2
Ash Gr Alloa FK10 .... 10 B3
Bathgate EH48 .... 145 E4
Blackburn EH47 .... 171 E4
Carnock KY12 .... 27 C3
Cowdenbeath KY4 .... 13 D2
Dunfermline KY11 .... 46 B4
Dunbar EH42 .... 78 A1
Livingston EH54 .... 148 A3
Stenhousemuir FK5 .... 38 C1
Westquarter FK2 .... 61 D1
Ash La EH20 .... 180 C4
Ash Terr FK8 .... 6 C3
Ashbank Ct EH48 .... 144 C3
Ashbank Terr EH53 .... 148 C2
Ashbrae Gdns FK7 .... 7 D1
Ashburnham Gdns EH30 .... 68 B1
Ashburnham Rd EH30 .... 89 E4
Ashfield Ct EH42 .... 78 C1
Ashfield Pl EH42 .... 78 C1
Ashgrove Mayfield EH22 .... 183 F4
Musselburgh EH21 .... 126 C3
Ashgrove Pl EH21 .... 126 C3
Ashgrove View EH21 .... 126 C3
Ashley Ct EH49 .... 84 C3
Ashley Dr EH11 .... 122 C2
Ashley Gdns EH11 .... 122 C2
Ashley Gr EH11 .... 122 C2
Ashley Hall Gdns EH49 .... 84 C3
Ashley Pl EH6 .... 93 F2
Ashley Rd EH6 .... 61 F2
Ashley St FK4 .... 57 F3
Ashley Terr Alloa FK10 .... 10 A4
Edinburgh EH11 .... 122 C2
Ashton Gr EH16 .... 124 A1
Ashville Terr EH6 .... 94 A2
Asquith St KY1 .... 17 D2
Assembly St FK5 .... 94 A3
Assynt Bank EH26 .... 204 A3
Astley Ainslie Hospl
EH9 .... 123 E2
Atheling Gr EH30 .... 89 E4
Athelstaneford Prim Sch
EH39 .... 101 F4
Athol Cres FK2 .... 61 D2
Athol Pl Bathgate EH48 .... 145 D4
Dunfermline KY12 .... 29 E2
Athol Terr EH48 .... 145 D4
Atholl Cres EH3 .... 232 A2
Atholl Crescent La
EH3 .... 232 A2
Atholl Pl FK8 .... 1 C1
Atholl Terr KY2 .... 16 B4
Atrium Way FK4 .... 58 A2
Attlee Cres EH22 .... 183 F3
Auchengray Rd ML11 .... 216 C1
Auchentyre Pl EH42 .... 39 E2
Auchinbaird FK10 .... 5 E1
Auchingane EH10 .... 153 F3
Auchinleck Ct EH6 .... 93 E3
Auchterderran Rd KY5 .... 14 A4
Auchtertool Prim Sch
KY2 .... 15 D1
Auction Mart EH41 .... 101 C1
Audenhard Terr EH47 .... 171 E1
Auld Brig Rd FK10 .... 10 A3
Auld Orch EH19 .... 182 B4
Auldcathie Pl EH52 .... 87 F2
Auldgate EH30 .... 89 D1
Auldhame Cotts EH39 .... 55 F3
Auldhill Ave EH49 .... 86 B2
Auldhill Cotts EH49 .... 86 B2
Auldhill Cres EH49 .... 86 B2
Auldhill Dr EH49 .... 86 B2
Auldhill Entry EH49 .... 86 B2
Auldhill Pl EH49 .... 86 B2
Auldhill Rd EH49 .... 86 B2
Auldhill Terr EH49 .... 86 B2
Ava St KY1 .... 17 D1
Avalon Gdns EH49 .... 84 B4
Aven Dr FK2 .... 60 C2
Avenue Pk Bridge of A FK9 .... 1 C4
Mid Calder EH53 .... 148 B2
Avenue Pk W EH53 .... 148 B2
Avenue The
Cockenzie & Port Seton
EH32 .... 97 E2
Dalkeith EH22 .... 156 C1
Avenue The Bridge of A FK9 .... 2 A4
Currie EH14 .... 151 F4
Dalgety Bay KY11 .... 47 F2
Falkirk FK1 .... 39 E1
Gifford EH41 .... 163 F2
Gorebridge EH23 .... 183 D1
Lochgelly KY5 .... 14 B4
Philpstoun EH49 .... 86 B4
Whitburn EH47 .... 170 A3
Avenue Villas EH4 .... 92 C1
Averton ML11 .... 215 D1
Avon Ct FK1 .... 60 B1
Avon Dr EH49 .... 84 B4
Avon Gr
Edinburgh EH4 .... 91 D2
Penicuik EH26 .... 204 A3
Avon Pk FK1 .... 111 F3

Avon Pl Bo'ness EH51 .... 63 F4
Edinburgh EH4 .... 91 D2
Avon Rd Bathgate EH48 .... 145 D4
Edinburgh EH4 .... 91 D2
Grangemouth FK3 .... 62 B4
Whitecross EH49 .... 83 F3
Avon St Denny FK6 .... 36 B2
Grangemouth FK3 .... 40 A1
Avon Terr FK1 .... 112 A3
Avonbank Ave FK3 .... 61 F3
Avonbridge Prim Sch
FK1 .... 112 A3
Avonbridge Rd FK1 .... 110 A4
Avondale Cres EH48 .... 143 F3
Avondale Dr EH48 .... 143 F3
Avondale Pl EH3 .... 93 D1
Avondale Rd FK2 .... 62 A2
Avondhu Gdns FK3 .... 61 F4
Avonlea Dr FK2 .... 61 F2
Avonmill Rd EH49 .... 84 B4
Avonmill View EH49 .... 84 B4
Avonside Dr FK6 .... 36 B3
Avontoun Cres EH49 .... 84 A3
Avontoun Pk EH49 .... 84 B3
Ayres Wynd EH32 .... 96 C1
Aytoun Cres FK5 .... 33 F1
Aytoun Gr KY12 .... 28 C3

Baads Rd ML7 .... 141 E1
Baberton Ave EH14 .... 152 C3
Baberton Cres EH14 .... 152 C3
Baberton Loan EH14 .... 152 B3
Baberton Mains EH14 .... 152 B4
Baberton Mains Ave
EH14 .... 152 B4
Baberton Mains Bank
EH14 .... 152 B4
Baberton Mains Brae
EH14 .... 152 B4
Baberton Mains Cres
EH14 .... 152 B4
Baberton Mains Ct
EH14 .... 152 B4
Baberton Mains Dell
EH14 .... 152 B4
Baberton Mains Dr
EH14 .... 152 B4
Baberton Mains Gdns
EH14 .... 152 B4
Baberton Mains Gn
EH14 .... 152 B4
Baberton Mains Gr
EH14 .... 152 B4
Baberton Mains Hill
EH14 .... 152 B4
Baberton Mains Lea
EH14 .... 152 B4
Baberton Mains Loan
EH14 .... 152 C4
Baberton Mains Pk
EH14 .... 152 B4
Baberton Mains Pl
EH14 .... 152 B4
Baberton Mains Rise
EH14 .... 152 B4
Baberton Mains Row
EH14 .... 152 B4
Baberton Mains Terr
EH14 .... 152 B4
Baberton Mains View
EH14 .... 152 C4
Baberton Mains Way EH14 152 B4
Baberton Mains Wood
EH14 .... 152 B4
Baberton Mains Wynd
EH14 .... 152 B4
Baberton Pk EH14 .... 152 B3
Bablins Wynd EH41 .... 163 F2
Back Cswy KY12 .... 42 B4
Back Dean EH4 .... 122 C4
Back O' Hill Ind Est FK8 .... 2 A1
Back O' Hill Rd FK8 .... 2 A1
Back O' Yds KY11 .... 47 D1
Back Rd Alva FK12 .... 4 C4
Dunbar EH42 .... 78 A1
Back St KY12 .... 42 B4
Back Station Rd EH49 .... 85 D4
Backdean Rd EH22 .... 156 A4
Backlee EH16 .... 155 D3
Backmarch Cres KY11 .... 46 C2
Backmarch Rd KY11 .... 46 C2
Backwood Ct FK10 .... 10 C3
Badallan Pl EH47 .... 193 F3
Badger Wood EH52 .... 116 B1
Baileyfield Cres EH15 .... 125 D4
Baileyfield Est EH15 .... 125 D4
Baileyfield Rd
Edinburgh, Northfield
EH15 .... 94 C1
Edinburgh, Portobello
EH15 .... 125 D4
Bailie Gr EH15 .... 125 D3
Bailie Path EH15 .... 125 D3
Bailie Pl EH15 .... 125 D3
Bailie Terr EH15 .... 125 D3
Bailielands EH49 .... 85 E4
Baillie St EH47 .... 170 A4
Baillie Waugh Rd FK7 .... 7 E2
Bain Sq EH54 .... 147 E1
Bain St KY5 .... 14 A4
Baingle Brae FK10 .... 4 A2
Baingle Cres FK10 .... 4 A2
Bainsford Prim Sch
FK2 .... 60 A4
Baird Ave EH12 .... 122 B3
Baird Dr Armadale EH48 .... 143 F4
Edinburgh EH12 .... 122 B3
Baird Gdns EH12 .... 122 B3

Baird Gr EH12 .... 122 B3
Baird Rd Armadale EH48 .... 143 F4
Livingston EH54 .... 147 D1
Ratho EH28 .... 119 E2
Baird St FK1 .... 59 F3
Baird Terr
Edinburgh EH12 .... 122 B3
Haddington EH41 .... 100 C1
Harthill ML7 .... 168 B3
Baird's Way EH39 .... 182 B3
Bairns Ford Ave FK2 .... 60 A4
Bairns Ford Ct FK2 .... 60 A4
Bairns Ford Dr FK2 .... 60 A4
Bakehouse Cl EH8 .... 233 E3
Baker St Bo'ness EH51 .... 63 F3
Stirling FK8 .... 7 D4
Balantyne Pl EH54 .... 147 D2
Balbakie Rd ML7 .... 168 C3
Balbardie Ave EH48 .... 145 D4
Balbardie Cres EH48 .... 145 D4
Balbardie Prim Sch
EH48 .... 145 D4
Balbardie Rd EH48 .... 145 D3
Balbirnie Pl EH12 .... 122 C4
Balcarres Ct EH10 .... 123 D1
Balcarres Pl EH21 .... 126 B4
Balcarres Rd EH21 .... 126 B4
Balcarres St EH10 .... 123 D1
Balcastle Rd FK1 .... 110 A3
Balderston Gdns EH16 .... 124 A1
Balderstone's Wynd
EH39 .... 54 B4
Baldridgeburn KY12 .... 28 C3
Baldwin Cres KY2 .... 17 D3
Balerno High Sch EH14 .... 151 E1
Balfour Cres Larbert FK5 .... 38 B1
Plean FK7 .... 20 B2
Balfour Ct
Dunfermline KY12 .... 29 E3
Edinburgh EH12 .... 91 D1
Balfour Pl EH6 .... 93 F2
Balfour St Alloa FK10 .... 10 B4
Bannockburn FK7 .... 7 E1
Bonnybridge FK4 .... 57 F3
Edinburgh EH6 .... 93 F2
Kirkaldy KY2 .... 17 D3
North Berwick EH39 .... 54 B4
Stirling FK8 .... 1 C1
Balfour Terr EH26 .... 180 A1
Balfour's Sq EH33 .... 128 B3
Balfron Loan EH4 .... 91 E1
Balgone Barns Cotts
EH39 .... 54 B1
Balgreen Ave EH12 .... 122 A3
Balgreen Gdns EH12 .... 122 A3
Balgreen Pk EH12 .... 122 A3
Balgreen Prim Sch
EH11 .... 122 B3
Balgreen Rd EH12 .... 122 A3
Baliol St KY3 .... 34 C1
Ballantyne Rd EH6 .... 93 F3
Ballast Bank KY1 .... 47 E1
Ballater Dr FK9 .... 2 B2
Ballencrieff Mill EH48 .... 144 C4
Ballencrieff Toll EH48 .... 114 A1
Ballengeich Pass FK8 .... 2 A1
Ballengeich Rd FK8 .... 1 C1
Ballingry La KY5 .... 14 A4
Ballingry St KY5 .... 14 A4
Balloch Rd ML7 .... 191 F3
Balm Well Ave EH16 .... 155 D3
Balm Well Gr EH16 .... 155 D3
Balm Well Pk EH16 .... 155 D3
Balm Well Terr EH16 .... 155 D3
Balmoral Dr Falkirk FK1 .... 59 F2
Kircaldy KY2 .... 16 B3
Balmoral Gdns
Brightons FK2 .... 82 B4
Livingston EH54 .... 173 D3
Balmoral Pl
Edinburgh EH3 .... 93 D1
Stenhousemuir FK5 .... 38 C2
Stirling FK7 .... 7 D4
Balmoral Rd EH51 .... 62 C3
Balmoral St FK1 .... 59 F2
Balmuir Rd EH48 .... 144 C4
Balmulzier Rd FK1 .... 110 A4
Balnacraig KY2 .... 28 A1
Balquhatstone Cres
FK1 .... 110 A3
Balquhidderock FK7 .... 7 E2
Balsusney Rd KY2 .... 17 D3
Baltic St EH6 .... 94 A3
Balure Cres FK7 .... 8 B2
Balvaird Pl KY12 .... 29 E3
Balwearie Cres KY2 .... 17 D1
Balwearie Gdns KY2 .... 16 C1
Balwearie Rd KY2 .... 17 D1
Balwearie Sch KY2 .... 17 D1
Banchory Cotts KY3 .... 34 C3
Banchory Pl FK10 .... 4 B2
Bancroft Ave EH54 .... 147 F2
Bandeath Ind Est FK7 .... 9 D3
Bandon Ave KY1 .... 17 F4
Bangholm Ave EH5 .... 93 D3
Bangholm Bower Ave
EH5 .... 93 D3
Bangholm Gr EH5 .... 93 E3
Bangholm Loan EH5 .... 93 E3
Bangholm Pk EH5 .... 93 D3
Bangholm Pl EH5 .... 93 D3
Bangholm Terr EH3 .... 93 D2
Bangholm View EH5 .... 93 E3
Bangly Brae EH41 .... 100 A2
Bangor Rd EH6 .... 93 F3

Bangour Village Hospl
EH52 .... 116 A1
Bank Pl ML7 .... 191 F2
Bank Rd East Linton EH40 .... 103 F4
Harthill ML7 .... 168 C3
Bank St Alloa FK10 .... 10 A3
Edinburgh EH1 .... 233 D3
Falkirk FK1 .... 60 A3
Grangemouth FK3 .... 40 A1
Inverkeithing KY11 .... 47 E1
Kincardine FK10 .... 23 E2
Kirkaldy KY1 .... 17 F4
Lochgelly KY5 .... 14 A4
Mid Calder EH53 .... 148 B2
North Berwick EH39 .... 54 A4
Penicuik EH26 .... 203 F2
Slamannan FK1 .... 110 A3
Stirling FK8 .... 7 D4
Whitburn EH47 .... 170 A4
Bankhead Ave EH11 .... 121 E2
Bankhead Broadway
EH11 .... 121 D2
Bankhead Cotts EH40 .... 75 E3
Bankhead Cres FK4 .... 57 E3
Bankhead Crossway N
EH11 .... 121 D2
Bankhead Crossway S
EH11 .... 121 E1
Bankhead Dr EH11 .... 121 D2
Bankhead Gr EH30 .... 68 B1
Bankhead Ind Est EH11 .... 121 E2
Bankhead Medway
EH11 .... 121 E1
Bankhead Pl EH11 .... 121 E1
Bankhead Rd
Fishcross FK10 .... 5 E2
Queensferry EH30 .... 89 F4
Bankhead St EH11 .... 121 E1
Bankhead Terr EH11 .... 121 D1
Bankhead Way EH11 .... 121 D1
Bankhill Ct FK1 .... 61 E3
Bankpark Brae EH33 .... 128 A4
Bankpark Cres EH33 .... 128 A4
Bankpark Gr EH33 .... 128 B4
Bankside FK2 .... 60 B4
Bankside Ct FK6 .... 36 C1
Bankside Ind Est FK2 .... 60 B4
Bankton Brae EH54 .... 173 F4
Bankton Ct
Livingston EH54 .... 174 A4
Tranent EH33 .... 128 B3
Bankton Dr EH54 .... 173 F4
Bankton Gdns EH54 .... 174 A4
Bankton Glade EH54 .... 174 A4
Bankton Gn EH54 .... 173 F4
Bankton Junc EH54 .... 128 B4
Bankton Pk E EH54 .... 148 A1
Bankton Pk W EH54 .... 148 A1
Bankton Prim Sch
EH54 .... 147 F1
Bankton Rd EH54 .... 173 F4
Bankton Sq EH54 .... 173 F4
Bankton Terr EH33 .... 128 A4
Bankton Way EH54 .... 173 F4
Bankton Wlk EH54 .... 173 F4
Bannerman Ave KY11 .... 47 E2
Bannerman St KY12 .... 29 D3
Bannoch Brae KY12 .... 29 E2
Bannock Br FK7 .... 8 B2
Bannockburn High Sch
FK7 .... 7 E2
Bannockburn Hospl FK7 .... 19 F4
Bannockburn Prim Sch
FK7 .... 7 F1
Bannockburn Rd
Cowie FK7 .... 20 B4
Stirling FK7 .... 7 E2
Bannockburn Station Rd
FK7 .... 8 A2
Bantaskin Prim Sch FK1 .... 59 F2
Bantaskin Dr FK1 .... 59 F2
Bantaskin Gdns FK1 .... 59 F2
Bantaskine St FK1 .... 59 F2
Banton Pl FK4 .... 58 A2
Baptie Pl EH51 .... 63 F3
Barassie Dr KY2 .... 17 D4
Barbauchlaw Ave EH48 .... 143 F3
Barbour Ave FK7 .... 7 E2
Barbour Gr KY12 .... 28 C3
Barclay Pl EH10 .... 232 B1
Barclay Rd KY3 .... 34 C2
Barclay St KY5 .... 13 D2
Barclay Terr EH10 .... 232 B1
Barclay Way EH54 .... 147 F4
Barham Rd KY11 .... 46 B1
Barkhill Rd EH49 .... 84 C3
Barkin Ct FK1 .... 60 A1
Barlaw Gdns EH48 .... 144 A3
Barleyhill FK4 .... 58 A3
Barleyknowe Cres
EH23 .... 183 E1
Barleyknowe Gdns
EH23 .... 183 E1
Barleyknowe La EH23 .... 183 E1
Barleyknowe Pl EH23 .... 183 E1
Barleyknowe Rd EH23 .... 183 E1
Barleyknowe St EH23 .... 183 E1
Barleyknowe Terr EH23 .... 183 E1
Barn Park Cres EH14 .... 152 C4
Barn Pk EH14 .... 152 C4
Barn Rd FK8 .... 7 D4
Barnbougle Ride EH30 .... 90 B4
Barnego Rd FK6 .... 36 B2
Barnes Gn EH54 .... 147 E4
Barnet Cres KY1 .... 17 D1
Barnhill Dr FK10 .... 4 B1
Barnhill Pl KY11 .... 48 B2

Barnhill Rd KY11 .... 48 B2
Barns Ct EH47 .... 170 C3
Barns Ness Terr EH42 .... 139 D4
Barns Pk KY11 .... 48 A1
Barnsdale Rd FK7 .... 7 D2
Barnshot Rd EH13 .... 153 D3
Barnton Ave EH4 .... 91 E2
Barnton Ave W EH4 .... 91 D2
Barnton Brae EH4 .... 91 D2
Barnton Ct EH4 .... 91 D2
Barnton Gdns EH4 .... 91 E2
Barnton Gr EH4 .... 91 D2
Barnton La FK1 .... 60 A2
Barnton Loan EH4 .... 91 E2
Barnton Park Ave EH4 .... 91 E2
Barnton Park Cres EH4 .... 91 E2
Barnton Park Dell EH4 .... 91 E2
Barnton Park Dr EH4 .... 91 E2
Barnton Park Gdns EH4 .... 91 E2
Barnton Park Gr EH4 .... 91 E2
Barnton Park Pl EH4 .... 91 E2
Barnton Park View EH4 .... 91 E2
Barnton Park Wood EH4 .... 91 D1
Barnton Pk FK8 .... 7 D4
Barntongate Ave EH4 .... 91 D1
Barntongate Dr EH4 .... 91 D1
Barntongate Terr EH4 .... 91 D1
Barnwell Rd FK9 .... 2 B2
Barons Hill Ave EH49 .... 85 D4
Barons Hill Ct EH49 .... 85 D4
Baronscourt Rd EH8 .... 94 B1
Baronscourt Terr EH8 .... 124 B4
Barony Ct EH51 .... 63 F3
Barony Pl EH3 .... 93 E1
Barony St EH3 .... 93 E1
Barony Terr EH12 .... 121 E4
Barr Cres KY11 .... 47 E1
Barra Pk FK5 .... 39 D2
Barracks Rdbt EH54 .... 146 C2
Barracks St FK32 .... 97 E2
Barrie Ct EH54 .... 148 B3
Barrie Pl
Dunfermline KY12 .... 28 C3
Grangemouth FK3 .... 61 E3
Barrie Rd FK5 .... 38 C2
Barrie St KY12 .... 28 C3
Barrie Terr EH48 .... 145 E3
Barton Rd KY11 .... 46 A1
Barton Terr EH47 .... 193 F3
Bass Rock View EH39 .... 55 D4
Bastion Wynd FK8 .... 7 D4
Bath Pl EH15 .... 95 D1
Bath Rd EH6 .... 94 A3
Bath St EH15 .... 125 D4
Bath Street La EH15 .... 125 D4
Bathfield EH6 .... 93 F3
Bathgate Acad EH48 .... 145 F3
Bathgate Rd
Blackburn EH47 .... 171 E4
East Whitburn EH47 .... 170 C4
Bathgate Sta EH48 .... 145 D3
Bathville Bsns Ctr EH48 .... 144 A3
Baton Rd ML7 .... 191 E2
Batterflats Gdns FK7 .... 6 C3
Battery Rd
Grangemouth FK3 .... 62 B4
North Queensferry KY11 .... 68 B3
Battock Rd FK2 .... 82 C4
Bavelaw Cres EH26 .... 203 E3
Bavelaw Gdns EH14 .... 151 E1
Bavelaw Rd EH14 .... 151 E1
Baxter Cres FK6 .... 36 B1
Baxter St FK7 .... 8 B2
Baxter's Pl EH1 .... 233 E4
Baxter's Wynd FK1 .... 60 A2
Bayne Gdns EH49 .... 84 A3
Bayne St FK8 .... 2 A1
Bayswell Pk EH42 .... 78 B2
Bayswell Rd EH42 .... 78 B2
Beach La Edinburgh EH15 .... 95 D1
Edinburgh EH15 .... 125 D4
Musselburgh EH21 .... 126 A4
Beach Rd Grangemouth FK9 .... 41 D1
North Berwick EH39 .... 54 A4
Beachmont Ct EH42 .... 78 C1
Beachmont Pl EH42 .... 78 C1
Beaconhurst Sch FK9 .... 2 B3
Bean Row FK1 .... 60 A2
Beancross Prim Sch FK3 .... 61 E3
Beancross Rd FK3 .... 61 D3
Beancross Rdbt FK3 .... 61 D3
Bearcroft Gdns FK3 .... 61 F4
Bearcroft Rd FK3 .... 62 B4
Bearford Pl EH41 .... 132 B4
Bearside Rd FK7 .... 7 D2
Beath High Sch KY4 .... 13 D2
Beath View KY11 .... 29 F2
Beath View Rd KY4 .... 13 D1
Beatlie Rd EH52 .... 88 A2
Beatlie Sch EH52 .... 88 A2
Beaton Ave FK7 .... 7 E1
Beatty Ave FK8 .... 2 A1
Beatty Cres KY1 .... 17 E4
Beatty Ct KY1 .... 17 E4
Beatty Pl KY12 .... 29 E3
Beauchamp Gr EH16 .... 155 D4
Beauchamp Rd EH16 .... 155 D4
Beauclerc St FK12 .... 5 D1
Beaufort Cres KY2 .... 16 B3
Beaufort Dr FK2 .... 39 D2
Beaufort Rd EH9 .... 123 D2
Beauly Ct Falkirk FK1 .... 60 B1
Grangemouth FK3 .... 61 E2
Beauly Dr EH54 .... 148 A2
Beauly Pl KY2 .... 16 C4
Beaumont Dr FK2 .... 39 D1
Beaverbank Pl EH7 .... 93 E2

Beaverhall Rd EH7 93 E2
Beck Cres KY12 29 E3
Beda Pl FK7 8 B3
Bedford Ct Alloa FK10 10 A3
Edinburgh 3 EH4 93 D1
Bedford Pl FK10 10 A3
Bedford St EH4 93 D1
Bedford Terr EH15 125 E4
Bedlormie Dr EH48 142 B1
Beech Ave Carrington EH23 206 C2
Dalgety Bay KY11 48 C3
Mid Calder EH53 148 A1
Plean FK7 20 B2
Beech Cres Denny FK6 36 B2
Larbert FK5 59 E4
Beech Gr Dunfermline KY11 46 B4
Livingston EH54 148 A3
Whitburn EH47 170 B3
Beech Gr Ave EH22 156 B1
Beech La FK9 2 A2
Beech Loan EH19 182 A3
Beech Pl Grangemouth FK3 61 E3
Livingston EH54 147 E2
Seafield EH47 146 A1
Beech Rd EH48 145 F3
Beech St EH42 78 A1
Beech Terr EH34 160 B3
Beech Way KY11 48 A3
Beechbank Cres EH53 148 C1
Beeches The
Dalgety Bay KY11 48 B2
Gullane EH31 52 A2
Newtongrange EH22 183 D4
Beechgrove Rd EH22 183 F3
Beechmount Cres EH12 122 A4
Beechmount Ct ML7 192 A1
Beechmount Pk EH12 122 A3
Beechwood Alloa FK10 5 E1
Crossford KY12 28 A1
Linlithgow EH49 85 D3
Beechwood Gdns EH47 145 E1
Beechwood Gr EH54 117 D1
Beechwood Mains EH12 122 A4
Beechwood Pk
Livingston EH54 146 C4
Newtongrange EH22 183 D3
Uphall Station EH54 117 D1
Beechwood Pl EH47 145 E1
Beechwood Rd
Blackburn EH47 145 E1
Haddington EH41 131 F4
Beechwood Terr EH6 94 A2
Beecraigs Ctry Pk EH49 85 D1
Beeslack High Sch EH26 204 A4
Begbie Pl EH54 147 D3
Begg Ave FK1 59 F2
Beldorney Pl KY12 29 E3
Belfield Ct EH21 126 A3
Belford Ave EH4 92 C1
Belford Gdns EH4 92 C1
Belford Pk EH4 122 C4
Belford Pl EH4 122 C4
Belford Rd EH4 122 C4
Belford Terr EH4 122 C4
Belfrange La EH3 232 C2
Belgrave Cres EH4 232 A4
Belgrave Crescent La
EH4 232 A4
Belgrave Gdns EH12 121 F4
Belgrave Mews 10 EH4 92 C1
Belgrave Pl EH4 92 C1
Belgrave Rd EH12 121 F3
Belhaven Hill (Boys Sch)
EH42 78 A1
Belhaven Hospl EH42 78 A1
Belhaven Pl EH10 123 D1
Belhaven Rd EH42 78 B1
Belhaven Terr EH10 123 D1
Bell Ct FK3 40 C1
Bell Pl EH3 93 D1
Bell Rd KY11 46 A1
Bell Sq EH54 173 E3
Bell Stane EH30 68 A1
Bell's Mill Terr EH52 87 F1
Bell's Mills EH4 122 C4
Bell's Wynd FK1 60 A2
Bellamond Cres EH47 170 C4
Belleknowes Ind Est KY11 47 D2
Bellenden Gdns EH16 124 B1
Bellerophon Dr EH26 203 F2
Bellevue Edinburgh EH7 93 E1
Maddiston FK2 82 C4
Bellevue Ave EH42 78 C1
Bellevue Cres EH3 93 E1
Bellevue Gdns EH7 93 E2
Bellevue Gr EH7 93 E1
Bellevue Pl EH7 93 E1
Bellevue Rd Alloa FK10 9 F3
Edinburgh EH7 93 E2
Bellevue St Edinburgh EH7 93 E1
Falkirk FK1 60 B2
Bellevue Terr EH7 93 E1
Bellfield Ave
Dalkeith EH22 156 C1
East Calder EH53 148 C1
Musselburgh EH21 126 A3
Bellfield Cres KY1 18 A4
Bellfield La EH15 125 D4
Bellfield Rd Bannockburn FK7 7 F1
Stirling FK8 7 D3
Bellfield Sq EH32 127 F4
Bellfield St EH15 125 D4
Bellfield Terr EH15 125 D4
Bellfield View EH19 182 B4
Bellhouse Rd KY3 49 D4
Bellman Way KY11 48 A3
Bellman's Rd EH26 203 F3
Bellona Terr EH47 193 F3
Bells Brae EH4 232 A3
Bells Burn Ave EH49 85 E4
Bellsdyke Hospl FK5 38 B3
Bellsdyke Rd Falkirk FK2 39 E3
Larbert FK5 38 B2
Bellsmains EH23 207 E3
Bellsmeadow Rd FK1 60 B2
Bellsquarry Prim Sch
EH54 173 E4
Bellsquarry South Rd
EH54 173 F3
Bellyeoman La KY12 29 E3
Bellyeoman Prim Sch
KY12 29 E3
Bellyeoman Rd KY12 29 E3
Bellyford Rd EH33 128 A1
Belmont Ave
Dennyloanhead FK4 57 E3
Edinburgh EH12 122 A4
Shieldhill FK1 81 F4
Belmont Cres EH12 122 A4
Belmont Dr ML7 192 A1
Belmont Gdns EH12 122 A4
Belmont Pk EH12 122 A4
Belmont Rd EH14 152 B3
Belmont St FK1 60 B2
Belmont Terr EH12 122 A4
Belmont View EH12 122 A4
Belstane Pk ML8 230 A2
Belstane Rd ML8 230 A2
Belsyde Ct EH49 84 B3
Belvedere Pk EH6 93 E3
Belvedere Rd EH48 144 C4
Belwood Cres EH26 180 A1
Belwood Rd EH26 179 F1
Ben Alder Pl KY2 16 C3
Ben Ledi Rd KY2 16 C3
Ben Lomond View KY12 27 D3
Ben Nevis Pl KY2 16 C3
Ben Sayers Pk EH39 54 C3
Benarty St KY2 16 C3
Bendachin Dr KY12 29 F3
Bendameer Rd KY3 33 E1
Benhar Prim Sch ML7 168 B3
Benhar Rd Harthill ML7 167 F1
Shotts ML7 192 A3
Benjamin Dr EH51 63 F3
Bennett Wood Terr EH52 87 F2
Bennie Mus EH48 145 D3
Bennochy Ave KY2 17 D3
Bennochy Ct KY2 17 D3
Bennochy Gdns KY2 17 D3
Bennochy Rd KY2 16 C3
Bentheads FK7 19 F4
Benview FK7 7 E1
Benview Terr FK10 5 F2
Beresford Ave EH5 93 E3
Beresford Gdns EH5 93 E3
Beresford Pl EH5 93 D3
Beresford Rise EH54 148 A1
Berkeley St FK7 7 D2
Bernard Shaw St KY12 28 C3
Bernard St EH6 94 A3
Bernard Terr EH8 233 E1
Berry St KY5 14 A4
Berryhill FK7 20 C4
Berryhill Cres FK3 61 F3
Berryhill Pl ML7 192 A1
Berrylaw Pl KY12 28 C2
Berrylaw Rd KY12 28 B2
Bertram Pl ML7 191 E3
Bertram St Harthill ML7 168 B3
Shotts ML7 191 F3
Bervie Dr EH54 173 F3
Berwick Pl Dysart KY1 18 A4
Kirkaldy KY1 17 E3
Bethesda Gr FK2 82 C3
Beulah EH21 126 C3
Bevan Dr FK12 5 E4
Bevan Pl KY11 46 C2
Bevan Rd EH22 183 E3
Bevan-lee Ct EH22 157 D2
Beveridge Ave EH22 183 F3
Beveridge Cl EH22 183 F3
Beveridge Rd KY1 17 D2
Beveridge Sq EH54 147 F1
Beveridge St KY11 29 E1
Bickerton Terr EH47 170 A3
Bickram Cres KY12 26 B4
Biggar Rd Edinburgh EH10 154 A2
Silverburn EH26 202 C3
Biggin Wa's KY1 17 F4
Bingham Ave EH15 124 C3
Bingham Broadway EH15 125 D3
Bingham Cres EH15 125 D3
Bingham Crossway EH15 124 C3
Bingham Dr EH15 125 D3
Bingham Medway EH15 124 C3
Bingham Pl EH15 124 C3
Bingham Way EH15 124 C3
Binn Ave KY3 33 F1
Binnie Pl FK2 39 F1
Binniehill Rd FK1 110 A2
Binning Rd KY11 47 D2
Binning Wood Rd EH42 75 F4
Binns The EH49 65 F1
Binny Pk EH52 116 C4
Birch Ave FK8 6 C3
Birch Cres EH20 180 C4
Birch Ct Edinburgh EH4 91 D1
Livingston EH54 147 E1
Birch Gr KY11 46 B4
Birchbank KY4 13 D1
Birchwood FK10 5 E1
Birk Hedges EH41 130 C3
Birkdale Dr EH52 116 C2
Birkdale Pk EH48 144 A3
Birkenshaw Way EH48 143 F3
Birkenside EH23 207 E3
Birkfield Loan ML8 230 B1
Birkfield Pl ML8 230 B1
Birkhill Clay Mine EH49 62 C1
Birkhill Cres EH51 63 F3
Birkhill Rd FK7 6 C3
Birkhill St EH51 63 F3
Birkhill Sta EH49 62 C2
Birnam Ct FK2 39 E1
Birnam Rd KY2 16 C4
Birnie Brae KY5 14 A4
Birnie St KY5 14 A4
Birniehill Ave EH48 144 C2
Birniehill Cres EH48 144 C2
Birniehill Rd EH48 144 C2
Birniehill Terr EH48 144 C2
Birniewell Rd FK1 110 A3
Birrell Dr KY11 29 E1
Birrell Street Wynd KY1 17 E3
Birrell's La KY1 17 F4
Birsley Rd EH33 128 B3
Bishops Pk EH53 148 B1
Black Craigs KY2 16 B4
Blackbarony Rd 1 EH16 124 A1
Blackburn Ave KY12 28 B3
Blackburn Dr KY4 13 D2
Blackburn Prim Sch EH47 145 E1
Blackburn Rd
Addiewell EH55 171 F1
Blackburn EH48 145 E2
Blackburnhall EH47 171 E3
Blackchapel Cl EH15 125 D2
Blackchapel Rd EH15 125 D2
Blackcot Ave EH22 183 E3
Blackcot Dr EH22 183 E3
Blackcot Pl EH22 183 E3
Blackcot Rd EH22 183 E3
Blacket Ave EH9 123 F3
Blacket Pl EH9 123 F3
Blackfaulds Ct EH47 193 F3
Blackfaulds Dr EH47 193 F3
Blackfaulds Pl EH47 193 F3
Blackford Ave EH9 123 E2
Blackford Bank EH9 123 E2
Blackford Gate EH9 123 E2
Blackford Glen Rd EH16 123 F1
Blackford Hill Gr EH9 123 E1
Blackford Hill Rise EH9 123 E1
Blackford Hill View EH9 123 E1
Blackford Rd EH9 123 E2
Blackfriars St EH1 233 E3
Blackhall Prim Sch EH4 92 A1
Blackhall St ML7 192 A2
Blackhill Rd EH48 142 C2
Blackie Rd EH6 94 A2
Blacklaw Prim Sch KY11 29 E1
Blacklaw Rd KY11 29 E1
Blackmill Cres FK2 39 D2
Blackmount Terr FK2 82 C3
Blackmuir Pl FK10 4 B2
Blackness Castle EH49 65 F3
Blackness Prim Sch EH49 65 E2
Blackness Rd EH49 85 D4
Blackridge Prim Sch EH48 142 B2
Blackston Rd FK1 112 A3
Blackthorn Ct EH4 91 D1
Blackwood Cres EH9 123 F3
Blackwood Gn KY11 46 C4
Blaeberry Gdns EH4 91 D1
Blaeberryhill Rd EH47 170 B3
Blaefaulds Cres FK6 57 E4
Blair Ave EH51 63 F3
Blair Dr Dunfermline KY12 29 D3
Kelty KY4 12 B4
Blair Pl KY2 16 B3
Blair St Edinburgh EH1 233 D3
Kelty KY4 12 B4
Blair Terr FK5 39 D2
Blair's Cotts FK2 61 E1
Blairdenon Cres FK1 59 F2
Blairdenon Dr FK10 5 D1
Blairdenon Rd FK12 4 C3
Blairforkie Dr FK9 1 C4
Blairhall Prim Sch KY12 26 A4
Blairlodge Ave FK2 82 B4
Blairmore Rd KY2 16 B4
Blairmuckhole
and Forrestdyke Rd
ML7 167 F4
Blairwood Wlk KY12 26 C4
Blake St KY11 29 E1
Blamey Cres KY4 13 D1
Blantyre Terr EH10 123 D2
Blawearie Rd EH33 128 B3
Bleachfield Edinburgh EH6 93 E2
Falkirk FK2 60 A3
Blenheim Ct Carluke ML8 230 A1
Penicuik EH26 204 A4
Blenheim Pl FK5 38 C3
Blindwell Brae EH41 133 F1
Blindwells FK12 4 C3
Blinkbonnie Terr FK1 110 A3
Blinkbonny Ave EH4 92 B1
Blinkbonny Cres EH4 92 B1
Blinkbonny Gdns EH4 92 B1
Blinkbonny Gr EH4 92 B1
Blinkbonny Gr W EH4 92 B1
Blinkbonny Rd Currie EH14 152 A2
Falkirk FK1 59 F2
Blinkbonny Terr EH4 92 B1
Blinny Ct ML7 192 A2
Bloom Ct EH54 147 D2
Bloom Pl EH54 147 D1
Bloom Rdbt EH54 147 E2
Bloomfield Pl EH48 145 D3
Blyth Rd EH52 117 E2
Blyth St KY1 17 F4
Bo'mains Ind Est EH51 63 F3
Bo'mains Rd EH51 63 F3
Bo'ness Hospl EH51 63 F4
Bo'ness & Kinneil Railway
EH51 63 E4
Bo'ness Public Sch (Prim)
EH51 63 F4
Bo'ness Rd
Grangemouth FK3, EH51 62 A3
Polmont FK2 61 F2
Queensferry EH30 67 F1
Bo'ness Sta EH51 64 A4
Boat Gn EH3 93 E2
Bog Rd Laurieston FK2 60 C2
Penicuik EH26 203 F3
Whitburn EH47 170 A3
Bog Rdbt FK2 60 C2
Bog Road Ind Est FK2 60 C2
Bog The EH51 64 A4
Bogend Rd Bannockburn FK7 19 F4
Larbert FK2 38 A4
Torwood FK5 37 F4
Boghall Dr EH48 145 F3
Boghall Prim Sch EH48 145 F3
Boghall Rdbt EH48 145 F3
Boghead Cres EH48 144 C3
Bogies Wynd KY1 17 E3
Boglily Rd KY2 16 C2
Bogpark Rd EH21 126 A3
Bogsmill Rd EH14 122 A1
Bogwood Ct EH22 183 E4
Bogwood Dr KY12 28 A1
Bogwood Rd EH22 183 F3
Bohun Ct FK7 7 E2
Bolam Dr KY3 33 F1
Bolan Sq KY5 14 A4
Bomar Ave EH51 64 A4
Bon Accord Cres ML7 191 F3
Bonaly Ave EH13 153 D3
Bonaly Brae EH13 153 D3
Bonaly Cres EH13 153 D3
Bonaly Ctry Pk EH13 152 C1
Bonaly Dr EH13 153 D3
Bonaly Gdns EH13 153 D3
Bonaly Gr EH13 153 D3
Bonaly Prim Sch EH13 153 D3
Bonaly Prim Sch (Annexe)
EH13 153 D3
Bonaly Rd EH13 153 D3
Bonaly Rise EH13 153 D3
Bonaly Steading EH13 153 D3
Bonaly Terr EH13 153 D3
Bonaly Wester EH13 153 D3
Bonar Pl EH6 93 E3
Bonhard Ct EH51 64 A3
Bonnar St KY12 29 D2
Bonnington EH27 150 A4
Bonnington Ave EH6 93 E3
Bonnington Gr EH6 93 E3
Bonnington Ind Est EH6 93 F2
Bonnington Prim Sch EH6 93 F2
Bonnington Rd
Edinburgh EH6 93 F2
Wilkieston EH27 150 A3
Bonnington Road La EH6 93 F2
Bonnington Terr EH6 93 E3
Bonnybank Ct EH23 207 E4
Bonnybank Rd EH23 207 E4
Bonnybridge Hospl FK4 58 B3
Bonnybridge Prim Sch
FK4 58 A3
Bonnybridge Rd FK4 57 F3
Bonnyfield Rd FK4 57 F3
Bonnyhaugh EH6 93 E2
Bonnyhaugh La EH6 93 E2
Bonnyhill Rd Falkirk FK1 59 D2
High Bonnybridge FK4 58 B2
Bonnyrigg Prim Sch EH19 182 B3
Bonnyrigg Rd EH22 156 C1
Bonnyside Rd FK4 58 A3
Bonnyton Pl KY11 29 E2
Bonnytoun Ave EH49 85 E4
Bonnytoun Terr EH49 85 E4
Bonnyview Gdns FK4 58 A3
Bonnywood Ave FK4 58 A4
Booth Ave KY11 46 B3
Booth Pl FK1 60 A2
Boothacre La EH6 94 B2
Boreland Pk KY11 47 E2
Boreland Rd Dysart KY1 18 A4
Inverkeithing KY11 47 E2
Borestone Cres FK7 7 D2
Borestone Ct FK7 7 D1
Borestone Pl FK7 7 D1
Borestone Prim Sch FK7 7 D1
Boroughdales EH42 78 B1
Boroughloch EH8 233 E1
Boroughloch Sq EH8 233 E1
Boroughmuir High Sch
EH10 123 D1
Boroughmuir Sec Sch (Annexe)
EH11 122 C3
Borrowlea Rd FK7 7 E4
Borrowmeadow Rd FK7 7 F4
Borrowstoun Cres EH51 63 F3
Borrowstoun Pl EH51 63 F3
Borrowstoun Rd EH51 64 A3
Borthwick Castle Pl EH23 207 F2
Borthwick Castle Rd
EH23 207 F1
Borthwick Castle Terr
EH23 207 F2
Borthwick Pl EH12 122 C4
Borthwick Prim Sch EH23 208 A2
Boswall Ave EH5 92 C3
Boswall Cres EH5 92 C3
Boswall Dr EH5 93 D3
Boswall Gdns EH5 92 C3
Boswall Gn EH5 93 D3
Boswall Gr EH5 92 C3
Boswall Loan EH5 92 C3
Boswall Parkway EH5 92 C3
Boswall Pl EH5 92 C3
Boswall Quadrant EH5 92 C3
Boswall Rd EH5 93 D3
Boswall Sq EH5 92 C3
Boswall Terr EH5 92 C3
Boswell Dr Kinghorn KY3 35 D2
Oakley KY12 26 C3
Boswell Rd KY5 14 A4
Bothkennar Prim Sch FK2 39 F2
Bothkennar Rd FK2 39 F2
Bothwell Gdns KY11 29 D1
Bothwell St
Dunfermline KY11 29 D1
Edinburgh EH7 94 A1
Boulevard Rdbt EH54 147 E1
Boundary Rd E EH14 151 F4
Boundary Rd N EH14 151 F4
Boundary St EH51 64 A4
Bouprie Rise KY11 48 A2
Bourtree Gr KY12 26 B4
Bow Butts KY12 29 D1
Bow St FK8 7 D4
Bowhill Terr EH5 93 D3
Bowhouse Dr KY1 35 D4
Bowhouse Gdns FK10 10 A3
Bowhouse Prim Sch FK3 61 F3
Bowhouse Rd Alloa FK10 10 A3
Grangemouth FK3 61 F3
Bowhouse Sq FK3 61 E3
Bowhousebog or Liquo
ML7 191 D1
Bowhousebog Rd ML7 191 D1
Bowling Green Rd
Kirkliston EH29 89 D1
Whitburn EH47 170 A3
Bowling Green St KY4 13 E2
Bowling Green The EH6 93 F3
Bowmont Pl EH8 233 E1
Bowmont Terr EH42 78 C1
Bowmore Wlk ML7 192 A2
Bowyett EH48 113 F3
Boyd Pl KY5 14 A4
Boyd St Falkirk FK2 60 A3
Laurieston FK2 61 D2
Boyd's Entry EH1 233 E3
Boyd-Orr Dr EH26 203 F4
Brackenlees Rd FK2 40 A3
Brackensbrae EH52 117 D3
Bradbury St FK2 39 D1
Brae Heads Loan EH40 103 E3
Brae Pk EH4 91 D2
Brae Rd EH51 62 B3
Brae The Bannockburn FK7 7 E1
Cambusbarron FK7 6 B3
Penicuik EH26 180 B1
Braefoot Gr KY11 48 A1
Braefoot Rd EH51 64 A3
Braefoot Terr 2 EH16 124 A1
Braehead Alloa FK10 4 B1
Alva FK12 5 D4
Bo'ness EH51 63 F4
Braehead Ave
Edinburgh EH4 91 D2
Linlithgow EH49 84 C3
Tullibody FK10 4 B1
Braehead Bank EH4 91 D2
Braehead Cres EH4 91 D2
Braehead Dr Edinburgh EH4 91 D2
Linlithgow EH49 84 C3
Braehead Gr Bo'ness EH51 63 F4
Edinburgh EH4 91 D2
Braehead Loan EH4 91 D2
Braehead Pk Edinburgh EH4 91 D2
Linlithgow EH49 84 C3
Braehead Pl EH49 84 C3
Braehead Prim Sch FK7 7 E2
Braehead Rd
Edinburgh EH4 91 D2
Linlithgow EH49 84 C3
Stirling FK7 7 E2
Braehead Rdbt EH54 147 E2
Braehead Row EH4 91 D2
Braehead Terr EH49 84 C3
Braehead View EH4 91 D2
Braekirk Ave EH27 149 E1
Braemar Cres
Carluke ML8 230 A2
Falkirk FK2 60 B3
Braemar Dr FK2 60 B3
Braemar Gdns
Brightons FK2 82 B4
Denny FK6 36 B2
Braemar Pl FK5 39 D2
Braemount KY4 13 D1
Braepark Rd EH4 91 D2
Braes The Lochgelly KY5 14 A4
Tullibody FK10 4 B2
Braes View Denny FK6 57 E4
Shieldhill FK1 81 F4
Braeside Alloa FK10 5 E1
Shieldhill FK1 81 E3
Braeside Cres EH47 193 E3
Braeside Gdns EH53 148 A1
Braeside Pk EH53 148 A2
Braeside Pl Laurieston FK2 61 D2
Redding FK2 61 D1
Reddingmuirhead FK2 82 A4
Braeside Rd
Gorebridge EH37 207 E4
Loanhead EH20 181 E4
Braeside Rd N EH23 207 E4
Braeside Rd S EH23 207 E4

Braeview
East Linton EH40 .... 103 E4
Laurieston KY2 .... 60 C2
Stenhousemuir FK5 .... 38 B1
Braewell Gdns EH49 .... 84 B4
Braid Ave EH10 .... 123 D1
Braid Cres EH10 .... 123 D1
Braid Farm Rd EH10 .... 123 D1
Braid Gn EH54 .... 147 E4
Braid Hills App EH10 .... 154 A4
Braid Hills Ave EH10 .... 123 D1
Braid Hills Cres EH10 .... 154 A4
Braid Hills Dr EH16 .... 154 B4
Braid Hills Rd EH10 .... 154 A4
Braid Mount EH10 .... 154 A4
Braid Mount Crest EH10 .... 154 A4
Braid Mount Rise EH10 .... 154 A4
Braid Mount View EH10 .... 154 A4
Braidburn Cres EH10 .... 123 D1
Braidburn Terr EH10 .... 123 D1
Braidlaw Pk EH26 .... 203 E3
Braigh Gdns KY12 .... 28 B3
Bramble Dr EH4 .... 91 D1
Bramdean Gr EH10 .... 154 A4
Bramdean Pl EH10 .... 154 A4
Bramdean Rise EH10 .... 154 A4
Bramdean View EH10 .... 154 A4
Brand Dr EH15 .... 125 D4
Brand Gdns EH15 .... 125 C4
Brandfield St EH3 .... 232 A1
Brandon St EH3 .... 93 E1
Brandon Terr EH3 .... 93 E2
Brands Row KY4 .... 30 C4
Brandy Riggs KY12 .... 27 E1
Brandy Wells KY12 .... 27 E1
Brandyhill FK10 .... 5 F2
Brankholm Brae KY11 .... 46 B2
Brankholm Cres KY11 .... 46 B3
Brankholm La KY11 .... 46 B1
Branning Ct KY1 .... 17 E3
Branshill Rd FK10 .... 10 A4
Branshill Rd FK10 .... 10 A4
Branxton Wynd KY1 .... 35 D4
Bravo St EH51 .... 62 C3
Bread St EH3 .... 232 A2
Bread Street La EH3 .... 232 B2
Breadalbane Pl FK2 .... 61 F1
Breadalbane St EH6 .... 93 F2
Breakers Way KY11 .... 47 F1
Brechin Dr FK2 .... 62 A1
Breck Terr EH26 .... 204 A4
Breich Sta EH55 .... 194 B3
Breich Terr EH55 .... 194 C3
Brentham Cres FK8 .... 7 D3
Brentham Cres FK8 .... 7 D3
Breslin Terr ML7 .... 168 B3
Breton Ct FK1 .... 60 B2
Brewary Cl EH30 .... 68 A1
Brewery La EH42 .... 78 A1
Brewery Pk EH41 .... 132 A4
Brewlands Ave EH51 .... 63 E3
Brewster Pl FK6 .... 36 B1
Brewster Sq EH54 .... 173 E3
Briar Brae FK2 .... 82 B4
Briar Cotts EH47 .... 171 E1
Briar Pl KY11 .... 29 E2
Briarbank EH54 .... 147 E3
Briarbank Terr EH11 .... 122 C2
Briarcliff St KY1 .... 17 F3
Briardene E 61 D2
Briarhill Ave KY11 .... 48 A3
Briars Rd KY12 .... 4 C1
Brickfield EH15 .... 95 D1
Brickworks Rd EH33 .... 128 A4
Bridge Cres FK6 .... 36 B1
Bridge End
East Whitburn EH47 .... 170 B4
Edinburgh EH16 .... 124 A2
Shotts ML7 .... 191 E3
Bridge End Cotts EH27 .... 150 B3
Bridge of Allan Prim Sch
FK9 .... 2 A3
Bridge of Allan Prim Sch FK9 ..... 1 C4
Bridge Pl Broxburn EH52 ..... 117 E3
Denny FK6 .... 36 B1
Edinburgh **4** EH3 .... 93 D1
Shotts ML7 .... 192 A2
Bridge Rd Balerno EH14 ...... 151 E1
Edinburgh EH13 .... 153 D3
Bridge St Bonnybridge FK4 .... 58 A3
Cowdenbeath KY4 .... 13 E2
Dunfermline KY12 .... 28 C2
East Linton EH40 .... 103 F4
Edinburgh EH15 .... 95 D1
Fauldhouse EH47 .... 193 F3
Haddington EH41 .... 132 B4
Kincardine FK10 .... 23 E2
Kirkcaldy KY1 .... 17 D1
Musselburgh EH21 .... 126 B3
Newbridge EH28 .... 119 D3
Penicuik EH26 .... 203 F2
Tranent EH33 .... 128 B3
Bridge Street La EH15 .... 95 D1
Bridge Terr FK10 .... 10 A3
Bridge View KY11 .... 68 B3
Bridgecastle Cotts EH48 ... 142 C3
Bridgecastle Rd EH48 .... 143 F4
Bridgehaugh Rd FK9 .... 2 A1
Bridgehill EH47 .... 112 A3
Bridgend Ct EH48 .... 144 C3
Bridgend Pk EH48 .... 144 C3
Bridgend Pl EH47 .... 170 B4
Bridgend Prim Sch EH49 .... 86 B2
Bridgend Rd FK1 .... 112 A3
Bridgeness Cres EH51 .... 64 B4

Bridgeness La EH51 .... 64 B4
Bridgeness Rd EH51 .... 64 B4
Bridges The KY11 .... 48 A1
Bridgeside Ave EH47 .... 170 A3
Bridgeton Cotts EH48 .... 112 C1
Brierbush Cres EH33 .... 129 E3
Brierbush Rd EH33 .... 129 E3
Briery Bank EH41 .... 132 B4
Briery Bauks EH8 .... 233 E2
Brig-O-Doon Gr FK7 .... 20 C4
Bright's Cres EH9 .... 123 F2
Brighton Pl EH15 .... 125 D4
Brighton St EH1 .... 233 D2
Brisbane St EH54 .... 148 A3
Bristo Pl EH1 .... 233 D2
Bristo Port EH1 .... 233 D2
Bristo Sq EH8 .... 233 D2
Britwell Cres EH7 .... 94 B1
Brixwold Bank EH19 .... 182 B3
Brixwold Dr EH19 .... 182 B3
Brixwold Neuk EH19 .... 182 B3
Brixwold Pk EH19 .... 182 B3
Brixwold Rise EH19 .... 182 B3
Brixwold View EH19 .... 182 B3
Broad Alloa FK10 .... 10 A3
Cowdenbeath KY4 .... 13 E1
Denny FK6 .... 36 C1
Stirling FK8 .... 7 D4
Broad Wynd Edinburgh EH6 .... 94 A1
Kirkcaldy KY1 .... 17 E3
Broadgait EH31 .... 52 A2
Broadgait Ct EH31 .... 52 A2
Broadgait Gn EH31 .... 52 A2
Broadhurst Rd EH22 .... 183 E4
Broadleys Rd EH7 .... 7 E4
Broadleys Rdbt FK7 .... 7 E3
Brock Pl FK7 .... 7 D1
Brock St KY11 .... 68 A3
Brocks Way EH52 .... 118 A4
Brockville Pk (Falkirk FC)
FK1 .... 60 A3
Brockwood Ave EH26 .... 203 E3
Brodick Pl FK1 .... 59 E2
Brodick Rd KY2 .... 16 C4
Brodie Ave EH39 .... 54 B3
Brodie St FK2 .... 60 A4
Broich The FK12 .... 4 C4
Bronte Pl FK5 .... 39 D2
Brook St Alva FK12 .... 5 D3
Menstrie FK11 .... 3 F3
Brookbank Terr ML8 .... 230 A1
Brooke La FK3 .... 61 E3
Brooke St FK3 .... 61 E3
Brookfield Pl FK12 .... 5 D3
Brookfield Terr EH25 .... 180 C3
Brookside 61 F1
Broom Ct FK7 .... 7 E2
Broom Gr KY11 .... 46 C4
Broom Pk E FK11 .... 4 A3
Broom Pk W FK11 .... 4 A3
Broom Pl KY2 .... 16 B4
Broom Rd Kircaldy KY2 .... 16 B4
Stirling FK7 .... 7 E2
Broom Wlk EH54 .... 148 A2
Broom Wynd ML7 .... 191 F3
Broomage Ave FK5 .... 38 A2
Broomage Cres FK5 .... 38 A2
Broomage Dr FK5 .... 38 A2
Broomage Pk FK5 .... 38 B1
Broombank Terr EH12 .... 121 E2
Broomburn Gr EH12 .... 121 F2
Broomfield Cres EH12 .... 121 F2
Broomfield Dr KY12 .... 29 D3
Broomfield Rd KY4 .... 13 E3
Broomfield Terr EH12 .... 121 F3
Broomhall Ave EH12 .... 121 E3
Broomhall Bank EH12 .... 121 E3
Broomhall Cres EH12 .... 121 E3
Broomhall Dr EH12 .... 121 E3
Broomhall Gdns EH12 .... 121 E3
Broomhall Loan EH12 .... 121 E3
Broomhall Pk EH12 .... 121 E3
Broomhall Pl EH12 .... 121 E3
Broomhall Rd EH12 .... 121 E3
Broomhall Terr EH12 .... 121 E3
Broomhead Dr KY12 .... 28 C3
Broomhead Pk KY12 .... 28 C3
Broomhill KY3 .... 50 C4
Broomhill Ave
Burntisland KY3 .... 33 F1
Larbert FK5 .... 38 A1
Penicuik EH26 .... 203 F2
Broomhill Dr EH22 .... 156 C1
Broomhill Rd EH22 .... 156 C1
Broomhill Pl Denny FK6 .... 36 B2
Stirling FK7 .... 6 C3
Broomhill St ML7 .... 168 B3
Broomhouse Ave EH11 .... 121 E2
Broomhouse Bank EH11 ...... 121 F2
Broomhouse Cres EH11 .... 121 F2
Broomhouse Ct EH11 .... 121 F2
Broomhouse Dr EH11 .... 121 E2
Broomhouse Gdns E EH11 .... 121 F2
Broomhouse Gdns W EH11 .. 121 E2
Broomhouse Gr EH11 .... 121 F2
Broomhouse Loan EH11 ...... 121 F2
Broomhouse Medway
EH11 .... 121 F2
Broomhouse Mkt EH11 .... 121 F2
Broomhouse Path EH11 ...... 121 F2
Broomhouse Pk EH11 .... 121 F2
Broomhouse Pl N EH11 .... 121 F2
Broomhouse Pl S EH11 .... 121 F2
Broomhouse Prim Sch
EH11 .... 121 F2

Broomhouse Rd EH11 .... 121 E2
Broomhouse Row EH11 .... 121 F2
Broomhouse Sq EH11 .... 121 F2
Broomhouse St N EH11 .... 121 F1
Broomhouse St S EH11 .... 121 F1
Broomhouse Terr EH11 .... 121 F2
Broomhouse Way EH11 .... 121 F2
Broomhouse Wlk EH11 .... 121 F2
Broomhouse Wynd EH11 ..... 121 F2
Broomieknowe
Bonnyrigg and
Lasswade EH18 .... 182 A4
Dunfermline KY11 .... 29 E2
Tullibody FK10 .... 4 B2
Broomieknowe Gdns
EH19 .... 182 A4
Broomieknowe Pk EH19 ...... 182 A4
Broomknowe Dr FK10 .... 23 E3
Broomlea EH41 .... 121 E3
Broompark Gdns
Denny FK6 .... 36 C1
East Calder EH53 .... 148 C2
Broompark Rd
East Calder EH53 .... 148 C2
Edinburgh EH12 .... 121 F3
Broompark View EH53 .... 148 C2
Broomridge Rd FK7 .... 7 E2
Broomside KY2 .... 16 B4
Broomside Pl FK5 .... 38 B1
Broomside Rd EH14 .... 58 A2
Broomside Terr EH12 .... 121 F2
Broomyknowe EH14 .... 153 D4
Broomyknowe Dr EH54 .... 146 C3
Brora Pl KY12 .... 28 B1
Brosdale Ct FK7 .... 60 A1
Brougham Pl EH3 .... 232 C1
Brougham St EH3 .... 232 B1
Broughton High Sch EH4 .... 92 C1
Broughton Market EH3 .... 93 E1
Broughton Pl EH1 .... 93 E1
Broughton Place EH1 .... 93 E1
Broughton Prim Sch EH7 ..... 93 E2
Broughton Rd EH7 .... 93 E2
Broughton St EH1 .... 93 E1
Broughton Street La EH1 ...... 93 E1
Brown Ave Alloa FK10 .... 4 C1
Stirling FK9 .... 2 A1
Brown St Armadale EH48 ..... 143 F2
Edinburgh EH8 .... 233 E2
Falkirk FK1 .... 59 E3
Haddington EH41 .... 132 A4
Shotts ML7 .... 192 A2
Whitburn EH47 .... 170 A3
Brown's Cl EH8 .... 233 F3
Brown's Pl
East Linton EH40 .... 103 E4
Edinburgh EH1 .... 232 C2
Brownrigg Farm Cotts
EH39 .... 74 B3
Broxburn Acad EH52 .... 117 E3
Broxburn Prim Sch EH52 ..... 117 E3
Bruart Ave FK5 .... 38 C2
Bruce Cres Falkirk FK2 .... 39 D2
Plean FK7 .... 20 B2
Bruce Dr Fallin FK7 .... 8 B3
Stenhousemuir FK5 .... 38 C2
Bruce Gdns Brighton FK2 .... 82 B4
Dalkeith EH22 .... 157 D1
Bruce Gr EH34 .... 160 C3
Bruce Pl FK3 .... 61 F4
Bruce Rd Bathgate EH48 ..... 145 E3
Grangemouth EH51 .... 62 C3
Bruce St Bannockburn KY3 .... 10 B4
Bannockburn FK7 .... 7 F1
Clackmannan KY3 .... 11 D2
Dunfermline KY12 .... 28 C2
Edinburgh KY12 .... 123 D1
Falkirk FK2 .... 60 B3
Kinghorn KY3 .... 35 D2
Plean FK7 .... 20 B2
Stirling FK8 .... 2 A1
Bruce Terr Cambusbarron FK7 . 6 B3
Kinghorn KY3 .... 35 D2
Bruce View FK7 .... 7 D1
Brucefield Ave KY11 .... 29 D1
Brucefield Cres FK10 .... 11 D2
Brucefield Dr EH47 .... 170 A3
Brucefield Feus KY11 .... 29 E2
Brucefield Ind Est EH54 .... 173 E3
Brucefield Pk E EH54 .... 173 E3
Brucefield Pk N EH54 .... 173 E3
Brucefield Pk W EH54 .... 173 E3
Brucefield Terr KY4 .... 13 F3
Brucehaven Cres KY11 .... 45 F2
Brucehaven Rd KY11 .... 45 E2
Brunstane Bank EH15 .... 125 E4
Brunstane Cres EH15 .... 125 E3
Brunstane Dr EH15 .... 125 E3
Brunstane Gardens Mews
EH15 .... 125 E4
Brunstane Gdns
Edinburgh EH15 .... 125 E4
Penicuik EH26 .... 203 E3
Brunstane Prim Sch EH15 .... 125 E3
Brunstane Rd EH15 .... 125 E4
Brunstane Rd N EH15 .... 125 E4
Brunstane Rd S EH15 .... 125 E3
Brunswick Rd EH7 .... 93 F1
Brunswick St EH7 .... 93 F1
Brunswick Street La EH7 .... 93 F1
Brunswick Terr EH7 .... 93 F1
Brunt Gr EH42 .... 106 B4
Brunt La EH42 .... 78 B1
Brunt Pl EH42 .... 106 C4
Brunton Pl **1** EH7 .... 93 F1
Brunton Terr EH7 .... 93 F1
Brunton's Cl EH22 .... 157 D2
Bruntsfield Ave EH10 .... 123 D3

Bruntsfield Cres EH10 .... 123 D3
Bruntsfield Gdns EH10 .... 123 D3
Bruntsfield Pl EH10 .... 232 B1
Bruntsfield Prim Sch
EH10 .... 123 D3
Bruntsfield Terr EH10 .... 123 D3
Bryans Ave EH22 .... 183 D3
Bryans Prim Sch EH22 .... 183 F4
Bryans Rd EH22 .... 183 D3
Bryce Ave Edinburgh EH7 ...... 94 C1
Falkirk FK2 .... 39 D1
Bryce Cres EH14 .... 152 A3
Bryce Gdns EH14 .... 152 A3
Bryce Gr EH7 .... 94 C1
Bryce Pl EH14 .... 152 A3
Bryce Rd EH14 .... 152 A3
Bryony The FK10 .... 4 A1
Bryson Rd EH11 .... 122 C3
Bryson St FK2 .... 60 A3
Bryson Street Ind Est FK2 .... 60 A3
Buccleuch Ct EH22 .... 156 C2
Buccleuch Pl EH8 .... 233 D1
Buccleuch St
Dalkeith EH22 .... 157 D2
Edinburgh EH8 .... 233 E1
Buccleuch Terr EH8 .... 233 D1
Buchan La EH52 .... 117 F3
Buchan Pl FK3 .... 61 E3
Buchan Rd Bathgate EH48 .... 144 C4
Broxburn EH52 .... 117 E3
Grangemouth EH51 .... 62 B3
Buchanan Cres EH48 .... 147 D3
Buchanan Ct Bo'ness EH51 ..... 63 F3
Falkirk FK2 .... 60 A4
Kirkcaldy KY1 .... 17 D1
Buchanan Dr FK9 .... 2 A2
Buchanan St
Dunfermline KY12 .... 29 D2
Edinburgh EH6 .... 93 F2
Buckie Rd EH22 .... 183 F3
Buckingham Terr EH4 .... 232 A4
Buckstane Pk EH10 .... 154 A4
Buckstone Ave EH10 .... 154 A3
Buckstone Bank EH10 .... 154 A4
Buckstone Circ EH10 .... 154 B3
Buckstone Cres EH10 .... 154 A4
Buckstone Crook EH10 .... 154 B3
Buckstone Ct EH10 .... 154 A3
Buckstone Dell EH10 .... 154 A4
Buckstone Dr EH10 .... 154 A4
Buckstone Gate EH10 .... 154 B3
Buckstone Gdns EH10 .... 154 A3
Buckstone Gn EH10 .... 154 A3
Buckstone Gr EH10 .... 154 A3
Buckstone Hill EH10 .... 154 B4
Buckstone Howe EH10 .... 154 B3
Buckstone Lea EH10 .... 154 B3
Buckstone Loan EH10 .... 154 A3
Buckstone Loan E EH10 .... 154 B3
Buckstone Neuk EH10 .... 154 B4
Buckstone Pl EH10 .... 154 A3
Buckstone Prim Sch
EH10 .... 154 B3
Buckstone Rd EH10 .... 154 A3
Buckstone Rise EH10 .... 154 B3
Buckstone Row EH10 .... 154 B4
Buckstone Shaw EH10 .... 154 B3
Buckstone Terr EH10 .... 154 A3
Buckstone View EH10 .... 154 A4
Buckstone Way EH10 .... 154 A4
Buckstone Wood EH10 .... 154 A4
Buckstone Wynd EH10 .... 154 B3
Buffies Brae KY12 .... 28 C2
Bughtknowes Dr EH48 .... 145 E4
Bughtlin Dr EH12 .... 91 D1
Bughtlin Gdns EH12 .... 121 D4
Bughtlin Gn EH12 .... 91 D1
Bughtlin Loan EH12 .... 121 D4
Bughtlin Mkt EH12 .... 121 D4
Bughtlin Pk EH12 .... 121 D4
Bughtlin Pl EH12 .... 91 D1
Builyeon Rd EH30 .... 89 D4
Buller St KY5 .... 14 A4
Bullet Loan EH41 .... 132 B4
Bulloch Cres FK6 .... 36 B1
Bungalows The FK5 .... 38 A1
Buntine Cres FK7 .... 7 D2
Burdiehouse Ave EH17 .... 155 D2
Burdiehouse Cres EH17 .... 155 D2
Burdiehouse Crossway
EH17 .... 155 D2
Burdiehouse Dr EH17 .... 155 D2
Burdiehouse Loan EH17 ...... 155 D2
Burdiehouse Medway
EH17 .... 155 D2
Burdiehouse Pl EH17 .... 155 D2
Burdiehouse Prim Sch
EH17 .... 155 D2
Burdiehouse Rd EH17 .... 155 D2
Burdiehouse Sq EH17 .... 155 D2
Burdiehouse St EH17 .... 155 D2
Burdiehouse Terr EH17 .... 155 D2
Burgess Hill EH49 .... 85 D3
Burgess Rd EH30 .... 89 E4
Burgess St EH6 .... 94 A3
Burgess Terr EH9 .... 124 A2
Burgh Mews FK10 .... 10 A3
Burgh Rd KY4 .... 13 E2
Burghlee Cres EH20 .... 181 D4
Burghlee Terr EH20 .... 181 E4
Burghmuir Ct EH49 .... 85 E4
Burghmuir Ind Est FK8 .... 7 D2
Burghmuir Rd FK7 .... 7 D3
Burghtoft EH17 .... 155 F3
Burleigh Cres KY11 .... 47 E2

Burleigh Way FK10 .... 10 B3
Burlington St EH6 .... 93 F3
Burn Dr FK7 .... 7 E2
Burnbank Carnock KY12 .... 27 E4
Livingston EH54 .... 147 E3
Loanhead EH20 .... 181 D4
Burnbank Rd Falkirk FK2 .... 60 A4
Grangemouth FK3 .... 61 E3
Burnbrae Alloa FK10 .... 10 B4
Edinburgh EH12 .... 121 D4
Fauldhouse EH47 .... 193 F3
Burnbrae Gdns Alva FK12 ...... 5 D4
Falkirk FK1 .... 60 A3
Burnbrae Pk FK10 .... 23 F2
Burnbrae Rd Falkirk FK1 .... 60 A3
Harthill ML7 .... 169 D3
Shotts ML7 .... 191 F2
Stoneyburn EH47 .... 171 D1
Burnbrae Terr EH47 .... 170 B3
Burndene Dr EH20 .... 155 D1
Burnee FK10 .... 5 F2
Burney Pl KY11 .... 46 C2
Burnfield EH54 .... 147 D1
Burnfield Pl FK2 .... 60 B4
Burnfoot Ct KY5 .... 61 E3
Burnfoot La 1 FK1 .... 60 A2
Burngrange Cotts EH55 .... 172 B1
Burngrange Ct EH55 .... 172 B1
Burngrange Gdns EH55 .... 172 A1
Burnhead Cres EH16 .... 155 D3
Burnhead Gr EH16 .... 155 D3
Burnhead La FK1 .... 60 B2
Burnhead Loan EH16 .... 155 D3
Burnhead Path E EH16 .... 155 D3
Burnhead Path W EH16 .... 155 D3
Burnhead Rd KY5 .... 38 B2
Burnhouse Dr
Dechmont EH52 .... 116 B1
Whitburn EH47 .... 169 F3
Burnhouse Ind Est EH47 .... 169 F3
Burnhouse Rd EH52 .... 116 B2
Burnhouse Sch EH47 .... 170 A3
Burnlea Dr EH47 .... 171 D1
Burnlea Pl EH47 .... 171 D1
Burns Ave Armadale EH48 .... 143 F3
Grangemouth FK3 .... 61 E3
Burns Cres Harthill ML7 .... 168 C3
Laurieston FK2 .... 60 C2
Whitburn EH47 .... 170 A3
Burns Ct EH54 .... 148 B3
Burns Pl ML7 .... 191 D3
Burns St Dunfermline KY12 ... 28 C3
Edinburgh EH6 .... 94 A2
High Valleyfield KY12 .... 26 A1
Stirling FK9 .... 2 A1
Burns Terr Bathgate EH48 ... 145 E3
Cowie FK7 .... 20 B4
Burnside Dechmont EH52 .... 116 A1
Edinburgh EH12 .... 121 D4
Haddington EH41 .... 131 F4
Prestonpans EH32 .... 96 C1
Burnside Ave
Armadale EH48 .... 143 E3
Easthouses EH22 .... 183 E4
Kinghorn KY3 .... 34 C2
Polbeth EH55 .... 172 C3
Burnside Bsns Ctr KY11 .... 47 E2
Burnside Cres
Clackmannan FK10 .... 11 D3
Easthouses EH22 .... 183 E4
Fauldhouse EH47 .... 193 F3
Plean FK7 .... 20 B2
Rosyth KY11 .... 47 E3
Shotts ML7 .... 191 E3
Burnside Ct EH41 .... 134 B1
Burnside Gdns EH49 .... 83 F3
Burnside La EH55 .... 172 C3
Burnside Pk EH14 .... 151 E1
Burnside Pl Falkirk FK2 .... 39 D2
Rosyth KY11 .... 47 D2
Burnside Rd
Bathgate EH48 .... 144 C4
Gorebridge EH23 .... 183 E1
Menstrie FK11 .... 3 F3
Polbeth EH55 .... 172 C3
Uphall EH52 .... 117 D2
Burnside St Alloa FK10 .... 5 E4
Rosyth KY11 .... 47 D3
Stirling FK7 .... 7 E3
Burnside Terr
Cowdenbeath KY4 .... 13 D3
East Calder EH53 .... 148 C3
Falkirk FK1 .... 59 F3
Fauldhouse EH47 .... 193 F3
Oakley KY12 .... 27 D4
Polbeth EH55 .... 172 C3
Redding FK2 .... 61 D2
Burnside View EH55 .... 171 E1
Burnsknowe EH54 .... 146 C3
Burntisland Prim Sch KY3 ...... 33 F1
Burntisland Rd KY3 .... 34 C1
Burntisland Sta KY3 .... 50 C4
Burnvale Broxburn EH52 ...... 118 A2
Livingston EH54 .... 147 E2
Burt Ave KY3 .... 34 C2
Burt Gr KY11 .... 29 F1
Burt St KY12 .... 29 D3
Bush St EH21 .... 126 A3
Bush Terr EH21 .... 126 A3
Bute EH15 .... 146 C3
Bute Cres Dunfermline KY11 .. 29 F2
Shotts ML7 .... 191 E3
Bute Pl FK3 .... 61 E3
Bute St FK2 .... 60 A3
Bute Wynd KY1 .... 17 D1
Butler's Pl EH54 .... 147 D2
Butterfield Ind Est EH19 .... 183 D2
Butterfly World EH18 .... 156 B2

Butts The EH41 .... 132 A4
Buxley Rd EH33 .... 128 A1
By-Pass Rd FK4 .... 57 F3
Byburn EH52 .... 116 C4
Byrehope Rd EH52 .... 117 D2
Byres The KY11 .... 46 B3
Byreside EH47 .... 146 A1
Byron Rd ML7 .... 191 D3

Cables Wynd EH6 .... 93 F3
Caddell's Row Cotts EH14 .... 91 D3
Cadell Dr EH3 .... 39 D3
Cadell Pl EH32 .... 97 E2
Cadiz St EH6 .... 94 A3
Cadogan Rd EH16 .... 155 D4
Cadzow Ave EH51 .... 63 F3
Cadzow Cres EH51 .... 63 F4
Cadzow La EH51 .... 63 F4
Cadzow Pl EH7 .... 94 A1
Caerketton Ave EH25 ..... 180 C3
Caerlaverock Ct EH12 .... 121 D4
Caesar Rd EH33 .... 128 B3
Caesar Way EH33 .... 128 B3
Caird's Row EH21 .... 126 A4
Cairn Gr KY12 .... 28 B1
Cairn's La EH51 .... 64 A4
Cairnbank Gdns EH26 .... 203 F2
Cairnbank Rd EH26 .... 203 F2
Cairncubie Rd KY12 .... 29 E4
Cairneyhill Prim Sch KY12 .. 27 E1
Cairneyhill Rd KY12 .... 28 A1
Cairneymount Ave FK2 .... 83 D3
Cairneymount Rd ML8 .... 230 A1
Cairngorm Cres KY2 .... 16 C3
Cairngorm Ho EH3 .... 93 F3
Cairngorm Rd FK3 .... 61 F3
Cairnhill St ML8 .... 230 A1
Cairnie Pl EH47 .... 170 A3
Cairnmuir Rd EH12 .... 121 F4
Cairnoch Way FK7 .... 7 F1
Cairnpapple Henge & Cairn
  EH48 .... 114 B2
Cairnpark Sch EH14 ...... 122 A1
Cairns Dr EH14 .... 177 D4
Cairns Gdns EH14 .... 177 D4
Cairns St E KY1 .... 17 F4
Cairns St W KY1 .... 17 E4
Cairns The
  Charlestown KY11 .... 45 D2
  Menstrie FK11 .... 4 A3
Cairntows Cl EH16 .... 124 B2
Cairnwell Pl
  Cairneyhill KY12 .... 27 E1
  Kirkcaldy KY2 .... 16 C4
Caithness Ct KY1 .... 17 F4
Caithness Pl Edinburgh EH5 .. 93 D3
  Kirkcaldy KY1 .... 17 F4
Caiyside EH10 .... 154 A2
Caiystane Ave EH10 ...... 154 A3
Caiystane Cres EH10 ..... 154 A3
Caiystane Dr EH10 .... 153 F3
Caiystane Gdns EH10 .... 154 A3
Caiystane Hill EH10 ...... 154 A3
Caiystane Terr EH10 ..... 154 A3
Caiystane View EH10 .... 154 A3
Calais View KY11 .... 29 F1
Calaisburn Pl KY11 .... 29 F1
Calder Cres
  Armadale EH48 .... 144 A3
  Edinburgh EH11 .... 121 D1
Calder Ct Edinburgh EH11 .. 121 E1
  Stirling FK7 .... 7 E3
  Shotts ML7 .... 192 A2
Calder Dr Edinburgh EH11 .. 121 E1
Calder Gdns EH11 .... 121 E1
Calder Gr EH11 .... 121 D1
Calder House Rd EH53 ... 148 C2
Calder Junc EH11 .... 121 D1
Calder Park Rd EH53 ..... 148 A1
Calder Pk EH11 .... 121 E1
Calder Pl Dalgety Bay KY11 .. 48 A2
  Edinburgh EH11 .... 121 E1
  Falkirk FK1 .... 60 B1
Calder Rd
  Edinburgh, East Hermiston
  EH14 .... 121 D1
  Edinburgh, Sighthill EH11 .. 121 E1
  Livingston EH54 .... 173 E3
Calder Rd Gdns EH11 .... 122 A2
Calder View EH11 .... 121 D1
Calder's Lawn EH41 ...... 101 D1
Calderburn Rd EH55 ..... 173 D3
Calderhall Ave EH53 ..... 148 C2
Calderhall Cres EH53 .... 148 C2
Calderhall Terr EH53 .... 148 C2
Calderhead High Sch
  ML7 .... 191 E4
Calderhead Rd ML7 ...... 191 E4
  Shotts ML7 .... 191 F3
Caledonia Rd Rosyth KY11 .. 46 A1
  Shotts ML7 .... 191 F3
Caledonia Way KY11 .... 46 A2
Caledonian Cres EH11 ... 232 A1
Caledonian Ct FK2 .... 60 B4
Caledonian Gdns FK10 ..... 9 F3
Caledonian Pl EH11 ...... 232 A1
Caledonian Rd Alloa FK10 .. 9 F3
  Edinburgh EH11 .... 232 A1
  Fauldhouse EH47 .... 193 E3
Caledonian Terr EH47 ... 193 E3
Calgary Ave EH54 .... 147 F2
California Prim Sch FK1 .... 81 F3
California Rd FK2 .... 82 C3
California Terr FK1 .... 81 F3
Callander Dr FK5 .... 59 E4
Callander Pl TD13 .... 140 C2

Callendar Ave FK1 .... 60 A1
Callendar Bsns Pk FK1 .... 60 C2
Callendar Bvd FK1 .... 60 C2
Callendar Ho FK1 .... 60 B2
Callendar Rd FK1 .... 60 B2
Callendar Riggs FK1 .... 60 B2
Callendar Square Sh Ctr 5
  FK1 .... 60 A2
Calliope St KY11 .... 46 A1
Calton Cres FK7 .... 7 D1
Calton Hill EH1 .... 233 E4
Calton Rd EH8 .... 233 E3
Caltrop Pl FK7 .... 7 F2
Calum Macdonald Ct KY11 .. 46 C2
Cambridge Ave EH6 .... 93 F3
Cambridge St EH6 .... 93 F2
Cambridge St EH1 .... 232 B2
Cambusbarron Prim Sch
  FK7 .... 6 B3
Cambusnethan St 7 EH7 .. 94 A1
Camdean Cres KY11 .... 46 B3
Camdean La KY11 .... 46 B3
Camdean Prim Sch KY11 .. 46 B2
Camelon Ed Ctr FK1 .... 59 F3
Camelon Rd FK1 .... 59 F3
Camelon Sta FK1 .... 59 E3
Cameron Cres
  Bonnyrigg and Lasswade
  EH19 .... 181 F3
  Edinburgh EH16 .... 124 C3
Cameron Gr KY11 .... 47 D2
Cameron House Ave
  EH16 .... 124 A2
Cameron Knowe EH49 .... 86 B3
Cameron March EH16 ... 124 C3
Cameron Pk EH16 .... 124 C3
Cameron Pl FK2 .... 39 D1
Cameron Smaill Rd EH14 .. 151 F4
Cameron St KY12 .... 28 C2
Cameron Terr
  Edinburgh EH16 .... 124 C3
  Slamannan FK1 .... 110 A2
Cameron Toll EH16 ...... 124 A2
Cameron Toll Gdns EH16 .. 124 A2
Cameron Toll (Sh Ctr)
  EH16 .... 124 A2
Cameron Way EH54 ...... 147 F4
Cameronian Dr ML8 ..... 230 A1
Cameronian St FK8 .... 7 D4
Camilla Gr KY2 .... 15 E1
Cammo Bank EH4 .... 91 D1
Cammo Brae EH4 .... 91 D1
Cammo Gdns EH4 .... 91 D1
Cammo Hill EH4 .... 90 C1
Cammo Parkway EH4 .... 91 D1
Cammo Pl EH4 .... 91 D1
Cammo Rd EH12 .... 90 C1
Cammo Wlk EH4 .... 90 C1
Camp Rd Crombie KY12 .... 44 B3
  Mayfield EH22 .... 183 F4
Camp Wood View EH22 .. 183 F3
Campbell Ave EH12 ...... 122 B4
Campbell Cres
  Laurieston FK2 .... 60 C2
  Lochgelly KY5 .... 14 A4
Campbell Ct
  Longniddry EH32 .... 98 B3
  Stirling FK7 .... 6 C2
Campbell Dr FK5 .... 38 A1
Campbell Park Cres EH13 .. 152 C3
Campbell Park Dr EH13 .. 152 C3
Campbell Rd
  Edinburgh EH12 .... 122 B4
  Longniddry EH32 .... 98 B3
Campbell St KY12 .... 29 D2
Campbell's Cl EH8 .... 233 E3
Camperdown Rd KY11 .... 46 B1
Campfield St FK2 .... 60 A3
Campie Gdns EH21 ...... 126 A3
Campie La EH21 .... 126 A3
Campie Prim Sch EH21 .. 126 A3
Campie Rd EH21 .... 126 A3
Campie Terr EH21 .... 39 F1
Camps Rd KY12 .... 27 C3
Camps Rigg EH54 .... 147 D4
Campsie Cres KY2 .... 16 C4
Campsie Rd FK3 .... 61 F3
Campus Rdbt EH54 ...... 147 E1
Campview EH22 .... 156 A4
Campview Ave EH22 ..... 156 A4
Campview Cres EH22 .... 156 B4
Campview Gdns EH22 ... 156 A4
Campview Gr EH22 .... 156 B4
Campview Rd EH19 ...... 182 A3
Campview Terr EH22 .... 156 A4
Camus Ave EH10 .... 154 A3
Camus Pk EH10 .... 154 A3
Camus Pl E EH10 .... 154 A3
Camus Rd E EH10 .... 154 A3
Camus Rd W EH10 .... 154 A3
Canaan La EH10 .... 123 D2
Canal St
  Falkirk, Camelon FK1 ...... 59 E3
  Falkirk, Grahamston FK2 .. 60 A4
Canal Wlk EH16 .... 61 E1
Canalyard Ind Est FK1 .... 60 A1
Canavan Ct FK7 .... 7 E2
Canberra St EH54 .... 148 A3
Candie Cres FK3 .... 61 F3
Candie Rd FK3 .... 62 A4
Candlemaker Row EH1 .. 233 D2
Candlemaker's Cres
  EH17 .... 155 F3
Candlemaker's Pk EH17 .. 155 F3
Candleriggs FK10 .... 10 A3
Candleriggs Ct FK10 ...... 10 A3
Caneluk Ave ML8 .... 230 A1

Canmore Dr FK5 .... 38 C2
Canmore Gr KY12 .... 29 D3
Canmore St
  Dunfermline KY12 .... 29 D2
  Kinghorn KY3 .... 34 C1
  Queensferry EH30 .... 89 D4
Canmore Terr KY12 .... 29 D4
Cannon Way KY12 .... 39 D1
Canning St EH3 .... 232 B2
Canning Street La EH3 .. 232 A2
Cannonmills Sch (Specl)
  EH7 .... 93 E1
Cannons Way KY12 .... 39 D1
Cannop Cres EH47 .... 170 C1
Canon La EH3 .... 93 E1
Canon Lynch Ct KY12 ..... 28 C2
Canon St EH3 .... 93 E1
Canongate EH8 .... 233 E3
Canonmills EH3 .... 93 E2
Canthill Gdns ML7 .... 191 D2
Cantlie Pl KY11 .... 46 C2
Cantsdam Rd KY4 .... 12 C4
Canty Gr EH32 .... 98 B2
Capelaw Rd EH13 .... 153 D3
Caplaw Way EH26 .... 203 E3
Caponflat Cres EH41 .... 100 C1
Caponhall Ct EH33 ...... 128 B3
Caponhall Dr EH33 ...... 128 B3
Caponhall Rd EH33 ...... 128 B3
Cappers Ct EH48 .... 143 F2
Captain's Dr EH16 ...... 155 D3
Captain's Loan EH16 ... 155 D3
Captain's Rd EH17 ...... 155 D3
Captain's Row EH16 .... 155 D3
Caputhall Rd EH54 ...... 146 B3
Carberry Ct EH21 .... 157 F4
Carberry Mains Cotts
  EH21 .... 127 D1
Carberry Pl EH12 .... 122 C4
Carberry Rd EH21 .... 126 C2
Carbrook Dr FK7 .... 20 B2
Carbrook Pl FK7 .... 61 F3
Carcraig Pl KY11 .... 48 A2
Cardross Ave EH12 ...... 117 D3
Cardross Cres EH52 .... 117 E3
Cardross Rd EH52 .... 117 E3
Cardrowan Rd FK7 .... 20 B1
Carfae Ave EH4 .... 92 A1
Carfae Gr EH4 .... 92 A1
Carfae Pk EH4 .... 92 A1
Carfae Rd EH4 .... 92 A1
Cargil Terr EH5 .... 93 D3
Cargilfield Sch EH4 .... 91 D2
Carhowden Rd FK2 .... 61 D2
Carlaverock Ave EH33 .. 128 B3
Carlaverock Cres EH33 .. 128 B3
Carlaverock Ct EH33 .... 128 C3
Carlaverock Dr EH33 ... 128 B3
Carlaverock Gr EH33 ... 128 B3
Carlaverock Terr EH33 .. 128 C2
Carlaverock View EH33 .. 128 B2
Carlaverock Wlk EH33 .. 128 B3
Carledubs Ave EH52 .... 117 D3
Carledubs Cres EH52 ... 117 D3
Carlie Ave FK9 .... 2 A3
Carlin Craig KY3 .... 34 C1
Carlin Cres KY3 .... 34 C1
Carlin La ML8 .... 230 A1
Carlingnose Ct KY11 ..... 68 B3
Carlingnose Pk KY11 ..... 68 B3
Carlingnose Point KY11 .. 68 B3
Carlingnose View KY11 .. 68 B3
Carlingnose Way KY11 ... 68 B3
Carlops Ave EH26 .... 203 F3
Carlops Cres EH26 ...... 203 F3
Carlops Rd EH26 .... 203 E3
Carlouk La ML8 .... 230 A1
Carlowrie Ave EH30 ...... 89 F4
Carlowrie Cres EH30 ..... 89 F4
Carlowrie Pl EH23 .... 207 E4
Carlton St EH4 .... 93 D1
Carlton Terr EH7 .... 233 F4
Carlton Terrace La EH7 .. 233 F4
Carlton Terrace Mews
  EH7 .... 233 F4
Carluke High Sch ML8 .. 230 A1
Carluke Prim Sch ML8 .. 230 A2
Carlyle Ct
  Haddington EH41 .... 132 A4
  Livingston EH54 .... 148 B3
Carlyle Gdns EH41 ...... 101 D1
Carlyle La KY12 .... 28 C3
Carlyle Pl Edinburgh EH7 .. 94 A1
  Musselburgh EH21 ...... 126 B3
Carlyle Rd KY1 .... 17 D2
Carlyle St KY12 .... 26 A1
Carlyle Terr EH48 .... 145 E3
Carmel Ave EH29 .... 89 D1
Carmel Rd EH29 .... 89 D1
Carmelaws EH49 .... 85 D3
Carmelite Rd EH30 .... 89 D4
Carmondean Centre Rd
  EH54 .... 147 D3
Carmondean Ctr EH54 .. 147 D3
Carmondean Prim Sch
  EH54 .... 147 D4
Carmuir ML11 .... 215 D1
Carmuirs Ave FK1 .... 59 E3
Carmuirs Dr FK1 .... 59 E3
Carmuirs Prim Sch FK1 .. 59 E3
Carmuirs St FK1 .... 59 E3
Carnaughton Pl FK12 ...... 4 C3
Carnbee Ave EH16 ...... 155 E3
Carnbee Cres EH16 ..... 155 E3
Carnbee Dell EH16 ...... 155 E3
Carnbee End EH16 ...... 155 E3
Carnbee Pk EH16 .... 155 E3

Carnbee Pl KY12 .... 29 E2
Carnegie Ave KY11 .... 46 C4
Carnegie Birthplace Mus
  KY12 .... 29 D2
Carnegie Campus (Bsns Pk)
  KY11 .... 46 C4
Carnegie Dr
  Dunfermline KY12 .... 29 D2
  Falkirk FK1 .... 59 E3
Carnegie Rd EH48 .... 146 A3
Carnegie St EH8 .... 233 E2
Carneil Rd KY12 .... 27 E4
Carneil Terr KY12 .... 27 E4
Carnethie St EH24 .... 181 F1
Carnethy Ave
  Edinburgh EH13 .... 153 D3
  Penicuik EH26 .... 203 F3
Carnethy Cres KY2 .... 16 C4
Carnethy Ct EH26 .... 203 F3
Carnock Rd KY12 .... 28 A3
Carnock St FK7 .... 20 C4
Carnwath Rd ML8 .... 230 A1
Caroline Cres FK12 .... 4 C3
Caroline Gdns
  Edinburgh EH12 .... 121 F4
  Mid Calder EH53 .... 148 A1
Caroline Park Ave EH5 ... 92 B3
Caroline Park Gr EH5 ..... 92 B3
Caroline Pk EH53 .... 148 A1
Caroline Pl EH12 .... 121 F4
Caroline Terr EH12 ...... 121 E4
Carpet La EH6 .... 94 A3
Carradale Ave FK1 .... 59 E2
Carribber Ave EH49 .... 84 A3
Carrick Cres EH22 .... 183 E4
Carrick Ct FK7 .... 7 E3
Carrick Dr KY11 .... 48 A2
Carrick Gdns EH54 ...... 173 F3
Carrick Gr KY11 .... 48 A2
Carrick Knowe Ave EH12 .. 121 F3
Carrick Knowe Dr EH12 .. 121 F3
Carrick Knowe Gdns EH12 .. 121 F3
Carrick Knowe Gr EH12 .. 121 F3
Carrick Knowe Hill EH12 .. 121 F3
Carrick Knowe Loan EH12 .. 121 F3
Carrick Knowe Parkway
  EH12 .... 121 F3
Carrick Knowe Pl EH12 .. 121 F3
Carrick Knowe Prim Sch
  EH12 .... 121 F3
Carrick Knowe Rd EH12 .. 121 F2
Carrick Knowe Terr EH12 .. 121 F3
Carrick Pl
  Falkirk, Roughlands FK2 .. 39 D2
  Falkirk, Tamfourhill FK1 .. 59 E2
Carriden Brae EH51 .... 64 B3
Carriden Glade EH51 ..... 64 B4
Carrington Cres EH4 ...... 92 C2
Carrington Mains Cotts
  EH23 .... 206 B3
Carrington Rd EH4 .... 92 C1
Carron Ind Est FK2 .... 39 E1
Carron La KY11 .... 29 F2
Carron Pl Edinburgh EH6 .. 94 A3
  Grangemouth FK3 .... 61 E2
  Kirkcaldy KY2 .... 16 C4
  Stirling FK7 .... 7 D1
Carron Prim Sch FK2 ..... 39 E1
Carron Rd FK2 .... 60 A4
Carron Terr FK2 .... 82 C4
Carron View FK2 .... 82 C4
Carron Wlk EH54 .... 148 A2
Carronbank Ave FK2 ...... 39 E1
Carronbank Cres FK6 ..... 36 C2
Carronbank Ct FK2 .... 39 E1
Carronflats Rd FK3 .... 61 F4
Carrongrove Ave FK2 ..... 39 E2
Carrongrove Rd FK2 ...... 39 E2
Carronhall Ave FK2 .... 39 E2
Carronlea Dr FK2 .... 39 E2
Carronshore Prim Sch FK2 .. 39 E2
Carronshore Rd FK2 ...... 39 E1
Carronside Pl FK6 .... 36 C2
Carronside St FK2 .... 60 A4
Carronvale Ave FK5 .... 38 B1
Carronvale Rd FK5 .... 38 B1
Carronview FK5 .... 38 B1
Carsaig Ct FK9 .... 2 A3
Carse Pl FK2 .... 61 D2
Carse Knowe EH49 .... 85 E4
Carse Terr FK10 .... 9 F4
Carse View Airth FK2 ...... 22 C2
Carseview Bannockburn FK7 .. 7 F1
  Tullibody FK10 .... 4 A1
Carson Pl KY11 .... 46 B3
Carswell Pl KY12 .... 28 C3
Cartmore Rd KY5 .... 14 A4
Cassel's La EH6 .... 93 F2
Casselbank St EH6 .... 93 F2
Cast The EH18 .... 181 E3
Castellau Cotts EH42 ..... 78 B1
Castings Ave FK2 .... 60 A4
Castings Ct
  Falkirk, Grahamston FK2 .. 60 A4
  Falkirk, Middlefield FK2 .. 60 C3
Castings Dr FK2 .... 60 A3
Castings Rd FK2 .... 60 C3
Castings The KY12 .... 28 B3
Castlandhill Rd KY11 ..... 47 D1
Castle Ave Airth FK2 ...... 22 C2
  Cockenzie & Port Seton EH32 .. 97 F2
  Edinburgh EH12 .... 121 E3
  Falkirk FK2 .... 39 E2
  Gorebridge EH23 .... 207 E4
Castle Bsns Pk The FK8 .... 1 C1

Castle Cres Denny FK6 .... 36 B1
  East Calder EH53 .... 148 C1
  Falkirk FK2 .... 60 B4
  Torwood FK5 .... 37 F4
Castle Ct Falkirk FK2 ...... 60 B4
  Menstrie FK11 .... 3 F3
  Stirling FK8 .... 7 D1
Castle Dr Airth FK2 .... 22 C2
  Dunfermline KY11 .... 46 C3
  Falkirk FK2 .... 60 B4
  Stenhousemuir FK5 ...... 38 C1
Castle Gate EH42 .... 78 B2
Castle Gogar EH12 ...... 120 B4
Castle Mains Pl EH39 .... 53 D3
Castle Moffat EH14 ..... 166 A4
Castle Pk EH39 .... 53 D2
Castle Pl Dunbar EH42 ... 78 B2
  Falkirk FK2 .... 60 B4
  Gorebridge EH23 .... 207 E4
Castle Row KY12 .... 28 B3
Castle St Alloa FK10 ...... 10 A3
  Clackmannan FK10 .... 11 D2
  Dunbar EH42 .... 78 B2
  Edinburgh EH2 .... 232 B3
Castle Terr
  Clackmannan FK10 .... 11 D2
  Cockenzie & Port Seton
  EH32 .... 97 F2
  Denny FK6 .... 36 B1
  Edinburgh EH2 .... 232 B2
  Winchburgh EH52 .... 88 A1
Castle View
  Cockenzie & Port Seton
  EH32 .... 97 F2
  Fallin FK7 .... 8 B2
  Gorebridge EH23 .... 207 E4
  Pencaitland EH34 .... 160 B3
Castle Wlk EH32 .... 97 F2
Castle Wynd FK8 .... 7 D4
Castle Wynd N EH1 ...... 232 C2
Castle Wynd S EH1 ...... 232 C2
Castleblair KY12 .... 28 C2
Castleblair La KY12 .... 28 C3
Castleblair Mews KY12 .. 28 C3
Castleblair Pk KY12 .... 28 C3
Castlebrae Bsns Ctr
  EH16 .... 124 C2
Castlebrae Com Sch
  EH16 .... 124 C2
Castlegait FK8 .... 7 D4
Castlehill Bo'ness EH51 .. 63 E4
  Edinburgh EH1 .... 232 C3
Castlehill Ave FK1 .... 110 A3
Castlelaurie St FK2 .... 60 B4
Castlelaw Cres EH25 .... 180 C3
Castlelaw Ct EH26 ...... 203 F3
Castlelaw Fort
  & Souterrain EH26 ...... 179 E2
Castlelaw Rd EH13 ...... 153 D3
Castlemains Pl EH39 ..... 53 E3
Castlemount Terr KY2 .... 16 B4
Castlepark FK10 .... 23 E3
Castlerig KY3 .... 34 C1
Castleton Cres FK3 .... 61 E3
Castleview FK9 .... 2 A2
Castleview Dr FK9 .... 2 A4
Castleview La EH54 ...... 173 F2
Castleview Terr FK4 .... 57 D2
Cath Church of St Mary
  EH12 .... 232 A3
Cathcart Pl EH11 .... 122 C3
Cathedral La EH1 .... 233 D4
Catherine St FK7 .... 7 E1
Catherine Terr EH47 .... 145 E1
Cathlaw La EH48 .... 114 A3
Cathrine Gr EH51 .... 64 A3
Catriona Terr EH26 ...... 180 A1
Cattle Market FK10 .... 11 D3
Cauldhame Cres FK7 .... 6 B3
Causeway The
  Bridge of A FK9 .... 2 B3
  Edinburgh EH15 .... 124 B3
Causewayhead Rd FK9 .... 2 B2
Causewayside EH9 ...... 123 F3
Cavalry Park Dr EH15 ... 124 B3
Cawder Gdns FK9 .... 1 C4
Cawder Rd FK9 .... 1 C4
Cawdor Cres KY2 .... 16 C3
Cecil St FK7 .... 7 D3
Cedar Ave Kirkcaldy KY1 .. 17 E4
  Stirling FK8 .... 6 C3
Cedar Cres
  Cowdenbeath KY4 .... 13 E3
  Westquarter FK2 .... 61 D1
  Whitburn EH47 .... 170 B3
Cedar Dr EH32 .... 97 E2
Cedar Gr
  Dunfermline KY11 .... 46 B4
  Stenhousemuir FK5 ...... 38 B1
Cedar Rd EH20 .... 180 C4
Cedar St Dunbar EH42 ... 78 A1
  Grangemouth FK3 .... 61 E4
Cedar Wynd ML7 .... 192 A3
Cedarbank EH54 .... 147 F3
Cedarbank Sch EH54 ... 147 F3
Cedars The FK10 .... 4 A1
Cedric Rise EH54 .... 148 A1

Cemetery Rd Dalkeith EH22 **156** C1
Fauldhouse EH47 .... **193** E3
Prestonpans EH32 .... **96** C1
Shotts ML7 .... **192** A2
Central Ave FK3 .... **61** E3
Central Bvd FK5 .... **38** A2
Central Dock Rd FK3 .... **40** C1
Central Dr FK5 .... **38** C2
Central Park Ave FK5 .... **38** A2
Central Park Bsns Pk FK5 .. **38** A2
Central Pk (Cowdenbeath FC)
KY4 .... **13** E2
Central Rd KY12 .... **44** B4
Central Ret Pk FK1 .... **60** B3
Central Way KY11 .... **48** B3
Centre Intc EH54 .... **148** A1
Chacefield St FK4 .... **58** A1
Chacefield Wood FK6 .... **57** F4
Chalmers Cres EH9 .... **123** E3
Chalmers Hospl EH3 .... **232** C2
Chalmers Sq EH54 .... **146** B3
Chalmers St
Dunfermline KY12 .... **28** C2
Edinburgh EH3 .... **232** C1
Chalmerston Rd FK9 .... **1** A2
Chalton Rd FK9 .... **2** A4
Chalybeate EH41 .... **131** F4
Chamberfield Rd KY12 ...... **29** E3
Chamberlain Rd EH10 .... **123** D2
Chambers Dr FK2 .... **39** D1
Chambers St EH1 .... **233** D2
Chamfron Gdns EH7 .... **7** F2
Champigny Ct EH21 .... **126** C3
Chancelot Cres EH6 .... **93** E3
Chancelot Gr EH5 .... **93** E3
Chancelot Terr EH6 .... **93** E3
Chandler's Rise KY11 .... **47** F2
Chandler's Wlk KY11 .... **47** F2
Channel Brae EH42 .... **136** B4
Chapel Bank EH22 .... **158** B3
Chapel Cres FK2 .... **39** D2
Chapel Ct EH16 .... **124** C2
Chapel Dr FK5 .... **38** C2
Chapel Gr KY2 .... **16** B4
Chapel La Edinburgh EH6 ... **94** A3
Falkirk FK1 .... **60** A3
Chapel Level KY2 .... **16** C4
Chapel Loan EH25 .... **181** D2
Chapel Pl
High Valleyfield KY12 .... **26** A1
Inverkeithing KY11 .... **47** E2
Kircaldy KY7 .... **16** B4
North Queensferry KY11 .... **68** B3
Pathhead EH37 .... **185** D3
Chapel Rd KY2 .... **16** B4
Chapel St Cowdenbeath KY4 .. **13** E2
Dunfermline KY12 .... **28** C2
Edinburgh EH8 .... **233** E1
High Valleyfield KY12 .... **26** A1
Kincardine FK10 .... **23** F2
Lochgelly KY5 .... **14** A4
Chapel Villas KY11 .... **48** A1
Chapel Wynd EH1 .... **232** C2
Chapelfauld Gn KY11 .... **29** F2
Chapelhill
Clackmannan FK10 .... **11** D2
Dirleton EH39 .... **53** D2
Kircaldy KY2 .... **16** B4
Chapelhill St KY11 .... **23** E3
Chapelton Ave EH55 .... **172** C2
Chapelton Dr EH55 .... **172** C2
Chapelton Gdns EH55 ...... **172** C2
Chapelton Gr EH55 .... **172** C2
Chapelton Pl EH55 .... **173** D2
Chapelton Terr EH55 .... **172** C3
Chapelwell Pl KY11 .... **29** F2
Charing Cross FK3 .... **40** B1
Charles Ave FK9 .... **2** A3
Charles Cres
Bathgate EH48 .... **145** F3
Carluke ML8 .... **230** A1
Charles Ct KY11 .... **45** F2
Charles Dr FK5 .... **59** E4
Charles La EH48 .... **145** F3
Charles Rodger Pl KY9 ...... **2** A2
Charles St Alloa FK10 .... **9** F4
Dunfermline KY11 .... **29** D1
Edinburgh EH8 .... **233** D1
Penicuik EH26 .... **203** F4
Shotts ML7 .... **192** A4
Stirling FK8 .... **7** D3
Charles Street La EH1 .... **233** D2
Charles Way KY11 .... **45** F2
Charles Way S KY11 .... **45** F2
Charlesfield EH8 .... **123** E4
Charlesfield La EH54 .... **147** D1
Charlesfield Rd EH54 .... **173** D4
Charlotte Dundas Ct FK3 ... **61** F3
Charlotte Hill Ct FK5 .... **38** A2
Charlotte La EH2 .... **232** B3
Charlotte Sq EH2 .... **232** B3
Charlotte St Brightons FK2 .. **82** B4
Kircaldy KY1 .... **17** D2
Shotts ML7 .... **192** A4
Charlton Gr EH25 .... **180** C2
Charter St FK7 .... **7** D2
Charterhall Gr EH9 .... **123** E1
Charterhall Rd EH9 .... **123** E1
Charteris Pk EH32 .... **98** B3
Charteris Rd EH32 .... **98** B3
Chartershall Rd FK7 .... **7** D1
Chattan Ave FK9 .... **2** A2
Chattan Ind Est FK4 .... **58** B2
Cherry Ave EH48 .... **145** F3

Cherry La EH22 .... **183** F3
Cherry Pl KY4 .... **13** E2
Cherry Rd EH19 .... **182** A3
Cherry Tree Ave EH14 .... **151** F2
Cherry Tree Cres EH14 ...... **151** F2
Cherry Tree Gdns EH14 ..... **151** F2
Cherry Tree Gr EH14 .... **151** F2
Cherry Tree Loan EH14 ..... **151** F2
Cherry Tree Pk EH14 .... **151** F2
Cherry Tree Pl EH14 .... **151** F2
Cherry Tree View EH14 ..... **151** F2
Cherrybank KY12 .... **29** E3
Cherryton Dr FK10 .... **11** D3
Chessel's Ct EH8 .... **233** E3
Chesser Ave EH14 .... **122** B2
Chesser Cres EH14 .... **122** B2
Chesser Gdns EH14 .... **122** A2
Chesser Gr EH14 .... **122** A2
Chesser Loan EH14 .... **122** A2
Chester Ct EH19 .... **182** A3
Chester Dr EH22 .... **183** E3
Chester Gr EH19 .... **182** A3
Chester St EH3 .... **232** A3
Chester View EH22 .... **183** E3
Chesters View EH19 .... **182** A3
Chestnut Ave Kirkaldy KY1 ... **17** E4
Whitburn EH47 .... **170** B3
Chestnut Cres FK6 .... **36** B2
Chestnut Gr Bo'ness EH51 .. **63** E3
Bonnyrigg and Lasswade
EH19 .... **182** A3
Dunfermline KY11 .... **46** C4
Livingston EH54 .... **148** A3
Stenhousemuir FK5 .... **38** C2
Winchburgh EH52 .... **87** F1
Chestnut St EH5 .... **92** C4
Cheviot Pl FK3 .... **61** F3
Cheviot Rd KY2 .... **16** C4
Cheyne St EH4 .... **93** D1
Chief's Cl KY1 .... **17** E3
Chisholm Ave FK9 .... **2** A2
Chisholm Cres KY5 .... **14** A4
Chisholm Pl FK3 .... **61** D3
Chisholm St KY11 .... **29** E4
Chisholm Terr EH26 .... **203** F4
Christian Cres EH15 .... **125** E4
Christian Gr EH15 .... **125** D4
Christie Pl KY1 .... **17** E4
Christie St KY12 .... **29** D3
Christie Terr FK5 .... **38** C2
Christiemiller Ave EH7 ...... **94** C1
Christiemiller Gr EH7 .... **94** C1
Christiemiller Pl EH7 .... **94** C1
Chuckie Pend EH3 .... **232** B2
Church Ct Kirkcaldy KY1 ..... **17** E2
Philpstoun EH49 .... **86** B3
Church Gdns EH32 .... **98** C3
Church Gr Alloa FK10 .... **5** E1
Burntisland KY3 .... **33** E1
Church Hill EH10 .... **123** D2
Church Hill Pl EH10 .... **123** D2
Church La Denny FK6 .... **36** B2
Kirkaldy KY2 .... **17** E2
Limekilns KY11 .... **45** E2
Church Pk EH48 .... **145** D3
Church Pl Armadale EH48 ... **144** A3
Bathgate EH48 .... **145** D3
Crossgates KY4 .... **30** C4
Falkirk FK2 .... **60** A3
Fauldhouse EH47 .... **193** F3
Longridge EH47 .... **170** B1
Church Rd Bo'ness EH51 .... **63** F4
Bonnyrigg and Lasswade
EH18 .... **155** F1
California FK1 .... **81** F3
North Berwick EH39 .... **54** B4
Church St Addiewell EH55 .. **171** E1
Alloa FK10 .... **10** A3
Broxburn EH52 .... **117** F3
Burntisland KY3 .... **33** E1
Cowdenbeath KY4 .... **13** E2
Dunbar EH42 .... **78** C1
Falkirk FK2 .... **39** E1
Haddington EH41 .... **132** A4
Harthill ML7 .... **168** B3
High Bonnybridge FK4 ...... **58** B2
Inverkeithing KY11 .... **47** E2
Kingseat KY12 .... **12** A1
Kirkaldy KY1 .... **17** E3
Limekilns KY11 .... **45** E2
Loanhead EH20 .... **181** E4
Lochgelly KY5 .... **14** A4
Stenhousemuir FK5 .... **38** C2
Tranent EH33 .... **128** B4
Church Wlk Denny FK6 ...... **36** C1
Kinghorn KY3 .... **35** D2
Church Wynd EH51 .... **63** F4
Churchill Dr EH10 .... **123** D2
Churchill Dr KY9 .... **2** A3
Churchill Pl KY11 .... **46** C2
Churchill St FK10 .... **9** F4
Churchill Way EH27 .... **149** F2
Churchway KY32 .... **98** C3
Cinderhall Pl EH33 .... **128** A1
Circle The EH22 .... **156** A4
Circus Gdns EH3 .... **232** B4
Circus La EH3 .... **93** D1
Circus Pl EH3 .... **232** B4
Citadel Pl EH6 .... **93** F3
Citadel St EH6 .... **93** F3
City Hospl EH14 .... **153** F4
City Mus EH8 .... **233** E3
City Of Edinburgh By-Pass
The Dalkeith EH22 .... **157** D4
Edinburgh EH14 .... **154** B2
Whitecraig EH21 .... **126** A1
Clackmae Gr EH16 .... **154** C4
Clackmae Rd EH16 .... **154** C4

Clackmannan Coll of F Ed
FK10 .... **10** A4
Clackmannan Prim Sch
FK10 .... **11** D2
Clanranald Pl FK1 .... **59** F1
Clare Ct EH39 .... **54** A4
Clarebank Cres EH6 .... **94** A3
Claremont Bank EH7 .... **93** E2
Claremont Cres EH7 .... **93** E2
Claremont Ct EH7 .... **93** E2
Claremont Dr FK9 .... **2** B4
Claremont Gdns EH6 .... **94** B2
Claremont Gr EH7 .... **93** E2
Claremont Ind Est FK10 ..... **10** A3
Claremont Pk EH6 .... **94** A2
Claremont Prim Sch FK10 .. **9** F4
Claremont Rd EH6 .... **94** A2
Claremont St FK4 .... **57** F3
Clarence St EH3 .... **93** D1
Clarendon Cres
Edinburgh EH4 .... **232** A4
Linlithgow EH49 .... **85** D3
Clarendon Pl FK8 .... **7** D4
Clarendon Rd
Linlithgow EH49 .... **85** D3
Stirling FK8 .... **7** D4
Claret Rd
Grangemouth, Bowhouse
FK3 .... **61** F2
Grangemouth, Oil Refinery
FK3 .... **62** B2
Clarinda Ave FK1 .... **59** D3
Clarinda Gdns EH22 .... **157** E2
Clarinda Terr EH16 .... **124** A1
Clark Ave EH5 .... **93** E3
Clark Bldgs EH35 .... **159** F4
Clark Pl Edinburgh EH5 ..... **93** D3
Kirkaldy KY2 .... **17** D3
Clark Rd Edinburgh EH5 ..... **93** D3
Inverkeithing KY11 .... **47** E1
Clarkson Rd EH17 .... **155** D4
Clarkson St EH17 .... **117** E3
Claverhouse Dr EH16 .... **155** D4
Claycrofts Pl FK7 .... **7** D3
Clayhills Gr EH14 .... **151** D1
Clayhills Pk EH14 .... **151** D1
Clayknowes Ave EH21 ...... **126** A3
Clayknowes Cres EH21 ..... **126** A3
Clayknowes Ct EH21 .... **126** A3
Clayknowes Dr EH21 .... **125** F3
Clayknowes Pl EH21 .... **126** A3
Clayknowes Way EH21 ...... **126** A3
Claymore Dr FK7 .... **7** E2
Clearburn Cres EH16 .... **124** A2
Clearburn Gdns EH16 .... **124** A2
Clearburn Rd
Edinburgh EH16 .... **124** A2
Gorebridge EH23 .... **183** D1
Cleaves The FK10 .... **4** A1
Cleekim Dr EH15 .... **125** D2
Cleekim Rd EH15 .... **125** D2
Cleghorn Dr EH52 .... **117** D3
Cleikiminrig EH15 .... **125** D2
Cleish Gdns KY2 .... **16** C3
Cleish Pl KY11 .... **29** F1
Cleish St KY11 .... **29** F1
Cleland St EH47 .... **170** A4
Clement Rise EH54 .... **148** A1
Clerics Hill EH29 .... **89** D1
Clerk Gr KY11 .... **29** F1
Clerk Rd EH26 .... **203** E3
Clerk St Edinburgh EH8 ..... **233** E1
Loanhead EH20 .... **181** E4
Clerkington Rd EH41 .... **131** E4
Clerkington Wlk EH41 .... **131** F4
Clermiston Ave EH4 .... **91** E1
Clermiston Cres EH4 .... **91** F1
Clermiston Dr EH4 .... **91** E1
Clermiston Gdns EH4 .... **91** E1
Clermiston Gn EH4 .... **91** E1
Clermiston Gr EH4 .... **91** E1
Clermiston Hill EH4 .... **91** F1
Clermiston Loan EH4 .... **91** E1
Clermiston Medway EH4 .... **91** E1
Clermiston Pk EH4 .... **91** E1
Clermiston Pl EH4 .... **91** E1
Clermiston Prim Sch EH4 ... **91** E1
Clermiston Rd EH12 .... **121** F4
Clermiston Rd N EH4 .... **91** F1
Clermiston View EH4 .... **91** F1
Clerwood Bank EH12 .... **121** E4
Clerwood Gdns EH12 .... **121** F4
Clerwood Gr EH12 .... **121** F4
Clerwood Loan EH12 .... **121** E4
Clerwood Pk EH12 .... **121** E4
Clerwood Pl EH12 .... **121** F4
Clerwood Row EH12 .... **121** E4
Clerwood Terr EH12 .... **121** F4
Clerwood View EH12 .... **121** F4
Clerwood Way EH12 .... **121** E4
Cleuch Ave FK10 .... **4** A1
Cleuch Dr FK12 .... **4** C4
Cleuch Rd EH23 .... **207** F1
Cleuchbrae FK5 .... **172** B2
Cleveland Dr KY11 .... **47** D3
Clifford Rd
North Berwick EH39 .... **54** B3
Stirling FK8 .... **7** D3
Clifton Rd EH28 .... **118** C1
Clifton Trad Est EH28 .... **118** C2
Clifton View EH52 .... **118** A3
Cliftonhall Rd EH28 .... **119** D3
Climpy Rd ML11 .... **214** B3
Clinkum Bank KY12 .... **26** B2
Clinton Rd EH9 .... **123** D2

Clive St ML7 .... **191** F3
Cloanden Pl KY2 .... **17** D2
Clockluine Rd KY11 .... **47** F3
Clockmill La EH7, EH8 .... **94** A1
Close The KY11 .... **46** B1
Clova Dr KY4 .... **173** F3
Clovenstone Dr EH14 .... **152** C4
Clovenstone Gdns EH14 .... **152** C4
Clovenstone Pk EH14 .... **152** C4
Clovenstone Prim Sch
EH14 .... **152** C4
Clovenstone Rd EH14 .... **152** C4
Clover Pl EH51 .... **63** F3
Cloverbank EH54 .... **147** F3
Cloverstone Rdbt EH14 ..... **152** C4
Cloves The FK13 .... **4** A3
Cluanie Ave ML7 .... **191** F3
Clufflatt EH30 .... **67** F1
Clufflatt Brae EH30 .... **67** F1
Clune Rd KY12 .... **27** F4
Clunie Rd KY11 .... **29** F2
Clunivar St KY12 .... **28** B3
Cluny Ave EH10 .... **123** D1
Cluny Dr Edinburgh EH10 ... **123** D1
Stenhousemuir FK5 .... **38** C2
Cluny Gdns EH10 .... **123** E1
Cluny Pl EH10 .... **123** E2
Cluny Terr EH10 .... **123** D1
Clyde Cres Dunfermline KY11 .. **29** F1
Larbert FK5 .... **38** A2
Clyde Dr Livingston EH54 ... **148** A2
Shotts ML7 .... **192** A4
Clyde St Edinburgh EH1 ..... **233** D4
Falkirk FK1 .... **59** F3
Grangemouth FK3 .... **40** A1
Clydesdale St EH51 .... **63** F3
Clydevale Pl EH54 .... **117** D3
Coal Neuk EH33 .... **128** B3
Coal Rd KY12 .... **28** C2
Coal Wynd Bannockburn FK7 .. **7** E1
Kirkaldy KY1 .... **17** E2
Coalgate FK10 .... **10** A3
Coalgate Ave EH33 .... **128** C4
Coalgate Rd EH33 .... **128** C4
Coalhill EH6 .... **93** F3
Coalpots Way KY10 .... **5** F2
Coates Cotts EH32 .... **99** F2
Coates Cres EH3 .... **232** A3
Coates Gdns EH12 .... **122** C4
Coatfield La EH6 .... **94** A3
Cobblebrae Cres FK2 .... **39** D1
Cobden Cres EH9 .... **123** F2
Cobden Rd EH9 .... **123** F2
Cobden St Alva FK12 .... **5** D4
Alva, The Boll FK12 .... **5** D3
Coblecrook Gdns FK12 ...... **4** C3
Coblecrook La FK12 .... **4** C3
Coblecrook Pl FK12 .... **4** C3
Coburg St EH6 .... **93** F3
Cochran Pl EH7 .... **93** E1
Cochran Terr EH7 .... **93** E1
Cochrane Ave Falkirk FK2 ... **60** A2
Inverkeithing KY11 .... **47** E1
Cochrane Cres FK12 .... **4** C4
Cochrane Pl EH6 .... **94** A2
Cochrane Rd KY11 .... **46** A1
Cochrane Sq EH54 .... **173** E3
Cochrane St
Bathgate EH48 .... **145** D4
Falkirk FK1 .... **60** A2
Cochrane Way KY11 .... **48** A3
Cochrane Wlk KY11 .... **29** F2
Cochranes The FK12 .... **5** D4
Cochrie Pl FK10 .... **4** B1
Cochrina Pl EH24 .... **181** D2
Cockburn Cres
Balerno EH14 .... **177** D4
Whitecross EH49 .... **84** A3
Cockburn Ct EH35 .... **159** F4
Cockburn Dr EH35 .... **159** E3
Cockburn Sq EH37 .... **185** D3
Cockburn St
Edinburgh EH1 .... **233** D3
Falkirk FK1 .... **60** A2
Cockburnhill Rd EH14 .... **177** D4
Cockburnspath Sch TD13 .. **140** C2
Cockenzie Prim Sch EH32 .. **97** E2
Cocklaw St KY4 .... **12** B4
Cockles Brae EH41 .... **132** C2
Cockmilane Brae EH41 ...... **132** B3
Cockmylane EH13, EH10 .... **153** F4
Cockpen Ave EH19 .... **182** A3
Cockpen Cres EH19 .... **182** A3
Cockpen Dr EH19 .... **182** A3
Cockpen Pl EH19 .... **182** A3
Cockpen Rd EH19 .... **182** B3
Cockpen Terr EH19 .... **182** A3
Cockpen View EH19 .... **182** A3
Coilesdene Ave EH15 .... **125** E4
Coilesdene Cres EH15 .... **125** E4
Coilesdene Dr EH15 .... **125** E4
Coilesdene Gdns EH15 ...... **125** E4
Coilesdene Loan EH15 .... **125** E4
Coilesdene Terr EH15 .... **125** E4
Coire Loan ML7 .... **192** A4
Coldingham Pl KY12 .... **29** E2
Colduie Circ FK2 .... **62** A1
Colegate Rd EH37 .... **208** B4
Coles Pl KY4 .... **31** D3
Colinshiel Ave EH48 .... **144** C4
Colinshiel St EH48 .... **144** C4
Colinshiel View EH48 .... **143** F4
Colinswell Rd KY3 .... **33** E1
Colinton Gr EH14 .... **122** B1
Colinton Gr W EH14 .... **122** B1
Colinton Mains Cres EH13 ... **153** F3

Colinton Mains Dr EH13 .... **153** E4
Colinton Mains Gdns
EH13 .... **153** E4
Colinton Mains Gn EH13 .... **153** E4
Colinton Mains Gr EH13 .... **153** F4
Colinton Mains Loan
EH13 .... **153** E4
Colinton Mains Pl EH13 ..... **153** F4
Colinton Mains Rd EH13 .... **153** E4
Colinton Mains Terr EH13 ... **153** F4
Colinton Prim Sch EH13 .... **153** F3
Colinton Rd EH10, EH13 .... **122** C2
Coll Pl FK3 .... **61** E3
College Cres FK2 .... **60** B4
College Wynd EH1 .... **233** D2
Colliers Rd FK7 .... **8** B2
Collingwood Ct FK1 .... **59** F3
Collins Cres KY11 .... **47** F1
Collins Pl EH3 .... **93** D1
Colliston Rd KY12 .... **29** E3
Collydand Rd KY11 .... **5** E2
Colmestone Gate EH10 ..... **154** A3
Colonsay Ave FK2 .... **61** E1
Colonsay Terr FK1 .... **60** A1
Colquhoun St FK7 .... **7** E3
Colquhoun Terr FK7 .... **7** E3
Colsnaur FK11 .... **4** A3
Coltbridge Ave EH12 .... **122** B4
Coltbridge Gdns EH12 ...... **122** C4
Coltbridge Millside EH12 ... **122** C4
Coltbridge Terr EH12 .... **122** B4
Coltbridge Vale EH12 .... **122** C4
Coltness Ave ML7 .... **212** A4
Colton Ct KY12 .... **28** C2
Columba Ave EH4 .... **92** A1
Columba Rd EH4 .... **92** A1
Columbia Ave EH54 .... **147** F2
Colvin St EH42 .... **78** C1
Combfoot Cotts EH53 .... **148** B2
Comeley Green Cres [10]
EH7 .... **94** A1
Comeley Green Pl [9] EH7 ... **94** A1
Comely Bank Ave EH4 ...... **92** C1
Comely Bank Gr EH4 .... **92** C1
Comely Bank Pl EH4 .... **93** C1
Comely Bank Place Mews [2]
EH4 .... **92** C1
Comely Bank Rd EH4 .... **92** C1
Comely Bank Row EH4 ...... **93** D1
Comely Bank St EH4 .... **92** C1
Comely Bank Terr [1] EH4 ... **93** D1
Comely Park La KY12 .... **29** D2
Comely Park Prim Sch
FK1 .... **60** A2
Comely Park Terr [15] FK1 ... **60** A2
Comely Pk Dunfermline KY12 .. **29** D2
Maddiston FK2 .... **82** C4
Comely Pl FK1 .... **60** A2
Comiston Dr EH10 .... **123** D1
Comiston Gdns EH10 .... **123** D1
Comiston Gr EH10 .... **154** A4
Comiston Pl EH10 .... **123** D1
Comiston Prim Sch EH13 ... **153** F3
Comiston Rd EH10 .... **154** A4
Comiston Rise EH10 .... **154** A4
Comiston Springs Ave
EH10 .... **154** A4
Comiston Terr EH10 .... **123** D1
Comiston View EH10 .... **154** A4
Commercial Prim Sch
KY11 .... **29** E2
Commercial Rd KY11 .... **47** E1
Commercial School La
KY12 .... **29** D2
Commercial St
Edinburgh EH6 .... **93** F3
Kirkaldy KY1 .... **17** E3
Commissioner St EH51 ...... **64** A4
Commodores Wlk KY11 ..... **46** B1
Compass Sch EH41 .... **131** F4
Compressor House Rd FK2 .. **62** B3
Compton Rd FK3 .... **61** E3
Comrie Terr EH51 .... **63** F3
Comyn Dr FK2 .... **82** B4
Concorde Way KY11 .... **47** E2
Coneyhill Rd FK9 .... **2** A4
Coneypark FK7 .... **6** C3
Conifer Rd EH22 .... **183** F4
Coningsby Pl FK10 .... **10** A3
Connaught Pl EH6 .... **93** E3
Conner Ave FK2 .... **60** A4
Considine Gdns [3] EH8 ..... **94** B1
Considine Terr [2] EH8 ...... **94** B1
Constable Rd FK7 .... **7** D3
Constitution Pl EH6 .... **94** A3
Constitution St EH6 .... **94** A3
Conway Ct FK1 .... **59** F2
Cook Cres EH22 .... **183** D3
Cook Pl KY1 .... **18** A4
Cook Sq KY5 .... **14** A4
Cook St KY1 .... **18** A4
Cooper's La FK10 .... **23** F2
Cooperage La FK1 .... **60** A3
Cope La EH32 .... **97** E2
Copeland Cres KY4 .... **13** D1
Copland Pl FK12 .... **4** C4
Copper Beech Wynd KY12 ... **27** E1
Corbett Pl KY11 .... **29** F1
Corbiehall EH51 .... **63** F4
Corbiehill Ave EH4 .... **92** A2
Corbiehill Cres EH4 .... **91** F2
Corbiehill Gdns EH4 .... **92** A2
Corbiehill Gr EH4 .... **92** A2
Corbiehill Pk EH4 .... **92** A2
Corbiehill Pl EH4 .... **91** F2
Corbiehill Terr EH4 .... **91** F2
Corbieshot EH15 .... **125** D3
Corbiewood Dr FK7 .... **19** F4

Cordiner's Land EH1 .... 232 C2
Corentin Ct FK1 .... 60 B2
Cormailin Pl KY12 .... 26 A1
Corn Exchange Rd FK8 .... 7 D4
Cornbank-St James'
　Prim Sch EH26 .... 203 E3
Cornfield Pl EH54 .... 147 D2
Cornhill Cres FK7 .... 7 D2
Cornhill Terr EH6 .... 94 A2
Cornton Bsns Pk FK9 .... 2 A2
Cornton Cres FK9 .... 2 A3
Cornton Prim Sch FK9 .... 2 A2
Cornton Rd FK9 .... 2 A2
Cornwall St EH1 .... 232 B2
Cornwallis Pl EH3 .... 93 E1
Coronation Pl
　Mayfield EH22 .... 183 E4
　Skinflats FK2 .... 39 F2
Corpach Dr KY12 .... 28 C1
Corporation St FK1 .... 60 B2
Corrennie Dr EH10 .... 123 D1
Corrennie Gdns EH10 .... 123 D1
Corrie Ave FK5 .... 38 C2
Corrie Ct EH22 .... 183 D2
Corrie Pl FK1 .... 59 E2
Corruna Rd ML8 .... 230 A1
Corslet Cres EH14 .... 152 A3
Corslet Pl EH14 .... 152 A3
Corslet Rd EH14 .... 152 A3
Corston Pk EH54 .... 148 A2
Corstorphine Bank Ave
　EH12 .... 121 E4
Corstorphine Bank Dr
　EH12 .... 121 E4
Corstorphine Bank Terr
　EH12 .... 121 E4
Corstorphine High St
　EH12 .... 121 E3
Corstorphine Hill Ave
　EH12 .... 121 F4
Corstorphine Hill Cres
　EH12 .... 121 F4
Corstorphine Hill Gdns
　EH12 .... 121 F4
Corstorphine Hill Rd
　EH12 .... 121 F4
Corstorphine Hospl EH12 ... 121 F3
Corstorphine House Ave
　EH12 .... 121 F3
Corstorphine Park Gdns
　EH12 .... 121 F3
Corstorphine Prim Sch
　EH12 .... 121 F3
Corstorphine Rd EH12 .... 122 A4
Cortachy Ave FK2 .... 39 D2
Cortleferry Dr EH22 .... 156 C1
Cortleferry Gr EH22 .... 156 C1
Cortleferry Pk EH22 .... 156 C1
Cortleferry Terr EH22 .... 156 C1
Corunna Pl EH6 .... 93 F3
Corunna Terr EH26 .... 204 A4
Cossars Wynd EH42 .... 78 B1
Cotburn Cres KY3 .... 33 F1
Cotlands Ave EH32 .... 98 B2
Cotlands Pk EH32 .... 98 B2
Cotlaws EH29 .... 89 D1
Cottage Gn EH4 .... 91 D2
Cottage Homes EH13 .... 153 D4
Cottage La EH21 .... 126 C3
Cottage Pk EH4 .... 92 A1
Cotton La FK2 .... 61 D2
Cotts The EH49 .... 86 C2
Coulport Pl KY12 .... 28 C1
Council Houses
　Athelstaneford EH39 .... 101 F4
　Bolton EH41 .... 162 C4
　Drem EH41 .... 73 D2
　Gifford EH41 .... 133 E3
Countess Ave EH42 .... 78 B1
Countess Cres EH42 .... 78 B1
Countess Rd EH42 .... 78 B1
County Hospl FK10 .... 10 A4
County Houses KY4 .... 31 D3
County Rd EH32 .... 96 C1
County Sq EH32 .... 96 C1
Couper Ave EH39 .... 54 B3
Couper St EH6 .... 93 F3
Court St EH41 .... 132 A4
Courthill FK1 .... 5 D4
Cousin's La KY12 .... 28 C2
Cousland Cres EH47 .... 146 A1
Cousland Intc EH54 .... 147 F3
Cousland Prim Sch EH22 ... 158 B3
Cousland Rd EH54 .... 147 E2
Cousland Terr EH47 .... 146 A1
Couston Ave KY11 .... 48 A2
Couston Pl KY11 .... 48 A2
Couston Rd KY11 .... 48 A2
Couston St KY12 .... 29 D2
Cove Cres ML7 .... 191 F3
Covenanter Rd ML7 .... 168 B2
Covenanters La EH30 .... 68 A1
Coville St EH6 .... 93 D1
Cow Wynd FK1 .... 60 A2
Cowan Rd EH11 .... 122 C2
Cowan St Bathgate EH48 ... 145 F3
　Bonnybridge FK4 .... 58 A3
Cowan Terr EH26 .... 203 F4
Cowan's Cl EH8 .... 233 E1
Cowane St FK8 .... 7 D4
Cowden Cres EH22 .... 157 E2
Cowden Gr EH22 .... 157 E2
Cowden La EH22 .... 157 E2
Cowden Pl EH22 .... 157 E2
Cowden Terr EH22 .... 157 E2
Cowden View EH22 .... 157 E2

Cowdenbeath Prim Sch
　KY4 .... 13 E2
Cowdenbeath Rd KY3 .... 33 F1
Cowdenbeath Sta KY4 .... 13 E2
Cowgate EH1 .... 233 D2
Cowgatehead EH1 .... 233 D2
Cowie Prim Sch FK7 .... 20 B4
Cowie Rd FK7 .... 20 A4
Cowiehall Rd FK7 .... 20 B4
Cowpits Ford Rd EH21 .... 126 B2
Cowpits Rd EH21 .... 126 B1
Coxfield EH11 .... 122 B2
Coxithall Rd FK7 .... 7 D2
Craig Ave Haddington EH41 ... 101 D1
　Whitburn EH47 .... 169 F3
Craig Cres FK9 .... 2 B2
Craig Ct Bridge of A FK9 ... 2 A3
　Burntisland KY3 .... 33 E1
Craig Leith Rd FK7 .... 7 E3
Craig St Blackridge EH48 ... 142 C2
　Rosyth KY11 .... 47 D2
Craigbank Alloa FK10 .... 5 E1
　Crossford KY12 .... 28 B1
Craigbank Prim Sch FK10 ... 5 E1
Craigbank Rd FK1 .... 112 A3
Craigbeath Ct KY4 .... 13 D3
Craigburn Ct FK1 .... 59 F1
Craigcrook Ave EH4 .... 92 A1
Craigcrook Gdns EH4 .... 92 A1
Craigcrook Pk EH4 .... 92 A1
Craigcrook Pl **5** EH4 .... 92 B1
Craigcrook Rd EH4 .... 92 A1
Craigcrook Sq EH4 .... 92 A1
Craigcrook Terr **4** EH4 .... 92 B1
Craigdimas Gr KY11 .... 48 A1
Craigearn Ave KY2 .... 16 A4
Craigend Dr FK2 .... 83 D3
Craigend Pk EH16 .... 124 B1
Craigend Rd FK7 .... 7 D2
Craigentinny Ave EH7 .... 94 C1
Craigentinny Ave N EH6 ... 94 B2
Craigentinny Cres EH7 .... 94 C1
Craigentinny Gr EH7 .... 94 C1
Craigentinny Pl EH7 .... 94 C1
Craigentinny Prim Sch
　EH7 .... 94 B1
Craigentinny Rd EH7 .... 94 B1
Craigford Dr FK7 .... 7 E1
Craigforth Cres FK8 .... 1 C1
Craighall Ave EH6 .... 93 E3
Craighall Bank EH6 .... 93 E3
Craighall Cres EH6 .... 93 E3
Craighall Gdns EH6 .... 93 E3
Craighall Rd EH6 .... 93 E3
Craighall St FK8 .... 1 C1
Craighall Terr
　Edinburgh EH6 .... 93 E3
　Musselburgh EH21 .... 126 C3
Craighill Gdns EH10 .... 122 C1
Craighill View EH48 .... 142 C2
Craigholm La KY3 .... 33 F1
Craighorn FK11 .... 4 A3
Craighorn Dr FK1 .... 59 F1
Craighorn Rd FK12 .... 4 C3
Craighouse Ave EH10 .... 122 C1
Craighouse Gdns EH10 .... 122 C1
Craighouse Pk EH10 .... 122 C1
Craighouse Rd EH10 .... 122 C1
Craighouse Terr EH10 .... 122 C1
Craigie Ct FK5 .... 38 A4
Craigiebield Cres EH26 .... 203 F2
Craigielaw Farm Cotts
　EH32 .... 71 D2
Craigievar Ave FK2 .... 39 D2
Craigievar Gdns KY2 .... 16 C3
Craigievar Sq EH12 .... 121 D4
Craigievar Wynd EH12 .... 121 D4
Craiginn Ct EH48 .... 142 B2
Craiginn Terr EH48 .... 142 B2
Craigkennochie Terr KY3 ... 33 F1
Craiglaw EH52 .... 116 B1
Craiglea Ct EH48 .... 142 B2
Craiglea Dr EH10 .... 123 D1
Craiglea Pl EH10 .... 122 C1
Craigleith **5** FK5 .... 38 A4
Craigleith Ave Falkirk FK1 ... 59 F1
　North Berwick EH39 .... 54 B3
Craigleith Ave N EH4 .... 122 B4
Craigleith Ave S EH4 .... 122 B4
Craigleith Bank EH4 .... 92 B1
Craigleith Cres EH4 .... 92 B1
Craigleith Dr EH4 .... 92 B1
Craigleith Gdns EH4 .... 92 B1
Craigleith Gr EH4 .... 92 B1
Craigleith Hill EH4 .... 92 B1
Craigleith Hill Ave EH4 .... 92 B1
Craigleith Hill Cres EH4 ... 92 B1
Craigleith Hill Gdns EH4 ... 92 C1
Craigleith Hill Gn EH4 .... 92 B1
Craigleith Hill Gr EH4 .... 92 B1
Craigleith Hill Loan EH4 ... 92 B1
Craigleith Hill Pk EH4 .... 92 B1
Craigleith Hill Row EH4 ... 92 B1
Craigleith Rd Edinburgh EH4 ... 92 C1
　Grangemouth FK3 .... 61 E3
Craigleith Ret Pk EH4 .... 92 B1
Craigleith Rise EH4 .... 122 B4
Craigleith View EH4 .... 122 B4
Craiglockhart Ave EH14 .... 122 B1
Craiglockhart Bank EH14 ... 122 B1
Craiglockhart Cres EH14 ... 122 B1
Craiglockhart Dell Rd
　EH14 .... 122 B1
Craiglockhart Dr N EH14 ... 122 B1
Craiglockhart Dr S EH14 ... 122 B1
Craiglockhart Gdns EH14 ... 122 B1

Craiglockhart Gr EH14 .... 153 E4
Craiglockhart Loan EH14 ... 122 B1
Craiglockhart Pk EH14 .... 122 B1
Craiglockhart Pl EH14 .... 122 B1
Craiglockhart Prim Sch
　EH11 .... 122 C2
Craiglockhart Quadrant
　EH14 .... 122 B1
Craiglockhart Rd N
　EH14 .... 122 B1
Craiglockhart Sports Ctr
　EH14 .... 122 B1
Craiglockhart Terr EH14 ... 122 C2
Craiglockhart View EH14 ... 122 B1
Craigmillar Castle EH16 .... 124 B1
Craigmillar Castle Ave
　EH16 .... 124 B2
Craigmillar Castle Gdns
　EH16 .... 124 B2
Craigmillar Castle Gr
　EH16 .... 124 B2
Craigmillar Castle Loan
　EH16 .... 124 C2
Craigmillar Castle Rd
　EH16 .... 124 B1
Craigmillar Castle Terr
　EH16 .... 124 B2
Craigmillar Pk EH16 .... 124 A2
Craigmillar Pl FK5 .... 38 C2
Craigmillar Prim Sch
　EH16 .... 124 C2
Craigmore Gdns KY12 .... 26 C1
Craigmount KY2 .... 16 A4
Craigmount App EH12 .... 121 E4
Craigmount Ave EH12 .... 121 E4
Craigmount Ave N EH12 ... 91 D1
Craigmount Bank EH4 .... 91 D1
Craigmount Bank W EH4 ... 91 D1
Craigmount Brae EH12 .... 91 D1
Craigmount Cres EH12 .... 121 E4
Craigmount Ct EH4 .... 91 D1
Craigmount Dr EH12 .... 121 E4
Craigmount Gdns EH12 .... 121 E4
Craigmount Gr EH12 .... 121 E4
Craigmount Gr N EH12 .... 121 D4
Craigmount Hill EH4 .... 91 D1
Craigmount Loan EH12 .... 121 D4
Craigmount Pk EH12 .... 121 E4
Craigmount Pl EH12 .... 121 E4
Craigmount Sec Sch
　EH12 .... 121 D4
Craigmount Terr EH12 .... 121 E4
Craigmount View EH12 .... 121 D4
Craigmount Way EH12 .... 91 E1
Craigmuir Prim Sch EH4 ... 92 B3
Craigmyle St KY12 .... 29 E3
Craigomus Cres FK11 .... 3 F3
Craigour Ave EH17 .... 155 F4
Craigour Cres EH17 .... 155 F4
Craigour Dr EH17 .... 155 F4
Craigour Gdns EH17 .... 155 F4
Craigour Gn EH17 .... 155 F4
Craigour Gr EH17 .... 155 F4
Craigour Loan EH17 .... 155 F4
Craigour Pl EH17 .... 155 F4
Craigour Terr EH17 .... 155 F4
Craigpark EH48 .... 113 F3
Craigpark Ave EH28 .... 119 E1
Craigpark Cres EH28 .... 119 E1
Craigridge Pl KY11 .... 48 B3
Craigrie Terr FK10 .... 11 D2
Craigrigg Cotts EH48 .... 112 C2
Craigroyston Com
　High Sch EH4 .... 92 A2
Craigs Ave EH12 .... 121 E3
Craigs Bank EH12 .... 121 D4
Craigs Chalet Pk EH49 .... 84 A2
Craigs Cres EH12 .... 121 E4
Craigs Ct EH48 .... 113 F3
Craigs Dr EH12 .... 121 D4
Craigs Gdns EH12 .... 121 E4
Craigs Gr EH12 .... 121 E4
Craigs Loan EH12 .... 121 E4
Craigs Pk EH12 .... 121 D4
Craigs Rd EH12 .... 121 D4
Craigseat Rd EH54 .... 148 A3
Craigshill Rd EH54 .... 148 A3
Craigshill West Rd EH54 ... 148 A3
Craigston Dr KY12 .... 29 E3
Craigswood EH54 .... 148 A3
Craigton Ct EH52 .... 87 F1
Craigton Pl KY4 .... 13 E1
Craigview Alloa FK10 .... 5 E1
　Bo'ness EH51 .... 64 B4
Craigward FK10 .... 10 A3
Craigwell Path KY12 .... 44 B4
Crame Terr EH16 .... 156 C1
Cramond Ave EH4 .... 91 E3
Cramond Bank EH4 .... 91 E3
Cramond Brig Toll EH4 .... 90 C2
Cramond Cres EH4 .... 91 E3
Cramond Ct FK1 .... 60 A1
Cramond Gdns
　Edinburgh EH4 .... 91 D3
　Kircaldy KY2 .... 16 C4
Cramond Glebe Gdns
　EH4 .... 91 E3
Cramond Glebe Rd EH4 ... 91 D3
Cramond Glebe Terr EH4 ... 91 D3
Cramond Gn EH4 .... 91 D3
Cramond Pk EH4 .... 91 D3

Cramond Pl
　Dalgety Bay KY11 .... 48 B2
　Edinburgh EH4 .... 91 E3
Cramond Prim Sch EH4 ... 91 D3
Cramond Rd N EH4 .... 91 E3
Cramond Rd S EH4 .... 91 F2
Cramond Regis EH4 .... 91 D3
Cramond Terr EH4 .... 91 D3
Cramond Vale EH4 .... 91 D3
Cramond Village EH4 .... 91 D4
Cranshaws Dr FK2 .... 61 E1
Cranston Dr EH22 .... 158 B3
Cranston Prim Sch EH37 ... 184 C3
Cranston St Edinburgh EH8 .. 233 E3
　Penicuik EH26 .... 203 F3
Crarae Ave EH4 .... 122 B4
Crathes Ave FK5 .... 39 D2
Crathes Gdns EH54 .... 173 F3
Crathie Dr FK6 .... 36 B2
Craufurdland EH4 .... 91 D3
Crawfield Ave EH51 .... 63 F3
Crawfield La EH51 .... 63 F3
Crawfield Rd EH51 .... 63 F3
Crawford Dr FK2 .... 82 A4
Crawford Pl KY12 .... 29 E4
Crawford Sq FK2 .... 22 B2
Crawfurd Rd EH16 .... 124 A2
Crawlees Cres EH22 .... 183 F3
Craws Knowe ML11 .... 215 D1
Creel Ct EH39 .... 54 B4
Creran Dr FK6 .... 57 E3
Crescent The
　Edinburgh EH10 .... 123 D1
　Gowkshill EH23 .... 183 E2
　Rosyth KY11 .... 46 A1
Creteil Ct FK1 .... 60 B2
Creteil Pl FK3 .... 61 E4
Crewe Bank EH5 .... 92 C3
Crewe Cres EH5 .... 92 C3
Crewe Gr EH5 .... 92 C3
Crewe Loan EH5 .... 92 B3
Crewe Pl EH5 .... 92 B3
Crewe Rd N EH5 .... 92 B3
Crewe Rd S EH4 .... 92 C2
Crewe Rd W EH5 .... 92 B3
Crewe Road Gdns EH5 .... 92 B3
Crewe Terr EH5 .... 92 C3
Crewe Toll EH4 .... 92 B2
Crichton Ave EH37 .... 185 D3
Crichton Castle EH37 .... 208 C4
Crichton Dr
　Grangemouth FK3 .... 61 F4
　Pathhead EH37 .... 185 D3
Crichton Rd EH37 .... 185 D3
Crichton St EH8 .... 233 D2
Crichton Terr EH37 .... 185 D3
Cricket Pl FK2 .... 61 E1
Crighton Pl EH6 .... 93 F2
Crimond Pl FK1 .... 81 F4
Cringate Gdns FK7 .... 7 F1
Crockett Gdns EH26 .... 203 E3
Croft An Righ KY3 .... 35 D2
Croft Pl EH54 .... 147 E3
Croft St Dalkeith EH22 .... 157 D2
　Penicuik EH26 .... 203 F2
Croft's Rd FK2 .... 4 A2
Croft-An-Righ EH8 .... 233 E4
Crofters Gate EH47 .... 170 C4
Crofters Way EH47 .... 170 C3
Croftfoot Dr EH47 .... 194 A3
Croftfoot Pl FK6 .... 36 B2
Crofthead Ct FK8 .... 2 A1
Crofthead Ct EH54 .... 173 E4
Crofthead Intc EH54 .... 173 F4
Crofthead Rd Stirling FK8 ... 2 A1
　Stoneyburn EH47 .... 171 D1
Croftmalloch Prim Sch
　EH47 .... 170 A3
Croftmalloch Rd EH47 .... 170 A3
Crofts Rd TD13 .... 140 C1
Crofts The EH42 .... 104 C1
Croftsacre TD13 .... 140 C1
Croftshaw Rd FK12 .... 5 D4
Croftside Ct FK3 .... 61 F3
Cromarty Pl KY1 .... 17 F4
Crombie Prim Sch KY12 ... 44 B4
Cromwell Pl FK1 .... 60 B2
Cromwell Pl EH6 .... 93 F3
Cromwell Rd
　Burntisland KY3 .... 33 F1
　Falkirk FK1 .... 60 B2
　North Berwick EH39 .... 54 A4
　Rosyth KY11 .... 46 C3
Cromwell Rd W FK1 .... 60 B2
Crookston Ct EH21 .... 126 C2
Crookston Rd EH21 .... 126 C2
Crophill FK10 .... 5 E1
Crosford Path KY12 .... 28 A1
Cross Brae FK1 .... 81 D2
Cross Loan EH35 .... 159 F4
Cross Row KY11 .... 45 D2
Cross St Dysart KY1 .... 18 A4
　Falkirk FK1 .... 39 D1
Cross The Linlithgow EH49 ... 85 D4
　Lochgelly KY5 .... 14 A4
Cross Way KY11 .... 48 B3
Cross Wynd KY12 .... 29 D2
Crossen La ML8 .... 230 A1
Crossgatehead Rd FK2 .... 60 A3
Crossgates Prim Sch KY4 ... 30 C3
Crossgreen Dr EH52 .... 117 D3
Crossgreen Pl EH52 .... 117 D3
Crosshill Dr
　Bathgate EH48 .... 145 E3
　Bo'ness EH51 .... 63 D3
Crossroads Pl KY11 .... 46 C2
Crosswood Ave EH14 .... 177 D4
Crosswood Cres EH14 .... 177 D4

Crosswood Terr EH55 .... 217 F2
Crowhill Rd KY11 .... 48 B2
Crown Gdns FK10 .... 9 F4
Crown Pl EH6 .... 93 F2
Crown St EH6 .... 93 F2
Crownest Loan FK5 .... 38 C1
Cruachan Ave FK9 .... 2 A2
Cruachan Ct Falkirk FK1 ... 60 B1
　Penicuik EH26 .... 204 A3
Cruachan Pl FK3 .... 61 F3
Cruckburn Wynd FK7 .... 6 C2
Cruickness Rd KY11 .... 68 B4
Cruickshank Dr FK1 .... 81 F4
Cruikshank's Ct FK6 .... 36 C1
Crum Cres FK7 .... 7 E1
Crusader Dr EH25 .... 180 C2
Crusader Rise EH54 .... 148 A1
Crystal Works EH26 .... 203 F3
Cuddy La EH10 .... 123 D2
Cuddyhouse Rd KY12 .... 12 B2
Cuffabouts EH51 .... 64 B4
Cuguen EH18 .... 156 A1
Cuiken Ave EH26 .... 203 E3
Cuiken Bank EH26 .... 203 E3
Cuiken Prim Sch EH26 .... 203 E3
Cuiken Terr EH26 .... 203 E3
Cuikenburn EH26 .... 203 F4
Cuil Gr KY12 .... 28 B3
Cuillin Ct FK1 .... 60 B1
Cuillin Pl FK1 .... 61 F3
Cullalo Cres KY3 .... 49 E4
Cullaloe Ct KY11 .... 48 B2
Cullaloe Nature Reserve
　KY3 .... 32 A2
Cullaloe View KY4 .... 13 E1
Cullen Cres KY2 .... 16 C4
Cullen Sq EH54 .... 146 B3
Culloch Rd FK1 .... 110 A3
Culmore Pl FK1 .... 60 C1
Culross Abbey KY12 .... 25 E1
Culross Palace KY12 .... 42 B4
Culross Prim Sch KY12 .... 42 B4
Cultenhove Cres
　Grangemouth FK3 .... 61 F3
　Stirling FK7 .... 6 C2
Cultenhove Pl FK7 .... 7 D2
Cultenhove Rd FK7 .... 7 D2
Cultins Rd EH11 .... 121 D2
Cultrig Dr EH47 .... 170 A3
Culvain Pl FK1 .... 60 B1
Culzean Cres KY2 .... 16 B4
Culzean Pl FK5 .... 38 C2
Cumberland St EH3 .... 93 E1
Cumbernauld Rd FK4 .... 57 D2
Cumbrae Dr FK1 .... 59 E2
Cumbrae Terr KY2 .... 17 D4
Cumin Pl EH9 .... 123 F2
Cumlodden Ave EH12 .... 122 B4
Cumnor Cres EH16 .... 124 A1
Cunnigar Gdns EH53 .... 148 B2
Cunnigar Hill View EH53 ... 148 B2
Cunningham Cres EH52 ... 117 E3
Cunningham Ct
　Longniddry EH32 .... 98 B2
　North Berwick EH39 .... 54 A3
Cunningham Dr ML7 .... 168 B3
Cunningham Gdns FK2 .... 60 C3
Cunningham Rd
　Rosyth KY11 .... 46 B1
　Stenhousemuir FK5 .... 39 D2
　Stirling FK7 .... 7 E4
Cunningham St FK3 .... 61 E3
Curling Knowe KY4 .... 31 D3
Curling Pk KY4 .... 30 C3
Curran Cres EH52 .... 117 F3
Currie High Sch EH14 .... 151 F2
Curriehill Castle Dr EH14 .. 151 E2
Curriehill Prim Sch EH14 .. 152 A2
Curriehill Rd EH14 .... 151 F3
Curriehill Sta EH14 .... 151 F3
Currieside Ave ML7 .... 191 E2
Currieside Pl ML7 .... 191 E2
Currievale Dr EH14 .... 151 F2
Currievale Park Gr EH14 ... 151 F2
Currievale Pk EH14 .... 151 F2
Cushenquarter Dr FK7 .... 20 B2
Custom House Sq EH42 ... 78 C2
Custonhall Pl FK6 .... 36 C1
Cuthill Cres ML7 .... 171 E1
Cuthill Terr EH47 .... 171 E1
Cuttyfield Pl FK2 .... 39 E2
Cypress Gr KY11 .... 46 B4

D'arcy Cres EH22 .... 183 F4
D'arcy Rd EH22 .... 183 F3
D'arcy Terr EH22 .... 183 F4
Daiches Braes EH15 .... 125 E3
Dairy Cotts EH39 .... 53 D1
Dairy Prim Sch EH11 .... 122 C3
Daisy Terr EH11 .... 122 C2
Dalachy Cotts KY3 .... 32 C1
Dalbeath Cres KY4 .... 13 D1
Dalbeath Gdns KY4 .... 12 C1
Dalcross Way KY12 .... 29 F3
Dalderse Ave FK2 .... 60 A3
Dalgety Ave EH7 .... 94 A1
Dalgety Bay Prim Sch
　KY11 .... 48 A2
Dalgety Bay Sta KY11 .... 47 F3
Dalgety Gdns KY11 .... 48 B3
Dalgety House View KY11 .. 48 B3
Dalgety Rd EH7 .... 94 A1
Dalgety St EH7 .... 94 A1
Dalgleish Ct FK8 .... 7 D4

Dalgrain Rd FK3 .... 40 A1
Dalhousie Ave EH19 .... 182 A3
Dalhousie Ave W EH19 ... 182 A3
Dalhousie Dr EH19 .... 182 A3
Dalhousie Gdns EH19 ...... 182 A3
Dalhousie Rd EH22 .... 156 C1
Dalhousie Rd E EH19 .... 182 A3
Dalhousie Rd W EH19 ...... 182 A3
Dalhousie Terr EH10 .... 123 D1
Dalkeith High Sch EH22 ... 157 D2
Dalkeith Rd EH16 .... 233 F1
Dalkeith St EH15 .... 125 E4
Dallas Ave KY3 .... 33 F1
Dalling Rd EH48 .... 144 C3
Dalmahoy Cres EH14 .... 151 E2
Dalmahoy Rd EH28 .... 119 E1
Dalmeny Ho EH30 .... 69 E1
Dalmeny Prim Sch EH30 ..... 89 F4
Dalmeny Rd EH6 .... 93 E3
Dalmeny St EH6 .... 93 F2
Dalmeny Sta EH30 .... 89 E4
Dalmeny View KY11 .... 48 B2
Dalmore Dr FK12 .... 4 C3
Dalmorglen Pk FK7 .... 6 C3
Dalratho Rd FK3 .... 61 F4
Dalry Pl EH11 .... 232 A2
Dalry Rd EH11 .... 122 C4
Dalrymple Cres
    Edinburgh EH9 .... 123 F2
    Musselburgh EH21 ..... 126 A3
Dalrymple Gdns EH22 ...... 158 B3
Dalrymple Loan EH21 ...... 126 B3
Dalton Ct EH22 .... 183 F3
Dalum Ct EH20 .... 181 D4
Dalum Dr EH20 .... 181 D4
Dalum Gr EH20 .... 181 D4
Dalum Loan EH20 .... 181 D4
Dalziel Ct EH47 .... 171 C1
Dalziel Pl EH7 .... 94 A1
Damhead
    Holdings Scheme EH10 .. 154 B1
Damside EH4 .... 232 A3
Danderhall Cres EH22 ...... 156 A4
Danderhall Prim Sch
    EH22 .... 156 A4
Dania Ct EH11 .... 121 F2
Daniel Pl KY11 .... 46 B3
Daniel Stewart's
    & Melville Coll EH4 ...... 92 C1
Danube St EH4 .... 232 A4
Dargai Pl EH52 .... 117 D3
Darian La EH51 .... 63 F4
Darmeid Pl ML7 .... 212 A4
Darnaway St EH3 .... 232 B4
Darnell Rd EH5 .... 93 D3
Darney Terr KY3 .... 34 C1
Darnley St FK8 .... 7 D4
Darrach Dr FK6 .... 36 A1
Darwin St EH54 .... 148 A3
Davaar Dr KY2 .... 16 C4
Davarr Pl FK1 .... 59 E2
Davenport Pl KY11 .... 46 C2
David Henderson Ct KY12 .. 29 D2
David Millar Pl KY12 .... 28 C3
David Scott Ave EH22 ...... 183 F4
David St Dunfermline KY12 ... 29 D3
    Kirkaldy KY1 .... 17 D2
    Lochgelly KY5 .... 14 A4
David The First St KY3 ...... 34 C1
David's Loan FK2 .... 39 E1
Davids Mains Prim Sch
    EH4 .... 91 F2
Davidson Gdns EH4 .... 92 A2
Davidson La ML8 .... 230 A1
Davidson Pk EH4 .... 92 C2
Davidson Rd EH4 .... 92 C2
Davidson St FK7 .... 7 E1
Davidson Terr EH41 .... 100 C1
Davidson Way EH54 .... 147 F4
Davie St EH8 .... 233 E2
Daviot Rd KY12 .... 29 F3
Dawson Ave Alloa FK10 .... 9 F4
    Livingston EH54 .... 147 F3
Dawson Park Sch FK2 .... 39 D1
Dawson Pl EH51 .... 63 F3
Dawson St FK2 .... 60 A4
De Quincey Path EH18 ..... 181 F3
De Quincey Rd EH18 .... 181 F3
Deacons Ct EH49 .... 85 D3
Dean Bank La EH3 .... 93 D1
Dean Cres FK8 .... 2 B1
Dean Ct EH32 .... 98 B2
Dean Dr KY12 .... 28 A1
Dean Gr KY12 .... 28 A1
Dean Park Cres EH4 .... 232 A4
Dean Park Mews EH4 .... 93 D1
Dean Park Prim Sch
    EH14 .... 151 E1
Dean Park Sch EH14 .... 177 E4
Dean Path EH4 .... 92 C1
Dean Pk Gowkhall KY12 ..... 27 F4
    Longniddry EH32 .... 98 B2
    Newtongrange EH22 ... 183 D3
Dean Park St EH4 .... 93 D1
Dean Pl Penicuik EH26 .... 203 E3
    Seafield EH47 .... 146 A1
Dean Rd Bo'ness EH51 ...... 63 F3
    Kirkaldy KY1 .... 17 D2
    Longniddry EH32 .... 98 B2
    Penicuik EH26 .... 203 E3
Dean Ridge KY12 .... 27 F4
Dean St Edinburgh EH4 ...... 93 D1
    Whitburn EH47 .... 170 A4

Dean Terr EH4 .... 232 A4
Dean The EH40 .... 75 F1
Deanburn EH26 .... 203 F4
Deanburn Cres EH51 .... 63 E3
Deanburn Pk EH49 .... 84 C3
Deanburn Prim Sch EH51 .. 63 E3
Deanburn Rd EH49 .... 84 C3
Deanburn Wlk EH51 .... 63 E3
Deanery Cl EH7 .... 94 B1
Deanfield Cres EH51 .... 63 F4
Deanfield Dr EH51 .... 63 F3
Deanfield Pl EH51 .... 63 F4
Deanfield Rd EH51 .... 63 F4
Deanfield Terr EH51 .... 63 F4
Deangate Gdns EH51 .... 63 E3
Deanhaugh St EH4 .... 93 D1
Deanpark Ave EH14 .... 151 E1
Deanpark Bank EH14 .... 151 E1
Deanpark Brae EH14 .... 151 E1
Deanpark Cres EH14 .... 151 E1
Deanpark Ct EH14 .... 151 D1
Deanpark Gdns EH14 .... 151 E1
Deanpark Gr EH14 .... 151 E1
Deanpark Pl EH14 .... 151 E1
Deans Com High Sch
    EH54 .... 147 D4
Deans Ind Est EH54 .... 146 B3
Deans North Rd EH54 ...... 146 C4
Deans Rd EH54 .... 146 C3
Deans Rd EH54 .... 146 B3
Deans Service Units EH54 . 146 C4
Deans South EH54 .... 146 C3
Deanswood Pk EH54 .... 146 C3
Deantown Ave EH21 .... 157 F4
Deantown Dr EH21 .... 126 C1
Deantown Path EH21 ...... 126 C1
Deas Rd Inverkeithing KY11 ... 47 D1
    Shotts ML7 .... 191 E3
Dechmont Inf Sch EH52 .. 116 A1
Dechmont Rd EH12 .... 121 D3
Dechmont Rdbt EH52 ...... 116 B1
Dedridge East Ind Est
    EH54 .... 148 A1
Dedridge East Rd EH54 ... 148 A1
Dedridge North Rd EH54 . 147 F1
Dedridge Prim Sch EH54 . 148 A1
Dedridge West Rd EH54 .. 173 A1
Dee Dr EH54 .... 148 A3
Dee Pl KY11 .... 29 F1
Dee St ML7 .... 191 E3
Deep Sea World KY11 .... 68 B3
Deer Park Bsns Campus
    EH54 .... 116 B1
Deer Park Dr EH54 .... 116 B1
Deer Park Rd Abercorn EH30 . 66 C1
    Dechmont EH54 .... 116 B1
Deerhill EH54 .... 116 B1
Deerpark KY10 .... 5 F1
Deerpark Prim Sch FK10 .... 5 F1
Deeside Dr ML8 .... 230 A1
Delisle St EH42 .... 78 B1
Dell Ave EH48 .... 143 F3
Dell Rd EH13 .... 153 D4
Delph Rd EH15 .... 4 B1
Delphwood Cres FK10 .... 4 B1
Delta Cres EH21 .... 127 C3
Delta Dr EH21 .... 127 D3
Delta Gdns EH21 .... 127 D3
Delta Pl EH21 .... 126 B2
Delta Rd EH21 .... 127 D3
Delta View EH21 .... 127 D3
Dempster Pl KY12 .... 28 C3
Den La ML7 .... 191 E3
Den Rd KY2, KY1 .... 17 E3
Denburn Pl KY2 .... 17 E3
Denburn Rd KY1 .... 17 E4
Denend Cres KY2 .... 17 D3
Denham Green Ave EH5 .... 93 D3
Denham Green Pl EH5 .... 93 D3
Denham Green Terr EH5 .... 93 D3
Denholm Ave EH21 .... 125 F2
Denholm Gr EH48 .... 143 F4
Denholm Rd EH21 .... 125 F3
Denholm Way EH21 .... 125 F3
Denny High Sch FK6 .... 57 F4
Denny Prim Sch FK6 .... 36 B1
Denny Rd Bankhead FK4 .... 57 F3
    Larbert FK5 .... 38 A1
Denovan Rd FK6 .... 36 C2
Dequincey Wlk EH33 .... 128 B3
Derby St EH6 .... 93 E3
Deroran Pl FK8 .... 6 C3
Derwent Ave FK1 .... 59 F2
Devon Ct KY10 .... 4 A1
Devon Dr FK10 .... 4 C2
Devon Pl Edinburgh EH12 .. 122 C4
    Tullibody FK10 .... 4 A1
Devon St KY10 .... 10 B3
Devon St FK3 .... 40 A1
Devon Terr KY11 .... 29 F1
Devon Village FK10 .... 5 F2
Devonbank FK10 .... 5 F2
Devonway FK10 .... 11 D3
Dewar Ave FK10 .... 23 F2
Dewar Pl EH3 .... 232 A2
Dewar Place La EH3 .... 232 A2
Dewar Sq EH54 .... 146 B3
Dewar St Dunfermline KY12 .. 28 C2
    Lochgelly KY5 .... 14 A4
Dewshill Cotts ML7 .... 167 D2
Dick Cres KY3 .... 33 F1
Dick Gdns EH47 .... 169 F3
Dick Pl Edinburgh EH9 ...... 123 E2
    Rosyth KY11 .... 46 C3
    Stoneyburn EH47 .... 171 E1
Dick St KY12 .... 29 E3

Dick Terr EH26 .... 203 F3
Dickburn Cres FK4 .... 57 F3
Dickies Wells FK12 .... 5 E4
Dickson Ct KY5 .... 14 A4
Dickson St
    Dunfermline KY12 .... 29 D1
    Edinburgh EH6 .... 93 F2
    West Calder EH55 .... 172 B1
Dicksons Gr EH19 .... 182 A4
Dinmont Dr EH16 .... 124 A1
Dirleton Ave EH39 .... 54 A4
Dirleton Castle EH39 .... 53 D2
Dirleton Gdns EH10 .... 9 F4
Dirleton Gr EH12 .... 121 F3
Dirleton La EH10 .... 9 F3
Dirleton Prim Sch EH39 .... 53 D2
Dirleton Rd Dirleton EH39 ... 53 D3
    North Berwick EH39 ...... 53 F3
Distillery La EH11 .... 122 C4
Diverswell FK10 .... 5 E1
Dixon Terr EH47 .... 170 A3
Dobbie Ave FK5 .... 38 B1
Dobbie's Rd EH19 .... 182 A4
Dobson's View EH41 .... 131 F4
Dobson's Wlk EH41 .... 131 F4
Dochart Cres FK2 .... 61 F1
Dochart Dr EH4 .... 91 E1
Dochart Path FK3 .... 61 E3
Dochart Pl FK1 .... 60 B1
Dock Pl EH6 .... 93 F3
Dock Rd EH6 .... 40 B1
Dock St Bo'ness EH51 .... 64 A4
    Edinburgh EH6 .... 93 F3
    Falkirk FK2 .... 39 E1
Doctor's Row KY1 .... 17 F4
Dog Well Wynd EH49 .... 85 D4
Dollar Ave FK2 .... 60 A4
Dollar Cres KY2 .... 16 B4
Dollar Ct KY12 .... 28 C3
Dollar Gdns FK2 .... 60 A4
Dollar Gr KY3 .... 33 F1
Dollar Ind Est FK1 .... 60 A3
Dollar Rd KY3 .... 33 F1
Dolphin Ave EH14 .... 151 F2
Dolphin Gdns E EH14 .... 151 F2
Dolphin Gdns W EH14 ...... 151 F2
Dolphin Rd EH14 .... 151 F2
Don Dr EH54 .... 148 A3
Don Rd KY11 .... 29 F1
Don St FK3 .... 40 A1
Donald St EH23 .... 29 E3
Donald St FK7 .... 6 B3
Donaldson Ct FK10 .... 23 F2
Donaldson Pl KY7 .... 6 B3
Donaldson's Sch
    for the Deaf
    Edinburgh, Coates EH12 .. 122 C4
    Edinburgh, Stockbridge EH4 .. 93 D1
Donibristle Gdns KY11 ...... 48 A1
Donibristle Ind Pk KY11 .... 48 A2
Donibristle Prim Sch
    KY11 .... 48 A1
Doo Dells La KY3 .... 34 C1
Doo'cot Brae KY10 .... 10 A4
Doocot Brae EH51 .... 64 A4
Doon Ave EH42 .... 78 B1
Doon Wlk EH54 .... 148 A2
Dora Ct KY3 .... 34 C1
Dornie Wynd ML7 .... 192 A2
Dorrator Rd FK1 .... 59 F3
Dorset Pl EH11 .... 123 D3
Double Dykes EH21 .... 126 B2
Double Hedges Pk EH16 .. 124 A1
Double Hedges Rd EH16 .. 124 A1
Double Row KY11 .... 45 D2
Dougall Ct EH22 .... 183 E3
Dougall Pl EH22 .... 183 E3
Dougall Rd EH22 .... 183 E3
Douglas Ave Brighons FK2 ... 82 B4
    Crossford KY12 .... 28 A1
    Grangemouth FK3 .... 61 F3
    Linlithgow EH49 .... 84 C3
Douglas Cres
    Bonnyrigg and Lasswade
    EH19 .... 182 A4
    Edinburgh EH12 .... 122 C4
    Longniddry EH32 .... 98 A3
Douglas Dr Bo'ness EH51 ... 63 F3
    Dunfermline KY12 .... 28 C3
    Stirling FK7 .... 7 E2
Douglas Gardens Mews
    EH4 .... 122 C4
Douglas Gdns EH4 .... 122 C4
Douglas Pk KY12 .... 28 C3
Douglas Pl Bo'ness EH51 ... 63 F3
    Linlithgow EH49 .... 84 C3
    Stenhousemuir FK5 .... 38 C2
Douglas Rd Bo'ness EH51 ... 63 F3
    Longniddry EH32 .... 98 C3
    Rosyth KY11 .... 46 B1
Douglas St Bannockburn FK7 ... 7 F2
    Dunfermline KY12 .... 29 D2
    Kirkaldy KY1 .... 17 D2
    Stirling FK8 .... 2 A1
Douglas Terr
    Bo'ness EH51 .... 63 F3
    Stirling FK7 .... 6 C3
Douglaswynd EH52 .... 117 D3
Doune Cres FK5 .... 39 D2
Doune Pk KY11 .... 48 B2
Doune Terr EH3 .... 232 B4
Dovecot Brae EH33 .... 128 B4
Dovecot Ct Aberdour KY3 .. 49 D3
Dovecot Loan EH14 .... 122 A1
Dovecot Pk Aberdour KY3 ... 49 D3
    Edinburgh EH14 .... 153 D4
    Linlithgow EH49 .... 85 E4
    Pencaitland EH34 .... 160 C3
Dovecot Pl FK10 .... 4 A2

Dovecot Rd
    Edinburgh EH12 .... 121 E3
    Tullibody FK10 .... 4 A2
    Westquarter FK2 .... 61 D1
Dovecot Way EH34 .... 160 C4
Dovecote Pl EH54 .... 147 E2
Dovehill FK10 .... 10 A4
Dowan Pl FK7 .... 6 C3
Dower Cres EH51 .... 64 A4
Dowie's Mill La EH4 .... 90 C2
Downfield KY4 .... 13 E3
Downfield Pl EH11 .... 122 C3
Downie Gr EH12 .... 121 F3
Downie Pl EH21 .... 126 B3
Downing Ct EH25 .... 181 D2
Downing Point KY11 .... 48 A1
Downs Cres KY10 .... 9 F3
Dreghorn Ave EH13 .... 153 F3
Dreghorn Dr EH13 .... 153 F3
Dreghorn Gdns EH13 ...... 153 F3
Dreghorn Gr EH13 .... 153 F3
Dreghorn Junc EH13 .... 153 F3
Dreghorn Link EH10 .... 153 F3
Dreghorn Pk EH13 .... 153 F3
Dreghorn Pl EH13 .... 153 F3
Drem Farm Cotts EH39 ..... 73 D2
Drem Sta EH39 .... 73 D2
Drip Rd FK9 .... 1 C1
Dronachy Rd KY2 .... 16 C2
Drossie Rd FK1 .... 60 A2
Drove Loan FK6 .... 57 F3
Drove Loan Cres FK6 .... 57 F4
Drove Rd EH48 .... 143 F4
Droverhall Ave KY4 .... 31 D3
Droverhall Pl KY4 .... 31 D3
Drovers Rd EH52 .... 118 A3
Drum Ave EH17 .... 155 F3
Drum Brae Ave EH12 .... 121 E4
Drum Brae Dr EH4 .... 91 E1
Drum Brae Gdns EH12 ..... 121 E4
Drum Brae Gr EH4 .... 91 E1
Drum Brae N EH4 .... 91 D1
Drum Brae Neuk EH12 ..... 121 E4
Drum Brae Park App
    EH12 .... 121 E4
Drum Brae Pk EH12 .... 121 E4
Drum Brae S EH12 .... 121 E4
Drum Brae Terr EH4 .... 91 E1
Drum Brae Wlk EH4 .... 91 D1
Drum Cotts EH17 .... 155 F3
Drum Cres EH17 .... 155 F3
Drum Pl
    East Whitburn EH47 ..... 170 C4
    Edinburgh EH17 .... 155 F3
Drum Rd Bo'ness EH51 ...... 64 B3
    Dunfermline KY11 .... 29 F1
Drum St EH17 .... 155 F3
Drum Terr EH7 .... 94 A1
Drum View Ave EH22 ...... 156 A4
Drumacre Rd EH51 .... 64 A3
Drumbowie Prim Sch
    FK1 .... 82 B2
Drumbrae Prim Sch EH4 .. 121 E4
Drumcross Rd EH48 .... 145 D4
Drumdryan St EH3 .... 232 B1
Drumlanrig Pl FK5 .... 38 C2
Drummohr Ave EH21 ...... 127 D3
Drummohr Gdns EH21 .... 127 D3
Drummond Com High Sch
    EH7 .... 93 E1
Drummond La FK8 .... 7 D3
Drummond Pk FK8 .... 7 D3
Drummond Pl
    Blackridge EH48 .... 142 B2
    Bonnybridge FK4 .... 58 A4
    Dunfermline KY12 .... 29 E3
    Edinburgh EH3 .... 93 E1
    Falkirk FK1 .... 59 F2
    Grangemouth FK3 .... 61 F4
    Stirling FK8 .... 7 D3
Drummond Place La FK8 .... 7 D3
Drummond Sq
    Livingston EH54 .... 173 E3
    Lochgelly KY5 .... 14 A4
Drummond St EH8 .... 233 E2
Drummore Dr EH32 .... 127 F4
Drummormie Rd KY12 ...... 27 C1
Drumpark Ave EH51 .... 64 A3
Drumpark St FK7 .... 7 D2
Drumsheugh Gdns EH3 ... 232 A3
Drumshoreland Ave
    EH53 .... 148 A4
Drumshoreland Cres
    EH53 .... 148 A4
Drumshoreland Pl EH53 .. 148 A4
Drumshoreland Rd EH53 .. 148 A4
Drumside Terr EH51 .... 64 B4
Drumview Gdns EH51 .... 64 A3
Dryburgh Ave KY5 .... 14 A4
Dryburgh Way FK3 .... 61 F3
Dryden Ave EH20 .... 181 D4
Dryden Cres EH20 .... 181 D4
Dryden Gdns EH7 .... 93 F2
Dryden Glen EH20 .... 180 C4
Dryden Gr EH25 .... 181 D3
Dryden Pl EH9 .... 123 F3
Dryden Rd EH20 .... 180 C4
Dryden St EH7 .... 93 F2
Dryden Terr Edinburgh EH7 .. 93 F2
    Loanhead EH20 .... 181 D4
Drylaw Ave EH4 .... 92 B1
Drylaw Cres EH4 .... 92 A1

Drylaw Gdns
    East Linton EH40 .... 103 E4
    Edinburgh EH4 .... 92 A2
Drylaw Gn EH4 .... 92 A1
Drylaw Gr EH4 .... 92 A1
Drylaw House Gdn EH4 ..... 92 A2
Drylaw House Paddock
    EH4 .... 92 A2
Drylaw Sch EH4 .... 92 B2
Drylaw Terr EH40 .... 103 E4
Drylawhill EH40 .... 75 E1
Drylie St KY4 .... 13 D2
Drysdale Ave EH47 .... 170 A4
Drysdale Cres FK10 .... 10 A3
Duart Cres EH4 .... 91 E1
Dublin Meuse EH3 .... 93 E1
Dublin St EH1 .... 233 D4
Dublin Street La N EH3 ..... 93 E1
Dublin Street La S EH1 .... 233 D4
Duddingston Ave EH15 .... 124 C4
Duddingston Cres EH52 .... 88 A4
Duddingston Gdns S EH15 . 125 C3
Duddingston Gr E EH15 ... 124 C3
Duddingston Gr W EH15 .. 125 C3
Duddingston Loan EH15 .. 124 C3
Duddingston Mills EH8 .... 124 C3
Duddingston Pk EH15 ..... 125 D4
Duddingston Pk S EH15 .. 125 D3
Duddingston Prim Sch
    EH15 .... 124 C4
Duddingston Rd EH15 ..... 124 C4
Duddingston Rd W EH15 .. 124 B3
Duddingston Rise EH15 .. 124 C3
Duddingston Row EH15 .. 124 C3
Duddingston Sq E EH15 .. 124 C4
Duddingston Sq W EH15 .. 124 C4
Duddingston View EH15 .. 124 C3
Duddingston Yds EH15 ... 125 D3
Duddingstone Terr EH52 .. 88 A4
Duddingston Gdns N EH15 . 124 C4
Dudgeon Pl EH29 .... 89 D1
Dudley Ave EH6 .... 93 E3
Dudley Ave S EH6 .... 93 F3
Dudley Bank EH6 .... 93 E3
Dudley Cres EH6 .... 93 E3
Dudley Gdns EH6 .... 93 E3
Dudley Gr EH6 .... 93 E3
Dudley Terr EH6 .... 93 E3
Duff Cres FK8 .... 1 C1
Duff Ct EH39 .... 54 A4
Duff St EH11 .... 122 C3
Duff Street La EH11 .... 122 C3
Duffy Pl KY11 .... 46 C2
Dugald Stewart Ave EH51 . 64 A4
Duglas Rise EH54 .... 148 A4
Duke Pl EH6 .... 94 A2
Duke St Alva FK12 .... 5 D4
    Bannockburn FK7 .... 7 E1
    Clackmannan FK10 ...... 11 D2
    Dalkeith EH22 .... 157 D2
    Denny FK6 .... 36 B1
    Dunbar EH42 .... 78 A1
    Edinburgh EH6 .... 94 A2
    Grangemouth FK3 .... 61 F4
    Rosewell EH24 .... 181 E1
    West Barns EH42 .... 77 F1
Duke's Wlk EH8 .... 94 A1
Dumbarton Rd FK8 .... 6 C4
Dumbeg FK14 .... 152 B4
Dumbiedykes Rd EH8 ...... 233 F2
Dumbryden Dr EH14 .... 121 F1
Dumbryden Gdns EH14 ... 121 F1
Dumbryden Gr EH14 .... 121 F1
Dumbryden Prim Sch
    EH14 .... 121 F1
Dumbryden Rd EH14 .... 121 F1
Dumyat Ave FK10 .... 4 A1
Dumyat Dr FK1 .... 59 F2
Dumyat Rd Alva FK12 .... 4 C3
    Menstrie FK11 .... 3 F3
    Stirling FK9 .... 2 B2
Dumyat St FK10 .... 4 C1
Dunard Gdn EH9 .... 123 E2
Dunbar Ave FK5 .... 38 C2
Dunbar Gate FK6 .... 36 C2
Dunbar Gram Sch EH42 .... 78 A1
Dunbar Pl KY2 .... 16 C3
Dunbar Prim Sch EH42 .... 78 B1
Dunbar Rd
    Haddington EH41 .... 101 D1
    North Berwick EH39 ...... 54 C3
Dunbar St EH3 .... 232 B1
Dunbar Sta EH42 .... 78 C1
Duncairn Ave FK4 .... 57 F3
Duncan Ave FK2 .... 39 D2
Duncan Cres KY11 .... 29 F1
Duncan Ct EH39 .... 54 A3
Duncan Gdns EH33 .... 128 B4
Duncan Gn EH54 .... 147 D4
Duncan Pl EH6 .... 94 A2
Duncan St Bonnybridge FK4 . 57 F3
    Edinburgh EH9 .... 123 F2
    Kirkaldy KY1 .... 17 D2
Duncanson Ave FK10 .... 10 A4
Duncanson Dr KY3 .... 34 A1
Duncarron Ind Est FK6 ...... 36 C1
Duncarron Pl FK6 .... 36 C1
Duncur Rd EH31 .... 52 B2
Dundaff St FK6 .... 36 B1
Dundarroch St FK5 .... 38 A1
Dundas Ave
    North Berwick EH39 ...... 54 B3
    Queensferry EH30 .... 89 E4
Dundas Cotts FK5 .... 57 D1
Dundas Cres
    Clackmannan FK10 ...... 11 D2
    Dalkeith EH22 .... 156 C1
    Laurieston FK2 .... 61 D2

Dundas Gdns EH23 .... **183** D1
Dundas Gr EH22 .... **156** C1
Dundas Pk EH19 .... **182** B4
Dundas Pl EH29 .... **89** D1
Dundas Rd Dalkeith EH22 .. **156** C1
  Laurieston FK2 .... **61** D2
  North Berwick EH39 .... **54** B3
  Rosyth KY11 .... **67** E4
  Stirling KY9 .... **2** A2
Dundas St Bathgate EH48 .. **145** D4
  Bo'ness EH51 .... **63** F4
  Bonnyrigg and Lasswade
  EH19 .... **182** B4
  Edinburgh EH3 .... **93** E1
  Grangemouth FK3 .... **61** E4
  Lochgelly KY5 .... **14** A4
  Townhill KY12 .... **29** E4
Dundee Ct FK2 .... **60** A4
Dundee Pl FK2 .... **60** A4
Dundee St EH11 .... **232** A1
Dundee Terr EH11 .... **122** C3
Dundonald Rd KY11 .... **46** B2
Dundonald St EH3 .... **93** E1
Dundrennan Cotts EH16 .. **124** B1
Dunearn Bank KY3 .... **33** E1
Dunearn Dr KY2 .... **16** C3
Dunearn Sch KY2 .... **16** C4
Dunedin St EH7 .... **93** E2
Dunfermline Abbey KY12 .. **28** C2
Dunfermline Bsns Ctr
  KY11 .... **29** D1
Dunfermline Bsns Pk
  KY11 .... **46** B3
Dunfermline High Sch
  KY11 .... **29** D1
Dunfermline Mus KY12 .. **29** D2
Dunfermline Rd
  Crossgates KY4 .... **30** C3
  Limekilns KY11 .... **45** F2
Dunfermline Sta KY12 .. **29** D2
Dunfermline Wynd KY11 .. **47** D1
Dunglass Church TD13 .. **140** B2
Dunimarle St KY12 .... **26** A1
Dunipace Cres KY12 .... **29** F3
Dunipace Prim Sch FK6 .. **36** B3
Dunkeld Pl FK2 .... **39** E1
Dunlin Brae EH54 .... **147** E3
Dunlop Sq EH54 .... **146** B3
Dunlop Terr EH26 .... **204** A3
Dunmar Cres FK10 .... **4** C1
Dunmar Dr FK10 .... **4** C1
Dunn Cres KY11 .... **29** F2
Dunn Pl EH52 .... **87** F1
Dunn St EH52 .... **117** D3
Dunn Terr ML7 .... **168** C3
Dunnet Way EH52 .... **118** A3
Dunnikier Prim Sch KY2 .. **17** D3
Dunnikier Rd KY1 .... **17** E3
Dunnikier Way KY1 .... **17** E4
Dunning Pl FK2 .... **39** E1
Dunnottar Dr FK5 .... **38** C2
Dunnottar Pl KY2 .... **16** C2
Dunollie Ct EH12 .... **121** D4
Dunollie Gdns EH41 .... **132** B4
Dunpender Dr EH41 .... **100** C1
Dunpender Rd EH40 .... **103** E4
Dunrobin Ave FK5 .... **38** C3
Dunrobin Pl EH3 .... **93** D1
Dunrobin Rd KY2 .... **16** C2
Duns Rd EH41 .... **163** F3
Dunsire St KY1 .... **17** F4
Dunsmuir Ct EH12 .... **121** E3
Dunster Rd FK9 .... **2** B2
Dunure Cres FK4 .... **58** A3
Dunure Pl KY2 .... **16** C2
Dunure St FK4 .... **58** A3
Dunvegan Ave Kircaldy KY2 .. **16** B3
  Stenhousemuir FK5 .... **38** C2
Dunvegan Ct Alloa FK10 .. **10** A3
  Crossford KY12 .... **28** A1
  Edinburgh EH4 .... **91** D2
Dunvegan Dr Falkirk FK2 .. **39** E1
  Stirling FK9 .... **2** A2
Dunvegan Gdns EH54 .... **173** F3
Dunvegan Pl
  Bonnybridge FK4 .... **57** F3
  Polmont FK2 .... **62** A1
Dura Rd ML7 .... **212** B3
Durar Dr EH4 .... **91** E1
Durham Ave
  Bathgate EH48 .... **144** C3
  Edinburgh EH15 .... **124** C4
Durham Bank EH19 .... **182** B3
Durham Dr Bathgate EH48 .. **144** C4
  Edinburgh EH15 .... **125** D3
Durham Gdns N EH15 .... **125** D4
Durham Gdns S EH15 .... **125** D3
Durham Gr
  Bonnyrigg and Lasswade
  EH19 .... **182** B3
  Edinburgh EH15 .... **125** D4
Durham Pl EH19 .... **182** B3
Durham Pl E EH15 .... **125** D4
Durham Pl W EH15 .... **124** C4
Durham Place La EH15 .... **125** D4
Durham Rd EH15 .... **125** D4
Durham Rd S EH15 .... **125** D3
Durham Sq EH15 .... **125** D4
Durham Terr
  Edinburgh EH15 .... **124** C4
  Newmills KY12 .... **26** B1
Durie Pk KY3 .... **50** B4
Durie Pl FK2 .... **29** F2
Durie's Pk EH33 .... **128** A1
Durward Rise EH54 .... **148** A1
Durwood Gr EH16 .... **124** A1
Dyfrig St ML7 .... **191** F3
Dyke Brow ML7 .... **169** D3

Dyke Rd ML7 .... **169** D3
Dykehead Prim Sch ML7 .. **191** F3
Dykes Rd EH26 .... **203** F4
Dykeside EH48 .... **144** C4
Dymond Gr KY11 .... **46** C4
Dysart Prim Sch KY1 .... **18** A4
Dysart Rd KY1 .... **17** F3

Eagle Brae EH54 .... **147** E2
Eagle Rock EH4 .... **91** D4
Earl Grey St EH3 .... **232** B2
Earl Haig Gdns EH5 .... **93** D3
Earl Of Mar Ct FK10 .... **10** A3
Earl's Gate Rdbt FK3 .... **61** D4
Earl's Rd FK3 .... **61** D4
Earls Ct FK10 .... **10** A3
Earls Pl EH47 .... **193** F3
Earlsburn Ave FK7 .... **7** D2
Earlshall Dr FK7 .... **7** F1
Earlston Pl EH7 .... **94** A1
Earn Ct Alloa FK10 .... **10** B3
  Grangemouth FK3 .... **61** E3
Earn Gr KY1 .... **29** F2
Earn Pl FK6 .... **57** E3
Earn Rd KY1 .... **17** E4
Earn Terr ML7 .... **191** F3
East Adam St EH8 .... **233** E2
East Albert Rd KY1 .... **17** E3
East Ave Blairhall KY12 .... **26** A4
  Dunfermline KY11 .... **46** C4
East Baldridge Dr KY12 .. **28** C3
East Bankton Pl EH54 .... **173** F4
East Barnton Ave EH4 .... **91** F2
East Barnton Gdns EH4 .... **91** F2
East Bay KY1 .... **68** B3
East Boreland Pl KY6 .... **36** C1
East Bridge St FK1 .... **60** B2
East Brighton Cres EH15 .. **125** D4
East Broomhill Rd KY3 .... **50** C4
East Caiystane Pl EH10 .. **154** A3
East Caiystane Rd EH10 .. **154** A3
East Calder Prim Sch
  EH53 .... **148** C2
East Campbell Ct EH52 .. **98** B3
East Castle Rd EH10 .... **123** D3
East Castle St FK10 .... **10** A3
East Champanyie EH9 .... **123** F2
East Clapperfield EH16 .. **124** A1
East Claremont St EH7 .... **93** E2
East Comiston EH10 .... **154** A3
East Craigs Prim Sch
  EH12 .... **121** D4
East Craigs Rigg EH12 .. **121** D4
East Croft EH28 .... **119** F1
East Cromwell St EH6 .... **93** F3
East Crosscauseway EH8 .. **233** E1
East Ct
  Edinburgh, Greendykes
  EH16 .... **124** C2
  Edinburgh, Ravelston 7 EH4 .. **92** B1
East Dr FK5 .... **38** B1
East End EH55 .... **172** B2
East End Park
  (Dunfermline Athletic FC)
  KY12 .... **29** E2
East Farm Of Gilmerton
  EH17 .... **155** F3
East Fenton Farm Cotts
  EH39 .... **73** E4
East Fergus Pl KY1 .... **17** D2
East Fettes Ave EH4 .... **92** C2
East Fountainbridge EH3 .. **232** B2
East Garleton Cotts EH39 .. **100** C3
East Glen Ave EH54 .... **146** C3
East Harbour Rd KY11 .... **45** D2
East Hermitage Pl EH6 .... **94** A1
East Leven St KY3 .... **50** C4
East Lillypot EH5 .... **93** D3
East Link Rd KY9 .... **2** B3
East Links Rd Dunbar EH42 .. **78** C1
  Gullane EH31 .... **52** A1
East Linton Prim Sch EH40 .. **103** E4
East Linton Station Ind Est
  EH40 .... **103** F4
East Loan EH32 .... **97** D1
East London St EH7 .... **93** E1
East Lorimer Pl EH32 .... **97** E2
East Main St
  Armadale EH48 .... **144** A3
  Blackburn EH47 .... **171** E4
  Broxburn EH52 .... **117** D3
  Harthill ML7 .... **168** C3
  Uphall EH52 .... **117** D2
  Whitburn EH47 .... **170** A4
East Mains FK11 .... **4** A3
East Mains Ind Est EH52 .. **118** A3
East March St KY1 .... **17** E4
East Market St EH8 .... **233** E3
East Mayfield EH9 .... **123** F2
East Montgomery Pl 4
  EH7 .... **93** E1
East Murrayfield KY1 .... **7** F1
East Newington Pl EH9 .. **123** F3
East Norton Pl 3 EH7 .... **93** F1
East Park Gr EH52 .... **117** D3
East Parkside EH16 .... **233** F1
East Pier St KY1 .... **63** F4
East Plean Prim Sch FK7 .. **20** B2
East Port KY12 .... **29** D2
East Port Ave EH41 .... **132** B4
East Preston St EH8 .... **233** F1
East Preston Street La 6
  EH8 .... **123** F3
East Quality St KY1 .... **18** A4
East Queensway EH26 .... **203** F3
East Restalrig Terr EH6 .... **94** A1

East Savile Rd EH16 .... **123** F2
East Sciennes St 2 EH9 .. **123** F3
East Scotland Street La 2
  EH3 .... **93** E1
East Seaside EH32 .... **96** C1
East Silvermills La EH3 .... **93** D1
East Stirling St FK12 .... **5** D4
East Suffolk Rd EH16 .... **124** A2
East Telferton EH7 .... **94** C1
East Terr EH30 .... **68** B1
East Toll KY11 .... **33** F1
East Trinity Rd EH5 .... **93** E3
East Vennel EH1 .... **10** A3
East Vows Wlk KY1 .... **35** D2
East Way KY11 .... **48** B3
East Werberside EH4 .... **92** C2
East Whitefield St KY12 .... **29** F3
Eastburn Dr FK1 .... **60** B2
Eastcroft Dr KY2 .... **62** A1
Easter Bankton EH54 .... **174** A4
Easter Belmont Rd EH12 .. **122** A4
Easter Carmuirs Prim Sch
  FK1 .... **59** D3
Easter Cornton Rd FK9 .... **2** A1
Easter Currie Cres EH14 .. **152** A3
Easter Currie Ct EH14 .... **152** A3
Easter Currie Pl EH14 .... **152** A3
Easter Currie Terr EH14 .. **152** A2
Easter Drylaw Ave EH4 .... **92** B2
Easter Drylaw Bank EH4 .. **92** B2
Easter Drylaw Dr EH4 .... **92** B2
Easter Drylaw Gdns EH4 .. **92** B2
Easter Drylaw Gr EH4 .... **92** B2
Easter Drylaw Loan EH4 .. **92** B2
Easter Drylaw Pl EH4 .... **92** B2
Easter Drylaw View EH4 .. **92** B2
Easter Drylaw Way EH4 .. **92** B2
Easter Ferrygate Pk EH39 .. **53** F4
Easter Haugh EH13 .... **153** F4
Easter Hermitage EH6 .... **94** A2
Easter Livilands FK7 .... **7** E2
Easter Park Dr EH4 .... **91** F2
Easter Rd Broxburn EH52 .. **117** F3
  Edinburgh EH6 .... **94** A2
  Shotts ML7 .... **191** E3
Easter Road Stad
  (Hibernian FC) EH7 .... **94** A1
Easter Steil EH10 .... **122** C1
Easter Warriston EH7 .... **93** E3
Easterfield Ct EH54 .... **147** E2
Eastern Ind Est EH15 .... **125** E2
Easterton Cres FK7 .... **20** C4
Easterton Dr FK7 .... **20** C4
Easterton Gr FK7 .... **20** C4
Eastertoun Gdns EH48 .... **143** F3
Eastertoun Prim Sch
  EH48 .... **143** F3
Eastfield EH15 .... **125** F4
Eastfield Dr EH26 .... **203** F3
Eastfield Farm Rd EH26 .. **203** F4
Eastfield Gdns EH15 .... **125** F4
Eastfield Ind Est EH26 .... **203** F3
Eastfield Park Rd EH26 .. **203** F3
Eastfield Pl EH15 .... **125** F4
Eastfield Rd Carluke ML8 .. **230** A1
  Edinburgh EH28 .... **120** A3
  Fauldhouse EH47 .... **193** F4
  North Berwick EH39 .... **54** B3
Eastfield View EH47 .... **193** F4
Easthouses Ct EH22 .... **183** E4
Easthouses Ind Est
  EH22 .... **183** E4
Easthouses Pl EH22 .... **157** E1
Easthouses Rd
  Dalkeith EH22 .... **157** E1
  Easthouses EH22 .... **183** E4
Easthouses Way EH22 .. **157** E1
Easton Ct EH8 .... **2** A1
Easton Dr FK1 .... **81** E4
Easton Rd EH48 .... **144** C4
Eastwood Pk
  Fauldhouse EH47 .... **193** F4
  Livingston EH47 .... **147** D4
Ebenezer Pl FK1 .... **81** E3
Eccles Ct FK7 .... **7** D2
Ecclesmachan Rd EH52 .. **116** C3
Echline Ave EH30 .... **89** D4
Echline Dr EH30 .... **88** C4
Echline Farm Cotts EH30 .. **88** C4
Echline Gdns EH30 .... **67** D1
Echline Gn EH30 .... **67** D1
Echline Gr EH30 .... **68** A1
Echline Pk EH30 .... **88** C4
Echline Prim Sch EH30 .. **68** A1
Echline Rigg EH30 .... **68** A1
Echline Steadings EH30 .. **88** C4
Echline Terr EH30 .... **89** D4
Echline View EH30 .... **89** D4
Echobank KY11 .... **47** D1
Eden Dr EH54 .... **148** A2
Eden La EH10 .... **123** D2
Eden Rd Alloa FK10 .... **9** F4
  Dunfermline KY11 .... **29** F1
Edenhall Bank EH21 .... **126** C3
Edenhall Cres EH21 .... **126** C3
Edenhall Hospl EH21 .... **126** C2
Edenhall Rd EH21 .... **126** C3
Edgefield Ind Est EH20 .. **155** E1
Edgefield Pl EH20 .... **181** E4
Edgefield Rd EH20 .... **155** E1
Edgehead Rd EH37 .... **184** B4
Edina Pl EH7 .... **94** A1
Edina St EH7 .... **93** F1
Edinburgh Acad EH3 .... **93** D1
Edinburgh Acad
  (Prep Sch) The EH3 .... **93** D2
Edinburgh Castle EH1 .... **232** C3

Edinburgh Fort Ret Pk
  EH11 .... **125** D2
Edinburgh Pk
  Edinburgh EH12 .... **120** C3
  Edinburgh EH12 .... **121** D2
Edinburgh Rd
  Bathgate EH48 .... **145** E3
  Cockenzie & Port Seton EH32 .. **97** D2
  Dalkeith EH22 .... **157** D2
  Harthill ML7 .... **168** B3
  Linlithgow EH49 .... **85** D4
  Musselburgh EH21 .... **126** A3
  Newbridge EH28 .... **119** D3
  Penicuik EH26 .... **204** A4
  Tranent EH33 .... **128** A3
  West Barns EH42 .... **77** F1
  West Linton EH46 .... **220** A1
Edinburgh West Off Pk
  EH12 .... **121** D2
Edinburgh Coll of Art
  EH3 .... **232** C2
Edinburgh Rd EH48 .... **145** E3
Edington Cottage Hospl
  EH39 .... **54** B4
Edington Pl KY1 .... **18** A4
Edmonstone Dr EH22 .... **156** A4
Edmonstone Rd EH22 .... **156** B4
Edmonstone Terr EH22 .. **156** A4
Edmonton Ave EH54 .... **147** F2
Edward Ave
  Stenhousemuir FK5 .... **38** C2
  Stirling FK9 .... **2** B1
Edward Pl FK2 .... **39** F2
Edward Rd FK3 .... **61** E4
Edward St EH48 .... **2** A1
Edward St Dunfermline KY12 .. **29** D1
  Kirkcaldy KY2 .... **17** D4
Eglinton Pl KY11 .... **47** E1
Eglintoun Dr KY12 .... **28** C3
Eglinton Cres EH12 .... **122** C4
Eighth St EH22 .... **183** D3
Eildon St EH3 .... **93** E2
Eildon Terr EH3 .... **93** E2
Eilean La KY12 .... **26** C1
Elam Terr EH51 .... **63** F4
Elbe St EH6 .... **94** A3
Elcho Ct EH32 .... **98** C3
Elcho Pl EH32 .... **97** E2
Elcho Rd EH32 .... **98** C3
Elcho Terr Aberlady EH32 .. **71** E2
  Edinburgh EH15 .... **125** F4
  Longniddry EH32 .... **98** C3
Elder Pl KY11 .... **46** C3
Elder St Dunbar EH42 .... **78** A1
  Edinburgh EH1 .... **233** D4
  Tranent EH33 .... **128** A4
Elder St E EH1 .... **233** D4
Elderslie Dr FK2 .... **82** A4
Eldin Ind Est EH20 .... **155** E1
Eldindean Rd EH19 .... **182** A4
Eldindean Pl EH19 .... **182** A4
Eldindean Terr EH19 .... **182** A4
Eldrick Ave EH47 .... **193** F3
Eldrick Cres EH47 .... **193** F3
Eldrick La EH47 .... **193** F3
Eldrick View EH47 .... **193** F3
Electra Pl EH15 .... **95** D1
Elgin Ct KY12 .... **29** D1
Elgin Dr FK7 .... **7** E2
Elgin Pl FK1 .... **60** B2
Elgin Rd KY4 .... **13** E2
Elgin St Dunfermline KY12 .. **29** D1
  Edinburgh EH7 .... **93** F1
  Kirkcaldy KY2 .... **17** D1
Elgin St N EH7 .... **93** F1
Elgin Terr EH7 .... **93** F1
Eliburn North Intc EH54 .. **147** D3
Eliburn Rd EH54 .... **146** C3
Eliburn South Rd EH54 .. **147** E2
Elie Ave EH54 .... **146** C3
Elim Dr FK1 .... **81** E3
Elizabeth Ave
  Grangemouth FK3 .... **61** F4
  Larbert FK5 .... **38** B1
Elizabeth Cres FK1 .... **59** D3
Elizabeth Dr EH48 .... **145** F3
Elizabeth Gdns EH47 .... **171** D1
Elizabeth La EH48 .... **145** F3
Elizabeth St Dunfermline KY11 .. **29** E1
  Stirling FK8 .... **7** D3
Elizafield EH6 .... **93** F2
Ellaleen Gr KY12 .... **28** A1
Ellangowan Terr EH16 .. **124** B1
Ellen St EH47 .... **170** A4
Ellen's Glen Loan EH17 .. **155** E4
Ellen's Glen Rd EH17 .... **155** E4
Ellersly Rd EH12 .... **122** B4
Elliot Gdns EH14 .... **153** E4
Elliot Pk EH14 .... **153** E4
Elliot Pl EH14 .... **153** E4
Elliot St Dunfermline KY11 .. **29** E1
  Edinburgh EH7 .... **93** F1
Elliot Terr FK2 .... **60** A4
Elliothill St KY11 .... **29** E1
Ellis Pl EH52 .... **117** D3
Ellon Pl KY12 .... **29** E1
Ellon Rd KY2 .... **16** B4
Elm Dr FK2 .... **61** D1
Elm Gr Alloa FK10 .... **10** B3
  Blackburn EH47 .... **171** F4
  Dunfermline KY11 .... **46** B4
  Larbert FK5 .... **38** B1
  Livingston EH54 .... **148** A3
Elm Pk EH47 .... **171** F4
Elm Pl Edinburgh EH6 .... **94** A2
  Kirkcaldy KY2 .... **16** C3
  Mayfield EH22 .... **183** E3

Elm Rd EH48 .... **145** F3
Elm Row
  Bonnyrigg and Lasswade
  EH18 .... **156** A1
  Edinburgh EH7 .... **93** F1
Elm Sq EH47 .... **170** B3
Elm St Dunbar EH42 .... **78** A1
  Stirling FK8 .... **1** A3
Elmbank FK11 .... **4** A3
Elmbank Cres FK4 .... **57** E3
Elmbank Rd FK7 .... **7** D2
Elmbank St FK3 .... **61** E3
Elmfield Ct EH22 .... **157** D2
Elmfield Pk EH22 .... **157** D2
Elmfield Rd EH22 .... **157** D2
Elms The EH10 .... **153** F4
Elmwood Pk EH54 .... **146** C4
Elmwood Rd ML7 .... **192** A1
Elmwood Terr EH6 .... **94** A2
Elphinstone Cres FK2 .... **22** C2
Elphinstone Prim Sch
  EH33 .... **128** A1
Elphinstone Rd EH33 .... **128** A3
Elphinstone Sq EH54 .... **146** B3
Elphinstone St FK10 .... **23** F2
Elphinstone Wlk EH33 .... **128** B3
Eltringham Gdns EH14 .. **122** B2
Eltringham Gr EH14 .... **122** B2
Eltringham Terr EH14 .... **122** B2
Emily St EH23 .... **183** E1
Emily Pl EH23 .... **183** E1
Empire St EH47 .... **170** A4
Endrick Dr FK6 .... **57** F3
Endrick Pl FK7 .... **7** D2
Engelen Dr FK10 .... **10** A3
Engine La EH48 .... **145** D3
Engine Pl EH48 .... **145** D3
Engine Rd Gorebridge EH23 .. **183** D1
  Loanhead EH20 .... **181** E4
Engineering Training Sch
  KY2 .... **17** D2
Ennis Pk EH55 .... **172** C3
Eppiestane Rd EH47 .... **170** B3
Epworth Gdns FK2 .... **82** A4
Erbach Ave FK2 .... **61** D2
Ercall Rd FK2 .... **82** C4
Erica Gr KY11 .... **46** C4
Ericht Pl ML7 .... **191** F3
Eriskay St FK1 .... **60** B1
Erngath Rd EH51 .... **64** A4
Erskine Brae KY12 .... **25** E1
Erskine Hill FK2 .... **61** F1
Erskine Loan EH31 .... **52** A2
Erskine Pl
  Clackmannan FK10 .... **10** C3
  Mid Calder EH53 .... **148** B3
Erskine Rd Broxburn EH52 .. **117** E3
  Gullane EH31 .... **52** A2
Erskine Sq KY11 .... **29** E1
Erskine St Alloa FK10 .... **10** A4
  Alva FK12 .... **5** D4
  Lochgelly KY5 .... **14** A3
Erskine Way
  Livingston EH54 .... **147** E4
  Shotts ML7 .... **191** F2
Erskine Wynd KY12 .... **27** D4
Esk Dr EH54 .... **148** A2
Esk Glades EH22 .... **157** D2
Esk Pl EH22 .... **156** C2
Eskbank Rd
  Bonnyrigg and Lasswade
  EH19 .... **182** B4
  Dalkeith EH22 .... **156** C1
Eskbank Road Rdbt EH22 .. **156** B1
Eskbank Terr EH22 .... **156** C1
Eskdaill Ct EH22 .... **157** D2
Eskdaill St EH22 .... **157** D2
Eskdale Ct EH19 .... **182** A4
Eskdale Dr EH19 .... **182** A4
Eskdale Mews EH21 .... **126** B3
Eskdale Terr EH19 .... **182** A4
Eskfield Gr EH22 .... **156** B1
Eskgrove Dr EH25 .... **180** C3
Eskhill EH26 .... **203** F3
Eskmill Ind Est EH26 .... **204** A3
Eskmill Rd EH26 .... **204** A3
Eskside E EH21 .... **126** B3
Eskside W EH21 .... **126** B3
Eskvale Cres EH26 .... **204** A3
Eskvale Dr EH26 .... **204** A3
Eskvale View EH26 .... **204** A3
Eskview Ave EH21 .... **126** A3
Eskview Cres EH21 .... **126** A3
Eskview Gr Dalkeith EH22 .. **156** C2
  Musselburgh EH21 .... **126** A3
Eskview Rd Mayfield EH22 .. **183** E3
  Musselburgh EH21 .... **126** A3
Eskview Terr EH21 .... **126** A3
Eskview Villas EH22 .... **156** C1
Esmonde Ct KY11 .... **46** C1
Esplanade Edinburgh EH1 .. **232** C3
  Kirkcaldy KY1 .... **17** E1
Esplanade Terr EH15 .... **125** E4
Essendean Pl EH4 .... **91** E1
Essendean Terr EH4 .... **91** E1
Essex Brae EH4 .... **91** D2
Essex Pk EH4 .... **91** D2
Essex Rd EH4 .... **91** D2
Esslemont Rd EH16 .... **124** A1
Estate Ave FK1 .... **60** B2
Ethel Terr EH10 .... **123** D1
Etive Pl Dalgety Bay KY11 .. **48** A1
  Stirling FK9 .... **2** A2
Etive Way Polmont FK2 .... **62** A1
  Shotts ML7 .... **192** A2

Etive Wlk EH54 ... 148 A2
Etna Ct FK2 ... 60 B4
Etna Rd FK2 ... 60 B4
Eton Terr EH4 ... 232 A4
Ettrick Cres KY11 ... 48 A2
Ettrick Ct Falkirk FK1 ... 60 B1
  Grangemouth FK3 ... 61 F3
Ettrick Dr EH48 ... 148 A3
Ettrick Gr EH10 ... 123 F3
Ettrick Rd EH10 ... 122 C2
Ettrickdale Pl EH3 ... 93 D2
Eva Pl EH9 ... 123 F1
Evans Gdns EH19 ... 182 B4
Evans St FK5 ... 38 B2
Evelyn Terr EH26 ... 180 B1
Everard Rise EH54 ... 148 A1
Evershed Ct KY11 ... 29 F1
Evershed Dr EH11 ... 29 F1
Ewart Ave EH48 ... 144 A3
Ewart Gr EH51 ... 63 F3
Ewerland EH4 ... 91 D2
Ewing Ave FK2 ... 60 A4
Ewing Ct FK7 ... 7 E2
Ewing Dr FK2 ... 60 A4
Ewing Pl FK2 ... 60 A4
Ewing St Cowdenbeath KY4 ... 13 D1
  Lochgelly KY5 ... 14 A3
  Penicuik EH26 ... 203 F4
Excise La FK10 ... 23 F2
Excise St FK10 ... 23 F2
Exmouth St EH54 ... 148 A3
Eyre Cres EH3 ... 93 E1
Eyre Pl EH3 ... 93 E1
Eyre Terr EH3 ... 93 E1

Fa'side Ave EH33 ... 128 B3
Fa'side Ave N EH21 ... 127 D2
Fa'side Ave S EH21 ... 127 D2
Fa'side Avenue Ct EH21 ... 127 D2
Fa'side Bldgs EH21 ... 127 D2
Fa'side Cres Tranent EH33 .. 128 B3
  Wallyford EH21 ... 127 D2
Fa'side Dr EH21 ... 127 D2
Fa'side Gdns EH21 ... 127 D2
Fa'side Rd EH33 ... 128 B3
Fa'side Terr EH21 ... 127 D2
Fa'side View EH33 ... 128 B3
Factory Rd Bathgate EH48 .. 144 C2
  Cowdenbeath KY4 ... 13 E2
  Kirkcaldy KY1 ... 17 E3
Fair Isle Prim Sch KY2 ... 16 C4
Fair Isle Rd KY2 ... 16 C4
Fair Pl KY11 ... 47 D2
Fair-a-Far EH4 ... 91 D3
Fair-a-Far Cotts EH4 ... 91 D3
Fair-a-Far Shot EH4 ... 91 D3
Fairbairn Rd EH54 ... 147 E2
Fairbrae EH11 ... 121 F2
Fairfax Ct KY3 ... 33 F1
Fairfield Alloa FK10 ... 5 E1
  Livingston EH54 ... 147 D2
Fairfield Ave FK4 ... 58 A3
Fairfield Pl FK2 ... 60 B3
Fairfield sch ... 5 D1
Fairford Gdns EH16 ... 124 C3
Fairgreen Pl FK7 ... 19 F4
Fairhill Rd FK7 ... 7 D1
Fairinsfell EH52 ... 117 D3
Fairley Ct KY12 ... 27 E1
Fairlie Dr FK1 ... 59 E3
Fairlie Gdns FK1 ... 59 E3
Fairlie St FK1 ... 59 E3
Fairmile Ave EH10 ... 154 A3
Fairmont Pk EH47 ... 169 F3
Fairmount Dr FK10 ... 5 D1
Fairspark Terr EH51 ... 63 E3
Fairview Rd EH28 ... 119 E4
Fairview Terr FK2 ... 82 A4
Fairway EH41 ... 131 F4
Fairway The KY1 ... 17 F4
Fairways KY12 ... 29 D3
Fairways Ave FK2 ... 82 C3
Fairways Pl FK4 ... 58 A4
Fairy Fa' Cres KY4 ... 30 C3
Fairyburn Rd FK10 ... 9 F4
Fairykirk Rd KY11 ... 47 D2
Faith Mission Coll The
  EH17 ... 155 F4
Falahill Cotts EH38 ... 228 A2
Falcon Ave EH10 ... 123 D2
Falcon Brae EH54 ... 147 E2
Falcon Ct EH10 ... 123 D2
Falcon Dr FK5 ... 38 A2
Falcon Gdns EH10 ... 123 D2
Falcon Rd EH10 ... 123 D2
Falcon Rd W EH10 ... 123 D2
Falconer Ct FK7 ... 7 E2
Falconer Rise EH54 ... 147 F1
Falcons The EH31 ... 52 A2
Falkirk Coll of F & H Ed
  Flexible Learning Ctr
  FK2 ... 60 C3
Falkirk & District
  Royal Infmy FK1 ... 60 A2
Falkirk High Sch FK1 ... 59 F2
Falkirk High Sta FK1 ... 60 A2
Falkirk Rd Bannockburn FK7 .. 19 F4
  Bonnybridge FK4 ... 58 B3
  Falkirk, Glen Village FK1 .. 60 A1
  Falkirk, Westfield FK1 ... 60 C3
  Grangemouth FK3 ... 61 D4
  Larbert FK5 ... 59 E4
  Linlithgow EH49 ... 84 C4
Falkland Gdns EH12 ... 91 F1

Falkland Pl FK5 ... 38 C2
Falla Hill Prim Sch EH47 .. 193 E3
Fallas Pl EH47 ... 193 E3
Fallin Prim Sch FK7 ... 8 B3
Fallodon Cres KY2 ... 17 D2
Falside Cres EH48 ... 144 C3
Falside Dr EH48 ... 144 C3
Falside Terr EH48 ... 144 C3
Faraday Pl EH55 ... 171 F1
Farm Ave EH18 ... 181 F3
Farm Cotts
  Pencaitland EH34 ... 160 B3
  Wallyford EH21 ... 127 E3
Farm Rd Cowdenbeath KY4 ... 13 D1
  Cowie FK7 ... 20 B4
  Crombie KY12 ... 44 B3
  Fallin FK7 ... 8 B3
  Roslin EH25 ... 204 C3
Farm Row KY12 ... 30 A3
Farm St FK2 ... 39 D1
Farmer's Bldgs EH37 ... 185 D3
Farne Ct KY2 ... 16 C4
Farnell Way KY12 ... 29 E3
Farquhar Sq EH48 ... 142 B2
Farquhar Terr EH30 ... 68 A1
Farquharson Way FK1 ... 59 F1
Farrer Gr EH7 ... 94 C1
Farrer Terr EH7 ... 94 C1
Farrier Ct EH47 ... 171 E4
Farteviot Royal Hospl
  for Sick Children EH9 .. 123 E2
Fauldburn EH12 ... 91 D1
Fauldburn Pk EH12 ... 91 D1
Fauldhouse Rd EH47 ... 170 A1
Fauldhouse Sta EH47 ... 193 E3
Featherhall Ave EH12 ... 121 E3
Featherhall Cres EH12 ... 121 E3
Featherhall Cres N EH12 .. 121 E3
Featherhall Cres S EH12 .. 121 E3
Featherhall Gdns EH12 ... 121 E3
Featherhall Pl EH12 ... 121 E3
Featherhall Rd EH12 ... 121 E3
Featherhall Terr EH12 ... 121 E3
Fell's Rd EH55 ... 172 C3
Fells Rigg EH54 ... 147 D4
Fendoch Rd FK3 ... 61 F4
Fenton St FK10 ... 10 A4
Fentoun Gait EH31 ... 52 B1
Fere Gait FK10 ... 23 F2
Fergus Ave EH54 ... 147 F2
Fergus Pl KY11 ... 29 E1
Fergus Wynd KY1 ... 17 D1
Ferguson Ct EH21 ... 126 B2
Ferguson Dr Denny FK6 ... 36 B1
  Falkirk FK2 ... 39 D3
  Musselburgh EH21 ... 126 A2
Ferguson Gdns EH21 ... 126 B2
Ferguson Gn EH21 ... 126 A2
Ferguson Gr FK4 ... 58 A3
Ferguson Pl KY3 ... 33 F1
Ferguson St FK8 ... 1 C1
Ferguson View EH21 ... 126 A2
Ferguson Way
  Livingston EH54 ... 147 E4
  Newtongrange EH22 ... 183 D1
Fergusson Rd EH52 ... 117 F3
Fern Lea Gr FK2 ... 39 E2
Fernbank EH54 ... 147 F3
Ferne Pl KY12 ... 28 C3
Ferniehill Ave EH17 ... 155 F4
Ferniehill Dr EH17 ... 155 F4
Ferniehill Gdns EH17 ... 155 F4
Ferniehill Gr EH17 ... 155 F4
Ferniehill Pl EH17 ... 155 F4
Ferniehill Rd EH17 ... 155 F4
Ferniehill Sq EH17 ... 155 F4
Ferniehill St EH17 ... 155 F4
Ferniehill Terr EH17 ... 155 F4
Ferniehill Way EH17 ... 155 F4
Fernielaw Ave
  Edinburgh EH13 ... 152 C2
  Edinburgh, Bonaly EH13 ... 153 D3
Fernieside Ave EH17 ... 155 F4
Fernieside Cres EH17 ... 155 F4
Fernieside Dr EH17 ... 155 F4
Fernieside Gdns EH17 ... 155 F4
Fernieside Gr EH17 ... 155 F4
Fernieside Prim Sch
  EH17 ... 155 F4
Fernlea EH52 ... 116 C3
Ferrard Rd KY2 ... 17 D2
Ferrier Cres EH48 ... 144 A3
Ferris Way KY11 ... 48 A2
Ferry La KY11 ... 68 A3
Ferry Muir Gait EH30 ... 89 D4
Ferry Orch FK9 ... 2 B1
Ferry Rd Edinburgh EH4, EH5 .. 92 B3
  South Alloa FK7 ... 9 F2
  Stirling FK9 ... 2 B1
Ferry Road Ave EH4 ... 92 B2
Ferry Road Dr EH4 ... 92 B3
Ferry Road Gdns EH4 ... 92 B2
Ferry Road Gr EH4 ... 92 B2
Ferry Road Pl EH4 ... 92 B2
Ferry Toll Pl KY11 ... 46 C1
Ferry Toll Rd KY11 ... 46 C1
Ferrybarns Ct KY11 ... 68 A3
Ferryburn Gn EH30 ... 89 D4
Ferryfield EH5 ... 93 D2
Ferrygate Cotts EH39 ... 53 E3
Ferryhill Prim Sch EH4 ... 92 B2
Ferryhill Rd KY11 ... 68 B4
Ferrymuir La EH30 ... 89 D4
Ferrymuir Rd EH30 ... 89 D4
Fetteresk Cotts EH26 ... 203 F2
Fettes Ave EH4 ... 92 C1
Fettes Coll EH4 ... 92 C2
Fettes Rise EH4 ... 92 C2

Fettes Row EH3 ... 93 E1
Fiddich Dr EH54 ... 173 F3
Fidra Ave EH39 ... 53 D3
Fidra Ct EH39 ... 53 F4
Fidra Rd EH39 ... 54 A4
Fife Coll of F & H Ed KY1 .. 17 D2
Fife Coll Priory Campus
  KY1 ... 17 E3
Fife Pl KY11 ... 46 A1
Fifth St EH22 ... 183 D3
Figgate Bank EH15 ... 95 D1
Figgate La EH15 ... 95 D1
Figgate St EH15 ... 95 D1
Fillyside Ave EH7 ... 94 C1
Fillyside Rd EH7 ... 94 C2
Fillyside Terr EH7 ... 94 C2
Finches The EH31 ... 52 A2
Findhorn Pl Edinburgh EH9 .. 123 F2
  Falkirk FK1 ... 60 B1
  Kircaldy KY2 ... 16 C4
Findlay Ave EH7 ... 94 B2
Findlay Cotts EH7 ... 94 B2
Findlay Cres KY11 ... 46 C2
Findlay Gdns EH7 ... 94 B2
Findlay Gr EH7 ... 94 B2
Findlay Medway EH7 ... 94 B2
Findlay St KY1 ... 17 F4
Fingal Pl EH9 ... 233 D1
Fingzies Pl EH6 ... 94 A2
Finistere Ave FK1 ... 60 A2
Finlaggan Ct EH12 ... 121 D4
Finlarig Ct FK5 ... 38 C2
Finlay Ave EH53 ... 148 C2
Finlay Pl EH22 ... 183 F3
Fintry Rd FK3 ... 61 F3
Fir Gr Dunfermline KY11 ... 46 C4
  Livingston EH54 ... 148 A3
  Westquarter FK2 ... 61 D1
Fir La FK5 ... 38 B1
Firbank Gr EH53 ... 148 C2
Firpark Terr FK7 ... 6 B3
Firr Hill High Sch EH14 .... 153 E4
Firrhill Cres EH13 ... 153 E4
Firrhill Dr EH13 ... 153 E4
Firrhill Loan EH13 ... 153 E4
Firs Cres EH26 ... 180 B1
Firs Entry FK7 ... 7 E1
Firs Pk
  (East Stirlingshire FC)
  FK2 ... 60 B3
Firs St FK2 ... 60 B3
Firs The Bannockburn FK7 ... 7 E1
  Dalgety Bay KY11 ... 48 A3
First Gait EH14 ... 151 F4
First St EH22 ... 183 D2
Firth Cres EH26 ... 180 B1
Firth Rd Auchendinny EH26 .. 180 B1
  Livingston EH54 ... 147 F4
  Roslin EH25 ... 204 C3
Firwood Dr EH51 ... 63 E3
Fishcross Prim Sch FK10 .... 5 E2
Fishergate Rd EH32 ... 97 F2
Fishernow Ind Est EH21 .... 126 A3
Fishers' Rd EH51 ... 63 E2
Fishers Rd EH32 ... 97 E2
Fishers Wynd EH21 ... 126 A3
Fishmarket Sq EH6 ... 93 E4
Fishwives' Cswy EH7, EH15 .. 94 C1
Fitzgerald Pl EH48 ... 113 F3
Fitzroy Sq KY1 ... 18 A4
Fitzroy St KY1 ... 18 A4
Five Gates EH42 ... 76 A3
Flare Rd FK2 ... 62 A3
Flax Mill Rd ML7 ... 168 C3
Fleets Gr EH33 ... 128 B2
Fleets Ind Est EH33 ... 128 B2
Fleets Rd EH33 ... 128 B3
Fleets View EH33 ... 128 B2
Fleming Dr FK5 ... 39 D2
Fleming Gdns FK1 ... 59 F3
Fleming Pl EH48 ... 142 C2
Fleming Rd EH54 ... 146 C1
Fleming Way KY3 ... 33 F1
Flemington Gdns EH47 ... 169 F3
Flesh Wynd KY1 ... 17 E3
Fleshmarket Cl EH1 ... 233 D3
Fletcher Gr EH26 ... 203 F4
Flint Cres EH7 ... 20 B4
Floors Pl KY2 ... 16 B3
Floors Terr EH42 ... 78 B1
Florabank Rd EH41 ... 101 D3
Flower Pl KY4 ... 12 C4
Fod St KY11 ... 30 A3
Fodbank View KY11 ... 29 F2
Foot Pl KY11 ... 46 C2
Foote St KY5 ... 14 A3
Forbes Cres FK5 ... 38 B1
Forbes Ct FK5 ... 60 C3
Forbes Rd Edinburgh EH10 .. 123 D3
  Falkirk FK1 ... 60 B2
  Rosyth KY11 ... 46 B1
Forbes St Alloa FK10 ... 9 F3
  Edinburgh EH8 ... 233 E1
Forbeslea Gdns KY12 ... 27 F4
Ford Rd Bonnybridge FK4 ... 58 A3
  Haddington EH41 ... 132 B4
Ford View KY12 ... 27 E1
Ford's Rd EH11 ... 122 A2
Fordell Bank KY11 ... 48 B2
Fordell Gdns KY2 ... 16 B3
Fordell Way KY11 ... 47 E1
Foredale Terr EH51 ... 64 B4
Forest Kirk ML8 ... 230 A1
Forest Pl KY12 ... 29 E4
Forest Rd KY12 ... 29 E4
Forest View FK2 ... 61 F1

Forestbank EH54 ... 147 F3
Forester Gr EH54 ... 4 C1
Forester High Sch EH12 .... 121 E2
Forester's Lea Cres KY12 .. 29 E3
Forester's View EH33 ... 128 B3
Forfar Pl EH47 ... 62 A1
Forgie Cres FK2 ... 83 D3
Forglen Cres FK9 ... 2 A3
Forglen Rd FK9 ... 2 A3
Forker Ave KY11 ... 46 B2
Forkneuk Rd EH52 ... 116 C2
Forkneuk Steadings
  EH52 ... 116 C3
Forman Gr KY11 ... 29 F1
Forres Dr KY2 ... 16 B4
Forres St EH3 ... 232 B4
Forrest Hill EH1 ... 233 D2
Forrest Pl ML7 ... 168 C3
Forrest Rd Edinburgh EH1 .. 233 D2
  Forrestfield ML6 ... 141 D1
  Salsburgh ML7 ... 167 D3
  Stirling FK8 ... 2 A1
Forrest St ML7 ... 191 F3
Forrest Wlk EH52 ... 116 C2
Forrester Ct KY5 ... 14 A4
Forrester Park Ave EH12 .. 121 E2
Forrester Park Dr EH12 ... 121 E2
Forrester Park Gdns
  EH12 ... 121 E2
Forrester Park Gn EH12 ... 121 E2
Forrester Park Gr EH12 ... 121 E2
Forrester Park Loan EH12 .. 121 E2
Forrester Park Rd EH12 ... 121 E2
Forrester Pl FK2 ... 22 B2
Forrester Rd
  Armadale EH48 ... 143 F4
  Edinburgh EH12 ... 121 E4
Forrestfield Rd ML6 ... 141 D3
Fort Ho EH6 ... 93 F3
Fort Prim Sch EH6 ... 93 F3
Forth Ave Kirkaldy KY2 ... 17 D2
  Larbert FK5 ... 38 A2
Forth Ave Ind Est KY2 ... 17 D2
Forth Cres Alloa FK10 ... 10 B3
  Dalgety Bay KY11 ... 48 A2
  High Valleyfield KY12 ... 26 A1
  Stirling FK8 ... 2 A1
Forth Ct
  Cockenzie & Port Seton EH32 .. 97 F2
  Dalgety Bay KY11 ... 48 A2
  Dunfermline KY12 ... 29 D1
  Stirling FK8 ... 2 A1
Forth Dr EH54 ... 148 A3
Forth Gdns
  Cockenzie & Port Seton EH32 .. 97 F2
  Oakley KY12 ... 26 C4
Forth Gr EH32 ... 97 F2
Forth Ind Est EH5 ... 92 C4
Forth Park Dr KY2 ... 17 D3
Forth Park Gdns KY2 ... 17 D3
Forth Park Maternity Hospl
  KY2 ... 17 D3
Forth Pk Bridge of A FK9 ... 2 A3
Forth Pl Burntisland KY3 ... 50 C4
  Queensferry EH30 ... 68 A1
Forth Prim Sch ML11 ... 215 D1
Forth Reach KY11 ... 47 F1
Forth Rd KY11 ... 46 A1
Forth Street La EH39 ... 54 B4
Forth Terr EH30 ... 89 E4
Forth View
  Dalgety Bay KY11 ... 48 A2
  Inverkeithing KY11 ... 47 D1
  Kincardine FK10 ... 23 F2
  Kirknewton EH27 ... 149 F2
  Stirling FK8 ... 2 A1
  West Barns EH42 ... 77 F1
Forth View Ave EH14 ... 151 F2
Forth View Cotts KY12 ... 26 A1
Forth View Cres
  Currie EH14 ... 151 F2
  Danderhall EH22 ... 156 A4
Forth View Rd KY12 ... 26 A1
Forth View Rd EH14 ... 151 F2
Forth Wynd EH32 ... 97 F2
Forthbank Ind Est FK10 .... 10 A2
Forthbank Pl KY12 ... 25 F1
Forthbank
  (Stirling Albion FC) FK7 .. 7 F4
Forthside Terr KY11 ... 68 B3
Forthvale FK11 ... 4 A3
Forthview FK7 ... 7 F1
Forthview Ave EH21 ... 127 D2
Forthview Cres
  Bo'ness EH51 ... 63 F3
  Musselburgh EH21 ... 127 D3
Forthview Dr EH21 ... 127 D3
Forthview Gdns FK2 ... 82 B4
Forthview Rd
  Edinburgh EH4 ... 92 B1
  Longniddry EH32 ... 98 C3
Forthview Terr
  Edinburgh EH4 ... 92 A1
  Reddingmuirhead FK2 ... 82 A4
  Wallyford EH21 ... 127 D2
Forties Rd EH51 ... 62 B3
Fortingall Cres FK2 ... 62 A1
Fortissat Ave ML7 ... 191 E3
Fortisset Rd ML7 ... 167 D1

Fortuna Ct FK1 ... 60 B2
Fortune Ave EH41 ... 101 D1
Foulden Pl KY12 ... 29 E2
Foulford Pl KY11 ... 13 D2
Foulford Prim Sch KY4 ... 13 D3
Foulford Rd KY11 ... 13 D2
Foulford St KY4 ... 13 E2
Foulis Cres EH14 ... 152 C3
Foulshiels Rd EH47 ... 171 E1
Foundry La EH20 ... 155 E1
Foundry Loan FK5 ... 38 A1
Foundry Rd
  Bonnybridge FK4 ... 58 A3
  Shotts ML7 ... 191 F2
Foundry St
  Dunfermline KY12 ... 29 D2
  Falkirk FK1 ... 60 A4
Fountain Pl EH20 ... 181 E4
Fountain Rd FK9 ... 2 A4
Fountainbridge EH3 ... 232 A1
Fountainhall Rd EH9 ... 123 F2
Fountainhead Rd EH48 ... 145 D4
Fourth Gait EH14 ... 151 F4
Fourth St EH22 ... 183 D3
Fowler Cres
  Loanhead EH20 ... 181 E4
  Maddiston FK2 ... 83 D3
Fowler Pl FK2 ... 61 F2
Fowler St EH33 ... 128 B4
Fowler Terr EH11 ... 122 C3
Fowlers Ct EH32 ... 96 C1
Fox Covert Ave EH12 ... 91 F1
Fox Covert Gr EH12 ... 91 F1
Fox Covert RC Prim Schs
  EH12 ... 91 F1
Fox Spring Cres EH10 ... 154 A4
Fox Spring Rise EH10 ... 154 A4
Fox St EH6 ... 94 A3
Foxknowe Pl EH54 ... 147 D2
Franchi Dr FK5 ... 38 C3
Francis Ct KY12 ... 28 B3
Francis St KY5 ... 14 A4
Frankfield Cres KY11 ... 48 B2
Frankfield Pl KY11 ... 48 B2
Frankfield Rd KY11 ... 48 B2
Fraser Ave Edinburgh EH5 .. 93 D3
  Inverkeithing KY11 ... 47 E1
Fraser Cres EH5 ... 93 D3
Fraser Dr KY5 ... 14 A4
Fraser Gdns EH5 ... 93 D3
Fraser Gr EH5 ... 93 D3
Fraser Pl Dysart KY1 ... 18 A4
  Grangemouth FK3 ... 61 E3
  Stirling FK9 ... 2 A2
Fraser Rd EH54 ... 146 C1
Frederick Cres KY11 ... 29 D1
Frederick St EH2 ... 232 C4
Freeland Ave EH52 ... 117 D3
Freelands Rd
  Edinburgh EH28 ... 120 A2
  Ratho EH28 ... 119 F2
Freeport Village EH55 ... 172 C3
Fremantle St EH54 ... 148 A3
Freskyn Pl EH52 ... 118 A3
Frew Ct KY11 ... 29 E1
Friar's Croft EH42 ... 78 B1
Friars Brae EH49 ... 85 D3
Friars Loan EH49 ... 85 D3
Friars St FK8 ... 7 D4
Friars Way EH49 ... 85 D3
Friarton Gdns EH26 ... 203 E3
Friendship Gdns FK2 ... 39 E2
Frobisher Ave FK1 ... 59 F2
Frogston Ave EH10 ... 154 A3
Frogston Brae EH17 ... 154 C2
Frogston Gdns EH10 ... 154 B3
Frogston Gr EH10 ... 154 B3
Frogston Rd E EH17 ... 154 C3
Frogston Rd W EH10 ... 154 B2
Frogston Terr EH10 ... 154 B3
Fullerton Dr FK2 ... 61 F2
Fulmar Brae EH54 ... 147 E3
Fulmar Way KY11 ... 48 A2
Furcheons Pk EH8 ... 124 C4
Furnace La EH51 ... 64 B4
Furnace Pl KY1 ... 13 F3
Furniss Ave KY11 ... 46 B3
Fyne La ML7 ... 191 F3

Gaberston Ave FK10 ... 10 B4
Gagarin Way KY4 ... 13 F3
Gair Cres ML8 ... 230 A2
Gair Rd ML8 ... 230 A3
Gair Wynd ML7 ... 192 A2
Gairdoch Dr FK2 ... 39 E2
Gairdoch St FK2 ... 60 A4
Gairloch Cres FK2 ... 61 E1
Gala Gn EH42 ... 78 A1
Galabraes Cres EH48 ... 145 E4
Galachlawshot EH10 ... 154 B3
Galachlawside EH10 ... 154 B3
Galadale EH22 ... 183 D3
Galadale Cres EH22 ... 183 D3
Galadale Dr EH22 ... 183 D3
Gallacher Pl KY4 ... 13 F3
Gallagher Gn EH54 ... 147 E4
Gallamuir Dr FK7 ... 20 B2
Gallamuir Rd FK7 ... 20 B3
Gallolee The EH13 ... 153 E3
Gallow View EH52 ... 88 A4
Galloway Ct FK1 ... 60 A3
Galloway St FK1 ... 60 A3
Gallows Loan KY12 ... 25 E1
Galmeilen EH52 ... 117 E3
Galt Ave EH21 ... 127 D3
Galt Cres EH21 ... 127 D3
Galt Dr EH21 ... 127 D3

Galt Rd EH21 .... 127 D3
Galt Terr EH21 .... 127 D3
Gambeson Cres FK7 .... 7 E2
Gamekeeper's Loan EH4 .... 91 D3
Gamekeeper's Pk EH4 .... 91 D3
Gamekeeper's Rd EH4 .... 91 D3
Garbett Rd EH54 .... 147 E1
Garden City EH47 .... 171 D1
Garden Ct KY12 .... 29 E4
Garden Pl Cairneyhill KY12 .... 27 E1
  Clackmannan FK10 .... 11 D2
  Livingston EH54 .... 147 E2
  Townhill KY12 .... 29 E4
Garden St FK1 .... 60 B3
Garden Terr
  Clackmannan FK10 .... 11 D2
  Edinburgh EH4 .... 91 F2
  Falkirk FK1 .... 60 B3
  Westquarter FK2 .... 61 D1
Gardener Rd EH42 .... 78 B1
Gardener St EH42 .... 78 B2
Gardener's Wlk EH26 .... 203 E3
Gardeners Ct KY12 .... 29 D2
Gardeners' St KY12 .... 29 D2
Gardenhead FK2 .... 61 F1
Gardens The Aberlady EH32 .... 71 E3
  Dirleton EH39 .... 53 D3
Gardiner Cres EH32 .... 97 D1
Gardiner Gr EH4 .... 92 A1
Gardiner Pl
  Cowdenbeath KY4 .... 13 D1
  Newtongrange EH22 .... 183 D3
Gardiner Rd
  Cowdenbeath KY4 .... 13 E1
  Edinburgh EH4 .... 92 A1
  Prestonpans EH32 .... 97 D1
Gardiner St KY5 .... 14 A4
Gardiner Terr
  Edinburgh EH4 .... 92 A1
  Tranent EH33 .... 128 A4
Gardner Cres EH47 .... 169 F3
Gardner Terr EH47 .... 171 D1
Gardner's Cres EH3 .... 232 B2
Gardners La EH48 .... 145 D3
Gardrum Gdns FK1 .... 81 E4
Gareloch Way EH47 .... 170 B4
Garleton Ct EH31 .... 52 A1
Garleton Dr EH41 .... 100 C1
Garngrew Rd FK4 .... 57 D2
Garrison Pl FK1 .... 60 A3
Garry Pl Falkirk FK1 .... 60 B1
  Grangemouth FK3 .... 61 F3
Garry St KY5 .... 14 A4
Garry Way ML7 .... 191 F3
Garry Wlk EH54 .... 148 A2
Garscube Terr EH12 .... 122 B4
Gartclush Gdns FK7 .... 19 F4
Gartcows Ave FK1 .... 60 A2
Gartcows Cres FK1 .... 60 A2
Gartcows Dr FK1 .... 60 A2
Gartcows Gdns FK1 .... 59 F2
Gartcows Pl FK1 .... 60 A2
Gartcows Rd FK1 .... 60 A2
Garten Dr ML7 .... 192 A2
Garthill Gdns FK1 .... 60 A2
Garthill La FK1 .... 60 A2
Gartmorn Rd FK10 .... 5 E1
Garvald La FK6 .... 36 B1
Garvald Rd FK6 .... 57 E4
Garvally Cres FK10 .... 10 A4
Garvock Bank KY11 .... 29 E2
Garvock Hill KY12 .... 29 E2
Garvock Terr KY12 .... 29 E2
Gas Wynd KY1 .... 17 D1
Gasworks La
  North Berwick EH39 .... 53 F3
  Whitburn EH47 .... 170 A4
Gateside Ave
  Bonnybridge FK4 .... 58 B3
  Haddington EH41 .... 100 B1
Gateside Ct KY4 .... 13 D2
Gateside Ind Est KY4 .... 13 D2
Gateside Rd
  Haddington EH41 .... 131 E4
  Kirkliston EH29 .... 89 D1
  Stirling FK7 .... 7 D2
  Whitburn EH47 .... 169 F3
Gauger's Bush EH42 .... 76 A4
Gauze Pl EH51 .... 64 A3
Gauze Rd EH51 .... 64 A3
Gavin Pl EH54 .... 147 D3
Gavins Rd FK10 .... 4 C1
Gayfield Pl EH7 .... 93 F1
Gayfield Place La EH1 .... 93 F1
Gayfield Sq EH1 .... 93 F1
Gayfield St EH1 .... 93 F1
Gayfield Street La [7] EH1 .... 93 F1
Gaynor Ave EH20 .... 181 D4
Gean Rd FK10 .... 9 F4
Gellatly Rd KY11 .... 29 E1
Gelnorchy Terr EH9 .... 123 F2
George Ave EH20 .... 181 D4
George Cres
  Loanhead EH20 .... 181 E4
  Ormiston EH35 .... 159 E4
George Dr EH20 .... 181 E4
George Heriot's Sch EH3 .... 232 C2
George IV Bridge EH1 .... 233 D1
George Sq EH8 .... 233 D1
George Square La EH8 .... 233 D1
George St Alva FK12 .... 5 D3
  Armadale EH48 .... 143 F1
  Bathgate EH48 .... 145 D3
  Bo'ness EH51 .... 63 F3
  Cowdenbeath KY4 .... 13 D2
  Dunfermline KY11 .... 29 D1
  Edinburgh EH2 .... 232 C3

George St continued
  Falkirk FK2 .... 60 A3
  Grangemouth FK3 .... 61 F4
  Kincardine FK10 .... 23 F2
  Kirkaldy KY1 .... 17 D2
  Larbert FK5 .... 38 B2
  Laurieston FK2 .... 60 C2
  Ormiston EH35 .... 159 F4
George Terr EH20 .... 181 D4
George Watson's Coll
  EH10 .... 122 C2
George Watson's Coll
  Lower Prim Sch EH10 .... 122 C2
George Watson's Coll
  Upper Prim Sch EH10 .... 122 C2
George Way EH33 .... 128 B3
George Wlk EH33 .... 128 B3
Gerald Terr FK5 .... 38 C2
Gib Gr KY11 .... 29 F1
Gibbdun Pl FK6 .... 57 F4
Gibbs Entry EH8 .... 233 E2
Gibbshill Pl ML7 .... 168 B3
Gibraltar Ct EH22 .... 157 D2
Gibraltar Gdns EH22 .... 157 D2
Gibraltar Rd EH22 .... 157 D2
Gibraltar Terr EH22 .... 157 D2
Gibson Dr EH22 .... 157 E2
Gibson St EH7 .... 93 F2
Gibson St EH11 .... 232 A1
Gibsongray St FK2 .... 60 A4
Gideon Ct EH48 .... 145 D4
Gideon St EH48 .... 145 D4
Gifford Pk EH8 .... 233 E1
Gifford Rd EH41 .... 132 B4
Giffordgate EH41 .... 132 A4
Gilberstoun EH15 .... 125 E3
Gilberstoun Brig EH15 .... 125 E3
Gilberstoun Loan EH15 .... 125 E3
Gilberstoun Pl EH15 .... 125 E3
Gilberstoun Wynd EH15 .... 125 E3
Gilbert Ave EH39 .... 54 B3
Gilburn Pl Bo'ness EH51 .... 63 E3
  Shotts ML7 .... 191 F2
Gilchrist Cres EH47 .... 170 A3
Gilchrist Dr FK1 .... 59 F2
Giles St EH6 .... 93 F3
Gilfillan Pl FK2 .... 39 E1
Gilfillan Rd KY11 .... 29 F2
Gill Pk FK6 .... 36 C1
Gill Way KY11 .... 46 B3
Gillespie Cres EH10 .... 232 B1
Gillespie Gr KY12 .... 26 C4
Gillespie Pl Bannockburn FK7 .... 7 D1
  Edinburgh EH11 .... 232 B1
Gillespie Rd EH13 .... 152 C3
Gillespie St EH3 .... 232 B1
Gillespie Terr EH20 .... 20 B1
Gillie Ct KY11 .... 29 E1
Gillies Dr FK7 .... 7 E2
Gillies Hill FK7 .... 6 B3
Gillsland Rd EH10 .... 122 C1
Gilmerton Dykes Ave EH17 .... 155 E3
Gilmerton Dykes Cres
  EH17 .... 155 E3
Gilmerton Dykes Dr EH17 .... 155 E3
Gilmerton Dykes Gr EH17 .... 155 E3
Gilmerton Dykes Loan
  EH17 .... 155 E3
Gilmerton Dykes Pl EH17 .... 155 E3
Gilmerton Dykes Rd EH17 .... 155 E3
Gilmerton Dykes St EH17 .... 155 E3
Gilmerton Dykes Terr
  EH17 .... 155 E3
Gilmerton Dykes View
  EH17 .... 155 E3
Gilmerton Pl EH17 .... 155 E3
Gilmerton Prim Sch EH17 .... 155 E3
Gilmerton Rd EH16, EH17 .... 155 E4
  EH17 .... 155 E3
Gilmerton Road Rdbt
  EH22 .... 156 B2
Gilmerton Station Rd
  EH17 .... 155 F2
Gilmore Pl EH11 .... 232 A1
Gilmore Pl EH3 .... 123 A1
Gilmour Rd EH16 .... 123 F2
Gilmour St
  Cowdenbeath KY4 .... 13 E3
  Edinburgh EH8 .... 233 E2
Gilsay Ct FK1 .... 60 B1
Gilston Cres FK2 .... 62 A1
Gladney Sq KY1 .... 17 D1
Gladsmuir ML11 .... 215 D1
Gladsmuir Junc EH33 .... 130 A4
Gladstone Pl
  Dunfermline KY12 .... 29 D3
  Edinburgh EH6 .... 94 A2
  Stirling FK8 .... 7 D3
Gladstone Rd FK5 .... 38 B2
Gladstone Terr EH9 .... 123 F3
Glaive Ave FK7 .... 7 E2
Glamis Gdns
  Dalgety Bay KY11 .... 48 A2
  Polmont FK2 .... 61 F1
Glamis Pl KY11 .... 48 A2
Glamis Pl Kinghorn KY3 .... 34 C2
  Kircaldy KY2 .... 16 B4
Glamis Terr KY3 .... 34 C2
Glasclune Ct EH4 .... 54 B4
Glasclune Gdns EH39 .... 54 B4
Glasgow Rd
  Bannockburn FK7 .... 19 E4
  Bathgate EH48 .... 144 C3
  Denny FK6 .... 36 C1
  Edinburgh EH12 .... 120 B3
  Falkirk FK1 .... 59 D1
  Longcroft FK4 .... 57 E2
  Ratho Station EH28 .... 119 E3
  Stirling FK7 .... 7 D1

Glaskhill Terr EH26 .... 203 F3
Glass Cres EH52 .... 87 F1
Glass Pl EH52 .... 87 F1
Glass Rd EH52 .... 87 F1
Glassel Park Rd EH32 .... 98 B2
Glasshouse Loan FK10 .... 10 A3
Glasswork St KY1 .... 17 D2
Glebe Ave
  Uphall EH52 .... 117 D2
Glebe Cres Alva FK12 .... 5 D4
  Athelstaneford EH39 .... 101 F4
  Stirling FK8 .... 7 D4
Glebe Ct EH47 .... 193 E3
Glebe Gdns
  Edinburgh EH12 .... 121 E3
  Prestonpans EH32 .... 96 C1
Glebe Gr EH12 .... 121 E3
Glebe Pk Inverkeithing KY11 .... 47 D1
  Kirkaldy KY1 .... 17 E3
Glebe Pl
  Bonnyrigg and Lasswade
  EH18 .... 155 F1
  Burntisland KY3 .... 33 F1
  Kinghorn KY3 .... 34 C2
Glebe Rd Bathgate EH48 .... 145 E3
  Edinburgh EH12 .... 121 E3
  Kincardine FK10 .... 23 F3
  Uphall EH52 .... 117 D2
  West Calder EH55 .... 172 B1
  Whitburn EH47 .... 170 A3
Glebe St Dalkeith EH22 .... 157 D2
  Denny FK6 .... 36 C1
  Falkirk FK1 .... 60 A3
Glebe Terr Alloa FK10 .... 10 A3
  Edinburgh EH12 .... 121 E3
  Haddington EH41 .... 101 D1
  Inverkeithing KY11 .... 47 D1
  Uphall EH52 .... 117 D2
Glebe The Aberdour KY3 .... 49 E4
  Alva FK12 .... 5 D4
  Clackmannan FK10 .... 11 D2
  East Linton EH40 .... 103 F4
  East Saltoun EH34 .... 161 F2
  Edinburgh EH4 .... 91 D3
  Kirklston EH29 .... 89 D1
  Linlithgow EH49 .... 85 D3
  Pencaitland EH34 .... 160 C4
  West Calder EH55 .... 172 B1
Gledhill Ave EH15 .... 64 B3
Glen Albyn Dr KY2 .... 16 A4
Glen Artney Gr KY11 .... 29 E1
Glen Avon Pl KY2 .... 82 C4
Glen Beasdale Ct KY11 .... 29 E1
Glen Brae FK1 .... 60 A2
Glen Bridge KY12 .... 28 C2
Glen Bruar Pl KY12 .... 16 A4
Glen Clova Cres KY12 .... 27 E1
Glen Cres Falkirk FK1 .... 60 A1
  Livingston EH54 .... 146 C3
Glen Ct EH54 .... 146 B3
Glen Fruin Gr KY11 .... 29 E1
Glen Gdns FK1 .... 60 A2
Glen Isla Gr KY11 .... 29 E1
Glen Isla Rd KY2 .... 16 B4
Glen Lyon Ct FK2 .... 62 A1
Glen Moriston Dr KY12 .... 27 E1
Glen Nevis Dr KY11 .... 29 E1
Glen Ogle Ct FK2 .... 62 A1
Glen Pl EH13 .... 203 F3
Glen Rd Armadale EH48 .... 143 F3
  Bathgate EH48 .... 145 D4
  Livingston EH54 .... 146 C3
  Plean FK7 .... 20 B1
  Shotts ML7 .... 191 F2
  Torwood FK5 .... 37 E4
Glen St EH3 .... 232 C1
Glen Terr Denny FK6 .... 36 B1
  Livingston EH54 .... 146 C3
Glen Tye Rd FK7 .... 7 E3
Glen View Bo'ness EH51 .... 63 E2
  Dennyloanhead FK4 .... 57 E3
Glen View Cres EH23 .... 207 E4
Glen View Ct EH23 .... 207 E4
Glen View Rd EH23 .... 207 E4
Glen Way [3] EH48 .... 145 D4
Glenafeoch Rd ML8 .... 230 A1
Glenallan Dr EH16 .... 124 A1
Glenallan Loan EH16 .... 124 A1
Glenalmond EH47 .... 170 B3
Glenalmond Ct
  Broxburn EH52 .... 117 D3
  Whitburn EH47 .... 170 B3
Glenalmond Terr EH48 .... 145 D4
Glenard View EH51 .... 64 B3
Glenavon Dr KY12 .... 27 E1
Glenavon Terr EH48 .... 145 D4
Glenbank FK1 .... 60 A1
Glenbervie Ave FK5 .... 38 A2
Glenbervie Cres FK5 .... 38 A2
Glenbervie Dr FK5 .... 38 A2
Glenbervie Gr KY11 .... 29 E1
Glenbervie Rd FK3 .... 61 F3
Glenbo Dr FK6 .... 57 F4
Glenbrae Ct FK1 .... 60 A1
Glenbridge Ct KY12 .... 28 C2
Glenbrook EH14 .... 176 C4
Glenburn Gdns EH47 .... 170 B3
Glenburn Gr KY12 .... 27 E1
Glenburn Rd Falkirk FK1 .... 60 B1
  North Berwick EH39 .... 54 B3
Glencairn Cres EH12 .... 122 C3
Glencairn St Falkirk FK1 .... 60 A1
  Stirling FK7 .... 7 D2
Glencairn Terr EH46 .... 89 D1
Glencoe Rd Carluke ML8 .... 230 A1
  Stirling FK8 .... 2 A1
Glencorse Pk EH26 .... 204 B4
Glencorse Prim Sch EH26 .... 180 A1

Glencoul Ave KY11 .... 48 A2
Glencross Gdns EH26 .... 203 E3
Glendenning Dr EH29 .... 89 D1
Glendevon Ave EH12 .... 122 A3
Glendevon Dr FK5 .... 1 C1
Glendevon Gdns EH12 .... 122 A3
Glendevon Gr EH12 .... 122 A3
Glendevon Pk
  Edinburgh EH12 .... 122 A3
  Winchburgh EH52 .... 87 F1
Glendevon Pl EH12 .... 122 A3
Glendevon Terr EH12 .... 122 A3
Glendinning Cres EH16 .... 155 D4
Glendinning Dr EH29 .... 88 C3
Glendinning Pl EH29 .... 88 C3
Gleneagles Ct EH47 .... 170 B3
Gleneagles Way EH54 .... 146 C3
Glenesk Cres EH22 .... 156 C1
Glenfield Carnock KY12 .... 27 E3
  Livingston EH54 .... 147 D2
Glenfield Ave EH13 .... 13 E3
Glenfield Cres KY4 .... 13 E3
Glenfield Ct EH13 .... 13 E3
Glenfield Gdns KY4 .... 13 E3
Glenfield Ind Est KY4 .... 13 E3
Glenfield Rd EH13 .... 13 E3
Glenfinlas St EH3 .... 232 B3
Glenfuir Rd FK1 .... 59 E3
Glenfuir St FK1 .... 59 E3
Glengairn Wlk KY11 .... 29 E1
Glengarry Cres FK1 .... 59 F1
Glengyle Terr EH3 .... 232 C1
Glenisla Gardens La EH9 .... 123 F2
Glenisla Gdns EH9 .... 123 E2
Glenkinchie Distillery
  EH34 .... 160 C1
Glenlee Ave EH8 .... 124 B4
Glenlee Gdns EH8 .... 124 B4
Glenlockhart Bank EH14 .... 122 B1
Glenlockhart Rd EH10 .... 122 C1
Glenlockhart Valley EH14 .... 122 B1
Glenmavis Cres ML8 .... 230 A1
Glenmavis Dr ML8 .... 230 A1
Glenmavis Dr EH48 .... 145 D4
Glenmore EH47 .... 170 B3
Glenmore Dr FK4 .... 57 F3
Glennie Gdns EH33 .... 128 B3
Glenochil Pk FK10 .... 4 C2
Glenochil Rd FK1 .... 60 A2
Glenochil Terr FK10 .... 4 C2
Glenogle Ct EH3 .... 93 D1
Glenogle Ho [7] EH3 .... 93 D1
Glenogle Pl [8] EH3 .... 93 D1
Glenogle Rd EH3 .... 93 D1
Glenogle Terr EH3 .... 93 D2
Glenorchy Rd EH34 .... 54 A3
Glensburgh Rd FK3 .... 61 D4
Glenshiel Gr KY11 .... 29 E1
Glenside Ct
  Armadale EH48 .... 143 F3
  Grangemouth FK3 .... 61 F3
Glenside Gdns EH48 .... 143 F3
Glentye Gdns FK1 .... 59 F1
Glenure Loan EH4 .... 91 E1
Glenvarloch Cres EH16 .... 155 D4
Glenview Denny FK6 .... 36 A2
  Menstrie FK11 .... 4 A3
  Penicuik EH26 .... 203 F3
Glenview Cres EH47 .... 171 D1
Glenview Dr FK1 .... 59 F1
Glenview Rd EH47 .... 171 D1
Glenwinnel Rd FK10 .... 4 C4
Glenwood Dr EH48 .... 143 D4
Glenyards Rd FK4 .... 58 A1
Gloag Pl EH55 .... 172 B2
Globe Rd KY11 .... 46 B1
Gloucester La EH3 .... 232 B4
Gloucester Pl EH3 .... 232 B4
Gloucester Sq EH3 .... 232 B4
Gloucester St EH3 .... 232 B4
Glover's Ct KY3 .... 35 D2
Glowrorum Dr FK6 .... 57 F4
Glynwed Ct FK2 .... 60 B4
Godfrey Ave FK6 .... 36 B1
Godfrey Cres FK5 .... 38 B1
Goff Ave EH7 .... 94 C1
Gogar Loan FK9 .... 3 E3
Gogar Pl FK7 .... 7 E1
Gogar Station Rd EH12 .... 120 C2
Gogar Rbdt HE12 .... 120 C3
Gogarbank Farm EH12 .... 120 B3
Gogarburn Hospl EH12 .... 120 B3
Gogarloch Haugh EH12 .... 121 D3
Gogarloch Muir EH12 .... 121 D3
Gogarloch Rd EH12 .... 121 D3
Gogarloch Syke EH12 .... 121 D3
Gogarstone Rd EH12 .... 120 A3
Goldenacre Terr EH3 .... 93 D2
Goldenstones Ave EH42 .... 78 C1
Goldpark Pl EH54 .... 147 D3
Golf Course Rd
  Bonnyrigg and Lasswade
  EH19 .... 182 A4
  Cowdenbeath KY4 .... 13 E3
  Linlithgow EH49 .... 84 C3
  Livingston EH54 .... 147 D4
Golf Ct EH32 .... 71 D2
Golf Dr EH39 .... 97 F2
Golf House Rd EH42 .... 78 C1
Goldfrum St KY12 .... 28 C2
Goodall Cres EH52 .... 116 B1
Goodall Pl KY11 .... 116 A1
Goodall's Pl EH41 .... 132 B4
Goodman Pl FK2 .... 82 C4
Goose Green Ave EH21 .... 126 B4
Goose Green Cres EH21 .... 126 B4

Goose Green Pl EH21 .... 126 B4
Goose Green Rd
  Gullane EH31 .... 52 A1
  Musselburgh EH21 .... 126 B4
Goosecroft Rd FK8 .... 7 D4
Gordon Ave
  Bathgate EH48 .... 145 D3
  Bonnyrigg and Lasswade
  EH19 .... 181 F3
Gordon Cres Bridge of A FK9 .... 2 A4
  Stirling FK8 .... 1 C1
Gordon Ct EH52 .... 117 F3
Gordon Dr FK10 .... 10 B4
Gordon Loan EH12 .... 121 F4
Gordon Pl FK1 .... 59 F3
Gordon Rd
  Edinburgh EH12 .... 121 F4
  Rosyth KY11 .... 46 A1
Gordon St
  Cowdenbeath KY4 .... 13 E3
  Easthouses EH22 .... 183 E4
  Edinburgh EH6 .... 94 A2
  Lochgelly KY5 .... 14 A4
Gordon Terr
  Dunfermline KY11 .... 29 D1
  Edinburgh EH16 .... 124 A1
Gordon Way EH54 .... 147 E4
Gore Ave EH23 .... 207 E4
Gorebridge Prim Sch
  EH23 .... 207 E4
Goremire Rd ML8 .... 230 A1
Gorgie Park Cl EH14 .... 122 B2
Gorgie Park Rd EH11 .... 122 B3
Gorgie Rd EH11 .... 122 B2
Gorrie St Denny FK6 .... 36 B1
  Dunfermline KY11 .... 29 E1
Gorsebank EH54 .... 147 F3
Gort Pl FK3 .... 61 E3
Gorton Loan EH24 .... 181 E1
Gorton Pl EH24 .... 181 E1
Gorton Rd EH24 .... 181 E1
Goschen Pl EH52 .... 117 D3
Goschen Terr EH52 .... 117 D3
Gosford Ho EH32 .... 71 D1
Gosford Pl EH6 .... 93 E3
Gosford Rd
  Cockenzie & Port Seton EH32 .... 97 E2
  Kircaldy KY2 .... 16 B4
  Longniddry EH32 .... 98 C3
Gote La EH30 .... 68 A1
Gourlaw Cotts EH24 .... 205 D4
Gourlay St KY2 .... 17 D2
Gourlaybank EH41 .... 101 D1
Gow Cres KY1 .... 17 D2
Gowan Ave FK2 .... 60 A3
Gowan La FK2 .... 60 A3
Gowanbank EH54 .... 147 E3
Gowanbrae EH47 .... 193 F3
Gowanbrae Dr KY12 .... 29 E2
Gowanbrae Rd KY12 .... 29 E2
Gowanbrae Terr KY12 .... 29 E2
Gowanhill Gdns FK8 .... 1 C1
Gowanlea Dr FK1 .... 110 B3
Grace St KY5 .... 14 B4
Gracefield Ct EH21 .... 126 A3
Gracemount Ave EH16 .... 155 D4
Gracemount Dr EH16 .... 155 D3
Gracemount High Sch
  EH16 .... 155 D3
Gracemount Pl EH16 .... 155 D3
Gracemount Prim Sch
  EH16 .... 155 D3
Gracemount Rd EH16 .... 155 D3
Gracemount Sq EH16 .... 155 D3
Gracie Cres FK7 .... 8 B2
Gracie's Wynd EH48 .... 144 A3
Gradlon Pl FK1 .... 60 A2
Graeme High Sch FK1 .... 60 B2
Graeme Pl FK1 .... 59 F1
Graham Ave Larbert FK5 .... 38 A2
  Stirling FK9 .... 2 B2
Graham Cres EH51 .... 64 A4
Graham Ct EH47 .... 171 F4
Graham St Bridge of A FK9 .... 2 A4
  Edinburgh EH6 .... 93 F3
Graham Terr FK2 .... 22 B2
Graham Way EH54 .... 147 E4
Graham's Rd EH26 .... 204 B4
Grahams Rd FK2 .... 60 A3
Grahamsdyke Ave EH51 .... 64 A4
Grahamsdyke Cres EH54 .... 58 A2
Grahamsdyke La EH51 .... 64 A4
Grahamsdyke Rd
  Bo'ness EH51 .... 64 B3
  Bonnybridge FK4 .... 58 A2
Grahamsdyke St EH51 .... 61 D2
Grahamsdyke Terr EH51 .... 64 A4
Grahamston Sta FK1 .... 60 A3
Graiglaw Pl EH52 .... 116 B1
Graigleith View FK10 .... 4 A4
Grainger St KY5 .... 14 A4
Grampian Cres FK3 .... 61 F3
Grampian Ct KY11 .... 46 C1
Grampian Gdns KY2 .... 16 C3
Grampian Ho EH6 .... 93 F3
Grampian Pl KY11 .... 46 C1
Grampian Rd Rosyth KY11 .... 6 C3
Grampion Ct EH54 .... 147 F1
Granary Rd FK2 .... 60 A4
Granary Sq FK2 .... 60 A4
Granby Ave EH54 .... 147 F2
Granby Rd EH16 .... 123 F2
Grandfield EH6 .... 93 E3
Granville EH6 .... 93 E3

Grange Ave FK2 ...... 60 B3
Grange Cotts KY3 ...... 34 C3
Grange Cres EH9 ...... 123 E2
Grange Cres E EH32 ...... 96 C1
Grange Cres W EH32 ...... 127 F4
Grange Ct
5 Edinburgh EH9 ...... 123 F3
North Berwick EH39 ...... 54 B3
Grange Dr
Dunfermline KY11 ...... 46 A4
Falkirk FK2 ...... 60 B3
Grange Gdns FK9 ...... 2 B4
Grange Gr EH32 ...... 96 C1
Grange Knowe EH49 ...... 85 E4
Grange La FK3 ...... 40 B1
Grange Loan Bo'ness EH51 ...... 64 A4
Edinburgh EH9 ...... 123 E2
Grange Loan Gdns EH9 ...... 123 E2
Grange Pk KY11 ...... 46 A4
Grange Pl Grangemouth FK3 ...... 61 E4
Redding FK2 ...... 61 E1
Grange Rd Alloa FK10 ...... 9 F3
Bridge of A FK9 ...... 2 B3
Broxburn EH52 ...... 117 F2
Burntisland KY3 ...... 33 E1
Dunfermline KY11 ...... 46 B3
Edinburgh EH9 ...... 123 E3
Livingston EH54 ...... 148 A4
North Berwick EH39 ...... 54 A3
Polmont FK2, FK3 ...... 61 F2
Prestonpans EH32 ...... 96 C1
Grange Sch EH51 ...... 64 A4
Grange Terr Bo'ness EH51 ...... 64 A4
Edinburgh EH9 ...... 123 E2
Grange The FK2 ...... 82 C4
Grange View EH49 ...... 85 E4
Grange Wynd KY11 ...... 46 B4
Grangeburn Rd FK3 ...... 40 C1
Grangemouth High Sch
FK3 ...... 61 F3
Grangemouth Rd FK2 ...... 60 C3
Grangepans EH51 ...... 64 A4
Grangeview FK5 ...... 38 C1
Grannies Park Ind Est
EH22 ...... 157 D2
Grant Ave EH13 ...... 153 D3
Grant Pl FK9 ...... 2 A2
Grant St Alloa FK10 ...... 9 F3
West Calder EH55 ...... 172 B2
Granton Cres EH5 ...... 92 C3
Granton Gdns EH5 ...... 92 C3
Granton Gr EH5 ...... 92 C3
Granton Mains Ave EH4 ...... 92 B3
Granton Mains Bank EH4 ...... 92 B3
Granton Mains Brae EH4 ...... 92 B3
Granton Mains Ct EH4 ...... 92 B3
Granton Mains E EH4 ...... 92 B3
Granton Mains Gait EH4 ...... 92 B3
Granton Mains Vale EH4 ...... 92 B3
Granton Mains Wynd EH4 ...... 92 B3
Granton Medway EH5 ...... 92 C3
Granton Park Ave EH5 ...... 92 C4
Granton Pl EH5 ...... 92 C3
Granton Prim Sch EH5 ...... 92 C3
Granton Rd EH5 ...... 93 D3
Granton Sq EH5 ...... 92 C4
Granton Terr EH5 ...... 92 C3
Granton View
Dalgety Bay KY11 ...... 47 F1
Edinburgh EH5 ...... 92 C3
Grants Bank KY12 ...... 29 D2
Grantully Pl EH9 ...... 123 F2
Granville Terr EH10 ...... 123 D3
Granville Way KY11 ...... 46 C2
Grassmarket EH1 ...... 232 C2
Gray Buchanan Ct FK2 ...... 61 E1
Gray Pk KY4 ...... 13 E3
Gray Pl KY11 ...... 47 E2
Gray St ML7 ...... 192 A2
Gray's Ct EH8 ...... 233 E2
Gray's Loan EH10 ...... 122 C2
Graysmill Sch EH14 ...... 122 B1
Graystale Rd FK7 ...... 7 D2
Graystonelee Rd ML7 ...... 191 E3
Great Cannon Bank EH15 ...... 95 D1
Great Carleton Pl EH16 ...... 125 D2
Great Carleton Sq EH16 ...... 125 D2
Great Junction St EH6 ...... 93 F3
Great King St EH3 ...... 93 E1
Great Michael Cl EH6 ...... 93 E4
Great Michael Rd KY11 ...... 46 A1
Great Michael Rise EH6 ...... 93 E3
Great Michael Sq EH6 ...... 93 E4
Great Stuart St EH3 ...... 232 A3
Green Apron Pk EH39 ...... 54 A3
Green La
Bonnyrigg and Lasswade
EH18 ...... 181 F4
Grangemouth FK3 ...... 61 F4
Townhill KY12 ...... 29 E4
Green St Edinburgh EH7 ...... 93 E1
Green The Alva FK12 ...... 5 D4
Bathgate EH48 ...... 145 E4
Edinburgh EH4 ...... 91 F4
Pencaitland EH34 ...... 160 C3
West Barns EH42 ...... 77 F1
Green Tree La EH51 ...... 63 E3
Greenacre EH14 ...... 152 C4
Greenacre Ct FK7 ...... 7 F1
Greenacre Pk FK7 ...... 7 F1
Greenbank Ave EH10 ...... 123 D1
Greenbank Cres EH10 ...... 154 A4
Greenbank Dr
Cowdenbeath KY4 ...... 13 D1
Edinburgh EH10 ...... 123 D1

Greenbank Gdns EH10 ...... 153 F4
Greenbank Gr EH10 ...... 153 F4
Greenbank La EH10 ...... 122 C1
Greenbank Loan EH10 ...... 122 C1
Greenbank Pk EH10 ...... 153 F4
Greenbank Pl
Edinburgh EH10 ...... 123 D1
Falkirk FK1 ...... 59 E2
Greenbank Rd
Edinburgh EH10 ...... 122 C1
Falkirk FK1 ...... 59 E2
Greenbank Rise EH10 ...... 153 F4
Greenbank Row EH10 ...... 153 F4
Greenbank Terr EH10 ...... 123 D1
Greenburn Rd EH47 ...... 193 F3
Greencraig Ave FK1 ...... 81 E3
Greendykes Ave EH16 ...... 124 C2
Greendykes Dr EH16 ...... 124 C2
Greendykes Gdns EH16 ...... 124 C2
Greendykes Ind Est EH52 ...... 117 E3
Greendykes Loan **7**
EH16 ...... 124 C2
Greendykes Prim Sch
EH16 ...... 124 C2
Greendykes Rd
Broxburn EH52 ...... 117 F3
Edinburgh EH16 ...... 124 C1
Greendykes Steadings
EH52 ...... 117 F3
Greendykes Terr EH16 ...... 124 C2
Greenend Dr EH17 ...... 155 E4
Greenend Gdns EH17 ...... 155 E4
Greenend Gr EH17 ...... 155 E4
Greenfield Cres EH14 ...... 177 E4
Greenfield Rd EH14 ...... 177 E4
Greenfield St Alloa FK10 ...... 10 A4
Bonnybridge FK4 ...... 58 A3
Greenhall Rd EH23 ...... 183 E1
Greenheads Rd EH39 ...... 54 C3
Greenhill Ct
Bonnybridge FK4 ...... 58 A1
Edinburgh EH10 ...... 123 D3
Fauldhouse EH47 ...... 193 F3
Greenhill Gdns EH10 ...... 123 D2
Greenhill Pk
Edinburgh EH10 ...... 123 D2
Penicuik EH26 ...... 203 E3
Greenhill Rd
Blackridge EH48 ...... 142 C2
Bonnybridge FK4 ...... 58 A2
Greenhill Terr EH10 ...... 123 D3
Greenhithe Terr FK2 ...... 82 C4
Greenhorn's Well Ave FK1 .. 59 F2
Greenhorn's Well Cres
FK1 ...... 59 F2
Greenhorn's Well Dr FK1 ...... 59 F2
Greenlaw Gr EH26 ...... 180 A1
Greenlaw Hedge EH13 ...... 153 F4
Greenlaw Rig EH13 ...... 153 F4
Greenloanings KY2 ...... 16 B4
Greenmantle Loan **9**
EH16 ...... 124 A1
Greenmount KY4 ...... 13 D1
Greenmount Dr
Burntisland KY3 ...... 33 F1
Shieldhill FK1 ...... 81 E3
Greenmount Rd N KY3 ...... 33 F1
Greenmount Rd S KY3 ...... 34 A1
Greenpark Dr FK2 ...... 61 F1
Greenrigg Cotts ML7 ...... 169 D3
Greenrigg Prim Sch ML7 ...... 168 C3
Greens The FK2 ...... 82 C4
Greenside EH48 ...... 113 F3
Greenside La EH1 ...... 233 E4
Greenside Pl
Edinburgh EH1 ...... 233 E4
Rosewell EH24 ...... 181 E1
Greenside Row EH1 ...... 233 E4
Greenside St FK10 ...... 10 A3
Greenvale Dr FK2 ...... 82 C4
Greenville Ct FK1 ...... 59 F2
Greenwell St EH47 ...... 193 F3
Greenwell Terr FK2 ...... 82 C4
Greenwells Dr FK2 ...... 82 C4
Greenwood Ave FK8 ...... 7 D4
Greenwood Pk EH54 ...... 147 E3
Greenwood St ML7 ...... 191 F3
Gregory Rd EH54 ...... 173 D4
Greig Cres EH48 ...... 144 A3
Greig Pl KY5 ...... 14 A4
Greig Rd KY11 ...... 46 A1
Grendon Ct FK8 ...... 7 D3
Grendon Gdns FK8 ...... 7 D3
Grey Craigs KY12 ...... 27 E1
Grey School Cnr EH32 ...... 96 C1
Greyfriar's Wlk KY11 ...... 47 E2
Greyfriars EH1 ...... 233 D2
Greyfriars Bobby Meml
EH1 ...... 233 D2
Greygoran FK10 ...... 5 E1
Grierson Ave EH5 ...... 93 D3
Grierson Cres
Cambusbarron FK7 ...... 6 B3
Edinburgh EH5 ...... 93 D3
Grierson Gdns EH5 ...... 93 D3
Grierson Rd EH5 ...... 92 C3
Grierson Sq EH5 ...... 93 D3
Grierson Villas EH5 ...... 93 D3
Grieve Ct EH26 ...... 203 F4
Grieve St Dunfermline KY12 .. 28 C2
Kirkcaldy KY2 ...... 17 D3
Griffith Dr EH47 ...... 170 A3
Griffiths St FK1 ...... 60 A2
Grigor Ave EH4 ...... 92 B2
Grigor Dr EH4 ...... 92 B2
Grigor Gdns EH4 ...... 92 B2

Grigor Terr EH4 ...... 92 B2
Grindlay St EH3 ...... 232 B2
Grindlay Street Ct EH3 ...... 232 B2
Groathill Ave EH4 ...... 92 B1
Groathill Gdns E **2** EH4 ...... 92 B1
Groathill Gdns W **1** EH4 ...... 92 B1
Groathill Rd N EH4 ...... 92 B2
Groathill Rd S EH4 ...... 92 B1
Grodwell Dr FK12 ...... 4 C4
Grosvenor Gdns EH12 ...... 122 C4
Grosvenor St EH12 ...... 232 A2
Grove Cres FK2 ...... 39 D1
Grove End EH4 ...... 182 A4
Grove St Denny FK6 ...... 36 B1
Edinburgh EH3 ...... 232 A2
Musselburgh EH21 ...... 126 B3
Grove The FK2 ...... 126 C3
Grundie's Well Rd EH17 ...... 155 F3
Guardians Wood EH12 ...... 122 B4
Guardwell Cres EH17 ...... 155 E4
Guildhall St KY12 ...... 29 D2
Guildie Howes Rd EH23 ...... 207 F1
Guildiehaugh Rdbt EH48 ...... 145 E2
Guildry Gr KY12 ...... 29 F2
Gullan's Cl EH1 ...... 233 E3
Gullane Prim Sch EH31 ...... 52 A1
Gunn Rd FK3 ...... 61 E3
Gunner Rd FK3 ...... 62 B4
Guthrie St EH1 ...... 233 D2
Guttergates Rd KY11 ...... 30 A3
Gyle Ave EH12 ...... 120 C3
Gyle Park Gdns EH12 ...... 121 D3
Gyle Rbdt EH12 ...... 121 D3
Gyle Sh Ctr EH12 ...... 121 D3
Gylemuir Prim Sch EH12 .. 121 E3
Gylemuir Rd EH12 ...... 121 E3
Gylers Rd EH39 ...... 53 D2

Haddington Inf Sch
EH41 ...... 132 A4
Haddington Pl EH7 ...... 93 F1
Haddington Rd
East Linton EH40 ...... 103 E4
Musselburgh EH21 ...... 127 D3
North Berwick EH39 ...... 54 B3
Tranent EH33 ...... 128 C3
Haddington Station
Ind Est EH41 ...... 131 F4
Haddon's Ct EH8 ...... 233 E2
Haddow Gr KY3 ...... 50 B4
Hadfast Rd EH22 ...... 158 B3
Hadrian Way EH51 ...... 64 A3
Haig Ave Kirkaldy KY1 ...... 17 E4
Stirling FK8 ...... 2 A1
Haig Cres Bathgate EH48 .. 145 E3
Dunfermline KY12 ...... 29 E3
Haig St FK1 ...... 61 E3
Hailes App EH13 ...... 153 D4
Hailes Ave EH13 ...... 153 D4
Hailes Bank EH13 ...... 153 D4
Hailes Castle EH41 ...... 103 D2
Hailes Cres EH13 ...... 153 D4
Hailes Gdns EH13 ...... 153 D4
Hailes Gr EH13 ...... 153 D4
Hailes Loan EH41 ...... 103 D2
Hailes Pk EH13 ...... 152 C4
Hailes Pl KY12 ...... 29 E2
Hailes St EH3 ...... 232 B1
Hailes Terr EH13 ...... 153 D4
Hailesland Gdns EH14 ...... 121 F1
Hailesland Gr EH14 ...... 121 F1
Hailesland Pk EH14 ...... 121 F1
Hailesland Pl EH14 ...... 121 F1
Hailesland Prim Sch
EH14 ...... 152 C4
Hailesland Rd EH14 ...... 121 F1
Hailstonegreen ML11 ...... 215 D1
Hailstones Cres EH48 ...... 143 F3
Hainburn Pk EH10 ...... 153 F3
Haining Gr FK2 ...... 83 D3
Haining Pl
Grangemouth FK3 ...... 61 F4
Livingston EH54 ...... 147 D3
Haining Rd EH49 ...... 83 F3
Haining Terr EH49 ...... 83 F3
Hakness Cres EH33 ...... 128 B3
Halbeath Dr KY11 ...... 29 F3
Halbeath Pl KY11 ...... 29 F3
Halbeath Rd
Dunfermline KY11 ...... 29 F3
Kirkcaldy KY11 ...... 30 A3
Halbeath Ret Pk KY11 ...... 30 A3
Halberts Cres FK7 ...... 7 F1
Haldane Ave Bridge of A FK9 .. 2 A1
Haddington EH41 ...... 100 C1
Haldane Gr KY12 ...... 26 B4
Haldane Sq EH54 ...... 173 E3
Halketshall KY11 ...... 45 E2
Halkett Cres KY11 ...... 29 E1
Hall Cres EH31 ...... 52 A1
Hall La KY5 ...... 14 A4
Hall Rd EH52 ...... 117 F3
Hall Row KY11 ...... 45 D2
Hall St Cowdenbeath KY4 ...... 13 E2
Lochgelly KY5 ...... 14 A4
Hallcraigs EH27 ...... 149 F2
Hallcroft Cl EH28 ...... 119 E1
Hallcroft Cres EH28 ...... 119 E1
Hallcroft Gdns EH28 ...... 119 E1
Hallcroft Gn EH28 ...... 119 E1
Hallcroft Neuk EH28 ...... 119 E1
Hallcroft Pk EH28 ...... 119 E1
Hallcroft Rise EH28 ...... 119 E1
Hallglen Prim Sch FK1 ...... 60 A1
Hallglen Rd FK1 ...... 60 A1
Hallglen Terr FK1 ...... 60 A1
Hallhead Rd EH16 ...... 123 F1
Hallhill EH42 ...... 106 B4

Halliburton Terr EH39 ...... 53 D2
Hallows The KY1 ...... 17 F4
Hallpark FK10 ...... 10 B4
Hallyards Rd
Newbridge HE29 ...... 119 D4
Ratho Station EH28 ...... 119 E3
Halmyre St EH6 ...... 94 A2
Halyard Rise KY11 ...... 47 F1
Halyard Terr KY2 ...... 15 D1
Hamburgh Pl EH6 ...... 93 F3
Hamilton Ave
Linlithgow EH49 ...... 84 C3
Stenhousemuir FK5 ...... 38 C2
Hamilton Cres
Gullane EH31 ...... 52 A1
Maddiston FK2 ...... 82 C3
Newtongrange EH22 ...... 183 D3
Hamilton Dr
Edinburgh EH15 ...... 124 C4
Falkirk FK1 ...... 60 A2
Stirling FK9 ...... 2 B2
Hamilton Dr W EH15 ...... 124 C4
Hamilton Gdns EH15 ...... 124 C4
Hamilton Gr EH15 ...... 124 C4
Hamilton La
Bathgate EH48 ...... 144 C4
Bo'ness EH51 ...... 63 F4
Hamilton Pk
Edinburgh EH15 ...... 124 C4
Linlithgow EH49 ...... 84 C3
Hamilton Pl Edinburgh EH3 .. 93 D1
Linlithgow EH49 ...... 84 C3
Rosyth KY11 ...... 46 C2
Hamilton Rd
Bathgate EH48 ...... 144 C4
Grangemouth FK3 ...... 61 F3
Gullane EH31 ...... 52 A1
Larbert FK2 ...... 38 B3
North Berwick EH39 ...... 54 A4
Hamilton Sq EH51 ...... 63 E3
Hamilton St Falkirk FK1 ...... 59 E3
Lochgelly KY5 ...... 14 A3
Hamilton Terr
Edinburgh EH15 ...... 125 D4
High Valleyfield KY12 ...... 26 A1
Inverkeithing KY11 ...... 47 E1
Hamilton Wynd EH6 ...... 93 F3
Hammermen's Entry EH8 .. 233 E3
Handax ML11 ...... 215 D1
Haney's Way EH51 ...... 64 A4
Hanover Ct Broxburn EH52 .. 117 F3
Livingston EH54 ...... 147 D2
Hanover Grange FK3 ...... 61 E4
Hanover St EH2 ...... 232 C4
Harbour Dr KY11 ...... 47 F2
Harbour Pl Burntisland KY3 .. 50 C4
Dalgety Bay KY11 ...... 47 F1
Edinburgh EH15 ...... 95 D1
Inverkeithing KY11 ...... 47 E1
Harbour Rd Bo'ness EH51 .. 64 B4
Edinburgh EH15 ...... 95 D1
Kinghorn KY3 ...... 35 D1
Musselburgh EH21 ...... 126 A3
Harburn Ave EH54 ...... 146 C3
Harburn Ave W EH54 ...... 146 C4
Harburn Dr EH55 ...... 172 C2
Harburn Gdns EH55 ...... 172 C2
Harburn La EH55 ...... 172 C2
Harburn Rd EH55 ...... 172 C2
Harcourt Rd KY2 ...... 17 D3
Harden Pl EH11 ...... 122 C3
Hardengreen Bsns Ctr
EH22 ...... 156 C1
Hardengreen Ind Est
EH22 ...... 156 C1
Hardengreen Junc EH22 .. 182 C4
Hardgate EH41 ...... 101 D1
Hardgate Ct EH41 ...... 101 D1
Hardhill Dr EH48 ...... 144 C3
Hardhill Pl EH48 ...... 144 A3
Hardhill Rd EH48 ...... 144 C3
Hardhill Terr EH48 ...... 144 C3
Hardie Cres FK7 ...... 8 B2
Hardie Ct FK7 ...... 7 F3
Hardie Rd EH54 ...... 146 B4
Hardie Terr EH40 ...... 103 E4
Hardwell Cl EH8 ...... 233 E2
Hardy Gdns EH48 ...... 145 F3
Hareburn Ave FK1 ...... 112 A3
Harelaw Rd EH13 ...... 153 D3
Hares Cl EH22 ...... 97 C2
Harestanes Rd EH48 ...... 143 F2
Harewood Cres EH16 ...... 124 C2
Harewood Dr EH16 ...... 124 C2
Harewood Rd EH16 ...... 124 C2
Harkenburn Gdns EH26 .. 203 E3
Harlaw Gr EH26 ...... 203 E3
Harlaw Hill EH32 ...... 96 C1
Harlaw March EH14 ...... 177 E4
Harlaw Rd Balerno EH14 ...... 177 F4
Currie EH14 ...... 152 A1
Harlawhill Gdns EH32 ...... 97 D1
Harley Ct FK2 ...... 60 A4
Harlow Ave FK2 ...... 61 E3
Harmeny Sch EH14 ...... 177 E4
Harness Ct EH20 ...... 181 E4
Harpenside Cres EH39 ...... 53 E3
Harper's Brae EH26 ...... 204 A3
Harpendean Terr EH41 ...... 100 C1
Harriebrae Pk KY12 ...... 28 C2
Harriet St KY1 ...... 17 F3
Harris Ct FK10 ...... 10 A3
Harris Dr KY2 ...... 16 C4
Harris Pl Dunfermline KY11 .. 29 E1
Grangemouth FK3 ...... 61 E3
Harrismith Pl EH7 ...... 94 A1

Harrison Gdns EH11 ...... 122 C2
Harrison La EH11 ...... 122 C3
Harrison Pl
Edinburgh EH11 ...... 122 C2
Falkirk FK1 ...... 59 F3
Harrison Rd EH11 ...... 122 C3
Harrysmuir Cres EH53 ...... 148 A4
Harrysmuir N EH53 ...... 148 A4
Harrysmuir Prim Sch EH54 147 F3
Harrysmuir Rd EH53 ...... 148 A4
Harrysmuir S EH53 ...... 148 A4
Harrysmuir Terr EH53 ...... 148 A4
Hart St EH1 ...... 93 E1
Hart Street La EH1 ...... 93 E1
Hart Wynd FK7 ...... 7 F1
Hartfield Terr ML7 ...... 212 A4
Harthill Rd
Blackridge EH48 ...... 142 B1
Fauldhouse EH47 ...... 193 E3
Hartington Gdns EH10 ...... 123 D3
Hartington Pl EH10 ...... 123 D3
Hartley Pl FK3 ...... 61 D3
Hartshill Prim Sch ML7 ...... 168 C3
Hartwood Gdns ML7 ...... 191 D2
Hartwood Rd Shotts ML7 ...... 191 D2
West Calder EH55 ...... 172 B1
Hartwoodhill Hospl ML7 .. 191 D4
Harvest Dr EH28 ...... 119 D3
Harvest Rd EH28 ...... 119 D3
Harvesters Way EH14 ...... 152 B4
Harvey Ave FK2 ...... 61 F1
Harvey Wynd FK8 ...... 2 A1
Harvieston Villas EH23 ...... 207 E4
Hatfield Pl **4** EH48 ...... 145 D4
Hatton Pl EH9 ...... 123 E3
Haugh Gdns FK2 ...... 39 D1
Haugh Park EH14 ...... 122 A1
Haugh Rd Burntisland KY3 .. 50 B4
Stirling FK9 ...... 2 A1
Haugh St Edinburgh EH4 ...... 93 D1
Falkirk FK2 ...... 39 D1
Haven The KY11 ...... 47 F1
Haven's Edge KY11 ...... 45 F2
Hawes Brae EH30 ...... 68 B1
Hawk Brae EH54 ...... 147 E3
Hawkcraig Rd KY3 ...... 49 E4
Hawkhead Cres EH16 ...... 155 D4
Hawkhead Gr EH16 ...... 155 D4
Hawkhill EH7 ...... 94 A2
Hawkhill Ave EH7 ...... 94 A2
Hawkhill Rd Alloa FK10 ...... 10 B3
Kincardine FK10 ...... 23 E3
Hawkins Terr EH26 ...... 204 A4
Hawksmuir KY1 ...... 17 E3
Hawkwood Terr ML11 ...... 215 D1
Hawley Rd FK1 ...... 60 B2
Hawthorn Bank
Carnock KY12 ...... 27 E3
Queensferry EH30 ...... 68 A1
Seafield EH47 ...... 172 A4
Hawthorn Cres
Easthouses EH22 ...... 183 E4
Fallin FK7 ...... 8 B2
Hill of B KY4 ...... 12 C1
Stirling FK8 ...... 1 C1
Hawthorn Dr Denny FK6 ...... 36 B2
Falkirk FK1 ...... 59 F2
Fallin FK7 ...... 8 B2
Harthill ML7 ...... 168 C3
Shotts ML7 ...... 192 B2
Hawthorn Gdns EH20 ...... 155 D1
Hawthorn Pl
Edinburgh EH17 ...... 155 F3
Ormiston EH35 ...... 159 E4
Shotts ML7 ...... 212 A4
Uphall EH52 ...... 116 C2
Hawthorn Rd EH32 ...... 97 D1
Hawthorn St FK3 ...... 61 E3
Hawthorn Terr EH32 ...... 97 D2
Hawthornbank La EH4 ...... 232 A3
Hawthornbank Pl EH6 ...... 93 E3
Hawthornbank Rd EH11 ...... 100 C1
Hawthornbank Terr EH6 ...... 93 F3
Hawthornden Ave EH19 .. 182 A4
Hawthornden Gdns EH19 . 182 A4
Hawthornden Prim Sch
EH19 ...... 181 F3
Hawthorne Pl FK5 ...... 38 B1
Hawthorns The EH31 ...... 52 A1
Hawthornvale EH6 ...... 93 E3
Hay Ave EH16 ...... 124 C2
Hay Dr EH16 ...... 125 D2
Hay Gr KY11 ...... 29 F1
Hay Pl EH16 ...... 124 C2
Hay Rd EH16 ...... 124 C2
Hay Terr EH16 ...... 124 C2
Hayfield Edinburgh EH12 ...... 121 D4
Falkirk FK2 ...... 60 B4
Hayfield Ind Est KY2 ...... 17 D4
Hayfield Pl KY2 ...... 17 D4
Hayfield Rd Falkirk FK2 ...... 60 B4
Kirkaldy KY1 ...... 17 E4
Hayfield Terr FK6 ...... 57 F4
Haygate Ave FK2 ...... 82 C4
Haymarket EH12 ...... 232 A2
Haymarket Sta EH12 ...... 232 A2
Haymarket Terr EH12 ...... 122 C3
Haypark Bsns Ctr FK2 ...... 61 F1
Haypark Rd FK6 ...... 57 E3
Hayworth Ave FK2 ...... 61 D2
Hazel Ave KY2 ...... 17 D1
Hazel Cres FK6 ...... 36 B2
Hazel Ct EH47 ...... 78 A1
Hazel Dr EH19 ...... 182 A3
Hazel Gr Dunfermline KY11 .. 46 C4
Falkirk FK2 ...... 60 B4
Livingston EH54 ...... 148 A3
Shotts ML7 ...... 192 A2

Hazel La EH20 ...... 180 C4
Hazel Rd EH3 ...... 61 E3
Hazelbank Gdns FK8 ...... 2 A1
Hazelbank Terr EH11 ...... 122 C2
Hazeldean Ave EH51 ...... 63 E3
Hazeldean Terr EH16 ...... 124 A1
Hazelhurst FK2 ...... 82 C4
Hazelwood Gr EH16 ...... 124 B1
Head of Muir Prim Sch
  FK6 ...... 57 E3
Headlesscross Rd ML7 ...... 192 C1
Headrig Rd EH30 ...... 67 F1
Headrigg Row EH16 ...... 124 A1
Headwell Ave KY12 ...... 29 D3
Headwell Rd KY12 ...... 29 D3
Heaney Ave KY53 ...... 148 A4
Heath Rd KY11 ...... 46 C2
Heather Ave FK1 ...... 81 E3
Heather Gr
  Dunfermline KY11 ...... 46 C4
  Maddiston FK2 ...... 83 D3
Heather Pk EH47 ...... 146 A1
Heatherbank EH54 ...... 147 E3
Heatherdale Gdns FK6 ...... 57 F4
Heathervale Wlk EH48 ...... 144 A3
Heatherwood EH47 ...... 146 A1
Heatherwood Pk EH53 ...... 148 A4
Heathery The KY11 ...... 46 C4
Hedge Row EH16 ...... 180 C4
Hedges The FK1 ...... 59 F3
Heggie's Wynd KY1 ...... 17 D1
Heights Rd EH48 ...... 142 B2
Helen Pl KY11 ...... 68 B3
Helmsdale Pk EH54 ...... 147 F1
Henderland Rd EH12 ...... 122 B4
Henderson Ave KY10 ...... 10 A4
Henderson Cres EH52 ...... 117 D3
Henderson Ct KY53 ...... 148 C2
Henderson Gdns
  Edinburgh EH3 ...... 93 F3
  Tranent EH33 ...... 128 B3
Henderson Pl Alva FK12 ...... 5 D4
  Broxburn EH52 ...... 117 D3
  Edinburgh EH3 ...... 93 E1
Henderson Place La EH3 ...... 93 D1
Henderson Row EH3 ...... 93 D1
Henderson St
  Bridge of A FK9 ...... 2 A4
  Edinburgh EH6 ...... 93 F3
  Kingseat KY12 ...... 12 A1
  Lochgelly KY5 ...... 14 A4
Henderson Terr EH11 ...... 122 C3
Hendry Cres KY2 ...... 17 D3
Hendry Rd KY2 ...... 17 D3
Hendry St FK2 ...... 60 A4
Hendry's Wynd KY1 ...... 17 D1
Hennings The FK10 ...... 5 E1
Henry Ross Pl EH30 ...... 68 A1
Henry St Alva FK12 ...... 5 D3
  Bo'ness EH51 ...... 64 A3
  Grangemouth FK3 ...... 61 F4
Henryson Rd KY11 ...... 29 F2
Hens Nest Rd EH47 ...... 170 C3
Hens Nest Road Crofts
  EH47 ...... 170 C2
Hepburn Dr EH22 ...... 157 E1
Hepburn Rd EH41 ...... 101 D1
Herald Rise EH54 ...... 147 F1
Herbertshire St FK6 ...... 36 C1
Hercus Loan EH21 ...... 126 A3
Herd Gn EH54 ...... 147 D4
Herd Terr EH20 ...... 181 D4
Herdmanflatt EH41 ...... 101 D1
Herdmanflatt Hospl
  EH41 ...... 101 D1
Herdshill Ave FK1 ...... 81 E3
Heriot Bridge EH1 ...... 232 C2
Heriot Gdns KY3 ...... 33 F1
Heriot Hill Terr EH7 ...... 93 E2
Heriot Pl EH1 ...... 232 C2
Heriot Row EH3 ...... 232 B4
Heriot St KY11 ...... 47 E1
Heriot Way EH38 ...... 228 B1
Heriot-Watt Univ EH14 ...... 151 F4
Heritage Dr FK2 ...... 39 D2
Hermand Cres EH11 ...... 122 C2
Hermand St EH11 ...... 122 B2
Hermand Terr EH11 ...... 122 B2
Hermiston Gait Ret Pk
  EH11 ...... 121 D2
Hermiston House Rd
  EH14 ...... 120 C1
Hermiston Junc EH11 ...... 121 D1
Hermitage Dr EH10 ...... 123 D1
Hermitage Gdns EH10 ...... 123 D1
Hermitage Park Gr EH6 ...... 94 A2
Hermitage Park Prim Sch
  EH6 ...... 94 A2
Hermitage Pk EH6 ...... 94 A2
Hermitage Pk S EH6 ...... 94 A2
Hermitage Pl EH6 ...... 94 A2
Hermitage Pl FK9 ...... 2 C3
Hermitage Terr EH10 ...... 123 D1
Hermits Croft EH8 ...... 233 F1
Heron Ind Complex EH54 ...... 146 B4
Hervey St FK10 ...... 10 A4
Heugh Brae EH39 ...... 54 C3
Heugh Rd EH39 ...... 54 C3
Heugh St FK1 ...... 60 A2
Heugh The EH33 ...... 128 B4
Hewitt Pl KY3 ...... 49 E4
Heyford FK7 ...... 6 B3
Higginson Loan EH22 ...... 183 F3
High Academy Gr EH48 ...... 143 F3
High Academy St EH48 ...... 143 F3
High Beveridgewell KY12 ...... 28 C3
High Brae EH10 ...... 113 F3
High Buckstone EH10 ...... 154 B3

High Meadow ML8 ...... 230 B1
High Mill Rd ML8 ...... 230 A1
High Park Rise EH26 ...... 203 F2
High Port EH49 ...... 85 D4
High Rd Maddiston FK2 ...... 83 D3
  Roslin EH25 ...... 204 C3
  Spott EH42 ...... 106 B2
High Riggs EH3 ...... 232 B2
High School Wynd EH1 ...... 233 E2
High School Yds EH1 ...... 233 E2
High St Aberdour KY3 ...... 49 D4
  Aberlady EH32 ...... 71 E2
  Airth FK2 ...... 22 B2
  Alloa FK10 ...... 10 A3
  Bathgate EH48 ...... 145 D4
  Bonnyrigg EH19 ...... 156 A1
  Bonnyrigg and Lasswade
  EH18 ...... 156 A1
  Bonnyrigg and Lasswade
  EH19 ...... 182 A4
  Burntisland KY3 ...... 50 C4
  Clackmannan FK10 ...... 10 C2
  Cockenzie & Port Seton EH32 ...... 97 E2
  Cowdenbeath KY4 ...... 13 E2
  Dalkeith EH22 ...... 157 D2
  Dunbar EH42 ...... 78 B1
  Dunbar, Belhaven EH42 ...... 78 A1
  Dunfermline KY12 ...... 29 D2
  Dysart KY1 ...... 18 A4
  East Linton EH40 ...... 103 E4
  Edinburgh EH1 ...... 233 D3
  Falkirk FK1 ...... 60 A2
  Gifford EH41 ...... 163 F2
  Haddington EH41 ...... 132 A4
  Inverkeithing KY11 ...... 47 D1
  Kincardine FK10 ...... 23 E2
  Kinghorn KY3 ...... 34 C1
  Kirkcaldy KY1 ...... 17 E2
  Kirkliston EH29 ...... 89 D1
  Linlithgow EH49 ...... 85 D4
  Loanhead EH20 ...... 181 E4
  Lochgelly KY5 ...... 14 A4
  Musselburgh EH21 ...... 126 B3
  North Berwick EH39 ...... 54 B4
  Ormiston EH35 ...... 159 F4
  Penicuik EH26 ...... 203 F2
  Prestonpans EH32 ...... 96 C1
  Queensferry EH30 ...... 68 B1
  Shotts ML7 ...... 191 F2
  Slamannan FK1 ...... 110 A4
  Tranent EH33 ...... 128 B3
High Station Rd FK1 ...... 60 A2
High View Gr FK1 ...... 81 E3
Highfield Livingston EH54 ...... 147 D2
  North Berwick EH39 ...... 54 C4
Highfield Cres EH49 ...... 84 C4
Highfield Rd EH39 ...... 54 A3
Highland Dr FK5 ...... 38 B2
Highland Dykes Cres FK4 ...... 58 A3
Highland Dykes Pk FK4 ...... 58 A3
Highlea Circ EH14 ...... 177 D4
Highlea Rd EH14 ...... 177 D4
Hill Cres EH48 ...... 145 D4
Hill Gr KY12 ...... 26 B4
Hill House Rd FK6 ...... 57 F4
Hill of Beath Prim Sch
  KY4 ...... 12 C1
Hill Pk KY11 ...... 10 A4
  Edinburgh EH8 ...... 233 E2
  Kirkaldy KY1 ...... 17 E2
  Mayfield EH22 ...... 183 F3
  Shotts ML7 ...... 191 F3
Hill Rd Gullane EH31 ...... 51 F1
  Harthill ML7 ...... 168 B3
  Pathhead EH37 ...... 185 D3
Hill Sq EH8 ...... 233 E2
Hill St Alloa FK10 ...... 10 A4
  Cowdenbeath KY4 ...... 13 E2
  Dunfermline KY12 ...... 29 D2
  Dysart KY1 ...... 18 A4
  Edinburgh EH2 ...... 232 C4
  Inverkeithing KY11 ...... 47 D1
  Kirkaldy KY1 ...... 17 D2
  Stirling FK7 ...... 7 D2
Hill Street La N EH2 ...... 232 C4
Hill Street La S EH2 ...... 232 C4
Hill View EH26 ...... 204 A3
Hillary Rd FK5 ...... 38 C1
Hillbank KY11 ...... 47 D2
Hillcoat Loan EH15 ...... 95 D1
Hillcoat Pl EH15 ...... 95 D1
Hillcrest Bo'ness EH51 ...... 63 F3
  Cowdenbeath KY4 ...... 13 D2
Hillcrest Ave KY2 ...... 16 C3
Hillcrest Dr FK10 ...... 10 B3
Hillcrest Pl FK6 ...... 57 E4
Hillcrest Rd FK1 ...... 59 F1
Hillend Ind Pk KY11 ...... 48 B3
Hillend Rd KY11 ...... 47 E2
Hillfield Rd KY11 ...... 47 D1
Hillfoot Terr ML8 ...... 230 A1
Hillfoots Rd FK9 ...... 2 C2
Hillhead EH19 ...... 182 A4
Hillhead Ave ML8 ...... 230 A1
Hillhead Dr FK1 ...... 59 F1
Hillhouse Ave EH48 ...... 144 C4
Hillhouse Cres EH27 ...... 149 F2
Hillhouse Rd EH4 ...... 92 A1
Hillhouse Terr EH27 ...... 149 F2
Hillhouseridge Rd ML7 ...... 191 E3
Hillock Ave FK1 ...... 61 E1
Hillpark Ave EH4 ...... 91 F1
Hillpark Brae EH4 ...... 91 F1
Hillpark Cres Bannockburn FK7 ...... 7 E1
  Edinburgh EH4 ...... 91 F1

Hillpark Ct EH4 ...... 91 F2
Hillpark Dr Bannockburn FK7 ...... 7 E1
  Edinburgh EH4 ...... 91 F2
Hillpark Gdns EH4 ...... 91 F1
Hillpark Gn EH4 ...... 91 F1
Hillpark Gr EH4 ...... 91 F1
Hillpark Loan EH4 ...... 92 A1
Hillpark Rd EH4 ...... 91 F1
Hillpark Terr EH4 ...... 91 F1
Hillpark Way EH4 ...... 92 A1
Hillpark Wood EH4 ...... 92 A1
Hillside EH1 ...... 5 E1
Hillside Ave EH11 ...... 48 A2
Hillside Camp Rd KY11 ...... 46 C1
Hillside Cres EH7 ...... 93 F1
Hillside Cres N EH23 ...... 207 E4
Hillside Cres S EH23 ...... 207 E4
Hillside Dr EH48 ...... 142 B2
Hillside Pl Blackridge EH48 ...... 142 B2
  Longridge EH47 ...... 170 B1
Hillside Rd EH30 ...... 90 B2
Hillside Sch KY3 ...... 49 E4
Hillside St EH7 ...... 93 F1
Hillside Terr Alloa FK10 ...... 10 A4
  Craigiehall FK2 ...... 90 B3
  Westquarter FK2 ...... 61 D2
Hillview Cowdenbeath KY4 ...... 13 D2
  Edinburgh EH4 ...... 92 A1
  Fauldhouse EH47 ...... 193 F3
  Oakley KY12 ...... 26 C4
Hillview Ave
  Crossgates KY4 ...... 30 C3
  Edinburgh EH12 ...... 121 E4
Hillview Cres
  Crossgates KY4 ...... 30 C3
  Edinburgh EH12 ...... 121 E4
Hillview Dr Bridge of A FK9 ...... 2 A3
  Edinburgh EH12 ...... 121 E4
Hillview La EH54 ...... 173 F2
Hillview Pl Broxburn EH52 ...... 117 E3
  Crossgates KY4 ...... 30 C3
  Fallin FK7 ...... 8 B2
Hillview Rd Brightons FK2 ...... 82 B4
  Edinburgh EH12 ...... 121 E4
  High Bonnybridge FK4 ...... 58 B2
  Larbert FK5 ...... 38 B2
  Ormiston EH35 ...... 159 F4
Hillview Terr Alloa FK10 ...... 10 B3
  Edinburgh EH12 ...... 121 E4
Hillwood Ave EH28 ...... 119 E3
Hillwood Cres EH28 ...... 119 E3
Hillwood Gdns EH28 ...... 119 E3
Hillwood Prim Sch EH28 ...... 119 E3
Hillwood Rd EH28 ...... 119 E3
Hillwood Rise EH28 ...... 119 E3
Hillwood Terr
  Ratho Station EH28 ...... 119 E3
  Rosyth KY11 ...... 47 D2
Hilton FK7 ...... 20 C4
Hilton Cres FK10 ...... 10 B4
Hilton Ct EH41 ...... 132 A4
Hilton Rd Alloa FK10 ...... 10 B4
  Cairneyhill KY12 ...... 27 F1
  Rosyth KY11 ...... 46 B1
Hilton Terr FK7 ...... 8 B2
Hilton View KY4 ...... 13 F3
Hirst Cres FK7 ...... 8 B2
Hirst Ct FK7 ...... 8 B2
Hirst Gdns ML7 ...... 191 E3
Hirst Rd ML7 ...... 167 E2
Hirstrigg Cotts ML7 ...... 167 D2
Hoban Sq EH52 ...... 117 F3
Hobart St EH54 ...... 148 A3
Hodge St FK1 ...... 60 A2
Hogarth Ave EH23 ...... 183 E1
Hoggan Cres KY11 ...... 29 E1
Hoghill Ct EH53 ...... 148 C2
Hoghill Pl EH53 ...... 148 C2
Holborn Pl KY11 ...... 46 C3
Holbourne Pl FK11 ...... 4 A4
Holden Way KY11 ...... 48 A3
Holly Ave FK5 ...... 38 C2
Holly Bank EH22 ...... 183 F4
Holly Cres KY11 ...... 46 C4
Holly Pl KY1 ...... 17 E4
Holly Terr EH19 ...... 182 A3
Holly Wlk EH20 ...... 180 C4
Hollybank Pl EH53 ...... 148 C1
Hollybank Terr EH11 ...... 122 C2
Holmes Farm La EH52 ...... 117 D3
Holmes Holdings EH52 ...... 117 E2
Holmes Rd EH52 ...... 117 D2
Holmlea Ave FK2 ...... 82 B4
Holton Cres FK10 ...... 5 E1
Holton Sq FK10 ...... 5 E1
Holy Cross Prim Sch
  EH6 ...... 93 E3
Holy Family RC Prim Sch
  EH52 ...... 87 F1
Holy Rood RC Sec Sch
  EH15 ...... 124 B3
Holy Trinity Episcopal Prim Sch
  FK8 ...... 7 D4
Holygate Pl EH52 ...... 117 E3
Holyrood Bsns Pk EH16 ...... 124 B2
Holyrood Park Rd EH16 ...... 233 F1
Holyrood Pl
  Dunfermline KY12 ...... 29 D2
  Stenhousemuir FK5 ...... 38 C2
Holyrood Rd EH8 ...... 233 F3
Home Farm Cotts FK6 ...... 57 F3
Home Pk KY3 ...... 49 E4
Home St EH3 ...... 232 B1
Homesteads The FK8 ...... 6 B4
Honeybank Cres ML8 ...... 230 A1
Honeyman Ct EH27 ...... 143 F4
Hookney Terr FK6 ...... 36 B1
Hope Cotts EH51 ...... 64 B3
Hope La EH15 ...... 125 D4

Hope Park Cres
  Edinburgh EH8 ...... 233 E1
  Haddington EH41 ...... 100 C1
Hope Park Gdns EH48 ...... 144 C3
Hope Park Sq EH8 ...... 233 E1
Hope Park Terr EH8 ...... 233 E1
Hope Pk EH41 ...... 101 D1
Hope Pl EH21 ...... 126 C3
Hope St Bo'ness EH51 ...... 63 F4
  Carluke ML8 ...... 230 A1
  Cowdenbeath KY4 ...... 13 F3
  Edinburgh EH2 ...... 232 B3
  Falkirk FK1 ...... 60 A3
  Inverkeithing KY11 ...... 47 D1
  Queensferry EH30 ...... 89 D4
  Stirling FK8 ...... 1 C1
Hope Street La EH2 ...... 232 B3
Hope Terr EH9 ...... 123 E2
Hopefield Dr EH47 ...... 171 E4
Hopefield Pk EH19 ...... 182 A3
Hopefield Pl
  Blackburn EH47 ...... 171 E4
  Bonnyrigg and Lasswade
  EH19 ...... 182 A3
Hopefield Prim Sch EH19 ...... 182 A3
Hopefield Rd EH47 ...... 171 E4
Hopefield Terr
  Bonnyrigg and Lasswade
  EH19 ...... 182 A3
  Edinburgh EH6 ...... 93 F3
Hopelands Rd EH26 ...... 202 C3
Hopepark EH48 ...... 144 C3
Hopepark Terr FK6 ...... 57 F3
Hopetoun Cres EH7 ...... 93 F1
Hopetoun Dr
  Bridge of A FK9 ...... 2 A4
  Haddington EH41 ...... 100 C1
Hopetoun Ho EH30 ...... 66 C1
Hopetoun La EH45 ...... 145 D3
Hopetoun Mews EH41 ...... 101 D1
Hopetoun Mon EH39 ...... 100 C3
Hopetoun Pl KY2 ...... 16 B3
Hopetoun Rd
  Queensferry EH30 ...... 68 A1
  Rosyth KY11 ...... 46 B1
Hopetoun St
  Bathgate EH48 ...... 145 D3
  Edinburgh EH7 ...... 93 F2
Hopetoun Terr
  Gullane EH31 ...... 52 A2
  Ormiston EH35 ...... 159 F4
Hopetoun View KY11 ...... 48 B2
Hopeward Ct KY11 ...... 48 B2
Hopeward Mews KY11 ...... 48 B1
Hoprig Pk TD13 ...... 140 C1
Hoprig Rd TD13 ...... 140 C1
Hornbeam Cres FK2 ...... 61 D2
Horne Terr EH11 ...... 232 A1
Horsburgh Bank EH14 ...... 151 E2
Horsburgh Gdns EH14 ...... 151 E2
Horsburgh Gr EH14 ...... 151 E2
Horse Wynd EH8 ...... 233 F3
Hoseason Gdns EH4 ...... 91 E1
Hosie Rigg EH15 ...... 125 D3
Hospital Hill KY11 ...... 29 D1
Hospital Intc EH54 ...... 147 E2
Hospital Rd EH41 ...... 100 C1
Hot Pot Wynd KY1 ...... 18 A3
Houldsworth Cres ML7 ...... 212 A4
Houldsworth St KY12 ...... 26 A4
Houliston Ave KY11 ...... 47 D2
House O' Muir Rd ML7 ...... 167 D2
House O'Hill Ave EH4 ...... 92 A2
House O'Hill Brae EH4 ...... 92 A2
House O'Hill Cres EH4 ...... 92 A2
House O'Hill Gdns EH4 ...... 92 A2
House O'Hill Gn EH4 ...... 92 A2
House O'Hill Gr EH4 ...... 92 A2
House O'Hill Pl EH4 ...... 92 A2
House O'Hill Rd EH4 ...... 92 A2
House O'Hill Row EH4 ...... 92 A2
House O'Hill Terr EH4 ...... 92 A1
Houston Ct KY12 ...... 28 C2
Houston Rd
  Livingston EH54 ...... 147 D3
  Uphall Station EH54 ...... 117 D1
Houstoun Gdns EH52 ...... 116 C2
Houstoun Ind Est
  Dechmont EH54 ...... 116 C1
  Livingston EH54 ...... 147 F4
Houstoun Intc EH54 ...... 147 E4
Houstoun Rd EH54 ...... 147 F3
Houstoun Rd W EH54 ...... 146 C3
Howard Cres KY11 ...... 29 E1
Howard Pl Dysart KY1 ...... 18 A4
  Edinburgh EH3 ...... 93 E2
Howard St Edinburgh EH3 ...... 93 E2
  Falkirk FK1 ...... 59 F2
Howburn Cres ML7 ...... 168 C3
Howburn Rd ML7 ...... 168 B3
Howden East Rd EH54 ...... 147 F2
Howden Hall Cres EH16 ...... 154 C3
Howden Hall Ct EH16 ...... 154 C3
Howden Hall Dr EH16 ...... 154 C3
Howden Hall Gdns EH16 ...... 155 D3
Howden Hall Loan EH16 ...... 154 C3
Howden Hall Pk EH16 ...... 154 C3
Howden Hall Rd EH16 ...... 155 D3
Howden Hall Way EH16 ...... 155 D3
Howden South Rd EH54 ...... 147 F2
Howden St EH8 ...... 233 E1
Howden St Andrew's
  RC Prim Sch EH54 ...... 147 F2
Howden West Rd EH54 ...... 147 F2
Howe Pk EH10 ...... 153 F3
Howe St EH3 ...... 232 C4
Howetown FK10 ...... 5 E2
Howgate Prim Sch EH26 ...... 204 A1

Howgate Sh Ctr **7** FK1 ...... 60 A2
Howie's Pl FK1 ...... 59 D2
Howieson Ave EH51 ...... 63 F3
Howieson Gn EH52 ...... 116 C2
Howlands Rd FK7 ...... 7 D2
Howley Ave EH54 ...... 147 F2
Hudson Rd KY11 ...... 46 C2
Hugh Ave KY5 ...... 14 A4
Hugh Miller Pl EH3 ...... 93 D1
Hugh Pl KY5 ...... 14 A4
Hugh Russell Pl EH30 ...... 89 D4
Hughes Cres EH22 ...... 183 F3
Humbie Prim Sch EH36 ...... 187 D1
Humbie Rd EH29 ...... 89 D1
Humbie Terr KY3 ...... 49 E4
Hume Cres FK9 ...... 2 A3
Hume Ct FK9 ...... 2 A3
Hummel Rd EH31 ...... 51 F1
Hungerage Sq EH33 ...... 128 B3
Hunt Cl EH22 ...... 157 D2
Hunt Pl KY12 ...... 28 A1
Hunter Ave EH20 ...... 181 E4
Hunter Ct EH20 ...... 181 E4
Hunter Gdns
  Bonnybridge FK4 ...... 58 A3
  Broxburn EH52 ...... 118 A3
  Denny FK6 ...... 36 B1
Hunter Gr Bathgate EH48 ...... 145 F3
  Whitburn EH47 ...... 169 F3
Hunter Hospl KY1 ...... 17 D2
Hunter Pl Dunfermline KY12 ...... 28 C3
  Kirkaldy KY1 ...... 17 D2
  Shotts ML7 ...... 191 F3
  Stenhousemuir FK2 ...... 39 D2
Hunter Rd EH54 ...... 147 E1
Hunter Sq Edinburgh EH1 ...... 233 D3
  Gorebridge EH23 ...... 207 E4
Hunter St Kirkaldy KY1 ...... 17 D2
  Shotts ML7 ...... 191 E3
Hunter Terr
  Bonnyrigg and Lasswade
  EH19 ...... 182 A4
  Loanhead EH20 ...... 181 E4
Hunter's Cl EH1 ...... 232 C2
Hunter's La EH47 ...... 170 A3
Hunter's Tryst Prim Sch
  EH13 ...... 153 F4
Hunterfield Ct EH23 ...... 207 E4
Hunterfield Pk EH23 ...... 183 E1
Hunterfield Rd EH23 ...... 207 E4
Hunterfield Terr EH23 ...... 183 D1
Hunters Hill EH26 ...... 203 E3
Hunting Pk EH54 ...... 116 C1
Huntingdon Pl EH7 ...... 93 F1
Huntlaw Rd EH34 ...... 160 C3
Huntley Cres FK8 ...... 1 C1
Huntley House Mus EH8 ...... 233 E3
Huntly Ave EH54 ...... 146 C3
Huntly Cres KY2 ...... 16 B4
Huntly St EH3 ...... 93 E2
Huntly Terr ML7 ...... 192 A2
Huron Ave EH54 ...... 147 F2
Hursted Ave EH22 ...... 183 E4
Hurworth St FK1 ...... 59 F2
Husband Pl KY11 ...... 29 F1
Hutchison Ave EH14 ...... 122 B2
Hutchison Cotts EH14 ...... 122 B2
Hutchison Crossway EH14 ...... 122 B2
Hutchison Gdns EH14 ...... 122 B2
Hutchison Loan EH14 ...... 122 B2
Hutchison Medway EH14 ...... 122 B2
Hutchison Pk EH14 ...... 122 B2
Hutchison Pl EH14 ...... 122 B2
Hutchison Rd EH14 ...... 122 B2
Hutchison Terr EH14 ...... 122 B2
Hutchison View EH14 ...... 122 B2
Hutton Pk FK10 ...... 10 B4
Hutton Sq EH54 ...... 173 E3
Hyndshaw Rd ML8 ...... 230 A2
Hyvot Bank Ave EH17 ...... 155 E3
Hyvot Ct EH17 ...... 155 E3
Hyvot Gdns EH17 ...... 155 E3
Hyvot Gn EH17 ...... 155 E3
Hyvot Gr EH17 ...... 155 E3
Hyvot Loan EH17 ...... 155 E3
Hyvot Pk EH17 ...... 155 E3
Hyvot Terr EH17 ...... 155 E3
Hyvot View EH17 ...... 155 E3

Ibris Pl EH39 ...... 54 A4
Icehouse Brae FK2 ...... 61 D2
Implement Rd EH42 ...... 77 F1
Imrie Pl EH26 ...... 203 F3
Inch Ave KY3 ...... 49 D3
Inch Cres EH48 ...... 145 E3
Inch View KY3 ...... 34 C1
Incholm Dr KY11 ...... 68 A3
Inchcolm Rd KY11 ...... 29 F2
Inchcolm Terr EH30 ...... 89 D4
Inchcorse Pl EH48 ...... 145 E1
Inchcross EH48 ...... 144 C2
Inchcross Ind Est EH48 ...... 144 C2
Inches The KY11 ...... 48 A1
Inchgarvie Cres KY11 ...... 29 F2
Inchgarvie Pk EH30 ...... 68 A1
Inchgarvie Rd KY2 ...... 16 C4
Inchkeith Ave EH30 ...... 89 E4
Inchkeith Ct EH7 ...... 93 F2
Inchkeith Dr KY11 ...... 29 F2
Inchkeith Pl FK1 ...... 60 A1
Inchkeith Sch KY12 ...... 42 B4
Inchmickery Ave KY11 ...... 48 B3
Inchmickery Rd KY11 ...... 48 B3

Inchmuir Rd EH48 .... 145 D1
Inchna FK11 .... 4 A3
Inchview EH32 .... 96 C1
Inchview Cres EH21 .... 127 E3
Inchview Gdns KY11 .... 48 A2
Inchview N EH21 .... 96 C1
Inchview Prim Sch
EH4 .... 92 B2
Inchview Rd EH21 .... 127 E3
Inchview Terr EH7 .... 94 C1
Inchyra Rd FK3 .... 61 F3
India Pl EH3 .... 232 B4
India St EH3 .... 232 B4
Industrial Rd EH6 .... 94 A2
Industry La EH1 .... 233 E2
Infirmary St EH1 .... 233 E2
Ingleston Ave FK6 .... 36 B3
Inglewood FK10 .... 9 F4
Inglewood Pl EH16 .... 155 D4
Inglewood Rd FK10 .... 9 F4
Inglewood St EH54 .... 147 F3
Inglis Ave EH32 .... 97 E2
Inglis Cres KY3 .... 34 C2
Inglis' Ct EH1 .... 232 C2
Inglis Dr FK2 .... 39 E1
Inglis Farm EH32 .... 97 E2
Inglis Green Rd EH14 .... 122 A1
Inglis Pl EH16 .... 82 C4
Inglis Pl EH16 .... 82 C4
Inglis St KY12 .... 29 D2
Ingram Pl FK2 .... 82 C3
Inkerman Ct EH26 .... 204 A4
Inn Pl EH14 .... 147 D1
Innerpeffray Dr FK2 .... 39 D2
Innerwick Prim Sch
EH42 .... 108 A1
Institution St KY1 .... 17 F4
Inver Ct FK2 .... 39 E1
Inverallan Ct FK9 .... 1 C4
Inverallan Dr FK9 .... 1 C4
Inverallan Rd FK9 .... 1 C4
Inveralmond
Com High Sch EH54 .... 147 F1
Inveralmond Dr EH4 .... 91 D3
Inveralmond Gdns EH4 ...... 91 D3
Inveralmond Gr EH4 .... 91 D3
Inverary Dr FK5 .... 38 C3
Inveravon Rd EH20 .... 155 D1
Inveravon Rdbt EH51 .... 62 B3
Inveravon Terr EH21 .... 126 B3
Inveresk Brae EH21 .... 126 B3
Inveresk Ind Est EH21 ...... 126 B3
Inveresk Mills Ind Pk
EH21 .... 126 A3
Inveresk Rd EH21 .... 126 B3
Inveresk Village Rd EH21 .. 126 B2
Inverkeithing High Sch
KY11 .... 47 E1
Inverkeithing Mus KY11 ..... 47 E1
Inverkeithing Prim Sch
KY11 .... 47 D2
Inverkeithing Rd
Aberdour KY3 .... 49 D4
Crossgates KY4 .... 30 C3
Inverkeithing Sta KY11 ...... 47 E2
Inverkip Dr ML7 .... 191 F3
Inverleith Ave EH3 .... 93 D2
Inverleith Ave S EH3 .... 93 D2
Inverleith Gr EH3 .... 92 C2
Inverleith Pl EH3 .... 93 D2
Inverleith Place La EH3 ...... 93 D2
Inverleith Row EH3 .... 93 D2
Inverleith Terr EH3 .... 93 D2
Inverleith Terrace La EH3 ... 93 E2
Invertiel Rd KY1 .... 35 D4
Invertiel Terr KY1 .... 17 D1
Inzievar Prim Sch KY12 ...... 26 C4
Inzievar Terr KY12 .... 27 D3
Iona Pl FK1 .... 60 A1
Iona Rd FK1 .... 29 F2
Iona St EH6 .... 93 F2
Ireland Ave EH47 .... 169 F3
Irene Terr FK1 .... 82 C1
Ironmills Rd FK2 .... 156 C2
Irvine Cres EH48 .... 144 C3
Irvine Pl FK8 .... 7 D4
Irving Pl FK1 .... 59 F3
Islands Cres FK1 .... 60 A1
Islay Ct FK3 .... 61 E3
Islay Rd KY11 .... 29 F1
Ivanhoe Cres EH16 .... 124 A1
Ivanhoe Pl FK8 .... 2 A1
Ivanhoe Rise EH54 .... 148 A1
Ivy Gr KY11 .... 46 C4
Ivy La KY1 .... 18 A4
Ivy Terr EH11 .... 122 C3
Ivybank Ct FK2 .... 61 F1
Izatt Ave KY11 .... 29 D1
Izatt St FK10 .... 10 A4
Izatt Terr FK10 .... 11 D2

Jacklin Gn EH54 .... 147 D4
Jackson Ave FK3 .... 61 E4
Jackson Pl EH54 .... 147 E2
Jackson St EH26 .... 203 F3
Jacob Pl FK1 .... 60 A2
Jail Wynd FK8 .... 7 D4
Jamaica Mews EH3 .... 232 B4
Jamaica St EH3 .... 232 B4
Jamaica St W EH3 .... 232 B4
Jamaica Street North La
EH3 .... 232 B4
Jamaica Street South La
EH3 .... 232 B4
James Croft Dr FK1 .... 59 F1
James Ct KY4 .... 13 E1

James Gillespie's High Sch
EH9 .... 123 E3
James Gillespie's High Sch
Annexe EH3 .... 232 B1
James Gillespie's Prim Sch
EH9 .... 123 E3
James Gr KY1 .... 17 E1
James Hog Cres KY12 .... 26 C3
James Lean Ave EH22 ...... 157 D2
James Leary Way EH19 .... 182 B4
James' Park La KY3 .... 33 F1
James' Pk KY3 .... 33 F1
James St Alva FK12 .... 5 D3
Armadale EH48 .... 143 F3
Bannockburn FK7 .... 7 E1
Cowdenbeath KY4 .... 13 E1
Dunfermline KY12 .... 29 D2
Edinburgh EH15 .... 125 E4
Falkirk FK2 .... 60 A3
Haggs FK4 .... 57 D2
Laurieston FK2 .... 60 C2
Musselburgh EH21 .... 126 B3
Stenhousemuir FK5 .... 38 B1
Stirling FK8 .... 2 A1
James Street La EH15 ...... 125 E4
James Watt Ave EH51 ...... 64 A4
James Wilson Dr FK2 .... 83 D3
James Young
High Sch The EH54 ...... 147 F1
Jameson Pl EH6 .... 93 F2
Jamieson Ave Bo'ness EH51 . 63 F3
Stenhousemuir FK5 .... 38 C2
Jamieson Gdns ML7 .... 191 F3
Jane St EH6 .... 93 F2
Janefield EH17 .... 155 D2
Jarnac Ct EH22 .... 157 D2
Jarvey St EH48 .... 145 D4
Jarvie Pl FK2 .... 60 A4
Jasper Ave FK2 .... 61 D2
Jawbanes Rd KY2 .... 35 D4
Jean Armour Ave ⑥
EH16 .... 124 A1
Jean Armour Dr EH22 ...... 157 E1
Jeffrey Ave EH4 .... 92 A1
Jeffrey Bank EH51 .... 63 F4
Jeffrey St EH1 .... 233 E3
Jeffrey Terr FK2 .... 61 F1
Jellyholm Rd FK10 .... 10 C4
Jennie Rennie's Rd KY11 ... 29 D1
Jessfield Pl EH51 .... 63 F3
Jessfield Terr EH6 .... 93 E3
Jewel & Esk Valley Coll
Dalkeith EH22 .... 156 C1
Edinburgh EH15 .... 125 E3
Jewel The EH15 .... 125 D3
Jock's Hill Cres EH54 .... 84 C4
John Bernard Way EH23 .. 207 E3
John Brown Ct EH41 .... 132 A4
John Cres EH33 .... 128 B3
John Davidson Dr KY12 ..... 36 B2
John Humble St EH3 .... 183 F1
John Knox Pl EH26 .... 203 F3
John Mason Ct EH30 .... 89 E4
John Muir Ctry Pk EH42 .... 77 E2
John Murray Dr FK9 .... 2 A4
John Row Pl KY12 .... 27 D4
John Rushforth Pl FK8 .... 1 C1
John Smith Way ML7 .... 191 F3
John St Dunfermline KY11 .. 29 D1
Edinburgh EH15 .... 125 E4
Falkirk FK2 .... 60 A4
Haggs FK4 .... 57 D2
Kincardine FK10 .... 23 E2
Kirkcaldy KY2 .... 17 D3
Penicuik EH26 .... 203 F3
Stirling FK8 .... 7 D4
John Street La
Edinburgh EH15 .... 125 E4
Penicuik EH26 .... 203 F3
John Street La E EH15 ..... 125 E4
John Street La W EH15 .... 125 E4
John Stuart Gait KY12 .... 26 C3
John Woods Pl KY4 .... 30 C4
John's La FK6 .... 94 A3
John's Pl EH6 .... 94 A3
Johnnie Cope's Rd EH33 .. 128 A4
Johnsburn Gn EH14 .... 151 D1
Johnsburn Haugh EH14 ... 151 D1
Johnsburn Pk EH14 .... 177 D4
Johnsburn Rd EH14 .... 151 D1
Johnston Ave
Stenhousemuir FK5 .... 38 C2
Stirling FK9 .... 2 A2
Uphall EH52 .... 116 C2
Johnston Cres
Dunfermline KY11 .... 29 D1
Lochgelly KY5 .... 14 A4
Johnston Ct EH52 .... 116 C2
Johnston Pk
Cowdenbeath KY4 .... 13 E3
Inverkeithing KY11 .... 47 D1
Johnston Pl Denny FK6 ...... 36 B1
Penicuik EH26 .... 203 F3
Kinghorn KY3 .... 7 E1
Johnston Terr
Cockenzie & Port Seton EH32 . 97 E2
Edinburgh EH1 .... 232 C2
Johnstone La ML8 .... 230 A1
Johnstone St Alva FK12 .... 5 D3
Menstrie FK11 .... 3 F3
Jones Ave FK5 .... 59 E4
Jones Gn EH54 .... 147 D4
Joppa Gdns EH15 .... 125 E4
Joppa Gr EH15 .... 125 E4
Joppa Pk EH15 .... 125 E4
Joppa Rd EH15 .... 125 E4

Joppa Terr EH15 .... 125 E4
Jordan La EH10 .... 123 D2
Joseph Scott Gdns
EH52 .... 117 F2
Jubilee Ave EH54 .... 146 C3
Jubilee Cres EH23 .... 183 E1
Jubilee Dr KY11 .... 46 A1
Jubilee Rd Denny FK6 .... 36 C2
Newbridge HE12 .... 119 F4
Whitburn EH47 .... 170 A3
Junction Pl EH6 .... 93 F3
Junction Rd KY1 .... 17 E4
Juner Pl EH23 .... 183 E1
Juniper Ave EH14 .... 152 B3
Juniper Gdns EH14 .... 152 B3
Juniper Gr
Dunfermline KY11 .... 46 B4
Edinburgh EH14 .... 152 B3
Livingston EH54 .... 148 A3
Juniper Green Prim Sch
EH14 .... 152 B3
Juniper Park Rd EH14 ...... 152 B3
Juniper Pl EH14 .... 152 B3
Juniper Terr EH14 .... 152 B3
Juniperlee EH14 .... 152 B3
Jura EH54 .... 146 C3
Jura Pl FK3 .... 61 E3
Justinhaugh Dr EH49 .... 84 B4

Kaemuir Ct EH48 .... 112 C3
Kaim Cres EH48 .... 145 D3
Kaimes Ave EH27 .... 149 F2
Kaimes Cres EH27 .... 149 F2
Kaimes Gdns EH27 .... 149 F2
Kaimes Gr EH27 .... 149 F2
Kaimes Rd EH12 .... 121 F4
Kaimes Sch EH16 .... 155 E3
Kaimes View EH27 .... 156 A4
Kaims Brae EH14 .... 147 E1
Kaims Ct EH54 .... 147 D1
Kaims Dr EH54 .... 147 E1
Kaims Gdns EH54 .... 147 E1
Kaims Gr EH54 .... 147 E1
Kaims Pl EH54 .... 147 E1
Kames Pl KY12 .... 29 E3
Kames Rd ML7 .... 191 F3
Katesmill Rd EH14 .... 153 D4
Katherine St
Kirkcaldy KY2 .... 17 D3
Livingston EH54 .... 148 A3
Katrine Cres KY2 .... 16 C4
Katrine Ct KY12 .... 10 B3
Katrine Dr KY12 .... 28 A1
Katrine Pl EH6 .... 57 E3
Katrine Rd Shotts ML7 ..... 191 F3
Whitburn EH47 .... 170 B4
Kay Gdns EH32 .... 97 E2
Keavil Pl KY12 .... 28 A1
Kedslie Pl EH16 .... 154 C4
Kedslie Rd EH16 .... 154 C4
Keilarsbrae FK10 .... 5 E1
Keir Ave FK7 .... 7 E2
Keir Hardie Ave FK2 .... 61 D2
Keir Hardie Dr EH22 .... 183 F3
Keir Hardie Rd FK12 .... 5 E4
Keir Hardie Terr KY11 .... 29 D1
Keir St Bridge of A FK9 ...... 2 A4
Cowdenbeath KY4 .... 13 D2
Edinburgh EH3 .... 232 C2
Keirsbeath Ct KY12 .... 12 A1
Keith Ave FK7 .... 7 E2
Keith Cres EH4 .... 92 A1
Keith Gdns EH51 .... 63 F4
Keith Pl Dunfermline KY12 . 29 E2
Inverkeithing KY11 .... 47 E2
Keith Rd KY11 .... 46 B1
Keith Row EH4 .... 92 B1
Keith St FK10 .... 23 F2
Keith Terr EH4 .... 92 A1
Kekewich Ave EH7 .... 94 C1
Kellie Pl FK10 .... 10 A4
Kelliebank FK10 .... 9 F3
Kelly Dr FK6 .... 36 C2
Kelly's La ML8 .... 230 A1
Kellywood Cres FK10 .... 23 F2
Kelso Dr ML8 .... 230 B1
Kelso Pl KY2 .... 17 D3
Kelso St EH52 .... 117 D3
Kelty Ave EH51 .... 64 A4
Kelvin Dr ML7 .... 192 A2
Kelvin Sq EH11 .... 148 A4
Kelvin St FK3 .... 40 A1
Kemp Pl EH3 .... 93 D1
Kemper Ave FK1 .... 60 B2
Kempston EH30 .... 89 E4
Kendieshill Ave FK2 .... 83 D3
Kenilworth Dr
Edinburgh EH16 .... 155 D4
Laurieston FK2 .... 60 C2
Kenilworth La EH3 .... 61 E3
Kenilworth Pl Denny FK6 ... 36 B1
Kenilworth Rise EH54 ...... 147 F1
Kenilworth St EH3 .... 61 E3
Kenmore Ave
Livingston EH54 .... 146 C3
Polmont FK2 .... 62 A1
Kenmore Terr KY2 .... 16 C4
Kenmure Ave EH8 .... 124 B4
Kenmure Pl
Dunfermline KY12 .... 29 E3
Stenhousemuir FK5 .... 38 C2
Kennard Rd FK2 .... 82 B4
Kennard St Falkirk FK2 ...... 60 B3
Lochgelly KY5 .... 14 A4
Kennedie Pk EH53 .... 148 B2

Kennedy Cres
Dunfermline KY12 .... 29 D3
Kirkcaldy KY2 .... 17 D3
Tranent EH33 .... 128 B4
Kenningknowes Rd KY7 ...... 6 C3
Kennington Ave EH20 ...... 181 D4
Kennington Terr EH20 ...... 181 D4
Kent Rd Alloa FK10 .... 9 F4
Stirling FK7 .... 7 D3
Kent St KY12 .... 29 E3
Kentigern Mall EH26 .... 203 F3
Keppel Rd EH39 .... 54 A3
Keppock Pl FK1 .... 59 F1
Kepscaith Cres EH47 ...... 170 A3
Kepscaith Gr EH47 .... 170 A3
Kepscaith Rd EH47 .... 170 A3
Kerr Ave EH22 .... 156 C1
Kerr Cres FK4 .... 57 D2
Kerr Pl Denny FK6 .... 36 B1
Dunfermline KY11 .... 29 F1
Kerr Rd EH33 .... 128 B3
Kerr St EH3 .... 93 D1
Kerr's Wynd EH21 .... 126 B3
Kerrisk Dr KY11 .... 29 F1
Kerse Gdns FK2 .... 60 C3
Kerse Green Rd FK10 .... 10 C3
Kerse La FK1 .... 60 B3
Kerse Pl FK1 .... 60 B3
Kerse Rd Grangemouth FK3 . 61 E4
Stirling FK7 .... 7 E3
Kersebonny Rd FK8 .... 6 B4
Kersie Rd FK7 .... 9 D2
Kersie Terr FK7 .... 9 F2
Kersiebank Ave FK3 .... 61 F3
Kestrel Brae EH54 .... 147 E3
Kestrel Dr EH54 .... 82 C4
Kettil'stoun Ct EH49 .... 84 B3
Kettil'stoun Gr EH49 .... 84 B3
Kettil'stoun Mains EH49 .... 84 B3
Kettilstoun Rd EH49 .... 84 B4
Keverkae FK10 .... 9 F3
Kevock Rd EH18 .... 181 F4
Kidd St KY1 .... 17 E4
Kilbagie St FK10 .... 23 E2
Kilbean Dr FK10 .... 59 F1
Kilbirnie Terr FK6 .... 36 B2
Kilbrennan Dr FK1 .... 59 D2
Kilburn Rd KY12 .... 28 A1
Kilchurn Ct EH12 .... 121 D4
Kilcruik Rd KY3 .... 34 C2
Kildean Hospl FK8 .... 1 C1
Kildean Sch FK8 .... 1 C1
Kildonan Pk KY12 .... 28 C1
Kildrummy Ave FK5 .... 38 C2
Kilduthie Pl FK10 .... 23 F3
Kilfinan Rd ML7 .... 191 E3
Kilgour Ave KY1 .... 17 E4
Kilgraston Rd EH9 .... 123 E2
Killin Ct KY12 .... 28 C1
Killin Dr FK5 .... 62 A1
Killochan Way KY12 .... 29 E3
Kilmartin Way KY12 .... 29 E3
Kilmaurs Rd EH16 .... 124 A2
Kilmaurs Terr EH16 .... 124 A2
Kilmory Ct FK1 .... 59 E2
Kilmory Gdns ML8 .... 230 A2
Kilmun Rd KY2 .... 16 B4
Kilmundy Dr KY3 .... 33 E1
Kilncraigs Ct FK10 .... 10 A3
Kilncraigs Rd FK10 .... 10 B3
Kilncroft Side EH14 .... 122 A1
Kilne Pl EH54 .... 147 D2
Kilns Pl FK2 .... 59 F3
Kilns Rd FK1 .... 60 A3
Kilpair St EH41 .... 132 A4
Kilpunt Gdns EH52 .... 118 A3
Kilpunt Rdbt EH52 .... 118 A3
Kilpunt View EH52 .... 118 A3
Kilrie Cotts KY2 .... 33 F4
Kilrymont ML11 .... 215 D1
Kilspindie Ct EH32 .... 71 E2
Kilsyth Rd FK4 .... 57 D2
Kilwinning Pl EH21 .... 126 B3
Kilwinning St EH21 .... 126 B3
Kilwinning Terr EH21 .... 126 B3
Kinacres Gr EH51 .... 64 B4
Kincairne Ct FK10 .... 23 F2
Kincardine Rd FK2 .... 39 E2
Kincraig Pl KY12 .... 28 C1
Kinellan Gdns EH12 .... 122 B4
Kinellan Rd EH12 .... 122 B4
King Cres EH55 .... 172 B2
King Edwards Way EH29 .... 89 D1
King James IV Rd KY11 ..... 46 B1
King Malcolm Cl EH10 ..... 154 B3
King O' Muirs Ave FK10 ...... 4 C2
King St Armadale EH48 .... 144 A3
Bathgate EH48 .... 145 D3
Cowdenbeath KY4 .... 13 E2
Edinburgh EH6 .... 93 F3
Falkirk FK2 .... 60 B3
Fallin FK7 .... 8 B2
Inverkeithing KY11 .... 47 E1
Kirkcaldy KY2 .... 17 D3
Musselburgh EH21 .... 126 B3
Shotts ML7 .... 191 F2
Stenhousemuir FK5 .... 38 C2
Stirling FK8 .... 7 D4
King's Ave EH32 .... 98 B2
King's Court FK2 .... 98 B2
King's Cramond EH4 .... 91 D2
King's Cres Carluke ML8 ... 231 A1
Rosyth KY11 .... 46 C2
King's Dr KY3 .... 34 C2
King's Gr EH32 .... 98 B2
King's Knoll Gdns EH39 .... 54 B3
King's Mdw EH16 .... 124 A2

King's Meadow Prim Sch
EH41 .... 132 A4
King's Park Prim Sch
EH22 .... 157 D1
King's Park Rd EH8 .... 7 D4
King's Pk FK10 .... 98 B3
King's Pl KY11 .... 46 C2
King's Rd Edinburgh EH15 . 95 D1
Longniddry EH32 .... 98 B3
Rosyth KY11 .... 46 C2
Tranent EH33 .... 128 B3
King's Rd EH47 .... 170 A1
King's Road Prim Sch KY11 . 46 C2
King's Stables La EH1 ...... 232 C2
King's Stables Rd EH1 ...... 232 C2
King's Terr EH15 .... 94 C1
Kingfisher Brae EH54 ...... 147 E3
Kinghorn Pl EH6 .... 93 E3
Kinghorn Prim Sch KY3 ..... 34 C1
Kinghorn Rd Burntisland KY3 . 34 A1
Kirkcaldy KY1, KY2 .... 35 D4
Kinghorn Sta KY3 .... 34 C1
Kinglass Ave EH51 .... 64 A4
Kinglass Ct EH51 .... 64 A3
Kinglass Dr EH51 .... 64 A3
Kinglass Pk EH51 .... 64 A3
Kings Bldgs
(Univ of Edinburgh) EH9 . 123 E1
Kings Ct Alloa FK10 .... 10 A4
⑧ Falkirk FK1 .... 60 A2
Stenhousemuir FK5 .... 38 B1
Kings Haugh EH16 .... 124 B2
Kings Park Hospl FK7 .... 6 C3
Kings Rd FK3 .... 61 F4
Kingsburgh EH40 .... 103 E4
Kingsburgh Gdns EH40 ... 103 E4
Kingsburgh Rd EH12 .... 122 B4
Kingseat Ave FK3 .... 61 E3
Kingseat Pl FK1 .... 59 F2
Kingseat Rd
Dunfermline KY12 .... 29 E3
Halbeath KY11, KY12 ..... 30 A3
Kingsfield EH49 .... 85 E4
Kingsgate KY12 .... 29 D2
Kingshill Rd ML7 .... 212 A4
Kingsinch Sch EH16 .... 124 A1
Kingsknowe Ave EH14 .... 122 A1
Kingsknowe Cres EH14 ... 122 A1
Kingsknowe Dr EH14 ...... 121 F1
Kingsknowe Gdns EH14 .. 153 D4
Kingsknowe Gr EH14 ...... 153 D4
Kingsknowe Pk EH14 ...... 153 D4
Kingsknowe Pl EH14 .... 121 F1
Kingsknowe Rd N EH14 ... 122 A1
Kingsknowe Rd S EH14 ... 122 A1
Kingsknowe Sta EH14 ..... 122 A1
Kingsknowe Terr EH14 .... 122 A1
Kingslaw Ct EH33 .... 128 B3
Kingslaw Farm Cotts EH33 . 128 C3
Kingsley Ave FK5 .... 38 C2
Kingsport Ave EH54 .... 147 F2
Kingstables La FK8 .... 7 D4
Kingsthorne Pk EH54 ...... 116 C1
Kingston Ave EH16 .... 124 B1
Kingston Cotts EH39 .... 53 F1
Kingswell Pk FK10 .... 10 B4
Kininmonth St KY1 .... 17 D1
Kinleith Ind Est EH14 ...... 152 A2
Kinloch Pl FK3 .... 61 F3
Kinloss Ct KY12 .... 26 A1
Kinnaird Ave FK2 .... 39 D2
Kinnaird Dr FK5 .... 38 C2
Kinnaird Pk EH15 .... 125 E2
Kinnaird Pl Dunfermline KY12 . 29 E3
Kirkcaldy KY2 .... 16 B2
Kinnear Rd EH3 .... 93 D2
Kinneil Dr EH51 .... 63 E3
Kinneil Prim Sch EH51 ...... 63 E3
Kinneil Rd EH51 .... 63 E4
Kinneil Sta EH51 .... 63 E4
Kinneil Rd KY11 .... 47 D1
Kinnis Ct KY11 .... 29 E1
Kinnonmonth Ave KY3 ...... 33 E1
Kintyre Pl EH22 .... 59 E2
Kippielaw Dr EH22 .... 157 E1
Kippielaw Gdns EH22 ...... 157 E1
Kippielaw Medway EH22 .. 157 E1
Kippielaw Pk EH22 .... 183 E4
Kippielaw Rd EH22 .... 157 E1
Kippielaw Wlk EH22 .... 157 E1
Kippithill EH36 .... 187 D1
Kirk Ave FK5 .... 38 C3
Kirk Brae Edinburgh EH16 . 155 D4
Innerwick EH42 .... 108 A1
Kincardine FK10 .... 23 F3
Longridge EH47 .... 170 B1
Kirk Cramond EH4 .... 91 E3
Kirk La EH54 .... 147 D1
Kirk Loan EH12 .... 121 F3
Kirk Pk Dunbar EH42 .... 78 A1
Edinburgh EH16 .... 155 D4
Kirk Ports EH39 .... 54 B4
Kirk Rd Aberlady EH32 ...... 71 E2
Bathgate EH48 .... 145 E3
Shotts ML7 .... 191 F2
Kirk St Culross KY12 .... 25 E1
Edinburgh EH6 .... 93 F2
Kincardine FK10 .... 23 F2
Prestonpans EH32 .... 96 C1
Kirk View EH41 .... 132 B4
Kirk Wynd
Clackmannan FK10 .... 11 D3
⑫ Falkirk FK1 .... 60 A2
Kirkcaldy KY1 .... 17 E2
Stirling FK7 .... 7 D2
Kirkcaldy High Sch KY1 .... 17 D4

Kirkcaldy Mus & Art Gallery KY1 ... 17 D2
Kirkbank Rd KY3 ... 33 F1
Kirkbrae FK10 ... 10 C2
Kirkbride Terr FK7 ... 20 B2
Kirkburn FK1 ... 110 A4
Kirkcaldy Rd
  Burntisland KY3 ... 33 F1
  Kinghorn KY3 ... 35 D2
Kirkcaldy Sta KY1 ... 17 D2
Kirkfield E EH54 ... 147 D2
Kirkfield View EH54 ... 147 E2
Kirkfield W EH54 ... 147 D2
Kirkflat FK7 ... 117 D3
Kirkford Ct KY4 ... 13 C3
Kirkgate Alloa FK10 ... 10 A3
  Burntisland KY3 ... 50 C4
  Currie EH14 ... 152 A2
  Dunfermline KY12 ... 28 C2
  Edinburgh EH16 ... 155 D4
  Inverkeithing KY11 ... 47 D2
  Linlithgow EH49 ... 85 D4
  West Calder EH55 ... 172 B2
Kirkhall Pl FK6 ... 36 C1
Kirkhill Ct Broxburn EH52 ... 117 E3
  Fauldhouse EH47 ... 193 F3
Kirkhill Dr EH16 ... 124 A2
Kirkhill Gdns
  Edinburgh EH16 ... 124 A3
  Penicuik EH26 ... 203 F3
Kirkhill Pk EH52 ... 117 E3
Kirkhill Rd Broxburn EH52 ... 117 E3
  Edinburgh EH16 ... 124 A2
  Penicuik EH26 ... 203 F3
Kirkhill Terr
  Broxburn EH52 ... 117 E3
  Edinburgh EH16 ... 124 A3
  Gorebridge EH23 ... 183 D1
Kirkhill Way EH26 ... 203 F3
Kirkland Dr FK6 ... 36 A1
Kirklands Dunfermline KY12 ... 29 D1
  Edinburgh EH12 ... 121 E2
  Penicuik EH26 ... 203 F3
Kirklands Park Cres EH29 ... 88 C1
Kirklands Park Gdns EH29 ... 88 C1
Kirklands Park Gr EH29 ... 88 C1
Kirklands Park St EH29 ... 88 C1
Kirkliston Prim Sch EH29 ... 89 D1
Kirkliston Rd EH30 ... 89 D4
Kirknewton Prim Sch EH27 ... 149 E2
Kirknewton Sta EH27 ... 149 E2
Kirkslap FK6 ... 36 C1
Kirkstyle Gdns EH29 ... 89 D1
Kirkton Ave EH48 ... 145 E3
Kirkton Bank EH26 ... 203 E3
Kirkton Bsns Pk EH54 ... 147 D2
Kirkton N EH54 ... 147 E4
Kirkton Pl Cowdenbeath KY4 ... 13 C3
  Falkirk FK2 ... 39 E2
Kirkton Rd KY3 ... 33 F1
Kirkton South Rd EH54 ... 147 E1
Kirkway FK2 ... 22 B2
Kirkwood Ave FK2 ... 61 E1
Kirkwood Cres KY12 ... 28 A1
Kisimul Ct EH12 ... 121 D4
Kitchener Cres EH32 ... 98 C3
Kittle Yds EH9 ... 123 F2
Knaphill KY11 ... 46 C4
Knights Way FK6 ... 36 B1
Knightsbridge Rd
  Livingston EH54 ... 147 E4
  Uphall EH52 ... 116 B1
Knightsiaw FK6 ... 36 C1
Knightsridge Ct EH52 ... 116 B1
Knightsridge East Rd EH54 ... 147 E4
Knightsridge Prim Sch EH54 ... 147 E4
Knightsridge Rdbt EH54 ... 147 E4
Knightsridge West Rd EH54 ... 147 D4
Knockenhair Rd EH42 ... 78 A1
Knockhill Ct KY5 ... 14 A4
Knockhouse Gdns KY12 ... 28 A1
Knockhouse Rd KY12 ... 28 A1
Knoll Croft Rd ML7 ... 192 A4
Knowe Park Rd EH47 ... 171 D1
Knowe The Alloa FK10 ... 5 E1
  Dalgety Bay KY11 ... 48 B2
Knowefaulds Rd FK10 ... 4 A2
Knowehead Rd FK2 ... 61 E1
Knowepark Ct EH47 ... 171 D1
Knowes Rd EH41 ... 131 F4
Knowetop EH54 ... 173 E4
Knowetop Pl EH25 ... 180 C2
Knowhead Rd KY12 ... 28 A1
Knox Acad EH41 ... 131 F4
Knox Pl EH41 ... 132 A4
Komarom EH22 ... 157 E2
Kyle Ave FK7 ... 20 C4
Kyle Pl EH7 ... 233 F4
Kyles The KY1 ... 17 F3

La Porte Prec FK3 ... 61 E4
Labrador EH54 ... 147 F2
Laburnum Dr KY1 ... 17 E4
Laburnum Gr
  Burntisland KY3 ... 33 F1
  Stirling FK8 ... 6 C3
Laburnum Pl EH22 ... 183 F3
Laburnum Rd
  Dunfermline KY11 ... 29 E1
  Whitburn EH47 ... 170 B3
Lade Braes KY11 ... 48 A2
Lade Ct EH49 ... 84 C4

Lade Dr FK5 ... 59 E4
Lade Gn KY11 ... 48 A2
Lade Mill FK7 ... 7 E1
Lade Rd FK4 ... 58 A3
Ladehead EH6 ... 93 E2
Ladeside Ave EH47 ... 171 E4
Ladeside Cres FK5 ... 38 C1
Ladeside Dr EH47 ... 171 E4
Ladeside Gdns EH47 ... 171 D4
Ladeside Prim Sch FK5 ... 59 E4
Ladeside Rd EH47 ... 171 E4
Ladiemeadow EH12 ... 121 F3
Lady Anne Ct KY4 ... 30 C3
Lady Brae EH23 ... 207 E4
Lady Brae Pl EH23 ... 207 F4
Lady Ct EH47 ... 170 B4
Lady Helen Cotts KY5 ... 15 D4
Lady Helen St KY1 ... 17 D1
Lady Jane Gdns EH39 ... 54 B3
Lady Jane Rd EH39 ... 54 B3
Lady Lawson St EH3 ... 232 C2
Lady Nairn Ave KY1 ... 17 F3
Lady Nairne Cres EH8 ... 124 B4
Lady Nairne Gr EH8 ... 124 B4
Lady Nairne Loan EH8 ... 124 B4
Lady Nairne Pl EH8 ... 124 B4
Lady Nairne Rd KY12 ... 28 C3
Lady Pl EH54 ... 147 D3
Lady Rd EH16 ... 124 A2
Lady Road Pl EH22 ... 183 D3
Lady Menzies Pl 3 EH7 ... 94 A1
Lady Victoria Bsns Ctr EH22 ... 183 D2
Lady Wood Pl EH54 ... 147 D3
Lady Wynd EH1 ... 232 C2
Ladyburn Pl KY3 ... 35 D2
Ladycroft EH14 ... 151 E1
Ladysgate Ct FK2 ... 39 E1
Ladysmill FK2 ... 60 B3
Ladysmill Ct KY12 ... 29 D1
Ladysmill Ind Est FK1 ... 60 B3
Ladysmith Rd EH9 ... 123 F1
Ladysneuk Rd FK9 ... 2 B1
Ladywell EH21 ... 126 B3
Ladywell Ct Edinburgh EH12 ... 121 E3
  Larbert FK5 ... 38 A2
Ladywell Dr FK10 ... 4 A2
Ladywell E EH54 ... 147 F3
Ladywell Gdns EH12 ... 121 E3
Ladywell Gr FK10 ... 11 D2
Ladywell Pl FK10 ... 4 A2
Ladywell Rd EH12 ... 121 E3
Ladywell View EH51 ... 63 E3
Ladywell Way EH21 ... 126 B3
Ladywell West Rd EH54 ... 147 E3
Ladywood FK10 ... 11 D2
Ladywood Prim Sch EH26 ... 204 A4
Lagan Rd ML8 ... 230 A1
Laggan Ave ML7 ... 192 A2
Laggan Path ML7 ... 191 F3
Laichfield EH14 ... 122 A2
Laichpark Pl EH14 ... 122 A2
Laichpark Rd EH14 ... 122 A2
Laing Gdns EH52 ... 116 B1
Laing Terr Edinburgh EH15 ... 125 E4
  Penicuik EH26 ... 203 F4
Laird Terr EH19 ... 182 B3
Laird's Entry EH37 ... 185 E2
Lakeside Rd KY2 ... 16 C2
Lamb's Cl EH8 ... 233 E1
Lamb's Pend EH26 ... 203 F2
Lambert Dr KY12 ... 29 E2
Lambert Terr FK10 ... 10 B4
Lamberton Ct EH34 ... 160 C3
Lambie St KY12 ... 78 C2
Lamer St EH42 ... 78 C1
Lamington Rd EH33 ... 130 B4
Lammerlaws Rd KY3 ... 50 C4
Lammermoor Gdns EH33 ... 128 A3
Lammermoor Terr
  Edinburgh EH16 ... 124 B1
  Tranent EH33 ... 128 A3
Lammermuir Cres
  Dunbar EH42 ... 78 B1
  Haddington EH41 ... 132 B4
Lammermuir Ct EH31 ... 52 A1
Lammermuir Pl KY2 ... 16 C3
Lammerview
  Gladsmuir EH33 ... 130 B4
  Tranent EH33 ... 128 B4
Lamond View KY5 ... 38 B1
Lamont Cres FK7 ... 8 B3
Lamont Way EH54 ... 147 E4
Lampacre Rd EH12 ... 121 F3
Lanark Ave EH54 ... 147 D3
Lanark Rd
  Edinburgh, Kingsknowe EH14 ... 122 A1
  Edinburgh, Westerhailes EH13 ... 152 C3
Landale Gdns KY3 ... 33 F1
Landale Pl KY3 ... 33 F1
Landale St KY5 ... 14 A4
Lane The EH21 ... 126 C1
Lang Loan EH17 ... 155 E2
Langfauld Gdns EH48 ... 144 C3
Langhill FK6 ... 36 B1
Langlaw Prim Sch EH22 ... 183 E4
Langlaw Rd EH22 ... 183 E4
Langlees Prim Sch FK2 ... 60 A4
Langlees St FK2 ... 39 E1
Langriggs EH41 ... 132 A4

Langside EH40 ... 103 E4
Langside Cres EH55 ... 173 D3
Langside Dr EH48 ... 142 A2
Langside Gdns EH55 ... 173 D3
Langton Ave EH53 ... 148 C2
Langton Gdns EH53 ... 148 C2
Langton Rd
  East Calder EH53 ... 148 C2
  Edinburgh EH9 ... 123 F2
  Westquarter EH47 ... 61 D2
Langton View EH53 ... 148 C2
Lanrigg Ave EH47 ... 193 F4
Lanrigg Rd EH47 ... 193 F4
Lansbury Ct EH22 ... 157 D2
Lansbury St KY1 ... 17 F4
Lansdowne Cres
  Edinburgh EH12 ... 232 A2
  Kincardine FK10 ... 23 F2
  Shotts ML7 ... 192 A2
Lapicide Pl EH6 ... 93 F3
Larbert Ave EH47 ... 147 D4
Larbert High Sch FK5 ... 38 C1
Larbert High Sch (Annexe) FK5 ... 38 C1
Larbert Rd FK4 ... 58 A3
Larbert St EH3 ... 38 B1
Larbert Village Prim Sch FK5 ... 38 A1
Larbourfield EH11 ... 121 E1
Larch Cres EH22 ... 183 F3
Larch Dr EH47 ... 170 B3
Larch Gr Dunfermline KY11 ... 46 B4
  Stenhousemuir FK5 ... 38 C2
Larch St FK3 ... 61 E3
Larchbank EH54 ... 147 F3
Larches The FK10 ... 10 A4
Larchfield EH14 ... 151 E1
Larchfield La ML7 ... 192 A1
Larchfield Neuk EH14 ... 151 E1
Largo Pl EH6 ... 93 F3
Larkfield Ct EH16 ... 156 C1
Larkfield Rd EH22 ... 156 C1
Lasswade Bank EH17 ... 155 E3
Lasswade Gr EH17 ... 155 E3
Lasswade High Sch EH19 ... 182 A4
Lasswade Prim Sch EH19 ... 182 B4
Lasswade Rd
  Bonnyrigg and Lasswade EH18 ... 156 A1
  Dalkeith EH22 ... 156 C1
  Edinburgh EH16, EH17 ... 155 E3
  Loanhead EH20 ... 181 E4
Latch Pk EH13 ... 153 E4
Latch The EH42 ... 78 C1
Latch The KY12 ... 27 E1
Lathallan Dr FK2 ... 61 F1
Lauder Coll KY11 ... 30 A3
Lauder Loan EH9 ... 123 F2
Lauder Lodge EH22 ... 157 D2
Lauder Pl EH40 ... 103 F4
Lauder Rd Dalkeith EH22 ... 157 E1
  Edinburgh EH9 ... 123 E2
  Kirkcaldy KY2 ... 17 E3
Lauder St KY1 ... 29 E3
Lauderdale Cres EH42 ... 78 B1
Lauderdale St EH9 ... 123 E3
Laurel Bank EH22 ... 157 E1
Laurel Bank Pl EH22 ... 183 F3
Laurel Bank Rd EH22 ... 183 F3
Laurel Cres KY2 ... 17 D4
Laurel Ct FK1 ... 59 E3
Laurel Gr Bonnyrigg FK4 ... 57 F2
  Westquarter FK2 ... 61 D1
Laurel Pl FK4 ... 57 F2
Laurel Rd KY11 ... 46 B1
Laurel Terr EH11 ... 122 C3
Laurelbank Ave FK4 ... 58 A2
Laurelbank Ct EH54 ... 148 C1
Laurelhill Gdns FK8 ... 6 C3
Laurelhill Pl FK8 ... 7 D3
Laurels The FK10 ... 4 A1
Laurencecroft Rd FK8 ... 2 A1
Laurie St EH6 ... 94 A2
Laurieston Prim Sch FK2 ... 61 D2
Lauriston Castle EH4 ... 91 F3
Lauriston Dr KY12 ... 29 E3
Lauriston Farm Rd EH4 ... 91 F2
Lauriston Gdns EH3 ... 232 C2
Lauriston Pk EH3 ... 232 C2
Lauriston Pl EH3 ... 232 C2
Lauriston St EH3 ... 232 C2
Lauriston Terr EH3 ... 232 C2
Laurmont Ct FK2 ... 61 D2
Laverock Dr EH26 ... 203 E3
Laverock Pk EH49 ... 85 D3
Laverockbank Ave EH5 ... 93 E3
Laverockbank Cres EH5 ... 93 E3
Laverockbank Gr EH5 ... 93 E3
Laverockbank Rd EH5 ... 93 E3
Laverockbank Terr EH5 ... 93 E3
Laverockdale Cres EH13 ... 153 D3
Laverockdale Loan EH13 ... 153 D3
Laverockdale Pk EH13 ... 153 D3
Law Pl EH15 ... 95 D1
Law Rd Dunfermline KY11 ... 29 F2
  North Berwick EH39 ... 54 B4
Lawers Cres FK2 ... 62 A1
Lawers Pl FK3 ... 61 F3
Lawers Sq EH26 ... 204 A4
Lawfield Rd EH22 ... 183 E4
Lawhead Cotts EH40 ... 75 F2
Lawhead Pl EH26 ... 203 E3
Lawmarket EH1 ... 233 D3
Lawrence St EH41 ... 131 F4
Lawrie Dr EH26 ... 203 F1
Lawson Cres EH30 ... 89 D4

Lawson Gdns KY1 ... 17 F4
Lawson Pl Dunbar EH42 ... 78 B1
  Maddiston FK2 ... 83 D3
Lawson St KY1 ... 17 F4
Lawswell KY6 ... 5 F2
Laxdale Dr FK6 ... 57 E4
Laxford Cres KY11 ... 48 A2
Leadburn Ave KY12 ... 29 D4
Leadervale Rd EH16 ... 154 C4
Leadervale Terr EH16 ... 154 C4
Leadside Cres KY12 ... 29 D4
Leamington Pl EH10 ... 232 B1
Leamington Rd EH3 ... 232 A1
Leamington Terr EH10 ... 123 D3
Learmonth Ave EH4 ... 92 C1
Learmonth Cres
  Edinburgh EH4 ... 92 C1
  West Calder EH55 ... 172 B2
Learmonth Ct EH4 ... 92 C1
Learmonth
  Gardens Mews 11 EH4 ... 93 D1
Learmonth Gdns 5 EH4 ... 92 C1
Learmonth Gr EH4 ... 92 C1
Learmonth Pk 2 EH4 ... 92 C1
Learmonth Pl EH4 ... 232 A4
Learmonth St FK1 ... 60 A2
Learmonth Terr EH4 ... 232 A4
Learmonth Terrace La EH4 ... 232 A4
Ledi Ave FK1 ... 4 A1
Ledi Pl KY1 ... 81 F4
Ledi Terr EH26 ... 204 A4
Ledi View FK9 ... 2 A2
Ledmore Pl FK1 ... 60 C1
Lee Cres EH15 ... 125 D4
Leighton Cres EH22 ... 183 E4
Leighton St KY1 ... 26 A1
Leith Acad EH6 ... 94 A2
Leith Ave KY3 ... 33 F1
Leith Pl FK6 ... 57 E4
Leith Prim Sch EH6 ... 94 A2
Leith St EH1 ... 233 D4
Leith Walk Prim Sch EH7 ... 93 F1
Leith Wlk EH6, EH7 ... 93 F2
Lempockwells Rd EH34 ... 160 C3
Lendrick Ave FK1 ... 59 F1
Lennel Ave EH12 ... 122 B4
Lenniemuir EH12 ... 90 A1
Lennox Ave FK7 ... 7 D2
Lennox Gdns EH49 ... 84 B4
Lennox Milne Ct EH41 ... 132 A4
Lennox Rd EH41 ... 132 B4
Lennox Row EH5 ... 93 D3
Lennox St EH4 ... 232 A4
Lennox Street La EH4 ... 232 A4
Lennox Terr FK3 ... 61 F3
Lennoxlove EH41 ... 132 A3
Lennoxlove Acredales
  EH41 ... 132 A4
Leny Pl KY12 ... 29 D3
Lenzie Ave EH54 ... 147 D3
Leopold Pl 6 EH7 ... 93 F1
Leslie Pl EH4 ... 93 D1
Leslie Rd KY11 ... 46 C3
Leslie St KY1 ... 35 D4
Lestrange Terr FK12 ... 5 D4
Letham Ave EH53 ... 148 A4
Letham Cotts FK2 ... 39 E4
Letham Cres EH53 ... 148 A4
Letham Dr EH41 ... 131 F4
Letham Gait KY11 ... 47 F2
Letham Gdns EH53 ... 148 A4
Letham Gr EH53 ... 148 A4
Letham Hill Ave KY11 ... 47 F2
Letham Hill Way KY11 ... 47 F2
Letham Pk Dunbar EH42 ... 78 B1
  Pumpherston EH53 ... 148 A4
Letham Pl Dunbar EH42 ... 78 B2
  Pumpherston EH53 ... 148 A4
Letham Prim Sch EH54 ... 148 A3
Letham Rd Dunbar EH42 ... 78 B1
  Livingston EH54 ... 148 A4
Letham Rise KY11 ... 47 F2
Letham Terrs FK2 ... 22 B1
Letham Way KY11 ... 47 F2
Leuchatsbeath Dr KY4 ... 13 D3
Leven Cl EH3 ... 232 B1
Leven Ct FK10 ... 10 B3
Leven Pl ML7 ... 191 F3
Leven St Edinburgh EH3 ... 232 B1
  Falkirk FK2 ... 60 A4
Leven Terr EH3 ... 232 C1
Leven Wlk EH54 ... 148 A2
Leving Pl EH54 ... 147 F2
Lewis Ct Alloa FK10 ... 10 A3
  Falkirk FK1 ... 60 A1
Lewis Rd FK2 ... 61 F1
Lewisvale Ave EH21 ... 126 C3
Lewisvale Ct EH21 ... 126 C3
Leyden Pk EH19 ... 182 A4
Leyden Pl EH19 ... 182 A4
Leys Park Rd KY12 ... 29 D2
Liberton Brae EH16 ... 155 D4
Liberton Dr EH16 ... 154 C4
Liberton Gdns EH16 ... 155 D3
Liberton High Sch EH17 ... 155 E4
Liberton Hospl EH16 ... 155 D4
Liberton Pl EH16 ... 155 D4
Liberton Prim Sch EH16 ... 124 A1
Liberton Rd EH16 ... 124 A1
Library La FK3 ... 40 B1
Liddesdale Pl EH3 ... 93 D1
Liddle Dr EH51 ... 63 F3
Lidgate Shot EH28 ... 119 F1
Liggar's Pl KY12 ... 28 C1
Liggat Pl EH52 ... 117 E3
Liggat Syke Pl EH52 ... 118 A3

Lighton Terr EH47 ... 171 D1
Lilac Ave EH22 ... 183 F3
Lilac Cres KY1 ... 17 E4
Lilac Gr KY11 ... 46 B4
Lillies La EH41 ... 163 F3
Lily Terr EH11 ... 122 C2
Lilybank Ct FK10 ... 5 E1
Lilyhill Terr EH8 ... 94 B1
Lime Ave EH30 ... 66 C1
Lime Gr Dunfermline KY11 ... 29 F1
  Larbert FK5 ... 38 B1
  Mayfield EH22 ... 183 F3
  North Berwick EH39 ... 54 C3
  Polmont FK2 ... 61 F1
Lime Pl EH19 ... 182 A3
Lime Rd FK1 ... 59 D2
Lime St EH6 ... 61 E3
Limebank Pk EH53 ... 148 C3
Limefield EH17 ... 155 F3
Limefield Ave EH55 ... 173 D3
Limefield Cres EH48 ... 145 F3
Limefield Gdns EH55 ... 173 D3
Limefield Pl EH48 ... 145 E3
Limefield Rd
  Bathgate EH48 ... 145 E4
  West Calder EH55 ... 173 D3
Limekilns EH34 ... 161 D3
Limekilns Gr EH53 ... 149 D2
Limekilns Prim Sch KY11 ... 45 F2
Limekilns Rd KY12 ... 28 C1
Limerigg Prim Sch FK1 ... 110 B1
Limes The EH10 ... 123 D2
Limetree Wlk EH42 ... 76 B3
Limeylands Cres EH35 ... 159 E4
Limeylands Rd EH35 ... 159 E4
Lina St KY2 ... 17 D3
Linburn Gr KY11 ... 29 F2
Linburn Pk EH27 ... 150 A4
Linburn Pl KY11 ... 29 F2
Linburn Rd KY11 ... 29 F2
Lindean Pl EH6 ... 94 A2
Lindean Terr EH27 ... 149 F3
Linden Ave Denny FK6 ... 36 B2
  Stirling FK7 ... 7 E3
Linden Gr EH54 ... 148 A3
Linden Pl EH20 ... 181 E4
Lindores Dr Kirkcaldy KY2 ... 16 C4
  Tranent EH33 ... 128 B3
Lindsay Dr FK9 ... 2 A2
Lindsay Pl Edinburgh EH6 ... 93 F3
  Lochgelly KY5 ... 14 A4
Lindsay Rd EH6 ... 93 F3
Lindsay Sq EH54 ... 146 B3
Lindsay St EH6 ... 93 F3
Lindsay Way EH54 ... 147 E4
Lindsay's Wynd KY12 ... 26 C3
Lingerwood Farm Cotts EH22 ... 183 D2
Lingerwood Rd EH22 ... 183 D2
Lingerwood Wlk EH22 ... 183 D2
Link Rd KY11 ... 47 F2
Linkfield Ct EH21 ... 126 C3
Linkfield Rd EH21 ... 126 C3
Links Ave EH21 ... 126 A4
Links Ct Bo'ness EH51 ... 64 A4
  Cockenzie & Port Seton EH32 ... 97 F2
Links Dr KY12 ... 28 A1
Links Gardens La EH6 ... 94 A3
Links Pl Bo'ness EH51 ... 64 A4
  Burntisland KY3 ... 50 C4
  Cockenzie & Port Seton EH32 ... 97 F2
  Edinburgh EH6 ... 94 A3
Links Rd Bo'ness EH51 ... 64 A4
  Cockenzie & Port Seton EH32 ... 97 F2
  Longniddry EH32 ... 98 C3
  North Berwick EH39 ... 54 A4
Links St Kirkaldy KY1 ... 17 D1
  Musselburgh EH21 ... 126 B3
Links View
  Cockenzie & Port Seton EH32 ... 97 F2
  Musselburgh EH21 ... 126 B4
Links Wlk EH32 ... 97 F2
Linlithgow Acad EH49 ... 84 C3
Linlithgow Canal Mus EH49 ... 85 D3
Linlithgow Palace EH49 ... 85 D4
Linlithgow Pl EH5 ... 38 C2
Linlithgow Prim Sch EH49 ... 84 C3
Linlithgow Prim Sch
  West Port Annexe EH49 ... 84 C3
Linlithgow Rd EH51 ... 63 F3
Linlithgow Sta EH49 ... 85 D4
Linlithgow Story (Mus) The EH49 ... 85 D4
Linlithgow Terr EH35 ... 159 F4
Linmill Rd FK1 ... 112 A3
Linn Mill EH30 ... 67 F1
Linn Pl EH52 ... 117 F2
Linnet Brae EH54 ... 147 E3
Linsay Macdonald Ct KY2 ... 29 E2
Lint Riggs FK1 ... 60 A3
Linton La KY2 ... 16 C3
Linton Pl KY11 ... 46 C2
Linty La EH26 ... 203 E3
Linview Ind Est EH54 ... 173 F2
Lion Well Wynd EH49 ... 84 C4
Lionthorn Rd FK1 ... 59 F1
Lipney FK11 ... 4 A3

Lismore Ave
4 Edinburgh EH8 .... **94** B1
Kirkcaldy KY2 .... **16** C4
Lismore Cres EH8 .... **94** B1
Lismore Ct FK1 .... **60** A1
Lismore Pl KY2 .... **16** C4
Lismore Prim Sch EH15 .. **124** C3
Lister Ct FK9 .... **2** A3
Lister Rd EH54 .... **147** D4
Listloaning Pl EH49 ...... **84** B4
Listloaning Rd EH49 ..... **84** B4
Liston Dr EH29 .... **89** D1
Liston Pl EH29 .... **89** D1
Liston Rd EH29 .... **89** D1
Little Acre EH22 .... **183** E4
Little Carriden EH51 ..... **64** B3
Little Cswy KY12 .... **42** B4
Little Denny Rd FK6 ...... **36** B1
Little Footworn KY12 .... **44** C3
Little France Mills EH16 . **124** C4
Little King St EH1 .... **233** D4
Little Rd EH16 .... **155** D4
Little Sandhaven KY12 ... **42** B4
Livery St KY4 .... **145** D4
Livesay Rd KY11 .... **46** B1
Livesay Terr EH26 .... **204** A4
Livilands Ct FK8 .... **7** D3
Livilands Gate FK8 .... **7** D3
Livilands La FK8 .... **7** D3
Livingston Mill EH54 ..... **147** D1
Livingston North Sta
EH54 .... **147** D3
Livingston Rd EH54 ...... **147** F3
Livingston South Sta
EH54 .... **174** A4
Livingstone Cres FK2 .... **60** C3
Livingstone Dr
Bo'ness EH51 .... **63** E3
Burntisland KY3 .... **33** F1
Laurieston FK2 .... **61** D1
Livingstone E Rdbt EH54 . **116** B1
Livingstone La KY3 .... **49** E4
Livingstone Pl EH9 ...... **123** E3
Livingstone Quadrant
ML7 .... **168** B2
Livingstone St ML7 ...... **171** F1
Livingstone Terr FK2 ..... **61** D1
Lixmount Ave EH5 .... **93** E3
Lixmount Gdns EH5 .... **93** E3
Lizzie Brice's Rdbt EH54 . **148** A1
Llynallan Rd ML7 .... **168** A3
Loan Pl ML7 .... **168** C3
Loan The Bo'ness EH51 .... **63** E3
Loanhead EH20 .... **181** D4
Pathhead EH37 .... **184** B4
Queensferry EH30 .... **68** A1
Torphichen EH48 .... **113** F3
Loanburn EH26 .... **203** F3
Loanburn Ave EH26 ...... **203** F3
Loanfoot Cres EH52 ..... **117** D3
Loanfoot Gdns FK7 .... **20** B2
Loanfoot Rd EH52 .... **117** D2
Loanhead Ave
Bankhead FK4 .... **57** E3
Grangemouth FK3 .... **61** F3
Loanhead Hospl EH20 .... **181** D4
Loanhead Pl KY2 .... **17** D3
Loanhead Prim Sch EH20 . **181** E4
Loanhead Prim Sch
(Annexe) EH20 .... **181** E4
Loanhead Rd EH20 .... **155** D1
Loaning Cres EH7 .... **94** B1
Loaning Rd EH7 .... **94** B1
Loaninghill Pk EH52 ...... **117** D2
Loaninghill Rd EH52 ...... **117** D2
Loch Awe Way EH47 ..... **170** B4
Loch Earn Way EH47 .... **170** B4
Loch Fyne Way EH47 ..... **170** B4
Loch Linnhe Ct EH47 .... **170** B4
Loch Maree Way EH47 ... **170** B4
Loch Pl EH30 .... **68** A1
Loch Rd Edinburgh EH4 .... **92** A1
Queensferry EH30 .... **68** A1
Tranent EH33 .... **128** B3
Loch Sq EH33 .... **128** B3
Loch St KY12 .... **29** E4
Loch Trool Way EH47 .... **170** B4
Lochaber Cres ML7 .... **192** A2
Lochaber Dr FK5 .... **38** C2
Lochbank EH54 .... **147** F3
Lochbrae FK10 .... **5** E1
Lochbridge Rd EH39 ...... **54** B3
Lochend Ave Dunbar EH42 . **78** C1
Edinburgh EH7 .... **94** A1
Lochend Castle Barns EH7 . **94** A1
Lochend Cl EH8 .... **233** F3
Lochend Cres Dunbar EH42 . **78** B1
Edinburgh EH7 .... **94** B1
Lochend Dr EH7 .... **94** B1
Lochend Gdns EH7 .... **94** A1
Lochend Gr EH7 .... **94** B1
Lochend Ind Est EH28 ... **119** D3
Lochend Pk EH7 .... **94** A1
Lochend Quadrant EH7 .. **94** B1
Lochend Rd Dunbar EH42 . **78** C1
Edinburgh EH6 .... **94** A2
Ratho Station EH28 .... **119** D4
Lochend Rd N EH21 ...... **126** A3
Lochend Rd S
Edinburgh EH7 .... **94** A1
Musselburgh EH21 .... **126** A3
Lochend Sq EH7 .... **94** A1
Lochgelly Ind Pk KY5 ...... **14** B4
Lochgelly North
Specl Sch (Prim) KY5 ..... **14** A4

Lochgelly Rd KY4 .... **13** E3
Lochgelly South Prim Sch
KY5 .... **14** A4
Lochgelly West Prim Sch
KY5 .... **14** A4
Lochgreen Hospl FK1 ...... **59** F1
Lochgreen Rd FK1 .... **59** F1
Lochhead Ave FK6 .... **36** C1
Lochhill Cotts KY4 .... **99** F4
Lochies Rd Burntisland KY3 . **34** A1
Clackmannan KY10 .... **11** D2
Lochinvar Pl FK4 .... **58** B2
Lochinvar Rd KY11 .... **46** B1
Lochlands Ind Est FK5 ..... **59** D4
Lochmaben Dr FK5 .... **38** C2
Lochpark Pl FK6 .... **36** C1
Lochridge Pl FK6 .... **36** B1
Lochrin EH3 .... **232** B1
Lochshot Pl EH54 .... **147** D2
Lochside Ave EH12 .... **120** C2
Lochside Cres
Edinburgh EH12 .... **120** C2
Redding FK2 .... **61** D1
Lochside Ct EH12 .... **121** D2
Lochside Pl EH12 .... **121** D2
Lochside Rd FK1 .... **110** B1
Lock Rd KY11 .... **67** D4
Lock Sixteen FK1 .... **59** E3
Lockerby Cotts EH16 ..... **155** E3
Lockerby Cres EH16 ...... **155** E3
Lockerby Gr EH16 .... **155** E3
Lockhart Terr EH25 .... **180** C2
Lockharton Ave EH10 .... **122** C1
Lockharton Cres EH10 ... **122** C1
Lockharton Gdns EH14 .. **122** C2
Lodge Dr FK5 .... **38** C1
Lodge St EH41 .... **132** A4
Logan St EH3 .... **93** E1
Logan Way EH54 .... **147** E4
Loganlea Ave EH7 .... **94** B1
Loganlea Cres EH55 ...... **171** E1
Loganlea Dr EH7 .... **94** B1
Loganlea Gdns EH7 .... **94** B1
Loganlea Loan EH7 .... **94** B1
Loganlea Pl EH7 .... **94** B1
Loganlea Rd
Addiewell EH55 .... **171** E1
Edinburgh EH7 .... **94** B1
Loganlea Terr
Addiewell EH55 .... **171** E1
Edinburgh EH7 .... **94** B1
Logie Dr FK5 .... **38** A2
Logie Green Gdns EH7 .... **93** E2
Logie Green Loan EH7 ..... **93** E2
Logie Green Rd EH7 .... **93** E2
Logie La FK9 .... **2** B4
Logie Mill EH7 .... **93** E2
Logie Pl KY12 .... **28** B3
Logie Rd FK9 .... **2** B2
Lomond Cres
Dunfermline KY11 .... **29** F1
Stenhousemuir FK5 .... **38** C2
Stirling FK9 .... **2** A2
Whitburn EH47 .... **170** A3
Lomond Ct FK10 .... **10** B3
Lomond Dr Bannockburn FK7 . **7** F1
Falkirk FK1 .... **39** E1
Lomond Gdns KY2 .... **16** C3
Lomond Rd Edinburgh EH5 . **93** D3
Grangemouth FK3 .... **61** F3
Shotts ML7 .... **191** F3
Lomond St FK10 .... **4** C1
Lomond Vale EH26 .... **204** A4
Lomond View EH48 .... **112** C2
Lomond Way FK6 .... **57** E3
Lomond Wlk EH54 .... **155** D1
London Rd Dalkeith EH22 . **157** D2
Edinburgh EH7 .... **94** A1
London St EH3 .... **93** E1
London Street Prim Sch
EH7 .... **93** E1
Loney Cres FK6 .... **57** F4
Long Byres EH52 .... **117** F3
Long Craig Wlk KY1 .... **35** D4
Long Craigs EH32 .... **97** F2
Long Craigs Terr KY3 ...... **35** D2
Long Cram EH41 .... **131** F4
Long Crook EH30 .... **89** D4
Long Dalmahoy Rd EH27 . **150** B2
Long Row Halbeath KY12 .. **30** A4
Menstrie FK11 .... **4** A4
Longannet Cotts KY10 .... **24** A1
Longbraes Gdns KY2 .... **16** B3
Longcroft Gdns EH49 ...... **84** C4
Longdales Ave FK2 .... **60** A4
Longdales Ct FK2 .... **60** A4
Longdales Pl FK2 .... **60** A4
Longdales Rd FK2 .... **60** A4
Longdykes Rd EH32 .... **97** D1
Longford ML11 .... **215** D1
Longformacus Rd EH16 .. **155** D4
Longhill Gdns KY11 .... **48** A2
Longniddry Prim Sch
EH32 .... **98** C3
Longniddry Sta EH32 ...... **98** C3
Longpark Pl EH54 .... **147** D2
Longridge Prim Sch
EH47 .... **170** B1
Longridge Rd EH47 .... **170** A3
Longstone Ave
East Linton EH40 .... **103** E4
Edinburgh EH14 .... **122** A1
Longstone Cres EH14 .... **122** A2
Longstone Gdns EH14 ... **121** F2
Longstone Gr EH14 .... **122** A1
Longstone Pk EH14 .... **122** A1
Longstone Pl EH14 .... **122** A1

Longstone Prim Sch
EH14 .... **122** A1
Longstone Rd EH14 .... **122** A1
Longstone St EH14 .... **122** A1
Longstone Terr EH14 ..... **121** F2
Longstone View EH14 .... **121** F2
Lonsdale Cres KY3 .... **33** F1
Lonsdale Terr EH3 .... **232** C1
Lookaboutye Brae FK10 ... **11** D2
Loom Rd KY2 .... **17** D3
Lord President Rd EH39 ... **54** A4
Loretto Ct EH21 .... **126** A2
Loretto RC Prim Sch
EH21 .... **126** B3
Loretto Sch EH21 .... **126** B3
Lorimar Pl FK2 .... **39** D1
Lorne Gdns FK2 .... **60** C2
Lorne Gr EH20 .... **155** D1
Lorne Pl EH6 .... **93** F2
Lorne Prim Sch EH6 .... **93** F2
Lorne Rd FK5 .... **38** B1
Lorne Sq Edinburgh EH6 .. **93** F2
North Berwick EH39 .... **54** B4
Lorne St Edinburgh EH6 ... **93** F2
Kirkcaldy KY1 .... **17** F4
Lornshill Acad FK10 .... **4** C1
Lornshill Cres FK10 .... **9** F4
Losshill FK11 .... **4** A3
Lothian Bank EH22 .... **157** D1
Lothian Coll of Nursing &
Midwifery EH3 .... **232** C2
Lothian Cres Bo'ness EH51 . **64** A3
Stirling FK9 .... **2** B2
Lothian Ct KY11 .... **47** E1
Lothian Dr EH22 .... **183** E4
Lothian Rd Dalkeith EH22 . **157** D2
Edinburgh EH1 .... **232** D2
Lothian St Bathgate EH48 . **145** D4
Bo'ness EH51 .... **64** A3
Bonnyrigg and Lasswade
EH19 .... **182** B4
Burntisland KY3 .... **50** C4
Dalkeith EH22 .... **157** D2
Edinburgh EH1 .... **123** E4
Rosewell EH24 .... **181** E1
Lothian Terr Kirkcaldy KY1 . **17** D4
Newtongrange EH22 ...... **183** D2
Lothian View KY11 .... **47** D1
Louburn EH41 .... **148** B2
Loudens Wlk FK6 .... **36** B3
Loughborough Rd KY1 ..... **17** F4
Loughrigg KY11 .... **47** D4
Louisa Sq EH24 .... **181** E1
Louise St KY11 .... **29** E1
Lovedale Ave EH14 .... **151** D1
Lovedale Cres EH14 .... **151** D1
Lovedale Gdns EH14 ...... **151** D1
Lovedale Gr EH14 .... **151** D1
Lovedale Rd EH14 .... **151** D1
Lovells Glen EH49 .... **84** B4
Lovers La EH30 .... **89** E4
Lovers Loan Alva FK12 ...... **5** D4
Dunfermline KY12 .... **28** C1
Lovers Wlk FK8 .... **2** A1
Low Brae EH27 .... **113** F3
Low Causewayside
Culross KY12 .... **42** B4
Newmills KY12 .... **26** B1
Low Cswy Culross KY12 ..... **25** F1
Torryburn KY12 .... **26** B1
Low Doors EH27 .... **149** F1
Low Port Prim Sch EH49 .. **85** D4
Lower Alderston Rd
EH41 .... **100** C1
Lower Bathville EH48 ..... **144** A3
Lower Bridge St FK8 .... **2** A1
Lower Broomieknowe
EH18 .... **182** A4
Lower Castlehill FK8 .... **2** A1
Lower Gilmore Pl EH3 ... **232** B1
Lower Glebe KY3 .... **49** E4
Lower Granton Rd EH5 ..... **93** D3
Lower Joppa EH15 .... **125** E4
Lower London Rd EH7 ...... **94** A1
Lower Valleyfield View
EH26 .... **203** F2
Lower Wellheads KY11 ..... **45** E2
Lowlands Crofts EH55 .... **196** B2
Lowrie Ave EH26 .... **203** E3
Lowry Pl KY11 .... **46** C2
Ludgate KY11 .... **10** A3
Luffness Ct EH32 .... **71** E2
Luffness Mains Cotts
EH39 .... **72** A2
Lugton Brae EH22 .... **156** C2
Lugton Sch EH22 .... **156** C2
Lumley Ct FK3 .... **61** E4
Lumley Pl FK3 .... **61** E4
Lumley St FK3 .... **61** E4
Lumphinnans
Prim & Com Sch KY4 ...... **13** E3
Lumphinnans Rd KY5 ...... **14** A4
Lumsdaine Dr KY11 .... **48** A1
Lumsden Ct
Broxburn EH52 .... **117** E3
Ratho EH28 .... **119** E1
Lundin Pl KY12 .... **28** A2
Lussielaw Rd EH9 .... **123** F2
Lutton Court Bsns Ctr
EH8 .... **233** E1
Lutton Pl EH8 .... **233** E1
Luvain Gdns EH48 .... **143** F2
Lyall Cres KY2 .... **61** E1
Lyars Rd EH32 .... **98** C3
Lyarthall EH52 .... **117** E3
Lychgate Rd FK10 .... **4** A1
Lydgait EH41 .... **101** D1
Lydgait Gdns EH41 .... **101** D1

Lyefield Pl EH54 .... **147** D2
Lygon Rd EH16 .... **123** F1
Lyle Gn EH54 .... **147** D4
Lynburn Rd KY11 .... **29** F1
Lyne Gr KY12 .... **28** B1
Lyne St EH7 .... **94** A1
Lyne Terr EH26 .... **204** A4
Lynebank
(Psychiatric) Hospl KY11 . **30** A3
Lyneburn Cres KY11 .... **30** A3
Lynedoch Pl EH3 .... **232** A3
Lynedoch Place La EH3 .. **232** A3
Lyness Ct KY11 .... **61** F1
Lynn Lea Ave EH41 .... **132** B4
Lyon Cres FK9 .... **2** A3
Lyon Cres KY11 .... **63** E3
Lyon Dr EH54 .... **173** F3

Mac Cormick Terr EH26 .. **203** F4
Macadam Pl FK1 .... **59** E3
Macarthur Cres FK2 .... **82** C3
Macbeth Moir Rd EH21 .. **127** D3
Macbeth Rd KY11 .... **29** F2
Macdonald Ave EH48 .... **143** F3
Macdonald Dr FK7 .... **7** D2
Macdonald Pl KY3 .... **34** A1
Macdonald Sq KY11 .... **30** A3
Macdowall Rd EH9 .... **123** F2
Macduff Cres KY3 .... **34** C1
Mace Ct FK7 .... **7** E2
Macfarlane Cres FK1 .... **60** A3
Macfarlane Pl EH52 .... **116** C2
Machrie Ct FK1 .... **59** E2
Macindoe Cres KY1 .... **17** E4
Macintosh Pl FK1 .... **60** A1
Macintosh Rd EH54 .... **146** C1
Mackenzie Cres KY5 .... **14** B4
Mackenzie Pl
Edinburgh EH3 .... **232** B4
Falkirk FK1 .... **60** A1
Mackenzie Terr FK3 .... **61** E3
Mackie Pl KY11 .... **29** F1
Maclachlan Ave FK6 .... **36** B1
Maclardy Ct EH52 .... **116** C2
Maclaren Terr FK2 .... **39** D1
Maclean Cres FK12 .... **5** D4
Maclean Ct FK7 .... **7** E2
Maclean Terr EH48 .... **142** B4
Macmerry Ind Est EH33 .. **129** F1
Macmerry Prim Sch
EH33 .... **129** E3
Macmillan Rd EH54 .... **147** E1
Macnair Ave EH39 .... **54** B3
Macpherson Pl FK1 .... **59** F1
Mactaggart Loan EH22 .. **183** D2
Madderfield Mews EH54 .. **85** D4
Maddiston Prim Sch FK2 .. **82** C3
Maddiston Rd FK2 .... **82** C4
Madeira Pl EH6 .... **93** F3
Madeira St EH6 .... **93** F3
Madill Pl FK5 .... **38** C2
Maesterten Pl EH22 ...... **183** D2
Mag's Bank EH41 .... **133** D1
Magdala Cres EH12 .... **122** C4
Magdala Mews EH12 ..... **122** C4
Magdalene Ave EH15 ..... **125** D3
Magdalene Ct EH15 .... **125** D3
Magdalene Dr EH15 .... **125** D3
Magdalene Gdns EH15 ... **125** D3
Magdalene Loan EH15 ... **125** D3
Magdalene Medway EH15 . **125** D3
Magdalene Pl EH15 .... **125** D3
Maggie Wood's Loan FK1 . **59** F3
Magnus Rd EH51 .... **62** B3
Maidencraig Cres EH4 ..... **92** B1
Maidencraig Gr EH4 .... **92** B1
Maidenpark Pl EH51 .... **63** F3
Maidlands EH49 .... **85** E4
Main Point EH3 .... **232** C1
Main Rd Charlestown KY11 . **45** D2
Crombie KY12 .... **44** C4
Grangemouth FK3 .... **62** A4
Macmerry EH33 .... **129** E3
Main St Aberdour KY3 .... **49** E4
Airth FK2 .... **22** B2
Alloa FK10 .... **5** E1
Auchtertool KY2 .... **15** D1
Avonbridge FK1 .... **112** A3
Balerno EH14 .... **151** E1
Bannockburn FK7 .... **7** E1
Bathgate EH48 .... **145** D4
Blackridge EH48 .... **142** B2
Bo'ness EH51 .... **64** A4
Bonnybridge FK4 .... **58** A3
Brightons FK2 .... **82** B4
Cairneyhill KY12 .... **27** E1
California FK1 .... **81** F3
Cambus FK10 .... **9** D4
Carnock KY12 .... **27** E4
Carrington EH23 .... **206** B3
Clackmannan FK10 .... **11** D2
Comrie KY12 .... **26** B4
Cowdenbeath, Hill of Beath
KY4 .... **13** D1
Cowdenbeath, Lumphinnans
KY4 .... **13** F3
Cowie FK7 .... **20** B4
Crossford KY12 .... **28** B1
Crossgates KY4 .... **30** C3
Dalmeny EH29, EH30 ...... **89** F4
Dechmont EH52 .... **116** B1
Edinburgh, Davidsons Mains
EH4 .... **91** F2
Elphinstone EH33 .... **128** A1

Main St continued
Falkirk FK1 .... **59** F3
Falkirk, Bainsford FK2 ...... **60** A4
Falkirk, Carronshore FK2 ... **39** E2
Fallin FK7 .... **8** C2
Fauldhouse EH47 .... **193** E3
Forth ML11 .... **215** D1
Gifford EH41 .... **163** F3
Gorebridge EH23 .... **207** E4
Gullane EH31 .... **52** A1
Halbeath KY11 .... **30** A3
High Valleyfield KY12 ...... **25** F1
Kirkliston EH29, EH30 ..... **89** D1
Kirknewton EH53, EH27 .. **149** F1
Larbert FK5 .... **38** B1
Limekilns KY11 .... **45** E2
Linlithgow EH49 .... **84** B4
Livingston, Deans EH54 .. **146** C3
Livingston, Livingston Village
EH54 .... **147** E1
Lochgelly KY5 .... **14** A4
Longniddry EH32 .... **98** C3
Longridge EH47 .... **170** B1
Mid Calder EH53 .... **148** B2
Newton EH52 .... **88** A4
Newtongrange EH22 ...... **183** D3
North Queensferry KY11 ... **68** B3
Ormiston EH35 .... **159** F4
Pathhead EH37 .... **185** D3
Pathhead, Dewartown EH37 . **184** B3
Philpstoun EH49 .... **86** B4
Plean FK7 .... **20** B2
Polmont FK2 .... **61** F1
Ratho EH28 .... **119** E1
Redding FK2 .... **61** E1
Roslin EH25 .... **181** D2
Shieldhill FK1 .... **81** E3
Shotts ML7 .... **192** A2
Slamannan FK1 .... **110** A4
Stenhousemuir FK5 .... **38** C1
Stirling, Cambusbarron FK7 . **6** B3
Stirling, St Ninians FK7 ...... **7** D2
Stoneyburn EH47 .... **171** D1
Torryburn KY12 .... **26** B1
Townhill KY12 .... **29** E4
Tullibody FK10 .... **4** A1
West Calder EH55 .... **172** B2
Westfield EH48 .... **112** C4
Winchburgh EH52 .... **87** F2
Main St E FK11 .... **4** A3
Main St W Hillend KY11 .... **47** F2
Menstrie FK11 .... **3** F3
Mains Of Craigmillar
EH16 .... **124** B1
Mains Rd Harthill ML7 .... **168** C3
Linlithgow EH49 .... **84** C3
Maitland Ave
Bannockburn FK7 .... **7** E1
Musselburgh EH21 .... **126** A3
Maitland Cres FK7 .... **7** D2
Maitland Hog La EH29 ..... **89** D1
Maitland Park Rd EH21 .. **126** A3
Maitland Rd
Kirkliston EH29 .... **89** D1
Rosyth KY11 .... **67** D4
Maitland St
Dunfermline KY12 .... **28** C2
Musselburgh EH21 .... **126** A3
Majors Loan FK1 .... **60** A2
Majors Pl FK1 .... **60** A2
Malbet Pl FK5 .... **155** D4
Malcolm Ct EH48 .... **144** C3
Malcolm Dr FK5 .... **38** C2
Malcolm St KY11 .... **29** E1
Mall Ave EH21 .... **126** A3
Mall The FK4 .... **148** A3
Mallard Brae EH54 .... **147** E3
Mallens Brae EH54 .... **114** A3
Malleny Millgate EH14 .. **177** E4
Malplaquet Ct ML8 .... **230** A1
Malta Gn EH4 .... **93** D1
Malta Terr EH4 .... **93** D1
Maltings The
Auchtertool KY2 .... **15** D1
Linlithgow EH49 .... **84** B3
Mamre Dr FK1 .... **81** F3
Man O' War Way EH51 ..... **64** A4
Mandel Rigg FK2 .... **82** C3
Mandela Ave FK2 .... **60** B4
Manderston St EH6 .... **93** F2
Mandora Ct ML8 .... **230** A1
Manitoba Ave EH54 .... **147** F2
Mannan Dr FK10 .... **11** D2
Mannering Pl EH16 .... **155** D4
Mannfield Ave FK4 .... **57** F2
Manor Cres FK10 .... **4** A1
Manor Gdns EH42 .... **78** A1
Manor Loan FK11 .... **3** D2
Manor Pl EH3 .... **232** A3
Manor Powis Cotts FK11 ... **3** D2
Manor St FK1 .... **60** A2
Manor Wynd FK2 .... **83** D3
Manse Ave
Armadale EH48 .... **143** F3
Whitburn EH47 .... **170** A3
Manse Cres FK7 .... **7** D2
Manse Ct EH53 .... **148** C2
Manse Gr EH47 .... **171** E1
Manse La Burntisland KY3 .. **33** F1
Cockenzie & Port Seton
EH32 .... **97** E2
Musselburgh EH21 .... **126** B3
Manse Pk EH52 .... **116** C3
Manse Pl Bannockburn FK7 .. **7** E1
Bathgate EH48 .... **145** D3
Falkirk FK1 .... **60** A2
Inverkeithing KY11 .... **47** D1
Slamannan FK1 .... **110** A4

Manse Rd Carrington EH23 .. 206 B3
Crossgates KY4 .... 30 C4
Dirleton EH39 .... 53 D3
Edinburgh EH12 .... 121 E3
Forth ML11 .... 215 D1
Inverkeithing KY11 .... 47 D1
Kincardine FK10 .... 23 F3
Kinghorn KY3 .... 34 C2
Kirkliston EH29 .... 89 D1
Linlithgow EH49 .... 85 D3
Roslin EH25 .... 181 D2
Shotts ML7 .... 192 A2
Torphichen EH48 .... 113 F3
Whitburn EH47 .... 170 A3
Manse St Aberdour KY3 ...... 49 E4
Edinburgh EH12 .... 121 E3
Manse View
Armadale EH48 .... 143 F3
Innerwick EH42 .... 107 F1
Mansfield
Athelstaneford EH39 .... 101 F4
East Calder EH53 .... 148 C2
Mansfield Ct
2 Bathgate EH48 .... 145 D4
Livingston EH54 .... 147 E2
Mansfield Gr EH48 .... 145 D3
Mansfield St EH48 .... 145 D4
Mansewood Cres EH47 ..... 170 A3
Mansfield Ave Alloa FK10 ... 5 E1
Musselburgh EH21 .... 126 A3
Newtongrange EH22 .... 183 D3
Mansfield Ct EH21 .... 126 B3
Mansfield Pl
Edinburgh EH3 .... 93 E1
Musselburgh EH21 .... 126 B3
Newtongrange EH22 .... 183 D3
Mansfield Rd
Balerno EH14 .... 177 E4
Musselburgh EH21 .... 126 B3
Newtongrange EH22 .... 183 D3
Mansionhouse Rd
Edinburgh EH9 .... 123 E3
Falkirk FK1 .... 59 E3
Manson Sq EH54 .... 146 B3
Manuel Terr EH49 .... 83 F3
Maple Ave FK5 .... 38 C2
Maple Ct FK10 .... 10 A3
Maple Gr EH54 .... 148 A3
Maple Pl FK6 .... 36 B2
Maple St KY2 .... 17 D4
Mar Pl Alloa FK10 .... 5 E1
Stirling FK8 .... 7 D4
Mar St FK10 .... 10 A3
Mar Terr FK10 .... 11 D2
Maranatha Cres FK2 .... 82 B4
March Gr EH4 .... 92 A1
March Pines EH4 .... 91 F1
March Rd EH4 .... 92 A1
Marchbank Dr EH14 .... 177 E4
Marchbank Gdns EH14 ..... 177 E4
Marchbank Pl EH14 .... 177 E4
Marchbank Way EH14 ...... 151 E1
Marchburn Dr EH26 .... 203 E3
Marches Dr EH48 .... 144 A3
Marches The
Armadale EH48 .... 144 A3
Stirling FK8 .... 7 D4
Marchfield Gr EH4 .... 92 A2
Marchfield Park La EH4 ...... 91 F2
Marchfield Pk EH4 .... 91 F2
Marchfield Terr EH4 .... 92 A2
Marchglen FK13 .... 5 F3
Marchhall Cres EH16 .... 124 A3
Marchhall Pl EH16 .... 124 A3
Marchhall Rd EH16 .... 124 A3
Marchlands Ave EH51 .... 64 A4
Marchlands La EH51 .... 64 A4
Marchmont Ave FK2 .... 61 E1
Marchmont Cres EH9 ...... 123 E3
Marchmont Ct FK2 .... 61 E1
Marchmont Rd EH9 .... 123 E3
Marchmont St EH9 .... 123 E3
Marchside Ct FK10 .... 5 E1
Marchwood Ave EH48 ...... 145 E3
Marchwood Cres EH48 ..... 145 E3
Marchwood Rd EH33 .... 128 A1
Mardale Cres EH10 .... 123 D2
Maree Ct FK10 .... 10 B3
Maree Pl Crossford KY12 .... 28 A1
Kircaldy KY2 .... 16 C4
Maree Wlk EH54 .... 148 A2
Margaret Ave
Bathgate EH48 .... 145 F3
Haggs FK4 .... 57 D2
Margaret Ct FK6 .... 36 C1
Margaret Dr FK4 .... 58 A3
Margaret Rd FK2 .... 7 E1
Margaret Terr FK5 .... 38 C2
Maria St KY1 .... 17 E3
Marina Rd EH48 .... 145 F3
Marine Dr EH4, EH5 .... 92 A3
Marine Espl EH6 .... 94 B3
Marine Par EH39 .... 54 B4
Marine Rd Dunbar EH42 ..... 78 B2
Gullane EH31 .... 52 A2
Marine Terr EH31 .... 52 A2
Mariner Ave FK1 .... 59 D3
Mariner Dr FK1 .... 59 D3
Mariner Gdns FK1 .... 59 E3
Mariner Rd FK1 .... 59 D3
Mariner St FK1 .... 59 D3
Mariners St KY2 .... 17 D3
Mariners Wlk KY11 .... 47 F2
Marion St KY1 .... 17 D1
Marionville Ave EH7 .... 94 B1
Marionville Cres EH7 .... 94 B1
Marionville Dr EH7 .... 94 B1

Marionville Gr EH7 .... 94 B1
Marionville Pk EH7 .... 94 A1
Marionville Rd EH7 .... 94 A1
Marischal Dr EH16 .... 124 C2
Marischal Pl **6** EH4 .... 92 B1
Maritime La EH6 .... 94 A3
Maritime St EH6 .... 94 A3
Marjoribanks St EH48 ...... 145 D3
Market Ct EH41 .... 101 D1
Market La EH49 .... 85 D4
Market Pl
North Berwick EH39 .... 54 B4
Whitburn EH47 .... 170 A4
Market St Bo'ness EH51 ..... 63 F4
Dunfermline KY12 .... 29 D2
Edinburgh EH1 .... 233 D3
Haddington EH41 .... 132 A4
Mid Calder EH53 .... 148 B2
Musselburgh EH21 .... 126 A3
Marketgate EH35 .... 159 F4
Markfield Rd KY11 .... 48 B2
Markle Steading EH40 ..... 103 D4
Marlborough Dr FK9 .... 2 B2
Marlborough St EH15 .... 125 D4
Marly Dr EH39 .... 54 A3
Marly Rise EH39 .... 54 A3
Marmion Ave EH25 .... 180 C2
Marmion Cres
Edinburgh EH16 .... 124 A1
North Berwick EH39 .... 54 A4
Marmion Rd
Bathgate EH48 .... 145 D4
Grangemouth FK3 .... 61 E3
North Berwick EH39 .... 54 A4
Marmion St FK2 .... 60 A4
Marquis Dr FK10 .... 11 D2
Marrfield Rd EH54 .... 117 C1
Marrfield Terr EH54 .... 117 D1
Marschal St FK2 .... 7 E2
Marshall Rd KY11 .... 29 D1
Marshall Rd EH29 .... 89 D1
Marshall St
Cockenzie & Port Seton EH32 . 97 D2
Cowdenbeath KY4 .... 13 E4
Edinburgh EH8 .... 233 D2
Grangemouth FK3 .... 61 E4
Marshall's Ct EH1 .... 233 E4
Marshill FK10 .... 10 A3
Martin Brae EH54 .... 147 E3
Martin Gr EH19 .... 182 B4
Martin Pl FK2 .... 156 C1
Stirling FK7 .... 7 D2
Mary Erskine
Sch for Girls The EH4 .... 92 A1
Mary Erskine & Stewart's
Melville Jun Sch The EH4 ... 92 C1
Mary Pl Clackmannan FK10 .. 11 D3
Dunfermline KY11 .... 29 D1
Mary Sq FK2 .... 61 D2
Mary St FK2 .... 60 C2
Mary Stevenson Dr FK10 .... 10 A4
Mary Street Rdbt FK2 .... 60 C2
Mary's Pl EH4 .... 93 D1
Maryburn Rd EH22 .... 183 E4
Maryfield **2** EH7 .... 93 F1
Maryfield Pk EH53 .... 148 B1
Maryfield Pl
Bonnyrigg and Lasswade
EH19 .... 182 B4
2 Edinburgh EH7 .... 94 A1
Falkirk FK1 .... 59 D2
Maryflats Pl FK3 .... 61 F4
Maryhall St KY1 .... 17 E3
Marywell KY1 .... 17 E3
Masefield Way EH12 .... 90 A1
Mason Pl EH18 .... 181 F3
Masserene Rd KY2 .... 16 C3
Masterton Rd KY11 .... 47 D4
Mather Terr FK2 .... 60 C2
Mathers Ave EH47 .... 169 F3
Mathieson Pl KY11 .... 29 E1
Matthew St KY2 .... 17 D3
Maukeshill Ct EH54 .... 147 E1
Maulsford Ave EH22 .... 156 A4
Maurice Ave FK7 .... 7 E2
Maurice Pl EH9 .... 123 E1
Mauricewood Ave EH26 .... 203 F4
Mauricewood Bank EH26 ... 203 F4
Mauricewood Gr EH26 ..... 203 F4
Mauricewood Pk EH26 ..... 203 F4
Mauricewood Prim Sch
EH26 .... 204 A4
Mauricewood Rd EH26 ..... 203 F4
Mauricewood Rise EH26 ... 203 F4
Mavisbank EH20 .... 181 E4
Mavisbank Ave FK1 .... 81 E3
Mavisbank Pl EH18 .... 181 F3
Maxton Cres FK12 .... 5 E4
Maxton Ct EH22 .... 157 D2
Maxton Pl KY11 .... 46 C2
Maxwell Cres KY4 .... 13 D1
Maxwell Pl FK8 .... 7 D4
Maxwell Rd EH39 .... 53 D2
Maxwell Sq EH54 .... 173 E3
Maxwell St EH10 .... 123 D2
May Terr EH39 .... 54 A4
Maybank Villas EH12 .... 121 E4
Mayburn Ave EH20 .... 155 D1
Mayburn Bank EH20 .... 181 D1
Mayburn Cres EH20 .... 155 D1
Mayburn Ct EH20 .... 181 D1
Mayburn Dr EH20 .... 155 D1
Mayburn Gr EH20 .... 181 D1
Mayburn Hill EH20 .... 181 D1
Mayburn Loan EH20 .... 155 D1
Mayburn Terr EH20 .... 155 D1
Mayburn Vale EH20 .... 181 D1
Mayburn Wlk EH20 .... 181 D1
Maybury Rd EH12 .... 121 D4

Mayfield Ave EH21 .... 126 A2
Mayfield Cres
Clackmannan FK10 .... 11 D3
Loanhead EH20 .... 181 E4
Musselburgh EH21 .... 126 A2
Mayfield Ct Armadale EH48 . 143 F2
Loanhead EH20 .... 181 E4
Stirling FK7 .... 7 D2
Mayfield Dr
Armadale EH48 .... 143 F3
Longcroft FK4 .... 57 D2
Mayfield Gdns EH9 .... 123 F2
Mayfield Gdns La EH9 ...... 123 F2
Mayfield Ind Est EH22 ..... 183 E3
Mayfield Mews FK1 .... 59 F2
Mayfield Pl Mayfield EH22 .. 183 D3
Musselburgh EH21 .... 126 A2
Mayfield Prim Sch EH22 ... 183 D3
Mayfield Rd
Easthouses EH22 .... 183 E4
Edinburgh EH9 .... 123 F2
Redding FK1 .... 61 E1
Mayfield St FK7 .... 7 D2
Mayfield Terr EH9 .... 123 F2
Mayflower St KY12 .... 29 E4
Maygate KY12 .... 29 D2
Mayne Ave FK9 .... 2 A3
Mayshade Rd EH20 .... 155 D1
Mayville Bank EH21 .... 127 D3
Mayville Gdns EH5 .... 93 E3
Mayville Gdns E EH5 .... 93 E3
Mayville Pk EH42 .... 78 B2
McAdam Sq EH54 .... 173 E3
McAlley St FK9 .... 1 C4
McAllister Ct FK7 .... 7 D1
McCall Gdns EH40 .... 103 E4
McCallum Ct EH48 .... 143 F4
McCann Ave EH52 .... 117 D3
McCathie Dr EH22 .... 183 D3
McClelland Cres KY11 .... 29 D1
McDiarmid Gr EH22 .... 183 D2
McDonald Pl EH7 .... 93 F2
McDonald Rd EH7 .... 93 F2
McDonald St EH7 .... 93 F2
McDouall Stewart Mus
KY1 .... 18 A4
McDouall Stuart Pl KY1 ...... 18 A4
McGinley Way EH49 .... 84 B3
McGregor Ave KY5 .... 14 A4
McGrigor Rd Rosyth KY11 .... 46 B1
Stirling FK7 .... 7 D2
McIntosh Ct EH52 .... 117 E3
McKane Pl KY12 .... 28 C1
McKay Dr KY11 .... 29 F1
McKell Ct KY4 .... 60 A2
McKenzie St KY1 .... 17 F4
McKinlay Cres FK10 .... 10 B4
McKinlay Terr EH20 .... 181 D4
McKinnon Dr EH22 .... 183 F3
McKinnon Rd EH47 .... 193 F4
McLachlan Ave FK7 .... 7 D1
McLachlan St FK5 .... 38 B1
McLaren Ave EH49 .... 84 A3
McLaren Ct FK5 .... 38 B1
McLaren Rd EH9 .... 124 A2
McLaren Terr FK7 .... 7 D1
McLauchlan Rise KY3 .... 49 D4
McLauchlan View ML7 ...... 168 C3
McLean Pl
Bonnyrigg and Lasswade
EH18 .... 181 F1
Gorebridge EH23 .... 207 E4
McLean Rd EH52 .... 28 C3
McLean Wlk EH22 .... 183 D2
McLeod Cres EH32 .... 96 C1
McLeod St Broxburn EH52 .. 117 F3
Edinburgh EH11 .... 122 C3
McMartin Ct EH47 .... 170 B4
McNeil Cres EH48 .... 144 A3
McNeil Path EH33 .... 128 B3
McNeil Way EH33 .... 128 B3
McNeill Ave EH20 .... 181 D4
McNeill Pl EH20 .... 181 D4
McNeill Terr EH20 .... 181 D4
McPhail Sq EH33 .... 128 B3
McPherson Dr FK8 .... 2 A1
McQuade St EH19 .... 182 B4
McRae Cres KY3 .... 33 F1
McTaggart Ave FK6 .... 36 C1
McVean Pl FK4 .... 57 D2
Meadow Cres EH47 .... 193 F3
Meadow Ct
Burntisland KY3 .... 33 F1
Carluke ML8 .... 230 B1
Meadow Dr EH47 .... 171 D1
Meadow Gn EH10 .... 5 D1
Meadow La EH8 .... 233 D1
Meadow Pk KY2 .... 17 D4
Meadow Pl Bilston EH25 ... 180 C3
Dunfermline KY11 .... 29 F2
Edinburgh EH9 .... 232 C1
Stirling FK8 .... 2 B1
Stoneyburn EH47 .... 171 D1
Meadow St FK1 .... 60 B1
Meadowbank
Edinburgh EH8 .... 94 A1
Livingston EH54 .... 147 F3
Ormiston EH35 .... 159 E4
Meadowbank Ave **13** EH8 . 94 A1
Meadowbank Cres
Edinburgh EH8 .... 94 A1
Ormiston EH35 .... 159 E4

Meadowbank Rd
Kirknewton EH27 .... 149 F2
Ormiston EH35 .... 159 F4
Meadowbank Sports Ctr
EH7 .... 94 A1
Meadowbank St FK2 .... 61 E1
Meadowbank View EH27 ... 149 F2
Meadowend KY12 .... 28 B1
Meadowfield
Burntisland KY3 .... 33 F1
Cowdenbeath KY4 .... 13 E1
Dalgety Bay KY11 .... 48 A2
Meadowfield Ave EH8 ...... 124 C4
Meadowfield Ct EH8 .... 124 B4
Meadowfield Dr EH8 .... 124 B4
Meadowfield Gdns EH8 ..... 124 B4
Meadowfield Ind Est KY3 .... 33 F1
Meadowfield Rd EH12 ...... 120 C4
Meadowfield Terr EH8 ...... 124 B3
Meadowforth Rd FK7 .... 7 E4
Meadowhead Ave EH55 .... 171 F1
Meadowhead Cres EH55 ... 171 F1
Meadowhead Gdns EH55 .. 171 F1
Meadowhead Gr EH55 ...... 171 F1
Meadowhead Loan EH55 ... 171 F1
Meadowhead Pl EH55 ...... 171 F1
Meadowhead Terr EH55 .... 171 F1
Meadowhouse Rd EH12 .... 121 F3
Meadowland Rd FK9 .... 2 A3
Meadowpark EH41 .... 132 A4
Meadowpark Rd EH48 ...... 144 C3
Meadowside EH33 .... 128 C3
Meadowspot EH10 .... 122 C1
Meadowview KY12 .... 28 A1
Mearenside EH12 .... 121 D4
Medwyn Pl KY10 .... 9 F3
Meeks Rd FK2 .... 60 A4
Meeting House Dr EH33 .... 128 B3
Meggat Pl EH26 .... 204 A4
Meggetland Terr EH14 ...... 122 C2
Meikle Rd EH54 .... 147 E1
Melbourne Pl EH39 .... 54 B4
Melbourne Rd
Broxburn EH52 .... 117 F3
North Berwick EH39 .... 54 B4
Melbourne St EH54 .... 148 A3
Meldrum Cres KY3 .... 33 E1
Meldrum Ct KY11 .... 29 F1
Meldrum Prim Sch EH54 .. 146 C4
Meldrum Rd KY2 .... 17 D3
Melford Ave ML7 .... 192 A2
Melfort Dr FK7 .... 7 D2
Melgund Pl KY5 .... 14 A4
Melgund Terr EH7 .... 93 E1
Mellerstain Rd KY2 .... 16 B3
Mellock Gdns FK1 .... 59 F1
Mellor Ct KY11 .... 46 C2
Melrose Cres KY2 .... 17 E3
Melrose Dr FK3 .... 61 F3
Melrose Pl **10** FK1 .... 60 A2
Melville Cotts EH18 .... 156 B2
Melville Cres EH3 .... 232 A3
Melville Dr EH9 .... 233 D1
Melville Dykes Rd EH18 .... 156 B1
Melville Gate EH22 .... 156 B2
Melville Gate Rd EH22 ..... 156 C2
Melville Pl Bridge of A FK9 .... 2 A4
Kircaldy KY1 .... 16 B3
Melville Rd EH22 .... 156 C1
Melville St Edinburgh EH3 .. 232 A3
Falkirk FK1 .... 60 A3
Lochgelly KY5 .... 14 A4
Melville Street La EH3 ..... 232 A3
Melville Terr
Dalkeith EH22 .... 156 C1
Edinburgh EH9 .... 233 E1
Stirling FK8 .... 7 D3
Melville View EH18 .... 182 A4
Menstrie Castle FK11 .... 3 F3
Menstrie Pl FK11 .... 4 A3
Menstrie Prim Sch FK11 ..... 4 A3
Menteith Ct FK10 .... 10 B3
Menteith Dr KY11 .... 29 F1
Menteith Pl KY11 .... 2 A2
Mentone Ave EH15 .... 95 D1
Mentone Gdns EH9 .... 123 F2
Mentone Terr EH9 .... 123 F2
Menzies Cres KY2 .... 16 C3
Menzies Dr FK8 .... 2 A1
Menzies Rd EH48 .... 145 D3
Mercat FK10 .... 11 D2
Mercat The KY1 .... 17 E2
Mercer Pl KY11 .... 29 F2
Mercer St FK10 .... 23 F2
Merchant St EH1 .... 233 D2
Merchiston Ave
Edinburgh EH10 .... 123 D3
Falkirk FK1 .... 60 A4
Merchiston Bank Ave
EH10 .... 123 D2
Merchiston Bank Gdns
EH10 .... 123 D2
Merchiston Castle Sch
EH14 .... 153 D4
Merchiston Cres EH10 ..... 123 D2
Merchiston Gdns
Edinburgh EH10 .... 122 C2
Falkirk FK1 .... 60 A3
Merchiston Gr EH11 .... 122 C2
Merchiston Ind Est FK2 ...... 60 B4
Merchiston Mews EH10 .... 123 D3
Merchiston Pk EH10 .... 123 D3
Merchiston Pl EH10 .... 123 D3
Merchiston Rd
Falkirk, Grahamston FK2 ..... 60 A3
Falkirk, Mungal FK2 .... 60 A4
Merchiston Terr FK2 .... 60 A4

Meredith Dr FK5 .... 38 C2
Merker Terr EH49 .... 84 C3
Merkland Cres KY11 .... 48 A2
Merkland Dr FK1 .... 60 C1
Merlin Way KY11 .... 48 B3
Merlyon Way EH26 .... 203 E4
Merrick Rd FK3 .... 61 F3
Merrick Way FK3 .... 61 F3
Merryfield Ave EH33 .... 129 E3
Mertoun Pl EH11 .... 122 C3
Merville Cres FK1 .... 81 F3
Merville Terr FK1 .... 81 F3
Methven Dr KY12 .... 29 D3
Methven Pl KY1 .... 17 D1
Methven Rd KY1 .... 17 D1
Methven Terr EH18 .... 181 F3
Meuse La EH2 .... 233 D3
Michaelson Sq EH54 .... 147 E1
Mid Beveridgewell KY12 .... 28 C3
Mid Brae KY12 .... 28 C3
Mid Cswy KY12 .... 42 B4
Mid Gogarloch Syke
EH12 .... 121 D3
Mid Liberton EH16 .... 124 A1
Mid New Cultins EH11 ..... 121 D1
Mid Rd KY3 .... 34 C2
Mid Road Ind Est EH32 .... 127 F4
Mid St Bathgate EH48 ...... 145 D3
Kirkaldy KY1 .... 17 E3
Livingston EH54 .... 146 C3
Lochgelly KY5 .... 14 A4
Mid Steil EH10 .... 122 C1
Midcalder Prim Sch EH53 . 148 B1
Middle Meadow Wlk EH8 .. 233 D1
Middle Street La FK3 .... 40 B1
Middlebank St KY11 .... 46 C3
Middleby St EH9 .... 123 F2
Middlefield EH7 .... 93 F2
Middlefield Ind Ctr FK2 ...... 60 B4
Middlefield Ind Est FK2 ...... 60 B4
Middlefield Rd FK2 .... 60 B3
Middleknowe EH14 .... 152 B4
Middlemass Ct KY2 .... 60 A3
Middlemuir Rd FK7 .... 7 E3
Middlepark EH14 .... 152 B4
Middleshot EH14 .... 152 B4
Middleshot Rd EH31 .... 52 A2
Middleshot Sq EH32 .... 97 D1
Middleton Dr KY11 .... 4 A3
Middleton Ave EH52 .... 117 D2
Middleton Rd EH52 .... 117 D2
Middlewood Pk EH54 ...... 146 C4
Midhope Pl EH52 .... 88 A1
Midmar Ave EH10 .... 123 E1
Midmar Dr EH10 .... 123 E1
Midmar Gdns EH10 .... 123 D1
Midthorn Cres FK2 .... 60 C3
Midtown FK11 .... 3 F3
Milburn Cres EH48 .... 143 E3
Milesmark Ct KY12 .... 28 B3
Milesmark Prim Sch KY12 .. 28 B3
Mill Farm KY3 .... 49 D4
Mill Hill FK7 .... 6 B3
Mill La Edinburgh EH6 .... 93 F3
Kincardine FK10 .... 23 F2
Mill Lade EH49 .... 84 C4
Mill Rd Alloa FK10 .... 10 A3
Armadale EH48 .... 143 F3
Bathgate EH48 .... 145 D4
Blackburn EH47 .... 171 E4
Cambusbarron FK7 .... 6 B3
Clackmannan FK10 .... 11 D3
Dunfermline KY11 .... 29 D1
Falkirk FK2 .... 39 D2
Harthill ML7 .... 168 C3
Linlithgow EH49 .... 84 B4
Stenton EH42 .... 104 B1
Mill Rdbt FK54 .... 147 D2
Mill St Alloa FK10 .... 10 A3
Dunfermline KY12 .... 28 C2
Kirkaldy KY1 .... 17 D1
Mill Wynd
East Linton EH40 .... 103 F4
Haddington EH41 .... 132 A4
Prestonpans EH32 .... 96 C1
Millar Cres EH10 .... 123 D2
Millar Pl Edinburgh EH10 ... 123 D2
High Bonnybridge FK4 .... 58 A2
Stenhousemuir FK2 .... 39 D3
Stirling FK8 .... 2 B1
Millar Place La EH10 .... 123 D2
Millar Rd EH33 .... 128 B3
Millars Wynd FK10 .... 5 E1
Millbank EH14 .... 151 E1
Millbank Gr EH23 .... 207 E4
Millbank Pl EH52 .... 116 C2
Millbank Sq EH47 .... 170 A4
Millbank Terr FK2 .... 82 C4
Millbrae EH53 .... 148 B3
Millbrae Wynd EH14 .... 122 A1
Millbrook Pl FK11 .... 3 F3
Millburn Rd
Bathgate EH48 .... 144 C3
Westfield EH48 .... 112 C3
Millburn St FK2 .... 60 B3
Milldean Gr KY12 .... 29 E3
Miller Ave KY12 .... 28 A1
Miller Cres EH51 .... 64 B3
Miller Pk FK2 .... 61 F1
Miller Pl Airth FK2 .... 22 C2
Harthill ML7 .... 168 C3
Miller Rd Dunfermline KY12 . 28 C3
Grangemouth EH51 .... 62 C3
Miller Row EH4 .... 232 A3

Miller St Carluke ML8 .... 230 A1
  Harthill ML7 .... 168 C3
  Kirkcaldy KY1 .... 17 F4
Millerfield EH49 .... 84 B4
Millerfield Pl EH9 .... 123 E3
Millerhill Rd Dalkeith EH22 125 D1
  Danderhall EH22 .... 156 B4
Millfield Haddington EH41 .. 132 A4
  Livingston EH54 .... 147 D1
Millfield Dr FK2 .... 61 F1
Millflats St FK2 .... 39 D1
Millgate EH52 .... 87 F1
Millhall Rd FK7 .... 7 E3
Millhaugh La EH48 .... 145 D4
Millhill EH21 .... 126 B3
Millhill La EH21 .... 126 B3
Millhill St KY11 .... 29 D1
Millhill Wynd EH21 .... 126 B3
Millie St KY1 .... 17 E3
Millway FK34 .... 161 D3
Miln-acre EH6 .... 93 E2
Milne Cres KY4 .... 13 E2
Milne Rd KY11 .... 46 C1
Milnepark Rd FK7 .... 19 F4
Milton Brae FK7 .... 7 D1
Milton Cl FK6 .... 36 B2
Milton Cres
  Bannockburn FK7 .... 7 E1
  Edinburgh EH15 .... 125 D3
Milton Dr EH15 .... 125 E4
Milton Gdns FK7 .... 7 D1
Milton Gdns N EH15 .... 125 D3
Milton Gdns S EH15 .... 125 D3
Milton Glen EH15 .... 125 F4
Milton Gn KY12 .... 29 D1
Milton Gr Bannockburn FK7 .. 7 E1
  Edinburgh EH15 .... 125 F4
Milton Link EH15 .... 125 E3
Milton Pl FK6 .... 36 B2
Milton Rd Bannockburn FK7 ... 7 E1
  Edinburgh EH15 .... 125 F4
  Kirkcaldy KY1 .... 17 D1
Milton Rd E EH15 .... 125 E4
Milton Rd W EH15 .... 124 C3
Milton Row KY12 .... 36 C2
Milton St EH8 .... 94 A1
Milton Terr
  Bannockburn FK7 .... 7 D1
  Edinburgh EH15 .... 125 F4
Minard Rd ML7 .... 191 E3
Mine Rd FK9 .... 2 A4
Miner's Terr EH21 .... 127 D3
Mingle Pl EH51 .... 64 A3
Minstrel Ct EH25 .... 181 D2
Minthill Pl ML7 .... 168 B3
Minto Ct FK12 .... 5 D3
Minto Gdns FK12 .... 5 D3
Minto Pl KY2 .... 17 D4
Minto St Edinburgh EH9 .... 123 F2
  Lochgelly KY5 .... 14 A4
Mission La **9** FK1 .... 60 A2
Mitchell Cres Alloa FK10 .... 9 F4
  Cowdenbeath KY4 .... 13 D1
Mitchell Pl Falkirk FK1 .... 59 F1
  Kirkcaldy KY1 .... 17 E3
Mitchell Rd KY11 .... 46 B1
Mitchell St Dalkeith EH22 ... 156 C2
  Edinburgh EH6 .... 94 A3
  Kirkcaldy KY1 .... 17 E2
Mitchell Way EH33 .... 128 B4
Mitchell Wlk KY11 .... 46 C2
Mitchellhall Brae EH41 .... 132 C3
Moat Dr EH14 .... 122 B2
Moat Pl EH14 .... 122 B2
Moat St EH14 .... 122 B2
Moat Terr EH14 .... 122 B2
Moat View EH25 .... 180 C2
Mochrum Dr KY12 .... 45 D4
Modan Rd FK7 .... 7 D2
Moffat Ave
  Bonnyrigg and Lasswade
  EH19 .... 182 A3
  Falkirk FK2 .... 39 E2
Moffat Cres KY5 .... 14 A4
Moffat Rd EH35 .... 159 E3
Moidart Rd EH47 .... 170 B4
Moir Ave EH21 .... 127 D3
Moir Cres EH21 .... 127 D3
Moir Ct KY4 .... 12 C4
Moir Dr EH21 .... 127 D3
Moir Pl EH21 .... 127 D3
Moir St FK10 .... 10 A4
Moir Terr EH21 .... 127 D3
Moira Pk EH7 .... 94 C1
Moira Terr EH7 .... 94 C1
Moira Terrace La EH7 .... 94 C1
Mollison Ave ML7 .... 168 C4
Monar Ct KY12 .... 48 A2
Monastery St KY12 .... 29 D2
Moncks Rd FK1 .... 60 B2
Moncrieff Terr EH9 .... 123 F3
Moncrieff Way EH54 .... 147 E4
Moncur St KY12 .... 29 E4
Monkbarns Gdns EH16 .... 155 D4
Monkland Rd EH41 .... 144 C3
Monkmains Rd EH41 .... 132 B4
Monkrigg Pl EH41 .... 132 B4
Monksrig Rd EH26 .... 203 E3
Monkswood Rd EH22 .... 183 D2
Monktonhall Pl EH21 .... 126 A2
Monktonhall Terr EH21 ...... 126 A2
Monkwood Ct EH9 .... 123 E2
Monmouth Terr EH3 .... 93 D2
Montagu Terr EH3 .... 93 D2
Montague St EH8 .... 233 E1

Monteith Wlk ML7 .... 191 F3
Montfort Pl FK1 .... 60 A2
Montgomery Cres FK2 .... 39 D1
Montgomery Dr FK2 .... 39 D1
Montgomery St
  Edinburgh EH7 .... 93 F1
  Falkirk FK2 .... 60 C3
  Grangemouth FK3 .... 61 E3
  Kirkcaldy KY2 .... 17 D3
Montgomery Street La
  EH7 .... 93 F1
Montgomery Way FK9 .... 2 A2
Montgomery Well FK2 .... 39 D1
Montpelier EH10 .... 123 D3
Montpelier Pk EH10 .... 123 D3
Montpelier Terr EH10 .... 123 D3
Montrose Dr Polmont FK2 ..... 62 A1
  Stirling FK9 .... 2 B2
Montrose Terr EH7 .... 233 F4
Montrose Way FK4 .... 57 F3
Moodie St KY12 .... 29 D2
Moor Rd Fala EH37 .... 210 B3
  Pathhead EH37 .... 185 E2
  Pencaitland EH35 .... 186 A3
Moore House Sch EH48 ...... 145 F3
Mooreland Gdns EH55 .... 171 E1
Moorelands EH55 .... 171 E1
Moorfield Cotts EH22 .... 156 B4
Moorfoot Ct EH19 .... 182 A4
Moorfoot Pl
  Bonnyrigg and Lasswade
  EH19 .... 182 A3
  Penicuik EH26 .... 203 F3
Moorfoot View
  Bilston EH26 .... 180 C3
  Bonnyrigg and Lasswade
  EH19 .... 182 A3
  Gorebridge EH23 .... 207 E4
Moorings The KY11 .... 47 F1
Moorside St ML8 .... 230 A1
Morar Ct FK3 .... 61 E3
Morar Dr FK2 .... 39 E1
Morar Pl FK3 .... 61 E3
Morar Rd KY12 .... 28 A1
Moray Ct Auchtertool KY2 .... 15 D1
  Dalgety Bay KY11 .... 48 A2
Moray Dr EH49 .... 84 C3
Moray House Coll
  Halls Of Residence
  EH16 .... 124 A2
Moray House Coll of Ed
  Edinburgh, Canongate EH8 .. 233 E3
  Edinburgh, Cramond EH4 .... 91 E3
Moray Park Terr EH7 .... 94 A1
Moray Pk KY11 .... 48 A2
Moray Pl Edinburgh EH3 .... 232 B4
  Grangemouth FK3 .... 61 F4
  Linlithgow EH49 .... 84 C3
Moray Prim Sch FK3 .... 61 F4
Moray Way N KY11 .... 48 B2
Moray Way S KY11 .... 48 A1
Morayvale KY3 .... 33 F1
Moredun Dykes Rd EH17 .... 155 E3
Moredun Park Ct EH17 .... 155 E4
Moredun Park Dr EH17 .... 155 E4
Moredun Park Gdns
  EH17 .... 155 E4
Moredun Park Gn EH17 ...... 155 F4
Moredun Park Gr EH17 .... 155 F4
Moredun Park Loan
  EH17 .... 155 E4
Moredun Park Rd EH17 ...... 155 F4
Moredun Park St EH17 .... 155 F4
Moredun Park View
  EH17 .... 155 E4
Moredun Park Way EH17 .... 155 E4
Moredun Park Wlk EH17 .... 155 E4
Moredun Prim Sch EH17 .... 155 E4
Moredunvale Bank EH17 .... 155 E4
Moredunvale Gn EH17 .... 155 E4
Moredunvale Gr EH17 .... 155 E4
Moredunvale Loan EH17 .... 155 E4
Moredunvale Pk EH17 .... 155 E4
Moredunvale Pl EH17 .... 155 E4
Moredunvale Rd EH17 .... 155 E4
Moredunvale View EH17 .... 155 E4
Moredunvale Way EH17 ..... 155 E4
Morgan Ct FK7 .... 7 E2
Morison Gdns EH30 .... 68 A1
Moriston Ct FK3 .... 61 F2
Moriston Dr EH54 .... 173 F3
Morley Cres FK7 .... 7 D2
Morlich Cres KY11 .... 48 A1
Morlich Ct KY11 .... 48 A1
Morlich Gr KY11 .... 48 A1
Morlich Pk KY11 .... 48 A1
Morlich Pl KY11 .... 48 A1
Morlich Rd KY11 .... 48 A1
Morlich Wlk EH54 .... 148 A2
Mornay Way ML7 .... 191 F3
Morningside Ct EH10 .... 123 D1
Morningside Dr EH10 .... 123 D1
Morningside Gdns EH10 ...... 122 C1
Morningside Gr EH10 .... 122 C1
Morningside Pk EH10 .... 123 D2
Morningside Pl EH10 .... 123 D2
Morningside Rd EH10 .... 123 D2
Morningside Terr EH10 .... 123 D2
Morris Ct KY11 .... 47 E1
Morris Rd EH47 .... 183 E3
Morris Sq EH54 .... 147 F1
Morris Terr FK8 .... 7 D4
Morrison Ave
  Bonnyrigg EH4 .... 57 F3
  Tranent EH33 .... 128 A2
Morrison Circ EH3 .... 232 A2
Morrison Cres EH3 .... 232 A2

Morrison Dr
  Bannockburn FK7 .... 7 E1
  Dunfermline KY11 .... 46 C4
Morrison Link EH3 .... 232 A2
Morrison St EH3 .... 232 A2
Morrison Way EH54 .... 147 E4
Mortimer Ct KY11 .... 48 A1
Morton St EH15 .... 125 E4
Mortonhall Gate EH16 .... 154 C3
Mortonhall Park Ave
  EH17 .... 154 C3
Mortonhall Park Bank
  EH17 .... 155 D3
Mortonhall Park Cres
  EH17 .... 155 D3
Mortonhall Park Dr
  EH17 .... 155 D3
Mortonhall Park Gdns
  EH17 .... 154 C3
Mortonhall Park Gr
  EH17 .... 154 C3
Mortonhall Park Pl
  EH17 .... 155 D3
Mortonhall Park Terr
  EH17 .... 155 D3
Mortonhall Park View
  EH17 .... 154 C3
Mortonhall Park Way
  EH17 .... 154 C3
Mortonhall Rd EH9 .... 123 E2
Morven Ct FK1 .... 60 B1
Morven Dr FK2 .... 61 E1
Morven Gr KY2 .... 16 C4
Morven Pl KY11 .... 48 A2
Morven St EH4 .... 91 E1
Morvenside EH14 .... 152 B4
Morvenside Cl EH14 .... 152 B4
Moss Intc EH54 .... 147 E3
Moss Rd FK7 .... 8 B2
Moss Way KY11 .... 48 A3
Moss-side Rd KY4 .... 13 D2
Mossband La ML7 .... 191 F3
Mossbank
  Cowdenbeath KY4 .... 13 D1
  Livingston EH54 .... 147 F3
  Rosyth KY11 .... 46 C3
Mossburn Ave ML7 .... 168 B3
Mosscastle Rd FK1 .... 110 A4
Mossend EH55 .... 172 B2
Mossend Terr KY4 .... 13 D1
Mossgiel Ave Cowie FK7 .... 20 B4
  Stirling FK8 .... 2 A1
Mossgiel Cotts EH54 .... 146 B4
Mossgiel St FK1 .... 59 D3
Mossgiel Terr FK2 .... 61 D3
Mossgiel Wlk **4** EH16 .... 124 A1
Mosshall Ind Est EH47 .... 171 D4
Mosshat Rd EH55 .... 216 C2
Mosshouse FK7 .... 6 C2
Mosside Dr EH47 .... 145 E1
Mosside Rd EH47 .... 171 E4
Mosside Terr EH47 .... 145 E1
Moston Terr EH9 .... 123 F2
Motion St KY5 .... 14 A4
Moubray Gr EH30 .... 89 E4
Moubray Rd KY11 .... 48 B3
Moulin Way KY12 .... 29 F3
Mound Pl EH1 .... 232 C3
Mound The EH2 .... 232 C3
Mount Grange EH9 .... 123 E2
Mount Hooly Cres KY11 .... 68 B3
Mount Hope FK9 .... 2 B4
Mount Lodge Pl EH15 .... 125 D4
Mount Oliphant FK7 .... 20 B4
Mount Pleasant EH48 .... 143 F3
Mount Vernon Rd EH16 ...... 155 D4
Mount William FK10 .... 5 F1
Mountbatten Pl KY11 .... 46 C2
Mountbatten St FK3 .... 61 E3
Mountcastle Bank EH8 .... 124 C4
Mountcastle Cres EH8 .... 124 C4
Mountcastle Dr N EH15 ...... 124 C4
Mountcastle Dr S EH15 .... 125 D3
Mountcastle Gdns EH8 .... 124 C4
Mountcastle Gn **1** EH8 .... 94 C1
Mountcastle Gr EH8 .... 124 C4
Mountcastle Loan EH8 .... 124 C4
Mountcastle Pk EH8 .... 94 C1
Mountcastle Pl **2** EH8 .... 94 C1
Mountcastle Terr EH8 .... 124 C4
Mountfair Gdns EH33 .... 129 E3
Mountfair Pl EH33 .... 129 E3
Mounthooly Loan EH10 ...... 154 B3
Mountjoy Terr EH21 .... 126 B4
Mowbray Ct KY7 .... 7 E2
Mowbray Gdns KY4 .... 30 C3
Mowbray Rise EH54 .... 147 F1
Moy Ct FK3 .... 61 E3
Muckle Hill Pk KY11 .... 47 D1
Mucklets Ave EH21 .... 126 A2
Mucklets Cres EH21 .... 126 A2
Mucklets Ct EH21 .... 126 A2
Mucklets Dr EH21 .... 126 A2
Mucklets Pl EH21 .... 126 A2
Mucklets Rd EH21 .... 125 F2
Mudale Ct FK1 .... 60 B1
Muia's Ct EH52 .... 116 C2
Muir Ct KY4 .... 30 C3
Muir Rd Bathgate EH48 ...... 144 C4
  Livingston EH54 .... 148 A4
  Townhill KY12 .... 29 E4
Muir St FK5 .... 38 B1
Muir Wood Cres EH14 .... 152 A3
Muir Wood Dr EH14 .... 152 A3
Muir Wood Gr EH14 .... 152 A3
Muir Wood Pl EH14 .... 152 A3
Muir Wood Rd EH14 .... 152 A3
Muiralehouse Rd FK7 .... 19 F4

Muiravonside Ctry Pk
  EH49 .... 83 F2
Muiredge & Jersey Rd
  ML7 .... 191 D4
Muiredge Ave EH14 .... 152 C4
Muiredge Ct EH51 .... 64 A3
Muiredge Rd FK7 .... 7 D3
Muirend Ave EH14 .... 152 C4
Muirfield Cres EH31 .... 52 A1
Muirfield Dr Gullane EH31 .... 52 A1
  Uphall EH52 .... 116 C2
Muirfield Gdns EH20 .... 181 E4
Muirfield Pk EH31 .... 52 A2
Muirfield Rd FK5 .... 38 C1
Muirfield Steading EH31 ..... 52 B2
Muirfield Terr EH31 .... 52 A1
Muirfield Way EH54 .... 146 C3
Muirhall Pl FK5 .... 38 B2
Muirhall Rd FK5 .... 38 B2
Muirhead Ave FK7 .... 60 A4
Muirhead Pl Harthill ML7 .... 168 B4
  Penicuik EH26 .... 203 F4
Muirhead Rd FK5 .... 38 C2
Muirhouse Ave EH4 .... 92 A2
Muirhouse Bank EH4 .... 92 A2
Muirhouse Cl EH4 .... 92 A3
Muirhouse Cres EH4 .... 92 A3
Muirhouse Dr EH4 .... 92 A3
Muirhouse Gdns EH4 .... 92 A3
Muirhouse Gn EH4 .... 92 A3
Muirhouse Gr EH4 .... 92 A3
Muirhouse Loan EH4 .... 92 A3
Muirhouse Medway EH4 .... 92 A3
Muirhouse Parkway EH4 ...... 92 A3
Muirhouse Pk EH4 .... 92 A2
Muirhouse Pl E EH4 .... 92 A2
Muirhouse Pl W EH4 .... 92 A2
Muirhouse Prim Sch EH4 ..... 92 A2
Muirhouse Terr EH4 .... 92 A2
Muirhouse View EH4 .... 92 A3
Muirhouse Way EH4 .... 92 A2
Muirlaun ML11 .... 215 D1
Muirlee Rd ML8 .... 230 A1
Muirpark EH22 .... 156 C1
Muirpark Ct EH33 .... 128 C3
Muirpark Dr Shieldhill FK1 ... 81 E3
  Tranent EH33 .... 128 C3
Muirpark Gdns
  Tranent EH33 .... 128 C3
  Tullibody FK10 .... 4 C2
Muirpark Gr EH33 .... 128 C3
Muirpark Pl EH33 .... 128 C3
Muirpark Rd EH33 .... 128 C3
Muirpark Terr EH33 .... 128 C3
Muirpark Wynd EH33 .... 128 C3
Muirside Ct KY12 .... 27 E1
Muirside Dr EH33 .... 128 B3
Muirside Gr KY12 .... 27 E1
Muirside La KY12 .... 44 B4
Muirside Rd EH10 .... 4 B2
Muirton Rd FK7 .... 7 F3
Muirton Rdbt FK7 .... 7 F4
Muirton Way KY11 .... 48 A3
Mulberry Dr KY1 .... 29 F1
Mulberry Pl EH6 .... 93 E3
Muldron Terr ML7 .... 192 A1
Mull Ct EH1 .... 232 C3
  Grangemouth FK3 .... 61 E3
Mumrills Rd FK2 .... 61 E2
Mungalend FK2 .... 60 A4
Mungalend Ct FK2 .... 60 A4
Mungalhead Rd FK2 .... 60 A4
Mungle St EH55 .... 172 B2
Munro Ave FK9 .... 2 A4
Munro Dr EH13 .... 153 D3
Munro Gdns FK2 .... 60 C2
Munro Pl FK10 .... 9 F3
Munro St Kirkcaldy KY1 .... 17 D1
  Stenhousemuir FK5 .... 38 C2
Munro Way EH54 .... 147 E4
Murano Pl EH7 .... 93 F1
Murderdean Rd EH22 .... 183 D3
Murdoch Terr EH11 .... 232 A1
Murdostoun Cres ML7 .... 168 C3
Murieston Cres EH11 .... 122 C3
Murieston Crescent La
  EH11 .... 122 C3
Murieston Ct EH54 .... 174 A3
Murieston Dr EH54 .... 174 A4
Murieston East Rd EH54 .... 174 A4
Murieston Gdns EH54 .... 174 A4
Murieston Gn EH54 .... 173 F3
Murieston Gr EH54 .... 174 A3
Murieston La EH11 .... 122 C3
Murieston Pk EH54 .... 173 F3
Murieston Pl EH11 .... 122 C3
Murieston Rd
  Edinburgh EH11 .... 122 C3
  Livingston EH54 .... 173 F2
Murieston Terr EH11 .... 122 C3
Murieston Vale EH54 .... 173 F3
Murieston Valley EH54 .... 173 F3
Murieston Way EH54 .... 174 A4
Murieston West Rd EH54 ... 173 F4
Murieston Wlk EH54 .... 173 F3
Murieston Wood EH54 .... 173 F3
Murnin Ct FK7 .... 7 E2
Murnin Rd FK4 .... 58 A2
Murnin Road Ind Est FK4 .... 58 A2
Murray Cotts EH12 .... 121 D3
Murray Cres FK2 .... 60 C3
Murray Pl Cambusbarron FK7 ... 6 B3
  Stirling FK8 .... 7 D4
Murray Rd KY11 .... 46 B1
Murray Way EH54 .... 147 E4
Murray Wlk KY11 .... 29 F2

Murrayburn App EH14 .... 121 E1
Murrayburn Dr EH14 .... 121 E1
Murrayburn Gate EH14 .... 152 B4
Murrayburn Gdns EH14 ...... 121 F1
Murrayburn Gn EH14 .... 121 F1
Murrayburn Gr EH14 .... 121 F1
Murrayburn Junc EH14 .... 152 B4
Murrayburn Pk EH14 .... 121 F1
Murrayburn Pl EH14 .... 121 E1
Murrayburn Prim Sch
  EH11 .... 121 F1
Murrayburn Rd EH14 .... 121 F1
Murrayfield Ave EH12 .... 122 B4
Murrayfield Dr
  Blackburn EH47 .... 171 E4
  Edinburgh EH12 .... 122 B4
Murrayfield Gdns EH12 ...... 122 B4
Murrayfield Hospl EH12 ..... 122 A4
Murrayfield Pl
  Bannockburn FK7 .... 7 E1
  Edinburgh EH12 .... 122 B4
Murrayfield Prim Sch
  EH47 .... 145 E3
Murrayfield Rd EH12 .... 122 B4
Murrayfield Rugby Gd
  EH12 .... 122 B3
Murrayfield Terr
  Bannockburn FK7 .... 7 E1
  Blackburn EH47 .... 171 E4
Murrays Brae EH17 .... 155 E2
Murrays The EH17 .... 155 E2
Murraysgate Cres EH49 ...... 169 F3
Murraysgate Ind Est
  EH47 .... 169 F3
Murrayshall Rd FK7 .... 7 D2
Murrel Rd KY3 .... 49 E4
Murrel Terr KY3 .... 49 E4
Mus of Childhood EH1 .... 233 E3
Mus of Flight EH39 .... 74 B1
Music Hall La KY12 .... 29 D2
Musselburgh Burgry
  Prim Sch EH21 .... 126 B3
Musselburgh Gram Sch
  EH21 .... 126 B3
Musselburgh Rd
  Dalkeith EH22 .... 157 D2
  Edinburgh EH15 .... 125 F4
Musselburgh Sta EH21 .... 126 A2
Myers Ct KY12 .... 29 E3
Mylne Pl FK2 .... 39 D1
Mylneburn Gdns KY11 .... 45 E2
Myothill Rd FK6 .... 57 E4
Myre Cres KY3 .... 35 D2
Myre Dale EH19 .... 182 B3
Myreside Ct EH10 .... 122 C1
Myreside Rd EH10 .... 122 C2
Myreton KY11 .... 4 A3
Myreton Dr KY7 .... 19 F4
Myreton Rd FK3 .... 61 E3
Myreton Way FK1 .... 59 F2
Myretoungate FK12 .... 4 C3
Myrtle Cres
  Bilston EH25 .... 180 C3
  Kirkcaldy KY1 .... 17 D4
Myrtle Gr EH22 .... 183 E4
Myrtle Terr EH11 .... 122 C3

Nailer Rd Falkirk FK1 .... 59 F3
  Stirling FK7 .... 7 D1
Nairn Ct FK1 .... 60 B1
Nairn Rd EH54 .... 146 C4
Nairn St KY1 .... 17 E3
Naismith Ct FK3 .... 40 C1
Namayo Ave FK2 .... 61 D2
Namur Rd EH26 .... 204 A4
Nantwich Dr EH7 .... 94 C2
Napier Ave EH54 .... 145 E3
Napier Cres FK2 .... 60 A4
Napier Pl FK2 .... 60 A4
Napier Rd
  Edinburgh EH10 .... 123 D2
  Rosyth KY11 .... 46 B1
Napier Sq EH54 .... 148 A4
Napier St KY1 .... 17 F4
Napier Univ
  Edinburgh EH10 .... 123 D2
  Edinburgh, Craiglockhart
  EH14 .... 122 B1
  Edinburgh, Sighthill EH11 .. 121 E1
Napier Univ
  (Craiglockhart Campus)
  EH10 .... 122 C1
Nasmyth Ct EH54 .... 148 A3
Nasmyth Rd KY11 .... 46 A1
Nasmyth Sq EH54 .... 148 A3
Natal Pl KY4 .... 13 E2
National Gallery EH2 .... 232 C2
National Liby of Scotland
  EH1 .... 233 D3
National Portrait Gallery
  EH2 .... 233 D4
Navar Ct ML7 .... 192 A2
Nebit The FK12 .... 4 C3
Neidpath Ct
  Edinburgh EH12 .... 121 D4
  Longniddry EH32 .... 98 C3
Neidpath Dr FK5 .... 38 C2
Neidpath Pl KY12 .... 29 E3
Neilson Gr KY3 .... 33 F1
Neilson Park Rd EH41 .... 132 A4
Neilson Sq EH54 .... 146 B3
Neilson St FK1 .... 60 A2
Neilburn EH54 .... 146 C3
Neilfield EH16 .... 155 D4
Nelson Ave EH54 .... 147 F2
Nelson Gdns FK3 .... 40 C3
Nelson Pl FK7 .... 7 E3
Nelson Rd EH51 .... 62 C3

Nelson St Edinburgh EH3 ..... 232 C4
Grangemouth FK3 .... 61 F4
Kirkcaldy KY2 .... 17 D3
Rosyth KY11 .... 46 C3
Ness The KY12 .... 26 C1
Nether Craigour EH17 .. 124 B1
Nether Currie Cres EH14 .. 152 A3
Nether Currie Pl EH14 .. 152 A3
Nether Currie Prim Sch
EH14 .... 152 A3
Nether Currie Rd EH14 .. 152 A3
Nether Dechmont Cotts
EH54 .... 147 D4
Nether St Dysart KY1 .... 18 A4
Kirkcaldy KY1 .... 17 E3
Netherbank EH16 .... 154 C3
Netherbank View EH16 .. 154 C3
Netherbeath Rd KY4 ...... 30 C4
Netherby Rd Airth FK2 .. 22 B2
Edinburgh EH5 .... 93 D3
Netherfield Rd FK2 .... 61 E1
Nethergate KY3 .... 35 D1
Nethergate The FK12 ...... 4 C3
Netherlaw EH39 .... 54 A3
Nethermains Prim Sch
FK6 .... 36 B1
Nethermains Rd FK6 ...... 36 B1
Nethershot Rd EH32 ...... 97 C1
Netherton Gr EH47 .... 170 A2
Netherton Pl EH47 .... 170 A2
Netherton St ML7 .... 168 B3
Nethertown Broad St
KY12 .... 29 D1
Netherwood Pk EH54 .... 147 D4
Nettlehill Dr EH54 .... 116 C1
Nettlehill Rd
Livingston EH54 .... 147 F4
Uphall Station EH54 ...... 117 D1
Neucks The FK1 .... 111 D3
Nevis Cres FK10 .... 10 A4
Nevis Dr EH54 .... 173 F3
Nevis Gdns EH26 .... 204 A4
Nevis Pl Falkirk FK1 ...... 60 B1
Grangemouth FK3 .... 61 E4
Shotts ML7 .... 192 A2
New Arthur Pl EH8 .... 233 D1
New Broompark EH5 ...... 92 C4
New Carron Rd FK5 .... 39 D2
New Coll EH1 .... 232 C1
New Hallglen Rd FK1 ...... 60 B1
New Halls Rd EH30 .... 68 B1
New Holygate EH52 .... 117 E3
New Houses EH39 .... 74 B2
New Hunterfield EH23 .. 183 D1
New John's Pl EH8 .... 233 E1
New La EH6 .... 93 E3
New Line Rd FK7 .... 19 D4
New Liston Rd EH29 ...... 89 D1
New Market Rd EH14 .... 122 B2
New Mart Rd EH14 .... 122 B2
New Meadowspott
EH22 .... 157 D1
New Rd FK7 .... 7 E1
New Row Dunfermline KY12 .. 29 D2
East Fortune EH39 .... 74 A2
Kincardine FK10 .... 24 A2
Tranent EH33 .... 128 B3
New Skinners Cl EH1 .... 233 E3
New St Bridge of A FK9 .... 1 C4
Cockenzie & Port Seton
EH32 .... 97 E2
Edinburgh EH8 .... 233 E3
Musselburgh EH21 .... 126 A3
Prestonpans EH32 .... 96 C1
Slamannan FK1 .... 110 A4
Tranent EH33 .... 128 B4
New Star Bank EH22 ...... 183 D3
New Swanston EH10 ...... 153 F3
New Tower Pl EH15 .... 95 D1
New Well Wynd EH49 .... 84 C3
Newbattle Abbey Cres
EH22 .... 182 C4
Newbattle Gdns EH22 .. 157 D1
Newbattle High Sch
EH22 .... 183 E4
Newbattle Terr EH10 .... 123 D2
Newbiggin Cres FK10 ...... 4 B1
Newbiggin Rd FK3 .... 61 F3
Newbigging
Auchtertool KY2 .... 15 E1
Musselburgh EH21 .... 126 B3
Newbigging Terr KY2 .... 15 E1
Newbridge Ind Est EH28 .. 118 C3
Newbridge Rdbt EH28 .. 119 D3
Newburn Pl KY12 .... 29 E2
Newbyres Ave EH23 ...... 183 E1
Newbyres Cres EH23 .... 207 E4
Newbyres Gdns EH23 .. 207 E4
Newcarron Ct KY2 .... 60 A4
Newcraighall Bsns Pk
EH15 .... 125 D2
Newcraighall Dr EH21 .. 125 E2
Newcraighall Prim sch
EH21 .... 125 D2
Newcraighall Rd EH15 .. 125 D2
Newhailes Ave EH21 .... 126 A3
Newhailes Cres EH21 .. 126 A3
Newhailes Rd EH15 ...... 125 F3
Newhaven Pl EH6 .... 93 E4
Newhaven Rd EH6 .... 93 E3
Newhouse FK8 .... 7 D3
Newhouse Ave EH54 ...... 78 C1
Newhouse Bsns Pk FK3 .. 61 E4
Newhouse Dr FK1 .... 59 F1
Newhouse Pl EH42 .... 78 C1
Newhouse Rd FK3 .... 61 E4

Newhouses Rd EH52 .... 118 A2
Newington Rd EH9 .... 123 F3
Newland Ave EH48 .... 145 D3
Newlands Pk
Dunfermline KY12 .... 29 D3
Edinburgh EH9 .... 123 F2
Newlands Pl FK10 .... 4 B2
Newlands Rd
Bannockburn FK7 .... 19 E4
Brightons FK2 .... 82 B4
Grangemouth FK3 .... 61 E3
Newliston Dr KY2 .... 16 B4
Newmains Farm La EH29 .. 89 D1
Newmains Rd EH29 .... 89 D1
Newmarket FK7 .... 7 F1
Newmarket Ctr FK1 .... 60 A3
Newmarket St FK1 .... 60 A3
Newmill & Canthill Rd
ML7 .... 191 D3
Newmills EH10 .... 4 A2
Newmills Ave EH14 ...... 151 E2
Newmills Cres EH14 ...... 151 E2
Newmills Gr EH14 .... 151 E2
Newmills Rd Currie EH14 .. 151 E2
Dalkeith EH22 .... 157 D2
Newmills Terr EH22 ...... 157 D2
Newpark Cres FK7 .... 7 D1
Newpark Rd
Livingston EH54 .... 173 E3
Stirling FK7 .... 7 D1
Newpark Rdbt EH54 ...... 173 E4
Newtoft St EH17 .... 155 F3
Newton Ave FK2 .... 40 A2
Newton Church Rd EH22 .. 156 B4
Newton Cres KY11 .... 47 D2
Newton Pl KY11 .... 46 C2
Newton Port EH41 .... 101 D1
Newton Rd FK3 .... 40 A1
Newton St
Easthouses EH22 .... 183 E4
Edinburgh EH11 .... 122 C1
Newtongrange Prim Sch
EH22 .... 183 D3
Newtonloan St Andrew's
Prim Sch EH22 .... 183 D2
Newtonshaw FK10 .... 5 E1
Newtown EH51 .... 63 F3
Newtown St EH51 .... 63 F3
Newyearfield Bsns Pk
EH54 .... 147 E3
Newyearfield Rdbt EH54 .. 147 E3
Nicholson Way EH54 .... 147 E4
Nicklaus Gn EH54 .... 147 D4
Nicol Pl EH52 .... 117 E3
Nicol Rd EH52 .... 117 E3
Nicol St KY1 .... 17 D2
Nicolson Sq EH8 .... 233 E2
Nicolson St EH8 .... 233 E2
Nicolton Ave FK2 .... 82 C4
Nicolton Rd FK2 .... 62 A1
Niddrie Farm Gr EH16 .. 124 C2
Niddrie House Ave EH16 .. 124 C2
Niddrie House Dr EH16 .. 125 D2
Niddrie House Gdns
EH16 .... 124 C2
Niddrie House Pk EH16 .. 124 C2
Niddrie House Sq EH16 .. 124 C2
Niddrie Mains Ct EH16 .. 125 D2
Niddrie Mains Dr EH16 .. 124 C2
Niddrie Mains Rd EH16 .. 124 C2
Niddrie Mains Terr EH16 .. 124 C2
Niddrie Marischal Cres
EH16 .... 124 C2
Niddrie Marischal Dr EH16 .. 124 C2
Niddrie Marischal Gdns
EH16 .... 124 C2
Niddrie Marischal Gn
EH16 .... 124 C2
Niddrie Marischal Gr
EH16 .... 125 D2
Niddrie Marischal Loan
EH16 .... 124 C2
Niddrie Marischal Pl
EH16 .... 124 C2
Niddrie Marischal Rd
EH16 .... 125 D2
Niddrie Marischal St
EH16 .... 124 C2
Niddrie Mill Ave EH15 .. 125 D2
Niddrie Mill Cres EH15 .. 125 D2
Niddrie Mill Dr EH15 .... 125 D2
Niddrie Mill Gr EH15 .... 125 D2
Niddrie Mill Pl EH15 .... 125 D2
Niddrie Mill Prim Sch
EH15 .... 125 D2
Niddrie Mill Terr EH15 .. 125 D2
Niddry Rd EH52 .... 87 F1
Niddry St EH1 .... 233 D3
Niddry St S EH1 .... 233 E2
Niddry View EH52 .... 87 F1
Nidrie Cotts EH15 .... 125 E2
Nielson Ct EH47 .... 171 D4
Nigel Loan EH16 .... 155 D4
Nigel Rise EH54 .... 147 F1
Nile Gr EH10 .... 123 D2
Nile St KY2 .... 17 D3
Nimmo Ave EH32 .... 97 D1
Ninian Rd EH51 .... 62 C3
Ninth St EH22 .... 183 D3
Nisbet Dr FK6 .... 36 B1
Nisbet Rd EH31 .... 51 F1
Nith St KY11 .... 29 F1
Nithsdale St ML7 .... 191 E3
Niven Rd KY11 .... 47 E2
Niven's Knowe Rd EH20 .. 180 C4
Niven017knowe Pk EH20 .. 180 C4

No 7 Pit Rd KY4 .... 13 E2
Nobel Pl EH25 .... 180 C2
Nobel View FK2 .... 82 A4
Noble Pl EH6 .... 94 A2
Norman Rise EH54 .... 147 F1
Normand Brae KY1 .... 18 A4
Normand Rd KY1 .... 18 A4
North Approach Rd FK10 .. 23 F2
North Ave FK2 .... 83 D4
North Bank Rd EH32 .... 127 F4
North Bank St EH1 .... 233 D3
North Berwick High Sch
EH39 .... 54 B3
North Bridge EH1 .... 233 D3
North Bridge St
Bathgate EH48 .... 145 D3
Grangemouth FK3 .... 40 B1
North Bughtlin Bank EH12 .. 91 D1
North Bughtlin Brae EH12 .. 91 D1
North Bughtlin Gate EH12 .. 91 D1
North Bughtlin Neuk
EH12 .... 91 D1
North Bughtlin Pl EH12 .. 91 D1
North Bughtlin Rd EH12 .. 91 D1
North Bughtlinfield EH12 .. 91 D1
North Bughtlinrig EH12 .. 91 D1
North Bughtlinside EH12 .. 91 D1
North Cairntow EH16 .. 124 B3
North Castle St Alloa FK10 .. 10 A3
Edinburgh EH2 .... 232 B4
North Charlotte St EH2 .. 232 B3
North Clyde Street La
EH3 .... 93 D1
North East Circus Pl EH3 .. 93 D1
North East Cumberland
Street La EH3 .... 93 E1
North East Thistle
Street La EH2 .... 232 C4
North Esk Lodge
(Loretto Jun Sch) EH21 .. 126 B3
North Esk Rd KY1 .... 46 B1
North Fort St EH6 .... 93 F3
North Gate EH48 .... 113 F3
North Grange Ave EH32 .. 96 C1
North Grange Gr EH32 .. 96 C1
North Grange Rd EH32 .. 96 C1
North Greendykes Rd
EH52 .... 117 F4
North Greens EH15 ...... 125 D3
North Gyle Ave EH12 .. 121 D3
North Gyle Dr EH12 ...... 121 D4
North Gyle Farm Ct
EH12 .... 121 D3
North Gyle Farm La
EH12 .... 121 D3
North Gyle Gr EH12 ...... 121 D3
North Gyle Loan EH12 .. 121 D4
North Gyle Pk EH12 ...... 121 D4
North Gyle Rd EH12 ...... 121 D4
North Gyle Terr EH12 .. 121 D3
North High St EH21 ...... 126 A3
North Hillhousefield EH6 .. 93 F3
North Junction St EH6 .. 93 F3
North Larches KY11 .... 29 F2
North Leith Sands EH6 .. 93 F3
North Loanhead KY11 .... 45 F2
North Lorimer Pl EH32 .. 97 D2
North Main St FK2 .... 39 E2
North Meggetland EH14 .. 122 C2
North Overgate KY3 ...... 34 C2
North Park Terr EH4 ...... 93 D1
North Peffer Pl EH16 .. 124 B2
North Prim Sch KY2 ...... 17 D3
North Queensferry Sta
KY11 .... 68 B3
North Rd Dunbar EH42 .. 78 B2
Fauldhouse EH47 .... 193 F4
Inverkeithing KY11 .... 47 E2
North Reeves Pl EH47 .. 170 A3
North Roundall KY11 .... 45 F2
North Row KY11 .... 45 D2
North Seton Pk EH32 .... 97 E2
North Shore Rd FK3 ...... 40 C1
North St Alloa FK10 .... 10 A4
Armadale EH48 .... 143 F3
Bo'ness EH51 .... 63 F4
Clackmannan FK10 .... 11 D2
Dunbar EH42 .... 78 A1
Falkirk FK2 .... 60 A4
Lochgelly KY5 .... 14 A4
Ratho EH28 .... 119 E1
Stirling FK9 .... 2 B1
North St Andrew La EH2 .. 233 D4
North St Andrew St EH2 .. 233 D4
North St David St EH2 .. 233 D4
North View Burntisland KY3 .. 50 C4
West Calder EH55 .... 172 B2
North Way KY11 .... 48 B3
North Werber Pk EH4 .... 92 C2
North Werber Pl EH4 .... 92 C2
North West Circus Pl
EH3 .... 93 D1
North West Cumberland
Street La EH3 .... 93 E1
North West Thistle
Street La
EH2 .... 232 C4
North Wood Rd FK10 ...... 4 B1
North Wynd EH22 .... 157 D2
Northbank Cl EH51 .... 64 A3
Northbank Dr EH51 ...... 64 A3
Northbank Pk EH51 ...... 63 F3
Northbank Rd KY12 ...... 27 E1
Northend FK7 .... 6 B3

Northfield
Cowdenbeath KY4 .... 13 E3
Tranent EH33 .... 128 C3
Northfield Ave
Edinburgh EH8 .... 124 B4
Shotts ML7 .... 192 A1
Northfield Broadway
EH8 .... 124 C4
Northfield Cir EH8 .... 124 B4
Northfield Cotts EH55 .. 172 B2
Northfield Cres
Edinburgh EH8 .... 124 C4
Longridge EH47 .... 170 B1
Northfield Ct EH32 ...... 127 F4
Northfield Dr EH8 .... 124 C4
Northfield E EH33 .... 128 C3
Northfield Farm Ave
EH8 .... 124 C4
Northfield Farm Rd EH8 .. 124 C4
Northfield Gdns
Clackmannan FK10 .... 11 D2
Edinburgh EH8 .... 124 C4
Prestonpans EH32 .... 127 F4
Northfield Gr EH8 .... 124 C4
Northfield Mdws EH47 .. 170 B1
Northfield Park Gr EH8 .. 124 C4
Northfield Pk EH8 .... 124 C4
Northfield Rd Denny FK6 .. 36 B2
Edinburgh EH8 .... 124 B4
Northfield Sq EH8 .... 124 C4
Northfield Terr
Edinburgh EH8 .... 124 B4
Longridge EH47 .... 170 B1
Northflat Pl ML8 .... 230 A1
Northlawn Ct EH4 .... 91 F2
Northlawn Terr EH4 ...... 91 F2
Northrig Cotts EH41 .... 133 D4
Northumberland
Place La EH3 .... 232 C4
Northumberland St EH3 .. 232 C4
Northumberland Street
North East La EH3 .... 93 E1
Northumberland Street
North West La EH3 ...... 232 C4
Northumberland Street
South East La EH3 ...... 232 C4
Northumberland Street
South West La EH3 ...... 232 C4
Northwood Pk EH54 .... 146 C4
Norton Pk EH7 .... 94 A1
Norton Pl KY11 .... 29 F1
Norton St KY12 .... 5 D4
Norval PI KY11 .... 46 C2
Norwood Ave Alloa FK10 .. 9 F4
Bonnybridge FK4 .... 58 A4
Whitburn EH47 .... 170 A3
Norwood Cres FK10 .... 9 F4
Norwood Ct
Bonnybridge FK4 .... 58 A4
Whitburn EH47 .... 170 A3
Norwood Gr FK10 .... 9 F4
Norwood Pl FK4 .... 58 A4
Novar Cres KY1 .... 17 D1
Nungate Rd EH39 .... 54 A4
Nunraw Abbey EH41 .... 134 C1
Nursery Rd FK1 .... 59 F2

Oak Ave EH20 .... 180 C4
Oak Bank FK2 .... 61 D1
Oak Cres Mayfield EH22 .. 183 F3
Plean FK7 .... 20 B2
Oak Dr Fallin FK7 .... 8 B2
Larbert FK5 .... 38 B1
Oak Gr Dunfermline KY11 .. 46 C4
Livingston EH54 .... 148 A3
Oak La EH12 .... 91 F1
Oak Pl EH22 .... 183 F3
Oak St FK3 .... 61 C1
Oakbank Ave EH53 ...... 148 C1
Oakbank Cotts EH53 .... 172 B3
Oakbank Park Dr EH53 .. 174 B4
Oakbank Park Rd EH53 .. 174 B4
Oakbank Park Way EH54 .. 174 A4
Oakbank Pk EH54 .... 174 A4
Oakbank Pl EH52 .... 88 A1
Oakbank Rd EH53 .... 148 C1
Oakbank Rdbt EH53 .... 174 B4
Oakfield Pl EH8 .... 233 E2
Oakfield St K 12 C4
Oakhill View FK2 .... 83 D3
Oaklands EH11 .... 121 F2
Oaktree Ct KY1 .... 17 E4
Oaktree Junc EH41 ...... 131 D4
Oaktree Sq KY1 .... 17 E4
Oakville Terr EH6 .... 94 A2
Oatlands Pk EH49 .... 85 D3
Oatridge Ag Coll EH52 .. 116 C4
Oberon FK10 .... 9 F4
Observatory Gn EH9 .... 123 F1
Observatory Rd EH9 .... 123 F1
Ochil Ave KY2 .... 16 C3
Ochil Cres FK8 .... 2 A1
Ochil Ct Queensferry EH30 .. 89 E4
Tullibody FK10 .... 4 B2
Ochil Dr Maddiston FK2 .. 83 D3
Stenhousemuir FK5 .... 38 C2
Ochil La EH47 .... 169 F3
Ochil Rd Alva FK12 .... 10 A4
Menstrie FK11 .... 4 A4
Stirling FK9 .... 2 B2
Ochil St Alloa FK10 .... 10 A4
Fallin FK7 .... 8 B2
Grangemouth FK3 .... 61 E4
Tullibody FK10 .... 4 B2
Ochil Terr KY11 .... 29 F1
Ochil View Denny FK6 .... 57 E4
Kincardine FK10 .... 23 E2
Shieldhill FK1 .... 81 E4

Ochilmount KY7 .... 7 F1
Ochiltree Cres EH53 .... 148 A1
Ochiltree Ct EH53 .... 148 A1
Ochiltree Dr EH53 .... 148 A1
Ochiltree Gdns EH16 .. 124 B1
Ochiltree Terr FK1 .... 59 D3
Ochilview Alva FK12 .... 5 D4
Cowdenbeath KY4 .... 13 E3
Cowie FK7 .... 20 C3
Ochilview Dr KY12 .... 26 A1
Ochilview Pk
(Stenhousemuir FC)
FK5 .... 38 B2
Ochilview Pl EH51 .... 63 F3
Ochilview Rd EH51 .... 63 F3
Ochilview Terr EH51 ...... 63 F3
Ochville Terr FK10 .... 5 E2
Octavia St KY2 .... 17 D3
Ogilface Cres EH48 .... 142 B1
Ogilvie Pl FK9 .... 2 A3
Ogilvie Rd FK8 .... 7 D3
Ogilvie Terr EH11 .... 122 C2
Ogilvie Way EH47 .... 147 E4
Ogilvy Cres EH47 .... 193 C3
Old Abbey Rd EH39 .... 54 A4
Old Bellsdyke Rd FK5 .... 38 A2
Old Bridge St FK10 .... 10 A3
Old Broughton EH3 ...... 93 E1
Old Burdiehouse Rd
EH17 .... 155 D2
Old Church La EH15 .... 124 B3
Old Craighall Junc EH21 .. 126 A1
Old Craighall Rd EH22 .. 156 C4
Old Dalkeith Rd EH22 .. 156 B3
Old Dean Rd EH32 .... 98 B2
Old Denny Rd FK5 .... 38 A2
Old Drove Rd
Cambusbarron FK7 .... 6 B3
West Linton EH46 .... 219 D2
Old Eastfield St ML7 .... 168 B3
Old Edinburgh Rd EH22 .. 156 C2
Old Farm Ave EH13 ...... 153 E4
Old Farm Pl EH13 .... 153 D4
Old Fishmarket Cl EH1 .. 233 D3
Old Forge Gr KY12 .... 26 C4
Old Hillview Pl KY4 .... 30 C3
Old Kirk Pl KY12 .... 29 E2
Old Kirk Rd
Dunfermline KY12 .... 29 E2
Edinburgh EH12 .... 121 F4
North Queensferry KY11 .. 68 B3
Old Linbun Rd KY12 ...... 29 F2
Old Liston Rd EH28 ...... 119 D3
Old Mill Ct EH47 .... 170 C4
Old Mill Ctyd The KY11 .. 29 D1
Old Mill Gr EH47 .... 170 C4
Old Mill La
Edinburgh EH16 .... 124 A1
Gifford EH41 .... 163 F3
Oakley KY12 .... 26 C3
Old Mill Rd
Broxburn EH52 .... 117 F3
Shotts ML7 .... 191 D1
Old Newmills Rd EH14 .. 151 E2
Old Orch The KY11 .... 45 E2
Old Perth Rd KY4 .... 13 D2
Old Redding Rd FK2 ...... 60 C2
Old Refinery Rd FK3 ...... 62 A4
Old School Ct FK10 .... 4 A1
Old Star Rd EH22 .... 183 D3
Old Tolbooth Wynd EH8 .. 233 E3
Old Town Bannockburn FK7 .. 7 E1
Broxburn EH52 .... 117 F3
Oldwalls Pl FK3 .... 61 F4
Oldwalls Rd FK3 .... 62 B4
Oldwood Pl EH54 .... 147 D2
Olive Bank Rd EH21 .... 126 A3
Oliver Rd FK1 .... 60 B2
Olympia Arc KY1 .... 17 D2
Onich Pl ML7 .... 192 A2
Onslow St EH54 .... 148 A3
Orchard Bank EH4 .... 92 C1
Orchard Brae EH4 .... 92 C1
Orchard Brae Ave EH4 .. 92 C1
Orchard Brae Gdns EH4 .. 92 C1
Orchard Brae Gdns W
EH4 .... 92 C1
Orchard Brae W EH4 .... 92 C1
Orchard Cres
Edinburgh EH4 .... 92 B1
Prestonpans EH32 .... 96 C1
Orchard Ct
East Linton EH40 .... 103 F4
Kinghorn KY3 .... 35 D2
Longniddry EH32 .... 98 B2
Orchard Dr EH4 .... 92 B1
Orchard Gdns KY3 .... 35 D2
Orchard Gr Edinburgh EH4 .. 92 C1
Haddington EH41 .... 101 D1
Kincardine FK10 .... 23 F2
Maddiston FK2 .... 83 D3
Polmont FK2 .... 61 F1
Orchard House Hospl FK8 .. 2 A1
Orchard La
Dunfermline KY11 .... 29 E1
Dysart KY1 .... 18 A4
Orchard Pl Dysart KY1 .. 18 A4
Edinburgh EH4 .... 92 C1
Livingston EH54 .... 147 D3
Orchard Rd Bridge of A FK9 .. 2 A3
Edinburgh EH4 .... 92 C1
Grangemouth FK3 .... 62 B4
Kinghorn KY3 .... 34 C2
Orchard Rd S EH4 .... 92 B1
Orchard Sq KY11 .... 45 E2

Orchard St Falkirk FK1 .... **60** A3
Grangemouth FK3 .... **61** E4
Orchard Terr
Clackmannan FK10 .... **11** E1
Edinburgh EH4 .... **92** C1
Kinghorn KY3 .... **34** C2
Torryburn KY12 .... **26** C1
Orchard The
Brightons FK2 .... **82** B4
Crossford KY12 .... **28** A1
Ormiston EH35 .... **159** F4
Tranent EH33 .... **128** B4
Tullibody FK10 .... **4** A1
Orchard Toll EH4 .... **92** C1
Orchard View EH22 .... **156** C1
Orchardcroft FK8 .... **7** D4
Orchardfield EH40 .... **103** E4
Orchardfield Ave EH12 ..... **121** E3
Orchardfield Terr EH27 ..... **150** A3
Orchardhead Loan EH16 ..... **155** D4
Orchardhead Rd EH16 ..... **155** D4
Ordnance Rd KY12 .... **44** B4
Oriel Cres KY2 .... **17** D2
Oriel Rd KY2 .... **16** C3
Orkney Ct FK10 .... **10** A3
Kirkcaldy KY1 .... **17** F4
Orkney Pl Falkirk FK1 ..... **60** A1
Orlit Cotts EH39 .... **74** B2
Ormelie Terr EH15 .... **125** E4
Ormidale Terr EH12 .... **122** B4
Ormiston Ave EH33 .... **128** C3
Ormiston Cres E EH33 ..... **128** C3
Ormiston Cres W EH33 ..... **128** C3
Ormiston Dr Alloa FK10 ..... **4** C1
East Calder EH53 .... **149** D2
Ormiston Pk KY12 .... **29** E3
Ormiston Pl EH32 .... **96** C1
Ormiston Prim Sch EH35 .. **159** F4
Ormiston Rd EH33 .... **128** B3
Orr Terr ML7 .... **168** B2
Orrin Gr KY11 .... **48** A2
Orrock Dr KY3 .... **33** F1
Orrock Pk EH16 .... **124** A1
Orwell Pl
Dunfermline KY12 .... **29** E2
Edinburgh EH11 .... **122** C4
Orwell Prim Sch EH10 .... **122** C3
Orwell Terr EH11 .... **122** C4
Osborne Ct EH32 .... **97** E2
Osborne Dr FK10 .... **23** F2
Osborne Gdns FK1 .... **59** F2
Osborne St FK1 .... **59** F2
Osborne Terr
Cockenzie & Port Seton
EH32 .... **97** E2
Edinburgh EH12 .... **122** C4
Ossian Dr EH54 .... **173** F3
Oswald Ave FK3 .... **61** F4
Oswald Ct EH9 .... **123** E2
Oswald Rd EH9 .... **123** E2
Oswald St FK1 .... **60** A2
Oswald Terr EH12 .... **121** E3
Oswalds Wynd KY1 .... **17** E2
Otterburn Pk EH14 .... **153** D4
Otterston Gr KY11 .... **48** A2
Otterston Pl KY2 .... **16** C3
Oudenarde Ct ML8 .... **230** A1
Our Lady of Lourdes
RC Prim Sch EH47 ..... **171** D1
Our Lady's RC Prim Sch
EH47 .... **171** D1
Overhaven KY11 .... **45** F2
Overton Cres Denny FK6 .. **36** B1
East Calder EH53 .... **149** D2
Redding FK2 .... **61** D1
Overton Mains KY1 .... **17** F4
Overton Rd
Grangemouth, Bowhouse
FK3 .... **61** E3
Grangemouth, Oil Refinery
FK3 .... **62** A4
Kirkcaldy KY1 .... **17** E4
Owen sq KY11 .... **147** E1
Oxcars Dr KY11 .... **48** A2
Oxcraig St EH5 .... **92** C4
Oxenfoord Ave EH37 ..... **185** D3
Oxenfoord Dr EH37 .... **185** D3
Oxford St EH8 .... **233** F1
Oxford Terr EH4 .... **232** A4
Oxgang Rd FK3 .... **61** F4
Oxgangs Ave EH13 .... **153** F3
Oxgangs Bank EH13 .... **153** F3
Oxgangs Brae EH13 .... **153** F3
Oxgangs Broadway EH13 .. **153** F3
Oxgangs Cres EH13 .... **153** F4
Oxgangs Dr EH13 .... **153** F4
Oxgangs Farm Ave EH13 .. **153** F3
Oxgangs Farm Dr EH13 .. **153** F3
Oxgangs Farm Gdns
EH13 .... **153** F3
Oxgangs Farm Gr EH13 .. **153** F3
Oxgangs Farm Loan
EH13 .... **153** F3
Oxgangs Farm Terr EH13 .. **153** F3
Oxgangs Gdns EH13 .... **153** F4
Oxgangs Gn EH13 .... **154** F3
Oxgangs Gr EH13 .... **154** F3
Oxgangs Hill EH13 .... **153** F4
Oxgangs Ho EH13 .... **153** F4
Oxgangs Loan EH13 .... **154** F4
Oxgangs Medway EH13 .. **153** F3
Oxgangs Path EH13 .... **153** F3
Oxgangs Pk EH13 .... **153** F3
Oxgangs Pl EH13 .... **153** F4
Oxgangs Prim Sch EH13 .. **153** E4

Oxgangs Rd EH10 .... **154** A3
Oxgangs Rd N EH13 .... **153** F4
Oxgangs Rise EH13 .... **153** F4
Oxgangs Row EH13 .... **153** F3
Oxgangs St EH13 .... **153** F3
Oxgangs Terr EH13 .... **153** F3
Oxgangs View EH13 .... **153** F3

Paddock The Gullane EH31 .. **52** A1
Musselburgh EH21 .... **126** B4
North Berwick EH39 .... **54** B3
Paddockholm The EH12 .. **121** F3
Page St KY5 .... **14** A4
Paisley Ave EH8 .... **124** B4
Paisley Cres EH8 .... **124** B4
Paisley Dr EH8 .... **124** B4
Paisley Gdns EH8 .... **124** B4
Paisley Gn EH8 .... **124** B4
Paisley Terr EH8 .... **124** B4
Palmer Pl EH14 .... **151** F2
Palmer Rd EH14 .... **151** F2
Palmer Rise EH54 .... **147** F1
Palmerston Pl EH12 .... **232** A3
Palmerston Place La
EH12 .... **232** A2
Palmerston Rd EH9 .... **123** E3
Pan Ha' KY1 .... **18** A3
Panbrae Rd EH51 .... **63** F4
Pankhurst Loan EH22 ..... **157** E2
Panmure Pl EH3 .... **232** C1
Pannie Rd KY1 .... **17** E4
Panstead St FK3 .... **61** F4
Panton Gn EH54 .... **147** D4
Papana Cotts EH41 .... **134** B1
Papple Farm Cotts EH41 .. **134** B3
Paradise La FK10 .... **23** F2
Paradykes Ave EH20 ..... **181** D4
Paradykes Prim Sch EH20 .. **181** D4
Pardovan Cres EH49 .... **86** B4
Pardovan Pl KY11 .... **59** F3
Pariothall **9** EH3 .... **93** D1
Paris Ave EH8 .... **124** B4
Paris St FK3 .... **61** F4
Park Ave Bankhead FK4 .. **57** F3
Bilston EH25 .... **180** B3
Brightons FK2 .... **82** B4
Cowdenbeath KY4 .... **13** E2
Dunbar EH42 .... **78** B1
Dunfermline KY12 .... **29** D2
Edinburgh EH15 .... **125** D4
Gorebridge EH23 .... **183** E1
Laurieston FK2 .... **60** C2
Loanhead EH20 .... **181** D4
Musselburgh EH21 .... **126** C3
Stenhousemuir FK5 .... **38** B1
Stirling FK8 .... **7** D4
Park Cres Alloa FK10 ..... **5** E1
Bannockburn FK7 .... **7** E1
Bonnyrigg and Lasswade
EH19 .... **182** A4
Easthouses EH22 .... **183** E4
Edinburgh EH16 .... **155** D4
Falkirk FK2 .... **39** D1
Gifford EH41 .... **163** F3
Loanhead EH20 .... **181** D4
Westquarter FK2 .... **61** D2
Park Ct Broxburn EH52 .. **117** D3
Musselburgh EH21 .... **126** C3
Park Dr Bannockburn FK7 .. **7** E1
Brightons FK2 .... **82** B4
Stenhousemuir FK5 .... **38** B1
West Calder EH55 .... **173** D3
Park Gdns Bannockburn FK7 .. **7** E1
Edinburgh EH16 .... **155** D4
Musselburgh EH21 .... **126** C3
Park Gr Broxburn EH52 .. **117** D3
Edinburgh EH16 .... **155** D4
Park Grove Pl EH21 .... **126** C3
Park Grove Terr EH21 ..... **126** C3
Park Hill EH23 .... **183** D1
Park La Aberdour KY3 .. **49** D4
Bo'ness EH51 .... **64** A4
Edinburgh EH15 .... **125** D4
Haddington EH41 .... **131** F4
Musselburgh EH21 .... **126** C3
Stirling FK8 .... **7** D4
Park Lea KY11 .... **47** D3
Park Par EH47 .... **193** F3
Park Pl Alloa FK10 .... **10** B4
Clackmannan FK10 .... **11** D2
Dunfermline KY12 .... **29** D2
Edinburgh EH6 .... **93** E3
Hill of B KY4 .... **30** C4
Kinghorn KY3 .... **34** C1
Kirkcaldy KY1 .... **17** D2
Livingston EH54 .... **147** D3
Stirling FK7 .... **7** D4
Park Prim Sch FK10 ..... **10** A3
Park Rd Blackridge EH48 .. **142** C2
Bonnyrigg and Lasswade
EH19 .... **182** A4
Broxburn EH52 .... **117** D3
Cockenzie & Port Seton
EH32 .... **97** E2
Cowdenbeath KY4 .... **13** D2
Dalkeith EH22 .... **156** C1
Edinburgh EH6 .... **93** E3
Falkirk FK2 .... **39** D1
Gifford EH41 .... **163** F3
Gorebridge EH23 .... **183** E1
Grangemouth FK3 .... **61** E4
Harthill ML7 .... **169** D3
Kirkcaldy KY1 .... **17** F4
Menstrie FK11 .... **4** A3
Newtongrange EH22 ..... **183** D3
Ormiston EH35 .... **159** D3
Rosyth KY11 .... **46** C3
Shotts ML7 .... **191** E3

Park Rd W KY11 .... **46** B3
Park Road Prim Sch KY11 .. **47** D2
Park St Alva FK12 .... **5** D4
Cowdenbeath KY4 .... **13** E2
Cowie FK7 .... **20** C4
Falkirk FK1 .... **60** A3
High Bonnybridge FK4 .. **58** B2
Lochgelly KY5 .... **14** A4
Park Terr Brightons FK2 .. **82** B4
Broxburn EH52 .... **117** D3
Kirknewton EH27 .... **149** F1
Newcraighall EH21 .... **125** F2
Stirling FK8 .... **7** D3
Tullibody FK10 .... **4** A1
Park View Brightons FK2 .. **82** C4
Broxburn EH52 .... **117** D3
Fauldhouse EH47 .... **193** F4
Kirkcaldy KY2 .... **16** C3
Loanhead EH20 .... **181** D4
Musselburgh EH21 .... **126** C3
Pencaitland EH34 .... **160** C4
Prestonpans EH32 .... **97** D1
Stoneyburn EH47 .... **171** E1
Westfield EH48 .... **112** C2
Whitburn EH47 .... **170** A4
Park View E EH32 .... **97** E2
Park View Terr KY11 .... **47** D1
Park View W EH32 .... **97** E2
Park-View EH32 .... **98** C3
Parkandarroch Cres
ML8 .... **230** A1
Parkdyke FK7 .... **6** C3
Parkend Cres FK1 .... **81** E3
Parker Ave EH7 .... **94** C1
Parker Rd EH7 .... **94** C1
Parker Terr EH7 .... **94** C1
Parkfoot Ct KY1 .... **60** A2
Parkgate Alva FK12 .... **4** C3
Rosyth KY11 .... **46** C2
Parkgrove Ave EH4 .... **91** E1
Parkgrove Bank EH4 .... **91** E1
Parkgrove Cres EH4 .... **91** E1
Parkgrove Dr EH4 .... **91** E1
Parkgrove Gdns EH4 .... **91** E1
Parkgrove Gn EH4 .... **91** E1
Parkgrove Loan EH4 .... **91** E1
Parkgrove Neuk EH4 .... **91** E1
Parkgrove Path EH4 .... **91** E1
Parkgrove Pl EH4 .... **91** E1
Parkgrove Rd EH4 .... **91** E1
Parkgrove Row EH4 .... **91** E1
Parkgrove St EH4 .... **91** E1
Parkgrove Terr EH4 .... **91** E1
Parkgrove View EH4 .... **91** E1
Parkhall Dr FK2 .... **83** D3
Parkhead Ave EH11 .... **121** F1
Parkhead Cotts EH55 ..... **172** C1
Parkhead Cres
Edinburgh EH11 .... **121** F1
West Calder EH55 .... **172** C2
Parkhead Ct FK10 .... **10** B4
Parkhead Dr EH11 .... **121** F1
Parkhead Gdns
Edinburgh EH11 .... **121** F1
West Calder EH55 .... **172** C2
Parkhead Loan EH11 ..... **121** F1
Parkhead Pk EH22 .... **183** E4
Parkhead Pl
Easthouses EH22 .... **183** E4
Edinburgh EH11 .... **121** F1
Parkhead Prim Sch
EH55 .... **172** C2
Parkhead Rd Alloa FK10 .. **10** B4
Linlithgow EH49 .... **84** C4
Parkhead St EH11 .... **121** F1
Parkhead Terr EH11 .... **121** F1
Parkhead View EH11 .... **121** F1
Parkland Gr Comrie KY12 .. **26** B4
Stoneyburn EH47 .... **170** C1
Parklands EH52 .... **117** E2
Parklands Cres KY11 .... **48** A2
Parkneuk Rd KY12 .... **28** B3
Parkside EH28 .... **119** D3
Parkside Ct Dalkeith EH22 .. **157** D2
Plean FK7 .... **20** B2
Parkside Pl EH22 .... **157** D2
Parkside Rd ML7 .... **191** E3
Parkside Sq KY11 .... **47** D2
Parkside St
Edinburgh EH8 .... **233** F1
Rosyth KY11 .... **46** C2
Parkside Terr EH16 .... **233** F1
Parkvale Pl EH47 .... **94** A2
Parkview Ave FK1 .... **59** F1
Parkway FK10 .... **10** A4
Parkwood Cres EH52 ..... **117** E2
Parkwood Gdns EH52 ..... **117** E3
Parliament Sq EH1 .... **233** D3
Parliament St EH6 .... **93** F3
Parrotshot EH15 .... **125** D3
Parsonage The EH21 ..... **126** B3
Parsons Green Prim Sch
EH8 .... **124** B4
Parsons Green Terr 1
EH8 .... **94** B1
Parsonspool
Bonnyrigg and Lasswade
EH19 .... **182** B3
Dunbar EH42 .... **78** B1
Paterson Dr FK1 .... **81** E3
Paterson Pl Bonnybridge
FK4 .... **58** B3
Bridge of A FK9 .... **2** A3
Paterson Way KY11 .... **29** D1
Paterson's Ct EH52 .... **117** F3
Path Brae EH29 .... **89** D1

Path The Bannockburn FK7 .. **7** E1
Kirkcaldy KY1 .... **17** E3
Pathead Prim Sch KY1 .. **17** D1
Pathfoot Ave FK9 .... **2** B4
Pathfoot Dr FK9 .... **2** B4
Pathfoot Rd KY1 .... **17** E3
Pathhead Ct KY1 .... **17** E3
Pathhead Prim Sch
EH37 .... **185** D2
Patie's Rd EH14 .... **153** E4
Paton Ct Alloa FK10 .... **10** A4
Dunfermline KY12 .... **29** E3
Patrick Dr FK1 .... **81** F4
Patterson La KY4 .... **13** E2
Patterson Pl KY2 .... **17** D3
Patterson St KY2 .... **17** D3
Pattison St EH6 .... **94** A3
Pattle Ct EH39 .... **54** A4
Paul Dr FK2 .... **22** C2
Paul Pl KY4 .... **13** E2
Paul St KY5 .... **14** A3
Pavilion View FK10 .... **9** F4
Paxstone Cl ML7 .... **168** C3
Paxstone Dr ML7 .... **168** C3
Paxton Cres KY5 .... **14** A4
Paxton Pl KY5 .... **14** A4
Peachdales EH41 .... **131** F4
Peacock Ct EH6 .... **93** E4
Peacocktail Cl EH15 .... **125** D2
Pearce Ave EH12 .... **121** E4
Pearce Gr EH12 .... **121** E4
Pearce Rd EH12 .... **121** E4
Pearson Ave FK4 .... **57** E3
Pearson Pl FK4 .... **57** E3
Peathill Rd FK4 .... **58** A3
Peatville Gdns EH14 ..... **122** A1
Peatville Terr EH14 .... **122** A1
Peddie Pl FK3 .... **61** F4
Peden St ML7 .... **168** B3
Peebles Rd EH26 .... **203** F2
Peebles St KY1 .... **35** D4
Peel Pentland Ctr
EH20 .... **155** D1
Peel Prim Sch EH54 ..... **147** E2
Peel Rdbt EH54 .... **147** E2
Peel Terr EH9 .... **123** F2
Peffer Bank EH16 .... **124** B2
Peffer Ind Est EH16 .... **124** B2
Peffer Pl EH16 .... **124** B2
Peffer St EH16 .... **124** B2
Peffer's Pl EH41 .... **132** A4
Peffermill Ind Est EH16 .. **124** B2
Peffermill Prim Sch
EH16 .... **124** B2
Peffermill Rd EH16 .... **124** B2
Peggy's Mill Rd EH4 .... **91** D2
Peirson Rd KY11 .... **29** F2
Pelstream Ave FK7 .... **7** D2
Pembroke Pl EH12 .... **122** C4
Pembroke St FK5 .... **38** B2
Pencaitland Prim Sch
EH34 .... **160** C3
Pencraig Brae EH40 .... **103** E3
Penders La FK1 .... **60** A3
Pendreich Ave EH19 ..... **182** B4
Pendreich Dr EH19 .... **182** B4
Pendreich Gr EH19 .... **182** B4
Pendreich Terr EH19 ..... **182** B4
Pendreich View EH19 ..... **182** B4
Pendreich Way FK9 .... **2** A2
Penicuik High Sch EH26 .. **203** F1
Penicuik St EH26 .... **180** C2
Pennelton Pl EH51 .... **63** F3
Pennyschool Pl FK10 ..... **11** D2
Pennywell Ct EH4 .... **92** A3
Pennywell Gdns EH4 ..... **92** A3
Pennywell Gr EH4 .... **92** A3
Pennywell Medway EH4 .. **92** A3
Pennywell Pl EH4 .... **92** A3
Pennywell Rd EH4 .... **92** A3
Pennywell Villas EH4 ..... **92** A3
Pentland Ave
Bathgate EH48 .... **145** F3
Currie EH14 .... **151** F2
Edinburgh EH13 .... **153** D4
Newton Grange EH23 ..... **183** D2
Penicuik EH26 .... **203** F1
Pentland Cres
Edinburgh EH10 .... **154** A4
Rosewell EH24 .... **181** F1
Pentland Ct Bilston EH25 .. **180** C3
Dalgety Bay KY11 .... **48** B2
Pentland Dr
Edinburgh EH10 .... **153** F3
Whitburn EH47 .... **170** B3
Pentland Gait Off Pk
EH11 .... **121** D1
Pentland Gr EH10 .... **154** A4
Pentland Hills
Regional Pk EH14, EH26 .. **201** E4
Pentland Ind Est EH20 .. **181** D4
Pentland Pk
Livingston EH54 .... **148** A2
Loanhead EH20 .... **180** C4
Pentland Pl Currie EH14 .. **151** F2
Kirkcaldy KY2 .... **16** C3
Pentland Rd
Bonnyrigg and Lasswade
EH19 .... **182** A4
Edinburgh EH13 .... **153** D4
Edinburgh, Old Pentland
EH10 .... **154** B1
Pentland Rise KY11 .... **48** B2
Pentland Terr
Dunfermline KY11 .... **29** F1
Edinburgh EH10 .... **154** A4
High Valleyfield KY12 ..... **26** A1
Penicuik EH26 .... **203** F3

Pentland View Currie EH14 . **151** F2
Dalkeith EH22 .... **157** E1
Edinburgh EH10 .... **154** A3
Uphall EH52 .... **117** D2
Pentland View Cres
EH25 .... **180** C2
Pentland View Ct EH54 .. **147** D3
Pentland View Pl EH25 .. **180** C2
Pentland View Rd
Kirkliston EH29 .... **89** D1
Roslin EH25 .... **180** C2
Pentland View Terr EH25 . **180** C2
Pentland Way FK3 .... **61** E2
Pentland Wlk EH47 .... **170** B3
Pentlands Gdns EH10 ..... **154** A4
Peppercraig Quarry
Ind Site EH41 .... **100** C1
Percival St KY2 .... **17** D3
Perdieus Mount KY12 ..... **29** D1
Perdrixknowe EH14 .... **122** B1
Perth Rd KY4 .... **13** E3
Perth St EH3 .... **93** D1
Petershill Gdns EH48 ..... **145** E4
Petershill Brae FK7 .... **7** E1
Pettigrew's Cl EH37 .... **157** D2
Pettycur Bay KY3 .... **34** C1
Pettycur Rd KY3 .... **34** C1
Peveril Rise EH54 .... **173** F4
Peveril Terr EH16 .... **155** D4
Phantassie Sq EH40 ..... **103** F4
Philip Ave Bathgate EH48 .. **145** F3
Linlithgow EH49 .... **84** C4
Philip Dr FK5 .... **38** B3
Philip Pl EH26 .... **203** F4
Philip St FK2 .... **60** A4
Philpingstone La EH51 .. **64** B4
Philpingstone Rd EH51 .. **64** B4
Phoenix La EH12 .... **28** C2
Picardy Pl EH1 .... **233** D4
Pier Pl EH6 .... **93** E4
Pier Rd EH6 .... **64** B4
Pierhead Bldgs KY11 ..... **68** B3
Piersfield Gr EH8 .... **94** B1
Piersfield Pl EH8 .... **94** B1
Piersfield Terr EH8 .... **94** B1
Piershill La **7** EH8 .... **94** B1
Piershill Pl **8** EH8 .... **94** B1
Piershill Sq E EH8 .... **124** B4
Piershill Sq E EH8 .... **94** B1
Piershill Sq W EH8 .... **94** B1
Piershill Terr **9** EH8 .... **94** B1
Pike Rd FK7 .... **7** E2
Pilgrims Hill EH49 .... **85** E4
Pilkham Ct KY4 .... **13** E2
Pilmuir St KY12 .... **29** D3
Pilrig Gdns EH6 .... **93** F2
Pilrig House Cl EH6 .... **93** F2
Pilrig Ind Est EH6 .... **93** F2
Pilrig Park Sch EH6 .... **93** F2
Pilrig St EH6 .... **93** F2
Pilton Ave EH5 .... **92** C3
Pilton Cres EH5 .... **92** C3
Pilton Dr EH5 .... **92** C3
Pilton Dr N EH5 .... **92** C3
Pilton Gdns EH5 .... **92** C3
Pilton Loan EH5 .... **92** C3
Pilton Pk EH5 .... **92** C3
Pilton Pl EH5 .... **92** C3
Pine Gn EH51 .... **63** E2
Pine Gr Alloa FK10 .... **10** B3
Dunfermline KY11 .... **46** C4
Livingston EH54 .... **148** A3
Westquarter FK2 .... **61** D1
Pine St EH42 .... **78** A1
Pine Wlk FK5 .... **38** B1
Pineapple The FK2 .... **22** A3
Pinebank EH54 .... **147** F3
Pines The EH31 .... **52** A2
Pinewood Dr KY11 .... **48** A2
Pinewood Pk EH54 .... **146** C4
Pinewood Pl EH22 .... **183** F3
Pinewood Rd EH22 .... **183** F3
Pinewood Sch EH47 ..... **171** F4
Pinewood View EH22 ..... **183** F3
Pinkerton Pl KY11 .... **46** C3
Pinkhill EH12 .... **122** A3
Pinkie Ave EH21 .... **126** C3
Pinkie Dr EH21 .... **126** C3
Pinkie Hill Cres EH21 ..... **126** C3
Pinkie Pl EH21 .... **126** C3
Pinkie Rd EH21 .... **126** C3
Pinkie St Peter's Prim Sch
EH21 .... **126** C3
Pinkie Terr EH21 .... **126** C3
Pinkie Wlk EH33 .... **128** B3
Pinnel Pl KY11 .... **48** B2
Pipe La EH15 .... **95** D1
Pipe St EH15 .... **95** D1
Piper Cres KY3 .... **33** F1
Pirig Cotts KY3 .... **93** F2
Pirleyhill Dr FK1 .... **81** E3
Pirleyhill Gdns FK1 .... **60** A1
Pirnhall Rd FK7 .... **19** D4
Pirniefield Bank EH6 ..... **94** B2
Pirniefield Gdns EH6 ..... **94** B2
Pirniefield Gr EH6 .... **94** B2
Pirniefield Pl EH6 .... **94** B2
Pirniefield Terr EH6 ..... **94** B2
Pirniehall Prim Sch EH4 .. **92** B3
Pirrie St EH6 .... **93** F2
Pitbauchlie Bank KY11 .. **29** E1
Pitcairn St KY11 .... **29** E1
Pitcorthie Dr KY11 .... **46** C4
Pitcorthie Prim Sch KY11 .. **29** F1
Pitcorthie Rd KY11 .... **29** E1
Pitdinnie Pl KY12 .... **27** E1
Pitdinnie Rd KY12 .... **27** E1
Pitfairn Rd FK10 .... **5** F2

Pitfirane Pk KY12 .... 28 A1
Pitfour Pl KY2 .... 16 B4
Pitlochry Pl **4** EH7 .... 94 A1
Pitreavie Bsns Pk KY11 .... 46 B4
Pitreavie Cres KY11 .... 46 B4
Pitreavie Dr KY11 .... 46 B3
Pitreavie Rd KY11 .... 46 B3
Pitreavie Prim Sch KY11 .... 46 B4
Pitsligo Rd EH10 .... 123 D2
Pitt St EH6 .... 93 F3
Pitt Terr FK8 .... 7 D3
Pittencrieff Ct EH21 .... 126 C3
Pittencrieff House Mus KY12 .... 28 C2
Pittencrieff Prim Sch KY12 .... 28 C2
Pittencrieff St KY12 .... 28 C2
Pittville St EH15 .... 125 E4
Pittville Street La EH15 .... 125 D4
Place Charente EH22 .... 157 E1
Plane Gr KY11 .... 46 C4
Plane Pl EH42 .... 78 A1
Plantation St KY5 .... 14 A4
Player Gn EH54 .... 147 D4
Players Pl FK7 .... 7 E4
Plean Ctry Pk FK7 .... 20 A1
Pleasance Edinburgh EH8 .... 233 E2
Falkirk FK1 .... 60 A2
Pleasance Brae KY12 .... 27 F1
Pleasance Ct
13 Falkirk FK2 .... 60 A2
Halbeath KY12 .... 30 A4
Pleasance Gdns FK1 .... 60 A2
Pleasance Rd
Dunfermline KY12 .... 29 F3
Falkirk FK2 .... 60 A2
Halbeath KY12 .... 30 A3
Pleasance Row ML15 .... 215 D2
Pleasance Sq **12** FK1 .... 60 A2
Pleasance The EH32 .... 71 E2
Plewlandcroft EH30 .... 68 A1
Plewlands Ave EH10 .... 122 C1
Plewlands Gdns EH10 .... 122 C1
Plewlands Pl EH30 .... 89 D4
Plewlands Terr EH10 .... 122 C1
Pleydell Pl EH16 .... 155 D4
Plough La EH33 .... 128 B3
Plover Brae EH54 .... 147 E3
Poachers Gn FK10 .... 11 D3
Pointgarry Rd EH39 .... 54 A4
Polbeth Ave EH55 .... 172 C3
Polbeth Cres EH55 .... 172 C3
Polbeth Gdns EH55 .... 172 C3
Polbeth Ind Est EH55 .... 172 C3
Polbeth Pl EH55 .... 172 C3
Polbeth Rd EH55 .... 172 C3
Polbeth West Calder Ind Est EH55 .... 172 C3
Poldrate EH41 .... 132 A4
Polkemmet Ctry Pk EH47 .... 169 E4
Polkemmet Dr ML7 .... 169 D3
Polkemmet La ML7 .... 168 C3
Polkemmet Prim Sch EH47 .... 170 A3
Polkemmet Rd
Harthill ML7 .... 168 C3
Whitburn EH47 .... 169 F3
Pollock Halls of Residence (Univ of Edinburgh) EH16 .... 124 A3
Pollock Wlk KY12 .... 28 C3
Polmaise Ave FK7 .... 7 D2
Polmaise Cres FK7 .... 8 B3
Polmaise Ct FK7 .... 7 D2
Polmaise Rd
Cambusbarron FK7 .... 6 C2
Stirling FK7 .... 6 C3
Polmont House Gdns FK2 .... 61 F1
Polmont Pk FK2 .... 61 F1
Polmont Rd FK2 .... 61 D2
Polmont Sta FK2 .... 61 F1
Polson Gdns EH33 .... 128 A3
Polton Avenue Rd EH19 .... 182 A3
Polton Bank EH18 .... 181 F3
Polton Bank Terr EH18 .... 181 F3
Polton Cotts EH18 .... 181 E3
Polton Ct EH19 .... 182 A4
Polton Gdns EH18 .... 182 A4
Polton Pl EH19 .... 182 A4
Polton Rd
Bonnyrigg and Lasswade EH18 .... 182 A4
Loanhead EH20, EH18 .... 181 E4
Polton Rd W EH18 .... 181 F3
Polton St EH19 .... 182 A3
Polton Terr EH18 .... 182 A4
Polwarth Ave FK2 .... 82 B4
Polwarth Cres
Edinburgh EH11 .... 123 D3
Prestonpans EH32 .... 97 D1
Polwarth Gdns EH11 .... 122 C3
Polwarth Gr EH11 .... 122 C3
Polwarth Pk EH11 .... 122 C3
Polwarth Pl EH11 .... 122 C3
Polwarth Terr
Edinburgh EH11 .... 122 C2
Prestonpans EH32 .... 97 D1
Polworth Pl KY4 .... 13 E2
Pomathorn Bank EH26 .... 203 F2
Pomathorn Rd EH26 .... 203 F2
Pompee Rd FK10 .... 5 D1
Ponton St EH3 .... 232 B1
Poolewe Dr FK2 .... 61 E1
Poplar Cres KY2 .... 17 D4
Poplar Gr
Dunfermline KY11 .... 46 C4
Livingston EH54 .... 148 A3

Poplar La EH6 .... 94 A3
Poplar St Dunbar EH42 .... 78 A1
Grangemouth FK3 .... 61 E4
Mayfield EH22 .... 183 F3
Poplar Terr EH19 .... 182 A3
Poplars The FK10 .... 4 A1
Port Buchan EH52 .... 117 E3
Port Edgar Water Sports Ctr EH30 .... 67 F1
Port Hamilton EH3 .... 232 B2
Port St Clackmannan FK10 .... 11 D2
Inverkeithing KY11 .... 47 E1
Stirling FK8 .... 7 D4
Portal Rd KY11 .... 61 E3
Portdownie FK1 .... 59 E3
Porteous' Pend EH1 .... 232 C2
Porterfield KY12 .... 26 C4
Porterfield Rd EH4 .... 92 C2
Portgower Pl EH4 .... 93 D1
Portland Pl Edinburgh EH6 .... 93 F3
Fauldhouse EH47 .... 193 E3
Portland St EH6 .... 93 F3
Portobello High Sch EH15 .... 124 C4
Portobello Rd EH6 .... 94 C1
Portree Cres FK2 .... 62 A1
Portsburgh Sq EH1 .... 232 C2
Post Office La KY11 .... 68 B3
Posthill FK10 .... 5 E1
Potter Pl FK2 .... 39 F2
Potterrow EH8 .... 233 D2
Potters Path FK33 .... 128 B3
Pottery St KY1 .... 17 F4
Pottery The Edinburgh EH15 .... 95 D1
Prestonpans EH32 .... 96 C1
Pottis Rd FK7 .... 7 E2
Pottishaw Pl EH48 .... 145 E1
Povert Rd EH19, EH23 .... 182 C1
Powderhall Brae EH23 .... 207 E3
Powdrake Rd FK3 .... 61 F4
Pratt St KY1 .... 17 D1
President Kennedy Dr FK7 .... 20 B2
Preston Ave Linlithgow EH49 .... 84 C3
Prestonpans EH32 .... 97 D1
Preston Cres Inverkeithing KY11 .... 47 E1
Linlithgow EH49 .... 84 C3
Prestonpans EH32 .... 97 D1
Preston Cross Cotts EH32 .... 97 D1
Preston Ct Linlithgow EH49 .... 84 C3
Prestonpans EH32 .... 127 F4
Preston Lodge High Sch EH32 .... 97 D1
Preston Mill EH40 .... 103 F4
Preston Pk EH49 .... 84 C3
Preston Rd East Linton EH40 .... 103 F4
Linlithgow EH49 .... 84 C3
Prestonpans EH32 .... 97 D1
Preston St High Valleyfield KY12 .... 26 A1
Rosewell EH24 .... 181 E1
Preston Street Prim Sch EH8 .... 233 F1
Preston Terr Inverkeithing KY11 .... 47 E1
Linlithgow EH49 .... 84 C3
Prestonpans EH32 .... 97 D1
Preston Tower EH32 .... 97 D1
Prestonfield Ave EH16 .... 124 A2
Prestonfield Bank EH16 .... 124 A2
Prestonfield Cres EH16 .... 124 A2
Prestonfield Gdns EH16 .... 124 A2
Prestonfield Prim Sch EH16 .... 124 A2
Prestonfield Rd EH16 .... 124 A2
Prestonfield Terr EH16 .... 124 A2
Prestongrange Rd EH32 .... 127 F4
Prestongrange Terr EH32 .... 96 C1
Prestonhall Cres EH24 .... 181 E1
Prestonhall Rd EH24 .... 181 E1
Prestonkirk Gdns EH40 .... 103 F4
Prestonpans Prim Sch Prestonpans, Cuthill EH32 .... 96 C1
Prestonpans, Preston EH32 .... 128 A4
Prestonpans Sta EH32 .... 128 A4
Pretoria Pl Cowdenbeath KY4 .... 13 D2
Polmont FK2 .... 61 F1
Pretoria Rd FK5 .... 38 A1
Priest Bank EH41 .... 134 B1
Priestfield Ave EH16 .... 124 A2
Priestfield Cres EH16 .... 124 A2
Priestfield Gdns EH16 .... 124 A2
Priestfield Gr EH16 .... 124 A3
Priestfield Rd EH16 .... 124 A3
Priestfield Rd N EH16 .... 124 A3
Prime Gilt Box St KY2 .... 17 D3
Primmer Pl KY4 .... 13 E2
Primrose Ave Grangemouth FK3 .... 61 D3
Rosyth KY11 .... 46 B3
Primrose Bank Rd EH5 .... 93 D3
Primrose Cres EH22 .... 157 E1
Primrose Ct Broxburn EH52 .... 117 F3
Rosyth KY11 .... 46 B3
Primrose Dr EH30 .... 90 B2
Primrose Gdns Carrington EH23 .... 206 B3
Queensferry EH30 .... 89 E4

Primrose La Cowdenbeath KY4 .... 13 E3
Kincardine FK10 .... 23 F2
Rosyth KY11 .... 46 B3
Primrose Pl Alloa FK10 .... 10 A3
Livingston EH54 .... 147 D3
Primrose Rd KY11 .... 46 A3
Primrose St Alloa FK10 .... 10 A4
Bonnybridge FK4 .... 58 A3
Edinburgh EH6 .... 94 A2
Primrose Terr Dalkeith EH22 .... 157 E1
Edinburgh EH11 .... 122 C3
Prince Regent St EH6 .... 93 F3
Princes St California FK1 .... 81 F3
Edinburgh EH2 .... 232 C3
Falkirk FK1 .... 60 A3
Grangemouth FK3 .... 61 E4
Stirling FK8 .... 7 D4
Princess Margaret Rose Hospl (Orthopaedic) EH10 .... 154 B3
Princess Mary Pl EH41 .... 101 D1
Princess Mary Rd EH41 .... 101 D1
Princess St FK4 .... 58 A3
Priors Grange EH48 .... 113 F3
Priorscroft EH48 .... 113 F3
Priory Gr EH30 .... 89 D4
Priory La KY12 .... 29 D2
Priory Rd Linlithgow EH49 .... 84 C3
Whitecross EH49 .... 83 F3
Priory Sq FK9 .... 1 C4
Priory Wlk EH41 .... 132 B4
Priory Wynd EH39 .... 54 A4
Promenade Edinburgh EH15 .... 95 D1
Limekilns KY11 .... 45 E2
Musselburgh EH21 .... 126 A4
Prora Cotts EH39 .... 73 E2
Prospect Bank Cres EH6 .... 94 A2
Prospect Bank Gdns EH6 .... 94 A2
Prospect Bank Gr EH6 .... 94 B2
Prospect Bank Pl EH6 .... 94 B2
Prospect Bank Rd EH6 .... 94 B2
Prospect Bank Sch EH6 .... 94 A2
Prospect Bank Terr EH6 .... 94 B2
Prospect St Cowdenbeath KY4 .... 13 D2
Falkirk FK1 .... 59 F3
Prospecthill Rd FK1 .... 60 A1
Providence Brae EH51 .... 63 F4
Provost Hunter Ave FK12 .... 5 E4
Provost Milne Gr EH30 .... 89 E4
Provost Rd Bo'ness EH51 .... 63 E3
Linlithgow EH49 .... 85 D4
Pryde Ave EH19 .... 182 A4
Pryde Terr EH19 .... 182 A4
Puir Wife's Brae EH48 .... 145 E3
Pullar Ave KY11 .... 2 A3
Pullar Ct FK9 .... 2 A3
Pumpherston Prim Sch EH53 .... 148 A4
Pumpherston Rd EH54, EH53 .... 148 B3
Pyothall Rd EH52 .... 117 E3
Pypers Wynd EH32 .... 96 C1

Quadrant EH39 .... 54 B4
Quadrant La EH39 .... 54 B4
Quadrant The EH26 .... 203 F3
Quakerfield FK7 .... 7 F1
Quality St Dysart KY1 .... 18 A4
Edinburgh EH4 .... 91 F2
North Berwick EH39 .... 54 B4
Quality Street Junc EH4 .... 91 F2
Quality Street La EH4 .... 91 F2
Quaraywood St KY11 .... 147 E2
Quarrolhall Cres FK2 .... 39 D2
Quarry Brae Brightons FK2 .... 82 C4
Kirkcaldy KY1 .... 17 F4
Quarry Cl EH18 .... 233 E1
Quarry Cotts EH15 .... 125 D2
Quarry Ct KY4 .... 13 D2
Quarry Howe EH14 .... 151 E4
Quarry Knowe FK7 .... 19 F4
Quarry Pl Alloa FK10 .... 10 B4
Shotts ML7 .... 191 E3
Quarry Rd Cambusbarron FK7 .... 6 B3
Fauldhouse EH47 .... 193 F3
Shotts ML7 .... 191 E3
Quarry St ML7 .... 191 E3
Quarrybank EH14 .... 152 B4
Quarrybank Cl EH14 .... 152 B4
Quarrybank Ct EH14 .... 152 B4
Quarrybank End EH14 .... 152 B4
Quarryfoot Gdns EH19 .... 182 B4
Quarryfoot Gn EH19 .... 182 B4
Quarryfoot Pl EH19 .... 182 A4
Quarryford Farm Cotts EH41 .... 190 C4
Quarryknowes The EH51 .... 63 F3
Quarryside Ct KY12 .... 28 B3
Quarryview EH54 .... 152 B4
Quayside St EH6 .... 93 F3
Quebec Ave EH54 .... 147 F2
Queen Anne Dr EH28 .... 119 D3
Queen Anne High Sch KY12 .... 28 C3
Queen Anne Pk EH28 .... 119 D3
Queen Anne St KY12 .... 29 D2
Queen Charlotte La EH6 .... 94 A3
Queen Charlotte St EH6 .... 94 A3
Queen Margaret Cl EH10 .... 154 B3
Queen Margaret Coll EH12 .... 121 E4
Queen Margaret Coll (Leith Campus) EH6 .... 94 A2

Queen Margaret Dr EH30 .... 89 E4
Queen Margaret Fauld KY12 .... 29 F3
Queen Margaret Hospl KY12 .... 29 F3
Queen Margaret St KY3 .... 34 C1
Queen Margaret's Pl KY11 .... 68 B3
Queen St Alloa FK10 .... 10 A4
Alva FK12 .... 5 D4
Bannockburn FK7 .... 7 E1
Edinburgh EH2 .... 232 C4
Fallin FK7 .... 8 B2
Grangemouth FK3 .... 61 F4
Inverkeithing KY11 .... 47 D1
Stirling FK8 .... 7 D4
Queen Street Gdns E EH3 .... 232 C4
Queen Street Gdns W EH3 .... 232 C4
Queen's Ave Bridge of A FK9 .... 2 A3
Edinburgh EH4 .... 92 A1
Queen's Ave S EH4 .... 92 B1
Queen's Bay Cres EH15 .... 125 E4
Queen's Bldgs KY11 .... 46 C3
Queen's Cres Carluke ML8 .... 230 A1
Edinburgh EH9 .... 123 F2
Falkirk FK1 .... 59 F3
Queen's Ct SK9 .... 1 C4
Queen's Dr EH8 .... 233 F2
Queen's Dr Larbert FK5 .... 38 B1
Pencaitland EH34 .... 160 C3
Queen's Gdns EH4 .... 92 B1
Queen's La K9 .... 2 A4
Queen's Park Ave EH8 .... 94 A1
Queen's Park Ct EH8 .... 124 B4
Queen's Pl EH42 .... 78 C1
Queen's Rd Broxburn EH52 .... 117 F2
Dunbar EH42 .... 78 C1
Edinburgh EH4 .... 92 B1
Stirling FK8 .... 6 C4
Queen's St FK1 .... 81 F3
Queen's Wlk EH16 .... 124 C2
Queens Ave Broxburn EH52 .... 117 F2
Haddington EH41 .... 100 C1
Queens Cres KY3 .... 34 C1
Queens Ct FK5 .... 38 B2
Queens Dr Denny FK6 .... 36 C2
Falkirk FK1 .... 59 F3
Queens Gdns EH53 .... 148 C2
Queens Terr EH53 .... 148 C2
Queens Way EH41 .... 46 A1
Queensferry High Sch EH30 .... 89 E4
Queensferry Mus EH30 .... 68 B1
Queensferry Rd Dunfermline KY11 .... 46 B4
Edinburgh, Braepark EH4 .... 91 D2
Edinburgh, Orchard Brae EH4 .... 92 B1
Kirkliston EH29 .... 89 D1
Rosyth KY11 .... 46 C3
Queensferry St EH2 .... 232 A3
Queensferry Street La EH2 .... 92 C1
Queensferry Terr EH4 .... 92 C1
Queenshaugh EH27 .... 27 E4
Queenshaugh Dr FK8 .... 2 B1
Queensway EH26 .... 203 F4
Quench Rd FK2 .... 62 A3
Quentin Rise EH54 .... 147 F1
Quidenham Ct EH39 .... 54 A3
Quilts The EH6 .... 93 F3
Quilts Wynd EH6 .... 93 F3
Quoiters Ct EH47 .... 171 E4

R L Stevenson's Birthplace & Mus EH3 .... 93 E2
Race Rd EH48 .... 144 C4
Rae Ct FK2 .... 39 E2
Rae St Cowdenbeath KY4 .... 13 E1
Stenhousemuir FK5 .... 38 B2
Rae's Ct EH16 .... 155 F3
Raeburn Cres Kirkcaldy KY2 .... 17 D2
Whitburn EH47 .... 170 A3
Raeburn Mews EH4 .... 93 D1
Raeburn Pl EH4 .... 93 D1
Raeburn Rigg EH54 .... 147 D3
Raeburn St EH4 .... 93 D1
Raes Gdns EH19 .... 182 B4
Rainhill Ave FK2 .... 82 C3
Raith Ave KY4 .... 13 E2
Raith Cres KY2 .... 17 D2
Raith Dr KY2 .... 17 D2
Raith Gdns KY2 .... 16 C2
Raleigh Ct FK1 .... 59 F3
Ramage Rd ML8 .... 230 A1
Ramillies Ct Carluke ML8 .... 230 A1
Penicuik EH26 .... 204 A4
Ramsay Ave EH19 .... 182 A2
Ramsay Cotts EH19 .... 182 C2
Ramsay Cres Bathgate EH48 .... 145 E3
Burntisland KY3 .... 34 A1
Mayfield EH22 .... 183 F3
Ramsay Ct EH54 .... 148 B3
Ramsay La Kincardine FK10 .... 23 F2
Limekilns KY11 .... 45 E2
Ramsay Pl Edinburgh EH15 .... 95 D1
Stirling FK8 .... 2 A1
Ramsay Rd KY1 .... 17 D1

Ramsay Terr EH18 .... 181 F2
Ramsay Wlk EH22 .... 183 F3
Ramsey Ct FK10 .... 23 F2
Ramsey Gdn EH1 .... 232 C3
Ramsey La EH1 .... 232 C3
Ramsey Pl Penicuik EH26 .... 203 E3
Rosyth KY11 .... 46 C2
Ramsey Tullis Ave FK10 .... 4 B1
Ramsey Tullis Dr FK10 .... 4 B1
Randolph Cliff EH3 .... 232 A3
Randolph Cres Bannockburn FK7 .... 7 E1
Brightons FK2 .... 82 B4
Edinburgh EH3 .... 232 A3
Randolph Ct FK8 .... 7 D3
Randolph Gdns EH6 .... 36 B1
Randolph Ind Est EH4 .... 18 A4
Randolph La EH3 .... 232 B3
Randolph Pl Bannockburn FK7 .... 7 E1
Edinburgh EH3 .... 232 B3
Kirkcaldy KY1 .... 18 A4
Randolph Rd FK8 .... 7 D3
Randolph St Cowdenbeath KY4 .... 13 E2
Dunfermline KY12 .... 29 D2
Randolph Terr FK7 .... 7 D2
Randyford Rd FK2 .... 60 B3
Randyford St FK2 .... 60 C3
Range Rd FK3 .... 62 B4
Rankeillor St EH8 .... 233 E1
Rankin Ave EH9 .... 123 F1
Rankin Cres FK4 .... 57 F3
Rankin Dr EH9 .... 123 F1
Rankin Rd EH9 .... 123 F2
Rannoch Ct FK10 .... 10 B3
Rannoch Dr Crossford KY12 .... 28 A1
Whitburn EH47 .... 170 B4
Rannoch Gr EH4 .... 91 E1
Rannoch Pl Edinburgh EH4 .... 91 E1
Shieldhill FK1 .... 81 F4
Shotts ML7 .... 191 F3
Stenhousemuir FK5 .... 38 C2
Rannoch Rd Edinburgh EH4 .... 91 E1
Grangemouth FK3 .... 61 E2
Kirkcaldy KY2 .... 16 C4
Rosyth KY11 .... 46 C1
Whitburn EH47 .... 170 B4
Rannoch Terr EH4 .... 91 E1
Rannoch Wlk Livingston EH54 .... 148 A2
Whitburn EH47 .... 170 B4
Ransome Gdns EH4 .... 91 E1
Raploch Prim Sch FK8 .... 1 C1
Raploch Rd FK8 .... 1 C1
Rashiehill Cres EH55 .... 194 C3
Rashiehill Rd FK1 .... 110 A3
Rashiehill Terr EH55 .... 194 C3
Rashienhill ML11 .... 215 D1
Rashierig EH52 .... 117 D3
Rashierigg Pl EH47 .... 170 A1
Ratcliffe Terr EH9 .... 123 F2
Rathbone Pl EH15 .... 95 D1
Ratho Park Rd EH28 .... 119 F1
Ratho Pl KY11 .... 29 E2
Ratho Prim Sch EH28 .... 119 E1
Rattray Gdns EH47 .... 171 F4
Rattray St EH51 .... 64 A3
Rattray Terr KY5 .... 14 A4
Ravelrig Hill EH14 .... 151 D1
Ravelrig Pk EH14 .... 151 D1
Ravelrig Rd EH14 .... 151 D2
Ravelston Dykes EH12 .... 122 B4
Ravelston Dykes La EH4 .... 122 A4
Ravelston Dykes Rd EH4 .... 122 A4
Ravelston Gdn EH4 .... 122 B4
Ravelston Hts EH4 .... 92 B1
Ravelston House Gr **9** EH4 .... 92 B1
Ravelston House Loan **8** EH4 .... 92 B1
Ravelston House Pk EH4 .... 92 B1
Ravelston House Rd EH4 .... 92 B1
Ravelston Pk EH4 .... 122 C4
Ravelston Rise EH4 .... 122 B4
Ravelston Terr EH4 .... 92 C1
Ravelsykes Rd EH26 .... 203 E3
Ravendean Gdns EH26 .... 203 E3
Ravens Craig KY1 .... 17 E3
Ravenscraig Park Nature Trail KY1 .... 17 F3
Ravenscraig St KY1 .... 17 F3
Ravenscroft Gdns EH17 .... 155 F3
Ravenscroft Pl EH17 .... 155 F3
Ravenscroft St EH17 .... 155 F3
Ravenshaugh Cres EH21 .... 127 D3
Ravenshaugh Rd EH21 .... 127 D4
Ravenswood Ave EH16 .... 124 B1
Ravenswood Rise EH54 .... 173 F4
Rectory La KY1 .... 18 A4
Red Craigs KY2 .... 16 B4
Red Fox Cres EH26 .... 180 A1
Red Row KY11 .... 45 E2
Redbrae Ave EH51 .... 64 A3
Redbrae Rd FK1 .... 59 D3
Redbraes Gr EH7 .... 93 E2
Redbraes Pl EH7 .... 93 E2
Redburn Rd Blackridge EH48 .... 142 A1
Prestonpans EH32 .... 96 C1
Redburn Rd N EH32 .... 96 C1
Redburn Wynd KY1 .... 17 E2
Redcraig Rd EH53 .... 148 C1

Redcroft Pl EH47 .... 171 D1
Redcroft St EH22 .... 156 A4
Redcroft Terr EH47 .... 171 D1
Redding Ind Est FK2 .... 61 D1
Redding Rd Brightons FK2 .... 82 B4
Redding FK2 .... 61 D1
Reddingmuirhead Rd
FK2 .... 61 D1
Reddoch Rd FK2 .... 62 A2
Redford Ave EH13 .... 153 E3
Redford Bank EH13 .... 153 E3
Redford Cres EH13 .... 153 E3
Redford Dr EH13 .... 153 D3
Redford Gdns EH13 .... 153 E3
Redford Gr EH13 .... 153 E3
Redford Loan EH13 .... 153 E3
Redford Neuk EH13 .... 153 E3
Redford Pl EH13 .... 153 E3
Redford Rd EH13 .... 153 E3
Redford Terr EH13 .... 153 E3
Redford Wlk EH13 .... 153 E3
Redgauntlet Terr EH16 .. 124 B1
Redhall Ave EH14 .... 122 A1
Redhall Bank Rd EH14 .. 122 A1
Redhall Cres EH14 .... 122 A1
Redhall Dr EH14 .... 122 A1
Redhall Gdns EH14 .... 122 A1
Redhall Gr EH14 .... 122 A1
Redhall House Dr
EH14 .... 122 A1
Redhall Pl EH14 .... 122 A1
Redhall Rd EH14 .... 122 A1
Redhall View EH14 .... 122 A1
Redhaws Rd ML7 .... 192 A2
Redheugh Loan EH23 .. 183 E4
Redheughs Ave EH12 .. 121 D2
Redheughs Rigg EH12 .. 121 D2
Redholm Pk EH39 .... 54 C3
Redhouse Cotts EH49 .. 86 C2
Redhouse Ct EH47 .... 171 F4
Redhouse Pl EH47 .... 145 E1
Redhouse Rd EH47 .... 172 A4
Redlands Ct EH47 .... 170 C4
Redlands Rd FK10 .... 4 A2
Redmill Cotts EH47 .... 170 C4
Redmill Ct EH47 .... 170 C4
Redmill View EH47 .... 170 C4
Redmire Cres ML7 .... 212 A4
Redpath Dr FK2 .... 39 D2
Redwell Pl FK10 .... 9 F4
Redwing Brae EH47 .... 147 E3
Redwood Gr EH22 .... 182 C3
Redwood Wlk EH22 .... 183 D3
Reed Dr EH22 .... 183 D4
Reedlands Dr FK6 .... 57 E4
Regal Gr ML7 .... 191 F2
Regent Pl EH7 .... 94 A1
Regent Rd EH7, EH8 .... 233 E4
Regent Sq EH49 .... 85 D4
Regent St
Edinburgh EH15 .... 125 D4
Kincardine FK10 .... 23 F2
Regent Street La EH15 .. 125 D4
Regent Terr EH7 .... 233 E4
Regent Terrace Mews
EH7 .... 233 F4
Regents Way KY11 .... 48 A2
Regis Ct EH4 .... 91 D2
Register Pl EH2 .... 233 D4
Register St EH51 .... 63 F4
Reid Ave KY4 .... 30 C3
Reid St
Dunfermline KY12 .... 29 D2
Lochgelly KY5 .... 14 A4
Reid Terr EH3 .... 93 D1
Reid's Cl EH8 .... 233 F3
Reilly Gdns FK4 .... 58 A2
Reilly Rd FK4 .... 58 A2
Relugas Gdns EH9 .... 123 F2
Relugas Pl EH9 .... 123 F2
Relugas Rd EH9 .... 123 F2
Rendall Gdns EH52 .... 117 F3
Rennie Pl EH40 .... 103 E4
Rennie Sq EH54 .... 173 E3
Rennie St FK1 .... 60 A2
Rennie's Isle EH6 .... 93 F3
Research Ave N
Currie EH14 .... 151 F4
Edinburgh EH14 .... 120 C1
Research Ave S EH14 .. 151 F4
Restalrig Ave EH7 .... 94 B1
Restalrig Cir EH7 .... 94 B2
Restalrig Cres EH7 .... 94 B2
Restalrig Dr EH7 .... 94 B1
Restalrig Gdns EH7 .... 94 B1
Restalrig Pk EH7 .... 94 A2
Restalrig Rd EH6 .... 94 A2
Restalrig Rd S EH7 .... 94 B1
Restalrig Sq EH7 .... 94 B2
Restalrig Terr EH6 .... 94 A2
Reveston La EH47 .... 170 A3
Reynard Gdns EH49 .... 84 A3
Rhodders Gr FK12 .... 5 D4
Rhodes Wlk KY11 .... 29 D1
Riccarton Ave EH14 .. 152 A3
Riccarton Cres EH14 .. 152 A2
Riccarton Dr EH14 .... 152 A3
Riccarton Gr EH14 .... 152 A3
Riccarton Mains Rd
EH14 .... 152 A3
Riccarton Prim Sch
EH14 .... 151 F2
Riccarton Rd EH49 .... 84 C3
Richmond Dr FK2 .... 82 B4
Richmond La EH8 .... 233 E2

Richmond Pl
Edinburgh EH8 .... 233 E2
Richmond Terr
Bo'ness EH51 .... 63 F4
Edinburgh EH11 .... 232 A2
Riddochhill Cres EH47 .. 171 E4
Riddochhill Ct EH47 .... 171 D4
Riddochhill Dr EH47 .... 171 E4
Riddochhill Rd EH47 .... 171 D4
Riddochhill View EH47 .. 171 D4
Ridge Way KY11 .... 48 A3
Riding Pk EH4 .... 91 D2
Ridley Dr KY11 .... 46 C2
Riego St EH3 .... 232 B2
Rifle Rd FK3 .... 62 B4
Rig Pl FK32 .... 71 E2
Rig St FK32 .... 71 E2
Rigg Pk KY12 .... 78 B1
Riggs View KY12 .... 27 E1
Rigley Terr FK32 .... 127 F4
Rillbank Cres EH9 .... 233 D1
Rillbank Terr EH9 .... 123 E3
Rimmon Cres ML7 .... 191 F3
Ring Rd FK10 .... 10 A4
Ringwood Pl EH16 .... 155 D4
Rintoul Ave KY12 .... 26 A4
Rintoul Pl Blairhall KY12 .. 26 A4
Edinburgh EH3 .... 93 D1
Riselaw Cres EH10 .... 154 A4
Riselaw Pl EH10 .... 154 A4
Riselaw Rd EH10 .... 154 A4
Riselaw Terr EH10 .... 154 A4
Ritchie St Bo'ness EH51 .. 64 A3
Edinburgh EH3 .... 122 C3
Grangemouth FK3 .... 61 E3
Rivaldsgreen Cres EH49 .. 85 D3
River St
Denny FK6 .... 39 D1
River View KY11 .... 48 A1
River Wlk KY11 .... 48 A1
Riverbank View FK8 .... 7 E4
Riversdale Cres EH12 .. 122 B4
Riversdale Gr EH12 .... 122 B4
Riversdale Rd EH12 .... 122 B4
Riverside Edinburgh EH4 .. 91 E4
Newbridge EH28 .... 118 C3
Riverside Ct EH54 .... 147 E2
Riverside Dr
Haddington EH41 .... 101 D1
Stirling FK8 .... 2 B1
Riverside Gdns EH21 .. 126 A3
Riverside Terr EH41 .... 101 E1
Riverside Prim Sch
Livingston EH54 .... 148 A2
Stirling FK8 .... 2 A1
Riverside Rd
Craigiehall EH30 .... 90 C2
Grangemouth FK2 .... 62 A3
Riverside Terr FK10 .... 23 F2
Riverside View FK10 .... 10 A2
Road 10 FK3 .... 62 B3
Road 11 FK3 .... 62 B3
Road 13 FK3 .... 62 B3
Road 15 FK3 .... 62 B3
Road 24 FK3 .... 62 A3
Road 25 FK3 .... 62 A3
Road 27 FK3 .... 62 A3
Road 28 FK3 .... 62 A3
Road 29 FK3 .... 62 A3
Road 30b FK3 .... 62 A3
Road 30c FK3 .... 62 A3
Road 31 FK3 .... 62 A3
Road 32 FK3 .... 62 A3
Road 33 FK2, FK3 .... 62 A3
Road 4 FK3 .... 62 B3
Road 4a FK3 .... 62 B3
Road 4b FK3 .... 62 B3
Road 6 FK3 .... 62 B3
Road 7 FK3 .... 62 B3
Road 9 FK3 .... 62 B3
Roanhead Terr FK10 .. 23 F2
Roanshead Rd EH22 .. 183 E4
Robb's Loan EH14 .... 122 B2
Robb's Loan Gr EH14 .. 122 B2
Robert Bruce Ct FK5 .. 38 A1
Robert Burns Dr EH16 .. 124 A1
Robert Burns Mews
EH22 .... 157 E2
Robert Dick Ct FK10 .. 4 B1
Robert Hardie Ct FK5 .. 38 B1
Robert Kinmond Ave EH10 .. 4 B1
Robert Knox Ave FK10 .. 4 B1
Robert Smilie Ave EH22 .. 183 F3
Robert Smith Ct KY4 .. 13 F3
Robert St ML7 .... 191 F2
Roberts Ave FK2 .... 61 E1
Roberts St KY1 .... 17 F4
Robertson Ave
Bathgate EH48 .... 144 C3
Bonnybridge FK4 .... 58 A3
Edinburgh EH11 .... 122 B3
Prestonpans EH32 .... 97 D1
Tranent EH33 .... 128 B3
Robertson Bank EH37 .. 207 E3
Robertson Ct EH48 .... 143 F2
Robertson Dr EH33 .... 128 B4
Robertson Pl FK7 .... 7 D2
Robertson Rd KY12 .... 29 E3
Robertson St FK12 .... 5 D4
Robertson Way EH54 .. 147 E4
Robertson's Cl
Dalkeith EH22 .... 157 D2
Edinburgh EH1 .... 233 E2
Robertsons Bank EH37 .. 207 E4
Robins Neuk EH33 .... 129 E3
Rocheid Pk EH4 .... 92 C2
Rochester Terr EH10 .. 123 D2
Rocks Rd KY11 .... 45 D2

Rockville Gr EH49 .... 85 D3
Rockville Terr EH19 .... 182 A4
Roddinglaw Rd EH12 .. 120 B2
Rodel Dr FK2 .... 61 F1
Rodney Pl EH7 .... 93 E1
Rodney St Edinburgh EH7 .. 93 E1
Grangemouth FK3 .... 61 E3
Roebuck Pl EH51 .... 63 E3
Rolland St KY12 .... 29 D2
Roman Camp EH37 .... 185 D2
Roman Camp Cotts
EH52 .... 117 E1
Roman Camp Way
EH37 .... 185 D2
Roman Dr FK1 .... 59 E3
Roman Rd
Bonnybridge FK4 .... 58 A2
Inverkeithing KY11 .... 47 D1
Roman Way EH51 .... 63 E3
Romero Pl EH16 .... 123 F3
Romyn Rd KY11 .... 46 B1
Ronades Rd FK2 .... 60 A4
Ronald Cres FK5 .... 38 A1
Ronald Pl FK8 .... 7 D4
Ronaldshay Cres FK3 .. 61 F4
Ronaldson Gr KY12 .... 29 E3
Ronaldson's Wharf EH6 .. 93 F3
Rood Well Cres EH42 .. 104 C1
Roodlands General Hospl
EH41 .... 100 C1
Roods Cres KY11 .... 47 D2
Roods Rd KY11 .... 47 D1
Roods Sq KY11 .... 47 E2
Roomlin Gdns KY1 .... 17 F4
Roosevelt Rd EH27 .... 149 F2
Rope Wlk EH32 .... 96 C1
Ropeway KY11 .... 46 A1
Rosabelle Rd EH25 .... 180 C2
Rosabelle St KY1 .... 17 F4
Rose Ave EH19 .... 182 B3
Rose Cotts EH19 .... 182 B3
Rose Cres KY12 .... 29 D2
Rose Ct EH4 .... 91 F2
Rose Gdns
Bonnyrigg and Lasswade
EH19 .... 182 B3
Cairneyhill KY12 .... 27 E1
Rose Gr EH19 .... 182 B3
Rose La Lochgelly KY5 .. 14 A4
Queensferry EH30 .... 68 A1
Torryburn KY12 .... 26 C1
Rose Pk EH5 .... 93 D3
Rose Pl EH19 .... 182 B3
Rose St Alloa FK10 .... 4 C1
Bonnybridge FK4 .... 58 A3
Burntisland KY3 .... 50 C4
Cowdenbeath KY4 .... 13 E2
Dunfermline KY12 .... 29 D2
Edinburgh EH2 .... 232 C3
Rose Street North La
EH2 .... 232 C3
Rose Street South La
EH2 .... 232 C3
Rose Terr
Bonnyrigg and Lasswade
EH19 .... 182 B3
Denny FK6 .... 36 B1
Stenhousemuir FK5 .... 38 C2
Rose Way EH19 .... 182 B3
Rosebank Alloa FK10 .... 5 E1
Cowdenbeath KY4 .... 13 E2
Dunfermline KY11 .... 29 E1
Rosebank Ave FK1 .... 59 F3
Rosebank Cotts EH3 .. 232 A2
Rosebank Gdns
Alloa FK10 .... 10 B4
Dunfermline KY12 .... 28 B3
Edinburgh EH5 .... 93 D3
Kincardine FK10 .... 23 F2
Rosebank Gr EH5 .... 93 D3
Rosebank Pl FK1 .... 59 F3
Rosebank Rd EH5 .... 93 D3
Rosebank Rdbt EH54 .. 173 D4
Roseberry Ct EH30 .... 89 E4
Roseberry Pl EH54 .... 147 D3
Roseberry Rd EH30 .... 89 E4
Rosebery Cres
Bathgate EH48 .... 145 D3
Edinburgh EH12 .... 122 C4
Gorebridge EH23 .... 207 E3
Rosebery Crescent La
EH12 .... 122 C4
Rosebery Ct
Dalgety Bay KY11 .... 47 F1
Kirkcaldy KY1 .... 17 D3
Rosebery Gr KY11 .... 47 F1
Rosebery Pl
Dalgety Bay KY11 .... 47 F1
Stirling FK8 .... 2 A1
Rosebery Terr KY1 .... 17 D3
Rosebery View KY11 .. 47 F1
Roseburn Ave EH12 .. 122 B4
Roseburn Cliff EH12 .. 122 C4
Roseburn Cres EH12 .. 122 B4
Roseburn Dr EH12 .... 122 B4
Roseburn Gdns EH12 .. 122 B4
Roseburn Maltings
EH12 .... 122 C4
Roseburn Pl EH12 .... 122 B4
Roseburn Prim Sch
EH12 .... 122 B3
Roseburn St EH12 .... 122 B3
Roseburn Terr EH12 .. 122 C4
Rosebush Cres KY11 .. 29 E2
Rosedale Ct EH24 .... 205 E4
Rosefield Ave EH15 .. 125 D4
Rosefield Avenue La EH15 .. 125 D4
Rosefield La EH15 .... 125 D4

Rosefield Pl EH15 .... 125 D4
Rosefield St EH15 .... 125 D4
Rosehall Pl EH41 .... 131 F4
Rosehall Rd ML7 .... 191 E2
Rosehall Terr FK1 .... 60 A2
Rosehall Wlk EH41 .... 131 F4
Rosehill Cres KY4 .... 13 D2
Rosehill Pl EH54 .... 147 D2
Rosehill Terr EH30 .... 89 E4
Roselea Dr FK2 .... 82 C4
Rosemead Terr FK1 .... 81 F3
Rosemill Ct KY12 .... 26 B1
Rosemount Ave KY2 .... 17 D4
Rosemount Bldgs EH3 .. 232 A2
Rosemount Ct EH48 .. 145 D3
Rosemount Rd EH52 .. 116 C2
Roseneath Pl EH9 .... 123 E3
Roseneath St EH9 .... 123 E3
Roseneath Terr EH9 .. 123 E3
Rosevale Pl EH6 .... 94 A2
Rosevale Terr EH6 .... 94 A2
Roseville Gdns EH5 .... 93 E3
Rosewell Prim Sch
EH24 .... 181 F1
Rosewell Rd EH19 .... 181 F2
Roslin Glen Ctry Pk
EH25 .... 180 C1
Roslin Prim Sch EH25 .. 180 C2
Roslin Prim Sch (Annexe)
EH25 .... 180 B3
Ross Ave KY11 .... 48 A1
Ross Cres Falkirk FK1 .. 59 E3
Tranent EH33 .... 128 B3
Ross Ct FK7 .... 7 D2
Ross Gdns Edinburgh EH9 .. 123 F2
Kirkcaldy KY1 .... 17 F4
Ross High Sch EH33 .. 128 B3
Ross La KY12 .... 28 C2
Ross Pl Edinburgh EH9 .. 123 F2
Kinghorn KY3 .... 34 C1
Newtongrange EH22 .. 183 D3
Ross Rd EH16 .... 123 F1
Ross St KY12 .... 29 D3
Rossend Terr KY3 .... 50 B4
Rossie Pl EH7 .... 94 A1
Rossland Pl KY3 .... 34 C1
Rosslyn Cres EH6 .... 93 F2
Rosslyn St KY1 .... 17 F4
Rosslyn Terr EH6 .... 93 F2
Rosslynlee Hospl EH25 .. 204 C3
Rossness Dr KY3 .... 34 C1
Rossvail St KY1 .... 59 E3
Rosyth Europarc
North Queensferry KY11 .. 68 A4
Rosyth KY11 .... 46 B1
Rosyth Sta KY11 .... 46 C3
Rothes Dr EH54 .... 173 F3
Rothesay Mews EH3 .. 122 C4
Rothesay Pl
Edinburgh EH3 .... 232 A3
Musselburgh EH21 .... 126 B3
Rothesay Terr EH3 .... 232 A3
Roughburn Rd KY9 .... 2 A2
Roughlands Cres FK2 .. 39 D2
Roughlands Dr FK2 .... 39 D2
Roull Gr EH12 .... 121 E3
Roull Pl EH12 .... 121 F3
Roull Rd EH12 .... 121 E3
Round The KY12 .... 29 E2
Roundel The FK2 .... 60 B4
Roundhouse KY7 .... 20 B4
Roundelwood FK10 .... 5 D1
Rowallan Ct EH12 .... 121 D4
Rowallan Dr FK7 .... 19 F4
Rowan Cres Falkirk FK1 .. 59 D2
Shotts ML7 .... 192 A2
Rowan Ct FK7 .... 7 F1
Rowan Dr EH47 .... 145 E1
Rowan Gdns EH19 .... 182 A3
Rowan Gr
Dunfermline KY11 .... 29 E1
Livingston EH54 .... 148 A3
Rowan La EH47 .... 145 E1
Rowan St Blackburn EH47 .. 145 E1
Rowan Terr
Blackburn EH47 .... 171 E4
Cowdenbeath KY4 .... 13 E2
Rowan Tree Ave EH14 .. 151 E2
Rowan Tree Gr EH14 .. 151 F2
Rowanhill Cl EH32 .... 97 E2
Rowanhill Dr EH32 .... 97 E2
Rowanhill Pk EH32 .... 97 E2
Rowanhill Way EH32 .. 97 E2
Rowans The Alloa FK10 .. 5 E1
Gullane EH31 .... 52 A2
Rowantree Rd EH22 .. 183 F4
Roxburgh Pl
Edinburgh EH8 .... 233 E2
Stenhousemuir FK5 .... 38 C2
Roxburgh St
Edinburgh EH8 .... 233 E2
Grangemouth FK3 .... 61 F4
Roxburghe Pl EH42 .... 78 C1
Roxburghe Terr EH42 .. 78 C1
Roy Dr EH54 .... 173 F3
Royal Blind Sch EH16 .. 123 F2
Royal Botanic Garden
EH3 .... 93 D2
Royal Cir EH3 .... 232 B4
Royal Coll of Physicians
EH2 .... 232 C4
Royal Cres EH3 .... 93 E1
Royal Ct EH26 .... 203 E4
Royal (Dick)
Veterinary Coll EH8 .. 233 e1
Royal Edinburgh Hospl
EH10 .... 123 D2

Royal Gdns FK8 .... 7 D4
Royal High Prim Sch
EH8 .... 124 B4
Royal High Sch The EH4 .. 91 E2
Royal Hospl
for Sick Children EH9 .. 123 E3
Royal Infirmary
of Edinburgh EH3 .. 233 D2
Royal Mile Prim Sch
EH8 .... 233 F3
Royal Mus of Scotland
EH1 .... 233 D2
Royal Observatory EH9 .. 123 E1
Royal Park Terr EH8 .. 94 A1
Royal Scot Way KY12 .. 29 D3
Royal Scottish Acad
EH2 .... 232 C3
Royal Scottish
National Hospl The
FK5 .... 37 F2
Royal Terr
Edinburgh EH7 .... 233 E4
Linlithgow EH49 .... 84 C3
Royal Victoria Hospl EH4 .. 92 C1
Royal Yacht Britannia
EH6 .... 93 F4
Royston Mains Ave EH5 .. 92 C3
Royston Mains Cl EH5 .. 92 C3
Royston Mains Cres EH5 .. 92 C3
Royston Mains Gdns EH5 .. 92 C3
Royston Mains Gn EH5 .. 92 C3
Royston Mains Pl EH5 .. 92 B3
Royston Mains Rd EH5 .. 92 C3
Royston Mains St EH5 .. 92 B3
Royston Prim Sch EH5 .. 92 C3
Royston Rd EH54 .... 146 C4
Royston Rdbt EH54 .... 146 B4
Royston Terr EH3 .... 93 D2
Rudolf Steiner Sch
EH10 .... 122 C2
Rulley View FK6 .... 36 B2
Rullion Green Ave EH26 .. 203 E4
Rullion Green Cres EH26 .. 203 E4
Rullion Green Gr EH26 .. 203 E4
Rullion Rd EH26 .... 203 E3
Rumblingwell KY12 .... 28 B3
Rumlie The FK1 .... 110 A3
Run The EH51 .... 64 B4
Rushbank EH54 .... 147 E3
Ruskie Rd KY9 .... 2 A2
Ruskin Pl EH22 .... 183 F3
Russel Ct KY5 .... 14 A4
Russel Pl EH5 .... 93 D3
Russel St FK2 .... 60 A3
Russell Ave EH48 .... 143 F4
Russell Ct KY11 .... 29 F1
Russell Gdns EH12 .... 122 C4
Russell Gr KY3 .... 33 F1
Russell Pl Kirkcaldy KY1 .. 17 E3
Oakley KY12 .... 26 C4
Russell Rd EH11 .... 122 C3
Russell St
Cowdenbeath KY4 .... 13 D2
Lochgelly KY5 .... 14 A4
Rutherford Ct
Bridge of Allan FK9 .. 2 A4
Kirkcaldy KY1 .... 17 F4
Rutherford Dr EH16 .. 124 A1
Rutherford Sq EH54 .. 173 E4
Ruthven St EH39 .... 53 D2
Rutland Court La EH3 .. 232 B2
Rutland Sq EH1 .... 232 B3
Rutland St EH1 .... 232 B3
Ryebank EH54 .... 147 F3
Ryehill Ave EH6 .... 94 A2
Ryehill Gdns EH6 .... 94 A2
Ryehill Gr EH6 .... 94 A2
Ryehill Pl EH6 .... 94 A2
Ryehill Terr EH6 .... 94 A2
Rymalton KY1 .... 17 E3

Sacred Heart RC Prim Sch
Grangemouth FK3 .... 61 F3
Penicuik EH26 .... 203 F3
Saddletree Loan EH16 .. 124 B1
Sailors' Wlk KY3 .... 50 B4
Sainford Cres FK2 .... 39 D1
Sainthill Ct EH39 .... 54 A4
St Alban's Rd EH9 .... 123 F2
St Andrew Pl EH6 .... 94 A2
St Andrew Sq EH2 .... 233 D4
St Andrew St
Dalkeith EH22 .... 157 D2
Dunfermline KY11 .... 29 E1
North Berwick EH39 .. 54 B4
St Andrew's Ct FK5 .... 38 A2
St Andrew's Dr Airth FK2 .. 22 A4
Armadale EH48 .... 143 F4
Uphall EH52 .... 116 C2
St Andrew's High Sch
KY2 .... 17 E4
St Andrew's Prim Sch
FK1 .... 60 B2
St Andrews Way EH54 .. 146 C3
St Andrews Pl 11 FK1 .. 60 A2
St Ann's Ave EH18 .... 181 F3
St Ann's Path EH18 .... 181 F3
St Anne's Cres FK7 .... 7 F1
St Anne's Ct EH22 .... 183 D3
St Anthony La EH6 .... 93 F3
St Anthony Pl EH6 .... 93 F3
St Anthony St EH6 .... 93 F3
St Anthony's RC Prim Sch
EH48 .... 143 F2
St Augustine's High Sch
EH12 .... 121 E2
St Baldred's Cres EH39 .. 54 B4
St Baldred's Rd EH39 .. 54 B3

St Bernadette's
RC Prim Sch FK10 .... 4 A1
St Bernard's Cres EH4 .... 93 D1
St Bernard's Row 5 EH4 .... 93 D1
St Bride's RC Prim Sch
KY4 .... 13 E2
St Bridget's Church KY11 .... 48 B2
St Bridgets Brae KY11 .... 48 B2
St Brycedale Ave KY1 .... 17 D2
St Brycedale Rd KY1 .... 17 D2
St Catherine FK2 .... 82 C4
St Catherine's Gdns
EH12 .... 122 A3
St Catherine's PI EH9 .... 123 F3
St Catherine's RC
Prim Sch EH16 .... 155 D3
St Catherine's Wynd
KY12 .... 28 C2
St Catherines Cres ML7 .... 191 E4
St Clair Ave EH6 .... 94 A2
St Clair Cres EH25 .... 181 D2
St Clair PI EH6 .... 94 A2
St Clair Rd EH6 .... 94 A2
St Clair St Edinburgh EH6 .. 94 A2
Kirkcaldy KY1 .... 17 F4
St Clair Terr EH10 .... 122 C1
St Clement's Cres EH21 .... 127 D2
St Clement's Gdns N
EH21 .... 127 D2
St Clement's Gdns S
EH21 .... 127 D2
St Clement's Terr EH21 .... 127 D2
St Colm's Abbey KY3 .... 49 D1
St Colm's Ed Ctr & Coll
EH3 .... 93 D2
St Colme Ave KY3 .... 49 D3
St Colme Cres KY3 .... 49 D4
St Colme Dr KY11 .... 48 B3
St Colme Rd KY11 .... 48 B2
St Colme St EH3 .... 232 B4
St Columba's High Sch
KY11 .... 29 F2
St Columba's RC
Prim Sch EH48 .... 145 E4
St Crispin's PI FK1 .... 60 A2
St Crispin's Sch EH16 ..... 123 F2
St Cuthbert's RC Prim Sch
EH14 .... 122 A3
St David's Bsns Pk KY11 .. 48 A2
St David's Ct
Dalgety Bay KY11 .... 48 A3
Larbert FK5 .... 38 A1
St David's PI EH3 .... 232 A2
EH22 .... 157 D1
St David's RC High Sch
Dalkeith EH22 .... 157 E1
Edinburgh EH4 .... 92 B2
St David's Terr EH3 .... 232 A2
St Davids EH22 .... 183 D2
St Davids Dr KY11 .... 48 A2
St Denis & Cranley Sch
EH10 .... 122 C2
St Fillan's Terr EH10 .... 123 D1
St Fillans Cres KY3 .... 49 E4
St Fillans Gr KY3 .... 49 E4
St Fillans PI KY2 .... 16 B3
St Fillans Rd KY2 .... 16 B3
St Francis' RC Prim Sch
FK2 .... 60 A3
St Francis's RC Prim Sch
EH16 .... 124 C2
St Gabrial's RC Prim Sch
EH32 .... 96 C1
St Gabriel's RC Prim Sch
EH47 .... 127 F4
St George's Ct FK5 .... 38 A1
St George's Sch EH4 .... 122 C4
St Georges Sch for girls
EH12 .... 122 B4
St Germains Terr EH33 .... 129 E3
St Giles' Cath EH1 .... 233 D3
St Giles Sq FK1 .... 59 D3
St Giles St EH1 .... 233 D3
St Giles Way FK1 .... 59 D3
St Helen's EH48 .... 143 F3
St James Ctr EH1 .... 233 D4
St James' Orch FK9 .... 2 B1
St James' PI EH1 .... 233 D4
St James PI KY3 .... 35 D1
St James Sq EH1 .... 233 D4
St James's Gdns EH26 .... 203 F2
St James's View EH26 .... 203 F2
St Joesph's Hospl EH24 .. 205 F4
St John Ogilvie
RC Prim Sch EH54 .... 146 C3
St John St
Edinburgh EH8 .... 233 E3
Spott EH42 .... 106 B2
Stirling FK8 .... 7 D4
St John the Baptist RC Sch
EH47 .... 193 F3
St John Vianney Prim Sch
EH16 .... 124 A1
St John's Ave
Edinburgh EH12 .... 121 F3
Falkirk FK2 .... 60 B3
Linlithgow EH49 .... 84 C3
St John's Cres EH12 .... 121 F3
St John's Ct KY11 .... 47 E2
St John's Dr KY12 .... 29 E2
St John's Gate FK6 .... 36 B1
St John's Gdns Denny FK6 .. 36 B1
Edinburgh EH12 .... 121 F3
St John's Gr FK6 .... 36 B1
St John's Hill EH8 .... 233 E2
St John's Hospl EH54 .... 147 E2
St John's PI KY12 .... 29 E2

St John's PI EH48 .... 113 F3
St John's Prim Sch
Edinburgh EH15 .... 125 D4
Rosyth KY11 .... 46 C2
St John's Rd
Broxburn EH52 .... 117 F2
Edinburgh EH12 .... 121 E3
St John's Terr EH12 .... 121 F3
St John's Way EH51 .... 63 F3
St Joseph's Cotts EH33 .. 128 B4
St Joseph's Prim Sch
Bonnybridge FK4 .... 58 A2
Edinburgh EH12 .... 121 F2
St Joseph's RC Prim Sch
EH49 .... 84 C3
Edinburgh EH32 .... 128 B4
St Joseph's Specl Sch
EH47 .... 181 A1
St Josephs RC Prim Sch
EH47 .... 169 F3
St Katharine's Brae
EH16 .... 155 D3
St Katharine's Cres
EH16 .... 155 D3
St Katharine's Loan
EH16 .... 155 D3
St Kenneth's RC Prim Sch
EH54 .... 147 E4
St Kentigern Rd EH26 .... 203 E3
St Kentigerns Acad
EH47 .... 171 D4
St Kilda Cres KY2 .... 16 C4
St Laurence Cres FK1 .... 110 A3
St Lawrence St KY11 .... 29 E1
St Leonard's Bank EH8 .. 233 F1
St Leonard's Crag EH8 .. 233 F1
St Leonard's Ct KY3 .... 35 D2
St Leonard's Hill EH8 .... 233 E1
St Leonard's La EH8 .... 233 E1
St Leonard's PI
Dunfermline KY11 .... 29 D1
Kinghorn KY3 .... 34 C2
St Leonard's Prim Sch
KY11 .... 29 D1
St Leonard's St
Dunfermline KY11 .... 29 D1
Edinburgh EH8 .... 233 E1
St Lukes Prim Sch EH22 .. 183 E3
St Magdalene's EH49 .... 85 D4
St Margaret St KY12 .... 29 D2
St Margaret's Cres FK2 .... 61 F1
St Margaret's Dr EH48 .... 143 F3
St Margaret's PI EH9 ...... 123 E2
St Margaret's Prep Sch
EH16 .... 124 A2
St Margaret's Prim Sch
KY11 .... 29 E2
St Margaret's RC Acad
EH54 .... 147 E2
St Margaret's RC Prim Sch
Cowie FK7 .... 20 B4
Loanhead EH20 .... 155 E1
Queensferry EH30 .... 68 B1
St Margaret's Rd
Edinburgh EH9 .... 123 D2
North Berwick EH39 .... 54 B4
St Margaret's Sch EH16 .. 124 A2
St Margaret's Sch
Sen Coll EH31 .... 52 A1
St Margarets Ct EH39 ...... 54 B4
St Margarets Dr KY12 .... 29 D2
St Marie's Prim Sch KY2 .. 17 E4
St Mark's La EH15 .... 125 D4
St Mark's PI EH15 .... 125 D4
St Mark's RC Prim Sch
EH14 .... 153 F4
St Martin's Ct EH41 .... 132 B4
St Martin's Gate EH41 .... 132 A4
St Martin's PI EH41 .... 132 B4
St Martin's RC Prim Sch
EH33 .... 128 B3
St Mary's (Leith)
RC Prim Sch EH6 .... 94 A3
St Mary's Music Sch
EH12 .... 122 C4
St Mary's PI
Edinburgh EH15 .... 125 E4
Kirkcaldy KY1 .... 17 E3
St Mary's Place La EH15 .. 125 E4
St Mary's RC Cath EH1 .. 233 D4
St Mary's RC Prim Sch
Bannockburn FK7 .... 7 E1
Bathgate EH48 .... 145 D3
Bo'ness EH51 .... 64 A4
Bonnyrigg and Lasswade
EH19 .... 182 A3
Edinburgh EH3 .... 93 E1
Polbeth EH55 .... 172 C3
Stirling FK8 .... 1 C1
St Mary's RC Sch EH41 .. 132 A4
St Mary's Rd KY1 .... 17 E3
St Mary's St EH1 .... 233 E3
St Mary's Wynd FK8 .... 7 D4
St Marys PI FK3 .... 61 F4
St Matthew's RC Prim Sch
EH24 .... 181 F1
St Michael's Ave EH21 .... 128 B3
St Michael's Hospl EH49 .. 85 E3
St Michael's Wynd EH49 .. 85 D4
St Michaels La EH49 .... 85 D4
St Modan's High Sch FK7 .. 7 D2
St Modans Ct 14 FK1 .... 60 A2
St Mungo's PI EH49 .... 60 A3
St Mungo's Prim Sch
FK10 .... 10 B3

St Mungo's View EH26 .... 203 F3
St Mungo's Wynd FK10 .... 10 A3
St Nicholas Prim Sch
EH52 .... 117 E2
St Nicholas (Specl Sch)
EH11 .... 122 B3
St Ninian's Ave EH49 .... 84 C4
St Ninian's Dr EH12 .... 121 E4
St Ninian's RC Prim Sch
Edinburgh EH7 .... 94 B1
Livingston EH54 .... 148 A1
St Ninian's Rd
Edinburgh EH12 .... 121 E4
Linlithgow EH49 .... 84 C4
St Ninian's Row EH1 ...... 233 D4
St Ninian's Terr EH10 .... 122 C1
St Ninian's Way EH49 ...... 84 C4
St Ninians Prim Sch FK7 ... 7 D2
St Ninians Rd
Cambusbarron FK7 .... 6 C3
Stirling FK8 .... 7 D3
St Ninians Row EH1 .... 93 E1
St Ninians Way
Blackness EH49 .... 65 F2
Musselburgh EH21 .... 127 D3
St Patrick Sq EH8 .... 233 E1
St Patrick St EH8 .... 233 E1
St Patrick's RC Prim Sch
FK6 .... 36 C2
St Patrick's RC Prim Sch
ML7 .... 191 F2
St Paul's Dr EH48 .... 144 A3
St Paul's RC Prim Sch
EH53 .... 148 C2
St Peter's Ct KY11 .... 47 E2
St Peter's RC Sch EH10 .. 123 D2
St Ronan's Terr EH10 .... 123 D1
St Serf's PI FK10 .... 4 A2
High Valleyfield KY12 .... 26 A1
Tullibody KY12 .... 4 A2
St Serf's Rd FK10 .... 4 A2
St Serf's Sch EH16 .... 122 C4
St Serfs Gr FK10 .... 11 D2
St Serfs Wlk FK12 .... 4 C3
St Stephen PI EH3 .... 93 D1
St Stephen St EH3 .... 93 D1
St Teresa PI EH11 .... 122 C2
St Thomas of Aquins
RC High Sch EH3 .... 232 C1
St Thomas Rd EH9 .... 123 E2
St Thomas's PI FK7 .... 6 C3
St Thomas's Well FK7 .... 6 B4
St Valery Dr FK7 .... 7 D2
St Vincent St EH3 .... 93 D1
Salamanca Cres EH26 .... 204 A4
Salamander PI EH6 .... 94 A3
Salamander St EH6 .... 94 A3
Salen Loan ML7 .... 192 A2
Salisbury PI EH9 .... 123 F3
Salisbury Rd EH16 .... 123 F3
Salisbury St KY2 .... 17 D3
Salisbury View EH22 ...... 183 E3
Salmon Dr FK1 .... 59 F1
Salmon Inn Rd FK2 .... 61 E1
Salmond PI 5 EH7 .... 94 A1
Salt Preston PI EH32 .... 96 C1
Saltcoats Dr FK3 .... 61 F4
Saltcoats Gdns EH54 ...... 173 F3
Saltcoats Rd
Grangemouth FK3 .... 62 A4
Gullane EH31 .... 52 A1
Salter's Rd Dalkeith EH22 .. 157 E3
Wallyford EH21 .... 127 D2
Salters'Gr EH22 .... 157 E2
Salters' Rd Dalkeith EH22 .. 157 E2
Pathhead EH37 .... 186 A1
Salters' Terr EH22 .... 157 E2
Saltire Gdns EH39 .... 101 F4
Saltoun Prim Sch EH34 .. 161 F3
Saltpans KY11 .... 45 D2
Salvage Rd KY11 .... 46 B1
Salvesen Cres EH4 .... 92 A3
Salvesen Gdns EH4 .... 92 A3
Salvesen Gr EH4 .... 92 A3
Salvesen Terr EH4 .... 92 A3
Samoa Terr EH26 .... 204 A4
Sand Port EH6 .... 94 A3
Sandport Trad Est EH6 .... 93 F3
Sandeman Ct FK10 .... 23 F2
Sanderson Terr KY2 .... 15 D1
Sanderson's Gr EH33 ..... 128 B4
Sandersons Wynd EH33 .. 128 B4
Sandford Gdns EH15 ...... 125 D4
Sandiland Dr EH53 .... 148 A1
Sandilands KY11 .... 45 E2
Sandport PI EH6 .... 93 F3
Sandport St EH6 .... 93 F3
Sands The EH41 .... 132 A4
Sandy Loan Gullane EH31 .. 52 A1
Laurieston FK2 .... 61 D2
Sandy Rd KY3 .... 32 B3
Sandyford Ave EH49 .... 84 A3
Sandyhill Ave ML7 .... 192 A2
Sandyloan Cres FK2 .... 61 D2
Sandyvale PI ML7 .... 192 A2
Sang PI KY1 .... 17 D2
Sang Rd KY1 .... 17 D2
Sarazen Ct EH54 .... 147 D4
Sarazen Gn EH54 .... 147 D4
Sauchenbush Rd KY2 ...... 16 C3
Sauchie Ct FK7 .... 7 F1
Sauchie Hospl FK10 .... 10 B4
Sauchie St FK7 .... 7 D1
Sauchiebank EH11 .... 122 C3
Saughbank EH52 .... 117 D3
Saughs The EH22 .... 183 D2
Saughton Ave EH11 .... 122 B2

Saughton Cres EH12 ...... 122 A3
Saughton Gdns EH12 ...... 122 A3
Saughton Gr EH12 .... 122 A3
Saughton Loan EH12 ...... 122 A3
Saughton Mains Ave
EH11 .... 121 F2
Saughton Mains Bank
EH11 .... 122 A2
Saughton Mains Dr
EH11 .... 121 F2
Saughton Mains Gdns
EH11 .... 121 F2
Saughton Mains Gr
EH11 .... 122 A2
Saughton Mains Loan
EH11 .... 121 F2
Saughton Mains Pk EH11 .. 121 F2
Saughton Mains PI EH11 .. 121 F2
Saughton Mains St EH11 .. 122 A2
Saughton Mains Terr
EH11 .... 121 F2
Saughton Pk EH12 .... 122 A3
Saughton Rd EH11 .... 121 F2
Saughton Rd N EH11 ...... 121 F2
Saughtonhall Ave EH12 .. 122 B3
Saughtonhall Ave W
EH12 .... 122 A3
Saughtonhall Cir EH12 ... 122 B3
Saughtonhall Cres EH12 .. 122 B3
Saughtonhall Dr EH12 .... 122 A3
Saughtonhall Gdns EH12 .. 122 B3
Saughtonhall Gr EH12 .... 122 B3
Saughtonhall Terr EH12 .. 122 B3
Saunders St
Edinburgh EH3 .... 232 B4
Kirkcaldy KY1 .... 17 D1
Savile PI EH9 .... 123 F2
Savile Terr EH9 .... 123 F2
Sawers Ave FK6 .... 36 B1
Saxe Coburg PI EH3 .... 93 D1
Saxe Coburg St EH3 .... 93 D1
Scarlett Pk EH21 .... 127 D3
Schaw Ct FK10 .... 5 E1
Schaw Rd EH32 .... 97 D1
Schawpark Ave FK10 .... 5 E1
Schiltron Way FK7 .... 7 D2
Scholars' Brae KY3 .... 50 C4
School Brae Bo'ness EH51 .. 63 F4
Bonnyrigg and Lasswade
EH18 .... 156 A1
Dysart KY1 .... 18 A4
Edinburgh EH4 .... 91 D3
West Barns EH42 .... 105 F4
School Gn
Bonnyrigg and Lasswade
EH18 .... 156 A1
Longniddry EH32 .... 98 C3
School La Bathgate EH48 .. 145 D3
Cockenzie & Port Seton
EH32 .... 97 E2
Menstrie FK11 .... 4 A4
Mid Calder EH53 .... 148 B2
Shotts ML7 .... 212 A4
School PI EH52 .... 116 C2
School Row FK10 .... 28 B3
School St
Cowdenbeath KY4 .... 13 E2
Shotts ML7 .... 191 F2
School Wlk FK5 .... 38 B2
School Wynd KY1 .... 17 D1
Schoolyard Ct EH25 .... 181 D2
Sciennes EH9 .... 123 F3
Sciennes Gdns EH9 .... 123 F3
Sciennes Hill PI 4 EH9 .. 123 F3
Sciennes House PI 3
EH9 .... 123 F3
Sciennes PI 1 EH9 .... 123 F3
Sciennes Prim Sch EH9 .. 123 E3
Sciennes Rd EH9 .... 123 F3
Sclandersburn Rd FK6 .... 57 E4
Scobie PI KY12 .... 29 E2
Scollon Ave EH19 .... 182 B4
Scone Gdns EH8 .... 94 B1
Scotch Whisky
Heritage Ctr The EH1 .. 123 E4
Scotia PI FK2 .... 60 B3
Scotland Dr KY12 .... 29 F2
Scotland St EH3 .... 93 E1
Scotlands CI EH51 .... 63 F4
Scotmill Way KY11 .... 47 F2
Scots Mill PI KY11 .... 47 F2
Scotstoun Ave EH30 .... 89 E4
Scotstoun Gn EH30 .... 89 D4
Scotstoun Pk EH30 .... 89 E4
Scotstoun Rd FK7 .... 20 C3
Scott Ave KY2 .... 61 F1
Scott Cres EH54 .... 148 B3
Scott PI EH47 .... 193 F2
Scott Rd EH26 .... 203 F4
Scott St Dunfermline KY12 .. 28 C3
Grangemouth FK3 .... 61 E3
Kirkcaldy KY1 .... 17 D1
Stirling FK8 .... 2 A1
Scott Terr EH48 .... 145 E3
Scottish Ag Mus EH28 .... 119 F3
Scottish Ag
Science Agency EH12 .... 121 D4
Scottish Mining Mus Lady
Victoria Colliery EH22 .. 183 D2

Scottish Nat Gall of Mod Art
EH4 .... 122 C4
Scottish Pol Coll FK10 ..... 23 F3
Scottish Prison Service
Coll FK2 .... 82 B4
Sea Wynd EH32 .... 71 E3
Seabegs Cres FK4 .... 58 A2
Seabegs PI FK4 .... 57 F2
Seabegs Rd FK4 .... 57 F2
Seacliff EH39 .... 56 A3
Seacot EH6 .... 94 B4
Seafield Ave EH6 .... 94 B2
Seafield Cres EH42 .... 78 C3
Seafield Ct FK1 .... 59 F1
Seafield Inf Sch EH54 .... 146 C3
Seafield Moor Rd EH25 .. 180 B3
Seafield PI
Dalgety Bay KY11 .... 48 A1
Edinburgh EH6 .... 94 B2
Seafield Rd Bilston EH25 .. 180 C3
Blackburn EH47 .... 171 F4
Edinburgh EH6 .... 94 B2
Kirkcaldy KY1 .... 35 D4
Seafield Rd E EH15 .... 94 C2
Seafield Rows EH47 .... 146 A1
Seafield St EH6 .... 94 B2
Seafield View
Kinghorn KY3 .... 35 D4
Kirkcaldy KY1 .... 35 D4
Seafield Way EH15 .... 94 C2
Seaforth Dr EH4 .... 92 B1
Seaforth PI Burntisland KY3 .. 50 C4
Kirkcaldy KY1 .... 17 F4
Stirling FK8 .... 7 D4
Seaforth Rd FK2 .... 39 E1
Seaforth Terr
Bonnyrigg and Lasswade
EH19 .... 181 F3
3 Edinburgh EH4 .... 92 B1
Sealcar St EH5 .... 92 C4
Sealock Ct FK3 .... 61 E3
Sealstrand KY11 .... 48 B2
Seaport St EH6 .... 94 A3
Seaside PI KY3 .... 49 E4
Seaton PI FK1 .... 60 B2
Seaview Cres EH15 .... 125 F4
Seaview PI EH51 .... 63 F4
Seaview Terr EH15 .... 125 F4
Seco PI KY4 .... 13 E2
Second Gait EH14 .... 151 F4
Second St EH22 .... 183 D2
Sedgebank EH54 .... 147 F3
Seggarsdean Ct EH41 .... 132 B4
Seggarsdean Pk EH41 .... 132 B4
Seggarsdean Terr EH41 .. 132 B4
Selkirk Ave EH54 .... 13 E1
Selkirk Rd KY11 .... 67 D4
Selm Pk EH54 .... 148 A2
Selvage PI KY11 .... 47 D2
Selvage St KY11 .... 47 D2
Semple St EH3 .... 232 B2
Seton Chapel EH32 .... 97 F2
Seton Ct
Cockenzie & Port Seton
EH32 .... 97 F2
Tranent EH33 .... 128 B3
Seton Dr FK7 .... 7 E2
Seton Mains EH32 .... 98 C2
Seton PI
Cockenzie & Port Seton
EH32 .... 97 E2
Dalgety Bay KY11 .... 48 B3
Edinburgh EH9 .... 123 F3
Kirkcaldy KY2 .... 16 B4
Seton Rd EH32 .... 98 C3
Seton Terr EH51 .... 64 A4
Seton View EH32 .... 97 F2
Seton Wynd EH32 .... 97 F2
Seventh St EH22 .... 183 D2
Shadepark Cres EH22 .... 157 D2
Shadepark Dr EH22 .... 157 D2
Shadepark Gdns EH22 ... 157 D2
Shaftesbury Pk EH11 ..... 122 C2
Shaftesbury St FK10 .... 10 A4
Shafto PI EH51 .... 63 F3
Shamrock St KY12 .... 29 D3
Shandon Cres EH11 .... 122 C2
Shandon PI EH11 .... 122 C2
Shandon Rd EH11 .... 122 C2
Shandon St EH11 .... 122 C2
Shandon Terr EH11 .... 122 C2
Shandwick PI EH2 .... 232 A3
Shanks Ave FK6 .... 57 F4
Shanks Rd EH47 .... 170 A4
Shannon Dr FK1 .... 59 F2
Shanter Way 7 EH16 ..... 124 A1
Sharp Terr FK3 .... 61 E3
Sharpdale Loan EH16 .... 124 A2
Shaw Ave EH48 .... 143 F3
Shaw Cres KY5 .... 14 A4
Shaw PI Armadale EH48 .. 143 F3
Grangemouth FK3 .... 61 E3
Mayfield EH22 .... 183 E3
Shaw St KY11 .... 29 E1
Shaw's PI EH7 .... 93 F1
Shaw's Sq EH7 .... 93 F1
Shaw's St EH7 .... 93 F2
Shaw's Terr EH7 .... 93 F2
Shaws Ct EH26 .... 180 A1
Sheephousehill ML7 .... 193 F3
Sheperdlands Gr KY12 ..... 26 B4
Shepherd Cres KY3 .... 50 B4
Sherbrooke Rd KY11 .... 46 B2
Sheriff Bank EH6 .... 93 F3
Sheriff Brae EH6 .... 93 F3

Sheriff Pk EH6 .... 93 F3
Sheriffhall Junc EH22 ...... 156 B3
Sheriffmuir Rd FK9 .... 2 B4
Sheriffmuirlands FK9 .... 2 B2
Sheriffs Pk EH49 .... 85 F4
Sherriff Hall Cotts EH39 ... 74 C4
Sherriff La FK5 .... 38 C2
Sherwood Ave EH19 .... 182 B3
Sherwood Cres EH19 .... 182 B3
Sherwood Ct EH19 .... 182 B3
Sherwood Dr EH19 .... 182 B3
Sherwood Gr EH19 .... 182 B3
Sherwood Ind Est EH19 .... 182 B4
Sherwood Loan EH19 ...... 182 B3
Sherwood Pk EH19 .... 182 B3
Sherwood Pl EH19 .... 182 B3
Sherwood Terr EH19 .... 182 B3
Sherwood View EH19 ...... 182 B3
Sherwood Way EH19 .... 182 B3
Sherwood Wlk EH19 .... 182 B3
Shetland Ct FK10 .... 10 A3
Shetland Pl KY1 .... 17 F4
Shiel Ct FK3 .... 61 E2
Shiel Gdns Falkirk FK2 ..... 39 E1
Shotts ML7 .... 192 A2
Shiel Wlk EH54 .... 148 A3
Shieldhill Prim Sch FK1 .... 81 E3
Shields Ct EH52 .... 117 F3
Shields Rd KY11 .... 29 F2
Shieling The KY12 .... 27 F1
Shillinghill FK10 .... 10 A3
Shinwell Pl KY11 .... 46 C2
Shiphaugh Pl FK8 .... 2 B1
Shire Way FK10 .... 9 F3
Shirra's Brae Rd FK7 .... 7 E2
Shoestanes Rd EH38 ...... 228 B1
Shoestanes Terr EH38 ..... 228 B1
Shore EH6 .... 94 A3
Shore Pl EH6 .... 94 A3
Shore Rd Aberdour KY3 ..... 49 E4
Airth FK2 .... 22 B2
Dysart KY1 .... 18 A3
Queensferry EH30 .... 68 A1
Stirling FK8 .... 7 D4
Shore St EH42 .... 78 C2
Shore The FK10 .... 10 A3
Shorthope St EH21 .... 126 B3
Shotts Rd
Fauldhouse EH47 .... 193 E2
Harthill ML7 .... 167 F1
Shotts Sta ML7 .... 191 F2
Shottsburn Rd ML7 .... 167 D2
Shottskirk Rd ML7 .... 191 E3
Shrub Mount EH15 .... 95 D1
Shrub Place La EH7 .... 93 F1
Sibbald Pl EH54 .... 147 D3
Sibbalds Brae EH48 .... 144 B3
Sidegate EH41 .... 132 A4
Sidehead Rd ML7 .... 168 C3
Sidlaw Pl FK3 .... 61 F3
Sidlaw St KY2 .... 16 C4
Sienna Gdns EH9 .... 123 F3
Sighthill Ave EH11 .... 121 F1
Sighthill Bank EH11 .... 121 E1
Sighthill Cres EH11 .... 121 E1
Sighthill Ct EH11 .... 121 E1
Sighthill Dr EH11 .... 121 E1
Sighthill Gdns EH11 .... 121 E1
Sighthill Gn EH11 .... 121 E1
Sighthill Gr EH11 .... 121 F1
Sighthill Ind Est EH11 ..... 121 D2
Sighthill Loan EH11 .... 121 E1
Sighthill Neuk EH11 .... 121 E1
Sighthill Pk EH11 .... 121 F1
Sighthill Pl EH11 .... 121 E1
Sighthill Prim Sch EH11 ... 121 E1
Sighthill Rd EH11 .... 121 E1
Sighthill Rise EH11 .... 121 E1
Sighthill St EH11 .... 121 E1
Sighthill Terr EH11 .... 121 E1
Sighthill View EH11 .... 121 E1
Sighthill Wynd EH11 ...... 121 E1
Silk Ho FK1 .... 60 A3
Silver St Dunbar EH42 ..... 78 B1
Kincardine FK10 .... 23 F2
Silverbarton Terr KY3 ...... 33 E1
Silverburn Dr EH26 .... 203 E3
Silverdale Rd FK2 .... 82 C4
Silverknowes Ave EH4 ..... 91 F2
Silverknowes Bank EH4 .... 91 F2
Silverknowes Brae EH4 .... 92 A2
Silverknowes Cres EH4 .... 91 F2
Silverknowes Ct EH4 ...... 91 F2
Silverknowes Dell EH4 ..... 91 F2
Silverknowes Dr EH4 ...... 91 F2
Silverknowes Eastway
EH4 .... 91 F2
Silverknowes Gdns EH4 .... 92 A2
Silverknowes Gn EH4 ...... 92 A2
Silverknowes Gr EH4 ...... 91 F2
Silverknowes Hill EH4 ..... 91 F2
Silverknowes Loan EH4 .... 91 F2
Silverknowes Midway
EH4 .... 92 A2
Silverknowes Neuk EH4 .... 92 A2
Silverknowes Parkway
EH4 .... 91 F3
Silverknowes Pl EH4 ...... 92 A2
Silverknowes Prim Sch
EH4 .... 92 A3
Silverknowes Rd EH4 ...... 91 F3
Silverknowes Rd E EH4 .... 92 A2
Silverknowes Rd S EH4 .... 91 F2
Silverknowes Southway
EH4 .... 92 A2

Silverknowes Terr EH4 ..... 91 F2
Silverknowes View EH4 .... 92 A2
Simon Sq EH8 .... 233 E2
Simpson Cres EH48 .... 145 E3
Simpson Dr FK2 .... 83 D3
Simpson Parkway FK54 .... 147 D1
Simpson Rd EH52 .... 118 A3
Simpson St FK1 .... 59 F3
Simpson Wlk KY11 .... 29 F1
Sinclair Cres FK6 .... 36 B1
Sinclair Ct Aberlady EH32 .. 71 E2
Bannockburn FK7 .... 7 F1
Sinclair Dr
Cowdenbeath KY4 .... 13 D1
Fallin FK7 .... 8 B2
Sinclair Gdns KY12 .... 29 D2
Sinclair Pl FK2 .... 39 D1
Sinclair Way FK54 .... 147 E3
Sinclairtown Prim Sch
KY1 .... 17 F4
Sir George Bruce Rd
KY12 .... 26 C4
Sir Harry Lauder Rd
EH15 .... 125 D4
Sir James Black Gait KY5 ... 14 A4
Sir Walter Scott Pend
EH32 .... 96 C1
Sir Walter Scott's Mon
EH2 .... 233 D3
Sir William Fraser Homes
EH13 .... 153 D4
Sir William Wallace Ct
FK5 .... 38 A2
Sivewright Ct FK10 .... 23 F2
Sixth St EH22 .... 183 D3
Skaithmuir Ave FK2 ...... 39 D2
Skaithmuir Cres FK2 ...... 39 D2
Skelmorlie Pl FK5 .... 38 C2
Skeltie Muir Ave EH19 .... 182 A3
Skeltiemuir Ct EH19 ...... 182 A3
Skeltiemuir Gr EH19 ...... 182 A3
Skene St FK4 .... 58 A3
Skibo Ct KY12 .... 29 D2
Skibo Pl KY2 .... 16 B3
Skye Ct FK3 .... 61 E3
Skye Dr FK2 .... 61 F1
Skye Rd KY11 .... 29 F1
Skylaw Terr ML11 .... 215 D1
Skythorn Way FK1 .... 59 F1
Slaeside EH14 .... 151 E1
Slamannan Prim Sch
FK1 .... 110 A4
Slamannan Rd
Avonbridge FK1 .... 112 A3
Falkirk FK1 .... 60 A1
Slamannan FK1 .... 110 A1
Slateford Rd EH14 .... 122 B2
Slateford Sta EH14 .... 122 B2
Sleigh Dr EH7 .... 94 B1
Sleigh Gdns EH7 .... 94 B1
Sligo St KY12 .... 26 C4
Sloan St EH6 .... 93 F2
Small St KY5 .... 14 A3
Smallburn Pl FK3 .... 61 F3
Smeaton Gdns KY2 .... 17 E3
Smeaton Gr EH21 .... 126 B2
Smeaton Ind Site KY1 ..... 17 E4
Smeaton Rd KY1 .... 17 E3
Smiddy Wynd FK12 .... 5 D3
Smileyknowes Ct EH39 .... 54 A3
Smith Art Gallery & Mus
FK8 .... 7 D4
Smith Ave KY4 .... 13 D2
Smith Pl FK6 .... 36 B1
Smith St FK2 .... 60 A4
Smith's Pl EH6 .... 93 F2
Smith's Terr KY1 .... 17 E3
Smithfield Loan FK10 ..... 9 F3
Smithfield St EH11 .... 122 B3
Smithy Brae EH27 .... 149 F1
Smithy Green Ave EH22 ... 156 A4
Smithy Row EH39 .... 74 A4
Snab Brae EH51 .... 63 E3
Snab La EH51 .... 63 E4
Snowden Sch Ltd FK8 ..... 7 D4
Snowdon Pl FK8 .... 7 D3
Snowdon Place La FK7 .... 7 D3
Society La EH55 .... 172 B2
Society Pl EH55 .... 172 B2
Society Rd EH30 .... 67 F1
Solway Dr FK6 .... 57 E4
Somerset Pl EH6 .... 94 A2
Somerville Rd KY11 ...... 46 B1
Somerville Sq KY3 .... 50 C4
Somerville St KY3 .... 50 C4
Sommers Pk EH53 .... 148 B1
Sommerville Gdns EH30 ... 89 E4
Somnerfield Ave EH41 .... 131 F4
Somnerfield Cres EH41 ... 131 F4
Somnerfield Ct EH41 ..... 131 F4
Somnerfield Gr EH41 ..... 131 F4
Somnerfield Pk EH41 ..... 131 F4
Souillac Dr FK6 .... 36 B1
South Acres KY12 .... 27 E1
South Approach Rd FK2 .... 23 D3
South Ave Blairhall KY12 ... 26 A4
Maddiston EH52 .... 83 D4
South Bantaskine Dr FK1 ... 60 A1
South Bantaskine Rd FK1 ... 60 A1
South Barnton Ave EH4 .... 91 F2
South Beechwood EH12 ... 122 A3
South Brae FK2 .... 83 D3
South Bridge EH1 .... 233 D3
South Bridge St
Bathgate EH48 .... 145 D3
Grangemouth FK3 .... 40 B1
South Broomage Ave FK5 .. 38 B1
South Charlotte St EH2 .... 232 B3

South Clerk St EH8 .... 233 E1
South College St EH8 ..... 233 D2
South Craigs Rd FK2 ...... 82 C4
South Cres EH32 .... 97 D1
South Dewar St KY12 ..... 28 C2
South Doors EH32 .... 97 E2
South Dr KY11 .... 46 C3
South East Circus Pl
EH3 .... 232 B4
South East Cumberland
Street La EH3 .... 93 E1
South East Thistle
Street La EH2 .... 232 C4
South Elixa Pl EH8 .... 124 B4
South Ettrick Rd EH10 .... 122 C2
South Fergus Pl KY1 ...... 17 D2
South Fort St EH6 .... 93 F3
South Gait EH39 .... 53 F4
South Gayfield La EH1 .... 93 F1
South Gillsland Rd EH10 ... 122 C2
South Grange Ave EH32 ... 127 F4
South Gray St EH9 .... 123 F2
South Gray's Cl EH1 ...... 233 E3
South Green Dr FK2 ...... 22 C2
South Groathill Ave EH4 ... 92 B1
South Gyle Access EH12 ... 121 E2
South Gyle Broadway
EH12 .... 121 D2
South Gyle Cres EH12 .... 121 D2
South Gyle Crescent La
EH12 .... 121 D2
South Gyle Gdns EH12 .... 121 D3
South Gyle Ind Est EH12 .. 121 D2
South Gyle Loan EH12 .... 121 D3
South Gyle Mains EH12 ... 121 D3
South Gyle Pk EH12 ..... 121 D3
South Gyle Rd EH12 ..... 121 D3
South Gyle Sta EH12 ..... 121 D3
South Gyle Wynd EH12 ... 121 E2
South Hamilton Rd EH39 .. 54 A4
South Hill St KY3 .... 50 C4
South Hirst Rd ML7 ...... 167 E2
South Knone KY4 .... 30 C3
South Larch Rd KY11 ..... 29 F2
South Lauder Rd EH9 ..... 123 F2
South Laverockbank Ave
EH5 .... 93 E3
South Learmonth Ave 7
EH4 .... 92 C1
South Loanhead KY11 .... 45 F2
South Loch Pk EH48 ..... 145 D3
South Lodge Ave EH53 ... 148 B1
South Lorimer Pl EH32 ... 97 E2
South Lorne Pl EH6 ..... 93 F2
South Lumley St FK3 ..... 61 E4
South Marshall St FK3 .... 61 E4
South Maybury EH12 .... 121 D3
South Mellis Pk EH8 ..... 124 C4
South Melville La FK1 .... 60 A3
South Mid St EH48 ...... 145 D3
South Morningside
Prim Sch EH10 .... 123 D1
South Morton St EH15 ... 125 E4
South Oswald Rd EH9 .... 123 E2
South Overgate KY3 ..... 35 D2
South Oxford St EH8 .... 123 F3
South Philpingstone La
EH51 .... 64 B4
South Pilmuir Rd FK10 ... 11 D2
South Pk EH48 Armadale EH48 . 143 F2
Edinburgh EH6 .... 93 E3
South Pleasance Ave FK1 .. 60 A2
South Queensferry
Prim Sch EH30 .... 68 B1
South Rd
Fauldhouse EH47 .... 193 F4
Grangemouth FK2 .... 62 A3
South Roundall KY11 .... 45 F2
South Row
Charlestown KY11 ...... 45 D2
Kirkcaldy KY1 .... 17 F4
South Scotstoun EH30 ... 89 E4
South Seton Pk EH32 .... 97 E2
South Shore Rd FK3 ..... 41 D1
South Sloan St EH6 ..... 93 F2
South St Armadale EH48 .. 143 F3
Bo'ness EH51 .... 63 F4
Cambus FK10 .... 9 D4
Cowdenbeath KY4 ...... 13 E1
Dalkeith EH22 .... 156 C1
Dunbar EH42 .... 78 A1
Lochgelly KY5 .... 14 A3
Musselburgh EH21 ..... 126 A3
Stirling FK9 .... 2 B1
South St Andrew St EH2 .. 233 D4
South St David St EH2 ... 233 D3
South Steil EH10 .... 122 C1
South Trinity Rd EH5 .... 93 D3
South View
Burntisland KY3 .... 50 C4
Stenhousemuir FK5 ..... 38 C2
South Village EH53 ..... 148 B3
South West Cumberland
Street La EH3 .... 93 E1
South West Thistle
Street La EH2 .... 232 C4
Southbank Ct EH4 ...... 91 F2
Southcroft KY2 .... 4 C3
Southerton Cres KY2 .... 16 C3
Southerton Gdns KY2 ... 16 C3
Southerton Rd KY2 ..... 16 C2
Southfield KY4 .... 13 E3
Southfield Ave ML7 ..... 192 A2
Southfield Bank EH15 ... 124 C3
Southfield Cres
Shotts ML7 .... 192 A2
Stirling FK8 .... 7 D3
Southfield Dr FK1 ...... 110 A3

Southfield Farm Gr
EH15 .... 124 C4
Southfield Gdns E EH15 .. 124 C4
Southfield Gdns W EH15 . 124 C3
Southfield Hospl EH17 ... 155 E4
Southfield Load EH15 ... 124 C3
Southfield Loan EH15 ... 124 C3
Southfield Pl EH15 ..... 125 D4
Southfield Rd
Cousland EH22 .... 158 B3
Shotts ML7 .... 192 A2
Southfield Rd E EH15 ... 124 C3
Southfield Rd W EH15 .. 124 C3
Southfield Sq EH15 .... 124 C3
Southfield Terr EH15 ... 124 C3
Southhouse Ave EH17 ... 155 D3
Southhouse Broadway
EH17 .... 155 D2
Southhouse Cres EH17 .. 155 E2
Southhouse Gdns EH17 . 155 D2
Southhouse Gr EH17 ... 155 D2
Southhouse Loan EH17 . 155 D3
Southhouse Medway
EH17 .... 155 D3
Southhouse Rd EH17 ... 155 D2
Southhouse Sq EH17 ... 155 D3
Southhouse Terr EH17 .. 155 E3
Southlawn Ct EH4 ..... 91 F2
Spa Pl EH15 .... 95 D1
Spalding Cres EH22 .... 157 D2
Speedwell Ave EH22 ... 156 A4
Spence Ave KY3 ...... 33 F1
Spence St
Bonnybridge FK4 ..... 58 A3
Edinburgh EH16 ...... 123 F3
Spencer Pl Edinburgh EH5 . 93 D3
Kirkcaldy KY1 .... 17 F4
Spencerfield Rd KY11 ... 47 E1
Spencerfield Steadings
KY11 .... 47 F2
Spens La KY11 .... 46 B1
Spey Ct Grangemouth FK3 . 61 E3
Stirling FK7 .... 7 E3
Spey Dr FK54 .... 148 A2
Spey St EH7 .... 93 F2
Spey Street La EH7 .... 93 F2
Spey Terr EH7 .... 93 F2
Spier's Pl EH6 .... 93 F3
Spinkhill FK2 .... 60 C1
Spinnaker Way KY11 ... 47 F1
Spinner's Ct KY12 ..... 27 E1
Spinney The EH17 ..... 155 E3
Spinneys The KY11 .... 48 B2
Spittal Hill FK9 .... 2 B2
Spittal St Edinburgh EH3 . 232 B2
Stirling FK8 .... 7 D4
Spittalfield Cres KY11 ... 47 E1
Spittalfield Rd KY11 .... 47 E1
Spott Ave EH42 .... 106 B2
Spott Loan EH42 ...... 106 B2
Spott Rd EH42 .... 78 C1
Spottiswoode Gdns
EH53 .... 148 B1
Spottiswoode Rd EH9 ... 123 E3
Spottiswoode St EH9 ... 123 E3
Sprig Way ML7 .... 168 C3
Spring Gdns EH8 ..... 94 A1
Springbank Gdns FK2 ... 60 B3
Springbank Rd
Shotts ML7 .... 191 E3
Stirling FK7 .... 7 E3
Springbank Terr KY12 ... 29 D3
Springfield Edinburgh EH6 . 93 F2
West Barns EH42 ...... 105 F4
Springfield Cres
North Berwick EH39 .... 54 A4
Queensferry EH30 ..... 67 F1
Springfield Ct EH49 .... 85 E4
Springfield Dr FK1 ..... 59 F3
Springfield Gdns EH39 .. 54 A4
Springfield Lea EH30 ... 67 F1
Springfield Pl
Gorebridge EH23 ...... 207 E4
Queensferry EH30 ..... 67 F1
Roslin EH25 .... 181 D2
Springfield Prim Sch
EH49 .... 85 E4
Springfield Rd Alloa FK10 . 10 B4
Denny FK6 .... 36 C1
Linlithgow EH49 ...... 85 E4
Penicuik EH26 .... 222 C3
Queensferry EH30 ..... 67 F1
Stirling FK7 .... 7 E3
Springfield St EH6 ..... 93 F2
Springfield Terr
Queensferry EH30 ..... 67 F1
West Barns EH42 ...... 77 F1
Springhead Rd ML7 .... 212 A4
Springhill Brae KY4 .... 30 C3
Springhill & Leadloch Rd
ML7 .... 192 C1
Springhill Rd ML7 ..... 192 A2
Springhill View ML7 ... 192 A2
Springkerse Ind Est FK7 .. 7 E3
Springkerse Rdbt FK7 ... 7 F4
Springvalley Gdns
EH10 .... 123 D2
Springvalley Terr EH10 . 123 D2
Springwell Pl EH11 .... 122 C3
Springwood KY11 ..... 47 D2
Springwood Ave FK8 ... 6 C3
Springwood Pk EH16 ... 155 D4
Sprinty Ave EH35 ..... 159 E4
Sprinty Dr EH35 ...... 159 E4
Sprotwell Terr FK10 .... 5 E1
Spruce Dr EH47 ...... 170 B3

Spruce Gr
Dunfermline KY11 ..... 46 B4
Livingston EH54 ...... 148 A3
Spylaw Ave EH13 ..... 152 C4
Spylaw Bank Rd EH13 .. 153 D4
Spylaw Pk EH13 ...... 152 C4
Spylaw Rd EH10 ...... 122 C2
Spylaw St EH13 ...... 153 D4
Square The
Cockburnspath TD13 ... 140 C2
Danderhall EH22 ..... 156 A4
East Linton EH40 ..... 103 F4
Fallin FK7 .... 8 B2
Gifford EH41 .... 163 F3
Kirkliston EH29 ...... 89 D1
Newtongrange EH22 ... 183 D3
Penicuik EH26 .... 203 F2
Spott EH42 .... 106 B2
Torphichen EH48 ..... 113 F3
Sraehouse Wynd ML8 .. 230 A1
Stable La EH10 ...... 123 D2
Stable Rd ML7 ...... 192 A4
Stables Rd KY11 ..... 46 B1
Staffa EH54 .... 146 C3
Staffa Pl FK1 .... 60 A1
Stafford St EH3 ..... 232 A3
Stair Pk Edinburgh EH12 . 122 B4
Tranent EH33 .... 128 A4
Standalane FK10 ..... 23 F2
Standhill Ct EH48 .... 144 C2
Standing Stone Wlk KY11 . 29 F1
Standingstane Rd EH30 .. 89 F3
Standrigg Rd FK2 .... 82 A3
Stane Prim Sch ML7 ... 192 A2
Stane Rd ML7 ...... 192 A1
Stanedykehead EH16 .. 154 C3
Stanhope Pl EH12 .... 122 C4
Stanhope St EH12 ... 122 C4
Stanistone Rd ML8 ... 230 A1
Stankards Rd EH52 .. 116 C2
Stanley Ave EH25 ... 180 C3
Stanley Dr Bridge of A FK9 . 2 A4
Harthill ML7 .... 169 D3
Stanley Gdns FK2 .... 82 C3
Stanley Pl Edinburgh EH7 . 94 A1
Ormiston EH35 ...... 159 F4
Stanley Rd Edinburgh EH6 . 93 E3
Harthill ML7 .... 169 D3
Stanley St EH15 ..... 125 D4
Stanley Terr KY12 ... 27 D3
Stanton Ave FK10 ... 9 F3
Stanwell St EH6 .... 93 F2
Stapeley Ave EH7 ... 94 C1
Starbank Rd EH5 .... 93 E3
Stark Ave FK1 ..... 59 E3
Stark's Brae EH51 ... 64 A4
Stark's Park
(Raith Rovers FC) KY1 . 17 D1
Starlaw Ave EH48 ... 145 F3
Starlaw Bsns Pk EH54 . 146 B2
Starlaw Cres EH48 .. 145 F3
Starlaw Gdns EH48 .. 145 F3
Starlaw Rd EH54, EH47 . 146 B2
Starlaw Terr EH48 .. 145 F3
Starlaw West Rdbt
EH47 .... 146 A2
Starlaw Wlk EH48 ... 145 F3
Starryshaw Rd ML7 .. 191 F3
Station Ave EH41 ... 131 F4
Station Brae
Edinburgh EH15 ..... 125 D4
Kinghorn KY3 .... 34 C1
Station Ct Addiewell EH55 . 171 F1
Haddington EH41 .... 131 F4
North Berwick EH39 .. 54 A4
Station Hill EH39 ... 54 A4
Station Loan EH14 .. 151 E2
Station Pl KY3 ..... 49 E4
Station Rd
Addiewell EH55 ..... 171 F1
Armadale EH48 ..... 143 F2
Bannockburn FK7 ... 7 F1
Blackridge EH48 .... 142 B1
Bridge of A FK9 ..... 1 C4
Brightons FK2 ...... 61 F1
Broxburn EH52 ..... 117 F3
Cambus FK10 ...... 4 A1
Cowdenbeath KY4 ... 13 E2
Cowie FK7 .... 20 B3
Dalkeith EH22 ..... 156 C1
Dirleton EH39 ..... 53 E2
Dunbar EH42 ...... 78 C1
Dysart KY1 .... 18 A4
East Linton EH40 ... 103 F4
Edinburgh EH12 .... 121 F3
Gifford EH41 ...... 163 F3
Gorebridge EH23 ... 207 E4
Grangemouth FK3 .. 40 B1
Gullane EH31 ..... 52 A1
Kincardine FK10 ... 23 E2
Kirkcaldy KY2, KY1 . 17 D2
Kirkliston EH29 .... 89 D1
Kirknewton EH27 .. 149 E2
Linlithgow EH49 ... 85 D4
Loanhead EH20 ... 181 E4
Lochgelly KY5 ..... 14 A4
Musselburgh EH21 . 126 B3
Newtongrange EH22 . 183 D3
North Berwick EH39 . 54 A4
Oakley KY12 ...... 26 C3
Prestonpans EH32 .. 128 A4
Queensferry EH30 .. 68 B1
Ratho Station EH28 . 119 E3
Roslin EH25 .... 181 D2
Shotts ML7 .... 191 F2
Slamannan FK1 .... 110 A3
Stirling FK8 .... 7 D4
Uphall EH52 ...... 116 C2

Station Rd continued
Uphall Station EH54 .... 117 D1
Whitecross EH49 .... 83 F3
Station Row FK1 .... 110 A3
Station Terr EH29 .... 89 D1
Staunton Rise EH54 .... 173 E4
Stead's Pl EH6 .... 93 F2
Steading The EH32 .... 98 B1
Steadings The EH49 .... 84 A4
Steel Gr KY12 .... 26 B4
Steel's Pl EH10 .... 123 D2
Steele Ave EH22 .... 183 F3
Steelyard The EH48 .... 145 D3
Steeple Cres KY11 .... 48 A2
Steil Gr EH33 .... 128 B3
Steils The EH10 .... 122 C1
Stein Sq FK7 .... 7 F1
Stein's Pl KY4 .... 13 E2
Stenhouse Ave EH11 .... 122 A2
Stenhouse Ave W EH11 .... 122 A2
Stenhouse Cotts EH11 .... 122 A2
Stenhouse Cres EH11 .... 122 A2
Stenhouse Cross EH11 .... 122 A2
Stenhouse Dr
Burntisland KY3 .... 33 E1
Edinburgh EH11 .... 122 A2
Stenhouse Gdns EH11 .... 122 A2
Stenhouse Gdns N EH11 .... 122 A2
Stenhouse Gr EH11 .... 122 A2
Stenhouse Mill Cres EH11 .... 122 A2
Stenhouse Mill La EH11 .... 122 A2
Stenhouse Mill Wynd
EH11 .... 122 A2
Stenhouse Pl E EH11 .... 122 A2
Stenhouse Pl W EH11 .... 122 A2
Stenhouse Prim Sch
EH11 .... 122 A2
Stenhouse Rd
Edinburgh EH11 .... 122 A2
Stenhousemuir FK5 .... 38 C1
Stenhouse St KY4 .... 13 D2
Stenhouse St E EH11 .... 122 A2
Stenhouse St W EH11 .... 121 F2
Stenhouse Terr EH11 .... 122 A2
Stenhousemuir Prim Sch
FK5 .... 38 B2
Stennis Gdns EH17 .... 155 E4
Stenton Loan EH42 .... 135 F4
Stenton Prim Sch EH42 .... 104 C1
Stenton Rd EH42 .... 105 F4
Stephen Pl KY5 .... 14 A4
Stephen's Dr KY11 .... 47 E2
Steps St FK5 .... 38 C2
Steuart Rd FK9 .... 1 C4
Stevenlaw's Cl EH1 .... 233 D3
Stevenson Ave EH11 .... 122 B3
Stevenson Coll of F Ed
EH11 .... 121 E2
Stevenson Ct Bridge of A FK9 .. 2 A3
Livingston EH54 .... 148 B3
Longniddry EH32 .... 98 B2
Stevenson Dr EH11 .... 122 A2
Stevenson Gr EH11 .... 122 B3
Stevenson La EH22 .... 183 D2
Stevenson Pk EH32 .... 98 B2
Stevenson Pl EH18 .... 181 E3
Stevenson Rd
Edinburgh EH11 .... 122 B3
Penicuik EH26 .... 204 A4
Stevenson St FK3 .... 61 E3
Stevenson Terr
Bathgate EH48 .... 145 E3
Edinburgh EH11 .... 122 B3
Stevenson Way EH32 .... 98 B2
Stewart Ave Bo'ness EH51 .... 63 F4
Currie EH14 .... 151 F2
Linlithgow EH49 .... 84 C3
Stewart Clark Ave EH30 .... 89 E4
Stewart Cres Currie EH14 .... 151 F2
Lochgelly KY5 .... 14 A4
Stewart Dr EH47 .... 169 F4
Stewart Gdns EH14 .... 151 F2
Stewart Gr
Danderhall EH22 .... 156 A4
Harthill ML7 .... 168 C3
Stewart Pk EH22 .... 158 B3
Stewart Pl Currie EH14 .... 151 F2
Kirkliston EH29 .... 89 D1
Stewart Sq EH54 .... 2 A1
Stewart St
Bonnybridge FK4 .... 57 F3
Cambusbarron FK7 .... 6 B3
Dysart KY1 .... 18 A4
Townhill KY12 .... 29 E4
West Calder EH55 .... 172 B1
Stewart Terr
Edinburgh EH11 .... 122 C3
Queensferry EH30 .... 68 A1
Stewart Way EH54 .... 147 E3
Stewartfield EH6 .... 93 E2
Stewartfield Cres EH52 .... 117 F3
Stewartfield Rd EH52 .... 117 F3
Stirling Castle FK8 .... 1 C1
Stirling Ent Pk FK7 .... 7 E4
Stirling F Ed Ctr FK7 .... 7 E3
Stirling High Sch FK8 .... 7 D3
Stirling Pl FK7 .... 20 B2
Stirling Rd Alloa FK10 .... 9 F4
Alva FK12 .... 4 C4
Edinburgh EH5 .... 93 D4
Falkirk FK2 .... 59 E4
Fallin FK7 .... 8 B2
Larbert FK5 .... 37 F3
Torwood FK5 .... 37 F3
Tullibody FK10 .... 4 A2
Stirling Royal Infmy FK8 .... 7 D3

Stirling St Alva FK12 .... 5 D4
Denny FK6 .... 36 B2
Stirling Sta FK8 .... 7 D4
Stobhill Prim Sch EH23 .... 207 E4
Stobhill Rd EH23 .... 183 D2
Stobie Pl KY12 .... 26 C4
Stobs Pl KY2 .... 16 B4
Stockbridge Prim Sch
EH3 .... 93 D1
Stone Ave EH22 .... 183 E3
Stone Cres EH22 .... 183 E3
Stone Pl EH22 .... 183 E3
Stonebank EH54 .... 147 F3
Stonedyke Cres ML8 .... 230 A2
Stonedyke Rd ML8 .... 230 A2
Stoneheap Crofts EH47 .... 194 C4
Stonelaws Cotts EH40 .... 75 D3
Stoneybank Ave EH21 .... 126 A3
Stoneybank Cres EH21 .... 126 A2
Stoneybank Ct EH21 .... 126 A3
Stoneybank Dr EH21 .... 126 A3
Stoneybank Gdns EH21 .... 126 A3
Stoneybank Gdns N
EH21 .... 126 A3
Stoneybank Gdns S
EH21 .... 126 A3
Stoneybank Gr EH21 .... 126 A3
Stoneybank Pl EH21 .... 126 A3
Stoneybank Rd EH21 .... 126 A3
Stoneybank Terr EH21 .... 126 A2
Stoneyburn Prim Sch
EH47 .... 171 E2
Stoneyflatts EH30 .... 89 D4
Stoneyflatts Cres EH30 .... 89 D4
Stoneyflatts Pk EH30 .... 89 D4
Stoneyhill Ave EH21 .... 126 A3
Stoneyhill Cres EH21 .... 126 A3
Stoneyhill Ct EH21 .... 126 A3
Stoneyhill Dr EH21 .... 126 A3
Stoneyhill Farm Rd
EH21 .... 126 A3
Stoneyhill Gr EH21 .... 126 A3
Stoneyhill Pl EH21 .... 126 A3
Stoneyhill Rd EH21 .... 126 A3
Stoneyhill Rise EH21 .... 126 A3
Stoneyhill Steading
EH21 .... 126 A3
Stoneyhill Terr EH21 .... 126 A3
Stoneyhill Wynd EH21 .... 126 A3
Stoneywood Pk FK6 .... 36 A1
Stony Brae FK10 .... 24 B1
Stony Croft Rd EH30 .... 68 B1
Stories Pk EH40 .... 103 F4
Strachan Gdns EH4 .... 92 A1
Strachan Rd EH4 .... 92 A1
Strachan St FK1 .... 59 F2
Straiton Mains EH20 .... 155 D1
Straiton Pk EH20 .... 155 D1
Straiton Pl EH15 .... 125 D4
Straiton Rd
Loanhead EH20 .... 180 C4
Straiton EH20 .... 155 D1
Strang's Pl FK1 .... 81 F3
Strathallan Ct FK9 .... 2 A3
Strathallan Dr KY2 .... 16 C3
Strathallan Rd FK9 .... 2 A3
Strathalmond Ct EH4 .... 90 C2
Strathalmond Gn EH4 .... 90 C2
Strathalmond Pk EH4 .... 90 C2
Strathalmond Rd EH4 .... 90 C2
Strathavon Terr EH48 .... 112 C3
Strathbeg Dr KY11 .... 47 F2
Strathbrock Pl
Broxburn EH52 .... 117 F3
Uphall EH52 .... 116 C2
Strathearn Pl EH9 .... 123 D2
Strathearn Rd
Edinburgh EH9 .... 123 E2
Kirkcaldy KY1 .... 17 F4
North Berwick EH39 .... 53 F4
Strathesk Pl EH26 .... 204 A3
Strathesk Pl EH26 .... 204 A3
Strathfillan Rd EH9 .... 123 E2
Strathkinnes Rd KY12 .... 17 D2
Strathlachlan Ave ML8 .... 230 A1
Strathlogie EH48 .... 112 C3
Strathmiglo Pl FK5 .... 38 C2
Strathmore Cres FK9 .... 2 A1
Strathmore Dr
Dunfermline KY12 .... 29 E2
Stirling FK9 .... 2 A2
Strathmore St KY3 .... 34 C2
Strathyre Dr FK1 .... 171 E1
Strawberry Bank
Dalkeith EH22 .... 156 C1
Linlithgow EH49 .... 85 D3
Streets Pl KY4 .... 29 E4
Stripehead FK10 .... 10 A3
Striven Dr FK2 .... 39 E1
Striven Pl KY2 .... 16 C4
Stromness Gdns EH54 .... 173 E3
Strowan Rd FK3 .... 61 F4
Strowan Sq FK3 .... 61 F4
Struan Dr KY11 .... 47 D2
Struan Pl KY11 .... 47 D2
Strude Howe FK12 .... 5 D4
Strude Mill FK12 .... 5 D4
Strude St FK12 .... 5 D4
Stuart Cres EH12 .... 121 D4
Stuart Ct EH12 .... 121 D4
Stuart Gn EH12 .... 121 D4
Stuart Gr EH12 .... 121 D4
Stuart Gr FK3 .... 61 D3
Stuart Pk EH12 .... 121 D4
Stuart Pl KY4 .... 13 E3
Stuart Rd KY11 .... 46 B1
Stuart Sq EH12 .... 121 D4
Stuart Terr EH48 .... 145 E4
Stuart Wynd EH12 .... 121 D4

Succoth Ave EH12 .... 122 B4
Succoth Ct EH12 .... 122 B4
Succoth Gdns EH12 .... 122 B4
Succoth Pk EH12 .... 122 B4
Succoth Pl EH12 .... 122 B4
Suffolk Rd EH16 .... 123 F2
Suilven Hts FK2 .... 61 D2
Summer Pl EH3 .... 93 E1
Summer Pl EH3 .... 93 E2
Summerfield Gdns EH6 .... 94 A2
Summerfield Pk EH42 .... 78 A1
Summerfield Rd EH6 .... 94 A2
Summerfield Rd EH42 .... 78 B1
Summerford FK1 .... 59 E2
Summerford Gdns FK1 .... 59 E2
Summerford Rd FK1 .... 59 E2
Summerhall EH9 .... 233 E1
Summerhall Cres EH9 .... 233 E1
Summerhall Pl EH9 .... 233 E1
Summerhall Sq EH9 .... 233 E1
Summerlee EH32 .... 96 C1
Summerside Pl EH6 .... 93 E3
Summerside St EH6 .... 93 E3
Summertrees Ct EH16 .... 124 A1
Summerville Ct EH54 .... 148 A4
Suna Path ML7 .... 192 A2
Sunart Pl FK3 .... 61 E3
Sunbury Mews EH4 .... 122 C4
Sunbury Pl EH4 .... 122 C4
Sunningdale La KY12 .... 28 B3
Sunnybank EH7 .... 94 A1
Sunnybank Pl **12** EH7 .... 94 A1
Sunnybank Rd FK7 .... 7 D2
Sunnybrae ML11 .... 215 D1
Sunnydale Dr EH48 .... 142 C2
Sunnydale Rd EH48 .... 142 C2
Sunnylaw Pl FK7 .... 59 F2
Sunnylaw Rd FK9 .... 2 A4
Sunnyside Edinburgh EH7 .... 94 A1
Stirling FK7 .... 7 D2
Stoneyburn EH47 .... 171 D1
Sunnyside Ave EH48 .... 145 E4
Sunnyside Ct FK10 .... 10 A4
Sunnyside Pl KY5 .... 14 A3
Sunnyside Prim Sch FK10 .... 10 A4
Sunnyside Rd Alloa FK10 .... 10 A4
Brightons FK2 .... 82 B4
Falkirk FK1 .... 59 F3
Sunnyside St FK1 .... 59 F3
Surcoat Loan FK7 .... 7 F2
Sutherland Ave Alloa FK10 .... 10 B4
Stirling FK8 .... 2 B1
Sutherland Cres EH48 .... 145 D3
Sutherland Dr FK6 .... 57 E4
Sutherland Pl KY1 .... 17 F4
Sutherland St EH12 .... 122 C4
Sutherland Way EH54 .... 147 E3
Suttie Way FK9 .... 1 C4
Suttieslea Cres EH22 .... 183 E3
Suttieslea Dr EH22 .... 183 E3
Suttieslea Pl EH22 .... 183 E3
Suttieslea Rd EH22 .... 183 E3
Suttieslea Wlk EH22 .... 183 E3
Sutton Park Cres FK5 .... 38 C2
Sutton Pl FK2 .... 60 B3
Swallow Craig KY11 .... 48 A1
Swallowdrum Rd KY12 .... 28 B3
Swan Cres EH23 .... 207 E4
Swan Pl FK3 .... 61 E3
Swan Rd Kirkcaldy KY1 .... 17 D2
Tranent EH33 .... 128 B3
Swan Spring Ave EH10 .... 154 A4
Swanfield EH6 .... 93 F3
Swanston Ave EH10 .... 154 A3
Swanston Cres EH10 .... 154 A3
Swanston Dr EH10 .... 154 A2
Swanston Gdns EH10 .... 154 A3
Swanston Gn EH10 .... 154 A3
Swanston Gr EH10 .... 154 A2
Swanston Loan EH10 .... 154 A3
Swanston Muir EH10 .... 153 F3
Swanston Pk EH10 .... 154 A3
Swanston Pl EH10 .... 154 A3
Swanston Rd EH10 .... 154 A2
Swanston Row EH10 .... 154 A3
Swanston Terr EH10 .... 154 A3
Swanston View EH10 .... 154 A3
Swanston Way EH10 .... 154 A3
Swinburne Dr FK10 .... 5 D1
Swintons Pl KY4 .... 12 C1
Sword's Way EH39 .... 39 D1
Sycamore Ave
Bo'ness EH51 .... 63 E3
Cockenzie & Port Seton
EH32 .... 97 C2
Kirkcaldy KY1 .... 17 F4
Sycamore Cres KY4 .... 13 E3
Sycamore Dr EH47 .... 170 B3
Sycamore Gdns EH12 .... 121 F3
Sycamore Gr
Dunfermline KY11 .... 46 B4
Winchburgh EH52 .... 87 F1
Sycamore Pl KY8 .... 6 C3
Sycamore Rd EH22 .... 183 F3
Sycamore Wlk EH47 .... 171 E4
Sycamores The FK10 .... 4 A1
Sydney Pk EH7 .... 94 C1
Sydney Pl EH7 .... 94 C1
Sydney St EH22 .... 148 S3 — Sydney St EH22 .... 183 D3
Sydney Terr EH7 .... 94 C1
Sylvan Gr EH51 .... 63 E3
Sylvan Pl EH9 .... 123 E1
Sylvan Way EH48 .... 144 C3
Syme Pl KY11 .... 46 B3
Symington Pl KY2 .... 39 D2
Ta-Verne La KY11 .... 29 E1
Tailend Ind Pk EH54 .... 146 B2

Tailend Rdbt EH54 .... 146 B2
Tait Dr Larbert FK5 .... 59 F4
Penicuik EH26 .... 203 F3
Tait St FK3 .... 157 D2
Talbot St FK3 .... 61 E4
Talisman Pl EH16 .... 124 A1
Talman Gdns FK2 .... 61 F2
Tam O'Shanter Dr FK7 .... 20 B4
Tamfourhill Ave FK1 .... 59 E2
Tamfourhill Ind Est FK1 .... 59 E2
Tamfourhill Rd FK1 .... 59 E2
Tanera Ct FK1 .... 60 A1
Tanhouse Brae KY12 .... 42 B4
Tanners Rd FK1 .... 60 A2
Tannery La FK1 .... 2 A1
Tantallon Castle EH39 .... 55 F4
Tantallon Dr FK2 .... 39 D2
Tantallon Gdns EH54 .... 173 E4
Tantallon Pl EH8 .... 123 E3
Tantallon Rd EH39 .... 54 C3
Tantallon Terr EH39 .... 54 C4
Tapitlaw Gr KY12 .... 26 B4
Tappoch Pl FK5 .... 38 A2
Taransay Dr FK2 .... 61 F1
Tarbert Pl FK2 .... 61 F1
Tarbert Terr KY10 .... 23 F2
Tarbet Pl ML8 .... 230 A1
Tarbrax Path ML7 .... 192 A2
Tarbrax Rd EH55 .... 217 F1
Tarduff Dr FK2 .... 83 D3
Tarduff Pl FK6 .... 36 A1
Targate Rd KY12 .... 28 B3
Target Wynd FK7 .... 7 F2
Target Rd FK3 .... 62 B4
Tartraven Pl EH52 .... 118 A3
Tarvit St EH3 .... 232 C1
Tashieburn Rd ML11 .... 215 F1
Tavern Cotts KY4 .... 30 C4
Taxi Way KY11 .... 48 B3
Tay Ct FK10 .... 10 B3
Tay Pl ML7 .... 191 F3
Tay St Edinburgh EH11 .... 122 C3
Falkirk FK2 .... 39 E1
Grangemouth FK3 .... 40 A1
Tay Terr KY11 .... 29 F1
Tay Wlk EH22 .... 148 A2
Taylor Ave KY4 .... 13 E2
Taylor Ct FK3 .... 40 C1
Taylor Gdns EH6 .... 93 F3
Taylor Gn EH22 .... 147 E4
Taylor Pl EH22 .... 157 E1
Taylor Rd EH47 .... 169 F3
Taylor's Rd FK5 .... 38 B1
Taymouth Rd KY2 .... 62 A1
Tedder St FK3 .... 61 E3
Telferton EH7 .... 94 C1
Telford Coll
Lochend Annexe EH6 .... 94 A2
Telford Coll North Campus
EH5 .... 92 C3
Telford Ct FK7 .... 7 E1
Telford Dr EH4 .... 92 B2
Telford Gdns EH4 .... 92 B2
Telford Pl Edinburgh EH4 .... 92 B2
Linlithgow EH49 .... 84 B4
Telford Rd EH4 .... 92 B2
Telford Sq Falkirk FK1 .... 59 F3
Livingston EH54 .... 147 F4
Telford View EH49 .... 84 B3
Telny Pl KY3 .... 49 E4
Templar La EH31 .... 52 A1
Templar Pl EH31 .... 52 A1
Templar Rise EH54 .... 173 E4
Templar's Cramond EH4 .... 91 D2
Templars Cres KY3 .... 34 C2
Temple Ave FK10 .... 5 D1
Temple Denny Rd FK6 .... 36 B1
Temple Park Cres EH11 .... 122 C3
Temple Pk EH23 .... 206 B1
Temple Prim Sch EH23 .... 206 B1
Templedean Pk EH41 .... 101 D1
Templehall Gr KY12 .... 121 E4
Templehall Ave KY2 .... 16 C4
Templeland Gr EH12 .... 121 E4
Templeland Rd EH12 .... 121 E4
Ten Acres EH1 .... 5 D1
Tenacres Pl FK3 .... 61 F3
Tenant's March EH55 .... 172 B2
Tennant St EH6 .... 93 F2
Tennent Pk EH53 .... 148 B1
Tenth St EH22 .... 183 D1
Tern Brae EH54 .... 147 E3
Terrace St KY1 .... 18 A4
Terrace The EH21 .... 126 C1
Terragies EH26 .... 203 E3
Terrars Croft EH8 .... 233 F1
Terris St KY4 .... 13 E2
Teviot Gr EH26 .... 203 F4
Teviot Pl EH1 .... 233 D2
Teviot St FK1 .... 59 F2
Teviotdale Pl EH3 .... 93 D1
Thane Pl KY11 .... 29 F1
Thimblehall Dr KY12 .... 29 E2
Thimblehall Pl KY12 .... 29 E2
Thimblehall Rd KY12 .... 29 F2
Third Gait EH14 .... 151 D4
Third St EH22 .... 183 D3
Thirlestane EH51 .... 64 A1
Thirlestane La EH9 .... 123 E2
Thirlestane Pl EH9 .... 123 E4
Thirlestane Rd EH9 .... 123 E3
Thistle Ave Denny FK6 .... 36 B2
Grangemouth FK3 .... 61 D3
Thistle Ind Est
Broxburn EH52 .... 118 A3
Cowdenbeath KY4 .... 13 F2
Stirling FK7 .... 7 E3

Thistle Pl EH11 .... 232 A1
Thistle St Alloa FK10 .... 10 B3
Burntisland KY3 .... 50 C4
Cowdenbeath KY4 .... 13 E2
Dunfermline KY12 .... 29 D3
Edinburgh EH2 .... 232 C4
Falkirk FK2 .... 60 B3
Kirkcaldy KY1 .... 17 E2
Thompson Pl FK1 .... 110 A2
Thomson Cres
Cockenzie & Port Seton
EH32 .... 97 C2
Currie EH14 .... 152 A3
Falkirk FK1 .... 59 F2
Thomson Ct EH52 .... 116 C2
Thomson Dr EH14 .... 152 B3
Thomson Gn EH54 .... 147 E3
Thomson Gr Currie EH14 .... 152 A3
Uphall EH52 .... 116 C2
Thomson Pl
Cambusbarron FK7 .... 6 B3
Rosyth KY11 .... 46 C2
Thomson Rd EH14 .... 152 A3
Thomson Terr ML7 .... 191 F3
Thorburn Gr EH13 .... 153 E3
Thorburn Rd EH13 .... 153 D3
Thorn Gr KY11 .... 46 C4
Thorn Tree Pl KY12 .... 26 C3
Thornbridge Gdns FK2 .... 60 C2
Thornbridge Rd FK2 .... 60 C2
Thornbridge Sq FK2 .... 60 C3
Thorndale Gdns FK4 .... 57 D1
Thorndene Ct FK1 .... 59 F1
Thorne Ct EH39 .... 54 A4
Thorne Rd FK10 .... 4 C1
Thornhill Dr KY2 .... 17 D3
Thornhill Rd Falkirk FK2 .... 60 B3
Kirkcaldy KY2 .... 17 E3
Thornton Ave FK4 .... 58 A3
Thornton Pl EH47 .... 193 E3
Thornton Rd EH24 .... 181 E1
Thorntree Cres EH32 .... 97 D1
Thorntree St EH6 .... 94 A2
Thorntreeside EH6 .... 94 A2
Thornville Terr EH6 .... 94 A2
Thorny Bank EH22 .... 157 E2
Thornybank Ind Est
EH22 .... 157 E2
Thornybauk EH3 .... 232 A1
Thornyhall EH22 .... 157 E2
Threipmuir Ave EH14 .... 177 E4
Threipmuir Gdns EH14 .... 177 E4
Threipmuir Pl EH14 .... 177 E4
Thrums The FK2 .... 61 D2
Thurston Pl EH54 .... 147 E3
Timber Bush EH6 .... 94 A3
Timmeryetts EH52 .... 117 E3
Timmons Pk KY5 .... 14 A4
Timmons Pl FK6 .... 36 B1
Tinian Cres KY12 .... 26 B1
Tinto Dr FK3 .... 61 F3
Tinto Pl Dunfermline KY11 .... 29 F1
Edinburgh EH6 .... 93 F2
Tipperlinn Rd EH10 .... 123 D2
Tippet Knowes Ct EH52 .... 87 F2
Tippet Knowes Pk EH52 .... 87 F2
Tippet Knowes Rd EH52 .... 87 F1
Tippethill Hospl EH48 .... 144 A1
Tiree Cres FK2 .... 61 E1
Tiree Pl Falkirk FK1 .... 60 A1
Kirkcaldy KY2 .... 16 C4
Titania FK10 .... 10 A4
Todd Sq EH54 .... 116 C1
Toddshill Rd EH29 .... 89 D1
Tolbooth St
3 Falkirk FK1 .... 60 A2
Kirkcaldy KY1 .... 17 E2
Tolbooth Wynd EH6 .... 94 A3
Toll Rd FK10 .... 23 F2
Toll Rdbt EH54 .... 146 C2
Toll View TD13 .... 140 C2
Tollcross EH3 .... 232 B1
Tollcross Prim Sch
EH3 .... 232 B1
Tollgate KY11 .... 29 E1
Tolmount Dr KY12 .... 29 E2
Tolsta Cres FK1 .... 61 F1
Tophill Entry FK1 .... 59 F3
Toravon Dr FK2 .... 83 D3
Torbain FK2 .... 16 B4
Torbain Prim Sch KY2 .... 16 B3
Torbain Rd KY2 .... 16 A3
Torbane Ave EH47 .... 170 C4
Torbane Dr EH47 .... 170 C4
Torbeith Gdns KY4 .... 12 C1
Torbothie Rd ML7 .... 192 A2
Torbrex Farm Rd FK7 .... 7 D2
Torbrex La FK7 .... 7 D3
Torbrex Rd FK7 .... 6 C2
Torburn Ave FK7 .... 20 B2
Torduff Rd EH13 .... 153 D2
Torlea Pl FK5 .... 38 A2
Torness Power Sta
Visitor Ctr EH42 .... 108 C2
Toronto Ave EH54 .... 147 F2
Toronto Prim Sch
EH54 .... 147 F2
Torosay Ave FK2 .... 82 C3
Torphichen Ave EH53 .... 148 A1
Torphichen Pl EH3 .... 232 A2
Torphichen Preceptory
EH48 .... 113 F3
Torphichen Prim Sch
EH48 .... 113 F3
Torphichen Rd EH48 .... 145 D4

Torphichen St
Bathgate EH48 .... 145 D4
Edinburgh EH3 .... 232 A2
Torphin Bank EH13 .... 152 C3
Torphin Rd EH13 .... 152 C3
Torrance Pk EH4 .... 91 E1
Torridon Ave FK2 .... 39 E1
Torridon Ct FK10 .... 10 B3
Torridon Dr KY11 .... 46 C1
Torridon La KY11 .... 46 C1
Torridon Pl Kirkcaldy KY2 .. 16 C4
Rosyth KY11 .... 46 C1
Torridon Rd EH47 .... 170 B4
Torridon Wlk EH54 .... 148 A2
Torrin Loan ML7 .... 192 A2
Torry Dr FK12 .... 4 C4
Torryburn Prim Sch KY12 .. 26 C1
Torsonce Rd EH22 .... 156 C1
Torvean Pl KY11 .... 29 E1
Torwood Ave
Grangemouth FK3 .... 61 F3
Larbert FK5 .... 38 A1
Torwood Pl KY12 .... 29 E3
Torwood Sch FK5 .... 37 F3
Touch Prim Sch KY11 ..... 29 F2
Touch Rd FK7 .... 6 A3
Touch Wards KY12 .... 29 F2
Touchhill Cres FK7 .... 20 B2
Tovey Rd KY11 .... 46 B1
Toward Ct EH12 .... 121 D4
Tower Gdns EH51 .... 64 B4
Tower Pl
Clackmannan FK10 ...... 10 C3
Edinburgh EH6 .... 94 A3
Tower St Alloa FK10 ...... 10 A4
Edinburgh EH6 .... 94 A3
Tower Terr KY1 .... 17 F4
Tower View FK10 .... 5 F1
Towerbank Prim Sch
EH15 .... 95 D1
Towers Ct FK2 .... 60 A3
Towers Pl FK9 .... 2 B2
Town Burn FK7 .... 6 C2
Town House St FK6 .... 36 C1
Townhall St KY11 .... 47 E1
Townhead Dysart KY1 ..... 18 A4
Kinghorn KY3 .... 34 C2
Townhead Gdns EH47 ..... 170 B3
Townhill Ctry Pk KY12 .... 29 E4
Townhill Prim Sch KY12 ... 29 E4
Townhill Rd KY12 .... 29 D3
Townsend Cres KY1 .... 17 E2
Townsend Pl KY1 .... 17 E2
Trafalgar La EH6 .... 93 F3
Trafalgar St EH6 .... 93 F3
Train Terr KY11 .... 46 B3
Tranent Inf Sch EH33 .... 128 B4
Tranent Prim Sch EH33 ... 128 A1
Tranent Rd EH33 .... 128 A1
Transy Gr KY12 .... 29 E2
Transy Pl KY12 .... 29 E2
Traprain Cres EH48 ...... 144 C4
Traprain Terr
Haddington EH41 .... 101 D1
Loanhead EH20 .... 181 E4
Traquair Pk E EH12 ...... 121 F3
Traquair Pk W EH12 ..... 121 F3
Trelawney Terr EH26 ..... 204 A4
Tremayne Pl KY12 .... 28 C3
Trench Knowe EH10 ...... 154 A3
Trenchard Pl KY12 ...... 28 C3
Tressilian Gdns 8 EH16 .. 124 A1
Trevelyan Cres EH34 ..... 160 C3
Trevelyan Pl EH34 ...... 160 C3
Trinity Acad EH6 .... 93 E3
Trinity Cres EH5 .... 93 D3
Trinity Ct EH5 .... 93 D3
Trinity Gr EH5 .... 93 D3
Trinity Prim Sch EH6 .... 93 E3
Trinity Rd EH5 .... 93 D3
Tron Cl FK10 .... 4 A1
Tron Sq EH1 .... 233 D3
Trondheim Parkway KY11 .. 29 F1
Trondheim Pl KY11 ...... 29 F1
Trongate KY3 .... 35 D2
Troup Ct FK3 .... 61 E4
Tryst Pk EH10 .... 153 F3
Tryst Rd FK5 .... 38 B2
Tudor Ct FK2 .... 61 E1
Tuke St KY12 .... 29 D3
Tulliallan Castle FK10 ... 23 E3
Tulliallan Pl FK5 ..... 39 D2
Tulliallan Prim Sch FK10 .. 23 F2
Tulliallan Terr FK10 .... 23 F3
Tullibody Rd FK10 ..... 4 C1
Tulligarth Pk FK10 .... 10 A4
Tulloch Ct KY4 .... 13 E3
Tulloch Rd ML7 .... 192 A2
Tummel Dr KY2 .... 16 B4
Tummel Pl
Grangemouth FK3 ...... 61 F2
Stenhousemuir FK5 .... 38 C2
Turnbull Gr KY11 ...... 29 E1
Turnbull Way EH54 ..... 147 E3
Turner Ave EH14 ...... 151 E2
Turner Pk EH14 ...... 151 E2
Turner St EH48 ...... 145 D4
Turnhigh Rd EH47 ..... 170 A2
Turnhouse Farm Rd EH12 .. 90 B1
Turnhouse Rd EH12 ..... 120 B4
Turret Ct FK10 .... 10 B3
Turret Dr FK2 .... 62 A1
Turret Gdns EH32 ..... 127 F3
Turret Rd FK3 .... 61 E4
Turriff Pl KY2 .... 16 C4

Twain Ave FK5 .... 39 D2
Tweed Dr EH54 .... 148 A3
Tweed St Dunfermline KY11 .. 29 F1
Grangemouth FK3 ...... 40 A1
Tweedale Cres EH41 .... 163 F3
Tweedale Ct EH41 ..... 163 F3
Tweeddale Ct EH1 ..... 233 E3
Tweeddale Dr KY11 .... 29 F1
Tweeddale Gr EH41 .... 163 F2
Tyhmebank EH54 ...... 147 F3
Tyler's Acre Ave EH12 .. 121 F3
Tyler's Acre Gdns EH12 .. 121 F3
Tyler's Acre Rd EH12 .. 121 F3
Tyndrum Pl KY2 ...... 16 C4
Tyne Cl East Linton EH40 .. 103 F4
Haddington EH41 ..... 132 A4
Tynebank Rd EH41 .... 132 A4
Tynecastle High Sch
EH11 .... 122 C3
Tynecastle La EH11 ... 122 C3
Tynecastle Pk (Heart of
Midlothian FC) EH11 .. 122 C3
Tynecastle Terr EH11 .. 122 C3
Tynemount Ave EH35 .. 159 E3
Tynemount Rd EH35 ... 159 E4
Tyneview EH35 .... 159 F4
Tyrwhitt Pl KY11 ..... 46 C2
Tytler Gdns EH8 ..... 94 A1

Ugston Cotts EH41 .... 100 B1
Ulg Way ML7 .... 192 A2
Ulster Cres EH8 ..... 124 B4
Ulster Dr EH8 ...... 124 B4
Ulster Gdns EH8 .... 124 B4
Ulster Gr EH8 ...... 124 B4
Ulster Terr EH8 .... 124 B4
Underwood Cotts FK7 .. 6 B3
Underwood Rd FK7 .... 6 B3
Union Dr EH47 ...... 170 A3
Union Pk EH19 ...... 182 A3
Union Pl Brightons FK2 .. 61 E1
Edinburgh EH1 ...... 233 E4
Larbert FK5 .... 38 A1
Union Rd Bathgate EH48 .. 145 D3
Broxburn EH52 ...... 117 E3
Falkirk FK1 .... 59 E3
Grangemouth FK3 .... 40 B1
Linlithgow EH49 .... 84 C3
Whitburn EH47 ...... 170 A3
Union St Alloa FK10 ... 10 A3
Bo'ness EH51 .... 64 A4
Bridge of A FK9 .... 2 A4
Burntisland KY3 .... 50 C4
Cowdenbeath KY4 .... 13 E2
Edinburgh EH1 ...... 93 F1
Falkirk FK2 .... 60 A4
Kirkcaldy KY1 ...... 17 F4
Lochgelly KY5 ...... 14 A4
Shotts ML7 .... 191 E3
Stenhousemuir FK5 .. 38 C2
Stirling FK8 .... 2 A1
Unity Pk ML7 .... 191 E2
Univ of Dundee Sch of
Nursing & Midwifery
Fife Campus KY2 .... 17 D2
Univ of Edinburgh EH8 .. 233 D2
Univ of Stirling
(Dept of Nursing &
Midwifery, Forth Valley
Campus) FK1 .... 60 A2
University of Stirling FK9 .. 2 B3
University Rd W EH9 .. 2 B3
Uphall Prim Sch EH52 .. 117 D3
Uphall Station Inf Sch
EH54 .... 117 D1
Uphall Station Rd EH53 .. 148 A4
Uphall Station Sta EH54 .. 117 D1
Upper Bathville EH48 .. 143 F2
Upper Bow EH1 ..... 233 D3
Upper Bridge St FK8 .. 2 A1
Upper Broomieknowe
EH18 .... 182 A4
Upper Castlehill EH7 .. 7 D4
Upper Coltbridge Terr
EH12 .... 122 C4
Upper Craigour EH17 .. 155 F4
Upper Craigour Way
EH17 .... 124 B1
Upper Craigs 3 FK8 .. 7 D4
Upper Cramond Ct EH4 .. 91 D4
Upper Dean Terr EH4 .. 232 A4
Upper Gilmore Pl EH3 .. 232 B1
Upper Gilmore Terr EH3 .. 232 B1
Upper Gray St EH9 .. 123 F3
Upper Grove Pl EH3 .. 232 A1
Upper Millhill St KY11 .. 29 D2
Upper Newmarket St FK1 .. 60 A4
Upper Wellheads KY11 .. 45 F2
Ure Cres FK4 .... 58 A3
Ure Ct FK3 .... 61 E4
Urquhart Cres KY12 .. 28 C2
Urquhart Ct KY2 .... 16 B3
Urquhart Cut KY2 ... 28 C2
Urquhart Farm Cotts KY12 .. 28 B1

Vale Gr FK9 .... 1 C3
Vale Pl FK6 .... 36 C2
Valeview FK5 ...... 38 B1
Valley Field View EH26 .. 203 F2
Valley Gdns KY2 .... 16 C3
Valley Gdns S KY2 .. 16 C3
Valley Prim Sch KY2 .. 17 D4
Valley View KY2 .... 16 C3
Valleyfield Ave KY12 .. 26 A1
Valleyfield Pl
Cowdenbeath KY4 .... 13 E3
Stirling FK7 .... 7 E3

Valleyfield Rd EH26 .. 203 F2
Valleyfield St EH3 ... 232 C1
Valleyfield Woodland Pk
KY12 .... 26 A1
Valleyview Dr FK2 ... 60 A4
Valleyview Pl FK2 ... 60 A4
Vancouver Ave EH54 .. 147 F2
Vandeleur Ave EH7 .. 94 C1
Vandeleur Gr EH7 ... 94 C1
Vandeleur Pl EH7 ... 94 C1
Vardon Rd EH31 .... 52 A2
Vaucluse Pl EH26 .. 203 F2
Veere Pk KY12 .... 25 F1
Veitch's Sq 6 EH4 .. 93 D1
Vellore Rd FK2 .... 83 D3
Venachar Pl KY12 .. 28 A1
Vennachar St ML7 .. 191 F3
Vennel The Denny FK6 .. 36 C1
Dunbar EH42 ...... 78 C1
Linlithgow EH49 ... 85 D4
Ventnor Pl EH9 .... 124 A2
Ventnor Terr EH9 .. 123 F2
Venturefair Ave KY12 .. 29 D3
Veronica Cres KY1 .. 17 E4
Vetch Pk EH41 .... 101 D1
Vexhim Pk EH15 ... 125 D3
Vicar St FK1 ...... 60 A4
Viceroy St KY7 .... 17 D3
Victor Park Terr EH12 .. 121 E4
Victoria Gdns
Kirkcaldy KY1 ..... 17 D2
Newtongrange EH22 .. 182 C3
Victoria Hospl KY2 .. 17 D4
Victoria Pk
Fauldhouse EH47 ... 193 F4
Haddington EH41 ... 101 D1
Victoria Pl Bo'ness EH51 .. 64 A4
Brightons FK2 ..... 61 E1
Dunbar EH42 ...... 78 B2
Stirling FK8 ...... 7 D4
Victoria Prim Sch
Edinburgh EH6 ..... 93 E4
Falkirk FK2 .... 60 B3
Victoria Rd Falkirk FK2 .. 60 B3
Fauldhouse EH47 ... 193 F4
Grangemouth FK3 ... 61 F4
Haddington EH41 ... 132 A4
Harthill ML7 ...... 168 C3
Kirkcaldy KY1 ..... 17 E3
Larbert FK5 .... 38 A1
Newtongrange EH22 .. 182 C3
North Berwick EH39 .. 54 B4
Victoria Sq FK8 .... 7 D4
Victoria St Alloa FK10 .. 10 A4
Dunbar EH42 ...... 78 B2
Dunfermline KY12 .. 29 D3
Dysart KY1 .... 18 A4
Edinburgh EH1 ..... 233 D3
Harthill ML7 ...... 168 C3
Livingston EH54 ... 148 A2
Rosewell EH24 ..... 181 E1
Victoria Terr
Dunfermline KY12 .. 29 D3
Edinburgh EH1 ..... 233 D3
Haddington EH41 ... 132 A4
Menstrie FK11 ..... 4 A4
Musselburgh EH21 .. 126 C3
Viewbank Dr EH19 .. 182 A4
Viewbank Rd EH19 .. 182 A4
Viewbank View EH19 .. 182 A4
Viewcraig Gdns EH8 .. 233 E2
Viewcraig St EH8 .. 233 E3
Viewfield EH19 .... 182 A4
Viewfield Dr FK12 .. 4 C3
Viewfield Rd
Edinburgh EH14 ... 152 C4
Tarbrax EH55 ..... 217 F2
Viewfield St Harthill ML7 .. 168 C3
Stirling FK8 ...... 7 D4
Viewforth Bo'ness EH51 .. 64 A4
Cockenzie & Port Seton
EH32 .... 97 E2
Dunbar EH42 ...... 78 B2
Edinburgh EH10 ... 123 D3
North Berwick EH39 .. 54 B4
Viewforth Ave KY1 .. 17 F4
Viewforth Dr FK2 .. 61 D2
Viewforth Gdns
Edinburgh EH10 ... 123 D3
Kirkcaldy KY1 ..... 17 F4
Tranent EH33 ..... 128 B3
Viewforth Pl EH30 .. 89 D4
Viewforth Rd EH30 .. 89 D4
Viewforth Sq EH10 .. 123 D3
Viewforth St KY1 .. 17 F4
Viewforth Terr
Edinburgh EH10 ... 123 D3
Kirkcaldy KY1 ..... 17 F4
Tranent EH33 ..... 128 B3
Viewpark Gdns EH19 .. 182 A4
Villa Bank FK6 .... 36 C1
Villa Rd EH30 .... 68 A1
Village La EH54 ... 147 D2
Vinefields EH34 ... 160 C3
Violet Terr EH11 .. 122 C3
Vivian Terr EH4 .. 92 A2
Vogrie Cres S EH23 .. 207 E4
Vogrie Estate Ctry Pk
EH23 .... 184 B2
Vogrie Pl EH23 .... 207 E4
Vogrie Rd EH23 ... 207 E4
Voil Rd FK9 ...... 2 A2
Volunteer's Gn KY1 .. 17 E2

Vorlich Cres EH26 .. 204 A4
Vorlich Dr FK1 .... 81 F4
Vorlich Pl FK9 .... 2 A2

Waddell St FK2 .... 39 E1
Wadingburn La KY11 .. 155 F1
Wadingburn Rd EH18 .. 181 F4
Waggon Rd Bo'ness EH51 .. 63 F4
Brightons FK2 ..... 82 B4
Crossford KY11 .... 45 E4
Falkirk FK2 .... 60 A4
Inverkeithing KY11 .. 47 E1
Wakefield Ave KY7 .. 94 C1
Walden Dr EH41 ... 163 F3
Walden Pl EH41 ... 163 F2
Walden Terr EH41 .. 163 F2
Waldie Ave EH49 .. 85 D3
Walk The Alloa FK10 .. 10 A3
Dysart KY1 .... 18 A4
Walker Cres EH22 .. 156 C1
Walker Dr
Dennyloanhead FK4 .. 57 E3
Queensferry EH30 .. 68 A1
Walker St
Cowdenbeath KY4 ... 13 D2
Edinburgh EH3 .... 232 A3
Kincardine FK10 ... 23 F2
Kirkcaldy KY2 ..... 17 D3
Lochgelly KY5 ..... 14 A3
Walker Terr EH40 .. 103 E4
Walkers Ct EH14 .. 121 F1
Walkers Rig EH14 .. 121 F1
Walkers Wynd EH14 .. 121 F1
Wall Gdns FK1 .... 59 E3
Wall St FK1 ...... 59 E3
Wallace Cres Brightons FK2 .. 82 B4
Denny FK6 .... 36 B1
Plean FK7 .... 20 B2
Roslin EH25 ...... 181 D2
Wallace Ct
Grangemouth FK3 ... 61 E4
Stirling FK8 ...... 2 A1
Wallace Gdns FK9 .. 2 B2
Wallace High Sch FK9 .. 2 A1
Wallace Mill Gdns EH53 .. 148 B2
Wallace Mon FK9 .. 2 C2
Wallace Pl
Cambusbarron FK7 .. 6 B3
Falkirk FK2 .... 60 B3
Fallin FK7 .... 8 B2
Tranent EH33 ..... 128 B4
Wallace Rd EH48 .. 145 E3
Wallace St Alloa FK10 .. 10 B4
Bannockburn FK7 ... 7 F1
Cowdenbeath KY4 ... 13 E2
Dunfermline KY11 .. 29 E1
Falkirk FK2 .... 60 B3
Grangemouth FK3 ... 61 E4
Stirling FK8 ...... 2 A1
Wallace View
Bo'ness EH51 ..... 63 E3
Shieldhill FK1 .... 81 E3
Tullibody FK10 ... 4 B2
Wallacelea FK2 ... 82 C4
Wallacestone Brae FK2 .. 82 B4
Wallacestone Prim Sch
FK2 .... 82 B4
Walls Pl KY11 ... 29 F1
Wallsend Ct KY12 .. 28 B3
Wallstale Rd FK7 .. 7 D2
Wallyford Ind Est EH21 .. 127 D2
Wallyford Prim Sch
EH21 .... 127 D1
Wallyford Sta EH21 .. 127 D1
Walmer Dr KY12 ... 29 D2
Walnut Gr KY11 ... 46 B4
Walter Hay Ct KY11 .. 46 C2
Walter Scott Ave EH16 .. 124 A1
Wanless Ct EH21 .. 126 B3
Ward Ave FK2 .... 61 E1
Ward St FK10 .... 10 A3
Warden's Cl EH1 .. 123 E4
Wardie Ave EH5 .. 93 D3
Wardie Cres EH5 .. 93 D3
Wardie Dell EH5 .. 93 D3
Wardie Gr EH5 ... 92 C3
Wardie House La EH5 .. 93 D3
Wardie Pk EH5 ... 93 D3
Wardie Prim Sch EH5 .. 93 D3
Wardie Rd EH5 ... 93 D3
Wardie Sq EH5 ... 93 D3
Wardieburn Dr EH5 .. 92 C3
Wardieburn Pl E EH5 .. 92 C3
Wardieburn Pl N EH5 .. 92 C3
Wardieburn Pl S EH5 .. 92 C3
Wardieburn Pl W EH5 .. 92 C3
Wardieburn Rd EH5 .. 92 C3
Wardieburn St E EH5 .. 92 C3
Wardieburn St W EH5 .. 92 C3
Wardieburn Terr EH5 .. 92 C3
Wardiefield EH5 .. 93 D3
Wardlaw Cres
Dunfermline KY11 .. 29 E1
Oakley KY12 ...... 26 C4
Wardlaw Pl
Edinburgh EH11 ... 122 C3
Falkirk FK2 .... 39 E1
Wardlaw St
Cowdenbeath KY4 ... 13 E2
Edinburgh EH11 ... 122 C3
Wardlaw Terr EH11 .. 122 C3
Wardlaw Way KY12 .. 26 C4

Wardrop Cres EH48 .. 143 F3
Ware Rd Dirleton EH39 .. 53 C2
North Berwick EH39 .. 54 A4
Warrender Cres EH42 .. 78 C3
Warrender Ct EH39 .. 54 A3
Warrender Park Cres
EH9 .... 123 E3
Warrender Park Rd EH9 .. 123 E3
Warrender Park Terr
EH9 .... 123 E3
Warriston Ave EH3 .. 93 E2
Warriston Cres EH3 .. 93 E2
Warriston Dr EH3 .. 93 E2
Warriston Gdns EH3 .. 93 E2
Warriston Gr EH3 .. 93 E2
Warriston Rd EH3, EH7 .. 93 E2
Warriston Terr EH3 .. 93 D2
Washington La EH11 .. 122 C3
Water St EH6 .... 94 A3
Water Yett EH49 .. 84 C4
Waterfall Wlk EH47 .. 157 D1
Waterlands Gdns ML8 .. 230 A4
Waterloo Bank EH26 .. 203 F2
Waterloo Pl
Edinburgh EH1 .... 233 D4
Elphinstone EH33 .. 128 A1
Waters' Cl EH6 .... 94 A3
Waterside EH41 ... 132 A4
Watertoun Rd EH9 .. 123 F2
Watling Ave FK1 .. 59 E3
Watling Dr FK1 ... 59 E3
Watling Gdns FK1 .. 59 E3
Watling St FK1 ... 59 E3
Watson Cres EH11 .. 122 C3
Watson Pl
Armadale EH48 .... 144 A3
Dennyloanhead FK4 .. 57 E2
Dunfermline KY12 .. 29 D3
Watson St
Cowdenbeath KY4 ... 13 E2
Falkirk FK1 .... 60 A3
Penicuik EH26 .... 203 F3
Watt Ave EH48 ... 144 A3
Watt Gdns FK1 ... 59 F3
Watt Gr EH22 .... 183 F3
Watt Pk EH22 .... 183 D2
Watt Rd KY11 .... 46 A1
Watt St KY1 ..... 18 A4
Watt's Cl EH21 .. 126 A3
Watters Cres KY5 .. 14 A3
Wauchope Ave EH16 .. 124 C2
Wauchope Cres EH16 .. 124 C2
Wauchope Pl EH16 .. 124 C2
Wauchope Rd EH16 .. 124 C2
Wauchope Sq EH16 .. 124 C2
Wauchope Terr EH16 .. 124 C2
Waugh Path EH19 .. 182 B4
Waughton Cotts EH40 .. 74 C3
Waulkmill Dr EH26 .. 204 A3
Waulkmill Loan EH14 .. 151 F2
Waulkmill Rd EH26 .. 204 A3
Waulkmill View EH26 .. 203 F3
Wavell St FK3 .... 61 E3
Waverley Bridge EH1 .. 233 D3
Waverley Cres
Bonnyrigg and Lasswade
EH19 .... 182 B4
Grangemouth FK3 ... 61 E3
High Bonnybridge FK4 .. 58 A2
Livingston EH54 ... 147 D3
Stirling FK8 ...... 2 B1
Waverley Dr EH19 .. 182 B4
Waverley Park Terr EH8 .. 94 A1
Waverley Pk
Bonnyrigg and Lasswade
EH19 .... 182 B4
Edinburgh EH8 .... 94 A1
Mayfield EH22 .... 183 E3
Redding FK2 ...... 61 D2
Waverley Pl EH7 .. 94 A1
Waverley Rd
Bonnyrigg and Lasswade
EH19 .... 182 B4
Dalkeith EH22 .... 156 C1
Stenhousemuir FK5 .. 38 B1
Waverley St
Bathgate EH48 .... 145 D4
Falkirk FK2 .... 60 A4
Mayfield EH22 .... 183 E3
Waverley St Ind Units 1
EH48 .... 145 D4
Waverley St EH1 .. 233 D3
Waverley Terr
Bonnyrigg and Lasswade
EH19 .... 182 B4
Mayfield EH22 .... 183 E3
Stenhousemuir FK5 .. 38 B1
Wayfarers Dr KY11 .. 47 F2
Wayfarers Pl KY11 .. 47 F2
Weaver Pl EH48 ... 145 D4
Weaver Row FK7 .. 7 D2
Weaver's Knowe Cres
EH14 .... 151 F4
Weavers Cres KY2 .. 17 F3
Weavers La EH47 .. 170 A3
Weavers Wlk KY12 .. 29 D1
Webster Ave KY4 .. 39 D2
Webster Ct EH52 .. 117 F3
Webster Pl KY11 .. 46 B3
Wedderburn Cres KY11 .. 29 F1
Wedderburn Pl KY11 .. 29 E1
Wedderburn Rd KY2 .. 16 B4
Wedderburn St KY11 .. 29 E1
Wedderburn Terr EH21 .. 126 B2
Wee Brae EH18 ... 156 A1
Wee Row FK2 .... 60 A3
Weir Ave KY4 .... 13 D1

Weir Cres EH22 .... 156 C1
Weir Dr FK7 .... 8 B2
Weir St Falkirk FK1 .... 60 B3
Stirling FK8 .... 1 C1
Well Rd Bridge of A FK9 .... 2 A4
Lochgelly KY5 .... 14 A4
Well Wynd EH33 .... 128 B3
Wellgate Dr FK9 .... 2 B4
Wellflats Rd EH29 .... 89 D1
Wellgate Dr FK9 .... 2 B4
Wellgreen Pl FK8 .... 7 D3
Wellhead Cl EH30 .... 89 E4
Wellington Pl EH6 .... 94 A3
Wellington Sch EH26 ...... 222 C3
Wellington St EH7 .... 93 F1
Wellmyre FK10 .... 11 D2
Wellpark FK52 .... 116 C4
Wellpark Cres FK7 .... 6 C2
Wellpark Terr FK4 .... 58 A3
Wellside EH41 .... 131 F4
Wellside Pl FK1 .... 60 A3
Welsh Gdns FK9 .... 2 A4
Welsh Rd EH17 .... 169 F3
Wemyss Ct KY11 .... 46 C3
Wemyss Gdns EH21 .... 127 E3
Wemyss Pl
Cockenzie & Port Seton
EH32 .... 97 E2
Edinburgh EH3 .... 232 B4
Haddington EH41 .... 132 A4
Wemyss Place Mews
EH3 .... 232 B4
Wemyss Rd EH32 .... 98 C3
Wemyss St
Cowdenbeath KY4 .... 13 E2
Rosyth KY11 .... 46 C3
Wemyss Terr EH32 .... 98 C3
Wemyssfield KY1 .... 17 D2
Werberside Mews KY4 ..... 92 C2
Wes Twindygoul Gdns
EH33 .... 128 B3
Wesley Pl FK2 .... 82 A4
West Adam St EH8 .... 233 E2
West Albert Rd KY1 .... 17 D2
West Annandale St EH7 .... 93 E2
West Approach Rd
EH3 EH11 .... 232 A2
West Baldridge Rd KY12 .. 28 C3
West Bankton EH54 .... 173 F4
West Barns Prim Sch
EH42 .... 77 F1
West Bay Rd EH39 .... 54 A4
West Benhar Rd ML7 ..... 168 A2
West Boreland Rd FK6 ..... 36 B1
West Bow EH1 .... 233 D2
West Bowling Green St
EH6 .... 93 F3
West Bridge St FK1 .... 60 A3
West Brighton Cres
EH15 .... 125 D4
West Broomhill Rd KY3 .. 50 C4
West Bryson Rd EH11 .... 122 C3
West Burnside FK52 ...... 117 F3
West Cairn Cres EH26 .... 203 F3
West Caiystane Rd EH10 . 154 A3
West Calder High Sch
EH55 .... 173 D3
West Carmuir Sta EH55 .. 172 B2
West Carmuirs Loan FK5 . 58 C3
West Carnethy Ave
EH13 .... 153 D3
West Castle Rd EH10 ..... 123 D3
West Catherine Pl EH12 . 122 C4
West Cherrybank EH6 ..... 93 E3
West Church La FK3 .... 40 A1
West Clifton Farm Cotts
EH53 .... 149 E4
West Coates EH12 .... 122 C4
West Colinton Ho EH13 .. 153 D3
West College St EH1 ...... 233 D2
West Craigs Ave EH12 .... 120 C3
West Craigs Cres EH12 ... 120 C4
West Cres EH34 .... 161 F2
West Croft EH28 .... 119 F1
West Cromwell St EH6 .... 93 F3
West Crosscauseway
EH8 .... 233 E1
West Ct
Edinburgh, Niddrie Mains
EH16 .... 124 C2
Edinburgh, Ravelston EH4 . 92 B1
West Dr Dunfermline KY12 . 29 D2
Larbert FK5 .... 38 B1
West End EH55 .... 172 B1
West End Gdns FK10 ..... 10 A3
West End Pl EH11 .... 122 C3
West Fenton Cotts EH32 .. 72 C4
West Fergus Pl KY1 .... 17 D2
West Ferryfield EH5 .... 92 C2
West Fountain Pl EH11 ... 122 C3
West Gate Rd FK3 .... 62 A4
West Glen Ave EH54 ..... 146 C3
West Gorgie Pl EH14 ..... 122 B2
West Gorgie Pl EH14 ..... 122 B2
West Grange Gdns EH9 .. 123 E2
West Granton Rd EH5 .... 92 B3
West Harbour Rd
Charlestown KY11 .... 45 D2
Cockenzie & Port Seton
EH32 .... 97 D2
Edinburgh EH5 .... 92 C4
West Harwood Crofts
EH55 .... 196 B3
West Holmes Gdns
EH21 .... 126 A3
West James St FK12 .... 5 D3
West Johnston St FK12 ..... 5 D3
West La KY4 .... 13 D1
West Leven St KY3 .... 50 C4

West Link Rd FK9 .... 2 B3
West Links Rd EH31 .... 51 F1
West Loan EH32 .... 96 C1
West Loan Ct EH32 .... 127 F4
West Lodge Gdns FK10 ..... 9 F4
West Lorimer Pl EH32 ..... 97 D2
West Lothian Coll of F Ed
EH48 .... 145 E3
West Main St
Armadale EH48 .... 143 F3
Blackburn EH47 .... 171 E4
Broxburn EH52 .... 117 E3
Harthill ML7 .... 168 C3
Uphall EH52 .... 116 C2
Whitburn EH47 .... 169 F3
West Mains Ind Est FK3 ... 61 D4
West Mains EH9 .... 123 F1
West Mains St EH32 .... 71 E2
West Maitland St EH12 .. 232 A2
West March St KY1 .... 17 E4
West Mayfield EH9 .... 123 F2
West Mill La EH4 .... 232 A3
West Mill Rd EH13 .... 153 D2
West Montgomery Pl 5
EH7 .... 93 F1
West Muir Rd EH55 .... 172 B1
West Murrayfield FK7 .... 7 E1
West Nethertown St
KY12 .... 29 D1
West Newington Pl EH9 .. 123 F3
West Nicolson St EH8 .... 233 E2
West Norton Pl EH7 ...... 233 F4
West Park Gr EH52 .... 117 D3
West Park Pl EH11 .... 122 C3
West Pilton Ave EH4 ...... 92 B3
West Pilton Bank EH4 ..... 92 B3
West Pilton Cres EH4 ..... 92 A3
West Pilton Crossway
EH4 .... 92 B3
West Pilton Dr EH4 .... 92 B3
West Pilton Gdns EH4 .... 92 B3
West Pilton Gn EH4 .... 92 B3
West Pilton Gr EH4 .... 92 B3
West Pilton Lea EH4 ...... 92 B3
West Pilton Loan EH4 .... 92 B3
West Pilton March EH4 ... 92 B3
West Pilton Pk EH4 .... 92 B3
West Pilton Pl EH4 .... 92 B3
West Pilton Rd EH4 .... 92 B3
West Pilton Rise EH4 ..... 92 B3
West Pilton Terr EH4 ...... 92 B3
West Pilton View EH4 ..... 92 B2
West Pk Carnock KY12 .... 27 E3
Lochgelly KY5 .... 14 A4
West Port Dunbar EH42 ... 78 B1
Dysart KY1 .... 18 A4
Edinburgh EH1 .... 232 C2
Linlithgow EH49 .... 84 C4
West Port Pl EH3 .... 84 C4
West Powburn EH9 .... 123 F2
West Preston St EH8 ..... 123 F3
West Quality St KY1 .... 17 D1
West Quality St KY1 .... 18 A4
West Rd Charlestown KY11 . 45 D2
Haddington EH41 .... 131 F4
West Register St EH2 .... 233 D4
West Register Street La
EH2 .... 233 D4
West Relugas Rd EH9 .... 123 E2
West Richmond St EH8 .. 233 E2
West Savile Rd EH16 ..... 123 F2
West Savile Terr EH9 ..... 123 F2
West Scotland Street La 1
EH3 .... 93 E1
West Seaside EH32 .... 96 C1
West Shore Rd EH5 .... 92 B4
West Shore Road Trad Est
EH5 .... 92 B4
West Silvermills La EH3 .. 93 D1
West Sq KY11 .... 46 C3
West St EH26 .... 203 F2
West Stirling St FK12 .... 4 C1
West Telferton EH7 .... 94 C1
West Tollcross EH3 .... 232 B1
West Torbain KY2 .... 16 B4
West Vennel EH10 .... 10 A3
West Way KY11 .... 48 A3
West Werberside EH4 ..... 92 C2
West Windygoul EH33 .... 128 A3
West Windygoul Gdns
EH33 .... 128 A2
West Winnelstrae EH5 .... 92 C2
West Woods EH4 .... 92 C2
West Wynd KY1 .... 17 E3
Westbank St EH33 .... 129 E3
Westbank Gdns EH33 .... 129 E3
Westbank Loan EH15 ..... 95 D1
Westbank Pl EH15 .... 95 D1
Westbank Rd EH33 .... 129 E3
Westbank St EH15 .... 95 D1
Westbank Terr EH33 ..... 129 E3
Westburn Ave
Cowdenbeath KY4 .... 13 D1
Edinburgh EH14 .... 152 B4
Falkirk FK1 .... 59 F2
Westburn Gdns EH14 .... 152 B4
Westburn Gr EH14 .... 152 B4
Westburn Middlefield
EH14 .... 152 B4
Westburn Pk EH14 .... 152 B4
Westburn Prim Sch
EH11 .... 121 E1
Westcliffe Ct EH33 .... 61 F3
Westcraigs Pk EH48 ...... 142 B2
Westcraigs Rd
Blackridge EH48 .... 142 B2
Harthill ML7 .... 168 A3

Westend Pl EH39 .... 54 A4
Wester Bankton EH54 ... 174 A4
Wester Bogie Rd KY2 ..... 16 A4
Wester Broom Ave EH12 . 121 E3
Wester Broom Dr EH12 .. 121 E3
Wester Broom Gdns
EH12 .... 121 E3
Wester Broom Gr EH12 .. 121 E3
Wester Broom Pl EH12 .. 121 E3
Wester Broom Terr EH12 . 121 E3
Wester Coates Ave EH12 . 122 C4
Wester Coates Gdns
EH12 .... 122 C4
Wester Coates Pl EH12 .. 122 C4
Wester Coates Rd EH12 . 122 C4
Wester Coates Terr EH12 . 122 C4
Wester Drylaw Ave EH4 .. 92 A2
Wester Drylaw Dr EH4 .... 92 B2
Wester Drylaw Pk EH4 .... 92 B2
Wester Drylaw Pl EH4 .... 92 A2
Wester Drylaw Row EH4 .. 92 B1
Wester Hailes Pk EH14 .. 152 B4
Wester Hailes Rd EH14 .. 152 B4
Wester Hailes Sta EH14 . 152 B4
Wester Row EH14 .... 120 C1
Wester Steil EH10 .... 122 C1
Westerdunes Pk EH39 .... 53 E4
Westerglen Rd FK1 .... 60 A1
Westerlands Dr FK8 .... 7 D3
Westerlea Ct KY9 .... 2 A3
Westerlea Dr KY9 .... 2 A3
Westerlea (Sch for
Spastic Children) EH12 . 122 B4
Westermains EH48 .... 143 F3
Western Ave Crossford KY12 . 28 A1
Falkirk FK3 .... 60 A3
Western Gdns EH12 ..... 122 B4
Western General Hospl
EH4 .... 92 B2
Western Pl EH12 .... 122 B4
Western Terr EH12 .... 122 B4
Westerton EH54 .... 147 D3
Westerton Dr FK9 .... 2 A4
Westerton Rd
Broxburn EH52 .... 118 A3
Grangemouth FK3 .... 61 F4
Westerton Terr FK2 .... 39 E2
Westfield FK10 .... 24 A2
Westfield Ave EH11 ...... 122 B3
Westfield Ct EH22 .... 156 C1
Westfield Dr EH22 .... 156 C1
Westfield Gr
Crossgates KY4 .... 30 C3
Dalkeith EH22 .... 156 C1
Westfield Pk EH22 .... 156 C1
Westfield Pl EH11 .... 122 B3
Westfield Prim Sch EH48 . 112 C2
Westfield Rd Edinburgh EH11 . 122 B3
Westfield Rdbt FK2 .... 60 C3
Westfield Sch EH52 ...... 157 D2
Westfield St
Edinburgh EH11 .... 122 B3
Falkirk FK2 .... 60 C3
Westgarth Ave EH13 .... 153 D3
Westgate Dunbar EH42 ... 78 B2
Mid Calder EH53 .... 148 A2
North Berwick EH39 ...... 54 A4
Westhall Cres KY12 .... 27 E1
Westhall Gdns
Edinburgh EH10 .... 123 D3
Uphall EH52 .... 117 D2
Westhall Rd FK2 .... 117 F2
Westhouse Ave EH22 .... 183 F3
Westhouse Dr EH22 ..... 183 F3
Westhouse St EH22 ..... 183 F3
Westhouses Rd EH22 ... 183 F3
Westmill Wynd EH18 .... 182 A4
Westminster Pl FK5 .... 38 C2
Westpoint EH42 .... 78 B1
Westquarter Ave FK2 .... 61 D1
Westquarter Prim Sch
FK2 .... 61 D1
Westray Terr FK1 .... 60 B1
Westside Plaza Sh Ctr
EH14 .... 152 B4
Westview EH49 .... 84 B4
Westview Cres FK10 .... 4 B1
Westwater St KY5 .... 14 A4
Westwood Ave FK1 .... 17 F4
Westwood Pk EH54 ..... 146 C4
Westwood Pl KY11 .... 29 F2
Westwood View EH55 ... 172 B2
Wharry Rd FK12 .... 5 D3
Wheatfield Gr EH20 ..... 181 D4
Wheatfield Loan EH20 .. 155 D1
Wheatfield Pl EH11 ...... 122 B3
Wheatfield Rd EH11 ..... 122 B3
Wheatfield St EH11 ...... 122 B3
Wheatfield Terr EH11 .... 122 B3
Wheatfield Wlk EH20 ... 181 D4
Wheatlands Ave FK4 ...... 58 A3
Wheatsheaf La EH22 .... 157 D2
Whim Rd EH31 .... 51 F1
Whin Park Ind Est EH32 .. 97 D2
Whin Pk EH32 .... 97 D2
Whinbank EH54 .... 147 F3
Whinhill KY11 .... 29 E2
Whinneyknowe KY11 .... 68 B3
Whinniehill Terr KY11 .... 27 E3
Whinny Hill Cres KY11 ... 47 D1
Whinnyburn Pl KY11 ..... 46 B3
Whinrig EH52 .... 117 F3
Whins of Milton Sch FK7 .. 7 D1
Whins Pl EH15 .... 95 D1
Whins Rd Alloa FK10 ..... 10 B4
Stirling FK7 .... 7 D1
Whinwell Rd FK8 .... 2 A1

Whirlbut Cres KY11 .... 29 D1
Whirlbut St KY11 .... 29 D1
Whitburn Acad EH47 .... 170 B4
Whitburn Rd
Bathgate EH48 .... 144 C2
Livingston EH54 .... 147 E2
White Castle EH14 ...... 166 B3
White Hart St EH22 ..... 157 D2
White Horse Cl EH8 ..... 233 F3
White Pk EH11 .... 122 C3
White St EH47 .... 170 A3
White's Cl EH22 .... 157 D2
Whitecraig Cres EH21 ... 126 C1
Whitecraig Cres EH21 ... 126 C1
Whitecraig Gdns EH21 .. 126 C1
Whitecraig Gdns E EH21 . 126 C1
Whitecraig Prim Sch
EH21 .... 126 C1
Whitecraig Rd EH21 ..... 126 C1
Whitecross Prim Sch
EH49 .... 83 F3
Whitedalehead Rd EH47 . 170 B3
Whitedales EH10 .... 154 B3
Whitefield Neuk KY12 ... 29 F3
Whitefield Rd KY12 ...... 29 F3
Whitefield St EH47 ...... 170 A3
Whitehead Gr EH30 ..... 89 E4
Whitehill Ave EH21 ..... 126 A2
Whitehill Dr
Blackburn EH47 .... 171 E4
Dalkeith EH22 .... 157 E1
Whitehill Farm Rd EH21 . 126 A2
Whitehill Gdns EH22 .... 126 A2
Whitehill Gr EH22 .... 157 E1
Whitehill Ind Est EH48 .. 145 E1
Whitehill Pl
Rosewell EH24 .... 181 E1
Stirling FK8 .... 7 D3
Whitehill Rd
Blackburn EH47 .... 145 E1
Edinburgh EH21 .... 125 E2
Whitehill St EH21 .... 125 E2
Whitehill View EH47 .... 171 E4
Whitehouse Loan EH9 .. 123 E3
Whitehouse Rd
Edinburgh EH4 .... 91 D2
Stirling FK8 .... 7 E4
Whitelaw Cres KY11 ..... 29 E1
Whitelaw Dr EH48 .... 145 F3
Whitelaw Pl KY11 .... 29 E1
Whitelaw Rd KY11 .... 29 E1
Whitelaw St EH48 .... 142 B1
Whitelea Cres EH14 ..... 177 E4
Whitelea Rd EH14 .... 177 E4
Whiteloch Rd EH33 ..... 129 E3
Whitemoss Rd EH27 .... 149 F1
Whitemyre Ct KY12 .... 28 B3
Whitequarries Ind Est
EH52 .... 87 E4
Whites Quay KY11 .... 47 F1
Whiteside Ind Est EH48 . 144 C2
Whitesideloan FK2 .... 82 C4
Whitestone Pl EH48 ..... 145 E1
Whitingford EH6 .... 93 E3
Whitson Cres EH11 ...... 122 A3
Whitson Gr EH11 .... 122 A3
Whitson Pl E EH11 ...... 122 A3
Whitson Pl W EH11 ..... 122 A3
Whitson Rd EH11 .... 122 A3
Whitson Terr EH11 ...... 122 A3
Whitson Way EH11 ...... 122 A3
Whitson Wlk EH11 ...... 122 A3
Whitten La EH49 .... 84 C4
Whittingehame Dr EH41 . 132 A4
Whittinghame Dr EH41 . 132 B4
Wholeflats Rd KY2 .... 61 F2
Wholequarter Ave FK2 ... 61 E1
Whyte Pl 11 EH7 .... 94 A1
Whyte St Harthill ML7 .. 168 C3
Lochgelly KY5 .... 14 A4
Whyte Wlk KY11 .... 29 F2
Whytehouse Ave KY1 .... 17 D2
Whyteman's Brae KY1 ... 17 E4
Whytemans Brae Hospl
KY1 .... 17 D4
Whytescauseway KY1 ... 17 D2
Wilderness Rdbt EH54 .. 173 E3
Wilderness The FK2 .... 22 B2
Wildridge Way KY5 .... 14 A4
Wilfred Terr 5 EH8 .... 94 B1
Wilkieston EH28 .... 119 E1
William Black Pl EH30 ... 89 E4
William Booth Pl FK7 .... 7 D2
William St
Dunfermline KY12 .... 28 C2
Edinburgh EH3 .... 232 A3
Kirkcaldy KY1 .... 17 D1
William Street La NE EH3 . 232 A3
William Street La NW EH3 . 232 A3
William Street La SE EH3 . 232 A3
William Street La SW EH3 . 232 A3
William Younger Ctr
(Mus) EH8 .... 233 D3
Williamfield Ave FK7 .... 7 D2
Williamfield Sq 2 EH15 . 125 D4
Williamson Ave FK1 ...... 39 D1
Williamson Pl FK4 .... 60 B4
Williamson St FK1 .... 60 A4
Williamston Intc EH54 .. 148 A3
Williamston Prim Sch
EH54 .... 173 F4
Willlamstone St EH39 ... 54 A3
Willow Ave EH19 .... 182 A3
Willow Brae EH47 .... 193 F3
Willow Dell EH51 .... 63 E3

Willow Dr KY1 .... 17 D3
Willow Gr Dunfermline KY11 . 46 C4
Livingston EH54 .... 148 A3
Willow Pk EH47 .... 193 F3
Willow Rd EH22 .... 183 F3
Willow Tree Pl EH14 .... 151 D4
Willowbank EH54 .... 147 F3
Willowbank Row EH6 .... 93 E3
Willowbrae FK2 .... 82 B4
Willowbrae Ave EH8 .... 124 B4
Willowbrae Gdns EH8 .. 124 B4
Willowbrae Rd EH8 ..... 124 B4
Willowdean EH49 .... 86 B2
Willowpark (Specl Sch)
EH11 .... 122 B3
Willows The
Cairneyhill KY12 .... 27 E1
Tullibody FK10 .... 4 A1
Wilson Ave Dalkeith EH22 . 157 E2
Denny FK6 .... 36 B1
Falkirk FK1 .... 59 E3
Kirkcaldy KY2 .... 17 D3
Polmont FK2 .... 61 F1
Prestonpans EH32 .... 96 C1
Wilson Dr Bannockburn FK7 . 7 E1
Falkirk FK1 .... 59 E3
Wilson Gdns FK1 .... 59 E3
Wilson Pl FK4 .... 58 B2
Wilson Rd Falkirk FK1 ... 59 E3
Gorebridge EH23 .... 183 E1
Livingston EH54 .... 146 C2
Shotts ML7 .... 212 A4
Wilson St Blairhall KY12 . 26 A4
Cowdenbeath KY4 .... 13 E2
Grangemouth FK3 .... 61 E3
Penicuik EH26 .... 203 F3
Townhill KY12 .... 29 E4
Wilson Terr
Broxburn EH52 .... 117 D3
Stoneyburn EH47 .... 171 D1
Wilson Way EH11 .... 46 B1
Wilson Wlk EH33 .... 128 B3
Wilson's Cl EH22 .... 29 D2
Wilson's Pk EH15 .... 95 D1
Wilsontown Rd ML11 ... 215 E1
Wilton Rd Carluke ML8 . 230 A1
Edinburgh EH16 .... 123 F2
Winchburgh Cotts EH52 . 87 F1
Winchburgh Prim Sch
EH52 .... 87 F1
Winchester Ave FK6 ...... 36 C2
Winchester Avenue
Ind Est FK6 .... 36 C2
Windlebrook EH54 .... 47 D4
Windmill Gn KY1 .... 17 D4
Windmill Knowe KY4 .... 30 C3
Windmill La EH8 .... 233 E1
Windmill Pl KY1 .... 18 A4
Windmill Rd KY1 .... 17 F4
Windmill St EH8 .... 233 E1
Windsor Ave FK1 .... 59 F2
Windsor Cres Falkirk FK1 . 59 F2
Maddiston FK2 .... 83 D3
Penicuik EH26 .... 204 A3
Windsor Dr Denny FK6 .. 36 B2
Falkirk FK1 .... 59 F2
Penicuik EH26 .... 204 A3
Windsor Gdns Alloa FK10 . 9 F4
Falkirk FK1 .... 59 F2
Musselburgh EH21 ...... 126 C3
Windsor Park Dr EH21 .. 126 C3
Windsor Park Pl EH21 .. 126 C3
Windsor Park Terr EH21 . 126 C3
Windsor Pl
Edinburgh EH15 .... 125 D4
Shotts ML7 .... 191 F3
Stirling FK8 .... 7 D4
Windsor Rd Falkirk FK1 . 59 F2
Penicuik EH26 .... 204 A3
Windsor Sq EH26 .... 204 A3
Windsor St Edinburgh EH7 . 93 F1
Menstrie FK11 .... 3 F3
Shotts ML7 .... 191 F3
Windsor Street La EH7 .. 93 F1
Windsor Terr EH26 ...... 204 A3
Windygate KY2 .... 16 C1
Windygates Rd EH39 .... 54 A3
Windygoul Cres EH33 .. 128 C3
Windyhill Ave FK10 .... 23 E3
Windyknowe Cres EH48 . 144 B3
Windyknowe Pk EH48 .. 144 B3
Windyknowe Prim Sch
EH48 .... 144 B3
Wingate Cres EH42 ...... 78 B1
Winifred Cres KY2 .... 17 D3
Winifred St KY2 .... 17 D3
Winterfield Mains EH42 . 78 A1
Winterfield Pl EH42 ...... 78 A1
Winton Cl EH33 .... 128 C2
Winton Ct
New Winton EH33 .... 129 D3
Tranent EH33 .... 128 C2
Winton Dr EH10 .... 154 B2
Winton Gdns EH10 ..... 154 B2
Winton Gr Edinburgh EH10 . 154 A3
Tranent EH33 .... 128 C2
Winton Loan
Edinburgh EH10 .... 154 B2
Macmerry EH33 .... 129 D3
Winton Pk
Cockenzie & Port Seton
EH32 .... 97 E2
Edinburgh EH10 .... 154 A2
Winton Pl EH33 .... 128 B3

Winton Terr
Edinburgh EH10 .... **154** A3
New Winton EH33 .... **129** D2
Winton Way EH33 .... **128** B2
Wishart Ave
Bonnyrigg and Lasswade
EH19 .... **182** B4
North Berwick EH39 .... **54** B3
Wishart Dr FK7 .... **7** E2
Wishart Pl
Dalkeith EH22 .... **156** C1
Kirkcaldy KY1 .... **17** F3
Wishaw Terr EH7 .... **94** A1
Wisp Gn EH15 .... **125** D2
Wisp The EH15 .... **125** D2
Witchbrae KY12 .... **29** D2
Wolfe Rd FK1 .... **60** B2
Wolrige Rd EH16 .... **155** D4
Wolseley Cres EH8 .... **94** B1
Wolseley Pl EH8 .... **94** B1
Wolsey Ave EH19 .... **182** B3
Wood Avens FK10 .... **4** B1
Wood Dr EH47 .... **169** F3
Wood Lea FK10 .... **23** F3
Wood Pl Livingston EH54 ... **147** E2
Rosyth KY11 .... **46** C3
Wood Rd KY11 .... **46** B1
Wood St FK3 .... **61** E4
Wood's Ct EH19 .... **182** A4
Woodbank KY4 .... **13** D1
Woodbank Gr KY12 .... **26** B4
Woodbine Terr EH6 .... **94** A2
Woodburn Ave
Dalkeith EH22 .... **157** E1
Redding FK2 .... **61** D1
Woodburn Bank EH22 ...... **157** E2
Woodburn Cres
Bonnybridge FK4 .... **57** F2
Oakley KY12 .... **26** C4
Redding FK2 .... **61** D1
Woodburn Dr
Alloa FK10 .... **4** C1
Dalkeith EH22 .... **157** D2

Woodburn Gdns
Dalkeith EH22 .... **157** E2
Falkirk FK2 .... **60** C3
Woodburn Gr EH22 .... **157** E1
Woodburn Loan EH22 ...... **157** E2
Woodburn Medway EH22 .. **157** E2
Woodburn Pk EH22 .... **157** E2
Woodburn Pl EH22 .... **157** E2
Woodburn Prim Sch
EH22 .... **157** E2
Woodburn Rd
Dalkeith EH22 .... **157** E2
Falkirk FK2 .... **60** B3
Woodburn St
Dalkeith EH22 .... **157** E2
Falkirk FK2 .... **60** C3
Woodburn Terr
Dalkeith EH22 .... **157** E2
Edinburgh EH10 .... **123** D2
Woodburn View EH22 ...... **157** E2
Woodburn Way FK12 .... **5** D3
Woodbush EH42 .... **78** C1
Woodbush Brae EH42 .... **78** C1
Woodbush Ct EH42 .... **78** C1
Woodbush Pl EH42 .... **78** C1
Woodend Ind Est KY4 ...... **13** D1
Woodend Pk EH25 .... **180** C2
Woodend Pl KY4 .... **13** D1
Woodend Rd ML8 .... **230** A1
Woodend Wlk EH48 .... **143** F3
Woodfield Ave EH13 .... **152** C3
Woodfield Pk
Bilston EH25 .... **180** B3
Edinburgh EH13 .... **152** C3
Woodhall Ave EH14 .... **152** B3
Woodhall Bank EH13 .... **152** C3
Woodhall Dr EH14 .... **152** B3
Woodhall Gr EH13 .... **152** C3
Woodhall Millbrae EH14 .. **152** C3
Woodhall Pl EH34 .... **160** C3
Woodhall Rd EH34 .... **160** B3
Woodhall Terr EH14 .... **152** B3
Woodhead Farm Rd KY12 ... **25** F1
Woodhead Gr EH48 .... **143** E3
Woodhead Pl EH48 .... **144** C3
Woodhead St KY12 .... **26** A1

Woodhill Ct FK3 .... **61** E3
Woodhill Gr KY12 .... **28** A1
Woodhill Rd EH48 .... **142** A2
Woodland Way FK6 .... **57** E4
Woodlands FK10 .... **5** F1
Woodlands Bank KY11 .... **48** A2
Woodlands Cotts EH48 ...... **144** A3
Woodlands Cres FK1 .... **60** A2
Woodlands Dr
Bo'ness EH51 .... **63** E3
Brightons FK2 .... **82** C4
Crossford KY12 .... **28** A1
Woodlands Gr
Armadale EH48 .... **144** A3
Edinburgh EH15 .... **124** C3
Townhill KY12 .... **29** E4
Woodlands Pk EH54 .... **146** C4
Woodlands Rd KY2 .... **16** B3
Woodlands Terr KY12 .... **26** A4
Woodlands The KY11 .... **46** C3
Woodlea Gdns FK10 .... **5** D1
Woodlea Pk FK10 .... **10** A4
Woodmill Cres KY11 .... **29** E2
Woodmill High Sch KY11 ... **29** F2
Woodmill Pl KY11 .... **29** F2
Woodmill Rd KY11 .... **29** E2
Woodmill St KY11 .... **29** D2
Woodmill Terr KY11 .... **29** D2
Woodmuir Pl EH55 .... **194** C3
Woodmuir Prim Sch
EH55 .... **194** C3
Woodmuir Rd
Breich EH55 .... **194** C3
Whitburn EH47 .... **170** B3
Woodrow EH23 .... **183** E1
Woodside KY4 .... **13** E2
Woodside Ave KY11 .... **46** C3
Woodside Ct
Cambusbarron FK7 .... **6** B3
Falkirk FK1 .... **60** A2
Woodside Dr EH26 .... **203** F3
Woodside Gdns
Brightons FK2 .... **82** C4
Musselburgh EH21 .... **126** C3
Woodside Gr FK5 .... **59** E4

Woodside Pl
Bridgend EH49 .... **86** B2
Fallin FK7 .... **8** B2
Woodside Rd Alloa FK10 ...... **4** C1
Forrestfield ML6 .... **141** D2
Stirling FK8 .... **2** A2
Tullibody FK10 .... **4** A1
Woodside St KY11 .... **46** C3
Woodside Terr
Bridgend EH49 .... **86** B2
Clackmannan FK10 .... **10** C2
Edinburgh EH15 .... **125** E4
Falkirk FK1 .... **60** A2
Tarbrax EH55 .... **217** F2
Woodstock Pl EH16 .... **124** A1
Woodville Ct EH52 .... **117** E2
Woodville Terr EH6 .... **94** A2
Wooer St ◫ FK1 .... **60** A2
Woolfords Cotts EH55 ...... **217** D4
Woolmet Cres EH22 .... **156** A4
Wordie Rd FK7 .... **6** C2
Wotherspoon Cres EH48 ... **143** F3
Wotherspoon Dr EH51 ...... **63** E3
Wright Pl Kirkcaldy KY1 ...... **17** E4
Lochgelly KY5 .... **14** A4
Wright St FK2 .... **60** A3
Writers Ct EH42 .... **78** B2
Wynd The Alva FK12 .... **5** D4
Dalgety Bay KY11 .... **48** B2
Gifford EH41 .... **163** F3
Ormiston EH35 .... **159** F2
Wyndford Ave EH52 .... **117** D3
Wyndford Pl EH52 .... **117** D3
Wyvern Pk EH9 .... **123** E2
Wyvis Pk EH26 .... **204** A4
Wyvis Pl ML7 .... **192** A2

Yardheads EH6 .... **93** F3
Yardley Pl FK2 .... **39** D1
Yarrow Ct EH26 .... **204** A4
Yarrow Pl FK3 .... **61** F3
Yeaman La EH11 .... **122** C3
Yeaman Pl EH11 .... **122** C3
Yester Pl EH41 .... **100** C1
Yester Prim Sch EH41 ...... **163** F2
Yetholm Pk KY12 .... **28** C1

Yetts The FK7 .... **6** B3
Yew Gr EH54 .... **148** A3
Yew Terr FK2 .... **61** D1
Yewlands Cres EH16 .... **155** D4
Yewlands Gdns EH16 .... **155** D4
Yieldshields Rd ML8 .... **231** E2
York Arc FK3 .... **40** B1
York Dr FK2 .... **60** B3
York La Edinburgh EH1 .... **233** D4
Grangemouth FK3 .... **40** B1
York Pl Dunfermline KY12 .... **29** E3
Edinburgh EH1 .... **233** D4
Kirkcaldy KY1 .... **17** F4
York Rd Edinburgh EH5 .... **93** E3
North Berwick EH39 .... **54** A4
York Sq FK3 .... **40** B1
York St FK2 .... **60** B3
Young Ave EH33 .... **128** B3
Young Cres EH48 .... **144** C3
Young Ct KY4 .... **13** E2
Young Gr EH54 .... **173** E3
Young St Edinburgh EH2 .... **232** B3
West Calder EH55 .... **172** B1
Young Street La N EH2 ...... **232** B3
Young Street La S EH2 ...... **232** B3
Young Terr KY4 .... **13** D2
Young's Terr KY1 .... **17** E3
Youngs Rd EH52 .... **118** A3
Yule Pl EH47 .... **145** E1
Yule Terr EH47 .... **171** E4

Zealandia Rd KY11 .... **46** A1
Zetland Dr
Grangemouth FK3 .... **61** D4
Laurieston FK2 .... **61** D2
Zetland Pl Edinburgh EH5 .. **93** D3
Lochgelly KY5 .... **14** A4
Skinflats FK2 .... **39** F2
Zetland Terr FK10 .... **11** D2
Zetland Terr FK2 .... **61** F1
**Zoo (Royal Zoological
Society of Scotland)**
EH12 .... **121** F4

The Street Atlases are available from all good bookshops or by mail order direct from the publisher. Orders can be made in the following ways. **By phone** Ring our special Credit Card Hotline on **01933 443863** during office hours (9am to 5pm) or leave a message on the answering machine, quoting your full credit card number plus expiry date and your full name and address. **By post or fax** Fill out the order form below (you may photocopy it) and post it to: **Philip's Direct, 27 Sanders Road, Wellingborough, Northants NN8 4NL** or fax it to: **01933 443849**. Before placing an order by post, by fax or on the answering machine, please telephone to check availability and prices.

STREET ATLASES ORDER FORM

COLOUR LOCAL ATLASES

	PAPERBACK	
	Quantity @ £3.50 each	£ Total
CANNOCK, LICHFIELD, RUGELEY	☐ 0 540 07625 2	➤
DERBY AND BELPER	☐ 0 540 07608 2	➤
NORTHWICH, WINSFORD, MIDDLEWICH	☐ 0 540 07589 2	➤
PEAK DISTRICT TOWNS	☐ 0 540 07609 0	➤
STAFFORD, STONE, UTTOXETER	☐ 0 540 07626 0	➤
WARRINGTON, WIDNES, RUNCORN	☐ 0 540 07588 4	➤

COLOUR REGIONAL ATLASES

	HARDBACK	SPIRAL	POCKET	
	Quantity @ £10.99 each	Quantity @ £8.99 each	Quantity @ £5.99 each	£ Total
BERKSHIRE	☐ 0 540 06170 0	☐ 0 540 06172 7	☐ 0 540 06173 5	➤
	Quantity @ £10.99 each	Quantity @ £8.99 each	Quantity @ £4.99 each	£ Total
MERSEYSIDE	☐ 0 540 06480 7	☐ 0 540 06481 5	☐ 0 540 06482 3	➤
	Quantity @ £12.99 each	Quantity @ £9.99 each	Quantity @ £4.99 each	£ Total
DURHAM	☐ 0 540 06365 7	☐ 0 540 06366 5	☐ 0 540 06367 3	➤
EAST KENT	☐ 0 540 07483 7	☐ 0 540 07276 1	☐ 0 540 07287 7	➤
WEST KENT	☐ 0 540 07366 0	☐ 0 540 07367 9	☐ 0 540 07369 5	➤
EAST SUSSEX	☐ 0 540 07306 7	☐ 0 540 07307 5	☐ 0 540 07312 1	➤
WEST SUSSEX	☐ 0 540 07319 9	☐ 0 540 07323 7	☐ 0 540 07327 X	➤
	Quantity @ £12.99 each	Quantity @ £9.99 each	Quantity @ £5.50 each	£ Total
GREATER MANCHESTER	☐ 0 540 06485 8	☐ 0 540 06486 6	☐ 0 540 06487 4	➤
TYNE AND WEAR	☐ 0 540 06370 3	☐ 0 540 06371 1	☐ 0 540 06372 X	➤
	Quantity @ £12.99 each	Quantity @ £9.99 each	Quantity @ £5.99 each	£ Total
BIRMINGHAM & WEST MIDLANDS	☐ 0 540 07603 1	☐ 0 540 07604 X	☐ 0 540 07605 8	➤
BUCKINGHAMSHIRE	☐ 0 540 07466 7	☐ 0 540 07467 5	☐ 0 540 07468 3	➤
CHESHIRE	☐ 0 540 07507 8	☐ 0 540 07508 6	☐ 0 540 07509 4	➤
DERBYSHIRE	☐ 0 540 07531 0	☐ 0 540 07532 9	☐ 0 540 07533 7	➤
EDINBURGH & East Central Scotland	☐ 0 540 07653 8	☐ 0 540 07654 6	☐ 0 540 07656 2	➤

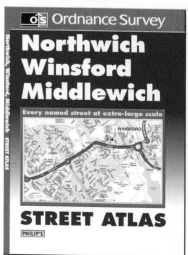

STREET ATLASES ORDER FORM

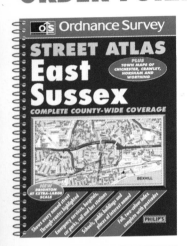

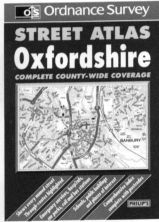

COLOUR REGIONAL ATLASES

	HARDBACK Quantity @ £12.99 each	SPIRAL Quantity @ £9.99 each	POCKET Quantity @ £5.99 each	£ Total
GLASGOW & West Central Scotland	☐ 0 540 07648 1	☐ 0 540 07649 X	☐ 0 540 07651 1	➤ ☐
NORTH HAMPSHIRE	☐ 0 540 07471 3	☐ 0 540 07472 1	☐ 0 540 07473 X	➤ ☐
SOUTH HAMPSHIRE	☐ 0 540 07476 4	☐ 0 540 07477 2	☐ 0 540 07478 0	➤ ☐
HERTFORDSHIRE	☐ 0 540 06174 3	☐ 0 540 06175 1	☐ 0 540 06176 X	➤ ☐
OXFORDSHIRE	☐ 0 540 07512 4	☐ 0 540 07513 2	☐ 0 540 07514 0	➤ ☐
SURREY	☐ 0 540 06435 1	☐ 0 540 06436 X	☐ 0 540 06438 6	➤ ☐
WARWICKSHIRE	☐ 0 540 07560 4	☐ 0 540 07561 2	☐ 0 540 07562 0	➤ ☐
SOUTH YORKSHIRE	☐ 0 540 06330 4	☐ 0 540 06331 2	☐ 0 540 06332 0	➤ ☐
WEST YORKSHIRE	☐ 0 540 06329 0	☐ 0 540 06327 4	☐ 0 540 06328 2	➤ ☐
	Quantity @ £14.99 each	Quantity @ £9.99 each	Quantity @ £5.99 each	£ Total
LANCASHIRE	☐ 0 540 06440 8	☐ 0 540 06441 6	☐ 0 540 06443 2	➤ ☐
NOTTINGHAMSHIRE	☐ 0 540 07541 8	☐ 0 540 075426 6	☐ 0 540 07543 4	➤ ☐
STAFFORDSHIRE	☐ 0 540 07549 3	☐ 0 540 07550 7	☐ 0 540 07551 5	➤ ☐

BLACK AND WHITE REGIONAL ATLASES

	HARDBACK Quantity @ £11.99 each	SOFTBACK Quantity @ £8.99 each	POCKET Quantity @ £3.99 each	£ Total
BRISTOL AND AVON	☐ 0 540 06140 9	☐ 0 540 06141 7	☐ 0 540 06142 5	➤ ☐
	Quantity @ £12.99 each	Quantity @ £9.99 each	Quantity @ £4.99 each	£ Total
CARDIFF, SWANSEA & GLAMORGAN	☐ 0 540 06186 7	☐ 0 540 06187 5	☐ 0 540 06207 3	➤ ☐
EAST ESSEX	☐ 0 540 05848 3	☐ 0 540 05866 1	☐ 0 540 05850 5	➤ ☐
WEST ESSEX	☐ 0 540 05849 1	☐ 0 540 05867 X	☐ 0 540 05851 3	➤ ☐

➤ ☐

Post to: Philip's Direct,
27 Sanders Road, Wellingborough,
Northants NN8 4NL

◆ Free postage and packing

◆ All available titles will normally be dispatched within 5 working days of receipt of order but please allow up to 28 days for delivery

☐ Please tick this box if you do not wish your name to be used by other carefully selected organisations that may wish to send you information about other products and services

Registered Office: Michelin House,
81 Fulham Road, London SW3 6RB

Registered in England
number: 3597451

I enclose a cheque / postal order, for a **total** of ☐
made payable to *Octopus Publishing Group Ltd*, or please debit my

☐ Access ☐ American Express ☐ Visa ☐ Diners

account by ☐

Account no

☐☐☐☐ ☐☐☐☐ ☐☐☐☐ ☐☐☐☐

Expiry date ☐☐ ☐☐

Signature...

Name...

Address...

....

....

....POSTCODE